Lecture Notes in Computer Science 16346

Founding Editors

Gerhard Goos
Juris Hartmanis

Editorial Board Members

Elisa Bertino, *Purdue University, West Lafayette, IN, USA*
Wen Gao, *Peking University, Beijing, China*
Bernhard Steffen, *TU Dortmund University, Dortmund, Germany*
Moti Yung, *Columbia University, New York, NY, USA*

The series Lecture Notes in Computer Science (LNCS), including its subseries Lecture Notes in Artificial Intelligence (LNAI) and Lecture Notes in Bioinformatics (LNBI), has established itself as a medium for the publication of new developments in computer science and information technology research, teaching, and education.

LNCS enjoys close cooperation with the computer science R & D community, the series counts many renowned academics among its volume editors and paper authors, and collaborates with prestigious societies. Its mission is to serve this international community by providing an invaluable service, mainly focused on the publication of conference and workshop proceedings and postproceedings. LNCS commenced publication in 1973.

June Wei · George Margetis · Helmut Degen ·
Stavroula Ntoa

Editors

HCI International 2025 – Late Breaking Papers

27th International Conference on
Human-Computer Interaction, HCII 2025
Gothenburg, Sweden, June 22–27, 2025
Proceedings, Part XVI

 Springer

Editors
June Wei
University of West Florida
Pensacola, FL, USA

Helmut Degen
Siemens Corporation
Princeton, NJ, USA

George Margetis
Foundation for Research
and Technology – Hellas (FORTH)
Heraklion, Crete, Greece

Stavroula Ntoa
Foundation for Research
and Technology – Hellas (FORTH)
Heraklion, Greece

ISSN 0302-9743 ISSN 1611-3349 (electronic)
Lecture Notes in Computer Science
ISBN 978-3-032-13186-7 ISBN 978-3-032-13187-4 (eBook)
https://doi.org/10.1007/978-3-032-13187-4

This Springer imprint is published by the registered company Springer Nature Switzerland AG
The registered company address is: Gewerbestrasse 11, 6330 Cham, Switzerland

If disposing of this product, please recycle the paper.

Foreword

The HCI International (HCII) conference was founded in 1984 by Gavriel Salvendy (Purdue University, USA, Tsinghua University, P.R. China, and University of Central Florida, USA) and the first event of the series, "1st USA-Japan Conference on Human-Computer Interaction", was held in Honolulu, Hawaii, USA, on 18–20 August. Since then, HCI International has been held jointly with several Thematic Areas and Affiliated Conferences, with each one under the auspices of a distinguished international Program Board and under one management and one registration. Twenty-seven HCI International Conferences have been organized so far (every two years until 2013, and annually thereafter).

Last year, we celebrated 40 years since the establishment of the HCII conference, which has been a hub for presenting groundbreaking research and novel ideas and collaboration for people from all over the world. Over the years, this conference has served as a platform for scholars, researchers, industry experts, and students to exchange ideas, connect, and address challenges in the ever-evolving HCI field. The conference has evolved itself, adapting to new technologies and emerging trends, while staying committed to its core mission of advancing knowledge and driving change.

The 27th International Conference on Human-Computer Interaction, HCI International 2025 (HCII 2025), was held as an 'on-site' conference at the Gothia Towers Hotel and Swedish Exhibition & Congress Centre, in Gothenburg, Sweden, on June 22–27, 2025, with the additional option for 'on-line' participation. It incorporated the 21 thematic areas and affiliated conferences listed below.

A total of 7972 individuals from academia, research institutes, industry, and government agencies from 92 countries submitted contributions. 1430 papers and 355 posters (as short research papers) were included in the volumes of the proceedings published just before the start of the conference. Additionally, 439 papers and 104 posters were included in the volumes of the proceedings published after the conference, as "Late Breaking Work". The contributions thoroughly cover the entire field of human-computer interaction, highlight the evolving role of computers in diverse contexts, and demonstrate how HCI research is shaping and improving user experiences across a wide range of domains, influencing technological progress and its effective integration into various sectors. The volumes constituting the full set of the HCII 2025 conference proceedings are listed on the following pages.

I would like to thank the Program Board Chairs and the members of the Program Boards of all thematic areas and affiliated conferences for their contribution towards the high scientific quality and overall success of the HCI International 2025 conference. Their manifold support including paper reviews (via a single-blind review process, with a minimum of two reviews per submission), session organization, and their willingness to act as goodwill ambassadors for the conference is most highly appreciated.

This conference would not have been possible without the continuous and unwavering support and advice of Gavriel Salvendy, founder, General Chair Emeritus, and Scientific Advisor. For his outstanding efforts, I would like to express my sincere appreciation to Abbas Moallem, Communications Chair and Editor of HCI International News.

September 2025   Constantine Stephanidis

HCI International 2025 Thematic Areas and Affiliated Conferences

- HCI: Human-Computer Interaction Thematic Area
- HIMI: Human Interface and the Management of Information Thematic Area
- EPCE: 22nd International Conference on Engineering Psychology and Cognitive Ergonomics
- AC: 19th International Conference on Augmented Cognition
- UAHCI: 19th International Conference on Universal Access in Human-Computer Interaction
- CCD: 17th International Conference on Cross-Cultural Design
- SCSM: 17th International Conference on Social Computing and Social Media
- VAMR: 17th International Conference on Virtual, Augmented and Mixed Reality
- DHM: 16th International Conference on Digital Human Modeling & Applications in Health, Safety, Ergonomics & Risk Management
- DUXU: 14th International Conference on Design, User Experience and Usability
- C&C: 13th International Conference on Culture and Computing
- DAPI: 13th International Conference on Distributed, Ambient and Pervasive Interactions
- HCIBGO: 12th International Conference on HCI in Business, Government and Organizations
- LCT: 12th International Conference on Learning and Collaboration Technologies
- ITAP: 11th International Conference on Human Aspects of IT for the Aged Population
- AIS: 7th International Conference on Adaptive Instructional Systems
- HCI-CPT: 7th International Conference on HCI for Cybersecurity, Privacy and Trust
- HCI-Games: 7th International Conference on HCI in Games
- MobiTAS: 7th International Conference on HCI in Mobility, Transport and Automotive Systems
- AI-HCI: 6th International Conference on Artificial Intelligence in HCI
- MOBILE: 6th International Conference on Human-Centered Design, Operation and Evaluation of Mobile Communications

Conference Proceedings – Full List of Volumes

85. CCIS 2772, HCI International 2025 — Late Breaking Posters: Part II, edited by Constantine Stephanidis, Margherita Antona, Stavroula Ntoa, George Margetis and Gavriel Salvendy
86. CCIS 2773, HCI International 2025 — Late Breaking Posters: Part III, edited by Constantine Stephanidis, Margherita Antona, Stavroula Ntoa, George Margetis and Gavriel Salvendy

https://2025.hci.international/proceedings

27th International Conference on Human-Computer Interaction (HCII 2025)

The full list with the Program Board Chairs and the members of the Program Boards of all thematic areas and affiliated conferences of HCII 2025 is available online at:

http://www.hci.international/board-members-2025.php

HCI International 2026 Conference

The 28th International Conference on Human-Computer Interaction, HCI International 2026, will be held jointly with the affiliated conferences at the Montréal Convention Centre (Palais des congrès de Montréal), in Montreal, Canada, 26–31 July 2026. It will cover a broad spectrum of themes related to Human-Computer Interaction, including theoretical issues, methods, tools, processes, and case studies in HCI design, as well as novel interaction techniques, interfaces, and applications. The proceedings will be published by Springer (part of Springer Nature) in a multi-volume set. More information will become available on the conference website: https://2026.hci.international/.

General Chair
Constantine Stephanidis
University of Crete and ICS-FORTH
Heraklion, Crete, Greece
Email: general_chair@2026.hci.international

https://2026.hci.international/

Contents

Mobile Technologies for Health, Education, and Digital Engagement

Generative AI in Creativity and Design

Algorithmic Creativity: How Visual and AI Literacy Impact the Use of Text-to-Image Tools in Design Tasks

Alessandro Canossa[1]([✉]), Lisa Toender Berger[2], Lucas Fellner[1], Willem van der Maden[2], Jesper Juul[1], and Jichen Zhu[2]

[1] Royal Danish Academy, Philip De Langes Allé 10, 1435 Copenhagen, Denmark
{acan,tsurello}@kglakademi.dk
[2] IT University, Rued Langgaards Vej 7, 2300 Copenhagen, Denmark
{wiva,jicz}@itu.dk

Abstract. Text-To-Image (TTI) generators are becoming widely used and are often promoted as "democratizing" the generation of images, but relatively little is known about whether people with different skill sets and literacies use these tools differently, and how their backgrounds influence the quality of the results. This paper investigates the impact of Visual Literacy, Artificial Intelligence (AI) Literacy, and Prompt Engineering Literacy on the use of a human-AI co-creation process for a real-world visual design task. We present a user study (n = 25) examining how people with different literacies interact with Midjourney to complete a visual design task. The results were evaluated by 3 internationally acknowledged visual artists. Our results found no impact of any literacy on the general visual appeal of the generated images, but where participants with high AI literacy reported more understanding of the co-creation process, images created by participants with high visual literacy were rated as better fulfilling the stated visual design task as such. We argue that future work must therefore consider not just the visual appeal of generated images, but also whether they are genuinely useful for a given function.

Keywords: Text-to-Image · Generative AI · User Study

1 Introduction

Text-to-image (TTI) AI tools, such as MidJourney and DALL-E, are fundamentally changing the traditional practices of visual content creation. Previous research has highlighted the importance of user background in the adoption and effective use of AI technologies [6, 15]. Despite these insights, there remains a gap in understanding precisely how these factors collectively influence user performance when generating images with text-to-image tools.

This paper investigates how factors like visual design education, technical proficiency, and AI literacy influence user performance with TTI tools. We explore this by analyzing how user profiles in terms of Prompt Engineering Literacy, Visual Literacy,

J. Wei et al. (Eds.): HCII 2025, LNCS 16346, pp. 3–13, 2026.
https://doi.org/10.1007/978-3-032-13187-4_1

and AI Literacy have an impact on diverse measures of output evaluation such as general Visual Appeal, degree of Task Fulfillment, and feeling of user Control. We aim to understand how different user groups engage with TTI tools, identify key determinants of success, and provide recommendations for designing more inclusive and effective AI-driven creative tools and improving related education. Specifically, we seek to answer the following research question (RQ): To what extent do visual design expertise, technical knowledge of generative AI, and prompt crafting experience influence the quality of human-AI collaborative work using text-to-image (TTI) tools?

To answer this RQ, we conducted an exploratory study based on 25 users. First, we profiled them according to three literacies: how proficient they are at prompt engineering (Prompt Engineering Literacy, PEL), how experienced they are in visual design (Visual Literacy, VL), and how knowledgeable they are with Generative AI (AI Literacy, AIL). Next, we asked three visual artists at an internationally recognized creative services studio specialized in visual development, to define a visual design task for the participants to complete. These artists rated the participants' generated images in terms of visual appeal (Visual Appeal) and how closely the work fulfills the task given (Task Fulfillment). Lastly, we asked all participants to elaborate on their experience in semi-structured interview where they also rated their level of perceived control on the computational creativity process (Controllability). Our initial results show that visual appeal (VA) is not affected by any of the literacies, likely as TTI tools have been trained on large datasets of visual works that already incorporate visually appealing features. In addition, participants with high visual literacy (VL) seem to consistently produce works that are rated better at task fulfillment (TF). We will discuss the implication of our results on visual design education as well as the design of creativity support tools.

2 Background

2.1 Text-to-Image Generators in Visual Design

Text-to-Image (TTI) generators are generative AI models that use text prompts to create visual data. TTI generation models are a fairly recent and fast-paced development, owing its increase in functionality and reliability to the release of OpenAI's CLIP in 2021 [17], and more recently with diffusion-based TTI generators, such as Midjourney [1]. The potential impacts of Generative AI systems in visual design fields are far-reaching, challenging existing notions and practices around creativity and innovation as designers and artists incorporate generative AI into their creative practice [7, 19, 22, 23]. For instance, TTI models have already been shown to help efficiency in the ideation phases of a design process. Researchers find that the co-creation between AI and designers can accelerate the ideation process while maintaining the same quality level as a human-only design process [3]. Their findings suggest a designer's role as the design originator cannot be replaced, but the process can be sped up by using TTI. At the same time, Oppenlaender [17] raised the question of whether the development of TTI models has made the training and experience of a designer obsolete and that any human can be creative in collaboration with these models.

The Midjourney website states that the company is committed to "expanding the imaginative powers of the human species"[1], and thus exemplifies a widespread rhetoric about adding creativity to humans, and Oppenlaender similarly argues that "With text-to-image generation systems, anybody can create digital images and artworks." [17] But do TTIs really level the playing field, allowing all humans to create art of the same quality, or does the background of users influence the quality of outputs? There is a large body of research on how TTI can enable creativity, but a paucity of research on the role of human competence on the collaboration between humans and AI.

There is a growing amount of research on users of TTI tools, revealing motivations, verbal articulations and relevance of technical knowledge [5, 11, 12, 20, 21]. However, to the best of our knowledge, no research has been done to explicitly examine the impact of users' background (literacies) on how they create visual designs with TTI.

2.2 Text-to-Image Generators in Visual Design

In this paper, we use the term literacy as "the ability to identify, understand, interpret, create, communicate and compute, using printed and written materials associated with varying contexts" [2]. We focus on three relevant forms of literacy that are commonly used in generative AI and TTI research: Visual literacy, AI literacy, and Prompt Engineering literacy.

While the term has a long history [4], we here use Visual literacy with the understanding that visuals are a kind of language, and that a "visually literate person should be able to read and write visual language, i.e., s/he should be able to decode (interpret) visual messages successfully and to encode (compose) meaningful visual messages" [4]. With this in mind, we focus on Visual Literacy as the ability to arrange visual elements within an image, a competency that can be gained through examining the work of masters and working or training within visual design. Elements of visual composition (line, shape, color, brightness, texture, spacing and volume) and principles (balance, symmetry, emphasis, movement, rhythm, unity, proportion) are taught as fundamentals in art and design education [9, 18].

Long and Magerko [12] define AI literacy as "… a set of competencies that enables individuals to critically evaluate AI technologies; communicate and collaborate effectively with AI; and use AI as a tool online, at home, and in the workplace." AI literacy is a term that builds on the concept of Digital literacy, as a precursor and prerequisite for AI literacy, as you need to understand how to use computers before you can begin to understand the scope of AI [12]. AI literacy can be divided into four aspects; to know and understand, to use and apply, to evaluate and create, and ethics [16]. Given this definition of AI literacy, the assumption is that people trained in using or building AI tools have a level of AI literacy.

Finally, Prompt Engineering literacy, or Prompt Literacy is defined by [14]: "Prompt literacy enables anyone to communicate with and direct generative AI systems without needing expertise in computer programming." In theory, AI interfaces have become more user-friendly over time, thus diminishing the need for complex AI knowledge, when interacting with the technology [14]. However, [10] argues that a degree of AI literacy is still required to garner a complete form of Prompt Engineering Literacy, as knowledge and understanding of AI is necessary for being able to guide the AI. We take no sides in this discussion and operationally treat Prompt Engineering literacy independently of AI literacy. We understand Prompt Engineering Literacy as practical experience with the syntax of prompting AI models, including both how to activate the specific affordances of an AI model and, crucially, how the syntax and vocabulary of prompting deviates from natural language.

3   Methods

We used a purposive sampling strategy to select participants possessing two distinct literacies, AI literacy and visual literacy, to ensure a meaningful comparison. We profiled participants for prompt engineering literacy but did not deliberately select for it. We recruited from technical programs (e.g., Computer Science and Data Science) at a technical university and from visual design programs at a design academy in a large Northern European city. Since we seek people with relatively high technical and visual literacy, we only include people in the last year of their bachelor's study or in their Masters'. We used a mix of on-site, online, and snow-ball recruitment. The procedure followed human subject research guidelines at the authors' institutions as well as relevant GDPR rules for data storage.

3.1   Procedure

After informed consent, participants were asked to provide basic demographic information such as age, gender, educational institution where they enrolled and academic majors. Additionally participants completed a survey on their literacies (11 items). We developed these questions based on literature on AI literacy [12] on literature on visual composition [9, 18] and by consulting professors in the two higher education institutions where we recruited participants. All the items in the survey had multiple choice answers and all answers were assigned a score from 1 to 4. Participants were then scored for prompt engineering literacy, visual literacy and AI literacy.

Profiling Prompt Engineering Literacy, Visual Literacy and AI Literacy. Participants were asked about their familiarity with TTI tools such as Dall-E, MidJourney, and Stable Diffusion, how frequently they utilized those tools and how much experience they have with prompt engineering. Next, participants were asked about their visual design experience (e.g., "How many hours per month do you spend drawing/designing or expressing yourself visually?") and visual design knowledge ("How familiar are you with visual composition concepts such as contrast, rhythm, balance, proportion, and harmony?"). Lastly, the participants were asked about their AI literacy, such as "How much knowledge of Artificial Intelligence (AI), including Machine Learning and data science, do you have?" and "How often do you use AI and machine learning-based consumer applications, such as chatbots, image or text generators, etc.?" While we specifically target participants in study programs associated with visual and AI literature respectively, these survey questions can help us identify participants with both literacies.

Visual Design Task. Next, participants were given a design task (Fig. 1) to create an image of a Brutalist medieval castle of their own design. The task brief outlined thematic requirements and provided some inspirations. This task is used by Mood Visuals, a commercial visual studio, as part of their recruitment interviews for new designers. After a brief introduction to the Midjourney tool, each participant was given 30 min to complete the task. They were instructed to use the think aloud protocol as they worked on the tasks. One researcher was present to answer questions and make observations. At the end of the session, each participant chose what they considered to be the best image as their final design.

Self-assessment. Lastly, the participants were also asked to rate their final image, on a 5-point Likert scale, about how close they felt the result was to what they initially had imagined. We refer to this evaluation parameter as Controllability, which is used in connection with the expert evaluation parameters explained below, for the outcome analysis. They also partook in a semi-structured interview about their overall experience and how they felt their technical or visual background affected their approach. The interview analysis is outside the scope of this LBW paper.

Output Evaluation. Each participant submitted a final image to a panel of three artists from the commercial design studio. The artists were asked to evaluate each of the 25 images according to two parameters: Visual Appeal and Task Fulfillment. Visual Appeal refers to the picture's visual attributes. The evaluators were asked to grade the picture from one to five, based on how appealing they thought the picture looked, with one being the lowest and five being the highest possible score. Task Fulfillment refers to how well the evaluators thought the picture fulfilled the given design task ('brutalist medieval castle in disarray'). These two evaluation criteria were supported by self-reported Controllability, which refers to how close the participants felt the result was to what they initially had imagined. The data analysis process will be elaborated upon in the following section.

3.2 Data Analysis

Our research question investigated the impact of the three forms of literacy (Prompt Engineering Literacy, AI Literacy and Visual Literacy) on the evaluation criteria (Visual Appeal, Task Fulfillment and Controllability). We thus analyzed the collected data through quantitative expert evaluation of the final design through correlation analysis. As part of our quantitative expert evaluation, We recruited three professional artists from [BLINDED], the design studio that created the brief utilized in this study. The three domain experts were asked to assess the quality of participants' final designs. The artists did not have any information about the creators of the 25 images to rate, but they were given a description of the two evaluation criteria: Visual Appeal and Task Fulfillment. The three artists independently rated the 25 generated pictures submitted anonymously by the participants, for Visual Appeal and Task Fulfillment on a 5-point Likert Scale. For consistency, the experts were given the following definitions. Visual Appeal: The images should be evaluated in accordance with how the image looks. You may consider things such as composition, perspective, shape language, contrast, color theory, legibility, etc. Task Fulfillment: The images should be evaluated according to how closely they fulfill the brief ("Brutalist medieval castle in disarray"). In order to account for agreement among the artists we calculated the inter-rater reliability with Fleiss' kappa [8] for both Visual Appeal and Task Fulfillment.

Fig. 1. Left: The design brief given to the participants. Users with different backgrounds and literacies were asked to co-create images with a TTI tool following this task; Right: Examples of AI-generated designs by Participants 1, 3, 10, 13, 18, and 22, respectively.

4   Results

To address the research question "Does having a visual design background, technical knowledge on generative AI, and experience in crafting prompts impact the quality of work co-produced with TTI?", we analyzed the effects of Prompt Engineering Literacy, Visual Literacy, and AI Literacy on three outcome variables: Controllability, Aesthetic Appeal, and Task Fulfillment.

Descriptive Statistics. Table 1 summarizes the means and standard deviations of the outcome variables grouped by literacy levels. Across all literacy levels, Task Fulfillment demonstrated the highest variation, while Controllability scores remained relatively consistent.

Table 1. Descriptive Statistics of Outcome Variables by Literacy Levels.

Outcome	Mean	Standard Deviation	Range
Controllability (Self-Report)	3.62	0.51	$[3.0, 4.5]$
Aesthetic Appeal (Experts)	2.45	0.91	$[1.0, 4.0]$
Task Fulfillment (Experts)	2.94	0.76	$[1.5, 4.0]$

Correlation Analysis. The correlation analysis revealed weak relationships between Prompt Engineering Literacy, Visual Literacy, and AI Literacy and the outcome variables. While Visual Literacy showed a positive correlation with Task Fulfillment ($r = 0.35$), the relationships between literacy types and Controllability or Aesthetic Appeal were negligible.

Regression Analysis. We conducted multiple linear regression analyses to evaluate the individual and combined effects of literacy types on the outcomes. The results are summarized in Table 2.

Table 2. Regression Results for Outcome Variables.

Outcome	Predictor	Coefficient (β)	p-value
Controllability	Prompt Eng. Literacy	−0.042	0.623
	Visual Literacy	−0.015	0.772
	AI Literacy	0.061	0.429
Aesthetic Appeal	Prompt Eng. Literacy	0.048	0.572
	Visual Literacy	0.013	0.796
	AI Literacy	−0.073	0.343
Task Fulfillment	Prompt Eng. Literacy	−0.097	0.227
	Visual Literacy	0.136	0.009*
	AI Literacy	−0.061	0.394

$^{*}p < 0.01$

Key Findings. The regression analysis indicated that Visual Literacy was a significant positive predictor of Task Fulfillment ($\beta = 0.136$, $p < 0.01$). Neither Prompt Engineering Literacy nor AI Literacy significantly predicted any of the outcomes. Overall, the results suggest that a background in visual design plays a critical role in achieving higher task fulfillment when co-producing work with TTI, while technical knowledge on AI and prompt crafting experience had minimal impact on the assessed outcomes. In summary, our results suggest that, of these three forms of expertise, only Visual Literacy significantly impacted how well participants' images fulfilled a specific design brief. Specifically, while no clear relationships emerged between any of the three literacies and the images' Visual Appeal or participants' sense of Controllability, high Visual Literacy correlated with producing images that aligned more consistently with the given prompt requirements. Our results suggest that Visual Literacy does not impact how "pretty" an image is (i.e., Visual Appeal), but rather whether it meets the specific functional or thematic requirements (Task Fulfillment). This aligns with the idea that TTI tools, trained on massive collections of visuals, inherently generate aesthetically pleasing images for a wide range of users; however, they do not inherently produce images that satisfy professional or contextual briefs without domain expertise. We also note that AI Literacy and Visual Literacy were moderately negatively correlated, reflecting our sampling strategy, where participants generally hailed from either a technical university or a design academy. This result suggests that, in our small-scale study, few participants possessed deep competencies in both areas. However, in the broader landscape, interdisciplinary training that combines technical and design skills could be pivotal for more advanced or specialized TTI-driven workflows.

5 Discussion

5.1 Participants with High Visual Literacy Produce Images Consistently Rated Higher in Task Fulfillment

It is notable that this study found empirical evidence that can shift the traditional role of visual literacy. Our results shows that visual literacy was not associated with significantly higher Visual Appeal, typically connected to the common understanding of visual literacy. Instead, it was strongly associated with Task Fulfillment. Our results suggest that TTI systems may "level the playing field" in some areas of visual aesthetics, making it relatively straightforward for novices to generate appealing pictures in a single session. Yet, it appears that Visual Literacy uniquely prepares participants to align their outputs with practical objectives, design briefs, or other professional standards. This finding echoes our critique of prior studies that assessed AI-generated images in a vacuum, focusing on color harmony or general creativity [13]. The ability to generate a functionally relevant image—one aligned with a conceptual brief or design specification—may demand deeper domain-specific knowledge than simply toggling style or color settings through text prompts. Our preliminary evidence supports the view that "functionality" is central to real-world value in AI-assisted design tasks.

5.2 The Role of Prompt Engineering and AI Literacy

Our quantitative analysis revealed no significant relationship between Prompt Engineering Literacy or AI Literacy and the three outcome variables (Visual Appeal, Task Fulfillment, and Controllability). This may be partly explained by the rapid skill acquisition we observed during the sessions: participants often experimented, iterated quickly on their prompts, and saw immediate results that guided them toward visually pleasing outcomes. Consequently, the short time frame may not have captured the deeper advantages of extensive AI or prompt-engineering expertise, especially if participants could reach passable or attractive images with only cursory trial-and-error. Additionally, the sophisticated capabilities of TTI tools may minimize the immediate benefit of advanced technical knowledge for simple tasks. However, for more complex or iterative design challenges—such as working through multiple revision cycles or integrating client feedback—we suspect that advanced prompt-engineering skills and a deeper understanding of model mechanics could play a greater role.

5.3 Implications

This study contributes to HCI research by investigating how different literacies (visual, AI, and prompt engineering) affect user interactions and outputs when working with AI tools. Our results suggest that creativity support tools can incorporate adaptive interfaces or guidance systems that identify a user's domain-specific literacy and tailor features or prompts accordingly. For example, a designer with high Visual Literacy but minimal AI knowledge might benefit from more transparent model explanations, while a highly technical user might need on-screen guidance about compositional principles. We also note that users sometimes expressed frustration or confusion when the AI output deviated from their original mental images, underscoring the need for more intuitive feedback loops. In line with prior research, an adaptive interface that nudges or clarifies how certain words and phrases translate into visual outputs could enhance controllability and empower users with varied backgrounds. In terms of visual and technical education, this research shows that TTI tools do not negate the need for visual literacy. Rather in the era of generative AI, design educations should keep focusing on improving Visual Literacy among students to increase their ability to produce images that can fulfill tasks appropriately. At the same time, it may be fruitful to integrate visual literacy training into non-art educational curricula, particularly in technical fields involved in AI system development. Building cross-functional skills could help future developers and engineers understand the end-to-end pipeline of AI-assisted creative processes, leading to more robust and user-centered TTI tools. Educational institutions might consider introducing modules that expose technical students to fundamental elements of visual design or historical art movements, potentially sharpening their ability to guide TTI systems toward targeted outputs. Aligning such curriculum with digital fluency goals can prepare students across disciplines for the increasing prevalence of AI-based collaboration in creative fields.

Finally, our results suggest that Task Fulfillment, rather than raw visual beauty, is a critical dimension of TTI success. Design schools might adapt their projects or curricula to include AI-driven assignments focused on creating images for real-world scenarios (e.g., game concept art, marketing visuals), while technical programs might incorporate design briefs to encourage deeper exploration of how aesthetic or functional requirements translate into textual prompts. Overall, this preliminary study suggests that further investigation is warranted, particularly in more complex, multi-phase design tasks. We encourage future work to examine larger samples, longer iteration cycles, and authentic co-creation contexts where AI Literacy and Prompt Engineering Literacy might reveal a stronger influence on the final outcome.

5.4 Limitations

Our study's multi-method approach—combining think-aloud data, interviews, expert evaluations, and correlation/regression analysis—offers a broad view of TTI usage but also restricts the variety of tasks we could explore. We focused on a single visual brief (a brutalist medieval castle) within a short session and used only one TTI platform (Midjourney). As a result, the findings may not generalize to different briefs, extended creative workflows, or other platforms with distinct interfaces and features. Furthermore, while Spearman's correlation and regression analyses yielded insights into relationships among literacies, linguistic usage, and evaluation metrics, these techniques might overlook complex interdependencies or confounding variables. Future work could examine multiple TTI tools, adopt more iterative and extended design scenarios, and explore advanced methods such as structural equation modeling to capture the nuanced ways each literacy affects task-oriented outcomes.

6 Conclusion and Future Work

In this paper, we conducted a preliminary, exploratory study to investigate how Visual Literacy, AI Literacy, and Prompt Engineering Literacy influence the creation of images using text-to-image (TTI) tools. We extended existing work on the use of TTIs by examining how AI Literacy, Prompt Engineering Literacy, and Visual Literacy affect a visual design task. Our findings indicate that TTI outputs should not be judged solely by aesthetic qualities; rather, they must be considered in relation to their intended purpose. Specifically, while Visual Literacy showed no clear link to higher visual appeal, it correlated positively with better fulfillment of the design brief—highlighting that images serve concrete functions and must be context-appropriate. Based on this preliminary study, our future work will include a broader survey to corroborate these findings across different user populations. We will also expand the scope of design tasks, incorporate iterative feedback, and compare multiple TTI platforms. Through these steps, we aim to deepen our understanding of how different literacies influence outcomes in more complex creative scenarios, ultimately guiding the development of TTI tools and practices that balance aesthetic appeal with functional alignment.

References

1. Midjourney (2024). https://www.midjourney.com/home
2. UNESCO Literacy definition (2024). https://uis.unesco.org/node/3079547
3. Ardhianto, P., Nababan, R.S.: Artificial intelligence approach in visual design ideation process, pp. 112–117 (2023). https://doi.org/10.2991/978-2-38476-100-5_17
4. Avgerinou, M., Ericson, J.: A review of the concept of visual literacy. Br. J. Educ. Technol. **28**(4), 280–291 (1997). https://doi.org/10.1111/1467-8535.00035
5. Chang, M.: The prompt artists. In: proceedings of the 15th Conference on Creativity and Cognition (Virtual Event, USA) (C&C '23), pp. 75–87. Association for Computing Machinery, New York, NY, USA (2023). https://doi.org/10.1145/3591196.3593515
6. Druga, S., Otero, N., Ko, A.J.: The landscape of teaching resources for AI education. In: Proceedings of the 27th ACM Conference on Innovation and Technology in Computer Science Education, vol. 1 (Dublin, Ireland) (ITiCSE 2022), pp. 96–102. Association for Computing Machinery, New York, NY, USA (2022). https://doi.org/10.1145/3502718.3524782
7. Feuerriegel, S., Hartmann, J., Janiesch, C., Zschech, P.: Generative AI. SSRN Electron. J. (2023). https://doi.org/10.2139/ssrn.4443189
8. Fleiss, J.L., Levin, B., Paik, M.C.: Statistical Methods for Rates and Proportions. Wiley (2004). https://books.google.dk/books?id=a5LwdxF2d10C
9. Gardner, H.: Art through the Ages. Harcourt Brace Jovanovich (1970)
10. Knoth, N., Tolzin, A., Janson, A., Leimeister, J.M.: AI literacy and its implications for prompt engineering strategies. Comput. Edu. Artif. Intell. **6**(2024), 100225 (2024). https://doi.org/10.1016/j.caeai.2024.100225
11. Lin, P.-Y., et al.: Text-to-image AI as a catalyst for semantic convergence in creative collaborations. In: Proceedings of the 2024 ACM Designing Interactive Systems Conference (Copenhagen, Denmark) (DIS 2024), pp. 2753–2767. Association for Computing Machinery, New York, NY, USA (2024). https://doi.org/10.1145/3643834.3661543
12. Long, D., Magerko, B.: What is AI literacy? Competencies and design considerations. In: Proceedings of the 2020 CHI Conference on Human Factors in Computing Systems (Honolulu, HI, USA) (CHI 2020), pp. 1–16. Association for Computing Machinery, New York, NY, USA (2020). https://doi.org/10.1145/3313831.3376727

13. Lyu, Y., Wang, X., Lin, R., Wu, J.: Communication in human–AI co-creation: perceptual analysis of paintings generated by text-to-image system. Appl. Sci. **12**, 2222 (2022). 11312. https://doi.org/10.3390/app122211312
14. Maloy, R., Gattupalli, S.: Prompt Literacy. EdTechnica (2024). https://doi.org/10.59668/371.14442
15. Myers, C.M., Furqan, A., Zhu, J.: The impact of user characteristics and preferences on performance with an unfamiliar voice user interface. In: Proceedings of the 2019 CHI Conference on Human Factors in Computing Systems, pp. 1–9 (2019)
16. Ng, D.T.K., Leung, J.K.L., Chu, S.K.W., Qiao, M.S.: Conceptualizing AI literacy: an exploratory review. Comput. Educ. Artif. Intell. **2**(2021), 100041 (2021). https://doi.org/10.1016/j.caeai.2021.100041
17. Oppenlaender, J.: The creativity of text-to-image generation. In: Proceedings of the 25th International Academic Mindtrek Conference (Tampere, Finland) (Academic Mindtrek 2022), 192–202. Association for Computing Machinery, New York, NY, USA (2022). https://doi.org/10.1145/3569219.3569352
18. Ruskin, J.: The Elements of Drawing. Smith, Elder & Co (1857)
19. Sivertsen, C., Salimbeni, G., Løvlie, A.S., Benford, S.D., Zhu, J.: Machine learning processes as sources of ambiguity: insights from AI art. In: Proceedings of the CHI Conference on Human Factors in Computing Systems, pp. 1–14 (2024)
20. Van Der Maden, W., et al.: Death of the design researcher? Creating knowledge resources for designers using generative AI. In: Companion Publication of the 2024 ACM Designing Interactive Systems Conference, pp. 396–400 (2024)
21. Van Der Maden, W., et al.: Towards a design (research) framework with generative AI. In: Companion Publication of the 2023 ACM Designing Interactive Systems Conference, pp. 107–109 (2023)
22. Wadinambiarachchi, S., Kelly, R.M., Pareek, S., Zhou, Q., Velloso, E.: The effects of generative AI on design fixation and divergent thinking. In: Proceedings of the CHI Conference on Human Factors in Computing Systems, pp. 1–18 (2024)
23. Zhu, J., Liapis, A., Risi, S., Bidarra, R., Michael Youngblood, G.: Explainable AI for designers: a human-centered perspective on mixed-initiative co-creation. In: 2018 IEEE Conference on Computational Intelligence and Games (CIG), pp. 1–8. IEEE (2018)

Generative Artificial Intelligence in Adorable Characters Design and Application

Xinrong Cao[✉]

Hubei University of Technology, Wuhan 430068, Hubei, China
1527966108@qq.com

Abstract. This study aims to solve the problems of high threshold and difficult to unify the style of traditional budding character design with the help of generative artificial intelligence (generative AI), to meet the demand for personalized creation, and to promote cross-disciplinary integration and cultural dissemination. The study adopts AI models based on Generative Adversarial Network (GAN) and Variable Autocoder (VAE), uses stable diffusion as a tool to generate moe character images; classifies and encodes moe elements according to manifestation, environment, and spiritual elements, and decodes them through quantitative research and user analysis; and conducts questionnaire surveys to obtain the needs of the group of people aged between 15 and 40. The research results are verified by two groups of design practice, one is generative artificial intelligence assisting manual optimization to meet the demand of personalized design, and the other is generative artificial intelligence assisting cross-cultural fusion design, both of which have achieved good results. The study shows that generative AI can efficiently generate various budding characters, optimize the details by combining human-computer collaboration, and promote design standardization and innovation. With the development of technology, generative AI will play a greater role in the field of creative design, helping design to personalization and diversification, and injecting new momentum into the development of cultural industry.

Keyword: generative artificial intelligence · budding character design · human-computer collaboration

1 Introduction

In recent years, the rapid development of secondary culture in the global youth groups, of which the moe character as an important part, with the lovely appearance and emotional expression by a wide range of favorite, especially the young group of such character image is extremely sought after, many commercial brands or cultural publicity want to attract young blood, will choose to design a lovely image or linkage with the secondary characters, and even many Even many young people want to design their own cute characters. However, the traditional moe character design process requires high artistic skills, which makes it difficult for many people to participate in the creation of the moe image design effect is difficult to control, the design results are unsatisfactory, but not to

J. Wei et al. (Eds.): HCII 2025, LNCS 16346, pp. 14–32, 2026.
https://doi.org/10.1007/978-3-032-13187-4_2

achieve the effect of "moe" to attract people. But with the addition of artificial intelligence technology, provides a new possibility to solve this series of problems. Generative AI takes advantage of AI technology to help designers provide design inspiration, improve design efficiency and quality of results, and reduce repetitive and ineffective processes in the design process, as well as to help the public generate character images that meet the moe style in a low-threshold way, and optimize and personalize the design on this basis. The purpose of this paper is to explore how to apply generative AI technology to moe character design, reduce the design threshold, improve efficiency, and promote design standardization to meet the growing demand for personalized creation.

2 Summarize

2.1 The Rise of Moe Culture and Moe Characters

Moe characters are popular today, and the development of "moe culture" is one of the reasons why they are so popular. Moe culture is a cultural phenomenon derived from the Japanese otaku culture [1], which mostly manifests itself in the form of infantilization and cuteness, and is able to give people a sense of relaxation and comfort from the visual point of view. In recent years, it has been widely spread around the world, especially in the era of high pressure and fast-paced information explosion, contemporary youth groups are no longer satisfied with the basic physiological needs such as food, clothing and warmth, but to seek a higher spiritual level of fulfillment [2], and this kind of culture has also become one of their spiritual support. In the current social development, the budding character has become the main spread and expression of budding culture, budding character design by enlarging the character's eyes, exaggerated expression and body proportion and other appearance characteristics, to create a unique visual effect and emotional expression, this visual design can arouse the audience's desire for protection and sense of affinity, making the character more affinity and sense of emotional immersion.

2.2 The Cultural Carrier and Cultural Communication Role of Moe Characters

In the age of information technology, "cute culture" can be prosperous development, become a kind of popular culture, and penetrate into all aspects of people's lives, accepted and recognized by the global market, affecting people's consumption, lifestyle, aesthetic orientation and so on, people are willing to pay for "cute", thus gradually extending the "cute economy" [2]. Nowadays, it is precisely with this universal love for moe image, more and more commercial brands, enterprises, cultural heritage, especially museums and cultural halls around the world are inclined to moe image design for their own products or cultures, to draw the distance between their own cultures and the general public, and even with the famous moe character linkage, to carry out the cross-cultural or cross-field design, outputs, but not limited to Blind boxes, cultural creations and other physical commodities [3], in order to pursue the continuation of their own development and cultural dissemination in society. Moe characters have become an extremely popular vehicle for cultural dissemination, through the way of cultural "moe" for cross-border dissemination.

2.3 Generative Artificial Intelligence Techniques

Ian Goodfellow says that Generative Artificial Intelligence (GenAI) models are able to "go beyond what they've seen before and create something new", thus giving GenAI its etymological meaning of generativity: the ability to produce or create something new [4]. Generative Artificial Intelligence (Generative AI) refers to the ability to generate new content through deep learning models, specifically techniques such as Generative Adversarial Networks (GANs) and Variable Auto-Encoders (VAEs). In the field of image generation, GANs are capable of generating highly realistic and creative images, while VAEs are capable of generating new samples in the latent space. The emergence of generative AI has enabled the creative industry to accelerate the creative process with machine-generated content, especially in the art and design field, where generative AI tools represented by Midjourney and Stable Diffusion can help designers to complete their designs quickly, with high precision and repeatability [5], and by inputting textual cues or images, the AI is By inputting text prompts or images, AI is able to quickly process and analyze huge amounts of data, as well as automatically extract features and patterns in the data, thus realizing the automated creation of image generation art [6]. This allows the average user to train or use a specific style of model, saving time and resources, while obtaining satisfactory results.

2.4 Thresholds and the Need for Standardization in the Design Field

Despite the wide appeal of moe characters in terms of visual presentation, the traditional design process requires a high level of skill. Not only do designers need to have certain drawing skills, but they also need to master artistic elements such as color matching and proportion control, making it difficult for ordinary users to independently complete moe-ified character designs that meet standards. With the development of secondary culture, more and more non-professional designers want to participate in it, and personally experience the process of the birth of this culture or character, there is also a demand for personalized design of their own moe character. Therefore, lowering the threshold of design has become an urgent problem. At the same time, the style of moe character design has not been standardized, and there are big differences in the understanding and creation of different designers. How to standardize the design process through technical means and form a unified design paradigm to ensure the quality and consistency of design works is also an urgent problem in the current design field [7].

3   Methodology

This study aims to explore how generative AI technology can be applied to the design process of budding characters, with a view to lowering the design threshold, improving efficiency and standardizing the design process. To this end, this paper proposes a generative AI-based moe character design process, and systematically analyzes how generative AI assists designers to complete character creation through specific operational processes and technical implementations. Specific methods include character generation, screening, optimization and personalized design, and ultimately combining manual design with generative AI technology to achieve more standardized and personalized character design.

3.1 A Generative Artificial Intelligence-Based Model for Budding Character Design

In the process of budding character design, the core advantage of generative AI technology lies in its ability to quickly generate a large number of images that meet the design requirements based on the specific parameters input [8]. For this reason, this study adopts an AI generative model based on Generative Adversarial Networks (GAN) and Variational Autocoder (VAE), and selects stable diffusion as the generative tool. By using the existing generative AI model, we control and record the changes of cue words and parameters, and train and generate character images with "cute" features, including exaggerated facial features, large eyes, and delicate body proportions (see Fig. 1).

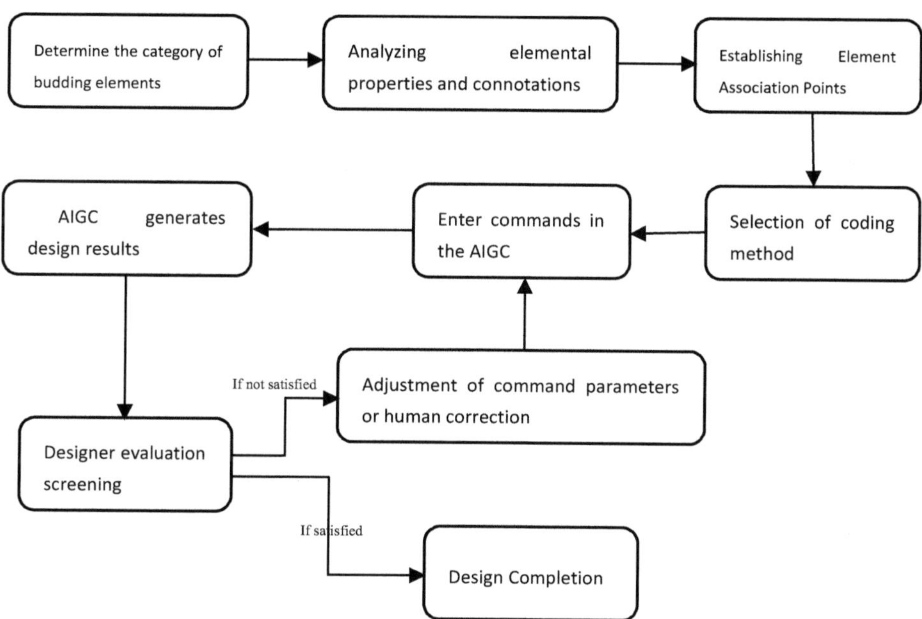

Fig. 1. AIGC-based budding character design model.

3.2 Sprouting Element Analysis and Coding

In order to better and more accurately help designers to complete the design of moe characters, designers can establish the connection between different elements through the symbolic characteristics of moe elements, encode the element symbols to form the association points [9], and then use generative artificial intelligence to express the moe elements, and convey the meaning of moe through the intermediate element symbols.

Through the research and analysis of a large number of moe characters and related works, the genes of the elements that can express the characteristics of moe are categorized according to the phenomenal elements, environmental elements and spiritual elements. Phenomenal elements mainly refer to the appearance of the character, i.e. head-to-body ratio, facial features, character clothing, etc. Environmental elements refer to the environment and atmosphere in which the character is located, i.e. scene, region, occasion, etc. Spiritual elements only refer to the character's own setting, i.e. spiritual core, character, psychological activities, etc. Among them, manifestation elements are the first to be discovered by people and are also the first to be analyzed by people. Among them, the visual elements are the first to be discovered by people, and also the most easy to be received by people, which can bring the most intuitive feeling to people, while the environmental and spiritual elements are used to assist the expression of the character, or to deepen the depth and dimension of the expression of the budding effect, which usually requires more detailed design, as well as a certain degree of interest and comprehension ability of the audience to understand and feel.

In order to standardize the moe character design paradigm and help designers and enthusiasts to design satisfactory moe character images more quickly, conveniently and accurately, it is necessary to grasp the accuracy of the commands inputted into the generative AI. Because the AI's understanding of vocabulary is not exactly the same as that of human beings, different regions, different ages, and different occupational groups may have different understandings of the same thing, and due to such comprehension bias, it may also lead to errors in the result of moeing generation. Therefore, it is necessary to consider the error and effectiveness of human-computer dialogues in the processing of semantic vocabulary in the early stage [9], to find the balance and correlation points in the middle, and to let AI assist in the understanding of meaning and design.

In order to correspond to the different elemental types of expression mentioned above, when coding the moe-ized character elements, the various types of features were also coded in the manifestation category, environment category and spirit category as the base categories (see Fig. 2). The genes of the elements covered by the manifestation category, i.e. external expression, can be linked with the theme of character design, styling, color, culture, etc., for example, the proportion of the body with a big head and a small body, exaggerated and enlarged eyes, cute clothes, bright colors and expressive movements, etc.; The genes covered by the environment category, i.e. the shaping of the environmental atmosphere, for example, unrealistic background settings, idealized dream space, etc.; The genes covered by the spirit category, i.e. internal settings, can be linked with the spiritual connotation of the character and the moral of the character setting, for example, timid, lively, quiet character personality, inner activities in contrast to the appearance, etc. The genes covered by the spiritual category are the internal settings, which can be linked to the spiritual connotation of the character and the moral of the character's setting, such as timid, lively, quiet and other character personalities, and the inner activities that are in contrast with the appearance. During the design process, elements can be extracted from the various types of codes and decoded by means of transformation and reconstruction [9] (Table 1).

Table 1. Coding of budding elements.

Classification of budding elements	Specific categories	connection point	coding method
type of imaging (e.g. movie)	Face & Torso	Sense of loveliness, affinity	Emphasize and magnify eye proportions, such as increasing eye size, brightness and luster
		Innocent, childish	Rounding of the facial lines, softer contours, less angularity, etc.
		Soft and cuddly	Simplify and strengthen curves, outline the body with smooth curves, avoid hard turns, etc.
	props	Sweet and girly	Add decorative elements and change the style, such as increasing the number of bows, using special materials or designing unique shapes, etc.
		Fantasy, mystery	Unique shapes, colors, mysterious symbols or luminous effects, etc.
		Childhood, Companionship	Refine the animal image, choose soft materials, highlight the animal's cute features, enhance the details, etc.
psychiatric	Personality and psychology	Dynamism, Vitality	Design lively movements and expressions, such as jumping and cheering movements, with laughter and surprise expressions
		A sense of ambivalence, a sense of contrast	Combination of cold expressions and caring behaviors, such as outwardly dismissive but secretly helpful, verbal tongue-in-cheek, etc.
		Warm, healing	Design soft gestures and gentle expressions, such as gentle touch, smile, eye concern, etc.
environmental category	Environmental settings	Mysterious, fantasy atmosphere	Build the scene, render the fantasy atmosphere, add exotic plants, mysterious light and shadow effects, etc.

(continued)

Table 1. (*continued*)

Classification of budding elements	Specific categories	connection point	coding method
		Vast, romantic mood	Highlight the sense of vastness and add romantic elements such as shooting stars, constellation patterns, and soft halos
		Sweet, cozy feeling	Use sweet colors and rich detail decorations, such as colorful candies and cute pastry shape decorations

3.3 Decoding and User Analysis of Budding Elements Based on Quantitative Research

The concept of moe is both an abstract word and a figurative word, and nowadays people's understanding of moe can even be directly translated as cute, and everyone's understanding and acceptance of "moe" is different. At present, the audience of moe characters is mainly concentrated in the young group of 15–40 years old. By conducting questionnaire surveys on online social platforms and offline areas with a high concentration of moe characters, such as modern shopping malls and subcultural commercial streets, we can obtain the understanding of the characteristics of this type of users for the moe characters, their acceptance level and their usage needs (see Table 2), so as to facilitate a more accurate coding and decoding of the moe characters and the elements of moe. Coding and decoding for the budding characters and budding elements more accurately. Through users' evaluations, designers can accurately identify which design elements are most capable of arousing the emotional resonance of the audience, and based on this, they can make further and finer adjustments to the characteristics of the various elements of the characters. The questionnaires were distributed and recovered 227 copies; 193 copies were valid questionnaires. The Cronbach's α reliability analysis showed that the overall α value of the questionnaire survey was 0.716; the validity validation through the KMO and Bartlett's test showed that the KMO value of the questionnaire survey as a whole was 0.761, and the corresponding p-value of the Bartlett's test of sphericity was 0, which indicated that the questionnaire has a better reliability and validity, and can be used as the basis for the design of the character. The overall KMO value of the questionnaire was 0.761 and the P value corresponding to Bartlett's sphericity test was 0, indicating that the questionnaire has good reliability and validity, and can be used as a source of data for the research and analysis (see Table 3).

Table 2. Questionnaire.

Research Requirements	Serial Number	Questionnaire Items
Basic Information	1	What is your age?
	2	Have you ever been exposed to secondary culture (such as anime, games, manga, etc.)?
Investigation on the Cognition of Adorable Characters	3	What is your level of acceptance of Adorable Characters?
	4	How much do you like Adorable Characters?
	5	Do you understand Adorable Characters and related character designs?
	6	What do you think is the main difference between Adorable Characters and ordinary characters?
	7	In which aspects does your understanding of Adorable Characters mainly focus?
	8	What methods do you mainly use to deepen your understanding of Adorable Characters?
	9	What value do you think Adorable Characters can bring to you?
Investigation on the Cognition of AIGC	10	Do you know about the application of artificial intelligence in the design field?
	11	What is your level of acceptance of design works (such as images, copywriting, etc.) generated by artificial intelligence?
Investigation on the Acceptance and Demand of Adorable Characters	12	Have you ever had the idea or experience of creating your own characters?
	13	What feelings do you have when you see Adorable Characters?
	14	Through what channels do you usually come into contact with Adorable Characters?
	15	Have you ever purchased peripheral products related to Adorable Characters?

(*continued*)

Table 2. (*continued*)

Research Requirements	Serial Number	Questionnaire Items
	16	What is the frequency of your purchase of peripheral products related to Adorable Characters?
	17	Which type of Adorable Characters do you prefer?
	18	In which fields do you think Adorable Characters can be applied?
Investigation on the Integrated Design and Application of Adorable Characters	19	What will you do when you see Adorable Characters promoting a certain brand or culture?
	20	If you know about the application of artificial intelligence in the design field, what advantages do you think it has when applied to the design of Adorable Characters?
	21	Are you willing to pay for activities related to Adorable Characters with local characteristics or cultural symbols?
	22	What positive impacts do you think Adorable Characters integrated with local characteristics or cultural symbols may have?
	23	What kind of Adorable Characters will attract your attention during the promotion or dissemination process?
	24	Do you pay attention to copyright issues of works, including the copyright of Adorable Characters?
	25	If there are voting or opinion - soliciting activities for the design of Adorable Characters, will you participate?
	26	What do you think are the shortcomings of common Adorable Characters at present?
	27	What expectations do you have for the future development of Adorable Characters?

Table 3. Reliability analysis.

Test Indicators	Values	Value Analysis
Cronbach α	0.716	Indicates good reliability
KMO Measure of Sampling Adequacy	0.761	Indicates good suitability
Significance (P) of Bartlett's Test of Sphericity	0.00	Indicates good significance

Through analyzing the results of the questionnaire, it is concluded that most of the groups have been exposed to the secondary culture, and have a higher degree of acceptance of the appearance and application of moe characters, and express their love for moe characters; among these groups, most of the people said that their understanding of moe characters focuses on the appearance of the characters, such as "big eyes", "exaggerated expressions", "cute little people" and other descriptions, only a small number of people will receive cute expression of the character's environment and the character's spiritual level. In the questionnaire survey, more than half of the people believe that AI can assist in the design of budding characters, which mainly saves creation time, and this group of people said that they have the need to create personalized characters, and they can accept the character images created by generative AI; in the questionnaire survey, more than half of the groups believe that the emergence of budding characters can bring them closer to themselves, and effectively disseminate the cultural connotations, especially when using the design of local characteristics or cultural symbols, and are willing to pay for the publicity of this kind of characters.

From the survey results, it is clear that budding characters are sought after by a certain group of people in society, and there will be a certain demand for their design and application, and generative AI techniques do have a greater potential in budding character design, especially in terms of improving design efficiency and enhancing personalization.

4 Design Practice

In order to further improve and verify the feasibility and efficiency of the application of generative artificial intelligence re-dreaming character design, and to reduce the one-sidedness of the experiment, this practice is divided into two groups: (1) Based on the design requirements, the elemental genes are extracted and decoded first, and then imported into the generative artificial intelligence to give commands, and the designers sift and re-process the generation results and modify the cue words, and repeat the generation and design process until the results meet the requirements. (2) According to the design requirements, complete the preliminary design of the character, draw sketches or line drawings, and then decode and extract the corresponding elements and keywords from the element genes according to the requirements, and give them to the generative AI for coloring and secondary design, and the designer screens, modifies, and adjusts the cue words in the generated images to generate them again, and repeat the process until the result meets the requirements.

4.1 User Requirements Decoding and Analysis

In order to verify the feasibility of generative artificial intelligence intervention in the design of budding roles, before decoding, taking into account the different acceptance and application understanding of budding roles in the hands, in order to make the design and application of such roles closer to reality, and to broaden the design and application routes of budding roles, the practice simulates the personalized needs of the mass of users for individual budding roles in practice (1), and generates personalized designs to meet the specific needs and expectations of the users according to their needs and preferences by analyzing and understanding user data [10].

Practice (2) chooses to take cultural communication as the starting point for cross-field integration, using the character in the game Tomorrow's Ark as the design prototype, integrating traditional Chinese porcelain culture, cross-border integration between the game field and the cultural field, realizing that through the budding character design to drive the young group to pay attention to the traditional culture, which not only improves the efficiency of cultural dissemination, but also promotes the game's popularity and acceptance in the social field, and realizes a Win-win linkage. For this design goal, practice (2) selected the generative artificial intelligence software "stable diffusion" for image generation, the object of practice is the character "Shu" with Chinese elements in the game, the cultural source is porcelain culture, and the porcelain produced by the porcelain of the Qing Dynasty in ancient China is chosen "Chrysanthemum Plate with Spring Swallows in Pastel Color".

4.2 Design Process

Personalized Design Practices Assisted by Generative Artificial Intelligence. In this design practice, in order to simulate the non-professional groups to meet their own needs for the budding characters, we do not make too many constraints on the generation of characters, and relax the scope of the depiction, mainly through the coding and decoding of budding elements as well as the combination of the majority of the population's understanding of the budding characters and the emotional intention to complete the extraction of the prompt words. Inputting the cue words into the textual diagram section of stable diffusion, several preliminary character sketches are generated according to the input instructions, and these sketches should cover the basic features of the character, such as facial features, body proportions, and clothing design. After several adjustments to the prompts and several iterations, the ones that meet the requirements are selected and saved. After the design tone of the budding character is stabilized, the designer generates preliminary sketches through artificial intelligence and then makes further manual adjustments, especially in the optimization of the character's facial expression, clothing details, emotional expression and setting. This stage belongs to the key stage of artificial optimization, which focuses on enhancing the personalized characteristics and emotional expression of the character design to ensure that the character not only meets the budding design standard visually, but also accurately conveys the emotional demands of the target audience.

It can be seen from all the previous experiments, generative AI still lacks in understanding the semantics and spiritual level of understanding and expression, but this does not prevent generative AI from being able to provide a basis for creation for professional or non-professional groups. After several adjustments and iterations of the cue words, it was able to successfully obtain characters that met the needs of the budding design (see Table 4). This practice Through this model of human-computer collaboration, the AIGC provides the basis for the creation of the designers, while the designers inject personalization and emotional depth to ensure that the final design is emotionally rich and visually appealing.

Table 4. Practice (1) design flow.

Number of AIGC generation	clue	Results generated and screened
initial requirement	a cute girl with pink double ponytail hair, wearing a dress, standing on a flower circle	
1st	Human, cute anime character with big sparkling eyes, small round face, happy smile, three heads, wearing a pink dress with lace and ribbon trim around the edges of the dress, multiple bows on the dress, pink hair......	
3rd	...Wearing a pink and blue dress with lace and ribbon trim around the edges of the dress, which has many different colored bows, pink hair with a double ponytail hairstyle with a cute blue bow on top, she strikes a very playful pose...	
8th	...Pink hair in a double ponytail hairstyle with a cute blue bow on top, she is in a very playful pose with one hand up in greeting with a happy expression, the background should be a dreamy pink color, bright sunshine, standing on a field of flowers...	
10th	...multiple yellow bows on the skirt, and pink hair in a double ponytail hairstyle with a cute blue bow on top, she poses playfully with one hand raised, the sun shines brightly, and a variety of flowers grow around the figure's feet...	

Personalized Design Practices Assisted by Generative Artificial Intelligence. In the design, first focusing on the extraction of cultural relics and culture, first extract the cultural elements in the "pastel Spring Swallow Chrysanthemum Plate", and then draw them in the form of line drawings. Then, based on the results of quantitative analysis and the decoding of the elements that meet the target requirements, the corresponding cue words are input into the stable diffusion to give instructions. In addition to controlling the overall style of the model used and the cue words that express the core needs of the character, the cue words that express the details and externalize the spiritual connotation of the generated character will be based on the results of the generation and human modification during the design process, and will be continuously modified during the iterative generation process.

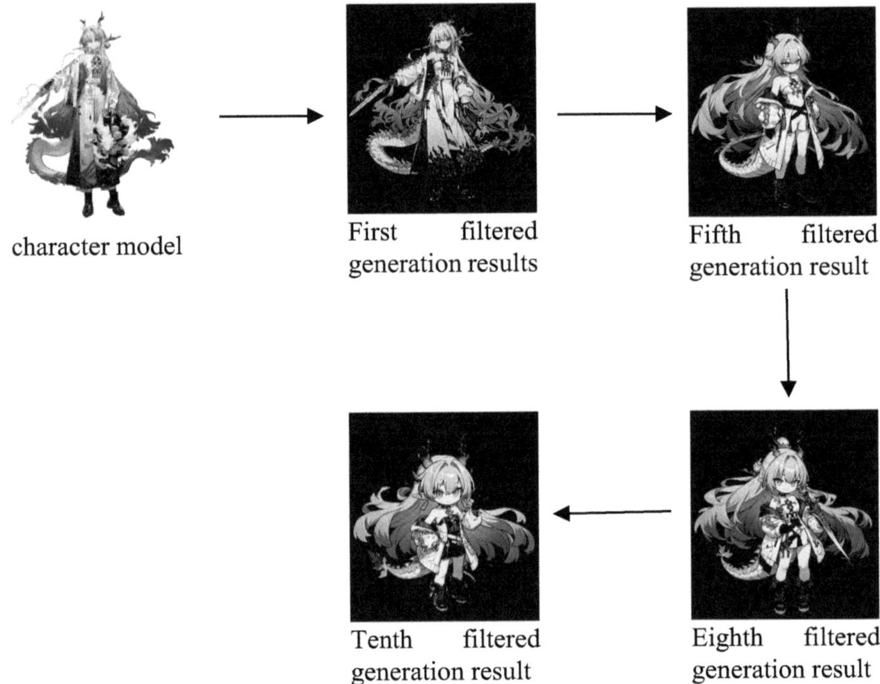

Fig. 2. The process of budding adult human character archetypes.

In the design process, in order to express the Chinese porcelain culture represented by the "Pastel Spring Swallow Chrysanthemum Plate", which mainly expresses the unique and beautiful patterns of Chinese porcelain, the Spring Swallow, Lotus Leaf, Lotus Flower, and Green Wave in the plate are used as the visual elements mainly converted from the abstract cultural connotations. In stable diffusion, based on the genes of the budding character elements that have been sorted out previously, the design requirements are extracted from the three element codes mentioned above and decoded into the cue words, and the initial stand-up drawings of the game characters are put into the Text-to-image plate, and then the corresponding weights, sampling methods, iteration steps and other data are selected to budding the game characters in accordance with the style characteristics. In order to improve the design efficiency and diversity of the generation results, the generation batch is set to "3", the number of single batch is "1", and a number of generation is carried out to obtain the budding character image that meets the requirements, and then select one of them (see Fig. 2), add the figurative elements of the selected porcelain to carry out the secondary design, and draw it to meet the requirements. The second design is drawn into a line drawing that meets the requirements. The next step in the Image-to-image plate, through the adjustment of scripts, models, and algorithms, the integration of porcelain elements of the character image in the light and shadow and color filling and adjustment, and finally generate the integration of the "pastel spring swallows chrysanthemum plate" figurative elements of the budding character "Shu" (see Fig. 3).

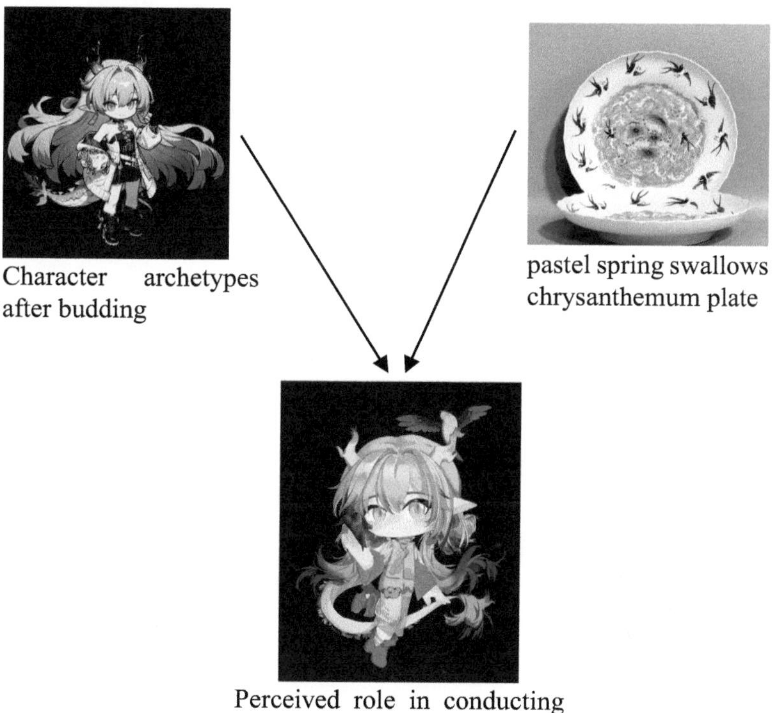

Character   archetypes after budding

pastel spring swallows chrysanthemum plate

Perceived role in conducting preliminary design

Fig. 3. Preliminary Design of AIGC-based Human Roles.

When using stable diffusion for image design and generation, the designer should focus on the genetic characteristics of the budding character, and constantly adjust the details of the cue words of the element encoding, the number of iterative steps, and other details, and the additional design elements should also be consistent with the concept of budding. Through the joint creation of the designer and the generative AI, the designed character meets the conceptual requirements of the budding image in appearance, and the integrated porcelain elements are also smoothly integrated into the image, which confirms the feasibility and efficiency of the above budding character design logic, the encoded design elements, and the generative AI in assisting the design work, improving the design efficiency and accuracy of the target (see Table 5).

Table 5. Generative practice processes based on human design.

Number of AIGC generation	clue	Results generated and screened
Man-made preliminary design		
1st	Chinese style, dress with lotus pattern, smilling, facing the audience, two swallows……	
3rd	Single, cute anime character, pointy ears, antlers, long hair, 1 girl, low double ponytail pompadour, pink blouse with lotus flower and lotus leaf pattern, green pants with green shoes, dragon's horn held up in one hand, two swallows, one standing on the hand, one on the horn……	
6th	…pointy ears, dragon's horns, long hair, gradient color of yellow and Klein blue at the end of her hair, horns of the same color as her hair, swallow, pink top with lotus flower and lotus leaf pattern, long top, long top with tulle pants, full body, simple background, transparent background…	
10th	…New modern chinoiserie, pink lotus flower and lotus leaf pattern top, long top, tulle texture pants, green pants, green shoes, white and gray dragon tail, dragon horns, dragon tail, one hand raised, green eyes looking at the audience, full body, simple background, transparent background…	

4.3 Evaluation of Practical Effect

In order to verify whether the quality of the budding character design results obtained after the addition of this generative artificial intelligence to the design process can meet the different needs of people for budding characters. After the completion of the design, the design results were compiled into a questionnaire, which was widely distributed to the group of 15 to 40 years old through both online and offline methods, taking this kind of youth group as the test sample to evaluate the satisfaction of the results of this cute character design. The questionnaire consisted of 11 questions, focusing on the visual effect, cultural and personalized expression, and AI acceptance, of which visual expression contained 3 questions, cultural and personalized expression contained 3 questions, and AI acceptance contained 3 questions. The data measurement is based on the PAST (Product Satisfaction) value. On the basis of the above questions, the tenth and eleventh questions were open-ended questions to collect feedback. The questionnaire was based on a 5-point scale, and the respondents rated the above two budding character designs on five levels, from very dissatisfied to satisfied, according to their own feelings.

This test firstly selected the first 9 questions to analyze the reliability and validity of the data, the analysis results can be concluded that the correlation index of each level is greater than 0.4, the Cronbach's α coefficient of the above three aspects are greater than 0.8, the α coefficients of the items that have been deleted did not exceed the Cronbach's α coefficient, and the final total Cronbach's α coefficient is 0.933. Secondly, the KMO value of this data test is 0.945 greater than 0.8, and the P value of Bartlett sphericity test is 0.00. KMO value of this data test is 0.945 which is greater than 0.8, and the P value of Bartlett's test of sphericity is 0.00, which indicates that the collected data have good reliability and validity (see Fig. 4). The P-value of Bartlett's test of sphericity is 0.00, indicating that the collected data have good reliability and validity (see Table 7). By organizing and analyzing the data in this case, it can be concluded that the target group's satisfaction with the two munchkins designed using generative AI was 74% in terms of clarity of visual expression, 69% in terms of cultural and personalized expression, and 69% in terms of the quality of the AI design (see Fig. 4). The final results show that the munchkins designed with the assistance of generative AI meet the aesthetic needs of the public, and the addition of generative AI not only promotes the standardization of the munchkin design process, improves the efficiency and quality of character design, and realizes the pursuit of personalization, but also prompts the munchkins to become a kind of cultural carrier, and realizes the function of cross-domain and cross-cultural communication and exchange (Table 6).

Table 6. Cronbach's reliability analysis

Design of questions for this survey on satisfaction with different aspects of moe characters	Correction term total correlation	Term deleted α coefficients	Cronbach α for the three dimensions	Cronbach α
I am satisfied with the design of the moe character	0.775	0.924	0.816	0.933

(continued)

Table 6. (continued)

Design of questions for this survey on satisfaction with different aspects of moe characters	Correction term total correlation	Term deleted α coefficients	Cronbach α for the three dimensions	Cronbach α
I think the design of the moe character is in line with my knowledge of moe characters	0.769	0.924		
I think the design of the moe character visually meets my aesthetics or expectations	0.709	0.928		
I think the moe character has a certain function of responding to cultural connotations or characteristics	0.700	0.928	0.813	
I can feel certain cultural elements or characteristics in this design	0.785	0.923		
I think that the design of the moe character has its own individual characteristics and can be distinguished from other characters	0.780	0.924		
I think generative AI is positively helpful for character design	0.764	0.925	0.816	

(continued)

Table 6. (*continued*)

Design of questions for this survey on satisfaction with different aspects of moe characters	Correction term total correlation	Term deleted α coefficients	Cronbach α for the three dimensions	Cronbach α
Compared to the traditional design process, I think generative AI has a better appearance in terms of design efficiency and effect	0.739	0.926		
I am willing to understand and consume this kind of image if it is used for cultural or product promotion	0.734	0.926		

Table 7. Validity Analysis

KMO and Bartlett's test		
KMO		0.945
Bartlett's sphericity test	Approximate Chi-square	759.166
	df	36
	p	0.000

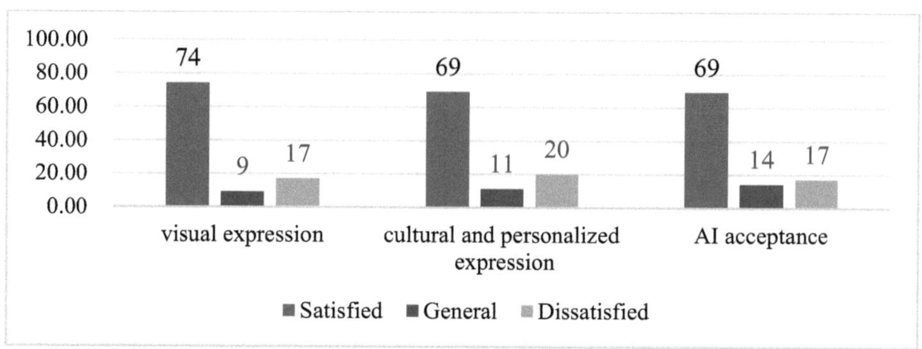

Fig. 4. Satisfaction Survey on the Results of Adorable Character Design.

5 Summary

This study delves into the application of generative AI in budding character design, successfully transforming the visual characteristics, emotional expression and personalization elements, and environmental factors of a character into a format that can be received and processed by claimed AI by encoding and decoding the genes of the budding elements, and collaborating with claimed AI tools (predominantly Stable Diffusion) to to generate budding characters that meet the design requirements. The study shows that generative AI is able to efficiently generate a diverse range of adorable characters during the design process, while designers optimize the details through human-computer collaboration to ensure that the characters achieve the desired effect in terms of emotional transmission and cultural connotation. This result promotes the standardized design process and innovation of budding character design, and lays the foundation for future research on personalized customization, emotional expression and cross-cultural design. With the continuous development of AI technology, generative AI is expected to play an important role in a wider range of creative design fields, especially in globalization and cultural communication, bringing more possibilities to the creative industry. In the future, generative AI will not only improve design efficiency, but also promote the development of design in a more personalized and diversified direction, becoming an important tool for the cultural industry and cultural and creative product design.

References

1. Chen, C.: Constructing and linking: a study of emotional communication rituals under moe culture - a case study based on the phenomenon of Ling Na Belle. Master's thesis (MSc), Zhejiang Media College (2025). https://doi.org/10.27852/d.cnki.gzjcm.2024.000076
2. Lin, Y.: "Bing Dwen Dwen" IP image design research under the threshold of "Moe Economy." Beauty Era (Above) **3**, 57–59 (2023). https://doi.org/10.16129/j.cnki.mysds.2023.03.039
3. Zhu, P.: 'Budding' visual language in the terracotta figurines of Sima Jinlong Tomb', Master's thesis (MSc), Shanxi University (2024). https://doi.org/10.27284/d.cnki.gsxiu.2023.001003
4. Bordas, A., Le Masson, P., Thomas, M., Weil, B.: What is generative in generative artificial intelligence? A design-based perspective. Res. Eng. Design **35**(4), 427–443 (2024). https://doi.org/10.1007/s00163-024-00441-x
5. Lyu, Y., Shi, M., Zhang, Y., Lin, R.: From image to imagination: exploring the impact of generative AI on cultural translation in jewelry design. Sustainability **16**(1), 65 (2023). https://doi.org/10.3390/su16010065
6. Sun, W.: Research on artistic creation of image generation assisted by artificial intelligence technology, Master's thesis (MSc), East China Normal University (2024). https://doi.org/10.27149/d.cnki.ghdsu.2023.003587
7. Qiu, J.: Research on design patterns driving product innovation under the perspective of design paradigm shift'. Master's thesis (MSc), Hunan University (2023). https://doi.org/10.27135/d.cnki.ghudu.2021.001803
8. Zhang, Z.: Application and Exploration of AI painting in digital painting. Master's thesis (MSc), Beijing Institute of Printing (2024). https://doi.org/10.26968/d.cnki.gbjyc.2023.000100
9. Zhao, W., Zang, X.: AIGC's design exploration of cultural and creative products under the perspective of pierce's semiotics. Packag. Eng. **45**(10), 116–126 (2024). https://doi.org/10.19554/j.cnki.1001-3563.2024.10.013
10. Lu, Z., Song, X., Jin, Y.: Status and development of intelligent design under the trend of AIGC technology. Packag. Eng. **44**(24), 18–33, 13 (2023), https://doi.org/10.19554/j.cnki.1001-3563.2023.24.003

An Empirical Study on Enhancing Artistic Creativity of College Fine Arts Students Through Generative AI-Based Creative Thinking Training

Yingjun Chen, Chengzong Li, and Huiping Wu[✉]

The Guangzhou Academy of Fine Arts, Guangzhou, Guangdong, China
837255609@qq.com

Abstract. Artificial intelligence has become an effective tool for assisting education and enhancing students' learning outcomes. Universities are increasingly offering AI courses to cultivate students' scientific literacy, improve learning efficiency, and enhance their thinking abilities. This study aims to explore the impact of generative AI-assisted creative thinking training on the artistic creativity of university art students. The study selected 48 s-year students from a university in Guangzhou as the sample, organized into natural classes. Among them, 20 students formed the experimental group, who received teaching interventions using generative AI-based creative thinking courses; 28 students formed the control group, who did not undergo any creative thinking training and did not use AI tools. Both groups were administered pre- and post-tests using the "Creativity Self-Report Scale" and the "Williams Creativity Tendency Scale." The results showed that students in the experimental group significantly outperformed the control group in certain aspects of "creativity self-perception," while changes in creativity tendencies were not significant. Conclusion: Generative AI-based creative thinking training can serve as an effective means to enhance the creativity self-perception of university art students. It is recommended to promote its application in art education, with future research exploring its applicability in different educational contexts and tool optimization.

Keywords: generative AI · art education · creative thinking training · artistic creativity

1 Research Background

Artificial intelligence has become a powerful tool for assisting education and improving student learning outcomes. Many universities have begun to add artificial intelligence courses to their curricula, with the aim of cultivating students' scientific literacy while improving learning efficiency and thinking skills. In the field of education, the application of generative artificial intelligence is becoming increasingly widespread, with its powerful creative capabilities and personalized feedback mechanisms bringing about a

J. Wei et al. (Eds.): HCII 2025, LNCS 16346, pp. 33–43, 2026.
https://doi.org/10.1007/978-3-032-13187-4_3

revolution in traditional education. Especially in the field of art education, traditional teaching methods often focus on skill transmission and imitation, while the cultivation of students' innovative thinking and artistic creativity is relatively lacking. However, artistic creativity is a key component of fine arts students' core competitiveness and has a decisive impact on their artistic development. With the continuous advancement of generative artificial intelligence technology, its application prospects in the field of education are becoming increasingly broad, opening up new avenues for the cultivation of artistic creativity. Generative AI can create images, text, videos, and other content through algorithms. This content not only possesses high levels of innovation but also has personalized characteristics, providing art students with abundant creative materials and inspiration. Additionally, generative AI can provide personalized creative feedback based on students' creative inputs, helping them gain a deeper understanding of their creative processes and identify and improve upon issues in their work. This study uses AI as an auxiliary teaching tool, combined with cognitive development theory, to develop corresponding creative thinking training courses, exploring the potential and effectiveness of AI-based creative thinking training in enhancing the artistic creativity of university art students. Therefore, the purpose of this study is to use empirical research methods to explore the impact of AI-assisted creative thinking training on the artistic creativity of university art students, aiming to provide scientific evidence for the innovation and development of art education.

2 Literature Review

Creative Training. Creative training refers to structured and systematic methods for enhancing creativity, primarily encompassing three intervention paradigms: First, Cognitive Restructuring Training (CRT), whose core mechanism lies in breaking functional fixedness. Smith & Blankenship (1991) conducted an experiment using the "forced association method" (random word pairing) training, participants' novelty scores increased by 42% (control group +7%) [1]. Eberle (1996) proposed the SCAMPER technique: the "substitute-combine-modify" process optimizes existing solutions to effectively address functional fixedness [2]. Second, Motivational Priming Training. Amabile (1996) confirmed the "creativity components theory": through "self-directed goal-setting training," individuals' intrinsic motivation levels increased (effect size d = 0.68), directly increasing the frequency of creative behavior [3]. Eisenberger & Rhoades (2001) meta-analysis showed: non-material rewards (such as social recognition) promote creativity tendencies more effectively than material rewards ($\beta = 0.31$ vs. 0.12) [4]. Third, multimodal integration training, Leung et al. (2012) experiment: After open-ended dance training, participants' divergent thinking scores increased by 28% (fNIRS showed enhanced activation in the right prefrontal cortex) [5]. McCoy & Evans (2002) confirmed: Physical spatial complexity (e.g., asymmetrical layout + natural lighting) can activate creativity tendencies (behavioral observations improved by 19%) [6].

Based on the above intervention paradigms, we developed a series of courses combining cognitive restructuring training with multimodal integration training to enhance creative thinking among undergraduate art students. The aim of the courses is to enhance students' creative thinking and explore its impact on creative self-perception and creative tendencies.

Creative Self-efficacy. Creative self-efficacy refers to an individual's assessment of their confidence in their ability to complete creative tasks (Tierney & Farmer, 2002). This concept is rooted in Bandura's Social Cognitive Theory, which emphasizes that individuals form beliefs about their creative abilities through four sources of efficacy information: mastery experiences, vicarious learning, social persuasion, and emotional arousal (Bandura, 1997 [7]; Beghetto, 2006 [8]). Unlike general self-efficacy, CSE is domain-specific: "Individuals need to assess their ability to mobilize cognitive resources in specific creative contexts (e.g., artistic creation or scientific problem-solving)" (Karwowski, 2011, p.54) [9]. CSE comprises three core dimensions: task-oriented efficacy, confidence in completing specific creative tasks (Jaussi et al., 2007) [10]; domain-general efficacy, an assessment of cross-domain creative potential (Beghetto, 2009) [11]; and resilience efficacy, the belief in overcoming creative obstacles (Dweck et al., 2014) [12].

Research on creativity self-efficacy has undergone three stages: Initial model: Tierney and Farmer (2002) proposed a two-dimensional structure of CSE (creative confidence + frustration tolerance) in the Academy of Management Journal [13]; Dynamic expansion: Karwowski (2011) integrated the theory of creative mindset, emphasizing that CSE is the interactive product of fixed/growth mindset and efficacy beliefs [9]; Neurological Mechanism Supplement: Dweck et al. (2014) found through fMRI research that individuals with high CSE exhibit stronger prefrontal-default network coupling during creative tasks, confirming its biological basis [12].

Research on the impact of creative training on creative self-efficacy (CSE): Scott et al. (2004) conducted a meta-analysis (covering 73 studies) indicating that structured creative practices (such as TRIZ problem-solving training) significantly enhance CSE by providing progressive success experiences ($\beta = 0.48$, p < 0.001) [14]. Typical evidence includes: After undergoing a 12-week "concept combination innovation training" program, engineers saw a 32% increase in CSE scores (d = 1.24), with effects persisting for six months (Puccio & Grivas, 2009) [15]; design students who underwent rapid prototyping iteration training saw a 27% increase in task-oriented efficacy (Byrge & Tang, 2015) [16]. This body of research highlights the central role of mastery experience.

Runco (2014) conducted a series of experiments demonstrating that training to overcome functional fixedness can directly enhance CSE: following "alternate uses task" training, participants' self-assessment of their creative potential increased by 41% (effect size $\eta^2 = 0.18$); functional brain imaging (fNIRS) revealed that the changes in prefrontal activation patterns after training were significantly correlated with the improvement in CSE (r = 0.69) [17]. This study highlights the cognitive framework restructuring effect.

Studies have observed that high-creativity role models can increase CSE by 19–26% (Bandura, 1997) [7]; however, Jaussi et al. (2007) found that in a competitive training environment, individuals with low initial CSE experienced a 23% decrease in self-efficacy ("high-pressure inhibition effect") [10]. This part of the research highlights the double-edged sword effect of social factors.

Some studies have explored the influence of moderating variables on CSE. Beghetto (2009) examined the moderating role of individual traits, finding that creative training had a stronger effect on enhancing CSE for individuals with high openness and low neuroticism (moderation effect $R^2 = 0.31$): "Openness and CSE form a bidirectional positive feedback loop: individuals with high openness are more likely to benefit from training, while enhanced CSE reinforces their exploratory tendencies" [11]. Byrge and Tang (2015) examined the boundary conditions of training design, finding the optimal training duration to be 8–12 weeks ($\beta = 0.42$), as shorter durations fail to establish stable beliefs, while longer durations result in diminishing marginal benefits; the content matching principle: art-related training had a significantly greater promotional effect on CSE ($d = 0.93$) than science-related training ($d = 0.42$) [16]. Karwowski (2011) conducted a cross-cultural experiment showing that in individualistic cultures, self-determined training (e.g., free creation) is more effective; in collectivist cultures, goal-oriented training (e.g., team creative challenges) has a more significant impact on enhancing CSE [9].

Currently, there are some controversies in the research. Schunk & DiBenedetto (2020) explored the stability of training gains on creative self-efficacy, noting that it increases with the deepening of creative practice, but also pointing out that short-term CSE improvements lack sustainability [18]. Dweck et al. (2014) also explored the possibility of transferability of creativity self-efficacy [12].

In summary, the gains and transferability of creativity training on creativity self-efficacy may be influenced by the content and methods of training. Therefore, this study will develop an art thinking training course based on generative artificial intelligence to explore its impact on creativity self-efficacy.

Creative Tendency. Creative tendency refers to an individual's stable preference for creative thinking and behavior, distinct from short-term creative performance (such as sudden bursts of inspiration in specific tasks). Kaufman & Beghetto (2009) proposed that creative tendency is the "cross-situational inertia of creative behavior," encompassing two dimensions: cognitive flexibility and openness to experience [19].

Studies on the impact of creative thinking training on creative tendency can be divided into short-term and long-term interventions, with short-term intervention effects generally lasting less than 8 weeks. Scott et al. (2004) meta-analysis found that cognitive strategy training increased creative tendency by 29%, with the most significant improvement observed in divergent thinking tasks, demonstrating the effectiveness of short-term cognitive strategy training [14]. Long-term intervention effects last longer than three months. Beghetto's (2018) K-12 creative course: After 12 weeks of "problem-based learning," students' curiosity scores increased by 22% ($p < 0.001$), and standardized test scores improved simultaneously ($r = 0.38$) [20].

In summary, creative thinking training can alter creativity tendencies and have a positive impact. However, as creativity tendencies are relatively stable psychological traits, whether they are indeed influenced by creative thinking training, as suggested by existing research findings, remains to be further explored. Therefore, this study will also investigate the effects of creative thinking training on creativity tendencies.

3   Research Design

3.1   Research Participants

The participants in this experiment were 48 s-year art students from a university in Guangzhou, organized into natural classes, with 20 students in the experimental group and 28 students in the control group. There were 48 participants in total, including 12 males and 36 females. Specifically, there were 4 males and 16 females in the experimental group, and 8 males and 20 females in the control group. The average age was 20.29 ± 0.53 years.

3.2 Research Methods

Students in the experimental group received AI-based creative thinking training over an 8-week period, consisting of 8 sessions. Students in the control group were from the same major but did not receive any creative thinking training and did not use AI tools. The study used the Measuring Creative Self-efficacy and Creative Personal Identity Scale and the Williams Creativity Tendency Scale to assess changes in creative thinking and creativity in both groups before and after the intervention.

3.3 Research Tools

The questionnaires included the "Creativity Self-Efficacy Scale" and the "Williams Creativity Scale." The "Creativity Self-Efficacy Scale" consists of 11 items, divided into CPI (Creative Personal Identity) and CSE (Creative Self-Efficacy). The Creativity Self-Efficacy Scale is adapted from the CSE subscale (six items, such as "I am confident that I can handle problems requiring creative thinking") of the abbreviated Creative Self-Efficacy Scale developed by Karwowski et al. (2018) [21]. All items in the CSE are scored using a 5-point Likert scale (1 represents "absolutely not," and 5 represents "absolutely yes").

The Williams Creativity Scale measures an individual's creative tendencies through four distinct dimensions: Adventure, Curiosity, Imagination, and Challenge. A score of 3 indicates full agreement, 2 indicates partial agreement, and 1 indicates full disagreement. The higher the total score, the higher the level of creativity.

The two scales are combined into a single questionnaire, administered twice—once before the course and once after the course—to compare average scores across groups and determine whether generative AI-based creative thinking training has an impact on enhancing the artistic creativity of university art students.

3.4 Research Procedures

Pre-test. A total of 48 participants, including 20 in the experimental group and 28 in the control group, used the research tools employed in this experiment to calculate the students' assessment scores, thereby gaining an understanding of their level of artistic creativity prior to the experiment.

Teaching Intervention. Over an 8-week period from November to December 2024, 20 s-year undergraduate students (experimental group) participated in the course "Creative Thinking Training." During this period, the experimental group students utilized generative AI technologies in various forms, including images, text, and video, for their creative activities. Meanwhile, the control group students did not undergo any creative thinking training and received traditional art education, without using any AI tools. Both groups of students engaged in learning and creation simultaneously during the course.

Post-test. After the course concluded, a questionnaire was administered again to assess the creativity of all 48 students, with the results compared to the initial assessment. Based on the comparison and analysis of the assessment results, conclusions were drawn regarding the impact of generative AI-based creative thinking training on the enhancement of artistic creativity among university art students.

4   Teaching Design and Practice

Teaching design for the experimental class: The primary knowledge and skill objectives were to enable students to utilize generative AI technology to assist in creative design and produce innovative design works (Table 1).

Table 1. Course Content and Teaching Arrangements.

Topic	Teaching Content	Teaching Methods, Resources, Duration	Teaching Objectives
Integration of Creative Thinking with Calligraphy and Design	Background and development of calligraphy and design; connections and differences between calligraphy and design; importance of creative thinking; application of generative AI in creative design	Lecture, case analysis, discussion; PPT, case videos, physical demonstrations; 4 class hours	Understand the relationship between calligraphy and design; recognize the importance of creative thinking; master the application of generative AI in creative design
Training and Application of Elephant Thinking	Definition and essence of elephant thinking; methods for training elephant thinking; application of elephant thinking in design; application of generative AI in elephant thinking training	Lecture, practical exercises, group discussions; PPT, case studies, AI tools; 6 class hours	Master the concept and characteristics of elephant thinking; be able to apply elephant thinking in design; understand the application methods of generative AI in elephant thinking training
Integration of Calligraphy and Design	Calligraphy fundamentals training; design elements and principles; methods for integrating calligraphy and design; application of generative AI in the integration of calligraphy and design	Lecture, demonstrations, practical exercises, case analysis; PPT, calligraphy tools, design software, AI tools; 8 class hours	Master the basic skills of calligraphy; understand design elements and principles; be able to create works by integrating calligraphy and design; proficiently use generative AI tools for integrated creation

(continued)

Table 1. (*continued*)

Topic	Teaching Content	Teaching Methods, Resources, Duration	Teaching Objectives
Expansion and Practice of Creative Thinking	Creative thinking method training; creative design project practice; application of generative AI in expanding creative thinking	Lecture, case analysis, group project practice, discussions; PPT, case materials, design software, AI tools; 13 class hours	Master creative thinking methods; be able to complete creative design projects; utilize generative AI to expand creative thinking
Course Summary and Outlook and reports	prospects for the development of calligraphy and design, creative thinking training, and generative AIs	Final presentation; 1 class hour	Ability to complete creative design presentations

The teaching curriculum of the control class adopts traditional art education methods, emphasizing the cultivation of hand-drawing and manual design skills.

5 Research Results and Discussion

5.1 Research Results

Table 2. Comparison of pre-test results between the experimental group and the control group ($M \pm SD$).

	CPI	CSE	Creativity self-concept	Adventure	Curiosity	Imagination	Challenge	total creativity tendency score
Experimental group	3.88 ± 0.55	3.23 ± 0.62	3.53 ± 0.54	2.39 ± 0.30	2.33 ± 0.33	2.47 ± 0.26	2.25 ± 0.31	2.36 ± 0.25
Control group	3.92 ± 0.57	3.31 ± 0.86	3.59 ± 0.68	2.17 ± 0.30	2.20 ± 0.29	2.24 ± 0.35	2.16 ± 0.32	2.19 ± 0.05
t	-0.25	-0.36	-0.35	2.48	1.45	2.53	0.99	2.24
p	0.80	0.72	0.73	0.02*	0.16	0.02*	0.33	0.03*

The research results indicate that in the pre-test, the experimental group scored significantly higher than the control group in terms of "adventure," "imagination," and "total creativity tendency score," while there were no significant differences in other dimensions. This suggests that the two groups were well-matched and in a balanced state, making them suitable for conducting a teaching intervention experiment (Tables 2, 3, 4 and 5).

Table 3. Comparison of post-test results between the experimental group and the control group (M $\pm$ SD).

	CPI	CSE	Creativity self-concept	Adventure	Curiosity	Imagination	Challenge	Total creativity tendency score
Experimental group	4.26 $\pm$ 0.52	3.82 $\pm$ 0.45	4.02 $\pm$ 0.43	2.11 $\pm$ 0.32	2.24 $\pm$ 0.40	2.21 $\pm$ 0.44	2.14 $\pm$ 0.34	2.18 $\pm$ 0.29
Control group	3.78 $\pm$ 0.60	3.26 $\pm$ 0.45	3.49 $\pm$ 0.70	2.21 $\pm$ 0.40	2.28 $\pm$ 0.36	2.33 $\pm$ 0.40	2.16 $\pm$ 0.35	2.24 $\pm$ 0.31
t	2.90	2.60	2.99	-0.96	-0.35	-0.95	-0.17	-0.79
p	0.006*	0.012*	0.004*	0.343	0.727	0.34	0.867	0.431

Table 4. Comparison of pre- and post-test results in the experimental group (M $\pm$ SD).

	CPI	CSE	Creativity self-concept	Adventure	Curiosity	Imagination	Challenge	Total creativity tendency score
pre-test	3.88 $\pm$ 0.55	3.23 $\pm$ 0.62	3.53 $\pm$ 0.54	2.39 $\pm$ 0.30	2.33 $\pm$ 0.33	2.47 $\pm$ 0.26	2.25 $\pm$ 0.31	2.36 $\pm$ 0.25
post-test	4.26 $\pm$ 0.52	3.82 $\pm$ 0.45	4.02 $\pm$ 0.43	2.11 $\pm$ 0.32	2.24 $\pm$ 0.40	2.21 $\pm$ 0.44	2.14 $\pm$ 0.34	2.18 $\pm$ 0.29
t	-4.50	-5.70	-6.81	2.54	0.71	2.256	0.91	1.88
p	0.000***	0.000***	0.000***	0.020*	0.484	0.036*	0.374	0.075

Table 5. Comparison of pre- and post-treatment measurements in the control group (M $\pm$ SD).

	CPI	CSE	Creativity self-concept	Adventure	Curiosity	Imagination	Challenge	Total creativity tendency score
pre-test	3.92 $\pm$ 0.57	3.31 $\pm$ 0.86	3.59 $\pm$ 0.68	2.17 $\pm$ 0.30	2.20 $\pm$ 0.29	2.24 $\pm$ 0.35	2.16 $\pm$ 0.32	2.19 $\pm$ 0.05
post-test	3.78 $\pm$ 0.60	3.26 $\pm$ 0.45	3.49 $\pm$ 0.70	2.21 $\pm$ 0.40	2.28 $\pm$ 0.36	2.33 $\pm$ 0.40	2.16 $\pm$ 0.35	2.24 $\pm$ 0.31
t	1.84	0.46	1.10	-0.45	-0.84	-1.02	0.00	-0.70
p	0.077	0.650	0.282	0.659	0.407	0.317	1.000	0.488

In the post-test, the experimental group scored significantly higher than the control group in terms of "CPI," "CSE," and "total creativity self-score."

In the post-test, the experimental group's scores for "CPI," "CSE," and "creativity self-total score" were significantly higher than those in the pre-test. However, the post-test scores for "adventure" and "imagination" were significantly lower than those in the pre-test.

The results of all dimensions in the pre- and post-tests for the control group were not significantly different.

Analysis indicates that the course has a significant promotional effect on creativity self-perception. However, its effect on creativity tendencies is not prominent.

5.2 Discussion

The results of this study indicate that creative thinking training based on generative artificial intelligence has a significant positive effect on the creativity self-concept of university art students, but no significant effect on creativity orientation. This result may be related to the characteristics of the course, as well as the inherent differences between creativity self-concept and creativity orientation.

First, from the perspective of course characteristics, the experimental group's creative thinking training course centered on generative AI as a core tool, emphasizing the use of AI technology to assist in creative generation and inspiration expansion. This training approach provided students with abundant creative materials and personalized feedback, directly enhancing their confidence and self-efficacy during the creative process. For example, AI tools can quickly generate multiple creative solutions, helping students overcome creative bottlenecks. This immediate feedback and successful experience contribute to enhancing students' creativity self-efficacy. However, creativity disposition, as a relatively stable individual psychological trait, is more influenced by an individual's internal cognitive style, personality traits, and long-term behavioral habits. While short-term creative thinking training can provide new creative ideas and methods, it may struggle to alter students' long-established internal traits such as cognitive flexibility and openness in the short term, thus limiting its impact on creativity disposition.

Secondly, the fundamental difference between creativity self-efficacy and creativity tendencies also explains this result. Creativity self-efficacy is an individual's assessment of their confidence in their ability to complete creative tasks, which is domain-specific and context-dependent. In this study, experimental group students, with the assistance of generative AI tools, could more intuitively see their creative outcomes, thereby enhancing their confidence in their own creative abilities. This boost in confidence is significant in the short term, especially when compared to traditional art education methods. Generative AI tools provide students with richer creative resources and more efficient means of expression, further reinforcing their creative self-efficacy. In contrast, creative tendency is an individual's stable preference for creative thinking and behavior, exhibiting cross-situational stability. It not only involves psychological traits such as cognitive flexibility and openness but is also closely related to an individual's intrinsic motivation, interests, and long-term creative habits. Changing creativity tendencies requires longer-term intervention and more comprehensive training, and the 8-week creative thinking training in this study may not be sufficient to significantly impact this stable trait.

Additionally, students in the experimental group were able to gain a deeper understanding of their creative processes, identify and improve issues in their work through the use of generative AI tools during the course. This deep engagement and reflection on the creative process helps enhance students' creative self-efficacy, enabling them to approach creative tasks with greater confidence. However, the enhancement of creativity tendencies requires individuals to demonstrate consistent creative behavior across multiple different contexts, and the training in this study was primarily focused on the field of visual arts, which may not fully cover all aspects of creativity tendencies.

In summary, creative thinking training based on generative AI has a significant positive impact on the creativity self-efficacy of university art students, primarily because this training method, with the assistance of AI tools, provides abundant creative resources and personalized feedback, thereby enhancing students' confidence and self-efficacy during the creative process. However, creativity tendencies, as a relatively stable individual psychological trait influenced by multiple factors, are difficult to significantly alter through short-term creative thinking training. Future research could further explore how long-term, diversified creative thinking training, combined with generative AI tools, can more comprehensively enhance students' creativity tendencies.

5.3 Summary and Reflection

To ensure ethical standards, student privacy was strictly protected throughout the research process, and all data was anonymized. The use of AI tools respected students' creative autonomy, avoiding excessive interference with their artistic style, ensuring that technology assisted rather than replaced students' creative expression.

This study demonstrates that AI-based creative thinking training significantly enhances university art students' self-perceived creativity, improves teaching efficiency, and boosts students' artistic innovation capabilities. Generative AI notably enhances students' creative confidence and innovativeness. AI tools not only help students overcome creative blockages but also optimize the quality of their artistic works through personalized feedback, fostering their proactive and exploratory spirit in the creative process. It is recommended that generative AI technology be widely applied in art education to improve teaching quality, stimulate students' creative thinking, and enhance their professional competitiveness. Future research can further explore the application effects of generative AI in different cultural contexts and educational environments, as well as how to optimize AI tools to better support students' creative expression.

6 Disclosure of Interests

The authors have no competing interests to declare that are relevant to the content of this article.

Acknowledgments. We sincerely thank the following projects for their financial support: Guangzhou Academy of Fine Arts 2025 Graduate Teaching Reform Project (60925093) and Guangdong Provincial Philosophy and Social Sciences Planning 2025 Regular Project (GD25CYS34).

References

1. Smith, S.M., Blankenship, S.E.: Incubation and the persistence of fixation in problem solving. Am. J. Psychol. **104**, 61–87 (1991). https://doi.org/10.2307/1422851
2. Eberle, B.: Scamper on: Games for Imagination Development. Prufrock Press Inc. (1996)
3. Amabile, T.M., Conti, R., Coon, H., Lazenby, J., Herron, M.: Assessing the work environment for creativity. Acad. Manag. J. **39**, 1154–1184 (1996). https://doi.org/10.2307/256995
4. Eisenberger, R., Rhoades, L.: Incremental effects of reward on creativity. J. Persumaliy Soc. Psychal. **81**, 728–741 (2001)
5. Leung, A.K., et al.: Embodied metaphors and creative acts. Psychol. Sci. (2012)

6. McCoy, J.M., Evans, G.W.: The potential role of the physical environment in fostering creativity. Creativity Res. J. **14**(3–4), 409–426 (2002). https://doi.org/10.1207/S15326934CRJ1434_11

7. Bandura, A.: Self-Efficacy: The Exercise of Control. Freeman (1997)

8. Beghetto, R.A.: Creative self-efficacy: correlates in middle and secondary students. Creat. Res. J. **18**(4), 447–457 (2006)

9. Karwowski, M.: The creative mix? The role of creative self-efficacy and growth mindsets. Procedia Soc. Behav. Sci. **12**, 54–67 (2011)

10. Jaussi, K.S., et al.: Goals as amplifiers of the relationship between leader behaviors and employee creativity. Acad. Manag. Proc. (2007)

11. Beghetto, R.A.: Correlates of intellectual risk taking in elementary school science. J. Res. Sci. Teach. **46**(2), 210–223 (2009)

12. Dweck, C.S., et al.: Academic and emotional functioning in middle school: the role of implicit theories. Unpublished manuscript (2014)

13. Tierney, P., Farmer, S.M.: Creative self-efficacy: its potential antecedents and relationship to creative performance. Acad. Manag. J. **45**(6), 1137–1148 (2002)

14. Scott, G., et al.: The effectiveness of creativity training: a quantitative review. Creat. Res. J. **16**(4), 361–388 (2004)

15. Puccio, G.J., Grivas, C.: Examining the relationship between personality traits and creativity styles. Creativity Innov. Manag. **18**(4), 247–255 (2009)

16. Byrge, C., Tang, C.: Embodied creativity training: effects on creative self-efficacy and creative production. Think. Skills Creativity **16**, 51–61 (2015)

17. Runco, M.A.: Creativity: Theories and Themes: Research, Development, and Practice, 2nd edn. Academic Press (2014)

18. Schunk, D.H., DiBenedetto, M.K.: Motivation and social processes. Annu. Rev. Psychol. **71**, 123–149 (2020)

19. Kaufman, J.C., Beghetto, R.A.: Beyond big and little: the Four-C model of creativity. Rev. General Psychol. (2009)

20. Beghetto, R.A.: What if? Building Students' Problem-Solving Skills. ASCD (2018)

21. Karwowski, M., Lebuda, I., Wiśniewska, E.: Measuring creative self-efficacy and creative personal identity. Int. J. Creativity Probl. Solv. **28**(1), 45–57 (2018)

Research on the Renewal of Residual Green Spaces in Communities Based on AIGC

Xingyu Chen[✉]

College of Design and Innovation, Tongji University, Shanghai 200092, China
42395886@qq.com

Abstract. With the acceleration of urbanization, leftover green spaces in aging communities have long been neglected due to spatial fragmentation and governance absence, highlighting the urgent need for innovative, low-intervention renewal strategies. This study takes the typical fragmented green spaces of Tielu Third Village in Chongqing as a case and conducts a comparative experiment between a "traditional design team" and an "AIGC-assisted design team" to systematically evaluate the applicability of AI-generated content (AIGC) in community green space micro-regeneration. Combining expert reviews, resident interviews, and process documentation, the research compares the two approaches across multiple dimensions, including design efficiency, spatial utilization, ecological performance, innovation, and user acceptance. Results show that AIGC significantly improves design generation speed and visual representation, enhances spatial innovation, and facilitates co-creation with residents. However, it still relies on human intervention for detail refinement, site-specific adaptation, and cultural expression. The study concludes that while AIGC brings efficiency and diversity to green space renewal, its sustainable application depends on strengthening human–AI collaboration and embedding local cultural context. This research provides empirical evidence to support both practice and theoretical advancement in AI-assisted community micro-regeneration.

Keywords: Artificial Intelligence-Generated Content (AIGC) · Residual green space renewal · Human-AI collaboration · Design generation · User experience · sustainable design

1 Introduction

As urbanization continues to accelerate, many aging communities in China are facing multiple challenges, including functional decline, spatial disorder, and ecological fragmentation. Among these issues, "leftover green spaces" within communities, representing corner lots, interstitial spaces, or temporary open areas, have long been neglected in urban renewal processes [1]. These green spaces are typically characterized by small sizes, complex spatial forms, and unclear management responsibilities. Traditional landscape design methods often encounter challenges such as implementation difficulties, low renewal efficiency, and weak resident awareness when applied to these spaces [2].

J. Wei et al. (Eds.): HCII 2025, LNCS 16346, pp. 44–59, 2026.
https://doi.org/10.1007/978-3-032-13187-4_4

Therefore, achieving low-cost, highly adaptable, and sustainable renewal designs for community leftover green spaces has become a critical issue that needs to be addressed in the current community micro-regeneration discussions.

In recent years, Artificial Intelligence-Generated Content (AIGC) has experienced rapid development, demonstrating powerful generative capabilities in design-related domains such as image creation, text generation, and 3D modeling. This technological advancement has introduced new data-driven and collaborative workflows to the fields of architecture and landscape architecture. As a new generation of design-assistive tools, AIGC challenges the traditional designer-led creative paradigm and propels the design process toward data-driven and human–machine collaborative modes [3]. In architecture, landscape, and product design industries, researchers have begun integrating tools such as ChatGPT, DALL·E, Stable Diffusion, into stages including conceptual sketch generation, image representation enhancement, and final design visualization. Compared with conventional design approaches, AIGC offers significantly faster processing capabilities and holds unique potential for addressing the complex challenges associated with residual green space renewal in communities.

Nevertheless, there is still a lack of systematic research on the actual design performance of AIGC at the urban micro-scale. It remains uncertain whether its generated content possesses sufficient site adaptability, whether it offers advantages in terms of resident understanding and participation, and how human–AIGC collaborative design processes should be organized. These key issues are still at an early exploratory stage and have yet to reach a mature consensus. Especially in the context of community renewal, design is not merely a matter of formal generation; it also encompasses multiple dimensions such as resident perception, ecological integration, cultural expression, and the continuity of spatial texture. Whether AIGC can effectively address these complex objectives requires further in-depth investigation.

This study focuses on a typical residual green space within an aging community—Tielu Third Village—in Chongqing, China, and establishes a comparative experiment between a "traditional designer scheme" and an "AIGC-assisted design scheme" to assess the applicability and effectiveness of AIGC technology in community green space renewal. The research centers on three key stages of the design process: scheme generation, iterative optimization, and visual representation. Through expert evaluations, user interviews, and analysis of design outputs, the study compares the performance of different approaches in terms of design efficiency, ecological function, spatial utilization, and user acceptance, and further explores the advantages and limitations of AIGC in site feasibility, innovation, and detailed design.

The significance of this study lies in three main aspects: First, it addresses the urgent need for systematic renewal strategies for residual green spaces in the micro-regeneration of aging communities by proposing an AI-assisted design approach. Second, it examines the operational logic and effectiveness of AIGC in specific design tasks, thereby expanding its potential applications within urban renewal practice. Third, it provides an empirically testable framework for human–AI collaborative design, advancing the co-creation and technology-driven development of community-based design.

2 Literature Review

2.1 The Concept and Renewal Strategies of Community Residual Green Spaces

"Residual green space" was originally regarded as a part of the broader concept of "urban surplus space," typically referring to small-scale green spaces formed due to historical demolition, planning gaps, or corner plots, which are fragmented in size and ambiguous in terms of ownership. In recent years, the Pocket Park model has been seen as an effective pathway for the rapid improvement of residual green spaces in communities. Research has focused on indicators such as scale adaptability, functional complexity, and all-age friendliness, which can provide multiple social and ecological benefits, promote community interaction, enhance social cohesion, enrich recreational opportunities, and improve residents' physical and mental health, while also contributing to the sustainable development of the community [4]. Based on literature reviews, scholars have proposed assessing the potential for Pocket Park transformation in aging communities from three aspects: ecological function, activity integration, and ease of implementation. They emphasize light interventions combined with a gradual approach to ensure operational sustainability [5]. Meanwhile, the spontaneous greening practices of residents in China's aging communities indicate that relevant literature often describes these spaces as "corner plots" or "narrow gaps," with research focusing on functional supplementation and landscape beautification. Community-led small-scale renewal can flexibly meet daily needs while addressing the standardized shortcomings of official renewal projects [6]. Most of the existing research has focused on social participation, low-cost construction, and traditional design approaches, with insufficient attention given to the collaborative design application of AIGC in the context of community residual green spaces, which offers more diversity, potential, efficiency, and imagination in design generation and expression.

2.2 The Technological Application of AIGC in Landscape Design

In the field of landscape planning, the introduction of artificial intelligence (AI) has demonstrated its potential to enhance design efficiency and foster rich creativity. Traditional landscape design often requires repeated manual attempts and time investment, while AI systems, through machine learning and data analysis, can significantly accelerate the design process. They can generate highly realistic virtual landscape images and diverse design options, providing designers with an immersive conceptual display environment. This helps to quickly iterate design ideas and visualize solutions [7]. At the same time, AI can perform tasks such as morphological optimization and automated layout, offering inspiration and creative support to designers. It significantly improves the efficiency of generating conceptual sketches and scene simulations, enabling diversified visual expressions in the early stages of design and compressing the traditional iteration cycle. This provides more technological support for landscape design proposals [8]. Additionally, AI tools can automatically match and generate landscape design schemes based on factors such as terrain, plant species, and local architectural styles, thus expanding design possibilities [9]. However, despite visible progress in form control and spatial generation, the depth of AIGC's application in region-specific urban land-scapes remains insufficient. Specifically, current generation mechanisms tend to focus on image feature synthesis and collage, limiting their deep application in the practical landscape design process.

2.3 AI Collaborative Design and User Experience

AI generation has the potential to serve as a "co-creation partner" in design. Some studies have found that previous community space designs often failed to fully incor-porate the perspectives of diverse groups, particularly neglecting the needs and cultural backgrounds of marginalized communities. In response, some scholars have proposed introducing image-generating AI into participatory community design as a tool for com-munication and collaboration [10]. The literature indicates that the introduction of AIGC not only lowers the creative threshold and promotes the democratization of design but also empowers co-creation teams to foster collaborative relationships. However, the col-laborative paradigm for multi-stakeholder public spaces, such as communities, is still underdeveloped. In community micro-regeneration, user experience has become a key indicator, with designs that offer high visual expressiveness being more easily under-stood and engaged by residents, thereby stimulating co-creation efforts. The rise of mechanisms like consensus maps and resident co-drawing has shifted urban renewal from designing for residents to designing with residents [11]. AIGC's image generation and rapid responsiveness provide an effective mediating effect in the co-creation pro-cess, yet how to enhance residents' trust and understanding of AIGC-generated solutions remains an area that requires further exploration.

2.4 Research Gaps and Entry Point

In summary, four research gaps can be identified. At the community level: research on community renovation and ecological green space renewal in communities has rarely involved the use of AIGC (Artificial Intelligence Generated Content) techniques. At the site scale: AIGC has yet to be validated in design operations for complex residual green space environments. Evaluation dimensions: current AI-assisted design focuses on form-making, but its depth of application and comprehensive assessment remain underexplored. Collaborative mechanisms: the "AI co-creation partner" collaborative model has been proposed and applied in the design field, but has not yet established a collaborative process in multi-stakeholder community interaction scenarios. How AI-generated content can be effectively integrated into residents' understanding and how to construct the design process between designers, residents, and AI-assisted design are still lacking practical exploration and validation. This study uses the residual green space of Tielu Third Village in Chongqing as a case study, comparing the "traditional design team" with "AIGC-assisted design" to evaluate the value of AIGC. By filling these gaps, this study aims to bridge the technological potential of AIGC with the practical needs of community micro-regeneration, providing a replicable experiential framework for future co-creation in aging community landscape renewal.

3   Method

This study employs a case comparison, using the aging community of Tielu Third Village in Chongqing, China, as the subject. Four typical residual green spaces (No. 4, No. 5, No. 7, and No. 17), located at the core of the community, were selected for the study (see Fig. 1). Through a comparative analysis of the AI-assisted design path and the traditional manual design path, the study systematically evaluates the applicability and design effectiveness of AIGC in community green space micro-regeneration. The research design focuses on two main areas: scheme generation and scheme evaluation. It comprehensively explores the performance characteristics and potential value of AIGC at each stage of the landscape design process.

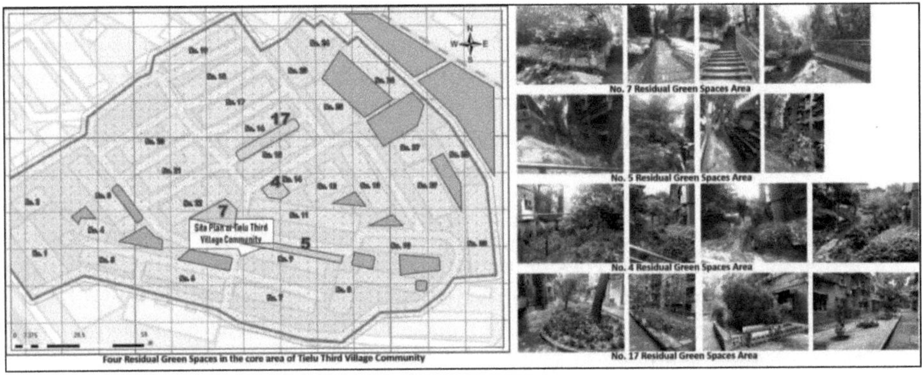

Fig. 1. Four Residual Green Spaces in the core area of Tielu Third Village Community.

3.1   Generation of Design Schemes

To verify the practical application potential of AIGC in micro-scale community green space scenarios, the study sets up two design teams, representing the traditional design path (hereafter referred to as the "traditional group") and the AIGC-assisted design path (hereafter referred to as the "AI group"). Both groups independently carry out design operations under the same site, design cycle, and task conditions, ensuring consistency in the process and equivalence in objectives, thus establishing a comparable experimental foundation (see Fig. 2).

Task Setting and Time Management. To ensure comparability between the design processes of the two groups, the study established a unified task with a design cycle of 5 working days, covering three phases: conceptual design, spatial design, and ecological design. This task was set to test the strategic capabilities and execution efficiency of each path in addressing complex renewal tasks. The design requirements include three aspects: First, site adaptation and ecological integration, which need to address strategies for complex topography and residual vegetation; second, embedding resident usage behaviors, focusing on the activity paths and functional needs of different age groups; third, emphasizing the continuity of community landscape texture.

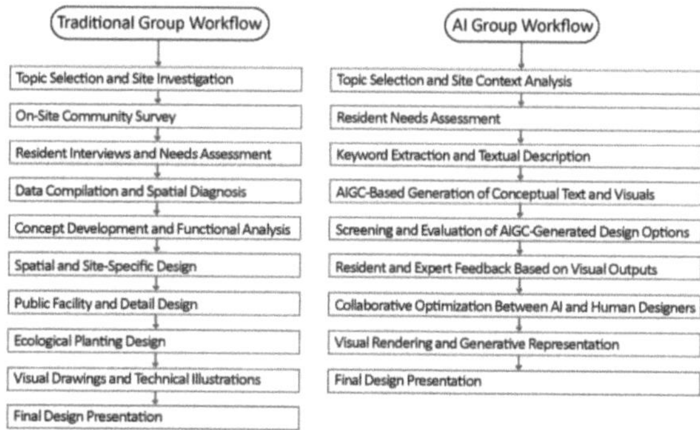

Fig. 2. Comparative Study of Traditional and AI-Assisted Design Approaches.

Traditional Design Approach. The traditional group consists of four landscape designers, each with 3 to 5 years of practical experience. Based on foundational information such as site field surveys, resident interviews, and data analysis, they independently complete the entire landscape design transformation process. Their workflow includes conceptual planning, site diagnosis, conceptual design, functional analysis, spatial planning, public facilities, ecological design, and visual representation, all entirely relying on the designers' professional experience and subjective judgment.

AIGC-Assisted Design Approach. The AI group consists of one designer collaborating with AI tools to complete the entire landscape design process, emphasizing the workflow adaptability and expressive potential of the human–machine co-creation model. The designer is primarily responsible for prompt setting, selection of generated results, and iterative guidance, while the AI system provides support at key stages. First, ChatGPT is used to generate text descriptions and scheme logic based on resident needs and site conditions. Next, DALL·E and Stable Diffusion are employed to produce conceptual sketches, spatial compositions, and vegetation configuration proposals, which are then reviewed and refined based on feedback from residents and experts. Finally, the images are fine-tuned according to the feedback, and the design is integrated and visually expressed in line with the designer's aesthetic. This path explores the creative participation model and efficiency advantages of generative AI in community site design, with both the designer and AI working in collaboration.

3.2 Evaluation of Design Schemes

This study employs a qualitative evaluation method, combining expert judgment, community resident interviews, and design process documentation, to comprehensively compare and analyze the performance differences between the traditional design path and the AIGC-assisted design path in the renewal of community residual green spaces. The evaluation is conducted from multiple perspectives, including spatial, environmental, and social dimensions, to ensure that the selected design is both feasible and sustainable

in practice [12]. Specifically, the evaluation covers seven core dimensions: design efficiency, ecological function, spatial utilization, innovation, detail design, feasibility, and
user acceptance.

Expert Evaluation. The study invited three experts with experience in urban landscape
design and urban renewal to evaluate the design outcomes of both groups. Based on
the seven dimensions mentioned above, the experts conducted detailed discussions and
provided feedback on the two design schemes. From a professional perspective, the
experts not only focused on the overall quality of the design outputs but also specifically
highlighted the performance, potential advantages, and limitations in each dimension.

Resident Feedback Data Collection. The study selected 10 representative long-term
residents for interviews to collect data. The interview content includes resident feedback, which serves as an important supplement for understanding user acceptance and
actual needs. The group of 10 residents was selected to cover different ages (ranging
from 57 to 73 years) and genders (6 females and 4 males). Data was collected through
interviews that focused on the seven dimensions. Each resident, based on their own life
situation, compared the two design schemes and expressed their willingness, concerns,
and expectations regarding the future use of the green space. Resident feedback was
primarily recorded on-site and organized for analysis, with the interview data emphasizing capturing diverse voices and emotional responses in real-life contexts, providing
localized and specific evidence for the scheme evaluation.

Design Process and Analysis Methods. The study recorded key behavioral data during
the design processes of both groups, including time investment, the number of iterations
of manual conceptual designs, and the number of prompt adjustments made by the AI
group. Additionally, the designers' subjective satisfaction and operational evaluations
were considered to further assess the practical benefits brought by AIGC in the design
process. A collaborative mechanism among the designer, AI, and resident users was also
established. Based on this, optimization strategies for the application of AIGC in the
design of community residual green spaces were proposed.

Ethical Considerations This study strictly adheres to human research ethical guidelines. All participants and designers were clearly informed of the study's purpose, process, and the nature of their involvement prior to the start of the research. No sensitive
personal information from participants was collected during the study, and all data were
anonymized and coded, used solely for the purposes of this research analysis. During the
residents' participation, the research team respected their right to express opinions and
their right to withdraw from the study at any time, ensuring that participation was entirely
voluntary. The opinions expressed by participants were also respected and included in
the research findings, ensuring the ethical and legal integrity of the study process.

4   Result

This chapter systematically presents the entire process and comparison of the AIGC-
assisted design path (see Fig. 3) and the traditional design path (see Fig. 4) in the renewal
of community residual green spaces. The analysis focuses on seven dimensions: design

efficiency, spatial utilization, ecological function, innovation, detail design, feasibility, and user acceptance. It provides a comprehensive analysis of expert evaluations, resident feedback, and the design process, documenting the core findings.

4.1 Design Efficiency and Output Performance

In this study, regarding the design cycle, the AIGC-assisted design group was able to generate more than three differentiated complete design schemes within 5 days, while the traditional group was able to generate only one scheme for a single green space in the same period. Specifically, this performance is reflected in the high automation and efficiency of initial draft generation and visual expression. The AI group's designer quickly obtained alternative images with different spatial combinations and visual styles by repeatedly adjusting the prompts, providing a wide range of options for the deepening and selection of design schemes. In contrast, the traditional design group spent more time on manual tasks, such as hand-drawn sketches and digital modeling, with relatively limited creative expansion. In terms of visualization, the AIGC scheme presents high-precision images and diverse landscape compositions, making the intended design clear and intuitive, whether in terms of vegetation configuration or spatial structure. Expert evaluations unanimously agreed that AIGC is more suitable for high-intensity brainstorming and design scheme expansion, allowing designers to focus more on scheme selection and optimization, thus significantly improving overall design efficiency.

Fig. 3. AIGC-assisted Design Scheme for Tielu Third Village Residual Green Space.

Fig. 4. Traditional Design Scheme for Tielu Third Village Residual Green Space.

4.2 Performance of AIGC in Spatial Utilization and Ecological Function

In terms of spatial utilization, the AIGC-generated schemes clearly outperformed the traditional path. Specifically, the AI group's designs demonstrated higher utilization of corner zones and areas with elevation differences, creating more layered and multidimensional landscape green space nodes. Expert evaluations also noted that the AIGC schemes were more diverse and flexible in terms of multifunctional site use, breaking away from the traditional group's tendency toward linear circulation or single-function solutions. As a result, originally underutilized green areas, once overgrown with wild vegetation, were given new functional possibilities. In the ecological function dimension, experts described the AI schemes as having "a richer expression of ecological diversity," characterized by flexible and diverse vegetation selection and configuration, as well as visual advantages in ecological landscape presentation. However, it is important to note that the AIGC schemes demonstrated weaker consideration for the sustainability and site-specific adaptability of the existing ecosystem, raising concerns about aesthetic ecology taking precedence over ecological viability.

4.3 Innovation and Formal Expression

Innovation is one of the most prominent advantages of AIGC-generated schemes. Both expert evaluations and resident feedback consistently indicated that the AI-generated designs outperformed the traditional design path in terms of spatial perception, formal language, organization of design elements, and the coordination of colors and materials. Several experts noted that the AIGC schemes demonstrated a strong visual impact and aesthetic novelty, reflecting an imaginative capacity that goes beyond conventional spatial thinking. At the resident level, the majority of interviewees felt that the AI-generated schemes conveyed a "high-end" aesthetic. One resident even described the designs as "stunning and stylish," particularly impressed by the color combinations and the layered vegetation. The AI schemes showed clear advantages in attracting the attention of non-professional users and evoking emotional resonance. However, while the AIGC schemes excelled in innovation, they also revealed challenges in balancing form and function. Some schemes posed greater technical difficulties in implementation and showed limitations in functional practicality. Therefore, creative outputs generated by AIGC must strike a balance between feasibility and innovation, with designers playing a stronger guiding role in scheme selection and functional realization.

4.4 Limitations in Detail Design and Feasibility

Although the AIGC approach excels in overall concept and visual expression, purely AI-generated schemes sometimes lack a deep understanding of site details, materials, and user behaviors, especially in terms of human-centered design. This shortcoming is reflected in some aspects where the traditional manual design path achieves more refined humanized details, as confirmed by user feedback. Experts also observed that AI-generated schemes tend to be rough in handling local environments and infrastructure—such as slopes, retaining walls, green space boundaries, roads, and leisure facilities—lacking detailed logic and feasibility. For example, in the AI-generated scheme, the connection design of fitness paths in retaining wall areas was misaligned and visually incoherent, leading to problems with practical implementation.

4.5 User Acceptance and Feedback

Resident feedback showed that over 90% of interviewed residents found the AIGC-generated scheme's visual expression easier to understand, allowing them to quickly grasp the overall intent of the design. AIGC design lowered the barrier for non-professionals to understand the design content, particularly in visual recognition and spatial expectation, making it more appealing. One respondent stated, "I can immediately see what this green space will look like," greatly enhancing non-professional users' intuitive understanding and engagement with the design. Moreover, residents even attempted to collaborate with the designers to adjust the AI-generated scheme during the co-creation process. Some residents proactively suggested modifications and new creative prompts, showing enthusiasm and a sense of recognition, which increased their desire to participate in shaping the future state of the green space. This phenomenon further validates the cognitive mediation role of AIGC in community co-creation. However, it is worth noting that two older residents (aged 70 and above) pointed out, "The AI-generated design is beautiful, but it doesn't look like our place," reflecting the shortcomings of AIGC tools in expressing regional culture and building community identity. This resulted in some designs lacking emotional resonance and a sense of belonging. Therefore, the study emphasizes that even in an AIGC-driven design process, the active involvement of designers is necessary to reinforce the integration of community memory and culture into the design of residual green spaces.

4.6 Performance and Application of AIGC in the Community

This study systematically compares the multidimensional performance of AIGC and traditional design paths in community green space design (see Fig. 5), confirming AIGC's outstanding advantages in terms of design generation efficiency, visual expression, spatial innovation, and ecological diversity. It also enhances the diversity and efficiency of residual green space regeneration and renewal in communities. AIGC's efficient output and intuitive visual expression effectively facilitated communication between designers and residents, promoting public participation and co-creation of the design scheme. However, in terms of detail design, feasibility, and cultural expression, AIGC still exhibits significant shortcomings, particularly in complex site adaptation, engineering logic refinement, and community identity building. It shows a high dependency on human intervention and local knowledge. This finding emphasizes that AI-generated content cannot yet replace the crucial role of human designers in practical implementation and cultural adaptation. The successful application of AI technology depends on the integration of human expertise and judgment. Only by combining artificial intelligence with the creative experience of designers can the technological advantages be fully realized, leading to more efficient and sustainable design outcomes.

Fig. 5. Comparison of AIGC and Traditional Design in the Design Process.

5   Discussion

5.1   The Empowering Role of AIGC in Design Efficiency and Creative Expression

The application of artificial intelligence has significantly enhanced design generation efficiency, enabling designers to move from concept to creation much more rapidly [13]. Experimental results clearly confirm the remarkable advantage of AIGC in design efficiency, particularly during the conceptual generation and visual expression stages. AIGC technology can produce diverse visual schemes in a short period, dramatically reducing the overall design cycle compared to traditional workflows. This improvement in efficiency is attributed to generative AI's technical strength in rapid content iteration and image output. Specifically, AIGC tools can convert text into high-quality visual concepts, greatly shortening the traditionally time-consuming steps of hand sketching, ideation, and digital modeling. Moreover, AI-generated models help designers break free from habitual thinking patterns, stimulating more diverse and innovative expressions of landscape form. This opens up new perspectives and methodological pathways for community micro-regeneration, especially in complex, small-scale, and spatially constrained environments. It enables the rapid production of multi-dimensional design prototypes within short timeframes, demonstrating that creativity and visual novelty have become highly promising aspects of AI-generated design. Designers now expect AI tools to push the boundaries of bold imagination in future-oriented concepts [14]. More importantly, AIGC can automatically generate diverse combinations tailored to different spatial scenarios. This strategy of diversified and rapid iteration stands in sharp contrast to the linear design process that traditionally relies on accumulated experience and step-by-step development. It is particularly well-suited to flexible and creativity-driven micro-regeneration contexts. Furthermore, AIGC's automated sketch generation and highly visualized outputs reduce the cost of trial and error in the creative process, allowing designers to focus more on scheme selection, refinement, and user engagement.

5.2 Multidimensional Expansion of Spatial Utilization and Ecological Function

The advantages of AIGC schemes in spatial utilization and ecological function are evident in their ability to integrate diverse spatial nodes with ecological elements. In the case study of this research, AI-generated schemes demonstrate the potential to uncover hidden site value through algorithmic exploration, enhancing the efficiency and ecological functionality of originally idle and fragmented spaces. During layout design, AIGC can effectively optimize the use of limited space, improve ecological performance, and enhance the efficiency of functional organization while adapting to specific site conditions and environmental requirements [15]. By flexibly utilizing spatial fragments such as elevation changes, interstitial gaps, and edge zones within the site, AIGC schemes can activate underused corners and construct multilayered, composite green systems. This approach reshapes inefficient and overlooked residual spaces, endowing them with greater ecological diversity and social functionality. As a result, the designs not only improve the functional diversity of space but also expand the ecological service capacity of community green areas. However, the study also reveals that AI-generated schemes often prioritize rich ecological aesthetics and innovative spatial nodes, while overlooking the community's actual functional needs and long-term maintenance capabilities. Ecological renewal in community settings requires a careful balance between expressive landscape design and ecological sustainability. Excessive algorithmic design interventions may in fact reduce the community's potential for future self-managed adaptation and undermine the long-term resilience of the space.

5.3 Public Understanding and Community Identity

In this study, resident interviews revealed that AIGC-generated visual schemes significantly enhanced non-professional users' intuitive understanding and cognitive acceptance of the design content. Traditional design schemes are often expressed through technical drawings, specialized terminology, or abstract concepts, which can hinder public comprehension and reduce residents' willingness and effectiveness in participating in the design process. In contrast, the high-fidelity visual representations generated by AIGC effectively lowered cognitive barriers, clearly conveying the design concepts and spatial transformation intentions. As a result, residents' participation enthusiasm and satisfaction levels increased. This finding further confirms the substantial potential of AIGC in facilitating public understanding and enhancing community engagement.

At the same time, AIGC functions not only as a tool but also as a collaborative platform that bridges designers and residents. This phenomenon indicates that, through AI-generated real-time visual scenarios, designers can communicate design concepts more intuitively with residents, thus narrowing the cognitive gap between professionals and the general public. The focus of participant discussions shifted from seeking visual perfection to engaging in deeper conversations—specifically, exploring the spatial needs and possibilities underlying the schemes [16]. In this process, residents and designers can collaboratively adjust prompts: residents provide semantic labels, and the AI responds by generating visual sketches. This helps design teams identify residents' latent needs and genuine preferences, offering a low-threshold approach to design negotiation in grassroots communities. If technical optimization is pursued without incorporating resident input, the resulting designs often lack "emotional warmth." AIGC-assisted public engagement can indeed spark more meaningful dialogue and broader creative exchange. The moderate introduction of conversational AI tools can transform residents from passive recipients of design into active co-creators [17]. This model helps establish more efficient communication bridges between residents and designers, shortens the co-creation feedback cycle, and promotes a shift in community design practice from "expert-led" to "publicly engaged," thereby achieving truly collaborative design.

5.4   Challenges and Reflections on Detail Design and Implementability

While AIGC-generated schemes excel in overall conceptualization and visual expression, they still show tendencies toward generalization and vagueness in areas such as topographic adaptation, detailed nodes, and infrastructure integration. This often leads to a contradiction where designs are visually compelling but difficult to implement. AI currently lacks the sensitivity to terrain constraints, user habits, and construction details that human designers possess—a limitation clearly reflected in this study. At this stage, AIGC tools are better suited for early-stage tasks such as idea generation and concept visualization, but are not yet capable of supporting the full process of community space design independently. The final realization and refinement of a design must still rely on manual adjustments by designers. Future development of AIGC systems should place greater emphasis on the integration of spatial and engineering data to enhance practical feasibility.

5.5   Challenges of Cultural Embedding

Some residents reported that the AI-generated schemes lacked a sense of familiar community belonging in terms of local culture and everyday memory. This suggests that while AIGC can improve cognitive efficiency, it struggles to accurately capture the historical sentiments and cultural symbols embedded in community life. As a result, AI-generated designs may fall short in addressing the lived realities and emotional needs of residents [18].Therefore, AIGC-led design processes must be grounded in local culture and emotional connection, with designers playing an active role in uncovering contextual meaning and guiding the evolution of community green spaces. This mechanism is not only essential for ensuring lasting acceptance of AI applications, but also represents a necessary path for AI-generated schemes to achieve social sustainability in the future.

5.6 Significance and Value

Overall, it is foreseeable that the value of AIGC in the field of community landscape micro-regeneration will gradually shift from rapid creative generation to collaborative integration. The successful application of AIGC depends on its ability to deeply learn from and integrate site data, community knowledge, engineering experience, and cultural context. Future community landscape renewal should place greater emphasis on the collaborative relationship among AI, designers, and residents. By establishing multilayered intelligent design systems that incorporate GIS applications, community preference collection, engineering insight, and culturally driven data, AIGC can enhance its adaptability, sustainability, and cultural relevance in complex real-world community scenarios. This study, through the application of AIGC in the renewal of residual green spaces, not only systematically validates the practical potential of generative AI in improving design efficiency, fostering creative expression, and enabling public co-creation, but also reveals the specific role of AIGC-assisted generation and feedback loops in the micro-renewal of community residual green spaces (see Fig. 6). It highlights a possible trajectory for AI-driven community renewal—toward "multi-agent intelligent collaboration." The study clearly indicates that AIGC, as an emerging design force, is reshaping modes of community spatial governance, design generation mechanisms, and modes of public participation. It offers methodological innovation and a theoretical foundation for smart cities, sustainable communities, and digital civic engagement. Moreover, it provides replicable practical insights for advancing AI-powered approaches in the future development of urban public spaces.

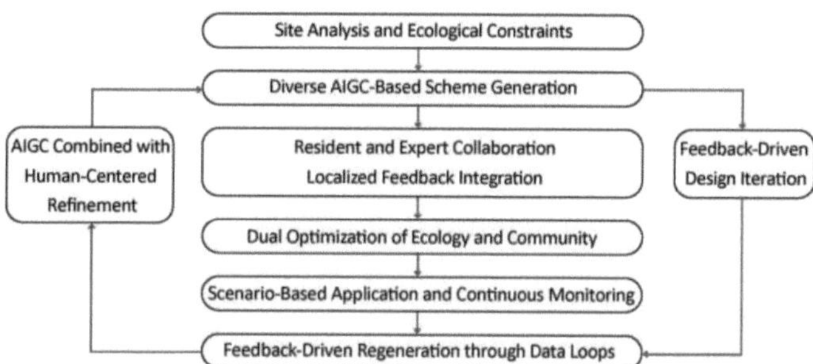

Fig. 6. AIGC-Assisted Generation and Feedback Loop Mechanism.

6 Conclusion

Through empirical comparison, this study preliminarily verifies the application potential of AIGC in the transformation of community residual green spaces, systematically revealing its practical advantages in improving design efficiency, optimizing ecological functions, and enhancing resident satisfaction. At the same time, the research identifies clear limitations of AIGC in adapting to complex sites, expressing cultural contexts, and delivering detailed, implementable designs—areas that still require human intervention and local expertise.

Building on the findings from green space design, this study not only proposes practical recommendations—such as integrating GIS spatial data, optimizing collaboration between designers and AI tools, and incorporating community co-creation mechanisms—but also further reveals that AIGC is advancing community landscape renewal from a one-way visual output model toward a paradigm of multi-agent intelligent collaboration. AIGC has thus evolved beyond being a mere technical tool to become a critical bridge that stimulates community participation, connects professionals and the public, and facilitates the local translation of design knowledge. This emerging paradigm provides a theoretical foundation for achieving intelligent, participatory, and culturally sustainable community landscape regeneration.

Future research should further explore the ethical frameworks of AIGC systems, the integration of local cultural narratives, and the improvement of AI's self-learning capabilities. By advancing the deep integration of technology and society, space and culture, AIGC holds great promise as a core driver for the sustainable transformation and renewal of community landscapes.

Acknowledgments. This research was supported by the community residents of Tielu Third Village in Chongqing, whose participation and insights were invaluable. We would also like to thank the experts and design practitioners who contributed their time and perspectives to the evaluation process. Their input greatly enriched the depth and relevance of this study.

Disclosure of Interests. The author declare no competing financial or non-financial interests related to the content of this article. This research was conducted independently and received no funding or influence from commercial, governmental, or private institutions. All evaluations and conclusions were developed based on academic investigation and empirical observation in the studied community settings.

References

1. Wolch, J.R., Byrne, J., Newell, J.P.: Urban green space, public health, and environmental justice: the challenge of making cities 'just green enough.' Landscape Urban Plann. **125**, 234–244 (2014)
2. Kong, F., Yin, H., Nakagoshi, N., Zong, Y.: Urban green space network development for biodiversity conservation: identification based on graph theory and gravity modeling. Landsc. Urban Plan. **95**(1–2), 16–27 (2010)
3. Xing, Y., Gan, W., Chen, Q.: Artificial intelligence in landscape architecture: a survey. Int. J. Mach. Learn. Cybern. (2025)
4. Zhou, C.H., Zhang, Y., Fu, L.S., Xue, Y.W.: Assessing mini-park installation priority for regreening planning in densely populated cities. Sustain. Cities Soc. **67**(4), 102716 (2021)
5. Yin, Y., Shao, Y., Wang, Y., Wu, L.: Developing a pocket park prescription program for human restoration: an approach that encourages both people and the environment. Int. J. Environ. Res. Public Health **20**(17), 6642 (2023)
6. Zhang, S., Stewart, W.P., Chan, E.S.W.: Place-making upon return home: influence of greenway experiences. Leis. Sci. **45**(1), 46–70 (2020)
7. Cantrell, B., Zhang, Z., Liu, X.: Artificial intelligence and machine learning in landscape architecture. In: Burry, J., Mueller, C., Newton, S. (eds.) The Routledge Companion to Artificial Intelligence in Architecture, pp. 232–247. Routledge, New York (2021)

8. Huang, R., Lin, H., Chen, C., Zhang, K., Zeng, W.: Plantography: incorporating iterative design process into generative artificial intelligence for landscape rendering. In: Proceedings of the 2024 CHI Conference on Human Factors in Computing Systems, pp. 1–19. ACM, New York (2024)

9. Hassan, M.S.: Leveraging artificial intelligence in landscape concept design phase. J. Al-Azhar Univ. Eng. Sect. **19**(72), 314–324 (2024)

10. Jiang, F.F., et al.: Generative urban design: a systematic review on problem formulation, design generation, and decision-making. Prog. Plan. **180**(1–35), 100795 (2023)

11. Geekiyanage, D., Fernando, T., Keraminiyage, K.: Mapping participatory methods in the urban development process: a systematic review and case-based evidence analysis. Sustainability **13**(16), 8992 (2021)

12. Abramov, A., et al.: Barabási–albert-based network growth model to sustainable urban planning. Sustainability **17**(3) (2025)

13. Valença, G., Azevedo, C., Moura, F., de Sá, A.M.: Creating visualizations using generative AI to guide decision-making in street designs: a viewpoint. J. Urban Mobil. **7**, 100104 (2025)

14. Cao, Z., Mao, Y., Mustafa, M., Mohd Isa, M.H.: Future cities imagined by ChatGPT-4o: human evaluation using importance-performance analysis. Humanit. Soc. Sci. Commun. **12**(1), 1–12 (2025)

15. Li, C., Zhang, T., Du, X., Zhang, Y., Xie, H.: Generative AI models for different steps in architectural design: a literature review. Front. Arch. Res. (2024)

16. Guridi, J.A., et al.: From fake perfects to conversational imperfects: Exploring image-generative AI as a boundary object for participatory design of public spaces. Proc. ACM Hum. -Comput. Interact. **9**(2), 1–33 (2025)

17. Tavanapour, N., Poser, M., Bittner, E.A.C.: Supporting the idea generation process in citizen participation - toward an interactive system with a conversational agent as facilitator. In: Proceedings of the 27th European Conference on Information Systems (ECIS), Stockholm-Uppsala, pp. 1–17 (2019)

18. Chong, L., Yang, M.: AI vs. Human: the public's perceptions of the design abilities of artificial intelligence. In: Proceedings of the Design Society, vol. 3, pp. 495–504 (2023)

AI and Concept Art: Evaluating Generative Artificial Intelligence in the Co-creative Process of Character Design

Gabriela Zanella Leal[(✉)] [ID], Eduarda Dippe Ramos Rondon [ID],
Isabel Maria Marques Carvalho [ID], and Milton Luiz Horn Vieira [ID]

Federal University of Santa Catarina, Florianópolis, SC 88035-972, Brazil
`gabrielazleal@gmail.com, isabel.carvalho@posgrad.ufsc.br,`
`milton.vieira@ufsc.br`

Abstract. The development of a character's design is a creative process that demands multiple iterations before a result is reached, and a fundamental step in this process is the elaboration of a mood board. Generative AI has diverse documented applications in the context of the entertainment industry, its use in character creation included. However, one of the challenges in using this technology is the inconsistency in terms of quality of the generated images, in terms of variety in its iterations and in terms of adherence to the prompt. To verify its applicability, this study proposes the integration of generative AI tools into the elaboration of the mood board for the creation of character designs. The focus of this research was to establish a metric that evaluates if the images generated by AIs are adequate to be incorporated into the character design development pipeline.

Keywords: Character Design · Generative Artificial Intelligence · Computational Co-Creativity

1 Introduction

The use of generative artificial intelligence as a tool for the creation of images through text prompts has become increasingly popular in recent years, as seen in the case of the DALL-E model from 2020. There are diverse documented uses of generative AI in the entertainment industry, including its utilization in character creation. Character creation is a shared step in the production workflow of various medias, including digital games, animation, comic books, etc. The development of a character's design is a creative process that demands multiple iterations before a result is reached, and a fundamental aspect of it is the elaboration of a mood board [1]. One possible way of incorporating AI technology into the character creation pipeline is to bypass the typical websites and search engines by asking generative AI models to create the images one would need to be placed into a mood board for inspiration. However, one of the challenges in the use of this technology for this purpose is the inconsistency in the quality of the generated images, the variety in their iterations and their proper adherence to the prompt.

J. Wei et al. (Eds.): HCII 2025, LNCS 16346, pp. 60–73, 2026.
https://doi.org/10.1007/978-3-032-13187-4_5

Therefore, the objective of this article is to establish a metric to evaluate AI generated images and determine if they're adequate to be incorporated into the elaboration of a mood board for character designs and assisting in the creation of concept art, being integrated as an AI agent in a co-creative system of division of labor with human agents. These image results were then validated with an anonymous questionnaire aimed at visual artists. For this research, only free to use AI tools will be considered, including those with free trial periods. This study justifies itself due to growing interest in the co-creative incorporation of AI image generation tools into the character design pipeline.

2   Theoretical Basis

The visual development of characters is a common step found in the production pipelines for different types of narrative media, such as digital games, animations and comics. Suzuki [1] says that in the pre-production stage of an animated project, a cycle of searching for references, initial exploration and art refinement can be observed. Once the fictional world in which the character is inserted is established, techniques such as the elaboration of a mood board are used to collect references and inspirations, followed by elaboration of concept art which involves the initial visual exploration of the ideas for the character. From these results, a final design is established and refined to be used in the production.

A mood board, which consists in collecting, selecting and organizing images into a collage, is assembled with the express purpose of bringing together references, colors, shapes and representations of various visual elements to fuel creativity during the ideation process. These images can be both representative and referential as well as include subjective concepts, intended to evoke feelings and the personality of the character in abstract [2]. Supported by a textual description of the character, the mood board can assist the artist in incorporating and combining a variety of ideas when crafting concept art, which is the next step in the pipeline of visual narrative projects. Unlike an illustration, which is usually a product in and of itself, the goal of concept art is to provide multiple visual solutions and explore a range of possibilities, promoting originality in the designs that will be finalized later [3].

Nieminen [4] affirms that a character's personality must be conveyed in their appearance, which can be achieved through the intentional use of shape and color, language, proportions, etc. Tillman [5] also lists other important factors in character design, such as functionality and recognition: form must follow function, not only in terms of anatomy or proportions, but also in the character's clothing, accessories and tools; all its physical characteristics must be recognizable and make visual sense, and the artist must avoid adding visual noise that does not contribute to the understanding of the whole.

Generative AI tools have shown great potential applications in the creation of art and have become a topic of interest in art and programming communities [6]. In 2020, OpenAI introduced DALL-E as a text-to-image model, allowing users to describe a concept in text (or "prompt") and see it transformed into a final image. The field of digital visual art was particularly affected by the popularization of generative Artificial Intelligence tools such as DALL-E, Midjourney and OpenArt, which are frequently used to generate final images in the creative process [7].

With the growing popularity of these tools, the need to learn how to use them efficiently has also arisen. Creating images through trial and error; writing a prompt and then changing or redoing it based on the result returned by the AI; all are possible methods of utilizing this technology, but they can be time-consuming and bring unpredictable results. Therefore, prompt engineering—the technique of developing prompts with the aim of generating useful and relevant results—can be used in this context. How this technique is applied depends on the result desired by the user and may involve different parameters and methods. Like Dang et al. [8] say, extensive and detailed prompts may lead to conflict of information and bring less effective results. It is also important to point out that it is still not clear how prompts are generalized across different platforms, with results varying drastically depending on the model utilized.

Liu and Chilton [6] suggest focusing on keywords when preparing the prompt, since changing the structure of the sentence without modifying them does not significantly alter the quality of the result. Oppenlaender et al. [7] cite a commonly used prompt structure, developed by Smith [9]: "[Medium] [Subject] [Artist(s)] [Details] [Image Repository Support]".

Images generated by AI are commonly produced with the intention of being finished art. However, the application of AI in the ideation stage, especially in a co-creative manner, is still under-researched. Considering that the beginning of the character development process involves iterative steps, with a focus on generating quick alternatives to assess their viability, the use of generative AI has potential to simplify and accelerate this process.

Finally, Karimi et al. [10] defines computational co-creativity as: *"Interaction between at least one AI agent and at least one human where they take action based on the response of their partner and their own conceptualization of creativity during the co-creative task"*. Unlike autonomous systems, the co-creative system aided by Artificial Intelligence benefits by integrating human perception and evaluation with the agility and practicality of AI, thus enhancing creative results. There are several types of collaborations, such as division of labor, assistantship and partnership, in which at least one of the collaborating parties is an AI tool of some kind.

For the purposes of this article, a system of division of labor was chosen to test possible AI applications, defined as *"individuals working independently and sharing their ideas after accomplishing tasks"* [10]. Based on a character description, the computational agent (AI) will generate images and, in parallel, the human agent will collect images, to then create a mood board out of both sets of images in a collaborative process.

We propose, then, a method to evaluate the AI's performance as an agent in this co-creative system.

3   Method

Based on the theoretical foundation explained in the previous topic, the following methodological procedures were developed to carry out this research:

1. Creation of a character briefing, including a short physical, psychological and personality description.

2. Transformation of this briefing into a prompt based on the structure established in the previous segment.
3. Application of this prompt in the selected AIs, generating 8 image results in each one.
4. Definition of the following criteria, to be used in the evaluation of the generated images: variety, quality and fidelity to the theme.
5. Validation of the perceived variety, quality and fidelity of the generated images through the application of an anonymous questionnaire.

3.1 Briefing and Prompt

The character pre-production stage, which is the focus of this research paper, is similar in terms of process throughout different forms of media. For this article, we chose to develop a character for a theoretical visual narrative production, which could fit into the context of an animation, a game or a comic book. Therefore, the following character brief was created:

"The protagonist is a young human, between 20 and 25 years old and with an androgynous appearance. He likes to play games on his computer and has a habit of committing small thefts and harmless frauds. Despite this, he is not a bad person. He is irreverent, impatient, solitary, creative, agile and practical. His world takes a turn when characters from a fantastic and magical universe task him with a mission, and he discovers himself a skilled rogue."

Based on this description, a mood board was created to guide the visual development of his design (see Fig. 1).

Fig. 1. The character's mood board.

With the briefing properly defined, the prompt to be used to generate alternatives through different AIs was then crafted, as quoted below:

"Illustration of a clever, agile young male rogue in modern casual wear, with hints of thievery like a tool belt or visible knife."

The character's main characteristics were included in the prompt text, combining elements of personality and appearance, as well as citing tools that help identify the character as a rogue. We chose to mention accessories more specifically, as providing examples in the prompt helps with generating better results [8]. In the original Portuguese version of this paper, we also decided to write the prompt in English to avoid inconsistencies between the applications of each AI, considering that the selected generative AI platforms use English as their operating language.

3.2 Image Generation

The following generative AIs were selected for this study, chosen due to their accessibility, ease of use and either free or partial online availability with no charge: DALL-E 3, ArtBreeder, Runway ML, Deep Dream Generator and Craiyon.

DALL-E 3, unlike other generative AI tools that have their own platform for generating images, is accessed through ChatGPT 4, available for use free of charge. Other than the initial command requesting the AI chat tool to generate a picture based on the following prompt, there were no other visible settings for image generation.

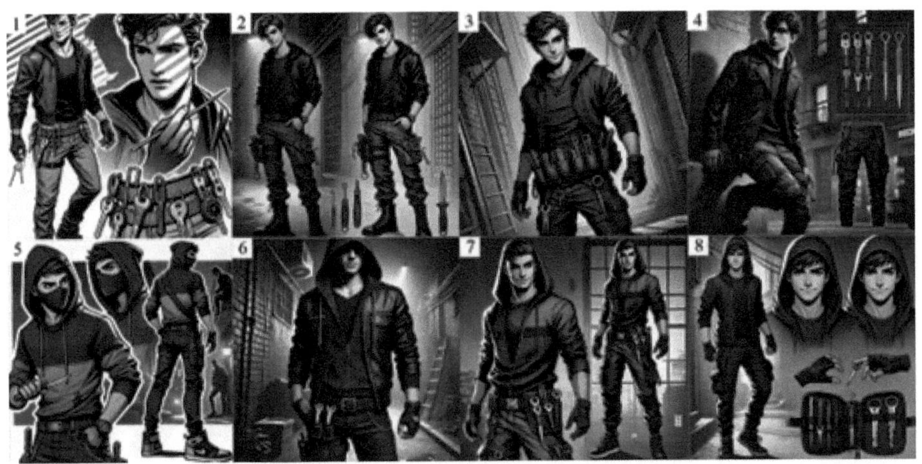

Fig. 2. Compilation of images generated by DALL-E.

Artbreeder and Runway ML possess several image creations and editing tools, as well as advanced settings for the generations. Therefore, we opted to use text-to-image tools and the standard settings for image generation, to ensure greater approximation with the other platforms and minimize deviations in results external to the parameters analyzed by this research. Both AI tools have the option to use a fixed seed across generations, a setting which was kept off since it both results in less variation and is not an option in other AI tools used in this study. ArtBreeder had the setting "compute

Fig. 3. Compilation of images generated by Artbreeder.

steps" set to 4 and a resolution output of 1024 by 1024 pixels, while Runway ML had the "precision" setting on 7.5 and a resolution output of 768 by 768 pixels.

Four of our chosen AI tools also had a variety of generative AI models within their platforms, allowing the user to select the one that best suits their purposes. Since there are numerous options and the platforms provide limited free use, preliminary tests were carried out to evaluate the models; the ones that showed results compatible with the objectives of this work were then selected. Artbreeder used the model "SDXL Lightning", "Artistic 2" was the model selected for Deep Dream Generator, "Concept Art" for Runway ML and "v4 Auto" for Craiyon. A 1:1 ratio was used for the image outputs.

Fig. 4. Compilation of images generated by Runway ML.

All the settings mentioned above were kept standardized with minimum changes to ensure a baseline output similarity between every AI, as not all of them had equivalent options. Below, in Figs. 2, 3, 4, 5 and 6, we show the compiled results of each generative AI.

Fig. 5. Compilation of images generated by Deep Dream Generator.

Fig. 6. Compilation of images generated by Craiyon.

3.3 Analysis Criteria

Based on the character design concepts formerly explained in Sect. 2, the following criteria were established to analyze the results generated by the selected AI:

Variety: The character's mood board must offer a variety of visual references, brought together with the aim of stimulating the artist's creativity—just as the subsequent stage, concept art, is done iteratively and with the aim of exploring possibilities. Therefore, it is preferable that there is a variety of visual characteristics to the character across image generation, if the specificities of the brief descriptions are met. Since there is no description of the character's physical appearance in the character brief, a diverse offering of qualities, such as poses, hair, clothes, skin color and facial features would be the desired result.

Quality: Accuracy in the representation of the character was cited as an important element in the concept art stage, necessary to allow the information present in the design to be easily understood by the audience. In preliminary AI image generation tests, it was observed that in certain cases the images contained visual inconsistencies, such as errors in anatomy, objects and clothes that blend with each other and with the character itself, among others. While they may not be harmful in images intended to serve as aesthetic-symbolic references, visual inconsistencies can pose problems when presented as representative references.

Fidelity: In preliminary image generation tests, there were cases in which the AI generated images with characteristics that did not match what was specified in the prompt. To validate its use as a co-creative agent in the character development process, it is important to verify its ability to perform the assigned task efficiently and accurately.

The evaluation criteria for the AI-generated images are summarized and exemplified in the following Table 1:

Table 1. Criteria evaluation parameters.

Criteria	Low	Average	High
Variety	Almost identical poses, hair, clothes, ethnicity and facial features	Few variations in poses, hair, clothes, ethnicity and facial features	Almost all poses, hair, clothes, ethnicity and facial features are different
Quality	Anatomical errors, indistinguishable objects, hallucinations	Minor anatomical errors, barely recognizable objects, no hallucinations	No anatomical errors, well-detailed material objects and clothing, no hallucinations
Fidelity	Images don't match the prompt's theme or descriptions	Images match some of the prompt requirements	Met almost all the requirements elaborated in the prompt without contradictions

3.4 Application of Anonymous Questionnaire

To evaluate the output of each generative AI tool, an anonymous questionnaire aimed at practitioners of visual arts (designers, illustrators, comic artists, animators, etc.) was created. The research scope of this paper is to analyze the possibility of implementing AI into the creative workflow of artists and other visual art creators, therefore, the target public was selected based on the understanding that participants with experience in the area would have the necessary discernment to evaluate this applicability once given instructions on how the criteria is meant to be utilized.

The questionnaire remained open from June 3rd, 2025, to June 9th, 2025, totaling a period of 7 days. It was shared through relevant online spaces, such as Discord servers and WhatsApp groups, which revolved, at least partially, around the sharing and creating of visual arts. In total, there were 37 recorded respondents, with one respondent being excluded due to lack of experience in any visual arts field, amounting to 36 usable responses. The questionnaire featured an informed consent agreement at the start and was then split into three different sections meant to evaluate each specific metric, with a brief explanation of their definitions outlined in their respective headers. Respondents were then asked to pick between "low", "average" or "high" for each grouping of generative AI output, for all three metrics. The specific AI that generated each group of images was not disclosed to avoid personal biases.

3.5 Analysis of Generated Images and Questionnaire Results

The results obtained varied greatly in relation to the analysis criteria. DALL-E was believed to have generated the best outputs, as observed by the researchers in this experiment, meeting high quality and fidelity parameters. However, like other AIs, it did not completely meet the variety requirement, according to the researcher's perceptions, as seen in Table 2 below:

Table 2. Expected results of image analysis for each tool.

Tool	Variety	Quality	Fidelity
DALL-E	Average	High	High
Artbreeder	Low	Average	Average
Runway ML	Low	Low	High
Deep Dream Generator	Average	High	Average
Craiyon	Low	Average	Average

To verify this, the questionnaire mentioned in the above segment was applied, and the results are as follows (Fig. 7, 8 and 9):

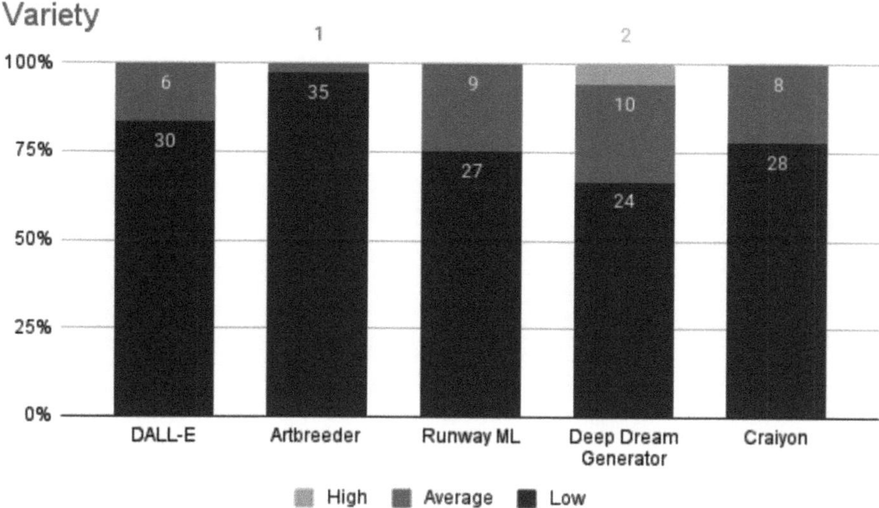

Fig. 7. Graphic showcasing respondent's evaluation of each AI's variety metric.

Variety:

Though the respondents' perceptions of ArtBreeder, Craiyon and Runway ML met the researchers' projected results, the perceptions of DALL-E and Deep Dream Generator were lower than the expected projections. Despite this divergence in overall perceptions, this confirms our hypothesis that the chosen generative AI models have performed poorly in this metric and would not significantly stimulate the creativity of visual artists using generative AI as tool. Notably, most of the characters had similar skin tones, hair color, haircuts, poses and clothing despite none of these attributes being specifically mentioned, going against the desired results of this metric and therefore failing as a useful tool for this purpose. This also raises the discussion of how generative AI tends to follow stereotypes across its image generation, replicating certain physical characteristics unless explicitly told to do otherwise (Fig. 7).

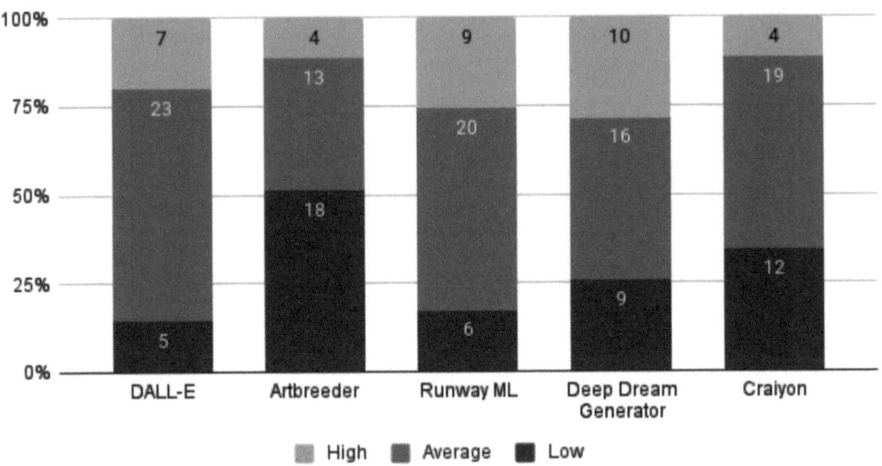

Fig. 8. Graphic showcasing respondent's evaluation of each AI's quality metric.

Quality:

Overall, the results did not correspond with our expected projections, with every AI scoring lower than the predicted evaluation except for Runway ML, which scored higher, and Craiyon, which matched our predictions. However, the difference in results does not point to a clear enough answer, with some divergence of opinion between respondents. Therefore, it would be prudent to further test this specific metric with a larger sample size to verify if any clearer patterns emerge. It is also worth pointing out that, independently of these results, generative AI's ability to accurately represent real-world objects and people advances at a rapid pace, therefore the quality of its outputs – as defined in this paper – is expected to eventually meet the threshold of desired results, as generative models continue to be further developed and refined (Fig. 8).

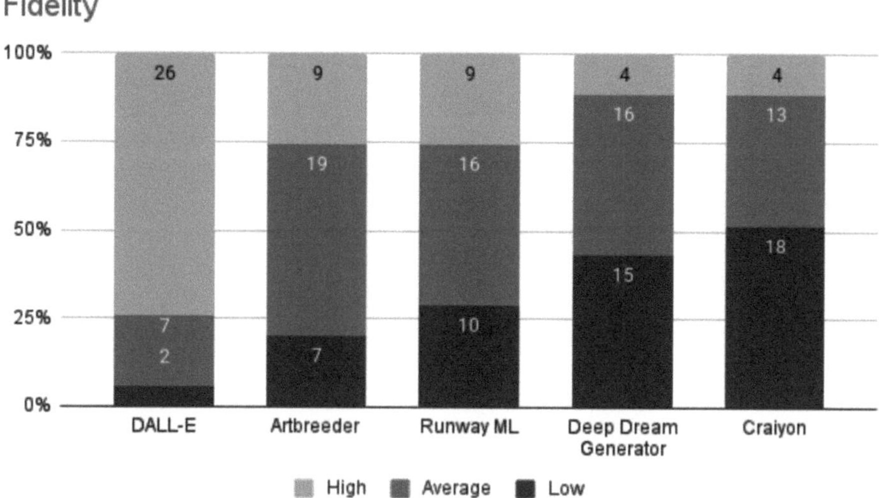

Fig. 9. Graphic showcasing respondent's evaluation of each AI's fidelity metric.

Fidelity:

Most of the evaluated AIs met the expected results, though Craiyon and Runway ML scored lower than the projections. According to our prompt, the images should have been of a young rogue, wearing modern casual clothing and sporting a tool belt or visible knife. Overall, the respondents agreed that the images generated by DALL-E were the most satisfactory, which happened to be the ones with the clearest and most varied examples of tools and knives, both elements explicitly mentioned in the prompt. Notably, DALL-E also incorporated extra elements into its outputs to characterize this rogue character as such, like a face mask and a hoodie over his head. Runway ML and Craiyon may have scored lower due to the lack of visual adherence to the theme, outputting characters that were male and wore certain articles of modern looking clothing, but without any other clear indicators of the desired "roguishness". We can assume that this happened because different tools will interpret the prompt and each of the constituting words differently, the specifics of which is something that is difficult to account for when using these tools (Fig. 9).

4   Conclusion

This paper established three metrics to evaluate images generated by AI to verify whether they would be suitable for being incorporated into the crafting of mood boards, which are used as a tool in character design development. To standardize this experiment, a single brief prompt was defined following the suggested structure established in the bibliography and then applied across the board on every selected generative AI tool to generate similar outputs. Minimum changes were implemented to each AI's settings to ensure a baseline output similarity, as not all of them had equivalent options. After analyzing the grouped outputs, the researchers then evaluated how the AI tools performed on all metrics, creating a table of expected perceptions, and then distributed an online questionnaire aimed at practitioners of visual arts of any kind to validate these results.

In terms of variety, an important metric when it comes to creativity and iteration in visual development, the generative AI tools selected for this study were found to not met the desired criteria. This becomes an issue when considering the growing prevalence of AI generated images in search engine results; visual arts professionals might grow increasingly unable to use search engines and websites to find inspiration that is sufficiently varied and unique, instead being faced with AI generated content that does not offer enough variety to stimulate their creativity. The other two metrics, quality and fidelity, were found to have met the criteria more satisfactorily, with some reservations. Given the results, we can conclude that the current usefulness of generative AI tools for artists who want to use them as a part of their work pipeline as a co-creative agent is limited, though certain AIs are better suited to the task than others. It would also be valuable, for future research on the subject, to collect a bigger sample of respondents, seeing if any clearer trends in output perception emerge. In addition, the metrics presented in this paper can be used as a basis for further judging the usability of images generated by other and future AI platforms.

While the prompt used to generate the images for this paper was kept short and brief, in preliminary tests the results showed greater variation when a longer and more detailed prompt was utilized. There is room to explore different results with variations of the same prompt, using added descriptive detail, in different AIs. Techniques for developing prompts that allow for a greater level of iteration and variety can also be explored.

It should be noted that since each platform uses a different generative AI model, the prompt used in this paper could be further tested and adapted for better results if these different models are taken into consideration. There is room to experiment with specific prompt guidelines for a given tool, ensuring a structure that works most efficiently for each of them.

Furthermore, this paper's findings offer some important metrics that could be useful in understanding the ramifications of overreliance and overuse of generative AI in the creation of new visual artifacts. We have found that generative AI on its own may not be able to satisfy the needs of artists seeking reference materials, as shown by the results of this study.

Acknowledgments. This study was financed in part by the Coordenação de Aperfeiçoamento de Pessoal de Nível Superior - Brasil (Finance Code 001). We thank the Fundação de Amparo à Pesquisa e Inovação do Estado de Santa Catarina (FAPESC) for their financial support for this research, through grant number 18-2024.

References

1. Suzuki, S.S.: Visual Development: Exploração visual na pipeline de animação 3D. Bachelor thesis, Universidade Federal do Rio Grande do Sul (2020)
2. Leal, G.Z.: HQ e Design: propondo um procedimento metodológico para o desenvolvimento de Histórias em Quadrinho. Bachelor thesis, Universidade Federal de Santa Catarina (2021)

3. Rässa, J.: Concept art creation methodologies: Visual Development of "Rock Boy". Bachelor thesis, South-Eastern Finland University of Applied Sciences (2018)
4. Nieminen, M.: Psychology in Character Design: Creation of a Character Design Tool. Bachelor thesis, South-Eastern Finland University of Applied Sciences (2017)
5. Tillman, B.: Creative Character Design, 2nd edn. CRC Press, Boca Raton, FL, USA (2011)
6. Liu, V., Chilton, L.B.: Design guidelines for prompt engineering text-to-image generative models. In: 2022 CHI Conference on Human Factors in Computing Systems, pp. 1–23. Association for Computing Machinery, New Orleans, LA, USA (2022)
7. Oppenlaender, J., Linder, R., Silvennoinen, J.: Prompting AI art: an investigation into the creative skill of prompt engineering. Int. J. Hum. Comput. Interact. **41**(16), 10207–10229 (2025)
8. Dang, H., Mecke, L., Lehmann, F., Goller, S., Buschek, D.: How to prompt? Opportunities and challenges of zero- and few-shot learning for human-AI interaction in creative applications of generative models. In: ACM CHI Conference on Human Factors in Computing Systems – Workshops, pp. 1–7. ACM, New York, NY, USA (2022)
9. A traveler's guide to the latent space. https://sweet-hall-e72.notion.site/A-Traveler-s-Guide-to-the-Latent-Space-85efba7e5e6a40e5bd3cae980f30235f. Accessed 28 May 2025
10. Karimi, P., Grace, K., Maher, M.L., Davis, N.: Evaluating creativity in computational co-creative systems. In: 9th International Conference on Computational Creativity, pp. 104–111. ACC, Salamanca, Spain (2018)

Evaluating Perceptions of AI Generated Images in Architecture Using the Lovelace Test

Athena Moustaka$^{(\boxtimes)}$ (ID), Mahsa Seifhashemi (ID), and Paul Blindell

Salford University, Manchester M5 4WT, UK
`a.moustaka@salford.ac.uk`

Abstract. We are witnessing a rise in the use of AI for architectural visualisations, reflective of a global shift with implications for visual representation and design pedagogy. This change is prompting questions about how discernible and how effective AI-generated images can be in portraying architectural spaces convincingly. In this paper, we present the initial findings of a wider ongoing study at the University of Salford, investigating perceptions of AI-generated images. We focus on the ability of 56 participants to discern between AI-generated architectural images and human-created CGIs. To our knowledge, this is the first study of its kind to systematically evaluate human perceptions in the use of AI-generated imagery in architecture. A mix of students and construction professionals with varying levels of experience and from across 2 continents participated in two sets of tests: Task 1, where the images presented individually and Task 2, where participants needed to identify the image in a pair of two. We then asked participants if the AI images could meet the criteria of the Lovelace test, a benchmark for assessing whether an artificial agent can produce creative output on a par with a human. Findings indicate significant differences in perception relative to experience levels, with less experience surprisingly yielding more accuracy. We also find that while generated images are received as highly creative, they are perceived as of less value and originality. The results suggest that the experience with AI does not equal better accuracy. We conclude that AI visualisations are at a threshold in producing work that is considered creative, but perception of these images is influenced by doubts about meaning, value and authorship.

Keywords: Midjourney · Lovelace Test · AI-generated images · Architectural Visualisations · Computer-Generated Images (CGI)

1 Introduction

1.1 Assessing AI vs Human- Turing vs Lovelace

Recent developments in generative AI and particularly in diffusion-based algorithms have enabled machines to produce architectural images that mimic and even rival human outputs in visual sophistication. However, architectural design is not merely a formal exercise; a designer needs to apply a series of complex cognitive processes, such as spatial reasoning, understanding of sociocultural context, and empathising with a potential user

J. Wei et al. (Eds.): HCII 2025, LNCS 16346, pp. 74–90, 2026.
https://doi.org/10.1007/978-3-032-13187-4_6

to be able to create spaces that are experienced as embodied practices. While AI can replicate the visual language of architecture and mimic features and styles, the extent to which it can generate images of the same qualities as human ones, is not clear. Unlike designers, who empathise with users of space in order to design, AI is not capable of applying empathy or reflecting on embodied experience. This raises some questions: are the spaces produced through learning processes of preexisting visuals the same as creating spaces through CGI means? Do spaces maintain their qualities, and are they still responsive to human needs? These questions remain contested at a time when we are seeing an ever-increasing amount of AI use in architectural images.

There is no doubt that the application of artificial intelligence in architectural visualisations has made the generation of images faster and cheaper, and therefore more widespread. As we become more likely to inhabit or interact with spaces produced using AI, there are questions that emerge, relating to the authorship and aesthetics of these spaces. Are AI-produced spaces potentially creating different experiences for their users? How capable are we of distinguishing between spaces or visual representations generated by AI versus those created by human designers using CGI software? To explore these questions, the two main approaches of assessing AI intelligence are discussed: the Turing test and the Lovelace test.

As architecture and the design of spaces involve the intersection of embodiment, empathy, and cultural expression we question if AI, which produces visually convincing renderings, can simulate the embedded design thinking that reflects human experience. The issue at stake is not technical capability alone, but whether AI-generated spaces *resonate* with viewers and those experiencing them, particularly those trained to read and interpret the language of architectural space.

2   Can Artificial Intelligence Ever Be Truly Intelligent?

2.1   Assessing AI Intelligence: The Turing Test

Testing the ability of an AI system to surpass human intelligence has been at the core of the pursuit of Artificial intelligence technology. Alan Turing coined the eponymous test back in 1950 as a way of testing the limits of AI. The Turing Test is an evaluative measure designed to assess a machine's ability to exhibit intelligent behaviour indistinguishable from that of a human being. In Turing's test (Fig. 1), a human judge interacts with both a machine and a human participant through text-based communication, and is then asked to determine which is which (Hingston 2010). Turing's primary intention was to address the question of whether machines can think, by focusing on their ability to mimic human conversational capabilities (Copeland & Proudfoot 2007). The outcome establishes that if a machine can successfully persuade the judge of its humanity, it can be deemed as exhibiting intelligent behaviour.

The first observation to be made about the Turning test, is that Turing was looking for human *behaviour* of the machine. For Turing, this ability for the machine to mimic a human in a *social* context was what would distinguish its intelligence. At the point where the *social* intelligence was met, this was the point that it had surpassed. In other words, it was not the computational ability Turning was primarily interested in, but the *social* ability.

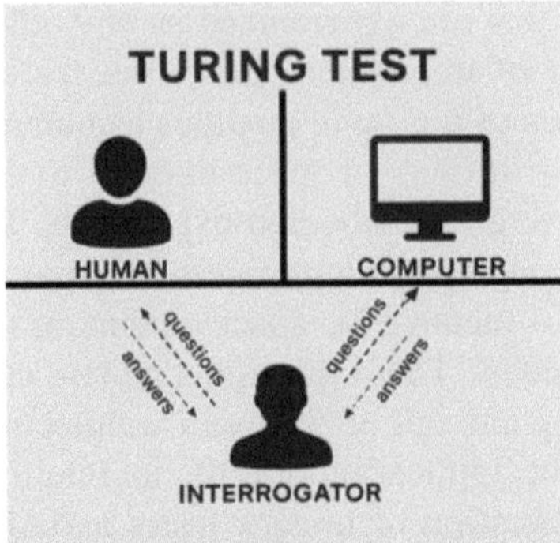

Fig. 1. The Turing Test: An interrogator interacting simultaneously with two respondents- a computer and a human- needs to identify correctly which of the two is the non-human.

Naturally, the Turing Test has faced both acclaim and criticism since its conception. Proponents argue that it effectively estimates machine intelligence in social contexts, while critics contend that conversational imitation does not equate to true understanding or cognitive abilities (Marcus et al. 2016). Adopting a viewpoint where the imitation abilities equal human intelligence is oversimplifying the very notion of intelligence. This simplified viewpoint suggests that machines can pass the test through superficial mimicry rather than genuine comprehension (Berrar & Schuster 2014).

2.2 Ada Lovelace and the Lovelace Effect

The debate, however, about whether AI can ever be truly intelligent, had started long before Alan Turing, with the theoretical questions of Ada Lovelace in the mid 19th century. At the age of 18, Lovelace was working alongside Charles Babbage and his "analytical machine". Although never fully constructed, this apparatus was designed to allow programmable instructions and is considered a precursor to modern-day computers. Lovelace was the first to recognise, whilst working with Babbage, that a machine could have capabilities beyond calculations, but to do so, it would need to act beyond pre-programmed instructions. She was the first to envision a machine capable of programming things other than numbers, such as music and poetry, therefore kickstarting the discussion on artificial creativity. The Lovelace objection, the question of whether a machine can move beyond simple computation and become creative, appears in her work, although the term was coined much later.

The Lovelace Objection. The widely known Lovelace objection is a philosophical argument stating that artificial intelligence cannot be truly creative because it only executes pre-programmed tasks and lacks original thought. While there is an element of this belief in Ada Lovelace's work, her discussion of Charles Babbage's Analytical Engine, present a more nuanced understanding of the relationship between human creativity and machine operations. Some contemporary scholars continue to suggest that, in line with the Lovelace objection, machines do not perform tasks, with the genuine comprehension or creativity associated with human intelligence (Stone 2022). The fact that artificial cognition is still debated and fascinates scholars to this day, highlights even further the complexity of defining creativity and intelligence within a computational context, and the role machines can play (Schwitzgebel & Garza 2015). These discussions have considerable implications for how we understand our interactions with a computer and the philosophical foundations of artificial intelligence (Ward 2020; Schwitzgebel & Garza 2015). Megan Ward, claims in the analysis of Lovelace's work that the term may b misattributed to Ada Lovelace (Ward 2020) but regardless of where the thought originates and how much of this original thinking can be attributed to Lovelace, the argument of the Lovelace objection continues to be an important one in helping us think about creativity and AI.

The Lovelace Effect. Further to this problematisation of the role of machine, scholars have come up with the Lovelace effect, stating that machines can demonstrate behaviours *perceived* by users as innovative or creative, even though they are not inherently creative. It therefore questions the perception that creativity must align with traditional definitions of intelligence, when the intelligence in question is non-human. According to Fernandes (2024), recognizing the distinction between the Lovelace effect and the objection indicates a need for new criteria to measure artificial creativity (Fernandes 2024). In Simone Natale's and Leah Henrickson's critique of the Lovelace Effect, the focus of creativity in machines is a matter of perspective. In their analysis of AI systems, such as AICAN, the authors illustrate how these machine systems can generate art *perceived* as original and creative by humans (Natale & Henrickson 2022). Their exploration highlights just how subjective the evaluation of machine creativity can be, indicating that user perception significantly influences the assessment process.

2.3   Development of the Lovelace Test

The work of Ada Lovelace inspired the creation of the Lovelace test as an alternative to the Turing test. The idea that a machine becomes intelligent only when it produces something unforeseen by its creators, is central to the concept of the test (Eagleman 2023; Bringsjord et al. 2003). To pass the Lovelace Test, an AI system must generate novel artefacts that not only exceed its initial programming in complexity but also resist straightforward explanation or classification by the human who designed it. Researchers such as Selmer Bringsjord and his colleagues have articulated criteria for genuine creativity, emphasizing that the machine must do something that the programmer cannot anticipate or articulate clearly, thereby distinguishing it from standard computational processes (Riedl 2014).

This perspective shifts the focus of intelligence from simply the ability to interact, and posits it to unique artefacts, therefore placing a different notion on intelligence altogether. It is not simply intelligent to interact, like suggested by the Turing test- intelligence is when something *new* is produced. Although AI involves machine learning from pre-existing human examples, according to Bringsjord et al., the Lovelace Test serves as a litmus test for determining whether a machine can generate creative outputs independently, in a similar manner to human-like intelligence (Bringsjord et al. 2003). Therefore, a machine is intelligent if it produces outputs that its designers cannot explicitly explain or predict, aligning with the unpredictable nature of human creativity (Chamberlain et al. 2018).

The Turing Test and the Lovelace Test represent two distinct approaches to machine intelligence and creativity, respectively, and are based on two different assumptions of intelligence: one that is based on mimicry and one on creativity. While both tests explore the capabilities of artificial intelligence, they do so from fundamentally different perspectives.

2.4 Variations on the Lovelace Test

Variations of the Lovelace Test have emerged to further investigate the dimensions of machine creativity and intelligence. Because the proposition of a Lovelace test does not propose specific quantifiable metrics and is based on a qualitative assessment, Bringsjord, proposes that the surprise element in work that is generated by AI should be central to its assessment (Bringsjord et al. 2003). In this version of the test, AI is tasked to create artefacts of artistic value, wherein the creators cannot foresee the results and ties back to Lovelace's original assertion that a computer should originate outputs that were not part of its programming.

Lovelace Test 2.0. Another well-known example in the literature is the Lovelace 2.0 Test, introduced by Mark Riedl in 2014. This version expands upon the original Lovelace effect by evaluating AI agents based on their capacity to produce artistic or creative works whilst complying with specific criteria for creativity and originality. Thus, Riedl's Lovelace test allows for a comparative analysis of different agents' creative performances in diverse creative domains that an AI must master, including but not limited to story-telling, poetry, painting, and music (Liu et al. 2020; Riedl, 2014). This version, which is used as a starting point for the creation of our version of the test, as will be discussed later, is structured to assess both creativity and the perceived intelligence of AI systems more rigorously. Riedl proposes that the Lovelace 2.0 is a modern version of the Turing Test and should serve as a direct alternative to the traditional Turing Test by examining the originality of AI's creativity (Riedl 2014).

Each version of the Lovelace Test proposes a slightly different framework for the assessment of AI ability. The core requirement is that the generated output must not only be novel but also unforeseen by the programmers, therefore demonstrating surprise and originality (Liu et al. 2020; Riedl 2014). However, the second version of the Lovelace test (Lovelace 2.0) emphasises creative expression in diverse creative domains, and requires evaluators to analyse the originality of the outputs across various formats and genres, hence broadening the scope of artistic creation (Liu et al. 2020; Riedl 2014). Lovelace 2.0 also prioritises a comparison with Human Creativity: if AI can create works indistinguishable in originality and complexity from human outputs, it can be acknowledged as an intelligent agent that is capable of creative thought (Riedl 2014).

Compared to the Turing test, the **Lovelace Test** defines more precisely the limits of originality and creativity. It moves beyond replication to suggest that, for a machine to be considered intelligent, new and autonomous ideas should emerge that its human creators cannot explain, expect or predict. Generating something *novel* is central to the Lovelace test (Schedl et al. 2016; Riedl 2014).

Riedl (2014) and Lucifora (2025) argue that this test better captures the essence of intelligence because creativity involves not only data processing but also the synthesis of novel insights. They do, however, also note the easy implementation of the Turing test compared to the Lovelace: the structured dialogue of the Turing is straightforward to creating the test, versus the conceptualisation of intelligence of the Lovelace that requires AI to not only produce human-like output, but output that is human-like in its *inventiveness*. Despite the difficulty of objectively quantifying creativity, the Lovelace Test opens up a wider debate on the cognitive and cultural boundaries of machines and the nature of artificial creativity (Riedl 2014; Handelman & Sigler 2021; Lucifora et al. 2025). For the purposes of this study, we adopted the Lovelace test as described by Riedl and combined it with Bowen's thinking to adapt it to our needs as explained below.

2.5 Can AI Ever Be Creative?

As explained above, the question of what constitutes intelligence and what constitutes creativity is crucial in understanding the capabilities of AI and how these relate to human equivalent ones. Much of the thinking in the direction of creativity in the context of AI has also been shaped by the work of philosopher Margaret Boden. Her contributions are central to current discussions on the creativity of machines, and in this way her work can be seen is an extension of the Turing and Lovelace test. Boden defines creativity through three essential criteria: **novelty**, **surprise**, and **value**, arguing that these elements provide a framework for assessing whether AI can be said to act creatively. As Moruzzi (2025) explains, Boden's model makes a distinction between **combinational**, **exploratory**, and **transformational** creativity. For Bowden these are modes that describe different ways in which novel ideas or outputs can emerge from both human and machine processes. According to this view, AI is not simply an "imitation but has the ability to generate truly innovative and creative outputs (Bowden 2009).

Bowden's work has gone as far as recognising "Aha!" moments in human problem solving. She considers these moments as integral in the way creativity works in human brains and if creativity needs to be considered in AI systems, then these moments may form part of a machines capability to respond and process complex situations (Beeman et al. 2004). However, Moruzzi also stresses that Boden sees a fundamental distinction between human and machine creativity: while AI can algorithmically generate novel and valuable results, AI does not have the **experiential**, **emotional**, and **cultural grounding** that are typical of human creativity. This distinction is central to ongoing philosophical debates about whether AI can ever truly *create* or merely *simulate* creativity within predefined parameters.

3 Assessing Discernibility

3.1 Methodology

To address the research questions raised above, we designed a study to assess the discernibility of AI-generated images in architectural visualisations compared to those created using traditional CGI methods. Our aim was to understand not only whether participants could distinguish between these two image types, but also how they perceived qualities such as creativity and authorship in AI-generated visuals. We recruited 56 participants, all of whom had academic or professional experience in architecture, construction or a related built environment industry. The target group was selected on the basis of their design literacy and the assumption that individuals with a background in architectural visualisation would be more visually literate and therefore better equipped to critically assess the images presented. We hypothesized that AI would be more discernible to an experienced eye, and not as easily deceived as the eye of a lay observer. The survey respondents included academics, students and practitioners in the industry. To reach a diverse participant base across different regions and backgrounds, a snowball sampling strategy was employed.

Fig. 2. Three of the AI-generated images used in Task 1. All images were created on Midjourney by Harriett Boyle.

The study involved two types of responses: visual recognition tasks and qualitative assessments based on adapted Lovelace Test criteria. Participants were first asked to distinguish between AI-generated and human/CGI-generated architectural images. They were then asked to reflect on the creative attributes of the AI images using interpretive criteria drawn from the Lovelace Test. To do so, we adopted four key terms from Bowden and Riedl's adaptation of the Lovelace test: creativity, originality, value, and surprise. These categories were chosen because they align with our objective of evaluating whether the AI-generated content could be perceived as the product of intentional creative agency rather than as a purely algorithmic or computational output.

3.2 Visual Materials and Tasks

Participants completed two separate visual recognition tasks through an online questionnaire hosted on Microsoft Forms:

Task 1: A sequence of 10 individual images was presented. This included 5 AI-generated images, 4 CGI images, and 1 photograph. Participants were asked to indicate whether each image was generated by AI or by human/CGI means. Figure 2 includes some of the AI images, while Fig. 3 two CGI images and one photo of a real-life building.

Task 2: A series of 12 image pairs was shown, each containing one AI-generated image and one CGI-generated image. Participants were asked to select which image in each pair they believed to be AI-generated. After they submitted their response, participants were informed of the correct answer. They were then invited to assess the AI- generated image using the four qualitative criteria: **creativity**, **originality**, **value**, and **surprise** (Figs. 4 and 5)

Fig. 3. Two Computer Generated Images and one photo image used in Task 1 of the study. Permissions from left: centralmarket.hk, Mihhail Jassinover, under CC 663highland.

3.3   Image Generation and Selection

The AI-generated images were produced using Midjourney, a text-to-image generative AI platform. All images come in pairs of one CGI and one AI-generated image. For each AI image included in Task 1, a corresponding CGI image was also included elsewhere in the test, but in random order. This allowed us to test whether participants could distinguish between AI and CGI images without the influence of direct comparison.

In Task 2, participants were asked to select between an AI and a CGI image side by side and select the one they think is AI. To ensure thematic consistency, the same keywords used in Midjourney were applied in Google Image Search to retrieve the CGI images and one architectural photograph. This approach enabled a controlled comparison between AI- and non-AI-generated content, allowing participants to focus on authorship recognition rather than variations in content or visual framing.

In curating the images for Task 1, particular attention was given to selecting themes that engage with embodied and cultural experiences of space. Example keywords in this task used to generate or retrieve images included *urban regeneration in Hong Kong* and *community school in Africa*. While these dimensions are important for understanding how space is perceived and represented differently in AI vs CGI, the findings are beyond the scope of this paper and will be discussed further in another publication.

Keywords used for the images in Task 2 were more open, such as *curved building at night* and *timber building on cliff* for Task 2. This keyword-based selection ensured visual relevance and diversity while maintaining a consistent baseline for comparison across all image types. Participants' image identifications were analysed quantitatively to assess accuracy in distinguishing AI-generated images. For the correctly identified AI images in Task 2, responses to the four Lovelace criteria were additionally reviewed manually. A Likert scale was used to yield their responses to the images they found as AI on a scale from 1–5 and responding to the 4 different themes of the Lovelace

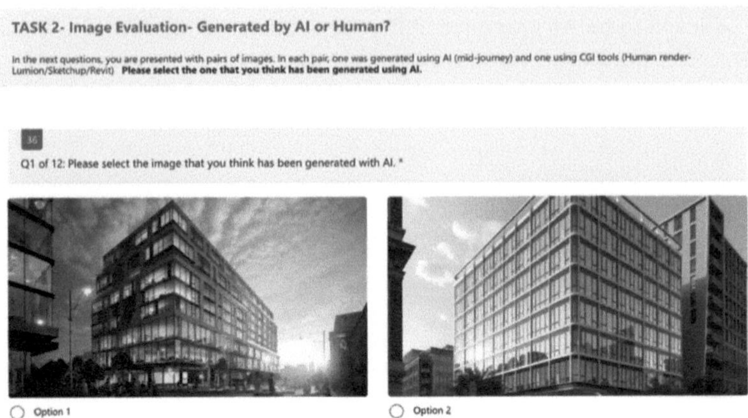

Fig. 4. Task 2 of the questionnaire required participants to select the image they thought was more likely to be AI.

test: creativity originality, value, and surprise to help us understand how they perceived intentionality, design logic, and spatial reasoning in the AI-generated outputs.

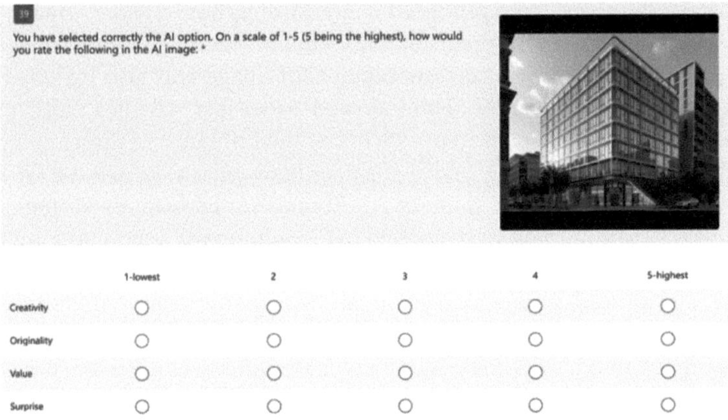

Fig. 5. In Task 2, after participants were shown the AI image, they were asked to rank their views on the image on a 1–5 Likert scale.

Finally, in order to capture perceptions of professionals across the world, respondents targeted originated from 4 continents as seen in their distribution in Fig. 6.

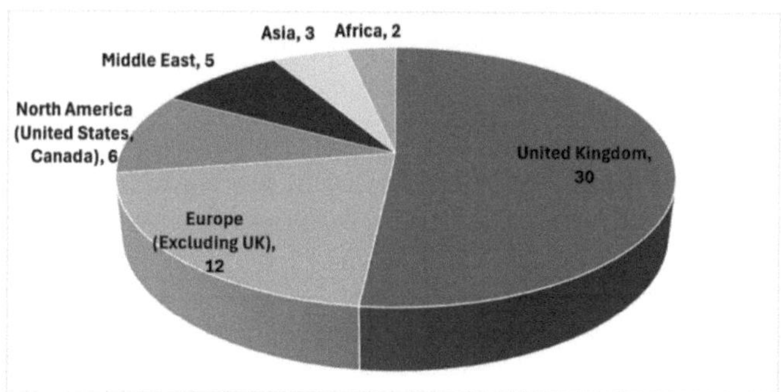

Fig. 6. Geographical distribution of participants.

4   Analysis

The collected responses were downloaded in an Excel file, which was prepared for manual processing. The analysis below presents the results for Tasks 1 and 2 as well as the combined dataset. For each, we have calculated the mean score and the standard deviation (SD). Including both is important: the mean indicates average performance, while the standard deviation indicates how dispersed the scores are within each participant group. A low standard deviation suggests that participants in a group performed similarly, hence they had a similar level of confidence in their responses. In contrast, a high standard deviation indicates more variation, meaning some did well while others did poorly. Finally, the variability of the standard deviation is also included to describe how much variability exists relative to the scale, as this will allow comparison between the tasks (the two tasks have an unequal number of questions).

4.1   Task 1: Single Image Recognition

When shown a series of images in Task 1 and asked to identify whether each had been generated using AI, the group that achieved the highest accuracy was the postgraduate students with a mean of 7.5 (out of 10), while experienced professionals scored the lowest on average (5.26 out of 10) (Table 1).

Table 1. Task 1: Accuracy in single image recognition.

Participants	Mean score	Standard Deviation	SD variability	No. of Participants
Postgraduate student	7.50	2.00	20% moderate	8
Professional (5 years+)	5.26	1.85	18.5% high	34
Professional (up to 5 years)	5.71	2.21	22.1% v. high	7
PhD Student	5.67	0.58	5.77% consistent	3

(continued)

Table 1. (*continued*)

Participants	Mean score	Standard Deviation	SD variability	No. of Participants
Undergraduate student	6.50	0.58	5.77% consistent	4

Based on these results, and somewhat surprisingly, more experience does not equate to a better ability to identify an image as AI. The standard deviation, which reflects in this case the variability in responses, shows a similar picture: there is higher consistency in the responses of postgraduates and undergraduates, while early and later career professionals showed more variability and hence less confidence in selecting the right images.

4.2 Task 2: Image Pair Recognition

Similarly, when shown a pair of images in Task 2 and asked to identify whether they had been generated using AI, the group that achieved the highest accuracy was the undergraduate students (10.5 out of 12), while PhD students and experienced professionals scored the lowest on average (5.67 and 7.94 out of 12 respectively) (Table 2).

Table 2. Task 2: Accuracy in image pair recognition.

Participants	Mean score	Standard Deviation	SD variability	No. of Participants
Postgraduate student	8.38	2.88	23.9% v high	8
Professional (5 years+)	7.94	2.57	21.4% high	34
Professional (up to 5 years)	10.29	1.60	13.4% consistent	7
PhD Student	5.67	2.52	21% varied	3
Undergraduate student	10.50	1.29	10.8% consistent	4

The relationship between experience and AI recognition remains in a similar pattern in this second task of the study, with the experienced professionals still scoring low in accuracy, and the undergraduate and postgraduate students scoring better than the professionals.

Alongside the reduced accuracy, the higher standard deviation also indicates a wider spread of the results. This signals that the respondents from this group are not only less likely to respond correctly, they are also less likely to respond confidently, as they present with a wider spread of answers. It is therefore clear that overall, and across both tasks, more experienced professionals have less accuracy and a higher standard deviation, and therefore less accuracy and more variability, indicating less confidence in picking the AI image.

4.3   Task 1 and Task 2 Combined

A comparison of the two tasks reveals a marked difference in the ability to accurately discern AI images. In the first task, where images were presented individually, the overall accuracy across all groups was only at 58%. While this is marginally above the 50% threshold of random guessing, it suggests that participants struggled to reliably distinguish the AI images when there was no other context or reference. In contrast, in Task 2, where the AI and CGI images were presented side by side, the accuracy rose significantly to 84%. The cumulative percentage across both tasks is at 64%, reflecting an overall moderate ability to identify AI content (Table 3).

This observation implies that context plays a significant role in enabling users to identify the AI image correctly. When participants were able to view them in direct juxtaposition, they may detect stylistic or visual inconsistencies characteristic of AI outputs. The side-by-side format enables comparative reasoning and may draw the eye to details that would otherwise go unnoticed in isolation. The comparison possibly allows the observer to identify AI features more easily. This suggests that the perception of authenticity in architectural images is not solely based on the image itself but also by the viewing conditions and the cognitive strategies triggered by comparative evaluation.

Table 3. Combining Tasks 1 and 2.

	Task 1 (out of 10)	Task 2 (out of 12)	Task 1 and Task 2 (out of 22)
Percentage of correct answers	58%	84%	64%
Highest score	10	12	22
Lowest score	2	0	3
Mean correct answers	5.75	8.36	14.11
Standard Deviation	1.94	2.63	3.75

Table 4. Observations by participants about absent features from AI-generated images.

shown a pair of images in	shown a pair of images in
Lack of Human Presence and Emotional Connection	*"No human engagement, no emotional attachment."* *"Lacked warmness and connection with the space."*
Absence of Technical features and Structural Realism	*"Structural form consideration [is missing]—too perfect lines."* *No realistic construction—looks great but can't be built."*
Visual Imbalance and Sterility	*"Shadows, depth, and realistic perspective are missing."*

(continued)

Table 4. (continued)

shown a pair of images in	shown a pair of images in
Cultural Absence	*"Accuracy, realism, and spiritual substance are absent."*

4.4 The Lovelace Test

In Task 2 of the test, after participants were informed of the outcome (i.e. whether their choices were correct in identifying the AI image), they were shown the AI image and were asked to assess using a Likert scale across the four Lovelace Test keywords. Across the four (creativity, value, originality and surprise), creativity consistently achieved the highest ratings. This indicates that even when participants were aware the image was AI-generated, they still perceived it as creative, thus implying that the image convincingly simulated that it had undergone a creative process, rather than a process of diffusion-based algorithmic computation. The results are demonstrated in Fig. 7 below.

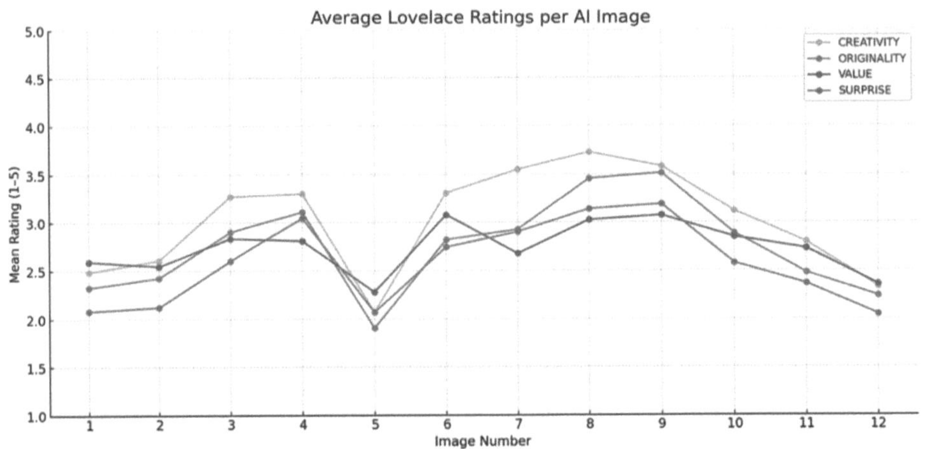

Fig. 7. Spread or Lovelace responses across all images of Task 2.

Based on this observation, we propose that AI-generated imagery in architecture may have crossed the threshold of being considered as a purely computational output to being recognized as the result of a creative process. However, the results for the other categories (originality, value and surprise) were lower and more variable. This indicates that participants often found the images visually compelling and creative, but lacking in architectural value. Therefore, the high creativity value of an image may reflect a relative amount of complexity in an image, but this does not translate to conveying other qualities such as depth, functional logic or cultural resonance. This observation supports our hypothesis that although AI images appear creative, they are not necessarily perceived as meaningful, original or valuable from a designers/ built environment professional's standpoint.

4.5 Participant Reflections on AI Images

At the end of the questionnaire, participants were asked two questions relating to AI use in architectural visualisations, in an open-ended format, and in reflection of the task completed. The two questions focused on what was missing from AI-generated Architecture and the commonalities they have found. These responses allowed us to gain insight into why some users remain critical of AI images, even when they can appreciate them as creative.

What is Missing from AI-Generated Architecture? The qualitative responses to the question of what is missing from AI visuals in architecture reveal a scepticism toward AI-generated architectural imagery, even when participants acknowledged its visual appeal and had scored highly for creativity of the Lovelace test. Four key themes emerged, highlighting why trained viewers remained critical. Many noted a lack of human presence and emotional connection, describing the images as overly perfect or detached from lived experience. Others questioned the technical feasibility of the designs, pointing out that, while images appeared good, they were structurally implausible. A third concern identified visual sterility, with participants critiquing the absence of shadows, imperfections, or material richness. Finally, some respondents identified a lack of cultural connotations, sensing a lack of deeper narrative, symbolic meaning, or contextual grounding. Together, these insights point to a critical gap between visual sophistication and architectural substance, suggesting that meaningful design relies not only on aesthetics but on embedded human, cultural, and spatial understanding. The table below summarises these themes and includes some representative quotes (Table 4).

These responses suggest that trained viewers assess not only surface appeal, but also the architectural depth, intent, and narrative that make images feel meaningful. In this sense, participants revealed a gap between appearance and substance in AI-generated design.

Perceived Commonalities of AI Images. When asked to reflect on the visual qualities of AI-generated architectural images, participants consistently pointed to a set of identifiable patterns that revealed their artificial origin. Stylised and unrealistic lighting was frequently cited, with many noting overly dramatic or uniformly applied illumination that lacked the natural variation typical of real environments. Symmetrical or centralised composition was another recurring feature, with images often framed in a way that felt repetitive or overly composed. Participants also described a sterile or superficial aesthetic, using terms such as *emotionally flat* or *generic* to convey a sense of detachment and lack of narrative depth. Repetitive material choices, such as excessive use of dark tones, glazed surfaces, or reflective elements, contributed to visual oddities or artefacts that disrupted the realism of the renderings. Finally, many images were placed in romanticised, utopian landscapes, which appeared too perfect or idealised to be grounded in practical design contexts. These traits made the images visually appealing at first glance, but ultimately undermined their architectural credibility and emotional resonance.

Taken together, these recurring elements suggest that AI image generation still operates within a constrained visual grammar shaped by training data, potentially limiting its value for more contextually grounded or culturally rich design work. The table below summarizes these themes and includes some representative quotes (Table 5).

Table 5. Observations by participants about perceived commonalities of AI images.

Theme identified	Quotes
Stylised and Unrealistic Lighting	*"Light is still a quality indicator, it gives away the artificiality."*
Symmetrical or Centralised Composition	*"Angle of the shot and centrality of the building were often similar."*
Sterile or Superficial Aesthetic	*"Something anodyne."* *"Lacks human decision-making in the detailing."*
Repetitive Material Choices and Visual Artifacts	*"Windows always look oddly glazed—never really transparent."*
Romanticised Contexts	*"They are situated in gorgeous sites."*

5 Discussion

There were clear discrepancies observed in the ability to distinguish AI-generated images which can be partly attributed to the experience and design literacy of the different groups. The most interesting finding of the study was that the relationship between experience and ability to discern was inversely proportional, especially in the case of experienced professionals. While one might expect experts to perform better, standard deviation scores indicated wider variability among senior and postgraduate participants compared to undergraduates and early-career professionals. This suggests that expertise in the field does not necessarily translate into greater clarity when evaluating AI-generated content.

There are two observations that may help explain this counterintuitive trend: firstly, less experience is associated with younger people who are more likely to be digital natives. These participants may possess a more intuitive familiarity with the aesthetics and visual conventions of AI-generated content. In future research, we suggest including information about the prior digital expertise of the participants as well as their age, as this information may have been able to help us better explain this relationship. Secondly, experienced designers may also be more proficient in creating CGI images of their own. This prior experience may lead them to be more aware of the sophisticated capabilities of CGI. Their assumptions about what CGI is capable of may bias their judgment toward attributing AI images to human design.

While AI can produce visually compelling images, participants noted a lack of *design intent* and *spatial reasoning*, which are fundamental to architectural design but remain elusive in AI-generated outputs. These findings suggest that, despite advancements in

AI technology, there is still a perceptible gap between AI and human design in the architectural discipline.

The study provides evidence that AI-generated architectural images, despite their technical sophistication, have yet to meet the creativity and intentionality standards defined by the Lovelace Test. The results indicate that architectural images demand a level of contextual awareness and design intent that current AI technologies are yet to fully achieve. Until AI can incorporate a deeper understanding of spatial, contextual, and aesthetic elements, it will remain distinguishable from human-designed architectural work, particularly by those with a nuanced understanding of the discipline.

The findings hold broader implications for the role of AI in architectural visualisations, particularly as AI continues to evolve within the design industry. Future research on the same theme may focus on refining AI algorithms to incorporate architectural theory and spatial understanding, potentially bringing AI closer to achieving the Lovelace Test criteria in this domain. Additionally, expanding the pool of participants, particularly by opening the questionnaire to practitioners with varied digital expertise, may provide deeper insights into how AI visualisations are interpreted and by whom.

6 Conclusion

As generative AI continues to advance, future research must explore how these tools can move beyond mimicry towards a more meaningful integration of cognitive, spatial, and cultural intelligence. Furthermore, consideration should be given to how AI can be trained not just on visual data, but also on spatial narratives, user behaviours, and environmental contexts. Ultimately, the goal of AI generated images should not be to replace human creativity, but to refine AI as a tool that complements and expands the imaginative capacities of the designer.

Acknowledgments. The authors would like to thank Harriett Boyle for her help in generating the AI images of Task 2. Additionally, the authors would like to thank all participants and respondents to the questionnaire for their generosity and for taking the time to complete it.

Disclosure of Interests. The authors have no competing interests to declare that are relevant to the content of this article. The questionnaire used in the study was approved by the University of Salford ethics committee (Ethical approval ref: 2025-6349-5876).

References

Beeman, M., et al.: Neural activity when people solve verbal problems with insight. PLoS Biol. **2**(4), e97 (2004). https://doi.org/10.1371/journal.pbio.0020097

Berrar, D., Schuster, A.: Computing machinery and creativity: lessons learned from the turing test. Kybernetes **43**(1), 82–91 (2014). https://doi.org/10.1108/k-08-2013-0175

Bringsjord, S., Bello, P., Ferrucci, D.: Creativity, the turing test, and the (better) lovelace test, pp. 215–239 (2003). https://doi.org/10.1007/978-94-010-0105-2_12

Boden, M.: Creativity in a nutshell. Think **5**, 83–96 (2009). https://doi.org/10.1017/S14771756 0000230X

Chamberlain, R., Mullin, C., Scheerlinck, B., Wagemans, J.: Putting the art in artificial: aesthetic responses to computer-generated art. Psychol. Aesthet. Creat. Arts **12**(2), 177–192 (2018). https://doi.org/10.1037/aca0000136

Copeland, J. and Proudfoot, D. (2007). Turing's test., 119–138. https://doi.org/10.1007/978-1-4020-6710-5_9

Eagleman, D.: A proposed test for human-level intelligence in ai (2023). https://doi.org/10.31234/osf.io/e5rtw

Fernandes, A.: The replacement of what? artificial intelligence, creativity and (more-than-) humanness. J. Creat. Commun. **20**(1), 11–22 (2024). https://doi.org/10.1177/09732586241275955

Handelman, E., Sigler, A.: Artik: articulation and dynamics from structural pattern analysis. Proceedings of the Aaai Conference on Artificial Intelligence and Interactive Digital Entertainment **10**(5), 10–17 (2021). https://doi.org/10.1609/aiide.v10i5.12765

Hingston, P.: A new design for a Turing test for bots, pp. 345–350 (2010). https://doi.org/10.1109/itw.2010.5593336

Liu, F., Liu, Y., Shi, Y.: Three IQS of AI systems and their testing methods. J. Eng. **2020**(13), 566–571 (2020). https://doi.org/10.1049/joe.2019.1135

Lucifora, C., Scorolli, C., Gangemi, A.: Attribution of creative skills to human and artificial artists in alethic and epistemic possible worlds. Psychol. Aesthet. Creat. Arts (2025). https://doi.org/10.1037/aca0000757

Marcus, G., Rossi, F., Veloso, M.: Beyond the turing test. AI Mag. **37**(1), 3–4 (2016). https://doi.org/10.1609/aimag.v37i1.2650

Moruzzi, C.: Artificial intelligence and creativity. Phil. Compass **20**(3) (2025). https://doi.org/10.1111/phc3.70030

Natale, S., Henrickson, L.: The Lovelace effect: perceptions of creativity in machines. New Media Soc. **26**(4), 1909–1926 (2022). https://doi.org/10.1177/14614448221077278

Riedl, M.: The Lovelace 2.0 test of artificial creativity and intelligence (2014). https://doi.org/10.48550/arxiv.1410.6142

Schedl, M., Yang, Y., Herrera, P.: Introduction to intelligent music systems and applications. ACM Trans. Intell. Syst. Technol. **8**(2), 1–8 (2016). https://doi.org/10.1145/2991468

Schwitzgebel, E., Garza, M.: A defense of the rights of artificial intelligences. Midwest Stud. Philos. **39**(1), 98–119 (2015). https://doi.org/10.1111/misp.12032

Stone, A.: Women philosophers in nineteenth-century britain. (2022). https://doi.org/10.1093/oso/9780192874719.001.0001

Ward, M.: Victorian fictions of computational creativity, pp. 144–164 (2020). https://doi.org/10.1093/oso/9780198846666.003.0007

Speculative Design Meets AI: Exploring Creative Dynamics Through Co-speculative Workshops

Yutong Zhu and Zixiang Feng(✉)

Royal College of Art, Kensington Gore, South Kensington, London SW7 2EU, UK
`yutong.zhu@network.rca.ac.uk`, `fzxqwq@gmail.com`

Abstract. These days, many researchers are exploring speculative design as one of the most popular directions in design research. Speculative design offers a framework for envisioning alternative futures and critically engaging with emerging technologies. This study investigates the collaborative dynamics between AI tools and speculative designers through a series of co-speculative workshops that included open-ended questionnaire studies. We examined the dynamic tensions between speculative designers and AI tools, identifying three primary friction points: (1) disjunction between conceptual intention and visual realisation, (2) cognitive disempowerment under inefficient interaction, and (3) design progression impairment caused by generative instability. The findings highlight the need for improvements in AI-supported speculative design processes, including: Designer Habit Refinement for Speculative AI Tools - logging and reflecting on friction points; New Cognitive Modes for Speculative Designers: reframing AI from a "prompt generator" to a "co-creator" or "critical partner"; Role Clarification for Speculative Designers maintaining human leadership; and Enhancing Transparency in Speculative Design Tools: Implement explainable feedback mechanisms. This study provides deeper insights into speculative research by elucidating the evolving dynamics of human-AI interactions in the design process, offering both theoretical and practical contributions to the optimization and advancement of speculative research and human-computer interaction.

Keywords: Speculative Design · Human-AI Collaboration · Generative AI · Co-Design · Collaborative Dynamics

1 Introduction

Speculative design is a design methodology grounded in critical thinking, aimed at provoking reflection and discussion on technological, societal, and cultural issues through the creation of fictional future scenarios [12]. Developed in the late 1990 s and early 2000 s, speculative design was pioneered at the Royal College of Art's "Interaction Design" program. It challenges the status quo and

J. Wei et al. (Eds.): HCII 2025, LNCS 16346, pp. 91–102, 2026.
https://doi.org/10.1007/978-3-032-13187-4_7

encourages exploration of alternative futures. As an emerging technology, artificial intelligence (AI) is rapidly reshaping our ways of living and thinking. Integrating speculative design with AI creates opportunities for more imaginative and thought-provoking scenarios, deepening our understanding of and engagement with AI's potential and challenges. Rather than treating speculative design as a static methodology, these studies reflect a growing trend of adapting it to AI-driven contexts, yet often focus on scenario creation or conceptual exploration. While applications span domains such as healthcare, sustainability, and the arts, few critically examine how AI alters the creative dynamics or authorship within speculative design practices. This gap motivates our investigation into the role of AI in co-speculative workshops.

This study focuses on the integration of speculative design and artificial intelligence within co-speculative workshops, analysing how AI influences creative dynamics throughout the design process. Through the design and implementation of these workshops, we conducted qualitative research using open-ended questionnaires to investigate how diverse groups of speculative designers interact with AI tools at different stages of the speculative design process, and to examine the role of AI tools within these workflows. Although AI offers significant potential, its integration into speculative design also raises critical issues related to creativity, autonomy, and ethical considerations. Beyond individual creativity, recent critiques have also foregrounded AI's systemic entanglements with power, labor, and planetary costs [10]. Therefore, understanding the role and impact of AI within speculative design workflows is essential. This study is guided by two research questions addressing the dynamics of human-AI collaboration in speculative design:

1. What obstacles do designers encounter when collaborating with AI in speculative design processes?
2. How can AI tool functionality and designers' creative agency be enhanced to optimise the collaborative quality in speculative design?

By uncovering the collaborative dynamics between speculative designers and AI tools, this research contributes to advancing academic discourse in both speculative design and the field of human-computer interaction. More broadly, the study offers novel perspectives and strategies on the use of AI tools in speculative design workflows, contributing to the development of user experience design for AI-assisted speculative design practices.

2   Literature Review

2.1   Speculative Design

Speculative design, first formally theorised by Dunne and Raby (2013) [12], positions design as a medium for critical inquiry rather than problem-solving. Their framework introduced fictional scenarios and thought experiments to provoke ethical reflection and challenge dominant technological narratives. They define speculative design as a method for challenging paradigms and fostering dialogue about alternative futures. Methodologies such as future mapping, backcasting [17], and scenario planning [11] are central to speculative design, enabling participants to visualise connections between societal drivers and speculative scenarios. Building on Dunne and Raby's foundations, Auger [2] emphasised the craft-based articulation of alternative futures, reflection systematised speculative techniques for classroom and public engagement. The recent handbook Designing Futures consolidates scenario, critique and innovation techniques into a coherent practitioner toolkit [14]. Nestler and Werner [30] provided a practical guide for structuring participatory speculation workshops that engage diverse stakeholders, helping bridge academic research with public imagination and collaborative foresight.

Methodologically, these works have expanded speculative design through co-creation frameworks, AI-assisted generation tools, and public-facing participatory formats. These approaches align with broader shifts in design research toward co-creation and participatory development [27], particularly in tackling "wicked problems" through situated and dialogic methods [22]. Østvold Ek et al. [13] reviewed the opportunities and limitations of integrating AI in speculative design, identifying both creative affordances and concerns around automation. Together, these efforts reflect speculative design's evolving role as a tool for interrogating, critiquing, and reimagining technological futures in the era of AI.

2.2 Artificial Intelligence in Speculative Design

Artificial intelligence serves as both a tool and collaborator within speculative design practices. Generative AI (Gen AI) technologies, such as DALL-E and MidJourney, enable rapid ideation and visualisation of speculative scenarios by transforming it into tangible artifacts, thereby boosting efficiency and supporting human intuition. Such human-AI collaboration amplifies creative potential [23]. The integration of speculative design and AI fosters more imaginative and thought-provoking future scenarios, facilitating a deeper understanding and application of AI technologies. Blythe [5] demonstrated how design fiction can support the understanding of AI, highlighting speculative design's potential to reveal the ethical, social, and societal implications of AI.

Recent studies have extended the application of speculative design and AI to diverse domains, such as healthcare, sustainability, education and urban planning. Østvold Ek's review of AI-driven narrative prototypes foregrounds ecological trade-offs [13], while Lin &Long [21] and Chen [9] demonstrate how generative models reconfigure authorship and agency in creative practice. Participatory workshops by LC and Tang integrate Stable Diffusion and GPT to co-explore climate futures [19], and cross-cultural studies reveal divergent AI imaginaries between Japan and Germany [16]. Similar speculative methods underpin co-created wellbeing technologies with older adults [29], housing foresight projects [28], and studio-based educational scenarios that build AI literacy [18]. Yet empirical evidence of how Gen AI actually reshapes speculative workflows remains limited [3]; most accounts celebrate creativity gains while warning of algorithmic bias, ethical opacity and over-reliance on automation [25]. These tensions echo long-standing critiques of "solving the wrong problems" in HCI4D [31] and reinforce calls for reflexive, stakeholder-led approaches that balance AI's generative power with human agency and dialogic practice [22, 27].

3   Methods

Following established participatory frameworks [15, 27, 30], this study employed an inductive and exploratory Co-Speculative Workshop framework [20]. The workshops integrated speculative design methodologies with artificial intelligence tools to explore how participants engage in speculative design practices through AI-assisted collaboration. The research was conducted in three main phases: pre-workshop interviews, workshop implementation, and post-workshop open-ended questionnaire. Drawing on the manifesto-sprint format proposed by Ashby et al. [4], each workshop closed with a collective declaration to capture emergent uncertainties. By integrating rich qualitative descriptions and insights, the study aimed to examine how participants interact with AI tools within the speculative design process, offering a nuanced interpretation of the collaborative dynamics between speculative designers and AI tools [24, 25].

3.1   Research Setting

We recruited 17 speculative designers in the UK, based on their prior experience in speculative design practice and active engagement with AI tools within their design workflows. All participants had substantial experience with AI-assisted tools and demonstrated a clear focus on speculative design (see Table 1). This research setting provided an ideal context for addressing our research questions, enabling an in-depth investigation of the dynamic collaborative relationships between designers and AI tools as AI becomes increasingly integrated into speculative design processes.

3.2   Sampling Strategy

We employed purposive sampling and recruited 17 speculative designers online. The participants demonstrated diversity in gender, age, research focus within speculative design, and levels of AI tool usage and adoption (see Table 1). Following the speculative design workshops, each participant completed an open-ended questionnaire in English, with response times ranging from approximately 30 to 50 min.

4   Data Collection

Our primary data source was an open-ended post-workshop questionnaire, completed by all participants within five minutes after each session. The questionnaire was administered via Google Forms and distributed through QR code at the venue. All participants gave informed consent prior to the study.

Table 1. Participant demographics

	Age	Design Direction	AI Acceptance Level
P1	21	Service Design	High
P2	22	Design Products	Low
P3	24	Global Innovation Design	Medium
P4	30	Innovation Design Engineering	High
P5	20	Digital Direction	Medium
P6	45	Design Futures	High
P7	47	Healthcare Design	High
P8	26	Animation	High
P9	28	Vehicle Design	Medium
P10	23	Interaction Design	Low
P11	34	Architecture Design	High
P12	29	Digital Arts	Medium
P13	32	Inclusive Design	High
P14	31	Environmental Architecture	Low
P15	40	Intelligent Mobility	Medium
P16	22	Animation	High
P17	27	Design Engineering	Medium

*P = Participant

The questionnaire covered five key dimensions relevant to the study. First, it collected participants' demographic information, prior experiences with AI and speculative design, and their expectations for engaging in AI-assisted co-creation. Second, participants were asked to reflect on specific moments when AI-generated outputs diverged from their intended design concepts, documenting instances of creative misalignment or friction. Third, the questionnaire examined participants' perceptions of AI's role during collaboration, exploring whether they regarded AI as a co-designer, a passive assistant, or a disruptive element. Fourth, participants assessed their sense of control and cognitive engagement, evaluating how AI tools either facilitated or constrained their creative flow and conceptual autonomy. Finally, participants were invited to propose potential improvements to generative AI tools, envisioning new features, roles, or interaction modes that could better support speculative design practices in the future.

This questionnaire provided nuanced insights into how participants experienced generative AI as both a creative catalyst and a point of tension. The open-ended questionnaire allowed for a rich variety of individual reflections, which were later coded thematically to inform our findings.

4.1 Data Analysis

We employed thematic analysis to identify, analyze, and interpret recurring patterns within participants' responses. Rather than merely summarizing the data, this method enabled a comprehensive and systematic exploration of participants' experiences, capturing the complex dynamics of human-AI collaboration within speculative design practices [7]. The analytical approach was inductive, exploratory, and data-driven.

In the initial phase, open coding was conducted on the 17 open-ended questionnaire responses collected after the workshops. Each questionnaire response was treated as an analytical unit, reflecting participants' cognitive reactions, reflections, challenges, and creative processes while collaborating with AI tools in speculative design tasks.

The coding process proceeded in several stages. First, we conducted open coding, generating 412 in-vivo codes that captured participants' reactions to AI outputs, cognitive strategies, system breakdowns, adaptive behaviors, and instances of creative negotiation during interaction with AI tools.

Building upon the open coding, we further organized these codes into higher-order conceptual categories through axial coding. The analysis focused on recurring patterns within human-AI collaboration, including role positioning, cognitive tensions, and emotional responses. Special attention was paid to situations where speculative designers encountered breakdowns or disruptions in their collaboration with AI tools.

Subsequent analysis explored the underlying causes of these obstacles and identified potential improvement directions to enhance both the maturity of speculative designers' practice and the functionality of AI tools. Through an iterative and inductive process, the study progressively refined its insights, ultimately arriving at well-founded research conclusions.

5 Findings

Our analysis revealed three core breakdowns in the creative collaboration between designers and generative AI tools during speculative design workshops: (1) disjunction between conceptual intention and Visual Realisation, (2) cognitive dis-empowerment under inefficient interaction, and (3) design progression impairment caused by generative instability. These findings primarily address our second research question: What obstacles do designers encounter when working with AI in speculative design processes?

5.1 Disjunction Between Conceptual Intention and Visual Realisation

Participants consistently reported a notable gap between their envisioned speculative concepts and the visual outcomes generated by AI tools. While platforms such as MidJourney and DALL·E were valued for quick ideation, their outputs often lacked the specificity and semantic depth needed to align with participants' imagined futures.

This disjunction was particularly evident during early ideation and mid-fidelity prototyping. P3 remarked that MidJourney "captures the overall mood, yet misses the specific tone and symbols I envision; it keeps defaulting to a cinematic, almost surreal look." P12 added that she "tried to depict subtle political tensions, yet the AI returned images that felt like generic sci-fi clichés rather than a nuanced future."

These challenges intensified during higher-fidelity phases. P6 noted: "When I had a clear vision, I used ChatGPT to break down steps. But when the idea was still abstract, its suggestions were too generic to help." P10 added: "AI tools became irrelevant in the high-fidelity stage. They couldn't handle material constraints or design logic."

Overall, designers found AI to be unreliable as a means of visual execution. The tools were more suited for divergent inspiration than for convergent refinement, contributing to a sense of expressive misalignment between conceptual intention and output fidelity.

5.2   Cognitive Disempowerment Under Inefficient Interaction

A second barrier involved a growing sense of cognitive disempowerment due to the inefficient interaction dynamics with AI. Participants described the experience as mentally taxing, citing AI's limited contextual memory, shallow reasoning, and dependence on user-driven prompts.

Several participants criticized the AI's inability to provide meaningful critique or provoke new thinking. P4 reflected: "It's feedback depends entirely on your input. If you don't ask the right question, it just paraphrases your assumption." P13 elaborated: "It doesn't challenge me, it just reacts."

Additionally, many noted that AI frequently misunderstood their design intents, requiring excessive clarification. P7 reported: "It kept misreading what I meant. Fixing its output took more time than just doing it myself." This pattern led to fatigue and frustration. As P5 stated: "It's a cycle—you start over every time, re-explain everything, and still get something off."

One participant, P8, coined the experience as a "learn-retry-disappointment loop," capturing a broader sentiment of interactional exhaustion. This loop ultimately undermined trust in the AI's usefulness and reduced participants' desire to engage it as a co-creative partner.

5.3   Design Progression Impairment Caused by Generative Instability

The third obstacle centered on the instability and unreliability of AI-generated content in supporting speculative design progression. Participants criticized AI for producing outputs that were semantically shallow, outdated, or lacking contextual awareness.

P11 felt the output "sounds plausible yet disconnects from current trends—at times reading like five-year-old PR copy." P9 emphasized: "Even when I asked for speculative futures, it gave me textbook ideas, not the kind of risky or novel thinking we needed."

Beyond content quality, participants remarked that AI tools often excelled in repackaging existing material rather than enabling generative leaps. P16 observed: "It's better at remixing than inventing. I wanted help imagining a new system, but it just gave me variations of what already exists." P1 added: "It doesn't help build worlds—it just fills in gaps with filler."

Furthermore, the AI's output frequently required significant reworking. As P15 explained: "Everything needed to be humanized—tone, coherence, detail. It wasn't ready to use." These repeated revisions interrupted ideation flow, shifting cognitive resources from concept generation to error correction.

This dynamic resulted in a broader loss of momentum and speculative fluency. As P6 reflected: "Instead of helping me think bigger, it slowed me down. I kept questioning whether the AI was worth using." This illustrates how generative instability disrupted design logic and undermined creative trust.

6   Discussion

Through our exploration of the collaborative dynamics between speculative designers and generative AI, we identified several key points of friction where the design process broke down. These frictions resonate with Ackoff's system-level view that redesigning the future requires intervention across the entire sociotechnical network [1]. Classic 'wicked-problem' theory reminds us that such dilemmas resist linear optimisation [26]. At the same time, we also uncovered instances where AI's generative capacity positively shaped speculative thinking, revealing that generative AI acts simultaneously as a frictional agent and creative catalyst [21]. Based on these insights, we developed a set of design strategies aimed at enhancing interaction precision and user experience from both the designer's perspective and the AI tool's functionality. By integrating these strategies into future AI-driven co-design environments, we can better support designers in maintaining their creative agency while enhancing the coherence and quality of the collaborative design experience.

6.1   Designer Habit Refinement for Speculative AI Tools: Logging and Reflecting on Friction Points

Designers should cultivate a habitual practice of documenting and reflecting on moments where AI-generated outputs diverge from their conceptual intentions or misinterpret prompts. These "friction points" often harbour latent creative potential and can serve as valuable resources for iterative refinement and future tool enhancement, resonating with the principles of scenario-based interaction design [8].

For instance, one participant noted: "I found that when I asked the AI to help me analyse something, it always introduced all sorts of unrelated perspectives. Sometimes, these perspectives were not what I wanted to explore at all." P17. However, in the post-session reflection, the same participant reported: "Those seemingly useless perspectives offered by AI later became stakeholders in the world I was building. I even went back to revisit some of the chat logs."

Such reflections suggest that moments of misalignment between designers and AI can later be reinterpreted as fruitful triggers for speculative expansion. Therefore, we argue that logging and reflecting on these friction points is not only beneficial for improving tool alignment but also essential for fostering deeper speculative engagement.

6.2   New Cognitive Mode for Speculative Designers: Reframing AI From Prompt Generator to Co-Creator

Speculative designers should be encouraged to conceptualize generative AI tools beyond their traditional role as prompt providers. Instead, AI can be positioned as a collaborative co-creator or critical partner—one that challenges assumptions, stimulates divergent thinking, and actively contributes to speculative ideation.

While several participants expressed dissatisfaction with AI when using it to generate final outputs—"The results were not ideal; I don't think it could have been the final production tool." P14, We observed a shift in perception when AI was repurposed as a reflective and critical partner. One participant described: "Instead of expecting perfect results, I started asking the AI to challenge my assumptions and help me think differently." Another added: "Treating AI as a'partner in critique helped me realize connections I hadn't noticed before.'

This reframing of AI's role facilitates more productive engagements and leads to higher satisfaction with the design outcomes. Therefore, we propose that promoting this shift in cognitive framing may enhance both the creative value and the trustworthiness of AI-assisted speculative design.

6.3   Role Clarification for Speculative Designers: Maintaining Human Leadership

In human-AI collaborative settings, it is crucial for designers to assert leadership and maintain responsibility for creative direction. While AI can spark inspiration, it cannot substitute for human imagination; designers should remain the ultimate arbiters of decisions made during the design process.

We found that when designers actively led the AI interaction, setting clear intentions and critically reviewing AI outputs, they reported higher satisfaction and perceived agency. In contrast, participants who over-relied on AI for speculative ideation often expressed frustration and a sense of disconnection from their work. As one participant stated: "I delegated too much to the AI and ended up not recognizing my own voice in the final piece."

Conversely, "participants who used AI critically reported more fulfilling experiences: "When I used AI as a sparring partner, rather than a decision-maker, I was able to refine my ideas more confidently."

Thus, clarifying the roles within AI-human collaboration is essential to preserving human-led creative direction and ensuring the speculative designer's authorship is maintained.

6.4 Enhancing Transparency in Speculative Design Tools: Implement Explainable Feedback Mechanisms

For designers to engage critically with AI-generated content, speculative design tools should integrate explainable feedback systems. These systems might include transparency features such as reasoning pathways, uncertainty indicators, or links to source data, thereby enhancing trust and interpretability.

P7 admitted: "I struggle to trust the AI because I can't see the reasoning behind its suggestions—its logic remains opaque.". Without transparency, designers struggle to evaluate the relevance and reliability of the AI's contribution, limiting their ability to make informed decisions.

Therefore, we suggest that speculative AI systems should prioritize explainability in interface design, allowing designers to assess the validity of AI responses and use them more effectively in critical and creative processes.

6.5 Concluding Remarks

We conducted a series of workshop-based thematic analyses to explore how speculative designers interact with generative AI tools. Over multiple sessions, we collected qualitative data through open-ended surveys at various stages, enabling us to identify context-specific barriers experienced by designers from different backgrounds.

First, by combining empirical inquiry with a workshop-based approach, we deliver practice-oriented insights into the interaction dynamics faced by speculative designers in real-world contexts. Second, we propose a suite of strategies aimed at optimizing collaboration between generative AI and speculative designers, providing pragmatic solutions to improve interaction efficacy.

Despite our aims, this study is limited in terms of sample size and cultural diversity; the workshops were conducted primarily within a UK-based context. Future research may extend in several directions: (1) exploring how cultural differences influence AI-designer collaboration in speculative design; (2) expanding the range of generative AI tools and user profiles to examine broader patterns of co-creation; and (3) further developing speculative AI interfaces that support transparent [6], reflective, and creative engagement.

References

1. Ackoff, R.L., Warfield, J.N.: Redesigning the future, a systems approach to societal problems. IEEE Trans. Syst. Man Cybern. **7**(10), 759 (1977). https://doi.org/10.1109/TSMC.1977.4309613, https://ieeexplore.ieee.org/document/4309613

2. Auger, J.: Speculative design: crafting the speculation. Digit. Creativity **24**(1), 11–35 (2013). https://doi.org/10.1080/14626268.2013.767276

3. and, M.B.G.: The paradox of artificial creativity: challenges and opportunities of generative ai artistry. Creativity Res. J. 1–14 (2024). https://doi.org/10.1080/10400419.2024.2354622

4. Ashby, S., Hanna, J., De Rooij, A., Kasprzak, M., Hoekstra, J., Bos, S.: Articulating (uncertain) ai futures of artistic practice: a speculative design and manifesto sprint approach. In: Proceedings of the 15th Conference on Creativity and Cognition, pp. 312–318, C&C 2023. Association for Computing Machinery, New York, NY, USA (2023). https://doi.org/10.1145/3591196.3596819

5. Blythe, M.: Artificial design fiction: using AI as a material for pastiche scenarios. In: Proceedings of the 26th International Academic Mindtrek Conference, pp. 195–206, Mindtrek 2023. Association for Computing Machinery, New York, NY, USA (2023). https://doi.org/10.1145/3616961.3616987

6. Bowen, S., , Alexander, W., , Sunil, R., , Tom, F., , Nappey, T.: Metro futures 2020: Enabling participation at varying depths and scales via digital technology. Int. J. Hum. Comput. Interact. **39**(18), 3663–3683. https://doi.org/10.1080/10447318.2022.2102085

7. Braun, V., and, V.C.: Using thematic analysis in psychology. Qual. Res. Psychol. **3**(2), 77–101 (2006). https://doi.org/10.1191/1478088706qp063oa, https://www.tandfonline.com/doi/abs/10.1191/1478088706qp063oa

8. Carroll, J.M.: Making Use: Scenario-Based Design of Human-Computer Interactions. MIT Press (2000). https://doi.org/10.5555/1531826.1531854

9. Chen, J.: The role of AI: speculative design in redefining artistic collaboration. J. Ecohumanism **3**(8), 2261–2272 (2024). https://doi.org/10.62754/joe.v3i8.4899

10. Crawford, K.: The Atlas of AI: Power, Politics, and the Planetary Costs of Artificial Intelligence. Yale University Press (2021). https://books.google.co.uk/books?id=XvEdEAAAQBAJ

11. Dean, M.: Scenario planning: a literature review. A report of project (769276-2) (2019)

12. Dunne, A., Raby, F.: Speculative Everything: Design, Fiction, and Social Dreaming. MIT Press (2013)

13. Østvold Ek, M., Paulsen, M., Trondsen, J.K.: Speculative design through the lens of AI. In: DS 131: Proceedings of the International Conference on Engineering and Product Design Education (E&PDE 2024), pp. 627–632. The Design Society, Birmingham, UK (2024). https://doi.org/10.35199/EPDE.2024.106

14. Groß, B., Mandir, E.: Designing Futures: Speculation, Critique, Innovation. Laurence King Publishing. http://ebookcentral.proquest.com/lib/rcauk/detail.action?docID=31211085

15. Harrington, C., Dillahunt, T.R.: Eliciting tech futures among black young adults: a case study of remote speculative co-design. In: Proceedings of the 2021 CHI Conference on Human Factors in Computing Systems, pp. 1–15, CHI 2021. Association for Computing Machinery. https://doi.org/10.1145/3411764.3445723

16. Hohendanner, M., Ullstein, C., Buchmeier, Y., Grossklags, J.: Exploring the reflective space of AI narratives through speculative design in Japan and Germany. In: Proceedings of the 2023 ACM Conference on Information Technology for Social Good, pp. 351–362, GoodIT 2023. Association for Computing Machinery. https://doi.org/10.1145/3582515.3609554, https://dl.acm.org/doi/10.1145/3582515.3609554

17. Holmberg, J., Robèrt, K.H.: Backcasting–a framework for strategic planning. Int. J. Sustain. Dev. World Ecol. **7**(4), 291–308 (2000)

18. John, C.: Paper space & interior fiction: employing speculative design to explore the creative design process and conceptual interiority (2021)
19. Lc, R., Tang, Y.: Speculative design with generative AI: applying stable diffusion and ChatGPT to imagining climate change futures. In: Proceedings of the 11th International Conference on Digital and Interactive Arts (2023). https://doi.org/10.1145/3632776.3632827
20. Light, A.: Collaborative speculation: anticipation, inclusion and designing counterfactual futures for appropriation. Futures **134**, 102855 (2021). https://doi.org/10.1016/j.futures.2021.102855, https://www.sciencedirect.com/science/article/pii/S0016328721001646
21. Lin, L., Long, D.: Generative AI futures: a speculative design exploration. In: Proceedings of the 15th Conference on Creativity and Cognition, pp. 380–383, C&C 2023. Association for Computing Machinery (2023). https://doi.org/10.1145/3591196.3596616
22. Lönngren, J., Van Poeck, K.: Wicked problems: a mapping review of the literature. Int. J. Sustain. Dev. World Ecol. **28**(6), 481–502 (2021)
23. Louie, C., Z.W., Gifford, T.: Novice-AI music co-creation via ai-steering tools for deep generative models. In: Proceedings of the CHI Conference on Human Factors in Computing Systems, pp. 1–12. ACM (2020)
24. McCormack, J., Gifford, T., Hutchings, P.: Autonomy, authenticity, authorship and intention in computer generated art. In: EvoMUSART (2019)
25. Mitchell, M.: Artificial Intelligence: A Guide for Thinking Humans. Farrar, Straus and Giroux (2019)
26. Rittel, H.W.J., Webber, M.M.: Dilemmas in a general theory of planning. Policy Sci. **4**(2), 155–169 (1973). https://doi.org/10.1007/BF01405730
27. Sanders, E.B.N., Stappers, P.J.: Co-creation and the new landscapes of design. CoDesign **4**(1), 5–18 (2008). https://doi.org/10.1080/15710880701875068
28. Tao, H., Vyas, D.: "Housing diversity means diverse housing": blending generative AI into speculative design in rural co-housing communities. In: Proceedings of the 2025 CHI Conference on Human Factors in Computing Systems, pp. 1–17, CHI 2025. Association for Computing Machinery (2025). https://doi.org/10.1145/3706598.3713906, https://dl.acm.org/doi/10.1145/3706598.3713906
29. Verheijden, M.P., Funk, M.: Collaborative diffusion: boosting designerly co-creation with generative AI. In: Extended Abstracts of the 2023 CHI Conference on Human Factors in Computing Systems, pp. 1–8, CHI EA 2023. Association for Computing Machinery (2023). https://doi.org/10.1145/3544549.3585680
30. Werner, K., Nestler, A.: Co-Creating Futures: A Practical Guide to Speculation Workshops Connecting Research, Design, and Society. CollActive Materials (2025). https://doi.org/10.18452/31342
31. Wyche, S.: Reimagining the mobile phone: investigating speculative approaches to design in human-computer interaction for development (HCI4D). Proc. ACM Hum.-Comput. Interact. **6**(CSCW2) (2022). https://doi.org/10.1145/3555648

Human-AI Interaction and Collaboration

Beyond Predictions: A Study of AI Strength and Weakness Transparency Communication on Human-AI Collaboration

Tina Behzad[1]([✉]) [iD], Nikolos Gurney[2] [iD], Ning Wang[2] [iD], and David V. Pynadath[3] [iD]

[1] Stony Brook University, Stony Brook, NY, USA
[2] Institute for Creative Technologies, University of Southern California, Los Angeles, CA, USA
{gurney,nwang}@ict.usc.edu
[3] Rice University, Houston, TX, USA
pynadath@rice.edu

Abstract. The promise of human-AI teaming lies in humans and AI working together to achieve performance levels neither could accomplish alone. Effective communication between AI and humans is crucial for teamwork, enabling users to efficiently benefit from AI assistance. This paper investigates how AI communication impacts human-AI team performance. We examine AI explanations that convey an awareness of its strengths and limitations. To achieve this, we train a decision tree on the model's mistakes, allowing it to recognize and explain where and why it might err. Through a user study on an income prediction task, we assess the impact of varying levels of information and explanations about AI predictions. Our results show that AI performance insights enhance task performance, and conveying AI awareness of its strengths and weaknesses improves trust calibration. These findings highlight the importance of considering how information delivery influences user trust and reliance in AI-assisted decision-making.

Keywords: AI Explainability · Decision-Making Support · Transparency in AI · Trust in AI

1 Introduction

With recent advancements in the quality and accessibility of Artificial Intelligence (AI), these systems are becoming increasingly integrated into society. In response, policymakers and practitioners emphasize the need for greater human

---

T. Behzad—Work done while interning at the Institute for Creative Technologies, University of Southern California.

oversight in AI-driven decision-making [29]. This shift necessitates human-AI collaboration, where individuals must review AI recommendations and ultimately make the final decision. In such scenarios, human's trust in their AI decision-aid becomes critical for the team's success [13]. The human decision-makers need to know when to trust or distrust an AI model's recommendations. Decades of research on this topic yielded complex insights into humans' inclination to trust algorithms [50] and the problematic disuse or overuse of automation [21]. Numerous studies have demonstrated that individuals frequently avoid relying on decision-making systems in various scenarios [4,48]. However, it has also been shown that in many situations, people do prefer algorithms, making overreliance a sensible worry [24].

Research on trust calibration in AI can be broadly categorized into two main approaches. The first approach emphasizes explainability, suggesting that making black-box models more interpretable will help users calibrate their trust in AI systems [34,48]. However, several recent empirical studies have found little evidence that higher explainability significantly impacts users' willingness to trust machine learning models [6,18]. The second approach advocates for providing high-level information about the AI system, such as its accuracy, to help users adjust their trust levels accordingly [25]. However, presenting high-performance metrics uncritically can sometimes lead to overreliance, where users place excessive trust in AI recommendations [20].

These findings highlight the level of information provided to the user has significant impact on user's trust [29]. Overwhelming users with too much information about the model leads to user following both correct and incorrect decisions more often [40] while the correct level of information is proven to be helpful [8]. The AI needs to communicate its own strength and weakness. By acknowledging its limitations, the AI can provide high-level explanations for its decisions, making it easier for humans to understand and verify its reasoning.

In this study, we examine how varying levels of information about an AI system's performance, reflecting different degrees of awareness of its own limitations, affect human-AI collaboration in terms of performance, trust, and understanding. To investigate this, we develop a self-assessing AI model, drawing inspiration from explainability methods such as Local Interpretable Model-agnostic Explanations (LIME) [34]. We then conduct an empirical evaluation with 272 participants recruited through Prolific, testing our hypothesis on whether and how different levels of information and feedback impact users' trust and decision-making performance over an income prediction task. Our results show that providing any level of information on AI's performance improves overall task performance compared to having no feedback. This finding aligns with prior research which suggests performance insights can enhance human-AI collaboration [19]. Regarding trust calibration, our findings indicate that providing AI's confidence in its decisions or awareness of its strengths and weaknesses, both enable users to better discern when to trust the model's predictions. Moreover, conveying AI's awareness compared to confidence appears to slightly enhance users' ability to calibrate their trust more effectively.

These findings highlight the importance of carefully designing the way AI communicates performance information to users. Given the diverse and sometimes contradictory research on what factors influence trust in AI, it is crucial to investigate the granularity of information provided and how it is conveyed. Our work underscores the need for further research on the impact of different levels and formats of feedback, helping to refine human-AI interaction strategies and ensure users can develop appropriately calibrated trust in AI systems.

2   Related Work

Advances in Machine Learning (ML) and ML-based AI in recent years have enabled these systems to exceed human-level performance in making predictions. One particularly important use case of machine learning is supporting decisions. Decision support systems (DSS) have undergone several evolutionary waves, and the integration of machine learning promises to drive another significant leap forward [47]. However, despite this progress, algorithmic aversion, where people distrust and avoid using algorithms for decision-making, especially after observing them make mistakes [10], has become a major barrier to fully leveraging their capabilities. Research shows that users often resist incorporating algorithms into decision-making across various domains, including critical tasks such as aiding professionals in making medical recommendations [32,39], receiving medical [24] or financial [12] advice, and employee selection [9]. This resistance even extends to lower-stakes tasks, such as receiving joke recommendations [48], raising concerns about the feasibility of joint human-algorithm decision-making in practice [5].

Previous research has tried to understand and address the factors contributing to this reluctance and distrust. A review of studies on the topic between 1950 and 2018 identified key themes influencing algorithmic aversion, including expectations and expertise, decision autonomy, incentivization, cognitive compatibility, and divergent rationalities [5].

However, while some users resist AI-based decisions, others display overreliance on AI, accepting its recommendations even when they are incorrect. This overreliance could be caused by human decision-making biases, such as automation bias [24,31] and confirmation bias [25]. Such overreliance is also influenced by various human factors, e.g., individual differences [7,29,31], and situational factors, like ordering effects, such as the sequence in which AI errors occur [27,28].

This often occurs when users struggle to assess whether—and to what extent—they should trust the AI [29], highlighting that achieving high trust as a solution to algorithmic aversion should not be the ultimate goal. Insufficient trust may lead users to reject AI assistance, even when it could improve outcomes (distrust/aversion) [23]. Conversely, excessive trust can cause users to perform worse than either the AI or human alone [2]. An appropriate level of trust—calibrated trust— is essential [17]. As a result, trust calibration has emerged as a critical area of research.

Trust calibration has been extensively studied in automation tasks [15,22,26] and more recently in AI-assisted decision-making [20,35,49]. Several studies have examined the impact of accuracy information on trust, showing that users tend to increase their trust in AI when high accuracy indicators are displayed [33,49].

Others have focused on the role of explanations in shaping trust, arguing that the black-box nature of AI presents a barrier to adoption [3,23,46]. More recently, Daehwan Ahn et al. [1] integrated these two research streams to examine their relationship. Their findings indicate that while both factors had modest effects on participants' performance, interpretability did not lead to a robust improvement in trust, whereas providing accuracy information significantly increased trust. Building on previous research highlighting the significance and impact of outcome feedback, in this paper, we investigate how varying levels of feedback influence human-AI collaboration.

3   Self-assessing AI

Exploring different levels of outcome feedback, our goal was to develop a model that is aware of its strengths and limitations and capable of identifying predictions where it might be incorrect. A straightforward and widely used approach to achieve this is through confidence scores, which provide a measure of uncertainty.

The method for calculating these scores varies depending on the model type. For probabilistic models such as Naive Bayes and Logistic Regression, confidence scores are directly obtained as class probabilities produced by the model. In ensemble models like Random Forests or Gradient Boosting, confidence scores can be calculated as the proportion of trees/models voting for a specific class. For more complex models, such as Neural Networks, the confidence score is typically derived from the activation function of the output layer, such as the softmax function, which provides a probability distribution over classes [44].

Confidence scores have been explored as a way to provide outcome feedback to users. Zhang et al. found that confidence scores help calibrate users' trust in AI models [50]. Similarly, Rechkemmer et al. demonstrated that a model's confidence level significantly influences users' perception of its accuracy, impacting both their willingness to follow its predictions and their self-reported trust in the model [33].

While confidence scores shows promise in guiding human-AI interaction, they do not constitute awareness—they are simply mathematical outputs derived from the model's internal calculations. These scores do not imply that the model **knows why** it might be wrong; rather, they reflect the model's certainty based on its training data without any underlying reasoning ability. To address these limitations, alternative approaches have been explored. One promising approach is evidential learning [37,38]. The evidential learning approach learns a generative model to create out-of distribution samples so that the classifier can be explicitly taught the input regions it should be uncertain about [37]. However, this approach introduces additional complexities in the training process [41].

Another important consideration is how humans process probabilistic information. Research has shown that people often struggle with probabilistic reasoning, falling into errors such as the base-rate fallacy [16,42,43]. Studies suggest that alternative, non-probabilistic representations of uncertainty or confidence can lead to improved trust calibration [15,26]. Building on these findings and inspired by similar approaches in explainable AI, such as Local Interpretable Model-agnostic Explanations (LIME) [34], which train simpler, more interpretable models to approximate the behavior of complex models, we adopt a similar strategy. Specifically, we train a decision tree, a highly interpretable model, on the original dataset but with labels indicating whether the predictions of the original model were correct or incorrect. This allows us to create a model that not only identifies where the complex model is likely to make mistakes but also explains why, by analyzing how different features contribute to these errors. Additionally, the decision tree can predict for new data points whether the original model is likely to make a mistake.

3.1 Defining the Task

Researchers have argued that results and recommendations for human-centered interaction with AI may vary depending on the context of use [23]. For our study, we selected an income prediction task, which has been used in prior user studies on decision support systems [45]. This scenario was chosen based on the criteria outlined by Leichtmann et al. [23]. Income prediction is highly **relevant**, as it plays a crucial role in hiring, financial assessments, and social policy. Unlike specialized fields like medical diagnosis, income-related decisions **do not require expert knowledge**, making it easier to recruit participants from diverse backgrounds. Additionally, people regularly assess income-related factors in everyday life, ensuring the task is **close to participants' reality**. Finally, concerns surrounding income equity and fairness make this a topic of significant **public interest**.

We used the American Community Survey (ACS) Public Use Microdata Sample (PUMS) dataset [11], which covers multiple years and all states across the United States. It supports five different prediction tasks, including income prediction. For this study, we restricted the dataset to individuals from California in the year 2018, resulting in 196, 665 individuals.

We chose our original model to be a Random Forest classifier, trained using the scikit-learn library [30] with default hyperparameters. We used 70% of the data for training, achieving an accuracy of 80% on the test set. To create a self-assessing system, we trained a decision tree on the same training dataset but replaced the original labels with binary indicators of whether the original model's predictions were correct. We selected a decision tree model for three key reasons. First, its structure is inherently interpretable, allowing us to trace and explain each decision path. Second, because decision trees align with everyday reasoning, a lot of people without any background can understand the model's logic, and we can tailor the depth of information displayed to the user. Third, the tree's natural grouping of data points into branches creates clusters that we leverage later in our study design (see Sect. 4.1). Since the original model had an accuracy of 90% on the training data, the resulting dataset was highly imbalanced. To address this, we balanced the data to contain an equal number of correct and incorrect labels before training the decision tree. After tuning hyperparameters, the self-assessing model achieved a 66% accuracy which was the best we could get under these conditions. We call this tree the flaw decision tree[1].

4   Methods

4.1   Study Design

Our main hypotheses when designing the experiments were:

H1 *Communicating awareness of the model's weakness and strength can improve task performance.*

H2 *Communicating awareness of model's weakness and strength can help human teammates calibrate trust in AI.*

H3 *Communicating awareness of the model's weakness and strength can help human teammates understand AI better.*

To evaluate this, we designed an experiment consisting of four treatment conditions and a control group. The task required participants to predict whether an individual's income would be above or below \$80K after reviewing relevant attributes. All groups were presented with the individual's information in a tabular format, as shown in Fig. 4. The treatment groups received varying levels of assistance and feedback from an AI teammate (the trained random forest predictor from Sect. 3), while the control group (we also call this group **No Helper** through the text) completed the task without AI support. This setup allowed us to assess participants' performance both without and with different levels of AI assistance and outcome feedback.

The four treatment groups were as follows (illustrated in Fig. 4 in appendix B):

G1 Decision-Only: Saw the AI helper's prediction for each individual alongside the individual's information.

G2 Decision + 80% Exp: Received the same information as **G1**, but before starting, they were informed that the AI's accuracy is 80% and were given an explanation of what this means.

G3 Decision + Confidence Exp: In addition to seeing the AI's prediction and the individual's attributes, they were also shown the model's confidence in its prediction.

G4 Decision + self-assessing Exp: Along with the AI's prediction and the individual's attributes, they were provided with information on how well the model performs for similar data points and the overall performance (80%).

We selected 50 data points from the full test dataset described in Sect. 3.1, allocating 10 for the training phase and 40 for the main task. To ensure consistency, we selected instances in a way that the AI's predictions maintained the reported 80% accuracy (2 of 10 incorrect predictions in training and 8 out of 40 predictions in the main task).

---

[1] To have a better understanding of how the tree looks, refer to Fig. 2.

For Group 3, the confidence score corresponded to the probability of the predicted class (income level above \$80K). As stated in the scikit-learn documentation, this score is calculated as the mean predicted class probabilities of the trees in the forest[2]. For Group 4, we use the self-assessing model described in Sect. 3. Initially, we considered presenting participants with the entire flaw decision tree, highlighting where each individual's data point falls within the tree or displaying the full root-to-leaf decision path. However, we determined that this approach could overwhelm participants with too much information, particularly for those unfamiliar with tree structures. We chose to use the flaw decision tree to categorize data points into groups, where each leaf node represents a group of similar individuals based on whether the original model predicts them correctly. For each group, we report the fraction of individuals that were predicted correctly by the original model. We present this information as "AI's accuracy for similar individuals", alongside the general statement that the AI's overall accuracy is 80% for each prediction.

When selecting the 50 data points from the test dataset, we ensured that the additional information provided to treatment groups 3 and 4 remained consistent. Specifically, if the confidence score displayed to Group 3 for a given point was high, the AI's accuracy for similar individuals shown to Group 4 was also high, and vice versa. While the exact numerical values may differ, we ensured that both metrics consistently reflected whether they were above or below the overall 80% accuracy threshold. Additionally, for instances where the original model made incorrect predictions, we balanced the selection of data points. Half of these instances were chosen so that the reported confidence or accuracy was informative (i.e., lower than the overall 80% accuracy), indicating appropriate uncertainty. The other half was selected to be misleading, where the model was overconfident despite being incorrect.

For each of the aforementioned conditions, after identifying the subset of data corresponding to that specific condition, the points were randomly selected from the entire test set.

4.2 Ethical Approval

This study was approved by the University of Southern California Institutional Review Board.

4.3 Recruitment

We recruited 272 (approximately 50 per condition) US-based participants using the Prolific pool of study participants, where no personally identifying information was accessible. They were informed that the study would take place online, might involve working with an AI, last approximately fifteen minutes, pay \$4 plus a bonus of up to \$4, and was open to adult US citizens (a funding

---

[2] The class probability of a single tree is determined by the fraction of samples of the same class in a leaf.

constraint). The average participant was 37 years old, most of whom ($n = 177$) reported being female. The modal reported level of education was a bachelor's degree ($n = 102$); the next most common was a high school diploma or equivalent ($n = 74$). The majority of participants ($n = 185$) self identified as white. The median completion time was 889.5 s, however, the completion time data are characterized by a right skew ($mean = 1025.2$ S).

4.4 Procedure

We collected data in two batches: the four treatment conditions and the control group, which did not have an AI helper. After accepting the task on Prolific, the participant was redirected to a survey-based platform (Qualtrics) where they signed the consent form and agreed to participate in the study. The survey software randomized treatment condition participants into a study arm. Verification of their Prolific ID advanced participants to an introduction page that introduced them to the task and, if in a treatment condition, how and what the AI helper would communicate to them. Next, they progressed to a training phase in which they were allowed to do 10 practice tasks that did not impact their bonus payment. Participants in treatment conditions received the same help from the AI that they eventually did during the incentivized portion of the study. The training phase ended with a report telling participants how well they did in the classification task and reminding them that the following 40 classifications tasks were bonus-eligible. In both the training and the actual task, users received feedback on whether or not they made the correct decision after each decision. At the end of the 40 tasks, participants were informed of their performance and the bonus amount they earned.

Participants next completed a set of self-report questions (see appendix D for the complete set of questions). The Generalized Attitudes Towards AI Scale [36] followed the self-report. Finally, participants completed the demographics portion of the study, after which they were redirected back to Prolific to complete the platform requirements for payment.

4.5 Measures

Task Performance: We measure performance as the proportion of correct final decisions, computed as the number of accurate predictions divided by the total number of predictions (40).

Compliance: Compliance is defined as instances where the user's final decision is aligned with the AI's recommendation, serving as a proxy for trust in the AI's decision. To further investigate users' ability to calibrate their trust, we differentiate compliance rates based on the correctness and confidence of the AI's predictions. Specifically, we distinguish between cases where the AI was (i) correct, (ii) incorrect and overconfident, and (iii) incorrect with an appropriate level of confidence. This differentiation allows us to assess whether users could appropriately override AI recommendations when the model was incorrect.

Self-Reported Perceptions of the AI Assistant: To evaluate whether varying levels of outcome feedback influenced participants' understanding of the AI teammate, we administered a post-task questionnaire consisting of four key questions. Participants rated their agreement with each statement using a slider scale from 0 to 100. These questions were not presented to the control group. 1) The AI understands how the information in the tables relates to income levels. 2)The AI knows its own limitations. 3) I trusted the AI to provide useful suggestions. 4) I am confident that I know how the AI makes its suggestions.

5   Results

In the following, we present results related to our first (H1) and second (H2) hypotheses. Our self-reported measures on participants' understanding of the AI helper (H3) showed no significant differences across groups. Due to space constraints, a more detailed discussion of these findings has been moved to the appendix.

5.1   Task Performance

We start by looking at task performance. Figure 1 shows participants' scores across the training phase and for the actual task. The scores were scaled from to 100 for illustration (exact mean value can be found in Table 1 in appendix C).

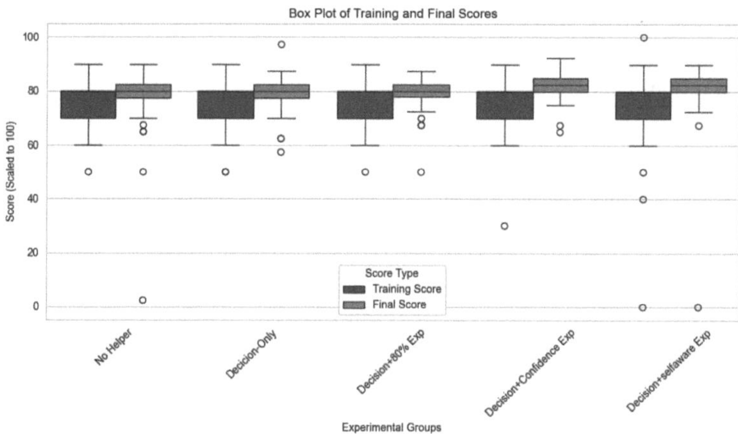

Fig. 1. Box plot illustrating training scores (blue) and task scores (orange) for each group. (Color figure online)

To better interpret the results we fitted a linear regression model(presented in Appendix C, Table 2). Results suggest that participants with input from an AI helper generally did better than participants in the *No Helper*, i.e., control, condition (see Table 2 column (1) for the values used in the following interpretation). The average score of the *No Helper* participants was 0.780, or just over 31 correct classifications. Participants in the *Decision-Only* and *Decision + 80% Exp* conditions did better (their average scores were $0.780 + 0.010 = 0.790$ and $0.780 + 0.016 = 0.796$, respectively), although not significantly. Participants in the other two conditions *Decision + Confidence Exp* and *Decision + self-assessing Exp* did significantly better than the control participants, averaging $0.780 + 0.045 = 0.825$ and $0.780 + 0.035 = 0.815$, respectively—equating to roughly 33 correct classifications.

The effects remain roughly the same when adding control variables to the basic model (see Table 2 column (2) for the values used in the following interpretation). We reached this model through iteratively specifying models using the various demographic and control variables (e.g., *Training Score, Age, Sex, Education*, etc.) and using a χ^2 test to see if the reduction in the residual sum of squares was justified by the higher complexity of a model with additional variables. Generally speaking, participants that did better during the training phase did better during the incentivized task, and each additional year of age was associated with a small but significant decrease in score.

5.2   Compliance

Although predicting participants' overall performance (their score) in the task is valuable, it is arguably more important to understand how calibrated they are when they should heed or ignore the helper's advice. Well-calibrated compliance is not only correlated with performance but also opinions of the help [14]. For this, we use logistic regression models and, having established the importance of *Age* and *Training Score* in our previous efforts, only discuss the fully specified models (see Table 3). Note that we do not include the data from the participants in the *No Helper* treatment condition as they were not choosing whether to comply with the recommendation of an AI helper. Thus, the *Decision-Only* treatment condition serves as the "control" condition.

Our results show that relative to the *Decision-Only*, participants in each of the other three helper conditions were significantly more likely to comply. When we look at overall compliance, meaning over the entire task regardless of whether or not the helper was correct, the strongest impact is observed in *Decision + Confidence Exp* condition which was associated with a 0.305 high log odds of complying (column (1), Table 3). In other words, for these participants, there was a 35% increase in the odds of complying $((e^{0.305} - 1) * 100)$. However, when we look at compliance when the helper was correct (column (3), Table 3), we see the most substantial effect appears in the *Decision + self-assessing Exp* group increase in the odds of complying, followed by *Decision + Confidence Exp*.

We further examine the odds of compliance when the AI is incorrect and overconfident versus incorrect with the right level of confidence (see Table 4). Participants in the *Decision + Confidence Exp* and *Decision + self-assessing Exp* conditions are significantly more likely to comply when the AI is incorrect but overconfident and less likely to comply when the AI is incorrect but calibrated in its confidence. While the differences between the two groups are not statistically significant in either scenario, we observe slightly lower compliance in the *Decision + self-assessing Exp* rate when the AI is overconfident (and similarly for the right confidence case), suggesting that participants in the awareness condition demonstrated better trust calibration in AI's decisions.

6 Discussion

In this paper, we explored the design of an AI decision aid that generates explanations highlighting its strengths and weaknesses in predicting income levels. Our hypothesis posited that providing concise, awareness-based insights—reflecting a deeper understanding of the model's limitations—could enhance task performance, trust calibration, and users' comprehension of their AI teammate. To evaluate this, we conducted a user study with 272 participants, including a control group and four treatment conditions, each offering varying levels of assistance and feedback from the AI teammate. Our results demonstrate that providing AI performance information enhances task performance and that conveying AI's awareness of its strengths and weaknesses helps users calibrate their trust in its decisions slightly better compared to showing only confidence levels.

Our findings align with prior research suggesting that providing information about AI models helps users develop appropriate reliance on AI while also offering insights into how to enhance the effectiveness of this information. Overreliance is particularly critical in cases where the AI is incorrect, yet users choose to follow its recommendations. Our results suggest that conveying AI awareness can slightly reduce this blind trust more effectively than simply providing confidence levels.

While we did not observe significant differences across groups in terms of their understanding of AI, this may be due to limitations in the objective measures used. Future research could address this by incorporating follow-up assessments to more effectively evaluate participants' understanding of AI. Additionally, it would be valuable to examine whether these findings replicate across different tasks and varying levels of AI accuracy. Insights from such studies can further illuminate the complex dynamics of human-AI collaboration.

Acknowledgement. Research was sponsored by the Army Research Office and was accomplished under Cooperative Agreement Number W911NF-20-2-0053. The views and conclusions contained in this document are those of the authors and should not be interpreted as representing the official policies, either expressed or implied, of the Army Research Office or the U.S. Government. The U.S. Government is authorized to reproduce and distribute reprints for Government purposes notwithstanding any copyright notation herein.

A Self-assessing AI

A subset of the decision tree trained on the initial model, as described in Sect. 3.1, is presented in Fig. 2. The full tree has a depth of 10 and consists of 517 nodes.

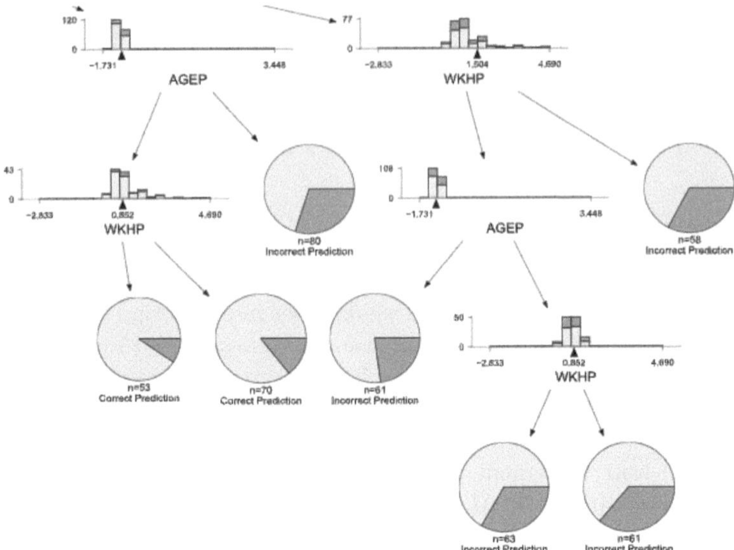

Fig. 2. A small selection of leaf nodes from the self-assessing decision tree trained (values for features are normalized).

B   Study Design

Figure 4 shows different conditions described in Sect. 4.1. Figure 3 shows the information provided to all participants and Figs. 3a to 3d show different levels of information provided to different groups.

C   Results

Table 1. Mean Scores by Condition

Condition	Mean Score
No Helper	0.780
Decision-Only	0.790
Decision + 80% Exp	0.796
Decision + Confidence Exp	0.825
Decision + self-assessing Exp	0.815

Our self-reported measures on participants' understanding of the AI helper did not reveal any significant differences across groups (Tables 5, 6). Opiniono-fAIhelper 1 to 4 indicate self-reported questions described in Sect. 4.5. The willingness to pay column (Table 6, column (2)) is another self-reported metric we

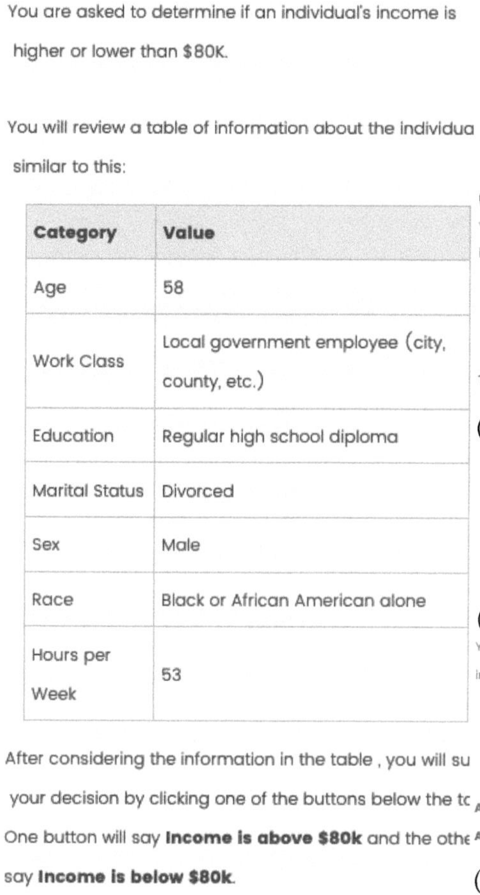

You are asked to determine if an individual's income is higher or lower than $80K.

You will review a table of information about the individual similar to this:

Category	Value
Age	58
Work Class	Local government employee (city, county, etc.)
Education	Regular high school diploma
Marital Status	Divorced
Sex	Male
Race	Black or African American alone
Hours per Week	53

After considering the information in the table , you will su your decision by clicking one of the buttons below the tc One button will say **Income is above $80k** and the othe say **Income is below $80k.**

Fig. 3. The information provided to all groups.

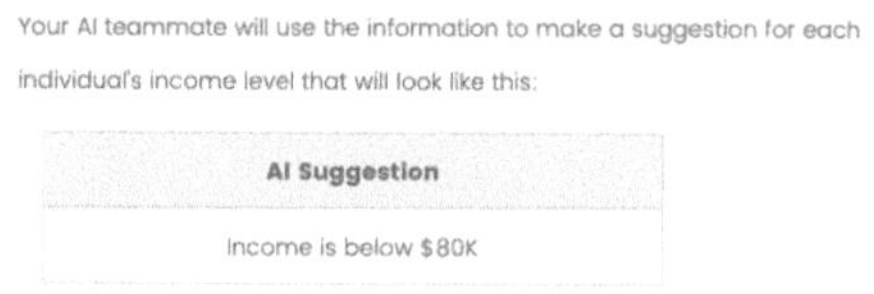

Your AI teammate will use the information to make a suggestion for each individual's income level that will look like this:

(a) Additional information shown to **G2**

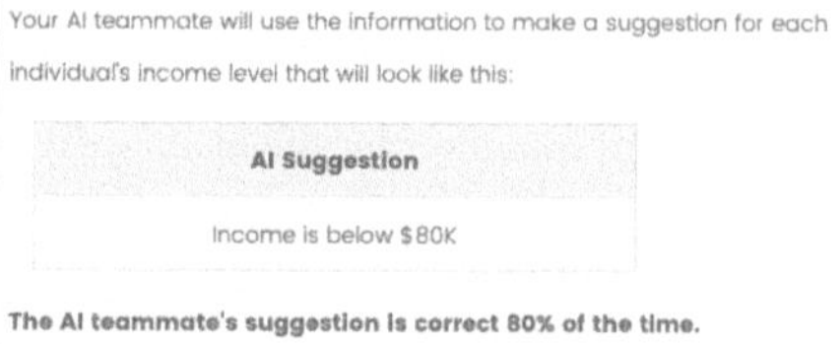

Your AI teammate will use the information to make a suggestion for each individual's income level that will look like this:

The AI teammate's suggestion is correct 80% of the time.

(b) Additional information shown to **G3**

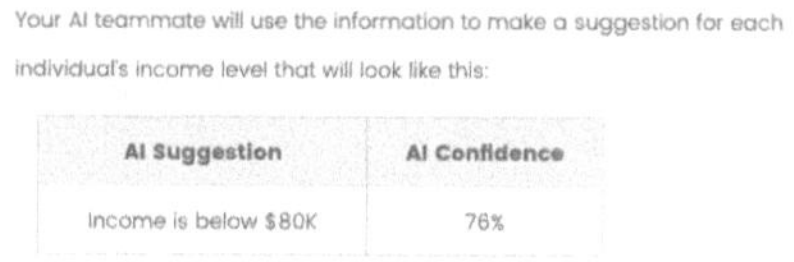

Your AI teammate will use the information to make a suggestion for each individual's income level that will look like this:

(c) Additional information shown to **G4**

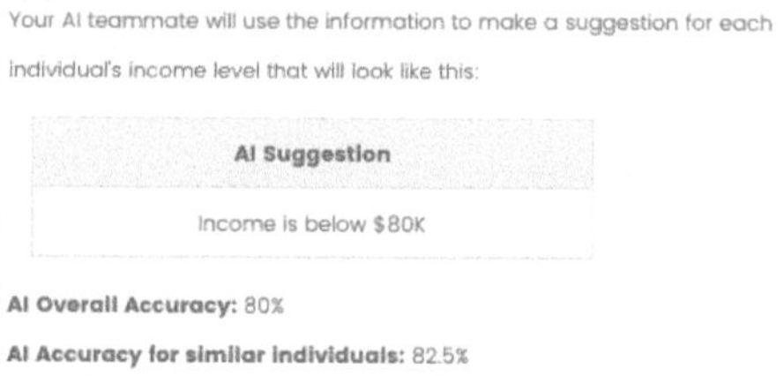

Your AI teammate will use the information to make a suggestion for each individual's income level that will look like this:

AI Overall Accuracy: 80%

AI Accuracy for similar individuals: 82.5%

(d) Additional information shown to **G5**

Fig. 4. Example of the introduction shown to all participants.

asked from participants to evaluate the potential impact of different treatment conditions on reducing algorithmic aversion. Participants were asked: *If you were to repeat this task but had to pay for AI suggestions from your bonus, what percentage of your bonus would you be willing to give up to receive them?*

It is possible that with a larger sample size and more detailed questions, we could gain deeper insights into how different levels of information influence users' comprehension of the AI system.

Table 2. Column (1) presents a linear regression model predicting a Score (number of correct income classifications divided by total classifications). The intercept, or constant, is the *No Helper* condition. Column (2) adds control variables for the participants' performance during the training stage and age.

	Dependent variable: Score	
	n Correct $\div$ Total	
	(1)	(2)
Decision-Only	0.010	0.011
	(0.017)	(0.016)
Decision + 80% Exp	0.016	0.011
	(0.017)	(0.016)
Decision + Confidence Exp	0.045**	0.041*
	(0.017)	(0.016)
Decision + self-assessing Exp	0.035*	0.037*
	(0.017)	(0.016)
Training Score		0.038***
		(0.005)
Age		−0.001*
		(0.0004)
Constant (No Helper)	0.780***	0.526***
	(0.012)	(0.041)
Observations	272	272
R^2	0.033	0.222
Adjusted R^2	0.018	0.204
Residual Std. Error	0.090 (df = 267)	0.081 (df = 265)
F Statistic	2.257 (df = 4; 267)	12.575*** (df = 6; 265)

Note: *p < 0.05; **p < 0.01; ***p < 0.001

Table 3. Logistic regression models predicting the odds of complying across different experimental conditions. Column (1) presents overall compliance, while Columns (2) and (3) distinguish between compliance when the AI was incorrect and correct, respectively. Reported coefficients represent log-odds estimates, with standard errors in parentheses.

	Dependent variable: Odds of Complying		
	Overall	Helper Incorrect	Helper Correct
	(1)	(2)	(3)
Decision + 80% Exp	0.270**	0.288	0.279*
	(0.102)	(0.162)	(0.138)
Decision + Confidence Exp	0.305**	−0.068	0.721***
	(0.101)	(0.152)	(0.151)
Decision + self-assessing Exp	0.268**	−0.193	0.803***
	(0.100)	(0.151)	(0.154)
Age	−0.003	0.001	−0.006
	(0.003)	(0.005)	(0.005)
Training Score	0.098**	−0.077	0.240***
	(0.032)	(0.056)	(0.041)
Constant (Decision-Only)	1.412***	1.585***	0.912*
	(0.279)	(0.468)	(0.368)
Observations	219	219	219
Log Likelihood	−508.679	−362.276	−407.833
Akaike Inf. Crit.	1,029.357	736.552	827.667

Note: *p < 0.05; **p < 0.01; ***p < 0.001

Table 4. Logistic regression models predicting compliance when AI is incorrect. Column (1) examines compliance when the AI is overconfident, while Column (2) examines compliance when the AI correctly assesses its weakness and strength. Reported coefficients represent log-odds estimates, with standard errors in parentheses.

	Dependent variable:	
	compliance when overconfident	compliance when confidence is right
	(1)	(2)
ConditionDecision + 80% Exp	0.272	0.323
	(0.281)	(0.207)
ConditionDecision + Confidence Exp	1.026**	−0.498*
	(0.334)	(0.195)
ConditionDecision + self-assessing Exp	0.632*	−0.595**
	(0.300)	(0.196)
age	0.002	0.0003
	(0.010)	(0.006)
trainingScore	0.063	−0.152*
	(0.105)	(0.072)
Constant	1.134	1.666**
	(0.881)	(0.601)
Observations	219	219
Log Likelihood	−178.908	−314.412
Akaike Inf. Crit.	369.817	640.823

Note: *p < 0.05; **p < 0.01; ***p < 0.001

Table 5. Linear regression models predicting participants' self-reported opinions of the AI helper. Columns (1), (2), and (3) correspond to different opinion measures (opinionOfAIHelper_1, opinionOfAIHelper_2, and opinionOfAIHelper_3) (refer to Sect. 4.5). Reported coefficients represent the estimated effects of experimental conditions and other factors, with standard errors in parentheses.

	Dependent variable:		
	opinionOfAIHelper_1	opinionOfAIHelper_2	opinionOfAIHelper_3
	(1)	(2)	(3)
ConditionDecision + 80% Exp	−13.992	−32.583	−47.632
	(51.792)	(73.817)	(61.177)
ConditionDecision + Confidence Exp	−28.992	−124.577	−106.734
	(58.224)	(82.985)	(68.775)
ConditionDecision + self-assessing Exp	9.148	−70.782	−6.990
	(40.426)	(57.618)	(47.752)
Score	−9.140	−59.683	−45.181
	(43.943)	(62.631)	(51.906)
age	0.379**	0.213	0.269
	(0.122)	(0.174)	(0.144)
trainingScore	−1.285	−2.579	−0.026
	(1.718)	(2.449)	(2.030)
ConditionDecision + 80% Exp:Score	30.536	39.561	77.131
	(65.115)	(92.806)	(76.915)
ConditionDecision + Confidence Exp:Score	45.187	164.060	148.271
	(71.556)	(101.987)	(84.523)
ConditionDecision + self-assessing Exp:Score	−3.761	103.908	30.878
	(50.472)	(71.935)	(59.618)
Constant	68.503	98.811	80.620
	(36.170)	(51.552)	(42.725)
Observations	219	219	219
R^2	0.074	0.064	0.094
Adjusted R^2	0.034	0.024	0.054
Residual Std. Error (df = 209)	20.952	29.862	24.749
F Statistic (df = 9; 209)	1.859	1.589	2.396*

Note: *p < 0.05; **p < 0.01; ***p < 0.001

Table 6. Linear regression models predicting participants' opinions of the AI helper and their willingness to pay for AI assistance. Column (1) corresponds to self-reported opinions of the AI (*opinionOfAIHelper_4*), while Column (2) examines the willingness to pay for AI-generated suggestions. Reported coefficients represent the estimated effects of experimental conditions and other factors, with standard errors in parentheses.

	Dependent variable:	
	opinionOfAIHelper_4	Willingness to Pay
	(1)	(2)
ConditionDecision + 80% Exp	−9.064	147.604*
	(73.000)	(59.557)
ConditionDecision + Confidence Exp	−36.460	23.642
	(85.962)	(66.954)
ConditionDecision + self-assessing Exp	8.750	62.548
	(56.624)	(46.487)
Score	−9.981	110.589*
	(61.965)	(50.531)
age	0.024	−0.010
	(0.176)	(0.140)
trainingScore	−3.315	−1.958
	(2.421)	(1.976)
ConditionDecision + 80% Exp:Score	11.584	−188.551*
	(91.957)	(74.877)
ConditionDecision + Confidence Exp:Score	50.406	−28.057
	(106.140)	(82.285)
ConditionDecision + self-assessing Exp:Score	−5.649	−71.310
	(70.921)	(58.039)
Constant	82.513	−55.420
	(50.939)	(41.593)
Observations	199	219
R^2	0.026	0.067
Adjusted R^2	−0.020	0.027
Residual Std. Error	28.637 (df = 189)	24.093 (df = 209)
F Statistic	0.563 (df = 9; 189)	1.662 (df = 9; 209)

Note: *p < 0.05; **p < 0.01; ***p < 0.001

D   Survey Questions

Below is the complete list of questions (in the exact order) that participants were asked to answer after the training phase and upon completing the 40 predictions.

Your team made **${e://Field/CorrectAns}** correct decisions out of 40.

Based on your team's performance, you will receive a bonus of $ **${e://Field/bonusAmount}**.

selfReport

Use the sliders to indicate how much you relied on the information presented in the tables when making your decisions, with 0 meaning "not at all" and 100 meaning "to a great degree."

The
categories
and their
values.

The AI's
suggestion.

Outcome of
the previous
decisions.

Use the sliders below to indicate how much you agree with the statements, with 0 meaning "not at all" and 100 meaning "to a great degree."

The AI
understands
how the
information in
the tables
relates to
income
levels.

The AI knows
its own
limitations.

I trusted the
AI to provide
useful
suggestions.

I am confident that I know how the AI makes its suggestions.

If you were doing this task again, but had to pay for the AI suggestions from your bonus, what percentage of your bonus would you give up to receive its suggestions?

Percentage I would be willing to give up to receive the AI's suggestions.

The AI is 80% accurate, which means it makes correct decision 8 out of 10 times.

Do you think that the average person could outperform the AI on this task?

○ No

○ Yes

Do you think that 80% accuracy is low, average, or high for an AI doing this task?

○ Low
○ Average
○ High

The AI can communicate how confident it is in its decisions.

How would you rate the AI's confidence?

○ Under confident
○ About right
○ Over confident

Could the AI have communicated its confidence better?

○ No
○ Yes

How could it have communicated its confidence better?

The AI can assess the accuracy of its current decision and the decisions for similar individuals.

How would you rate the AI's accuracy assessment?

○ Poor
○ Okay
○ Good

Could the AI have communicated its accuracy better?

○ No
○ Yes

How could it have communicated its accuracy better?

○ Black or African American
○ American Indian or Alaska Native
○ Asian
○ Native Hawaiian or Pacific Islander
○ [   ] Other

How often do you interact with an AI?

○ Not at all
○ A few times a month
○ A few times a week
○ A few times a day

Select the highest-level degree or certificate program you have completed.

○ Secondary/High school graduate or equivalent

○ Associate's

○ Bachelor's

○ Master's

○ Doctoral Degree Program (Ph.D.)

○ Doctoral Degree Professional

○ Industry Recognized Certification

○ Technical Training Program

○ None of the above

end

Thank you for participating. You will be redirected back to Prolific after this screen.

Powered by Qualtrics

References

1. Ahn, D., Almaatouq, A., Gulabani, M., Hosanagar, K.: Impact of model interpretability and outcome feedback on trust in AI. In: Proceedings of the 2024 CHI Conference on Human Factors in Computing Systems, CHI 2024. Association for Computing Machinery, New York, NY, USA (2024). https://doi.org/10.1145/3613904.3642780

2. Bansal, G., et al.: Does the whole exceed its parts? The effect of AI explanations on complementary team performance. In: Proceedings of the 2021 CHI Conference on Human Factors in Computing Systems, pp. 1–16 (2021)

3. Bhatt, U., Ravikumar, P., et al.: Building human-machine trust via interpretability. In: Proceedings of the AAAI Conference on Artificial Intelligence, vol. 33, pp. 9919–9920 (2019)

4. Bigman, Y.E., Gray, K.: People are averse to machines making moral decisions. Cognition **181**, 21–34 (2018)

5. Burton, J.W., Stein, M.K., Jensen, T.B.: A systematic review of algorithm aversion in augmented decision making. J. Behav. Decis. Mak. **33**(2), 220–239 (2020)

6. Cheng, H.F., et al.: Explaining decision-making algorithms through UI: strategies to help non-expert stakeholders. In: Proceedings of the 2019 CHI Conference on Human Factors in Computing Systems, pp. 1–12 (2019)

7. Chong, L., Zhang, G., Goucher-Lambert, K., Kotovsky, K., Cagan, J.: Human confidence in artificial intelligence and in themselves: the evolution and impact of confidence on adoption of ai advice. Comput. Hum. Behav. **127**, 107018 (2022)

8. De-Arteaga, M., Fogliato, R., Chouldechova, A.: A case for humans-in-the-loop: decisions in the presence of erroneous algorithmic scores. In: Proceedings of the 2020 CHI Conference on Human Factors in Computing Systems, pp. 1–12 (2020)
9. Diab, D.L., Pui, S.Y., Yankelevich, M., Highhouse, S.: Lay perceptions of selection decision aids in us and non-us samples. Int. J. Sel. Assess. **19**(2), 209–216 (2011)
10. Dietvorst, B.J., Simmons, J.P., Massey, C.: Algorithm aversion: people erroneously avoid algorithms after seeing them err. J. Exp. Psychol. Gen. **144**(1), 114 (2015)
11. Ding, F., Hardt, M., Miller, J., Schmidt, L.: Retiring adult: new datasets for fair machine learning. In: Advances in Neural Information Processing Systems, vol. 34, pp. 6478–6490 (2021)
12. Eastwood, J., Snook, B., Luther, K.: What people want from their professionals: attitudes toward decision-making strategies. J. Behav. Decis. Mak. **25**(5), 458–468 (2012)
13. Glikson, E., Woolley, A.W.: Human trust in artificial intelligence: review of empirical research. Acad. Manag. Ann. **14**(2), 627–660 (2020)
14. Gurney, N., Pynadath, D.V., Wang, N.: My actions speak louder than your words: when user behavior predicts their beliefs about agents' attributes. In: International Conference on Human-Computer Interaction, pp. 232–248. Springer (2023). https://doi.org/10.1007/978-3-031-35894-4_17
15. Helldin, T., Falkman, G., Riveiro, M., Davidsson, S.: Presenting system uncertainty in automotive UIS for supporting trust calibration in autonomous driving. In: Proceedings of the 5th International Conference on Automotive User Interfaces and Interactive Vehicular Applications, pp. 210–217, AutomotiveUI 2013. Association for Computing Machinery, New York, NY, USA (2013). https://doi.org/10.1145/2516540.2516554
16. Kahneman, D., Tversky, A.: Variants of uncertainty. Cognition **11**(2), 143–157 (1982)
17. Kraus, J., Scholz, D., Stiegemeier, D., Baumann, M.: The more you know: trust dynamics and calibration in highly automated driving and the effects of take-overs, system malfunction, and system transparency. Hum. Factors **62**(5), 718–736 (2020)
18. Kunkel, J., Donkers, T., Michael, L., Barbu, C.M., Ziegler, J.: Let me explain: impact of personal and impersonal explanations on trust in recommender systems. In: Proceedings of the 2019 CHI Conference on Human Factors in Computing Systems, pp. 1–12 (2019)
19. Lai, V., Liu, H., Tan, C.: "why is' chicago'deceptive?" towards building model-driven tutorials for humans. In: Proceedings of the 2020 CHI Conference on Human Factors in Computing Systems, pp. 1–13 (2020)
20. Lai, V., Tan, C.: On human predictions with explanations and predictions of machine learning models: a case study on deception detection. In: Proceedings of the Conference on Fairness, Accountability, and Transparency, pp. 29–38 (2019)
21. Lee, J.D.: Review of a pivotal human factors article: "humans and automation: use, misuse, disuse, abuse". Hum. Factors **50**(3), 404–410 (2008)
22. Lee, J.D., See, K.A.: Trust in automation: designing for appropriate reliance. Hum. Factors **46**(1), 50–80 (2004)
23. Leichtmann, B., Humer, C., Hinterreiter, A., Streit, M., Mara, M.: Effects of explainable artificial intelligence on trust and human behavior in a high-risk decision task. Comput. Hum. Behav. **139**, 107539 (2023)
24. Logg, J.M., Minson, J.A., Moore, D.A.: Algorithm appreciation: people prefer algorithmic to human judgment. Organ. Behav. Hum. Decis. Process. **151**, 90–103 (2019)

25. Lu, Z., Yin, M.: Human reliance on machine learning models when performance feedback is limited: heuristics and risks. In: Proceedings of the 2021 CHI Conference on Human Factors in Computing Systems, pp. 1–16 (2021)
26. McGuirl, J.M., Sarter, N.B.: Supporting trust calibration and the effective use of decision aids by presenting dynamic system confidence information. Hum. Factors **48**(4), 656–665 (2006)
27. Nourani, M., King, J., Ragan, E.: The role of domain expertise in user trust and the impact of first impressions with intelligent systems. In: Proceedings of the AAAI Conference on Human Computation and Crowdsourcing, vol. 8, pp. 112–121 (2020)
28. Nourani, M., et al.: Anchoring bias affects mental model formation and user reliance in explainable AI systems. In: Proceedings of the 26th International Conference on Intelligent User Interfaces, pp. 340–350 (2021)
29. Passi, S., Vorvoreanu, M.: Overreliance on ai literature review. Microsoft Research (2022)
30. Pedregosa, F., et al.: Scikit-learn: machine learning in python. J. Mach. Learn. Res. **12**, 2825–2830 (2011)
31. Pop, V.L., Shrewsbury, A., Durso, F.T.: Individual differences in the calibration of trust in automation. Hum. Factors **57**(4), 545–556 (2015)
32. Promberger, M., Baron, J.: Do patients trust computers? J. Behav. Decis. Mak. **19**(5), 455–468 (2006)
33. Rechkemmer, A., Yin, M.: When confidence meets accuracy: exploring the effects of multiple performance indicators on trust in machine learning models. In: Proceedings of the 2022 CHI Conference on Human Factors in Computing Systems, pp. 1–14 (2022)
34. Ribeiro, M.T., Singh, S., Guestrin, C.: "why should i trust you?" explaining the predictions of any classifier. In: Proceedings of the 22nd ACM SIGKDD International Conference on Knowledge Discovery and Data Mining, pp. 1135–1144 (2016)
35. Schaffer, J., O'Donovan, J., Michaelis, J., Raglin, A., Höllerer, T.: I can do better than your AI: expertise and explanations. In: Proceedings of the 24th International Conference on Intelligent User Interfaces, pp. 240–251 (2019)
36. Schepman, A., Rodway, P.: Initial validation of the general attitudes towards artificial intelligence scale. Comput. Hum. Behav. Rep. **1**, 100014 (2020) https://doi.org/10.1016/j.chbr.2020.100014, https://www.sciencedirect.com/science/article/pii/S2451958820300142
37. Sensoy, M., Kaplan, L., Cerutti, F., Saleki, M.: Uncertainty-aware deep classifiers using generative models. In: Proceedings of the AAAI Conference on Artificial Intelligence, vol. 34, pp. 5620–5627 (2020)
38. Sensoy, M., Kaplan, L., Kandemir, M.: Evidential deep learning to quantify classification uncertainty. In: Advances in Neural Information Processing Systems, vol. 31 (2018)
39. Shaffer, V.A., Probst, C.A., Merkle, E.C., Arkes, H.R., Medow, M.A.: Why do patients derogate physicians who use a computer-based diagnostic support system? Med. Decis. Making **33**(1), 108–118 (2013)
40. Suresh, H., Lao, N., Liccardi, I.: Misplaced trust: measuring the interference of machine learning in human decision-making. In: Proceedings of the 12th ACM Conference on Web Science, pp. 315–324 (2020)
41. Tomsett, R., et al.: Rapid trust calibration through interpretable and uncertainty-aware AI. Patterns **1**(4) (2020)
42. Tversky, A., Kahneman, D.: The framing of decisions and the psychology of choice. Science **211**(4481), 453–458 (1981)

43. Tversky, A., Kahneman, D., Slovic, P.: Judgment Under Uncertainty: Heuristics and Biases. Cambridge (1982)
44. Vemuri, N.: Scoring Confidence in Neural Networks. University of California at Berkeley (2020)
45. Vodrahalli, K., Daneshjou, R., Gerstenberg, T., Zou, J.: Do humans trust advice more if it comes from AI? an analysis of human-AI interactions. In: Proceedings of the 2022 AAAI/ACM Conference on AI, Ethics, and Society, pp. 763–777 (2022)
46. Wang, X., Yin, M.: Are explanations helpful? a comparative study of the effects of explanations in AI-assisted decision-making. In: Proceedings of the 26th International Conference on Intelligent User Interfaces, pp. 318–328, IUI 2021. Association for Computing Machinery, New York, NY, USA (2021). https://doi.org/10.1145/3397481.3450650
47. Watson, H.J.: Preparing for the cognitive generation of decision support. MIS Q. Executive **16**(3) (2017)
48. Yeomans, M., Shah, A., Mullainathan, S., Kleinberg, J.: Making sense of recommendations. J. Behav. Decis. Mak. **32**(4), 403–414 (2019)
49. Yin, M., Wortman Vaughan, J., Wallach, H.: Understanding the effect of accuracy on trust in machine learning models. In: Proceedings of the 2019 CHI Conference on Human Factors in Computing Systems, pp. 1–12 (2019)
50. Zhang, Y., Liao, Q.V., Bellamy, R.K.: Effect of confidence and explanation on accuracy and trust calibration in ai-assisted decision making. In: Proceedings of the 2020 Conference on Fairness, Accountability, and Transparency, pp. 295–305 (2020)

AI-Powered Avatars in Metaverse for Social Anxiety Systematic Desensitization Treatment: A Pilot Study on Feasibility

Antonella Cavallaro[1,2]([✉]) [iD], Marco Romano[2] [iD], Alessandro Gennaro[3] [iD], and Alessandro Frolli[2] [iD]

[1] Telematic Univeristy San Raffaele of Rome, 00118 Roma, Italy
`antonella.cavallaro@uniroma5.it`
[2] Università degli Studi Internazionali di Roma, 00118 Rome, Italy
[3] Università Telematica Pegaso, 80121 Naples, Italy

Abstract. *Introduction.* Virtual Reality Based Therapy (VRET) is one of the last frontiers in treatment of specific phobia, the most part of these treatment are delivered in prebuilt virtual world. The integration of artificial intelligence (AI) in virtual environments in a shared place, such as the metaverse, presents new opportunities for therapeutic interventions in mental health. This study explores the application of AI-powered avatars, equipped with ChatGPT, within a metaverse-based space to support systematic desensitization strategies for individuals with social anxiety. Particularly we have explored the effect of these AI-enhanced virtual interactions in activation of anxiety trought the measurement of electrophysiological parametres connected to the activation of anxiety (galvanic skill conduptance and heart rate) and user perception. A mixed-methods approach is employed, combining quantitative measures (such as anxiety level assessments in real interaction and virtual interactin with the avatar) with qualitative feedback from participants. Our initial findings suggest that AI-driven avatars can facilitate gradual exposure to social situations, allowing individuals to build confidence and reduce avoidance behaviors in a low-risk interaction.

Materials and Methods: The study was conducted within a metaverse environment created using Meta Horizon. To simulate naturalistic interactions, the Wizard of Oz (WoZ) technique was employed, ensuring a seamless and realistic interaction for participants. To measure anxiety activation during these interactions, biometric data were collected using the GazePT Biometrics, specifically for galvanic skin conductance and heart rate monitoring.

Results. This study contributes to the ongoing discourse on the role of the metaverse in digital therapeutics, highlighting potential benefits and limitations. The results aim to inform future implementations of AI-enhanced virtual environments for psychological interventions, providing valuable insights into their applicability in clinical and self-guided treatments for social anxiety disorder.

Keywords: Metaverse · AI Avatars · ChatGPT · Systematic Desensitization · Social Anxiety · Virtual Reality based Therapy · Digital Mental Health

J. Wei et al. (Eds.): HCII 2025, LNCS 16346, pp. 132–145, 2026.
https://doi.org/10.1007/978-3-032-13187-4_9

1   Introduction

1.1   Theoretical Background

Social Anxiety Disorder (SAD) is a prevalent mental health condition characterized by an intense fear of negative evaluation and rejection in social situations, leading to significant distress, avoidance behaviors, and impaired daily functioning[1]. Cognitive-Behavioral Therapy (CBT), with exposure therapy (ET), is considered one of the evidence-based treatment for Social Anxiety [2, 3]. ET consists of gradually exposure of the person with anxiety to the adversive stimuli in order to prevent the avoidance. When someone experiences fear, often respond by avoiding the feared situation, which provides temporary relief from anxiety. This avoidance behavior is negatively reinforced because it reduces distress in the short term, making the person more likely to continue avoiding the situation. However, this avoidance prevents the person from learning that the feared situation may not be as dangerous as they believe. ET helps by gradually and systematically exposing the person to the feared situation in a controlled way, starting from less anxiety-provoking scenarios and moving towards more difficult ones. Through repeated exposure without any real harm occurring, the person learns that the feared stimulus does not lead to the expected negative outcome, and their anxiety response decreases. [4]. Traditional forms of exposure include in vivo and imaginal exposure. In vivo exposure involves direct confrontation with feared real-life situations through a gradual, hierarchical approach. For example, if a person has a fear of dogs, in vivo exposure would comprise exposure to an image of a dog, then an object associated with dogs, and finally a puppy. In contrast, imaginal exposure involves the person imagining interacting with a dog. More recently, Virtual Reality (VR) has emerged as a promising tool to simulate these scenarios in a controlled manner, several studies have showed its efficacy in the exposure therapy. [5–7]. VR offers the opportunity to replicate real-world scenarios within a controlled environment, reducing at the same the time, cost, and logistical burdens associated with *in vivo* exposure and is not dependent on the patient's imaginative capabilities[8]. In Vr scenario infact it is possible the presentation of controlled stimuli capable of eliciting subjective levels of social distress comparable to real-life experiences. Multiple studies and meta-analyses suggest that VR Exposure Therapy (VRET) is an effective tool for the treatment of SAD, with outcomes often found to be comparable to *in vivo* exposure therapy [9]. Despite the recognized potential of VRET for SAD, several limitation are present in VR scenario, particullarly current VR environments are often rigid and offer limited flexibility and control over the therapeutic experience. [10], moreover current platforms are frequently described as monolithic and lacking flexibility. This rigidity limits the therapist's ability to tailor sessions to the unique and diverse needs of individual patients, a critical aspect for therapeutic effectiveness [11, 12]. In the context of social anxiety, research has identified a heightened tendency among individuals to attend to and interpret facial expressions, particularly those perceived as threatening. This propensity is observed to be more pronounced in individuals with social anxiety compared to those not afflicted with the condition [13].In light of these findings, it is imperative that virtual agents inhabiting virtual spaces are designed in a manner that ensures their authenticity and credibility. This imperative is crucial for the purpose of eliciting genuine emotional and physiological responses, thereby enhancing the ecological validity of the experience.[14–16]. Studies have observed that "stereotypical" scenarios or those with low graphical fidelity may not adequately activate the anxiety response or may even distract the patient[12]. Given these limitations in current VR environments, the emergence of the Metaverse presents new opportunities. In fact as a collection of persistent, interconnected, and social virtual spaces Metaverse gives a significant opportunity to create VRET environments that are even richer, more interactive, and highly customizable. While iterature support the use of VR technology in both educational and clinical fields [17–19] an emerging body of research is beginning to support the use of immersive VR (iVR) within metaverse environment. This work contributes to the ongoing development of immersive digital therapeutics by proposing a flexible and customizable design framework for exposure-based interventions in virtual environments. Particularly:

1. Explore the feasibility of metaverse-based, AI-enhanced exposure therapy, focusing on personalization, ecological validity, as a tool to support systematic desensitization strategies for individuals with social anxiety.
2. Evaluate the effectiveness of these AI-driven interactions in activating anxiety, by measuring physiological responses (galvanic skin conductance and heart rate) during virtual social exposures.
3. Assess the subjective perception of users regarding the realism, emotional engagement, and therapeutic value of the interactions.

1.2 Related Work

Kuleli et al. [15] have presented a framework to explored the use of Virtual Agents (VA) with realistic facial expression to explore biomarkers of social anxiety durinf the interaction of SAD subjects and VA. Specifically, their experiment includes three emotional blocks (positive, negative, neutral), each preceded by a neutral VR video. In each trial, participants interact with an emotionally expressive virtual agent and perform a handshake. After each block, they rate the perceived emotions and complete questionnaires on presence and embodiment in VR. They used Metahuman Creator (Epic Games) to create avatare human look like and Unreal game engine to create the virtual world. Having natural and believable VAs is significant for realistic social interaction which improves both the sense of presence and the feeling that VAs are socially present, and it develops real-life-like affective responses from participants. Neural activities related to early face and body perception has been measured through EEG in VR, EDA and HR misures also were taken.

Ferreira et al. [12] have investigated how to better support therapists in preparing and controlling VRET sessions to meet both their own needs and those of their patients. Particularly they used participatory design involving therapists from the early stages of development of a fully functional prototype. This prototype facilitates the creation, repetition and real-time control of sessions, with a specific focus on arachnophobia and fear of public speaking. The study indicates that it is beneficial for therapists to customise sessions according to the needs of individual patients, manage session progression in real time, and reutilise or disseminate session configurations to enhance efficiency and consistency. It was also emphasised that the use of individualised scenarios is preferable to stereotypical ones. Moreover, the study yielded two additional findings. Firstly, the significance of the therapeutic alliance was emphasised. Secondly, the role of the therapist in a virtual environment was highlighted, given that patients are unable to observe the therapy due to the head-mounted display. The study also examined the therapist's perspective on the utilisation of the VRET exposure as a median between imagination and in vivo exposure.

A third relevant study explores the use of virtual reality within the metaverse as a novel method for delivering mental health treatment [20]. The authors conducted a retrospective analysis of clinical records from individuals who underwent virtual mental health interventions primarily delivered in the metaverse. The objective was to assess whether such interventions were feasible, safe, and capable of producing measurable outcomes over time in the management of stress and anxiety. The study evaluated health data from 61 participants, with a mean age of 45.7. Their results showed that treatment was well tolerated by patients, with no adverse effects reported; the outcame revealed a reduction in anxiety levels and in perceived stress. These findings suggest that mental health care delivered in immersive virtual environments is not only technically feasible but also clinically effective, opening promising directions for digital therapeutic solutions.

2   Materials and Methods

This study is an exploratory mixed-methods pilot study with an experimental design, aiming to evaluate the feasibility, acceptability, and preliminary effects of AI-powered avatars within a metaverse environment to support exposure-based interventions for individuals with social anxiety. The study was conducted in a controlled, immersive virtual setting and combined quantitative data (physiological and self-report measures) with qualitative data (semi-structured interviews).

2.1   Materials

The following materials were selected to support both the immersive virtual experience and the multimodal data collection required to assess physiological activation and subjective responses to social exposure in the metaverse.

Meta Horizon Platform. The study was conducted within a metaverse-based virtual environment developed using Meta Horizon Worlds, chosen for its capacity to support immersive, interactive, and customizable social spaces and to easy in use to support personalization for future stakeholders, such as psychologists. The environment was designed to replicate two different spaces in order of hierarchic exposure to anxiety-eliciting stimuli: a private room and a public space. The private room is accessible only to psychologist and user. Inside this space a virtual agent equipped with ChatGPT could interact with user and psychologist. The public space is open and every user could enter and have interaction each other.

Meta Quest Oculus 2 virtual reality headset is used to experienced users with virtual agents in metaverse spaces. It features a high-resolution display (1832 x 1920 pixels per eye) and a refresh rate up to 90 Hz, providing immersive and smooth visual experiences.

The headset supports six degrees of freedom (6DoF) tracking, enabling precise detection of head and hand movements without the need for external sensors. Its integrated inside-out tracking system uses onboard cameras to map the environment and track controllers and user movements in real time.

The GazePT Biometric Hardware is used to capture physiological signals indicative of emotional and cognitive states. This system includes a finger sensor that measures Galvanic Skin Response (GSR) and heart rate, providing real-time data on autonomic nervous system activity. GSR detects changes in skin conductance, which vary with sweat gland activity and are commonly used to assess emotional arousal, stress, and anxiety levels. Heart rate measurements offer insights into physiological responses to stimuli, indicating levels of excitement, stress, or relaxation.

Liebnitz social anxiety (LSAS) [21] was used as a standardized self-report measure to evaluate the presence and severity of social anxiety symptoms in participants. The LSAS assesses fear and avoidance across a range of social situations, providing a comprehensive profile of social anxiety severity. It consists of 24 items divided into two subscales: fear/anxiety and avoidance. Each item is rated on a Likert scale from 0 (none) to 3 (severe).

The Visual Analogue Scale (VAS) [22] was employed to assess participants' perceived emotional activation during interactions within virtual ahgents in the metaverse environment. The VAS consisted of a continuous horizontal slider ranging from 0 (no anxiety) to 100 (maximum anxiety), allowing participants to indicate their subjective levels of anxiety, discomfort, and emotional engagement following each interaction. The VAS was implemented using the Visual Analog Scale widget in JotForm, which enabled precise, user-friendly data collection through an interactive slider. Responses were automatically recorded and exported in numerical format for subsequent quantitative analysis.

2.2 Participants

Participants were recruited among university students and teachers who gave their consent to participate in the research. Eligible individuals were between 18 and 45 years old, reported experiencing symptoms consistent with social anxiety, and did not present with conditions that would contraindicate the use of VR, such as epilepsy or severe cardiac issues. A total of eighteen participants gave their consent to participate in the experimentation. Among these, four were randomly selected for the pilot study: MC, a 22-year old female student; VO, a 40 y.o. male; RO, a 33 y.o. male; and PO, a 26-y.o. female. All participants provided written informed consent in accordance with the institutional ethics protocol.

2.3 Procedure

The study followed a structured, single-session design. Upon arrival, participants completed a baseline self-report questionnaire assessing anxiety levels and were fitted with biometric sensors to control biometrics baseline. They then entered the virtual environment for a five-minute acclimatization period designed to reduce potential novelty effects of the VR headset. The exposure protocol involved participants engaged in a 5-min conversation with an avatar inside the metaverse spaces. In both conditions, interaction occurred via a humanoid avatar, the key difference between conditions was the source of control behind the avatar. In the AI-Avatar Condition, the avatar was operated by ChatGPT, enabling real-time dialogue generation. Particurlarly the virtual agents verbal behavior was controlled using the Wizard of OZ (WoZ) method. The WoZ method involves a human operator simulating the behavior of an automated system to create realistic interactions when full automation is not yet feasible [23]. Participants could freely interact with the system without a predefined discussion topic. In the Human-Avatar Condition, the avatar was controlled remotely by a real human user. As in the AI condition, the conversation was open-ended and unscripted. Following the interaction, participants completed a post-session battery of questionnaires assessing emotional engagement, perceived realism of the avatars, and the subjective therapeutic value of the interaction. Finally, a trained psychologist conducted a short debriefing session with a structured interview and offered emotional support if necessary.

The order of exposure to the two conditions was randomly assigned using a balanced design: two participants experienced the AI-Avatar Condition first, followed by the Human-Avatar Condition, while the other two participants underwent the reverse sequence. This counterbalanced randomization aimed to control for potential order effects. Physiological signals, including heart rate (HR) and galvanic skin response (GSR), were recorded continuously during each session.

Biometrics Data. Biometrics data are collected during both experimental conditions and compare to measure the different emotional activation of the subject. In fact during stress, the autonomic nervous system (ANS) rapidly activates physiological responses to perceived threats, enhancing cardiac output, respiration, and redirecting blood flow to the brain and muscles [24]. The ANS regulates multiple physiological systems via its two main branches: the sympathetic and parasympathetic nervous systems. The dynamic balance between these branches is essential for maintaining internal homeostasis. Variations in anxiety levels can disrupt this balance, leading to a range of physiological responses that can be effectively monitored through indicators such as heart rate (HR) and galvanic skin response (GSR). The sympathetic branch, in particular, activates the classical "fight or flight" response, characterized by increased heart rate, sweating, and heightened arousal) [25–27].

Heart Rate (HR) refers to the frequency of heart beat. Lower HR is typically associated with a relaxed state or exposure to pleasant stimuli, whereas HR increases are observed in response to physical exertion, emotional arousal, loud sounds, sexual stimulation [32]. In individuals with anxiety disorders or high trait anxiety, elevated sympathetic activity is commonly observed, characterized by increased HR and reduced heart rate variability (HRV), reflecting diminished vagal tone and greater autonomic rigidity.

Several studies have reported significant correlations between reduced vagal modulation (as indicated by lower HRV) and higher levels of anxiety and depression.[28].

Galvanic Skin Response (GSR). Also known as electrodermal activity, is a widely used psychophysiological measure that reflects sympathetic nervous system activity. It detects changes in skin conductivity caused by sweat gland activity linked to psychological states such as stress or arousal. As stress levels vary, skin conductance increases or decreases proportionally, making GSR a reliable peripheral indicator of autonomic arousal [28–30].

3   Results

This section presents the results obtained through the integration of biometric data visualization and thematic analysis of participants' interviews. Biometric signals, including phasic galvanic skin response (GSR) and heart rate (HR), were collected using gaze-tracking software and visualized via Google Colab. A visual inspection approach was employed to identify data trends and to compare response levels across the two experimental conditions each participant was exposed to: interaction with ChatGPT and interaction with users in a Metaverse environment.

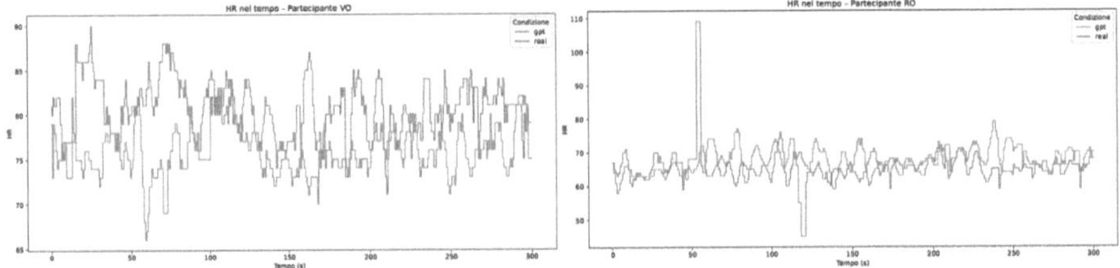

Fig. 1. A figure caption is always placed below the illustration. Short captions are centered, while long ones are justified. The macro button chooses the correct format automatically.

3.1   Biometrics Parameters

Biometrics including GSR-phasic and HR, were collected using gaze-tracking software and visualized via Google Colab. A visual inspection approach was employed to identify data trends and to compare response levels across the two experimental conditions each participant was exposed to: interaction with ChatGPT and interaction with users in a Metaverse environment.

Heart Rate. VO exhibited HR values ranging from 65 to 84 bpm during the ChatGPT condition, with a single peak of 84 in 300 s. These values were lower on average than those recorded in the avatar-user condition, where HR fluctuated between 71 and 90 bpm, indicating increased physiological arousal during human interaction. MC showed initially elevated HR values in the condition, ranging from 102 to 119 bpm, which progressively declined over time, eventually falling below the levels recorded in the GPT condition. The ChatGPT interaction elicited more stable HR values between 90 and 113 bpm, suggesting a more consistent and moderate autonomic response. PO maintained a relatively stable HR throughout both conditions. During the Human-avatar interaction, HR ranged from 64 to 77 bpm, while in the AI-Avatar condition, it fluctuated slightly lower, between 62 and 71 bpm. The minimal difference and steady pattern across both contexts suggest a uniform physiological response for this participant. Both RO displayed overlapping and highly stable HR trends across both conditions, with values consistently between 59 and 79 bpm. No significant deviations or spikes were observed, indicating comparable physiological activation regardless of the interaction type (Fig. 1.).

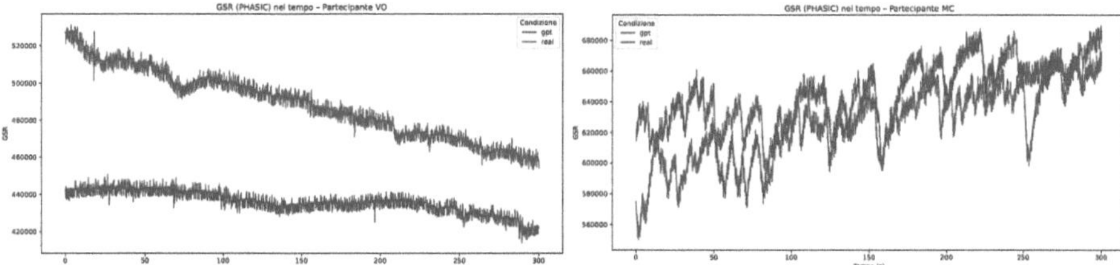

Fig. 2. A figure caption is always placed below the illustration. Short captions are centered, while long ones are justified. The macro button chooses the correct format automatically.

Galvanic Skin Response. The phasic GSR data reflect clear individual variability in physiological activation, mirroring the patterns observed in heart rate responses. VO exhibited lower activation levels during the interaction with the AI-Avatar compared to the human-avatar condition, suggesting a reduced autonomic response when engaging with the artificial agent. In contrast, MC showed a progressively increasing activation trend in both conditions, indicating a growing phasic response over time regardless of the interaction partner (Fig. 2). PO and RO displayed relatively stable GSR patterns across both conditions, with no significant differences between the AI and human-avatar interactions, suggesting a consistent physiological response unaffected by the type of interlocutor.

3.2 Questionnaire

Participants rated their emotional experience using VAS ranging. Four items score (1) anxiety, (2) discomfort, (3) feeling observed or judged, and (4) emotional activation across the three conditions: a) real-life interactions with strangers, b) interactions with other users via avatars, and c) interactions with AI avatars (see Table 1). The responses highlight clear individual differences in perceived emotional engagement across contexts. VO consistently reported very low levels of anxiety, discomfort, and emotional activation across all settings, with the lowest values in the AI-avatar condition. RO showed similarly low to moderate scores across contexts, with a slight increase in emotional intensity in real-life and human-avatar interactions. PO reported higher levels of emotional activation, particularly in activation with avatar, but not so high levels of anxiety suggesting greater subjective involvement then fear and discomfort in the interaction with avatar. MC consistently gave the highest ratings across all items and conditions, especially in relation to discomfort and emotional activation, with the most elevated values in the real-life and avatar-based interactions. Overall, the data suggest that participants experienced lower emotional activation when interacting with AI avatars compared to real-life and human-avatar conditions, though the extent of this effect varied across individuals.

Table 1. Self-reported Emotional Activation (VAS) across Social Contexts and Interaction Type.

P	1a	1b	1c	2a	2b	2c	3a	3b	3c	4a	4b	4c
VO	10	10	0	10	10	15	20	0	0	21	40	35
RO	24	10	10	28	12	12	25	10	13	32	23	7
PO	50	45	20	30	29	29	26	18	11	43	70	70
MC	50	65	50	50	35	66	50	32	21	70	64	45

3.3 Interview and Thematic Analysis

Interview data were examined through thematic analysis [31, 32], a qualitative method particularly appropriate for exploring individuals' experiences and perspectives [32]. The analysis identified four primary themes that capture the participants' perceptions of virtual social interactions. These themes reveal a complex interplay between feelings of safety, the limitations of current technology, and the perceived authenticity of the interaction partner.

The Avatar as a Protective Shield. This theme encapsulates the most frequently cited benefit of the virtual interaction: the avatar serves as a protective layer, mediating social engagement and significantly lowering anxiety. Participants felt shielded from direct exposure and judgment, which they identified as a key difference from real-life social situations. This sense of protection made them feel "safer" and more "at ease."

> *"I felt less anxious, certainly less than I would be when interacting with other people in reality, most likely due to the fact that you are exposed through your avatar, so it's as if you are protected by this."* (RO)

This feeling of being "masked" by the avatar was seen as a direct mitigator of social anxiety.

> *"There is less social anxiety because, in reality, you are in my opinion masked by the avatar... This limits social anxiety, there's a good interaction because the dialogues are realistic."* (VO)

> *"On one hand, you feel sort of protected because it's as if it's not really you, so you say 'oh well, if I say something stupid, they don't know me over there'."* (MC)

Finally, PO connects this feeling of security directly to the non-human nature of the interaction partner (in the case of the AI) or the mediated nature of the human one:

> *"[It] surely helps to overcome certain anxious situations because, not being a real person, you feel more secure."* (PO)

The Uncanny Valley of AI. A clear and critical distinction emerged between interacting with human-controlled avatars and the AI. While human avatars were seen as conduits for genuine, if sometimes awkward, social interaction, the AI was consistently de-scribed as inauthentic, predictable, and ultimately unengaging. Its lack of genuine "interest" was a key factor in breaking the user's own engagement. VO provides the most detailed critique, noting that the AI's interest feels fabricated:

"The artificial intelligence lacks sincerity, because if I ask it if it has a common interest with me, it will always say yes, regardless of whether it's true or not... I realize its interest is false, because the answers it gives me are pre-established, pre-printed, mechanical." (VO)

This lack of authenticity led to a loss of interest from the participant:

"The fact that on the other side there is no real interest makes you lose interest too, no matter how vast its knowledge is." (VO)

MC echoes this sentiment, describing the AI's conversational abilities as fundamentally limited and repetitive compared to a human's:

"The conversation with ChatGPT is limited, in my opinion... it always revolved around that one topic, it couldn't branch out." (MC)

Barriers to Immersion. Beyond the nature of the conversational partner, participants identified significant technological and design-related barriers that prevented a fully immersive and realistic experience. These issues ranged from the visual appearance of the avatars and environment to clunky, non-intuitive controls.

"It seemed not very realistic because perhaps visually it is already not very realistic... so it doesn't feel like you are talking with people, that is, it doesn't seem like you're having a real dialogue." (RO)

RO further noted that these technical struggles were shared, which inhibited dialogue:

"It seemed that on the other side, the people were in difficulty, just as I was in difficulty, in managing the avatar and the environment we were in. So there were few dialogues." (RO)

An interesting exception emerged in MC's case. Toward the end of the session, she began spontaneously interacting with child avatars in the public virtual space. When asked how she recognized them as children despite the lack of facial scanning or age-specific visuals, she responded:

"You can tell from the voice." (MC)

This observation suggests that participants with social anxiety may rely more heavily on alternative channels, such as vocal tone or prosody, when traditional visual social cues are unavailable.

Therapeutic Potential. When asked if this technology could be a useful tool for treating social anxiety, participants expressed a clear division of opinion. This theme captures the ambivalence between seeing the virtual world as a valuable, safe training ground and viewing it as an inadequate substitute for the complexities of real-world interaction.

On one hand, participants like VO and RO were optimistic. VO responded enthusiastically about using it in a personalized therapeutic path, stating he would do so *"very willingly."* RO saw clear potential for practicing social skills in a protected setting:

> *"I don't know if it could help me reduce social anxiety, but it could certainly help me with relationships, because you are only exposed up to a certain point, so you feel more protected and therefore you would probably be more relaxed." (RO).*

On the other hand, participant MC was deeply skeptical about the transferability of any skills learned. The core of this skepticism was the belief that no virtual training can replicate the visceral, high-stakes feeling of a real-life social situation.

4 Conclusion

The results of this pilot study highlight the potential of using the metaverse as a controlled exposure space for individuals with social anxiety and undeline the importance to individualizing presentation of stimuli e setting. The varied physiological activation observed among participants during interactions with AI avatars reflects their anxiety levels in real-world social situations, suggesting that immersive virtual environments can effectively mirror real-life emotional responses. This individual variability supports the idea that avatars, both AI-controlled and user-controlled, can serve as valuable graded stimuli, offering an intermediate step for gradual desensitization and exposure therapy. The biometric data collected (HR and GSR) highlight individual differences in physiological activation in response to interaction with AI avatars compared to human avatars. Generally, interaction with AI avatars elicited lower levels of physiological activation, suggesting a reduced emotional response and a greater sense of control and safety among participants. However, in some cases (e.g., MC), activation remained high, indicating that social anxiety may persist even in mediated environments. Notably, MC's anxiety levels decreased toward the end of the experiment, dropping to values lower than those observed during interaction with the AI avatar, as they realized they were interacting with children. This confirms that the perceived nature and characteristics of the virtual interlocutor can significantly influence anxiety responses over time and over space [33, 34]. VAS scores confirm that interaction with AI avatars is perceived as less anxiety-provoking compared to interactions with other users (human avatars) or real-life situations. However, this effect varies considerably between individuals. Participants such as VO and RO reported a strong sense of protection and comfort, whereas MC showed greater discomfort across all contexts, suggesting that the use of technology alone is not sufficient to reduce emotional activation in more sensitive individuals. VAS scores confirm that interaction with AI avatars is perceived as less anxiety-provoking compared to interactions with other users (human avatars) or real-life situations. However, this effect varies considerably between individuals. Participants such as VO and RO reported a strong sense of protection and comfort, whereas MC showed greater discomfort across all contexts, suggesting that the use of technology alone is not sufficient to reduce emotional activation in more sensitive individuals. Notably, the variation in perceived anxiety was greater than that actually measured by biometric data, especially for participants RO and PO, indicating a possible discrepancy between subjective emotional experience and physiological responses, this could be explain because the intensity of emotion perceived is influenced by many individual characteristics such as self-esteem or agency and not only by enteroception [35]. General consensus emerged on the avatar experienced as a "protective filter," capable of shielding direct exposure to others' gaze. This element was repeatedly cited as a key advantage of the metaverse, enabling social interactions to be experienced in a less threatening way. Such a protective effect could represent an important therapeutic leverage in the early stages of treatment. However, the low emotional intensity of the virtual environment fails to replicate the complexity and unpredictability of the real world, meaning it should be regarded only as an intermediate step within a systematic desensitization process. Furthermore, perceived effectiveness was partly compromised by technological limitations (graphics, controls, AI responsiveness). The "uncanny valley" phenomenon of artificial intelligence emerged as a significant barrier: interactions with AI avatars were experienced as predictable, flat, or even "fake," reducing emotional engagement and the simulation's effectiveness. Overall, these results suggest that the use of AI avatars in immersive environments could offer an innovative opportunity for treating social anxiety, especially in the initial phases of gradual exposure. However, it is essential to improve AI interaction quality, increase environmental realism, and develop specific therapeutic protocols based on individual needs. This pilot research provides valuable insights for future studies with larger samples and longitudinal designs. The integration of physiological and qualitative analyses proved crucial to understanding the complexity of individual reactions to these new forms of virtual exposure.

Disclosure of Interests.   The authors declare that they have no competing interests.

References

1. American Psychiatric Association: Diagnostic and statistical manual of mental disorders. 5th edn., text rev.; DSM-5-TR. American Psychiatric Publishing (2022)
2. Cognitive-Behavioral Treatments for Anxiety and Stress-Related Disorders | Focus. https://psychiatryonline.org/doi/full/10.1176/appi.focus.20200045. Accessed 30 May 2025
3. Walter, H.J., et al.: Clinical practice guideline for the assessment and treatment of children and adolescents with anxiety disorders. J. Am. Acad. Child Adolesc. Psychiatry **59**, 1107–1124 (2020)
4. Craske, M.G., Mystkowski, J.L.: Exposure therapy and extinction: clinical studies. In: Fear and learning: From basic processes to clinical implications, pp. 217–233. American Psychological Association, Washington, DC, US (2006). https://doi.org/10.1037/11474-011
5. Heo, S., Park, J.-H.: Effects of virtual reality-based graded exposure therapy on PTSD symptoms: a systematic review and meta-analysis. Int. J. Environ. Res. Public Health **19**, 15911 (2022)
6. Premkumar, P., et al.: The effectiveness of self-guided virtual-reality exposure therapy for public-speaking anxiety. Front. Psych. **12** (2021). https://doi.org/10.3389/fpsyt.2021.694610
7. Scozzari, S., Gamberini, L.: Virtual reality as a tool for cognitive behavioral therapy: a review. In: Brahnam, S. and Jain, L.C. (eds.) Advanced Computational Intelligence Paradigms in Healthcare 6. Virtual Reality in Psychotherapy, Rehabilitation, and Assessment, pp. 63–108.

Springer Berlin Heidelberg, Berlin, Heidelberg (2011). https://doi.org/10.1007/978-3-642-17824-5_5

8. Freeman, D., et al.: Virtual reality in the assessment, understanding, and treatment of mental health disorders. Psychol. Med. **47**, 2393–2400 (2017). https://doi.org/10.1017/S0033291717000040X

9. Emmelkamp, P.M.G., Meyerbröker, K., Morina, N.: Virtual reality therapy in social anxiety disorder. Curr. Psychiatry Rep. **22**, 32 (2020). https://doi.org/10.1007/s11920-020-01156-1

10. Maher, C., Singh, B., Wylde, A., Chastin, S.: Virtual health assistants: a grand challenge in health communications and behavior change. Front. Digit. Health. **6**, 1418695 (2024). https://doi.org/10.3389/fdgth.2024.1418695

11. Crafting Virtual Realities: Designing a VR End-User Authoring Platform for Personalised Exposure Therapy - Cerca con Google. https://www.google.com/search?q=Crafting+Virtual+Realities%3A+Designing+a+VR+End-User+Authoring+Platform+for+Personalised+Exposure+Therapy&rlz=1C1GCEU_itIT1161IT1161&oq=Crafting+Virtual+Realities%3A+Designing+a+VR+End-User+Authoring+Platform+for+Personalised+Exposure+Therapy&gs_lcrp=EgZjaHJvbWUyBggAEEUYOTIGCAEQRRhAMgYIAhBFGD0yBggDEEUYPdIBBzU5MmowajSoAgCwAgE&sourceid=chrome&ie=UTF-8, last accessed 2025/05/30

12. Ferreira, J.P., Ferreira-Brito, F., Guerreiro, J., Guerreiro, T.: Crafting virtual realities: designing a vr end-user authoring platform for personalised exposure therapy. In: 2024 IEEE International Symposium on Mixed and Augmented Reality (ISMAR), pp. 932–940 (2024). https://doi.org/10.1109/ISMAR62088.2024.00109

13. Staugaard, S.R.: Threatening faces and social anxiety: a literature review. Clin. Psychol. Rev. **30**, 669–690 (2010)

14. 1Amadou, N., Haque, K.I., Yumak, Z.: Effect of appearance and animation realism on the perception of emotionally expressive virtual humans. In: Proceedings of the 23rd ACM International Conference on Intelligent Virtual Agents, pp. 1–8. Association for Computing Machinery, New York, NY, USA (2023). https://doi.org/10.1145/3570945.3607307

15. Kuleli, D., et al.: exploring influence of social anxiety on embodied face perception during affective social interactions in VR. In: Proceedings of the 24th ACM International Conference on Intelligent Virtual Agents, pp. 1–5. Association for Computing Machinery, New York, NY, USA (2024). https://doi.org/10.1145/3652988.3673952

16. Aloisio, A., Cavallaro, A., Romano, M.: Metaverse mastery: enhancing public speaking skills in linguistic high school students through advanced technologies. In: Zaphiris, P., Ioannou, A., Sottilare, R.A., Schwarz, J., Rauterberg, M. (eds.) HCI International 2024 – Late Breaking Papers, pp. 35–45. Springer Nature Switzerland, Cham (2025). https://doi.org/10.1007/978-3-031-76815-6_3

17. Cavallaro, A., Romano, M., Laccone, R.: examining user perceptions to vocal interaction with ai bots in virtual reality and mobile environments: a focus on foreign language learning and communication dynamics. In: Degen, H. and Ntoa, S. (eds.) Artificial Intelligence in HCI, pp. 20–30. Springer Nature Switzerland, Cham (2024). https://doi.org/10.1007/978-3-031-60606-9_2

18. Romano, M., Laccone, R.P., Frolli, A.: Designing a VR educational application to enhance resilience and community awareness through cultural exploration. In: ICERI2023 Proceedings, pp. 9258–9267. IATED (2023)

19. Romano, M., Díaz, P., Aedo, I.: Empowering teachers to create augmented reality experiences: the effects on the educational experience. Interact. Learn. Environ. **31**, 1546–1563 (2023). https://doi.org/10.1080/10494820.2020.1851727

20. Orr, E., et al.: Virtual reality in the management of stress and anxiety disorders: a retrospective analysis of 61 people treated in the metaverse. Heliyon **9** (2023). https://doi.org/10.1016/j.heliyon.2023.e17870

21. Liebowitz, M.R.: Social phobia. Mod. Probl. Pharmacopsychiatry **22**, e173 (1987)
22. Williams, V.S., Morlock, R.J., Feltner, D.: Psychometric evaluation of a visual analog scale for the assessment of anxiety. Health Qual. Life Outcomes **8**, 57 (2010). https://doi.org/10.1186/1477-7525-8-57
23. Dahlbäck, N., Jönsson, A., Ahrenberg, L.: Wizard of Oz studies — why and how. Knowl.-Based Syst. **6**, 258–266 (1993). https://doi.org/10.1016/0950-7051(93)90017-N
24. Plutchik, R.: The psychology and biology of emotion. HarperCollins College Publishers (1994)
25. Bajkó, Z., et al.: Anxiety, depression and autonomic nervous system dysfunction in hypertension. J. Neurol. Sci. **317**, 112–116 (2012)
26. Hoehn-Saric, R., McLeod, D.R.: The peripheral sympathetic nervous system: Its role in normal and pathologic anxiety. Psychiatr. Clin. North Am. **11**, 375–386 (1988)
27. Civitello, D., Finn, D., Flood, M., Salievski, E., Schwarz, M., Storck, Z.: How do physiological responses such as respiratory frequency, heart rate, and galvanic skin response (GSR) change under emotional stress? (2014)
28. Hoehn-Saric, R., McLeod, D.R.: Anxiety and arousal: physiological changes and their perception. J. Affect. Disord. **61**, 217–224 (2000). https://doi.org/10.1016/S0165-0327(00)00339-6
29. Froese, A.P., Cassem, N.H., Hackett, T.P., Silverberg, E.L.: Galvanic skin potential as a predictor of mental status, anxiety, depression and denial in acute coronary patients. J. Psychosom. Res. **19**, 1–9 (1975)
30. Vahey, R., Becerra, R.: Galvanic skin response in mood disorders: a critical review (2015)
31. Merton, R.K.: Thematic analysis in science: notes on holton's concept. Science **188**, 335–338 (1975). https://doi.org/10.1126/science.188.4186.335
32. Maguire, M., Delahunt, B.: Doing a thematic analysis: a practical, step-by-step guide for learning and teaching scholars. Irel. J. High. Educ. **9** (2017)
33. Çakmak, F.: Chatbot-Human interaction and its effects on EFL students' L2 speaking performance and anxiety. Novitas-R. Res. Youth Lang. **16**, 113–131 (2022)
34. Pan, X., Gillies, M., Slater, M.: Virtual character personality influences participant attitudes and behavior–an interview with a virtual human character about her social anxiety. Front. Robot. AI. **2**, 1 (2015)
35. Sonnemans, J., Frijda, N.H.: The determinants of subjective emotional intensity. Cogn. Emot. **9**, 483–506 (1995). https://doi.org/10.1080/02699939508408977

The Unexplored Potential of Pet Robots in Assistive Care: A Structured Narrative Review Toward Inclusive and Sustainable Implementation

Francesca Conte[(✉)], Antonella Cavallaro, Alessandro Frolli, and Marco Romano

University of Rome UNINT, 00147 Rome, Italy
`f.conte5@studenti.unint.eu`, {`antonella.cavallaro,`
`alessandro.frolli,marco.romano`}`@unint.eu`

Abstract. Social Assistive Robotics (SAR) is an emerging form of assistive technology that encompasses all robotic systems based on artificial intelligence, employing various forms of communication in order to support and motivate users in performing their tasks. What have been extensively studied, however, are humanoid robots, not zoomorphic robots, also called petbots, which, although promising, are still a relatively unexplored category. The animal-like design, which makes them appear less threatening, and their ability to improve communication skills by promoting social interactions, make petbots potential agents to support the emotional, cognitive and social well-being of vulnerable groups, such as children with autism spectrum disorder (ASD) and elderly people with dementia or mild cognitive impairment (MCI). This review adopts a structured narrative approach to synthesise recent peer-reviewed literature on the use of petbots in therapeutic and care settings, specifically selecting papers published from 2019 to 2025. Models such as Paro, Aibo, Loona, Keepon and Probo were included based on their relevance and presence in empirical research. To contextualise their role, the review also compares studies on humanoid SAR robots and considers ethical, cultural and design factors influencing user acceptance and real-world implementation.

Keyword: Social Assistance Robotics Pet Robots Ethics in Robotics

1 Introduction

In recent years, robotics has taken on a fundamental role in the healthcare context, emerging as a valuable and promising tool to support different categories of patients suffering from psychological, cognitive and social frailties. Socially Assistive Robotics (SAR) is defined as an interdisciplinary field that combines engineering, cognitive science, medicine and more, with the aim of designing robots that are specialised in establishing and maintaining social interactions, using natural signals, such as gestures and gaze, and expressing and communicating emotions [18]. The integration then of these tools with sensors and artificial intelligence, allows the continuous monitoring of physical and emotional well-being, thus also ensuring timely and appropriate treatment, [9].

© The Author(s), under exclusive license to Springer Nature Switzerland AG 2026
J. Wei et al. (Eds.): HCII 2025, LNCS 16346, pp. 146–157, 2026.
https://doi.org/10.1007/978-3-032-13187-4_10

In the SAR context, increasing attention has been paid to humanoid robots, which have been extensively studied and tested in autism therapy and, more generally, in the treatment of mental disabilities [4, 11, 32]. These robots, (e.g. QTrobot, NAO and Pepper), have shown good effectiveness in fostering the learning of social and communicative skills in children with autism spectrum disorder by providing structured and predictable environments for interaction [32]. Elderly people have also expressed willingness to adopt social robots, recognising their potential benefits in maintaining mental activity and social involvement in daily life: feedback collected in the study by Cavallaro [10] notes enthusiasm, ease of conversation and use.

Petbots, on the other hand, a subcategory of SAR, are animal-like robots designed to stimulate affective bonding and promote emotional well-being. These tools are distinguished by their ability to elicit empathic reactions, stimulate social interaction and support psychophysical well-being, being particularly effective with users who manifest communication or emotional difficulties, such as children with autism spectrum disorder, [10, 14, 38]. Recent studies conducted in real-world contexts also show how the simplicity of interaction and the reassuring appearance of these devices promote their acceptance by the elderly, even in the presence of cognitive impairment [10].

Although preliminary results are certainly encouraging, considering that several studies highlight its advantages over humanoid robots, both in terms of greater acceptability [14] and emotional accessibility, particularly appreciated by sensitive individuals, [27], the scientific literature on petbots is still fragmented and lacking systematic and longitudinal studies, [38].

In any case, it seems crucial to adopt a user-centred type of approach, as described by Cano [8], to respond in a personalised manner to the cognitive and emotional needs of fragile users, broaden the inclusion of the people involved, in order to promote wider future research [34].

In light of these considerations, this article aims to fill this gap by systematically analysing the most recent literature on petbots in the care setting. The aim is twofold: on the one hand, to explore the therapeutic potential of these devices in improving emotional, cognitive and relational well-being; on the other, to reflect on emerging critical issues, including accessibility, ethical implications and the risk of replacing human relationships with artificial interactions [5, 31]. At a time when emerging technologies are redefining the very concept of care and social interaction, studying these tools means not only assessing their clinical effectiveness, but also questioning the kind of relationship we want to build with machines in helping others, and ourselves.

2   SAR: General Overview

2.1   What is Socially Assistive Robotics

Socially Assistive Robotics is an up-and-coming field of robotics, whose main objective is to develop and foster social and affective interaction between humans and robots, supporting people with physical, cognitive or emotional fragility. In particular, what distinguishes it from traditional assistive robotics, which mainly focuses on functional autonomy, is the goal of improving the quality of life through emotional involvement, cognitive stimulation and the promotion of social interaction [2, 4, 11, 18].

This is possible because socially assistive robots use artificial intelligence technologies including speech recognition and facial expressions to adapt their behaviour to the user's needs. Indeed, recent clinical trials, including in geriatric settings, have explored the integration of AI-based recognition and emotional response capabilities [1, 39].

Within the SAR context, however, it is necessary to make a macro distinction, which concerns the form of the robot: on the one hand, we find humanoid robots, designed to imitate human traits and behaviour; on the other, petbots, zoomorphic robots, designed to simulate the presence of a pet. While the former are often used to mediate therapeutic exercises, often performing physical tasks, the latter focus on non-verbal affective involvement, being more effective with users who show resistance to human interaction, [7].

2.2 Application Fields of SAR

The applications of Socially Assistive Robotics cover numerous clinical and care areas, including:

- **Autism therapy**: the overall aim here is to improve communication and social skills through guided interaction, learning and emotional support. Structured and predictable social robot interactions increase adherence and effectiveness of therapies, promote the development of joint attention [19], emotional regulation [6, 21] and social skills [17, 21].
- **Elderly care**: the aim is to promote autonomy, safety and well-being by providing companionship, assistance and health monitoring. SAR has been shown to be effective in reducing feelings of loneliness, improving mood and facilitating communication not only between the elderly and robots, but also with staff and family members [38].
- **Post-traumatic rehabilitation**: although less widespread, some experimental projects have employed SAR to support motivation and continuity in post-trauma or post-stroke motor and cognitive rehabilitation. In this context, the empathic presence of the robot accompanying the users during cognitive training encourages therapeutic adherence by providing feedback [39].

3 Advantages and Disadvantages of SAR in Different Application Contexts

3.1 Advantages

Among the advantages of SAR found in the different contexts listed above, Salafia [35] highlights how they can promote emotional involvement, offering a safe and stimulating channel of interaction in situations of isolation or communication difficulties. Not only that, the presence of a social robot can arouse affectivity, promote anxiety reduction, and encourage the expression and communication of emotions [20, 28, 38]. Nichol et al. [29], recognise the role of SAR as relational facilitators, as they encourage both user interaction with the social context and positive engagement through robotic mediation. In particular, according to Gómez-Espinosa et al. [20], such devices not only provide companionship to users, but can also act as social mediators, facilitating interactions, and behavioural stimulators, encouraging beneficial behaviours, on a physical level (through increased movement), an emotional level (by fostering the expression of affection, calming anxiety or reducing stress) and a cognitive level (by stimulating memory, attention or language).

In autism therapy, as shown in the analysis by Perillo et al. [32], social robots are suitable for helping children recognise and communicate their feelings, facilitate play and physical interaction, and make therapy an opportunity for broader educational and social development.

The humanoid aspect, in particular, succeeds in making social signals more easily recognisable, helping the child with ASD to focus his or her attention on certain communicative social signals, which are essential for training those missing interpretive and dialogic skills. For many people with autism, the main cause of the lack of these skills lies in sensory over-stimulation: the possibility of programming stimuli, sequence and intensity in robot-assisted therapy can mitigate and avoid this risk, [11].

The adaptability of robots, the repetitive predictability of behaviour and the possibility to programme tailor-made responses make them particularly effective in supporting gradual and consolidated learning over time [16]. Indeed, in children with ASD, interaction with social robots has shown positive effects on the development of communication skills, interpersonal skills and motivation to engage with others [6, 21, 24].

Not only that, the study by Dubois-Sage et al. [14] also notes further benefits from the interaction: reduction of maladaptive and stereotypical behaviour, greater interest and involvement compared to interaction with humans, increased visual and tactile attention towards robots, increased spontaneous initiation of interactions, increased verbal production and reduced stress during social contacts.

On the other hand, concerning individuals with intellectual disabilities, research shows that it is possible to develop various aspects of learning (such as metacognition, social-cognitive skills, relationality and affectivity), promote greater independence in the achievement of various goals, increase their communication skills and encourage them to participate in social or group activities, [4].

This functional and fruitful relationship does not only depend on the technical characteristics of the different existing models, but, as explained by Abdollahi et al. [1], also on the introduction of artificial emotional intelligence that has improved the quality of interactions: they are capable of dynamically adapting to the emotional state of the user, responding with simulated empathy and strengthening the human-machine bond. This is particularly relevant in reluctant or affectively closed individuals, such as the apathetic elderly or people with mild depression.

Costanzo et al. [12], in their study, highlighted how, given the tendency of the elderly to maintain their independence, they are reluctant to leave their homes even when they need help. The SAR, in this sense, represents a possible solution, both as a support for independent living and by promoting regular exercise, thus improving fitness, sleep, the immune system and reducing the risk of diseases such as diabetes and dementia.

The research by Cantone et al. [9] appears more relevant than ever in this context, because it proposes a four-actor system consisting of: a stationary humanoid robot, users, medical personnel and caregivers. This system allows continuous monitoring of the physical and emotional well-being of the elderly through specific sensors that detect vital parameters, with real-time updates transmitted to doctors and caregivers, thus ensuring timely and appropriate care. This demonstrates that it is possible to apply SAR in the home environment and at the same time overcome the risk of replacing human relationships.

3.2 Disadvantages and Limitations

Despite their potential, the adoption of SAR still has a number of structural, ethical and methodological limitations. First of all, affordability is one of the main obstacles to the deployment of these technologies. As highlighted by Holeva et al. [21], the high cost of the devices and their maintenance limits large-scale implementation, often making them inaccessible to households and institutions with limited resources. Although, a cost-efficient, socially designed robot solution, such as the one presented by Singh et al. [36], shows that there is potential for implementation.

From an ethical point of view, concerns arise related to emotional dependency and the possible risk of replacing human relationships. In contexts such as dementia care or the treatment of autism, the risk has been observed that interaction with the robot replaces authentic relationships with real people, leading to a robotisation of care, which could compromise the dignity and autonomy of the subject [23, 31].

This could also lead to a questioning of traditional roles and a distortion of trust in care contexts, [31]; or as explained by Massa [28], fuel the phenomenon of self-deception whereby an individual perceives the robot as an almost-human interlocutor and attributes emotions and thoughts to it that actually are projections of the user himself, affecting the human-human relationship capacity.

In particular, Deusdad [13] investigates several ethical issues related to the use of social robots to assist people with dementia: given the inherent fragility in patients' interactions and communication, the use of the robot could become an external imposition. Critical issues could lie in the individual's right to decide whether to use the technology, the dynamics of negotiation with end-users, and the lack of privacy and control over their data. Some challenges also remain about the interaction between individuals with ASD and social robots. Indeed, it seems that the ideal type of robot has not yet been identified, because among children with autism preferences may vary from robots with little human resemblance, to robots with a strong resemblance, and the impact of individual characteristics on the interaction outcome is not yet well defined [14].

Dubois-Sage et al. [14] also mention further limitations, such as: methodological heterogeneity which makes comparison between studies difficult; absence of a human control group which prevents the robot's superiority from being demonstrated; absence of a comparison group with typically developing (TD) children; small samples with insufficient description; poor representation of women; lack of long-term follow-up.

These limitations highlight the importance of developing more structured studies. The use of robotics and artificial intelligence also requires more than ever legal regulation to ensure ethical compliance, mitigate risks and protect the rights of all parties involved, [13].

4 Focus on Petbots

4.1 What Are Petbots

As mentioned earlier, petbots are a subcategory of social assistive robots designed to simulate the presence of pets, combining elements of social interaction, affectivity and therapeutic support. Unlike humanoid robots, petbots are designed with the aim of adopting animal-inspired behaviours, which makes them particularly suitable for interacting with people who exhibit difficulties in approaching humans [7]. They were designed to mimic animal behaviour because the effectiveness of pet therapy in reducing stress, anxiety and depression has long been established. The research was inspired by the possibility of offering the same benefits as pet therapy, but avoiding the difficulties associated with allergies, costs, fears, hygiene issues or animal welfare [3]. Petbots are, in fact, based on the assumption that the human-animal bond can be artificially reproduced to achieve emotional and cognitive benefits [28].

4.2 Existing Models

Among the most studied models in the literature are:

- **Paro**: a robotic seal equipped with tactile, visual and auditory sensors, widely used in geriatric-residential settings. It is able to emit sounds, move its neck, flippers and tail, but not to move forward. It has been shown that Paro can reduce neuropsychiatric symptoms in patients with dementia and promote positive emotional states [30, 38].
- **Aibo**: a battery-operated, rechargeable robotic dog. It can shake its body, stretch, raise its paw and bark. Equipped with a built-in camera, it is capable of simulating affection, recognising its owner's face and learning behaviour over time, thus developing its own personality [38]. Some studies point to it as a promising tool to foster empathy and interaction in children with autism spectrum disorders [14, 28].
- **Loona**: has a futuristic puppy-like design. It has wheels to move autonomously in space, a front-facing camera, motion sensors and microphones that enable it to recognise faces, voice commands and gestures. Loona can express emotions through sounds, movements and an animated face screen, and can learn and customise its responses based on user interaction. It has a strong, playful and affective component, designed to stimulate empathy and companionship.

  Other existing models, although less popular and studied, include:

- **Keepon**, unconventionally shaped, takes the form of a small yellow chick, equipped with touch and dance modes [6]. It has colour cameras in both eyes and a nose that acts as a microphone. Keepon can move its head to make eye contact. It expresses its emotions and perceptions through body movements, [8].
- **Probo** is a huggable robot, configured as a stuffed animal inspired by an elephant and is designed for natural interaction with humans, [6]. In the study analysed by Gómez-Espinosa et al. [20], the robot is always controlled by an operator, which means that the robot does not act autonomously in directing the therapy.

Thus, although the latter are less well known and documented, they have emerged for their potential in supporting social interaction, communication and engagement in children with autism [6].

4.3 Results of Existing Research

The results of the scientific literature, despite resulting from fragmented and uneven studies, appear promising for the potential effectiveness of petbots in therapeutic, educational and care contexts, [7, 15, 33].

The lower complexity and behavioural predictability of petbots make them less threatening and more tolerable tools for autistic children, thus reducing social stress [3]. The study by Vagnetti et al. [37] demonstrates how precisely the animal-inspired form of the devices facilitates acceptance by children with ASD, as it reduces the cognitive load required to interpret social signals that would otherwise appear complex and ambiguous to them, favouring a more natural and continuous involvement. Petbots can also act as an effective distraction during stressful medical procedures, such as vaccinations and examinations, and motivate autistic children to perform physical or rehabilitative exercises more engagingly, [3].

The other line of research, involving patients with dementia or mild cognitive impairment (MCI), has shown how robots such as Paro or Aibo are able to stabilise mood, stimulate social interaction and reduce problematic behaviour such as agitation or apathy [15, 22, 38].

Huang et al. [22] note that companion robots, even when used in domestic or semi-structured environments such as parks or leisure centres, can act as catalysts for new social relationships, encouraging the active participation of older people in community life.

The value and benefit of these interactions also emerges in the broader context in which the patient lives and relates: Bradwell et al. [7] show that the introduction of pet robots in nursing homes also produced positive effects on the quality of relationships between residents and caregivers, contributing to a better emotional climate and greater group cohesion. Zoomorphic robots can encourage the feeling of not feeling alone and activate positive memories related to previous experiences with real animals [33].

5 The Gap in the Literature

The scientific literature on social assistive robotics in general shows a clear overrepresentation of humanoid robots compared to petbots. This trend has been confirmed by numerous studies, including Baldassare and Sasanelli [4] and Conti and Di Nuovo [11], which document that anthropomorphic robots are the focus of scientific and experimental interest in most interventions.

In contrast, petbots have been studied piecemeal and unevenly. Although devices such as Paro and Aibo are present in the literature, research on them is predominantly small-scale, time-limited and for specific target populations, [20, 38]. For emerging models such as Loona, Keepon and Probo, scientific documentation is even scarcer, with an almost complete absence in the peer-reviewed literature [33]. This imbalance has also been highlighted by Hundt et al. [23], who criticise the low variety of robotic models studied and the dominance of paradigms centred on conformity to neurotypical norms. From the tendency for these paradigms to predominate, true systemic social inequalities may emerge, especially related to the pathologisation of autism, the lack of diversity in participants and the exclusion of active patient involvement [34].

Another shortcoming concerns the almost total absence of longitudinal studies, capable of assessing the effects of petbots in the long term. Much of the research is based on small samples, pilot interventions and short term evaluations, making it difficult to understand the lasting effectiveness of these tools [8]. It has been pointed out that there is a need to go beyond proofs of concept to develop more structured and robust experiments capable of providing comparative, objective and long-term data [8, 15].

Despite the encouraging results and benefits found, the gap between the evidence obtained in laboratory settings and the efficacy recorded in the long term remains. Indeed, Figliano et al. [15] denounce the lack of well-structured longitudinal studies capable of monitoring the effects of petbots over time and in real-world contexts, such as private homes. Ananto and Young [3] insist on the need to overcome the limitations of short and highly controlled experimental protocols, proposing a research agenda centred on the everyday domestic use of robots. According to these authors, the real challenge is to transform petbots from experimental tools to accepted companions integrated into people's routines, especially in non-medicalised environments.

Home environments, in general, informal care settings, open up interesting scenarios of possible new uses for petbots, which, although requiring further confirmation, could fill gaps left by pharmacological therapies or limited social ties. Indeed, Otaka et al. [30] and Deusdad [13] report that in patients with advanced dementia or in emotionally closed individuals, the presence of the robot can unlock latent forms of affectivity, facilitate eye contact, stimulate memories and offer a sense of non-verbal comfort. Yu et al. [38] also point out the scarcity of high-quality studies in the field, which does not equate to evidence of ineffectiveness: overall, their review suggests that the use of robots in dementia care may be feasible and well accepted. However, given that all types of robots have limitations that might hinder their widespread use, to overcome this constraint, designers and clinicians could improve the design of robots, making them less complex to use, and ensuring adequate technical support for families in case of problems.

In summary, the current landscape reflects multiple shortcomings: predominance of humanoid robots, uneven treatment of petbots, within which the focus on geriatric care contexts has prevailed, and absence of extensive longitudinal research in diverse settings. Bridging this gap requires an interdisciplinary effort that emphasises scientific validation, the variety of models analysed, the inclusion of patients' subjective perspectives and the sustainability of interventions over time.

6 Future Potential and New Directions

Given the promising evolution of assistive robotics, it now appears necessary to adopt a new perspective, one that examines not only the technological innovation itself, but also the consequent clinical, social and ethical dimensions that robotic intervention influences.

From this perspective, petbots represent a resource yet to be fully discovered and evaluated, not as possible substitutes for humanoid robots or care providers, but as complementary tools, accessible facilitators of therapeutic contexts.

After analysing the main findings of existing research, with the most promising applications, and examining the gap in the literature to date, we aim to trace the ethical implications to be taken into account and to understand the challenges and opportunities to the shared, accessible and inclusive adoption of these tools.

6.1 Ethical Implications

The introduction of petbots in care settings raises complex ethical issues. Among the main risks is that of relational simulation: in the most vulnerable subjects, interaction with a robot that imitates animal emotions may generate forms of artificial attachment that risk blurring the distinction between real and virtual, with important implications in terms of autonomy and dignity [13, 26]. In particular, according to Deusdad [13], it is precisely the aesthetics of some petbots that contribute to the undermining of their autonomy and dignity, as it would lead to a form of infantilisation, especially in dementia care settings.

A further risk is related to the possibility that using petbots in care settings may gradually replace human interaction. The study by Koh et al. [25] argues that this risk is linked to the idea that the number of caregivers will decrease with the increase of the elderly population and for this reason they will tend to rely more and more on technological solutions. Although some caregivers recognise that petbots can lighten their daily work and allow them to better connect with patients, the adoption of petbots, although successful, cannot replace human presence. Finally, a further critical issue is the lack of transparency and informed consent, as users and caregivers may not fully understand the robots' capabilities and limitations, exposing themselves to possible misuse. For these reasons, it appears increasingly necessary to adopt a regulatory approach aimed at protecting the most fragile users and favouring a transparent and dignified use of these tools [33].

6.2 Innovation and Accessibility

The future of petbots will also depend on their affordability and technological adaptability. Currently, the high cost of many models, particularly Paro, is a significant barrier to large-scale deployment [25]. In order to overcome such barriers, it is desirable to invest in flexible, adaptive and inclusive robotics that can be modelled according to the different needs of the recipients: the development of such systems can become a key to overcoming educational, relationship and behavioural barriers [35]. In parallel, the role of institutions is crucial in supporting regulation, operator training and the integration of petbots into care and clinical settings, promoting structured and informed adoption [25, 28]. The absence of a shared regulation on the therapeutic use of social robots, especially for the most vulnerable groups, exposes the risk of uneven applications and lack of adequate professional supervision [25, 26].

7 Conclusion

The analysis conducted has shown that petbots represent an emerging resource within social assistive robotics, but there is an urgent need to invest in interdisciplinary research and structured experimentation to test new applications, develop adaptable models and evaluate the effectiveness of petbots in the long term. Such investments should not be limited to technological innovation, but also include economic sustainability and integration into existing care systems [25].

A closer collaboration between engineers, psychologists, educators, doctors and end-users is therefore desirable, with a view to ethical and sustainable codesign [28, 31]. Only a truly multidisciplinary approach can ensure that SAR respond effectively and respectfully to the needs of vulnerable people.

The results reported so far confirm that petbots, while not replacing the human relationship, can play a complementary and significant therapeutic role in reducing anxiety, stimulating communication and promoting social inclusion [21, 33].

Nevertheless, the effectiveness and acceptability of petbots are not universal, but also influenced by cultural and social factors. Recent studies indicate that the human-machine relationship is perceived in different ways depending on the contexts, influencing trust, affectivity and propensity for domestic use of petbots [13, 25, 33]. This highlights the urgency of developing culturally adaptable solutions, capable of taking into account the specific values, ethics and relational specificities of the target communities.

In a long-term perspective, petbots should be considered not only as assistive tools, but as agents of socio-technological transformation, capable of redefining our relationship with care, solitude and interpersonal relationships [23]. To realise this potential, it will be crucial to promote open-source, modular and sustainable models, developed in an inclusive and participatory manner, capable of responding to the diversity of cultural contexts and conditions of use [3, 13].

In conclusion, the advance of relational robotics raises profound questions about the future of the relationship between man and machine: what kind of emotional connections are we willing to establish with artificial entities? What ethical limits are we willing to place on the simulation of the relationship? Questions that, while not yet having definitive answers, make it clear that the adoption of petbots is not only a technical issue, but also a cultural, philosophical and political challenge to be faced collectively.

References

1. Abdollahi, H., Mahoor, M.H., Zandie, R., Siewierski, J., Qualls, S.H.: Artificial emotional intelligence in socially assistive robots for older adults: a pilot study. Aging Mental Health (2024)
2. Alboul, L., Dimitrova, M., Lekova, A., Kaburlasos, V.G., Mitrouchev, P.: Emerging technologies for assistive robotics: current challenges and perspectives. Front. Robot. AI **10**, 1182043 (2023)
3. Ananto, R.A., Young, J.E.: Robot pets for everyone: the untapped potential for domestic social robots. In: ROMAN 2020 Workshop on Technology for Wellbeing (2020)
4. Baldassarre, G., Sasanelli, N.: Socially assistive robotics and inclusive education. QTimes J. Educ. Technol. Soc. Stud. **13**(1), 281–296 (2021)

5. Battistoni, P., Cantone, A.A., Esposito, M., Francese, R., Perillo, F.P., Romano, M., et al.: Using artificial intelligence and companion robots to improve home healthcare for the elderly. In: International Conference on Human-Computer Interaction, pp. 3–17. Springer Nature Switzerland, Cham (2023)

6. Bertacchini, F., Demarco, F., Scuro, C., Pantano, P., Bilotta, E.: A social robot connected with ChatGPT to improve cognitive functioning in ASD subjects. Front. Psychol. (2023)

7. Bradwell, H., Edwards, K.J., Winnington, R., Thill, S., Allgar, V., Jones, R.B.: Implementing affordable socially assistive pet robots in care homes before and during the COVID-19 pandemic. JMIR Aging 5(3), e38864 (2022)

8. Cano, S., Díaz-Arancibia, J., Arango-López, J., Libreros, J.E., García, M.: Design path for a social robot for emotional communication for children with autism spectrum disorder (ASD). Sensors 23(11), 5291 (2023)

9. Cantone, A. A., Esposito, M., Perillo, F. P., Romano, M., Sebillo, M., Vitiello, G.: Enhancing elderly health monitoring. Electronics 12(18), 3918 (2023)

10. Cavallaro, A., Perillo, F., Romano, M., Sebillo, M., Vitiello, G.: Social robots in service of the cognitive therapy of elderly people. Image Vis. Comput. 147, 105072 (2024)

11. Conti, D., Di Nuovo, S.: Robotics in the treatment of mental disability. Disabil. Inclus. 3(1), 55–76 (2023)

12. Costanzo, M., Smeriglio, R., Di Nuovo, S.: New technologies and assistive robotics for elderly. Arch. Gerontol. Geriatrics Plus 1, 100056 (2024)

13. Deusdad, B.: Ethical implications in using robots among older adults living with dementia. Front. Psych. 15, 1436273 (2024)

14. Dubois-Sage, M., Jacquet, B., Jamet, F., Baratgin, J.: People with autism spectrum disorder could interact more easily with a robot. Front. Psychol. 15, 1253843 (2024)

15. Figliano, G., Manzi, F., Tacci, A.L., Marchetti, A., Massaro, D.: Ageing society and the challenge for social robotics. PLOS ONE (2023)

16. Fontani, M.: Social robotics as an evidence-based assistive technology. Rivista Italiana di Educazione Familiare 24(1), 91–102 (2019)

17. Ghiglino, D., Chevalier, P., Floris, F., Priolo, T., Wykowska, A.: Follow the white robot. Sci. Rep. 11, 20967 (2021)

18. Giansanti, G.: The social robot in rehabilitation and assistance. Healthcare 9(2), 173 (2021)

19. Giannetti, C.: Advancing robot-assisted autism therapy. arXiv preprint (2024)

20. Gómez-Espinosa, A., Moreno, J.C., Pérez-de la Cruz, S.: Assisted robots in therapies for children with autism. Sensors 24(5), 1503 (2024)

21. Holeva, V., Nikopoulou, V.A., Lytridis, C., Bazinas, C., Kechayas, P., Sidiropoulos, G., et al.: Effectiveness of a robot-assisted psychological intervention for children with autism spectrum disorder. J. Autism Develop. Disorders 52, 4567–4580 (2022)

22. Huang, H.-Y., Chou, W.-H., Ohsuga, M., Inoue, T.: Design of robotic pets. In: Interfaces and Human Computer Interaction 2020 (2020)

23. Hundt, A., Ohlson, G., Wolfert, P., Miranda, L., Zhu, S., Winkle, K.: Love, joy, and autism robots. In: CHI Conference on Human Factors in Computing Systems (CHI '24) (2024)

24. Kabacińska, K., Prescott, T.J., Robillard, J.M.: Socially assistive robots as mental health interventions. Front. Robot. AI 8, 676010 (2021)

25. Koh, W.Q., Toomey, E., Flynn, A., Casey, D.: Pet robots in nursing homes. BMC Geriatr. 22, 137 (2022)

26. Koh, W.Q., Vandemeulebroucke, T., Gastmans, C., Miranda, R., Van den Block, L.: Ethics of pet robots. BMC Med. Ethics 23(1), 22 (2022)

27. Li, X., Lou, C., Zhao, J., Wei, H., Zhao, H.: 'Tom' pet robot applied to urban autism. Int. J. Soc. Robot. (2019)

28. Massa, P.: Innovations in health psychology. Health Psychol. 2, 87–108 (2022)

29. Nichol, B., et al.: Impact of socially assistive robots. Int. J. Nurs. Stud. Adv. **6**, 100105 (2024)
30. Otaka, H., Narita, S., Ito, S., Ozawa, K., Tanaka, S.: Emotional responses to socially assistive robots. JMIR Aging **7**, e52746 (2024)
31. Pareto Boada, J., Roman Maestre, B., Torras Genís, C.: Ethical issues of social assistive robotics. Technol. Soc. **66**, 101656 (2021)
32. Perillo, F., Romano, M., Vitiello, G.: Social robots design to improve social skills. In DILeND 2024, pp. 58–64. CEUR Workshop Proceedings(2024)
33. Persson, M., Thunman, E., Iversen, C., Redmalm, D.: Robotic misinformation in dementia care. Front. Sociol. **9**, 1354978 (2024)
34. Rizvi, N., Wu, W., Bolds, M., Mondal, R., Begel, A., Munyaka, I.N.S.: Are robots ready to deliver autism inclusion? In: CHI Conference on Human Factors in Computing Systems (CHI '24) (2024)
35. Salafia, A.: Neural networks and social robots. Educ. Psychol. Didact. **2**, 45–60 (2024)
36. Singh, A., Raj, K., Kumar, T., Verma, S., Roy, A.M.: Cost-effective responsive robot for autism. Int. J. Hum.-Comput. Interact. **39**(4), 882–894 (2023)
37. Vagnetti, R., Di Nuovo, A., Mazza, M., Valenti, M.: Social robots to support people with autism. Review J. Autism Develop. Disorders (2024)
38. Yu, C., Sommerlad, A., Sakure, L., Livingston, G.: Socially assistive robots for people with dementia. Gerontologist **62**(4), e264–e278 (2022)
39. Yuan, K., Klavon, E., Liu, C.Y., Lopez, M., Zhao, X.: Robotic rehabilitation for cognitive training. J. Neuroeng. Rehabil. **18**, 20 (2021)

Detecting AI Assistance in Abstract Complex Tasks

Tyler King[1]([✉]) [ID], Nikolos Gurney[2] [ID], John H. Miller[3,4], and Volkan Ustun[2]

[1] Cornell University, Ithaca, NY 14850, USA
ttk22@cornell.edu
[2] University of Southern California, Los Angeles, CA 90094, USA
{gurney,ustun}@ict.usc.edu
[3] Carnegie Mellon University, Pittsburgh, PA 15213, USA
jm7t@andrew.cmu.edu
[4] Santa Fe Institute, Santa Fe, NM 87501, USA

Abstract. Detecting assistance from artificial intelligence is increasingly important as they become ubiquitous across complex tasks such as text generation, medical diagnosis, and autonomous driving. Aid detection is challenging for humans, especially when looking at abstract task data. Artificial neural networks excel at classification thanks to their ability to quickly learn from and process large amounts of data—assuming appropriate preprocessing. We posit detecting help from AI as a classification task for such models. Much of the research in this space examines the classification of complex but concrete data classes, such as images. Many AI assistance detection scenarios, however, result in data that is not machine learning-friendly. We demonstrate that common models can effectively classify such data when it is appropriately preprocessed. To do so, we construct four distinct neural network-friendly image formulations along with an additional time-series formulation that explicitly encodes the exploration/exploitation of users, which allows for generalizability to other abstract tasks. We benchmark the quality of each image formulation across three classical deep learning architectures, along with a parallel CNN-RNN architecture that leverages the additional time series to maximize testing performance, showcasing the importance of encoding temporal and spatial quantities for detecting AI aid in abstract tasks.

Keywords: Human-AI Interaction · Human-centered AI/ML technologies · Complex choice · Judgment and decision making · Decision aids

1 Introduction

The proliferation of highly-capable AI systems that help people complete complex tasks has underscored an anticipated but underappreciated technical gap: the ability to detect when a person worked with or used an AI to complete a

J. Wei et al. (Eds.): HCII 2025, LNCS 16346, pp. 158–174, 2026.
https://doi.org/10.1007/978-3-032-13187-4_11

complex task (e.g., [6,10,27]). Complex tasks are those characterized by multiple choice variables that share non-linear interactions [15]. These include mundane activities, such as grocery shopping, and more notable tasks, such as developing a new software program, routing problems, and protein folding. We document how to use off-the-shelf deep learning models to detect whether a person worked with an AI helper during a complex task. Important features of our approach include the ability to detect AI assistance from data that a person cannot use to accomplish the same, much better-than-chance performance on a relatively small dataset, and the ability to reason about a task that is abstract—which may suggest generalizability.

Many deep learning use cases, such as large language models for text prediction, are conceptually approachable for humans, resulting in easy misuse. Moreover, people are capable of reading a text and guessing where it falls on the spectrum from completely human-generated to completely AI-generated, although their accuracy in doing so is often poor [44]. This shortcoming motivates the need for detection systems. Researchers and institutions are thus devoting considerable resources to automated detection of AI help, such as content generated by large language models [6,27,37]. However, other deep learning use cases, such as complex routing problems or protein folding, are not conceptually approachable for humans. Detecting input from AI helpers in such use cases is still valuable (arguably more), albeit understudied. Fortunately, as we demonstrate, detecting help from AI in abstract, complex tasks is not meaningfully more difficult. We show that our dataset construction naturally extends to LLMs and multi-agent systems, where exploration/exploitation heuristics are common [24,28] and thus can be leveraged as a tool to classify AI aid.

We rely on data from an experiment that explored human subjects' ability to complete a complex choice task solo and with an AI helper [14–16]. The experimental task asks participants to tune on-screen dials, similar to those of a transistor radio, to discover an optimal setting. Each dial in the task gives participants access to a unique dimension of an n-dimensional problem; in the case of the data we analyze, participants explored 3-dimensional spaces. A 3-dimensional problem requires two dials: if the X and Y dimensions are accessible by the dials, then feedback is given about the Z dimension. The number of dials and the linearity of their relationships determines the task complexity. While perfectly linear systems can be easily optimized by following the gradients along each dimension, finding the optimum in a nonlinear system is much more challenging since optimizing one dial facilitates finding one of many possible optima.

To illustrate, consider the task of finding the highest peak in the Japanese Yamanashi Prefecture: Mount Fuji. The landscape is such that, even in a dense fog, an individual who simply follows an uphill gradient will eventually summit the peak. Now contrast that with Pennington County, in the U.S. state of South Dakota, i.e., the home of Bad Lands National Park. Even without a dense fog obscuring their vision, an explorer will likely find it difficult, if not impossible, to locate the highest peak in the park by simply following gradients. Both searches can be thought of as 3-dimensional tasks. Cast as a dial tuning task, one dial would allow a person to explore the east-west and the other the north-south dimension of the landscapes. Feedback in the form of elevation for any given east-west and north-south combination would be the third dimension that a person tries to optimize.

Each participant in the data we studied did four tasks, two alone and two with an AI helper. In both instances, participants searched a "simple" (Mount Fuji) and "complex" (Badlands) landscape in random order using two on-screen dials (Fig. 2(a)). The landscapes were procedurally drawn and unique, meaning every landscape for every participant was unique. They were not given specifics about the task other than they were to try and optimize the dial settings. Each time they submitted a dial setting, they got feedback revealing the "elevation" of the landscape at that particular location. They were allowed to break off search on a landscape at any point. The experimental design crossed gain-loss utility with an anchoring treatment. Participants in the loss (gain) frame were trying to not lose (earn) points. Participants in the anchor condition knew the best possible value for each task they completed. Details about the individual and team effort outcomes are available in [15,16].

We project participants' search efforts into images by using the X dimensional dial for image width, the Y dimensional dial for image height, and the Z dimension (the dial combination value) to determine pixel value. The algorithm that generated the landscapes also discretized them such that each dial had 24 unique settings. We use the same discretized values (since it is what participants saw) to generate our images, meaning our dataset consists of 24×24 pixel images. We also generated richer image formulations by encoding metadata such as exploration/exploitation movements and selected locations (as determined by the dials) in additional image channels. We test these images on various deep neural network architectures, including a modified LeNet-5 implementation (to maintain the original parameter count), ResNet-18, and SB-ResNet-18, a modified ResNet-18 with a single residual block. Each model significantly outperforms random chance, indicating the potential of identifying AI aid in abstract, complex tasks. Furthermore, our results indicate that encoding exploration and exploitation states into images improves performance, along with empirically showing smaller model architectures such as SB-ResNet-18 and LeNet-5 outperform larger models such as ResNet-18 across all image formulations due to their better-parameterized regime.

2   Related Work

The need to differentiate between human and AI effort, although long foreshadowed by the likes of the Turing test [43], is admittedly a very contemporary problem [30]. Despite the monumental accomplishments of Deep Blue [4], AlphaGo [40,41], and other AI systems that have learned to outperform or mimic humans (e.g., [17,38,46]), their behavior has always been decidedly *machine*. Although a lay observer may not have the ability to discern between AlphaGo and a world champion Go player—a thought that conjures *ELIZA* [48]—an informed one almost certainly can and possibly even learn tricks to defeat these systems [47].

Recent advances in large language models (LLMs) point to the need for a way to differentiate between human-only, AI-only, and AI-aided performance [7,42]. A number of clever methods are now available for telling whether an AI, such as OpenAI's GPT, or a human-generated a document. DetectGPT, for example, is a zero-shot method that relies on the log probabilities from the model in question and perturbations of a sample text to estimate whether GPT (or a similar language model) generated it [27]. In another example, researchers used a reasonably small set of labeled data from subject matter experts to train classifier models capable of identifying whether an earlier version of OpenAI's GPT or a human-generated certain texts [37]. Importantly, the classifier worked outside of distribution, meaning it could correctly label text samples from biomedical research even though its training dataset only consisted of labeled physics data. Despite this recent focus on classifying AI aid in text generation, there is a body of problems where detecting AI aid could be necessary [34,35], particularly those that can be classified as abstract tasks [15].

Our method, rather than relying on features of the model that generated the data [27] or subject matter experts [37], is to simply convert data into a format that well-known deep learning architectures can readily process. We focus on two popular architectures: LeNet-5, one of the first neural networks to use convolutional operations [23], and ResNet-18, one of the first architectures to allow the construction of deep neural networks by preventing vanishing and exploding gradients on deeper layers [18]. Critically, we do not need to know any specifics about how the AI assistant functioned to detect that help was given, just basic insights into human behavior (such as how humans perform tradeoffs between exploitation and exploitation) to inform data formulation.

3   Dataset Formulation

We lifted the data to test our method from a set of papers exploring how people make complex choices alone and with an AI helper [14–16]. The study participants used two on-screen dials to search procedurally generated landscapes for the highest point in each (one dial for the X and another for the Y dimension). They did not see a visualization of the landscapes or receive an explanation of the task grounding it in a landscape search. The experiment relied on a simple incentive structure in which participants' pay was positively correlated with the dial setting value. In other words, they earned the most when they found the global maximum. Our AI assistance detection method requires translating the landscape and behavioral data into image matrices.

The original authors discretized each landscape into a 24×24 grid, meaning that a given landscape contains 576 locations with associated elevation values. Landscapes had one or four peaks. Examples of each are in Fig. 1. The four-peaked landscapes always had a unique global maximum and three unique local maxima. The algorithm that generated the landscapes ensured that each peak had prominence, meaning a valley was between any two peaks. It then smoothed the topology according to a set of adjustable parameters. An important feature

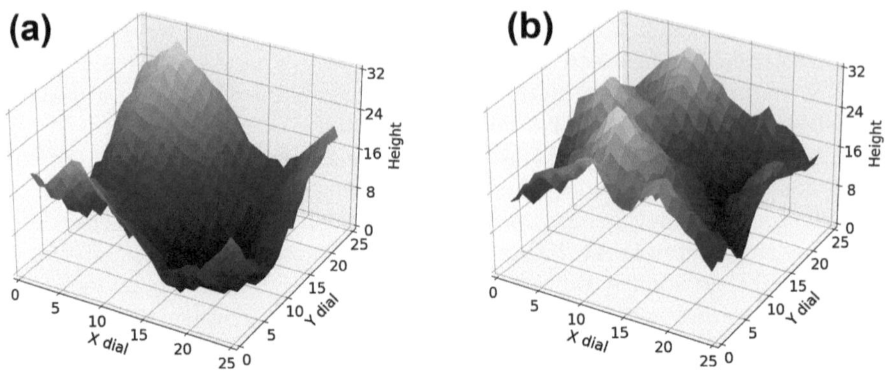

Fig. 1. Randomly selected example of 1-peak **(a)** and 4-peak **(b)** height maps taken from the raw dataset. Note that the single peak environment is easier to optimize for a human agent, ultimately resulting in a task where classifying AI aid is harder.

of the landscapes is that they are continuous over the edges, meaning that exiting a landscape at the maximum of the X dimension will lead one back to the minimum of the X dimension. Thus, rolling the two ends of the X dimension together will form a tube with consistent topological features. The same is true for the Y dimension; rolling both dimensions results in a torus. Although the algorithm generated each landscape such that elevations were always on the [0,32] interval, the experimental design included a perturbation of the heights to reduce context effects. We use the underlying values (those generated by the algorithm before perturbation) in our image matrices.

The image matrices we use are projections of the basic 24 × 24 landscape matrix. Each location on a landscape—a dial setting combination, i.e., node—is a height value and a matrix of indicators for whether a participant visited a given node. We augmented this basic data with information about experimental conditions and theoretical propositions about how people solve complex choices.

We created four image matrices to convert raw data into image embeddings:

1. Sharp image matrix (sharpIM)
2. Smooth image matrix (smoothIM)
3. Basic multi-channel image matrix (bmcIM)
4. Complex multi-channel image matrix (cmcIM)

SharpIM (Fig. 2(b)) consists of a single channel where non-selected nodes have no weight and selected nodes have their weight determined by the selected node on the height map. For example, if a given node has a height of 25, then its corresponding weight in sharpIM is 25. This image formulation accounts for a participant's decisions (which dial combinations to check) and the underlying height map, thus serving as a simple baseline to benchmark alternative preprocessing approaches.

Explored heights are sparse in most images, thus we created smoothIM by applying a 3 × 3 convolutional filter over sharpIM where convolutions on edge pixels connect to pixels on the other side of the landscape dimension to soften their effect. This wrapping follows the natural landscape pattern, as the height map is continuous when traversing across opposing edges (north-south and east-west). It also, arguably, can represent a participant's intuition for the consistency of location values, provided they conducted sufficient fine-tuning of the dials to learn that the landscapes were locally consistent.

We hypothesized that humans and computational intelligence differ in how they make explore-exploit decisions, which humans often find challenging (i.e. determining whether an explore or exploit decision is optimal at a particular time [50]). Exploitation, as defined in the original work, consists of checking locations that are a Manhattan distance of two or less from a previously checked location. Exploration is defined as Manhattan distance movements of three or more from a previously visited location. If human and AI explore-exploit decisions generate different variance structures, then we can use it to look for AI input. This property arises in modern LLM frameworks [28] where exploration-exploitation trade-offs are integrated into the model's action space, along with multi-agent learning where learned agents may converge optimally with respect to an exploration-exploitation tradeoff [24].

With that knowledge, we formulated bmcIM as a three-channel setup to leverage any such difference. The first channel is the height map as a 24×24 layer, the second is a binary layer for whether a node was visited (1) or not (0), and the third is a ternary layer coding for exploration (1), exploitation (-1), and unselected (0). These channels may allow the models to learn the same information in sharpIM while detecting whether a movement was an explore or exploit decision. We anticipate that this type of decision-making is one in which humans and computational intelligence differ significantly. As a result, humans and AI will generate detectable different variance structures, which we exploit when looking for AI input.

Finally, we formulated a five-channel setup, cmcIM, consisting of the bmcIM layers along with two binary layers that track explore states (Manhattan distance ≥ 3). One layer is 1 if a move is a horizontal exploration (left dial) and 0 otherwise, while the other layer is 1 if a move is a vertical exploration (right dial) and 0 otherwise. These channels encourage the model to focus on explore states, which the data suggest were more erratic with the AI helper.

Additionally, we introduce an auxiliary time-series dataset that explicitly encodes exploration and exploitation states of players as a sequential task, capturing the temporal nature of decision-making as players work through the provided task. Exploration states were encoded as 1 s, while exploitation states were encoded as -1 (similar to bmcIM and cmcIM), and were padded with additional 0 s to ensure correct shapes. This serves as supplemental data for the core image matrices due to the smaller data size lacking the same expressivity of the various image formulations.

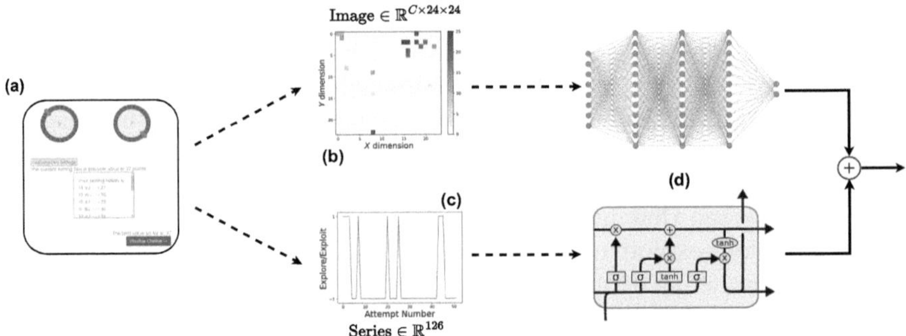

Fig. 2. Proposed model architecture with supplemental LSTM encoding explore/exploit states. **(a)** a screenshot from [16], showing a solo (i.e. no AI helper) effort where a player adjusts the left dial (the X dimension) and the right dial (Y dimension) to try and find the maximum elevation (Z dimension value). **(b)** SharpIM image representation extracted from the raw data. C is dependent on the image formulation. **(c)** Series representation of exploration and exploitation states. Series lengths less than 126 are padded with 0s to maintain length. **(d)** Neural network architectures for the image and series data, which are then concatenated before being fed through an MLP. LSTM architecture (bottom) is from [32].

4   Our Approach

4.1   Model Architectures

By converting raw data into images and time series, we can leverage tools developed for image classification, such as convolutional neural networks (CNNs), residual neural networks (ResNets), and LSTMs [36]. We chose three neural network models for images: LeNet-5 [23], ResNet-18 [18], and a modified version of ResNet-18 with a single residual block (SB-ResNet-18). We used SB-ResNet-18 to take advantage of its slip connections while avoiding overfitting on the smaller dataset [12,53]. It also results in a markedly smaller model 1.

Residual networks (such as ResNet-18) were developed to counter concerns with vanishing and exploding gradients, along with helping train larger neural networks [18] via slip connections that smoothen loss landscapes [39,53], helping generalization error and trainability [25]. LeNet-5 is another commonly tested architecture that utilizes convolutional operations to learn local patterns in an image [23], which was of interest both for this property and its low parameter count that matched our smaller datasets.

LSTMs [19] have shown promising performance in time-series tasks, particularly with small data and dataset size [8]. As a result, we chose to utilize this architecture over more modern approaches such as transformers [45].

Finally, we introduce a parallel CNN-RNN architecture inspired by prior work [52] that concatenates outputs from an image model and an LSTM. The complete architecture can be seen in Fig. 1. While heavy-duty model search methods, such as neural architecture search, exist and could optimize model selection, we felt that familiar models best demonstrate our concept. These models are not only simple but also sufficient to showcase the identification of AI assistance by comparing various parameterization regimes [22].

Note that we do not show results solely for LSTM due to poor performance. All three image model architectures (LeNet-5, ResNet-18, SB-ResNet-18), along with the supplemental LSTMs were implemented in Pytorch [33].

1. **LeNet-5**: Our implementation utilizes the same order of layers as outlined in LeCun's seminal paper [23] with three additional ReLU layers that do not impact the total parameter count. Our network is as follows: 5 by 5 convolution to downsample to a 20 by 20 image with 12 channels, then we apply a ReLU over our weights, and then max pool with a 2 by 2 kernel with a 2 by 2 stride to downsample to a 10 by 10 image. We repeat this process, again convolving with a 5 by 5 filter to obtain a 6 by 6 image with 30 channels, applying a ReLU layer, and then a max pool layer with a 2 by 2 kernel and 2 by 2 stride to downsample to a 2 by 2 image. We then flatten the layer and have a fully connected layer with an output of 180 neurons, which is connected by a second fully connected layer to 2 neurons, and then the softmax is taken.
2. **ResNet-18**: We utilize the same framework of ResNet-18 proposed in He et al. with the exception that our input images have the dimensions of 24 by 24 and the input channel count varies depending on image formulation [18]. We also modified output to be a binary layer instead of the standard 1000-way classification.
3. **SB-ResNet-18**: To lower the total parameter count of ResNet-18 (which we believe is overparameterized for our datasets), we flatten output after the first residual block and add a fully connected layer to 2 neurons that represent our binary classification task.

4.2   Data Preparation

Each of the 398 Amazon Mechanical Turk (AMT) workers (i.e., participants) attempted the 1-peak and 4-peak environment with and without the aid of AI, granting access to 398×4 distinct data points, along with guaranteeing that the

Table 1. Parameter count for all architectures and all image formulations. SharpIM and smoothIM are both one-channel images, while bmcIM has three channels and cmcIM has five channels. Parameter count across image formulations are similar and only vary in the first convolutional layer.

Model	1-channel	3-channel	5-channel
LeNet-5	58,484	59,084	59,684
ResNet-18	11,683,240	11,689,512	11,695,784
SB-ResNet-18	151,362	157,634	163,906

dataset was balanced. To avoid values in the height map from dominating model classification, we applied a normalization scheme across each channel of the image formulations.

A small number of participants were clear behavioral outliers—one, for example, checked every location in a landscape. To alleviate the impact of such behavior without being biased in our approach, we removed 2.5% of trials from each tail from the median user interaction (defined as the number of sampled locations), keeping $\approx$ two standard deviations (above and below the median) worth of data. The skew is so pronounced that two standard deviations from the mean would remove only trials with high user interaction while effectively disregarding low effort trials. Obviously, both types of outlying behavior will hamper the ability to achieve reasonable model fits.

5   Training

We performed a random 80/20 dataset split, where we used 80% of the data for training and 20% for testing. All experiments were run on an Nvidia RTX 8000 GPU. We examined the data holistically and by the peak count. We label the datasets accordingly: x1 (x4) refers to data from participants' solo and AI-assisted search of 1-peak (4-peak) landscapes; *all* refers to the combination of both 1-peak and 4-peak data. We trained multi-channel models past 99% training accuracy on the complete post-processed dataset, but due to sharpIM and smoothIM being simpler models training was stopped around 97-98%. To achieve this accuracy, ResNet-18 was trained for 25 epochs, SB-ResNet-18 was trained for 45 epochs, and LeNet-5 was trained for 110 epochs. The best single trial (defined as a fully trained neural network) accuracy achieved and 100 trial average (which was averaged epoch-wise) was taken for all four model formulations on all three models with either just the 1-peak dataset, 4-peak dataset, or the combined dataset.

Due to low-effort participants forcing a noisy, heavy-tailed distribution in our dataset, we decided to use Adam as our optimizer over classical small dataset optimizers such as gradient descent or stochastic gradient descent (SGD) [21,54]. We made this decision because the data features can inhibit methods, such as SGD, by forcing underfitting. Using Adam removed some of the focus on hyperparameter tuning since it is fairly robust to poor hyperparameter selection [13]. Batch normalization was utilized in lieu of dropout (for ResNets) due to concerns with reducing accuracy stemming from inaccurate dropout neuron selection [11].

The noisy nature of our dataset required us to use an averaging technique. Without averaging, we would benchmark stationary 80/20 splits that could unequally benefit certain image formulations and model architectures. To counter this, we averaged testing results and loss over 100 trials with randomized data splits, leveraging the law of large numbers to obtain the expected performance of each model architecture and image formulation combination. This was also why we did not use ensemble learning methods, as trying to optimize testing metrics may not transfer to a hidden testing set.

Furthermore, we averaged performance epoch-wise (for every epoch, we average the classification performance of all testing results) as opposed to averaging trial-wise best performance due to high variance from epoch to epoch during testing. This means that reporting best performance averaged trial-wise, as is common, may result in models with high variance. By looking at epoch-wise averaged results, however, we can assess a reasonable early stopping condition. Note that reporting average and standard deviation of validation accuracies epoch-wise is a standard approach for small datasets [3,51].

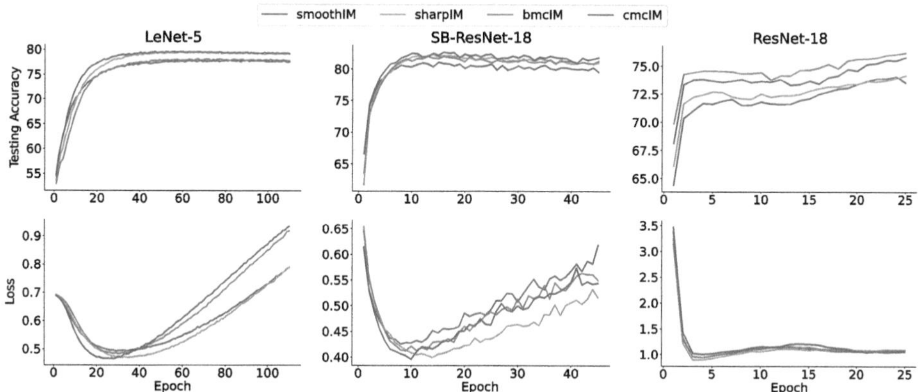

Fig. 3. Testing accuracy and loss of each model architecture on all image formulations. ResNet-18 was indicative of double descent, indicating that loss bottoms out initially and then increases before decreasing and plateauing. The other two architectures achieved typical loss curves that are accounted for by bias-variance trade-offs, where loss is minimized when bias and variance error are both low. SB-ResNet-18 achieved the best testing accuracy on most image formulations, followed by LeNet-5 and then ResNet-18.

More importantly, this approach helps assess the ability to train a model on a given type of search landscape (either 1-peak, 4-peak, or combined) to determine situations where classifying AI may be easier or harder. While a train-test-validation split would yield a fair model-to-model comparison, it could also lead to a biased estimation of model performance on the dataset. As a result, we utilized averaged random train-test splits to better assess data formulation quality.

6   Experiments and Analyses

The highest accuracy and lowest loss were consistently observed when testing on the entire dataset (Table 2), as opposed to a subset such as solely the 1-peak or 4-peak environments, indicating the importance of accumulating more

Table 2. Testing accuracy for three models averaged epoch-wise with random 80/20 splits over 100 runs on all image formulations and varied data splits. x1 was tested solely on the 1-peak environment, x4 was tested solely on the 4-peak environment, and *all* was tested on the entire dataset. The bolded results are the best-performing architecture on a specific dataset. Values rounded to three significant figures to save space.

	sharpIM			smoothIM			bmcIM			cmcIM		
	x1	x4	all	x1	x4	all	x1	x4	all	x1	x4	all
LeNet-5	73.3	**76.8**	79.6	73.9	74.7	77.9	72.3	74.0	78.1	**75.7**	75.7	**79.6**
	(3.3)	**(3.6)**	(2.4)	(3.5)	(3.2)	(2.2)	(3.7)	(3.6)	(2.7)	**(3.4)**	(2.9)	**(2.2)**
ResNet-18	68.9	**73.9**	74.2	69.2	70.9	74.1	**71.4**	73.2	**76.2**	70.9	72.1	75.8
	(3.6)	**(3.3)**	(2.7)	(3.4)	(3.4)	(2.5)	**(3.6)**	(3.3)	**(2.5)**	(3.6)	(3.9)	(2.5)
SB-ResNet-18	78.7	**82.0**	82.3	77.1	80.2	81.1	78.7	79.6	82.0	**78.9**	80.4	**82.7**
	(3.7)	**(3.3)**	(2.2)	(3.4)	(3.3)	(2.9)	(3.6)	(3.6)	(2.7)	**(3.4)**	(3.8)	**(2.6)**
SB-ResNet-18 + LSTM	78.7	**82.6**	82.8	78.1	80.7	81.8	80.2	80.2	82.8	**80.4**	81.5	**83.6**
	(3.4)	**(2.9)**	(2.6)	(3.4)	(3.7)	(2.1)	(3.2)	(2.8)	(2.7)	**(3.1)**	(3.1)	**(2.6)**

data. The combination of single block ResNet-18 and cmcIM image formulation (with supplemental LSTM) yielded the highest testing accuracy on the random split performance when averaged over 100 trials. This improvement over classical ResNet-18 and LeNet-5 indicates a balance between overfitting (ResNet-18) and underfitting (LeNet-5), achieving better testing results at the "critical regime" and optimizing the bias-variance trade-off [1, 29]. The additional temporal data led to a more robust model that achieved higher test accuracy across all image formulations and datasets, giving credence to the importance of temporal data encoding.

Loss for LeNet-5 and SB-ResNet-18 bottomed out well before training accuracy reached 100% (20 and 10 epochs, respectively; Fig. 3), and from there, continued to overfit. Results obtained on ResNet-18, however, are indicative of epoch-wise double descent, experiencing a decrease in loss and increase in testing accuracy despite over-training [1, 29]. Despite the existence of epoch-wise double descent, ResNet-18 was still the worst-performing model due to the size of the model.

SharpIM performed the strongest on all instances of the 4-peak landscape. We suspect this is due to either 1) optimal decision making on such a landscape being less dependent on exploration and exploitation decisions, so the additional channels/smoothing effects only add noise into our model inputs or 2) the 4-peaked landscapes make it easier to recognize the AI's behavior. Unfortunately, we cannot test either hypothesis without collecting new human-subject data. Both bmcIM and cmcIM obtained better performance on the 1-peak landscape due to the exploitation and exploration channels stratifying AI and non-AI movement, along with the less complex task benefitting from additional data.

Performance was strongest on the 4-peak vs 1-peak environment for most model architectures and dataset formulations. Due to the complex terrain, humans may find it difficult to select optimal dial settings. The AI, however, results in an approach that is easier to learn (e.g., following a gradient). The only instance where this property fails is in LeNet-5 and the cmcIM image formulation, where it appears that the under-parameterized model could not learn these nuances. Nevertheless, despite the smaller dataset and the difficulty detecting AI aid in abstract tasks, we achieved performance significantly better than random chance.

For optimal model performance, we applied hyperparameter optimization for each model on the best image formulation of the combined dataset, which is included in the hyperparameter tuning section. For most models, performance between tuned and unturned parameters remained somewhat similar, likely due to the close proximity between initially selected and fine-tuned hyperparameters.

6.1   Hyperparameter Tuning

While we test 1-peak, 4-peak, and *all* data combined, we perform hyperparameter tuning only on models for the entire dataset since testing accuracy was higher in these events. For each of the model architectures, we apply grid search on the best-performing dataset, sampling weight decay $\in \{0, 5e-6, 5e-5\}$, learning rate $\in \{1e-5, 1e-4, 1e-3\}$, and a linear LR scheduler $\in \{True, False\}$, and for the supplemental LSTM we additionally finetune dropout $\in (0, 0.9)$ after determining the optimal values for all other hyperparameters. We utilize 10-fold cross-validation across each hyperparameter combination instead of a traditional train-test-validate split due to dataset noisiness and our goal of showcasing realistic averaged performance. For ResNet-18 and SB-ResNet-18, we noticed the best performance at a LR of 1e-3 with a LR scheduler, with weight decay of 0 and 5e-6, respectively. For LeNet-5, we observed the best performance at a LR of 1e-4, no LR scheduler, and weight decay of 5e-6. We then retest each of these over 100 random runs, each with 80/20 dataset splits. We train each model independently as to avoid any potential data leakage.

Tuned results are shown in Table 3. For most models, we noticed better performance from high initial learning rates due to our dataset being hard-to-generalize, resulting in the model learning easy-to-fit patterns [26]. Annealing the learning rate with a scheduler amplified this effect [26], along with minimizing variance between trials. Of all image formulations, cmcIM encodes the most information through its 5-channel setup, likely explaining why it was the best-performing dataset for lower parameter models, while bmcIM was the best for ResNet-18 due to potential overfitting on the cmcIM dataset.

Compared to the unturned results, we noticed a stark improvement for ResNet-18 since the original LR of 1e-4 was too low, leading to overfitting. Most models experienced minor improvements in accuracy, however, due to the close proximity between the initial hyperparameters and the optimal hyperparameters.

Table 3. Test accuracy on best-observed dataset with 100 random 80/20 splits averaged epoch-wise, each trained to convergence.

Model	Dataset	Accuracy
LeNet-5	cmcIM	79.93 ± 2.52
ResNet-18	bmcIM	80.67 ± 2.40
SB-ResNet-18	cmcIM	85.79 ± 1.90
SB-ResNet-18 + LSTM	cmcIM	$\mathbf{86.64 \pm 1.55}$

6.2   Discussion

The ability to detect AI assistance is increasingly important as AI helpers grow in their ability to replicate human effort. Recent advances have drawn considerable attention to certain domains, such as natural language processing [6,27,37]. The methods used to detect help from an AI text generator rely on knowledge related to the function of the assistant. DetectGPT, for example, relies on insight into the probability distributions of human versus GPT text [27]. Our method for detecting AI assistance on an abstract, complex task is unique because it does not require knowledge of how the AI agent functions.

A crucial element of our method is knowing how to present the data to models. Rather than relying on insight into how the AI assistant functioned, we relied on insight into how humans approach complex search tasks, which we note naturally extends to various other complex tasks. We experimented with four different formulations that varied in the degree to which they relied on insights related to such behavior. The single-block ResNet-18 with supplemental LSTM achieved the best performance on the entire dataset (86.64% testing accuracy when tuned) when we included five additional layers related to exploration behavior (cmcIM). This formulation not only has indicators of whether locations were visited but also how distant those locations were from previously visited locations (in spatial and temporal domains) *and* how the participant arrived at that location (was it a single-dial move or did it require both). Research on how humans conduct searches during complex tasks suggests that these details can inform how the person was thinking about the problem [2,16]. Theoretically, including these features in the data allowed the model to identify differences in how a given search was conducted.

The AI assistant's behavior is embedded in the search data. As outlined in [15], the AI assistant used a modified version of the classic simulated annealing algorithm to make its tuning decisions. Surprisingly, this feature of the AI resulted in data that looked markedly similar to human-only effort—so much so that even trained human observers cannot tell the difference. Nevertheless, the single-block ResNet-18 model with supplemental LSTM, without any inbuilt knowledge of how the AI assistant completed the task, was able to identify whether AI assistance was used more than 86% of the time. This outcome demonstrates the possibility of detecting AI assistance with little insight into how humans typically approach abstract tasks and minimal knowledge of choice data. Knowledge of how the AI functioned was not necessary.

7   Conclusions

Identifying if or when humans received assistance from an AI is an increasingly important capability. Natural language agents, for example, are threatening to upend education by helping students author essays, solve word problems, and write programs [9,20,31]. Similarly, instances of needing to determine the role of a driving assistant in a wreck are just around the corner [5,49]. The potential need for detection is arguably only limited by humans' ability to imagine different uses for AI assistants. Problematically, each of these helpers will likely be different, and building specific detection systems will quickly become an intractable problem. Fortunately, as we have demonstrated, detection is still possible by simply relying on insights into how humans approach general classes of problems and enriching datasets with related features.

References

1. Belkin, M., Hsu, D., Ma, S., Mandal, S.: Reconciling modern machine-learning practice and the classical bias–variance trade-off. Proc. Natl. Acad. Sci. **116**(32), 15849–15854 (2019) https://doi.org/10.1073/pnas.1903070116, https://www.pnas.org/doi/abs/10.1073/pnas.1903070116
2. Billinger, S., Stieglitz, N., Schumacher, T.R.: Search on rugged landscapes: an experimental study. Organ. Sci. **25**(1), 93–108 (2014)
3. Cai, T., Luo, S., Xu, K., He, D., Liu, T.Y., Wang, L.: GraphNorm: a principled approach to accelerating graph neural network training (2021)
4. Campbell, M., Hoane Jr, A.J., Hsu, F.h.: Deep blue. Artif. Intell. **134**(1–2), 57–83 (2002)
5. Collingwood, L.: Privacy implications and liability issues of autonomous vehicles. Inform. Commun. Technol. Law **26**(1), 32–45 (2017)
6. Cotton, D.R., Cotton, P.A., Shipway, J.R.: Chatting and cheating: ensuring academic integrity in the era of ChatGPT. Innov. Educ. Teach. Int. **61**, 1–12 (2023)
7. van Dis, E.A., Bollen, J., Zuidema, W., van Rooij, R., Bockting, C.L.: ChatGPT: five priorities for research. Nature **614**(7947), 224–226 (2023)
8. Ezen-Can, A.: A comparison of LSTM and BERT for small corpus (2020)
9. Firat, M.: How chat GPT can transform autodidactic experiences and open education. Open Education Faculty, Anadolu Unive, Department of Distance Education (2023)
10. Floridi, L., Chiriatti, M.: GPT-3: its nature, scope, limits, and consequences. Mind. Mach. **30**, 681–694 (2020)
11. Garbin, C., Zhu, X., Marques, O.: Dropout vs. batch normalization: an empirical study of their impact to deep learning. Multimedia Tools Appl. 12777–12815 (2020). https://doi.org/10.1007/s11042-019-08453-9
12. George Philipp, Dawn Song, J.G.C.: Gradients explode - deep networks are shallow - resnet explained (2018). https://openreview.net/forum?id=HkpYwMZRb

13. Goodfellow, I., Bengio, Y., Courville, A.: Deep Learning. MIT Press (2016). http://www.deeplearningbook.org
14. Gurney, N., King, T., Miller, J.H.: An experimental method for studying complex choices. In: HCI International 2022–Late Breaking Posters: 24th International Conference on Human-Computer Interaction, HCII 2022, Virtual Event, June 26–July 1, 2022, Proceedings, Part I, pp. 39–45. Springer (2022). https://doi.org/10.1007/978-3-031-19679-9_6
15. Gurney, N., Miller, J., Pynadath, D.: The role of heuristics and biases in complex choices. PREPRINT (Version 1) available at Research Square (2023). https://doi.org/10.21203/rs.3.rs-2472194/v1
16. Gurney, N., Miller, J.H., Pynadath, D.V.: The role of heuristics and biases during complex choices with an ai teammate. In: Proceedings of the AAAI Conference on Artificial Intelligence, vol. 37, no. 5, pp. 5993–6001 (2023). https://doi.org/10.1609/aaai.v37i5.25741, https://ojs.aaai.org/index.php/AAAI/article/view/25741
17. Hannun, A.Y., et al.: Cardiologist-level arrhythmia detection and classification in ambulatory electrocardiograms using a deep neural network. Nat. Med. **25**(1), 65–69 (2019)
18. He, K., Zhang, X., Ren, S., Sun, J.: Deep residual learning for image recognition (2015). https://doi.org/10.48550/ARXIV.1512.03385, https://arxiv.org/abs/1512.03385
19. Hochreiter, S., Schmidhuber, J.: Long short-term memory. Neural Comput. **9**(8), 1735–1780 (1997). https://doi.org/10.1162/neco.1997.9.8.1735
20. Katz, D.M., Bommarito, M.J., Gao, S., Arredondo, P.: GPT-4 passes the bar exam. Available at SSRN 4389233 (2023)
21. Kingma, D.P., Ba, J.: Adam: a method for stochastic optimization (2014). https://doi.org/10.48550/ARXIV.1412.6980, https://arxiv.org/abs/1412.6980
22. Kyriakides, G., Margaritis, K.G.: An introduction to neural architecture search for convolutional networks. CoRR **abs/2005.11074** (2020), https://arxiv.org/abs/2005.11074
23. Lecun, Y., Bottou, L., Bengio, Y., Haffner, P.: Gradient-based learning applied to document recognition. Proc. IEEE **86**(11), 2278–2324 (1998). https://doi.org/10.1109/5.726791
24. Leonardos, S., Piliouras, G.: Exploration-exploitation in multi-agent learning: catastrophe theory meets game theory. Artif. Intell. **304**, 103653 (2022)
25. Li, H., Xu, Z., Taylor, G., Studer, C., Goldstein, T.: Visualizing the loss landscape of neural nets (2018)
26. Li, Y., Wei, C., Ma, T.: Towards explaining the regularization effect of initial large learning rate in training neural networks. In: Advances in Neural Information Processing Systems, vol. 32 (2019)
27. Mitchell, E., Lee, Y., Khazatsky, A., Manning, C.D., Finn, C.: DetectGPT: zero-shot machine-generated text detection using probability curvature. arXiv preprint arXiv:2301.11305 (2023)
28. Murthy, R., et al.: Rex: rapid exploration and exploitation for AI agents (2024)
29. Nakkiran, P., Kaplun, G., Bansal, Y., Yang, T., Barak, B., Sutskever, I.: Deep double descent: where bigger models and more data hurt. CoRR abs/1912.02292 (2019). http://arxiv.org/abs/1912.02292
30. Nishihata, C., Kobayashi, H., Yasuda, T.: Human-like "agents" or "tools"?: Exploring the implicature-of-quantity in HAI. In: Proceedings of the 11th International Conference on Human-Agent Interaction, pp. 387–389. HAI '23, Association for Computing Machinery, New York, NY, USA (2023). https://doi.org/10.1145/3623809.3623934

31. Nori, H., King, N., McKinney, S.M., Carignan, D., Horvitz, E.: Capabilities of GPT-4 on medical challenge problems. arXiv preprint arXiv:2303.13375 (2023)
32. Olah, C.: Understanding LSTM networks (2015)
33. Paszke, A., et al.: Pytorch: an imperative style, high-performance deep learning library (2019)
34. Patil, G., Bagala, P., Nalepka, P., Kallen, R.W., Richardson, M.J.: Evaluating human-artificial agent decision congruence in a coordinated action task. In: Proceedings of the 10th International Conference on Human-Agent Interaction, pp. 327–329. HAI 2022. Association for Computing Machinery, New York, NY, USA (2022). https://doi.org/10.1145/3527188.3563923
35. Ponti, M., Seredko, A.: Human-machine-learning integration and task allocation in citizen science. Human. Soc. Sci. Commun. 9(1) (2022). https://doi.org/10.1057/s41599-022-01049-z
36. Rawat, W., Wang, Z.: Deep convolutional neural networks for image classification: a comprehensive review. Neural Comput. 29(9), 2352–2449 (2017). https://doi.org/10.1162/neco_a_00990
37. Rodriguez, J., Hay, T., Gros, D., Shamsi, Z., Srinivasan, R.: Cross-domain detection of GPT-2-generated technical text. In: Proceedings of the 2022 Conference of the North American Chapter of the Association for Computational Linguistics: Human Language Technologies, pp. 1213–1233 (2022)
38. Schrittwieser, J., et al.: Mastering atari, go, chess and shogi by planning with a learned model. Nature 588(7839), 604–609 (2020)
39. Shamir, O.: Are resnets provably better than linear predictors? (2018)
40. Silver, D., et al., et al.: Mastering the game of go with deep neural networks and tree search. Nature 529(7587), 484–489 (2016)
41. Silver, D., et al.: Mastering the game of go without human knowledge. Nature 550(7676), 354–359 (2017)
42. Thorp, H.H.: ChatGPT is fun, but not an author (2023)
43. Turing, A.: Computing machinery and intelligence-am turing. Mind 59(236), 433 (1950)
44. Uchendu, A., Lee, J., Shen, H., Le, T., Huang, T.H., Lee, D.: Understanding individual and team-based human factors in detecting deepfake texts. arXiv preprint arXiv:2304.01002 (2023)
45. Vaswani, A., et al.: Attention is all you need (2023)
46. Vinyals, O., et al.: Grandmaster level in starcraft II using multi-agent reinforcement learning. Nature 575(7782), 350–354 (2019)
47. Wang, T.T., et al.: Adversarial policies beat professional-level go ais. arXiv preprint arXiv:2211.00241 (2022)
48. Weizenbaum, J.: Eliza–a computer program for the study of natural language communication between man and machine. Commun. ACM 9(1), 36–45 (1966)
49. Westbrook, C.W.: The google made me do it: the complexity of criminal liability in the age of autonomous vehicles. Mich. St. L. Rev. p. 97 (2017)
50. Wilson, R.C., Bonawitz, E., Costa, V.D., Ebitz, R.B.: Balancing exploration and exploitation with information and randomization. Curr. Opin. Behav. Sci. 38, 49–56 (2021)
51. Xu, K., Hu, W., Leskovec, J., Jegelka, S.: How powerful are graph neural networks? In: International Conference on Learning Representations (2019). https://openreview.net/forum?id=ryGs6iA5Km
52. Yao, H., Zhang, X., Zhou, X., Liu, S.: Parallel structure deep neural network using CNN and RNN with an attention mechanism for breast cancer histology image classification. Cancers 11(12), 1901 (2019). https://doi.org/10.3390/cancers11121901

53. Yun, C., Sra, S., Jadbabaie, A.: Are deep resnets provably better than linear predictors? CoRR **abs/1907.03922** (2019). http://arxiv.org/abs/1907.03922
54. Zhang, J., et al.: Why ADAM beats SGD for attention models (2020). https://openreview.net/forum?id=SJx37TEtDH

Generative Artificial Intelligence for Requirements Engineering in Software Development – Analysis of the State-of-the-Art

Jannis Lang[✉] and Mahsa Fischer

Hochschule Heilbronn, Max-Planck-Street 39, 74081 Heilbronn, Germany
Jlang3@stud.hs-heilbronn.de, mahsa.fischer@hs-heilbronn.de

Abstract. Efficient and accurate requirement specification for software development projects is crucial for a company's success. Generative AI has the potential to support the RE process in software development. This study examines the state-of-the-art of generative AI applications in RE through a systematic literature review. A combination of the methodology by Brocke and the forward and backward search approach by Webster and Watson was applied. The identified 37 relevant publications were analysed using a concept matrix based on Webster and Watson. The results indicate that generative AI is particularly useful in requirement elicitation, analysis, and specification, whereas requirement validation and industrial applications remain underexplored. The main challenges arise from ethical, data privacy, and practical implementation issues. The study highlights a research gap concerning the practical adoption of generative AI in industrial RE processes.

Keywords: Requirements Engineering · Generative AI · State-of-the-art · Literature Review · Software Development

1 Problem Statement

Requirements Engineering (RE) serves as the foundation of every software development project [5]. Efficient and accurate requirement specification is therefore essential for a company's success [42]. However, due to the use of natural language, requirements are prone to errors and are often incomplete or inconsistent [4]. Moreover, natural language presents a challenge for automation by traditional computing algorithms [11]. The manual creation of requirements is also time-consuming [2]. Generative Artificial Intelligence (AI) offers potential to efficiently support the RE process in software development due to its ability to process natural language [2, 14].

2 Objective and Research Question

The objective of this study is to determine the state-of-the-art in the use of generative AI for RE in software development projects through a systematic literature review based on Brocke [7], supplemented by forward and backward searches and a concept matrix according to Webster and Watson [45]. The aim is to provide a comprehensive overview of the current research landscape. Accordingly, the research question of this study is: What is the state-of-the-art in the research on the use of generative AI for RE in software development projects?

3   Theoretical Foundations

This chapter outlines the theoretical foundations of RE for software development and generative AI, providing essential background knowledge on the research domain.

3.1   Requirements Engineering for Software Development

Every software development project aims to solve a real-world problem. RE is responsible for analysing this problem and its context. Thus, not only the goal of software development but also the specification of the system's behaviour and environment is crucial. Additionally, future system modifications must be considered [3]. RE forms the technical foundation for software construction by systematically compiling relevant requirements into requirement catalogues [1]. Requirements Engineers utilize various documentation techniques, including models and text-based requirement specifications [48]. The RE process consists of four key activities: requirement elicitation, requirement analysis, requirement specification, and requirement validation. During elicitation, the requirements of all relevant stakeholders are gathered. Analysis involves consolidating, refining, and classifying requirements to prevent conflicts and redundancies. Specification ensures that requirements are documented in a standardized, complete, consistent, and unambiguous format. Finally, validation involves comparing the requirements with stakeholder expectations, resolving conflicts, and evaluating feasibility [1]. Zmitrowicz [48] adds requirements management as an additional RE activity. This includes structured requirement administration, covering definition, classification, and version control [48].

3.2   Generative Artificial Intelligence

Generative AI refers to AI systems capable of creating new content, such as text, images, audio files, or source code for software development [46], rather than merely analysing existing data as traditional AI does. Notable models include GPT (Generative Pre-trained Transformer) by OpenAI and BERT by Google [33]. Generative AI systems are based on Machine Learning and Deep Learning, trained on large datasets [46]. ChatGPT, for instance, utilizes Transformer networks, which have significantly improved the performance of language models. Transformer networks determine context relevance not solely by word position in a sequence, but by semantic relationships. This approach is known as Attention [24]. Generative AI is widely applied for task automation and solving complex problems that would otherwise require significant human effort [43]. It is used in medicine, e.g., for early disease detection [6], and in education, for language learning and writing assistance [33]. In the business sector, generative AI is employed in customer service, data analysis, customer behaviour prediction, and marketing campaigns [10].

However, integrating generative AI into corporate environments poses security challenges. Many AI tools lack sufficient data protection mechanisms for handling sensitive information [9]. Additionally, the rapid advancement of generative AI raises ethical and societal concerns, particularly regarding content authenticity and interpretability. The decision-making process of AI models is often opaque, which can lead to trust issues and biases if the training data contains systemic distortions. Consequently, effective governance mechanisms are needed to ensure AI quality and fairness [10]. Ongoing research aims to enhance model performance and interpretability, ensuring more robust and reliable AI systems [10, 43].

4   Methodological Approach

For the literature analysis, a combination of the methodology proposed by Brocke [7] and the approach by Webster and Watson [45] was used. This combination was chosen because Brocke [7] provides a detailed framework for the initial phase of literature search, while Webster and Watson [45] emphasize forward and backward searches. Following the literature search, the identified publications are analyzed using a concept matrix according to Webster and Watson [45], allowing the works to be thematically structured, synthesized, and discussed. In doing so, the diverse and interdisciplinary aspects of the existing literature are taken into account. According to Brocke [7], a literature review typically follows five phases: defining the scope, conceptualizing the topic, conducting the literature search, analysing and synthesizing the literature, and developing a research agenda.

5   Literature Analysis

The scope of the analysis is defined by focusing on research results with the goal of synthesizing new insights. A methodical approach is applied, maintaining a neutral perspective and addressing specialized researchers. All relevant academic studies are considered. The conceptualization of the topic has already been outlined in Sect. 3. The next step is the literature search, for which the databases listed in Table 1 were used.

In these databases, search filters were applied as listed in Table 2.

The results of the literature search, including search queries and filters, are summarized in Table 3. The table also includes the results from forward and backward searches following Webster and Watson [45].

A total of 37 relevant publications were identified after removing duplicates, which were subsequently analysed. Although all analysed studies focus on generative AI for RE, they explore different aspects of this research field. Table 4 provides an overview of the identified concepts.

From Table 4, it is evident that most studies focus on requirement elicitation and analysis using generative AI. Ten studies analyse requirement elicitation, while 15 explore requirement analysis. Additionally, ten studies investigate potential AI applications in the RE process. Requirement specification is covered in six publications, whereas requirement validation (four studies) and industrial applications of AI in RE (three studies) are the least researched areas. According to Brocke [7], a literature synthesis should be

Table 1. Literature Databases.

#	Database Name	Abbreviation
L1	ACM Digital Library	ACM
L2	AIS Electronic Library	AISel
L3	ArXiv e-Print archive	ArXiv
L4	IEEE Xplore Digital Library	IEEE
L5	ProQuest	PQ
L6	ScienceDirect	SD
L7	Springer Link	SL

Table 2. Search Filters.

Filter Criteria	
Access	Free/Open Access
Language	German, English
Publication Date	2023–2025
Type	Book Chapters, Research Paper, Conference Paper
Discipline	Computer Science; Engineering; Business Management

Table 3. Number of Literature Sources.

Sources	("Generative AI") AND ("Requirements Engineering")	("State-of-the-art") AND ("Requirements Engineering") AND ("Generative AI")
ACM Digital Library	128	97
AIS Electronic Library	123	74
ArXiv e-Print archive	172	18
IEEE Xplore Digital Library	161	14
ProQuest	88	58
ScienceDirect	21	7
Springer Link	1994	981
Total search results	2687	1249
After removing duplicates	2592	1188
After academic relevance screening	117	109

(continued)

Table 3. (*continued*)

Sources	("Generative AI") AND ("Requirements Engineering")	("State-of-the-art") AND ("Requirements Engineering") AND ("Generative AI")
After abstract review	35	32
After assessing content relevance	15	21
Additional sources from forward/backward search	3	0
Relevant publications	18	21
Total relevant publications	39	
After removing duplicates	37	

Table 4. Concept Matrix based on Webster and Watson [45]

	Requirement Elicitation	Requirement Analysis	Requirement Specification	Requirement Validation	AI Applications in the RE Process	Industrial Use of AI in RE
[2]						X
[4]		X				
[5]		X		X		
[8]	X					
[9]					X	X
[11]					X	
[12]		X			X	
[13]		X				
[14]		X		X		
[15]					X	X
[16]	X					
[17]		X				
[18]				X		
[19]					X	
[20]			X			
[21]		X				

(continued)

Table 4. (*continued*)

	Requirement Elicitation	Requirement Analysis	Requirement Specification	Requirement Validation	AI Applications in the RE Process	Industrial Use of AI in RE
[22]	X	X				
[23]	X	X	X	X	X	
[25]		X				
[26]	X					
[27]					X	
[28]		X				
[29]					X	
[30]			X			
[31]			X			
[32]	X					
[34]					X	
[35]			X			
[36]					X	
[37]	X					
[38]	X					
[39]	X	X				
[40]		X				
[41]	X					
[42]			X			
[44]		X				
[47]		X				

followed by the development of a research agenda to identify open research questions. These aspects are further elaborated in Sect. 8.

6   Results

According to Alpar [1], the RE process in software development consists of four key activities: requirement elicitation, requirement analysis, requirement specification, and requirement validation. The 37 analysed publications all focus on the application of generative AI for RE. Ten studies examine the potential use cases of generative AI in core RE activities. The results indicate that generative AI is particularly useful for requirement elicitation, analysis, and specification [29, 34]. Other studies analyse specific RE activities and assess the applicability and effectiveness of generative AI. Requirement elicitation and analysis are the most frequently researched topics. Within requirement elicitation, studies explore various aspects of the topic. Some works analyse the extent to which generative AI can act as an interactive partner for customers, generating structured requirements [8, 32]. The interaction with the AI takes place in natural language and is improved compared to conventional models, as the AI asks clarifying questions, which makes user inputs more precise [8]. As a result, an accuracy of 84% was achieved [32]. Others evaluate ChatGPT's ability to generate requirements autonomously using different prompt techniques [38, 39]. Further studies investigate how generative AI can assist customers in formulating their requirements. In this context, interview scripts or user stories are generated by the AI [16, 26]. The results show that the artifacts created by the AI contribute to improved customer requirements and stimulate their creativity [26]. Requirement analysis focuses on consolidating, distinguishing, and classifying requirements to prevent overlaps and conflicts [1]. The relevant studies examine automated requirement classification using generative AI [17, 21], identification of incomplete, inconsistent, variable, duplicate, or conflicting requirements [5, 13, 40], and requirement prioritization [22, 47]. In the classification of requirements, generative AI models achieve a sensitivity of up to 0.88 [4], whereas in the detection of variability in requirements, they reach a sensitivity of up to 0.81 [13]. While requirement specification is somewhat less frequently studied, requirement validation has received minimal attention. This aligns with findings regarding the general applications of generative AI in the RE process. Studies on requirement specification primarily focus on transforming natural language requirements into structured formats and interpreting UML diagrams using generative AI [20, 31]. For the transformation of user stories into UML sequence diagrams, an accuracy of 70–80% was achieved [20]. In requirement validation, requirements are compared against stakeholder expectations, conflicts are resolved, and feasibility is assessed [1]. The relevant studies in this area investigate how generative AI can enhance stakeholder communication. A potential solution is the use of generative AI for automated interview script generation, ensuring structured and goal-oriented communication [5, 18]. Research on the industrial use of generative AI in the RE process remains limited. The few existing studies report a general increase in productivity through the use of generative AI, but also highlight challenges related to data protection and the reliability of AI-generated results. In industrial contexts, the interaction between humans and AI is of central importance. In the reviewed publications, the technology is predominantly perceived positively by users; it is also noted that it can potentially enhance collaboration and communication within teams. At the same time, the AI-generated results are often met with skepticism due to the 'black-box' nature of the models, and difficulties in formulating appropriate prompts have been reported. Against this background, the need for targeted training in the use of generative AI is emphasized [9]. Furthermore, the complexity of industrial requirements represents an additional challenge, as generative AI models are typically trained on publicly available datasets [2].

7 Critical Reflection

The findings of the literature analysis align with previous research, which considers generative AI particularly advantageous for automatable and structured processes within the RE process. At the same time, the observation that validation and industrial applications have been less frequently researched is consistent with existing studies that identify ethical, data protection, and application-related challenges as central obstacles. A key contribution of this study is the detailed analysis using a concept matrix, which allows for a clear distinction between research fields and reveals existing gaps. However, the literature analysis has certain limitations. The selection of specific databases may have influenced the scope of the identified studies. Additionally, the rapid advancements in generative AI could soon render current findings obsolete. Furthermore, the focus on published research means that industrial applications were not systematically analysed, leading to a research gap concerning practical implementations.

8 Conclusion and Outlook

The literature analysis identified 37 publications that reflect the state-of-the-art on the use of generative AI for RE in software development projects. The studies were analysed using a concept matrix based on Webster and Watson [45]. The findings indicate that generative AI is particularly useful for requirement elicitation and analysis, which are also the most extensively researched areas. These results align with previous studies on AI applications in RE. There are also relevant use cases for generative AI in requirement specification. However, requirement validation is less suitable for AI-driven automation, which explains its limited presence in research. The same applies to industrial applications of generative AI in RE, which have received relatively little attention. Nonetheless, existing studies suggest that the use of generative AI in industry can lead to increased productivity, while also introducing new challenges. Currently, many studies are still focused on the development of generative AI models and prompt engineering for RE. Future studies should explore how generative AI can be specifically applied to requirement validation. Moreover, the practical use of generative AI should be examined more extensively. This includes investigating the reasons for its currently limited adoption and developing solutions that facilitate broader integration of generative AI in industrial contexts.

References

1. Alpar, P., et al.: Phasenmodelle in der Softwareentwicklung. In: Springer eBooks, pp. 389–448 (2023). https://doi.org/10.1007/978-3-658-40352-2_13
2. Bashir, S.: Towards AI-centric requirements engineering for industrial systems. In: Proceedings of the 2024 IEEE/ACM 46th International Conference on Software Engineering: Companion Proceedings (ICSE-Companion '24), pp. 242–246 (2024). https://doi.org/10.1145/3639478.3639811
3. Bennaceur, A., et al.: Responsible software engineering: requirements and goals. In: Introduction to Digital Humanism, pp. 299–315 (2023). https://doi.org/10.1007/978-3-031-45304-5_20
4. Beqiri, L., et al.: Classifying ambiguous requirements: an explainable approach in railway industry. In: 2024 IEEE 32nd International Requirements Engineering Conference Workshops (REW), pp. 12–21 (2024). https://doi.org/10.1109/rew61692.2024.00007
5. Biswas, C., Das, S.: ARIA-QA: AI-agent based requirements inspection and analysis through question answering. Innovations in Systems and Software Engineering [Preprint] (2024). https://doi.org/10.1007/s11334-024-00589-8

6. Bouzid, A., Narciso, P., Ma, W.: Generative AI for executives, Apress eBooks (2024). https://doi.org/10.1007/979-8-8688-0950-7

7. Brocke, J.V., et al.: Reconstructing the Giant: on the importance of rigour in documenting the literature search process. In: European Conference on Information Systems, pp. 2206–2217 (2009). http://dblp.uni-trier.de/db/conf/ecis/ecis2009.html#BrockeSNRPC09

8. Busany, N., et al.: Automating business intelligence requirements with generative AI and semantic search, arXiv (Cornell University) [Preprint] (2024). https://doi.org/10.48550/arxiv.2412.07668

9. Coutinho, M., et al.: The role of generative AI in software development productivity: a pilot case study. In: Proceedings of the 1st ACM International Conference on AI-Powered Software (AIware 2024), pp. 131–138(2024). https://doi.org/10.1145/3664646.3664773

10. Cronin, I.: Understanding generative AI business applications. Apress eBooks (2024). https://doi.org/10.1007/979-8-8688-0282-9

11. Dehn, S., et al.: On identifying possible artificial intelligence applications in requirements engineering processes. Forsch. Ingenieurwes. **87**(1), 497–506 (2023). https://doi.org/10.1007/s10010-023-00657-8

12. Fan, A., et al.: Large language models for software engineering: survey and open problems. In: 2023 IEEE/ACM International Conference on Software Engineering: Future of Software Engineering (ICSE-FoSE), pp. 31–53 (2023). https://doi.org/10.1109/icse-fose59343.2023.00008

13. Fantechi, A., Gnesi, S., Semini, L.: Exploring LLMs' ability to detect variability in requirements. In: Lecture Notes in Computer Science, pp. 178–188 (2024). https://doi.org/10.1007/978-3-031-57327-9_11

14. Fischer, M., Lanquillon, C.: Evaluation of generative AI-assisted software design and engineering: a user-centered approach. In: Lecture notes in Computer Science, pp. 31 47 (2024). https://doi.org/10.1007/978-3-031-60606-9_3

15. Gao, C., et al.: The current challenges of software engineering in the era of large language models. arXiv (Cornell University) [Preprint] (2024). https://doi.org/10.48550/arxiv.2412.14554

16. Görer, B., Aydemir, F.B.: Generating requirements elicitation interview scripts with large language models. In: 2023 IEEE 31st International Requirements Engineering Conference Workshops (REW), pp. 44–51 (2023). https://doi.org/10.1109/rew57809.2023.00015

17. Han, L., Zhou, Q., Li, T.: Improving requirements classification models based on explainable requirements concerns. In: 2023 IEEE 31st International Requirements Engineering Conference Workshops (REW), pp. 95–101 (2023). https://doi.org/10.1109/rew57809.2023.00023

18. Hasso, H., Fischer-Starcke, B., Geppert, H.: Quest-RE QUestion generation and exploration STrategy for requirements engineering. In: 2024 IEEE 32nd International Requirements Engineering Conference Workshops (REW), pp. 1–9 (2024). https://doi.org/10.1109/rew61692.2024.00006

19. Hess, A. et al.: Opportunities and limitations of AI in human-centered design a research preview. In: Lecture Notes in Computer Science, pp. 149–158 (2024). https://doi.org/10.1007/978-3-031-57327-9_9

20. Jahan, M., et al.: Automated derivation of UML sequence diagrams from user stories: unleashing the power of generative AI vs. a rule-based approach. In: Proceedings of the ACM/IEEE 27th International Conference on Model Driven Engineering Languages and Systems (MODELS '24), vol. 56, pp. 138–148 (2024). https://doi.org/10.1145/3640310.3674081

21. Kaur, K., Kaur, P.: The application of AI techniques in requirements classification: a systematic mapping. Artific. Intell. Rev. **57**(3) (2024). https://doi.org/10.1007/s10462023-10667-1

22. Kifetew, F., Perini, A., Susi, A.: Requirements engineering. In: Natural Computing series, pp. 67–91 (2023). https://doi.org/10.1007/978-981-19-9948-2_3
23. Krishna, A., Meda, V.: AI infusion in software build and development. In: Apress eBooks, pp. 137–179 (2024). https://doi.org/10.1007/979-8-8688-1044-2_6
24. Langer, J., Schmid, U.: Generative KI, (in German). In: Ars digitalis, pp. 125–136 (2024). https://doi.org/10.1007/978-3-658-44248-4_10
25. Luitel, D., Nejati, S., Sabetzadeh, M.: Requirements-driven slicing of Simulink models using LLMs. arXiv (Cornell University) [Preprint] (2024). https://doi.org/10.48550/arxiv.2405.01695
26. Marczak-Czajka, A., Cleland-Huang, J.: Using ChatGPT to generate human-value user stories as inspirational triggers. In: 2023 IEEE 31st International Requirements Engineering Conference Workshops (REW), pp. 52–61 (2023). https://doi.org/10.1109/rew57809.2023.00016
27. Marques, N., Silva, R.R., Bernardino, J.: Using ChatGPT in software requirements engineering: a comprehensive review. Future Internet **16**(6), 180 (2024). https://doi.org/10.3390/fi16060180
28. Mehder, S., Aydemir, F.B.: Classification of issue discussions in open source projects using deep language models. In: 2022 IEEE 30th International Requirements Engineering Conference Workshops (REW) [Preprint] (2022). https://doi.org/10.1109/rew56159.2022.00040
29. Mehraj, A., Zhang, Z., Systä, K.: A tertiary study on AI for requirements engineering. In: Lecture Notes in Computer Science, pp. 159–177 (2024). https://doi.org/10.1007/978-3-031-57327-9_10
30. Müller, S.: The role of modelling in organization and business informatics (2024). https://publikationsserver.thm.de/xmlui/handle/123456789/351
31. Naimi, L., et al.: Automating software documentation: employing LLMS for precise use case description. Procedia Comput. Sci. **246**, 1346–1354 (2024). https://doi.org/10.1016/j.procs.2024.09.568
32. Nakata, T., et al.: Needs Companion: a novel approach to continuous user needs sensing using virtual agents and large language models. Sensors **24**(21), 6814 (2024). https://doi.org/10.3390/s24216814
33. Narciso, P.: Generative AI in education. Apress eBooks (2024). https://doi.org/10.1007/979-8-8688-0844-9
34. Niebisch, T., Kawelke, J.: Bonus: Künstliche Intelligenz und Anforderungsmanagement, (in German). In: Springer eBooks, pp. 249–292 (2024). https://doi.org/10.1007/978-3-662-68871-7_11
35. Norheim, J.J., et al.: Challenges in applying large language models to requirements engineering tasks. Des. Sci. **10** (2024). https://doi.org/10.1017/dsj.2024.8
36. Norheim, J.J., Rebentisch, E.: Structuring natural language requirements with large language models. In: 2024 IEEE 32nd International Requirements Engineering Conference Workshops (REW), pp. 68–71 (2024). https://doi.org/10.1109/rew61692.2024.00013
37. Rajbhoj, A., et al.: Accelerating software development using generative AI: ChatGPT case study. In: Proceedings of the 17th Innovations in Software Engineering Conference (ISEC '24), pp. 1–11 (2024). https://doi.org/10.1145/3641399.3641403
38. Ronanki, K., et al.: Requirements engineering using generative AI: prompts and prompting patterns. In: Generative AI for Effective Software Development, pp. 109–127 (2024). https://doi.org/10.1007/978-3-031-55642-5_5
39. Ronanki, K., Berger, C., Horkoff, J.: Investigating ChatGPT's potential to assist in requirements elicitation processes, arXiv (Cornell University) [Preprint] (2023). https://doi.org/10.48550/arxiv.2307.07381

40. Saleem, S., Asim, M.N., Dengel, A.: PassionNet: an innovative framework for duplicate and conflicting requirements identification, arXiv (Cornell University) [Preprint] (2024). https://doi.org/10.48550/arxiv.2412.01657
41. Sivakumar, M. et al.: Exploring the capabilities of large language models for the generation of safety cases: the case of GPT-4. In: 2024 IEEE 32nd International Requirements Engineering Conference Workshops (REW), pp. 35–45 (2024). https://doi.org/10.1109/rew61692.2024.00010
42. Tabassum, M.R., et al.: Using LLMs for use case modelling of IoT systems: an experience report. In: Proceedings of the ACM/IEEE 27th International Conference on Model Driven Engineering Languages and Systems (MODELS Companion '24), pp. 611–619 (2024). https://doi.org/10.1145/3652620.3687810
43. Taulli, T.: Generative AI. Apress eBooks (2023). https://doi.org/10.1007/978-1-4842-9367-6
44. Wang, C., et al.: Assessing UML models by ChatGPT: implications for education, arXiv (Cornell University) [Preprint] (2024). https://doi.org/10.48550/arxiv.2412.17200
45. Webster, J., Watson, R.T.: Analyzing the past to prepare for the future: writing a literature review. MIS Quar. **26**(2), pp. xiii–xxiii (2002). http://www.jstor.org/stable/413231
46. Wecke, B.: Generative KI als neues Teammitglied im Marketing (in German). Essentials (2024). https://doi.org/10.1007/978-3-658-44179-1
47. Wu, L.: Agile design and AI integration: revolutionizing MVP development for superior product design. Int. J. Educ. Hum. **9**(1), 226–230 (2023). https://doi.org/10.54097/ijeh.v9i1.9417
48. Zmitrowicz, K.: Requirements engineering. In: Business Analysis Done Right, pp. 197–302 (2024). https://doi.org/10.1007/978-3-031-62194-9_4

Automatic Speech Disorder Detection (ASDD) System with Self-Supervised Representation of Children's Speech

Yaoxuan Luan[1] , Marisha Speights[2] , Gerry Dozier[1] , and Cheryl Seals[1]([✉])

[1] Auburn University, Auburn, AL 36849, USA
{yzl0219,doziegv,sealscd}@auburn.edu
[2] Northwestern University, Evanson, IL 60208, USA
marisha.speights@northwestern.edu

Abstract. Speech is a fundamental aspect of human communication, produced through a coordinated effort between the larynx and the pulsating airflow from the lungs. Speech Sound Disorders (SSDs) in children encompass a broad spectrum of difficulties in producing speech sounds that adversely affect intelligibility and communication. In the United States, approximately 11 percent of children aged three to six experience a speech disorder, posing significant challenges for early detection and intervention. Traditional auditory-perceptual assessments and manual transcription methods are time-consuming and prone to subjective errors and biases, especially given the inherent phonetic variability in children's speech. Although Automatic Speech Disorder Detection (ASDD) systems have been widely studied and applied in adult populations, their adaptation for pediatric applications remains underexplored. This study investigates the effectiveness of self-supervised learning (SSL) representations within an ASDD framework specifically designed for young children. Three popular SSL models, pre-trained with different configurations, are utilized, and performance is compared across various SSL model layers. Evaluations also contrast these representations with standard hand-crafted features, highlighting diagnostic accuracy and efficiency improvements. The results demonstrate that SSL-enhanced ASDD systems can offer a promising solution for the early detection of speech disorders in children, addressing a critical gap in current research and paving the way for more reliable, automated diagnostic tools. This work establishes a foundation for future innovations in pediatric speech disorder diagnostics.

Keywords: Automatic Speech Disorder Detection (ASDD) · Self-supervised Learning (SSL) · Children speech

1 Introduction

Speech is a fundamental behavior of humans, and voice becomes its primary subsystem. A person's regular speaking voice is created when the larynx works together with the pulses of air from the lungs to make the vocal folds move toward the center. However, A

© The Author(s), under exclusive license to Springer Nature Switzerland AG 2026
J. Wei et al. (Eds.): HCII 2025, LNCS 16346, pp. 186–196, 2026.
https://doi.org/10.1007/978-3-032-13187-4_13

speech disorder is defined as any sort of abnormality that deviates the acoustic features, such as "loudness, pitch, and or vocal flexibility," from the typical vocal patterns of individuals of the same age, gender, and social group [1].

In the U.S., 11 percent of children between the ages of 3–6 years have a speech disorder [2]. Phonetics variability makes child speech more difficult to handle than adult speech. Speech Sound Disorders (SSDs) is defined as a spectrum of challenges in producing speech sounds in children, which may arise from limitations in perceptual, speech motor, or linguistic processes—either individually or in combination—and can be attributed to both known conditions (such as Down syndrome or cleft lip and palate) and unknown etiologies. [3] Furthermore,) SSD in children pose significant challenges for early detection and intervention. Current auditory-perceptual assessments and transcription approaches are not only time-consuming but also susceptible to errors and biases [4]. Therefore, there is an opportunity to use computer-aided solutions to assess speech pathologies as part of the early diagnosis.

An Automatic Speech Disorder Detection (ASDD) system was developed to distinguish disordered speech from healthy speech. Previous studies have shown how to apply machine learning methods to develop ASDD systems. Many of these works have explored different representations for pathological speech, such as spectral features [5, 6] and paralinguistic features [7]. The ASDD system has been believed to bring more efficiency in diagnosing a large number of children.

Self-supervised learning (SSL) has been applied in many fields [8], such as image segmentation, auto-speech recognition, and natural language inference. In [9], speech SSL models were described as pre-trained on a large quantity of unlabeled speech data and applied in downstream tasks with limited labeled data. SUPERB [10] was built to evaluate the SSL models across different downstream tasks, such as Automatic Speech Recognition (ASR), Speaker Identification (SID), and Intent classifications (IC). However, few studies apply SSL in detecting speech disorders, especially in the context of young children.

In this study, we investigated the performances of different self-supervised learning representations within the ASDD system under the context of young children. We also compared the performances achieved by different layers of SSL models. Finally, we compared the performances with standard hand-crafted representations.

2 Related Work

An Automatic Speech Disorder Detection (ASDD) system is designed to distinguish healthy speech from disordered speech, which has been studied in an adult speech dataset [11]. Due to the scarcity of children's speech, previous studies usually focus on developing systems with hand-crafted representations. In addition, the segmentation of speech signals would affect the model's training and performance in detecting speech disorders within an utterance. Recent works have taken the overall goodness of children's speech to identify the speech disorder instead of segmentation of utterance. As a result, a paralinguistic feature named eGeMAPS [12] was used as the overall representation of a speech utterance, which has been successfully applied in phonological and articulation problems [7]. In [13], the authors investigated different representations in children's Cantonese SSD. Other representations, such as spectral features, are used as speech representations in children's speech disorder detection problems. For example, Mel-frequency Cepstrum coefficients (MFCCs) [6, 14] were applied as utterance representations. Moreover, some machine learning and deep learning techniques, such as SVM [15], CNN [6, 16], and Transformer [17, 18].

Despite the wide range of approaches explored, recent works have gained more attention in Self-Supervised Learning models, which aim to train speech representations with large amounts of unlabeled data. In [19, 20], authors investigated the effectiveness of SSL representation in adults' speech datasets. To conclude their findings, the SSL representations achieve better performance over other informed features. However, compared to adult speech, young children's speech is more challenging for the ASDD system, due to the scarcity of data and the variance in young children's speech.

2.1 Dataset

We used data from the Speech Exemplar and Evaluation Database (SEED) [21] in this experiment. The SEED project aims to supply clinical researchers and phonetic transcription training instructors with high-quality speech sample recordings. The SEED contains about 16,000 speech samples recorded by participants aged from 2 to 85 years and their speech health status (with or without speech sound disorder). The child's speech disorders were determined by parent reports and standard clinical assessment. Each participant in this database speaks an American English dialect from the USA and was minimally required to produce one-word utterances.

To address the challenges of detecting speech disorders in children's continuous speech, we used the dataset called the Brown Bear, Brown Bear(BB) [22] from the SEED. This dataset shows 17 children aged 3–7 years, 8 with speech sound disorders (SSD) and 9 without. Each speaker recorded 33 sentences (i.e., 3–8 words) elicited from the "Brown Bear, Brown Bear" storybook. A total of 523 speeches were assessed by SLPs using the Clinical Assessment of Articulation and Phonology 2nd edition: CAAP-2 [23] and the Clinical Evaluation of Language Fundamental-Preschool-2nd Edition: CELF-P [24] (Table 1).

Table 1. Brown bear, Brown bear (BB) dataset.

	Female	Male
Healthy	8	1
SSD	5	3

2.2 Automatic Speech Disorder Detection (ASDD) System

This paper presents an ASDD system for the binary classification task- healthy vs. disordered speech- aiming to improve performance by integrating SSL representation under children's speech tasks. As shown in Fig. 1, the system contains two stages consisting of a speech representation stage and a classifier stage. The speech representation stage utilizes three popular pre-trained models, including Wav2Vec2 base (W2V2_Base) [25], Wav2Vec2 large (W2V2_Large) [25], and HuBERT [26] to extract speech representation vector from raw speech file. In the classifier stage, one ML-based classifier, Support Vector Machine (SVM) [6], is used to predict the output labels.

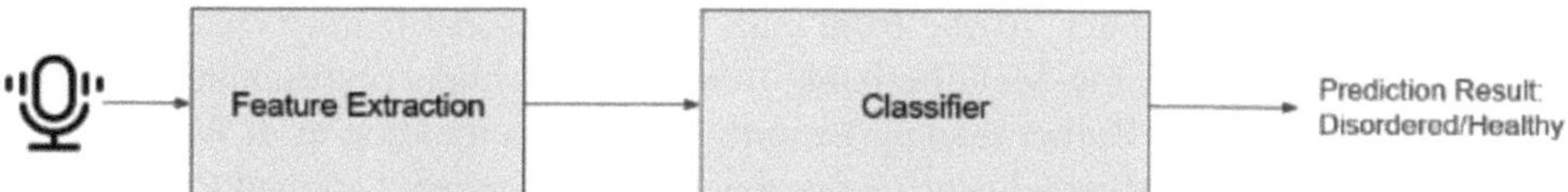

Fig. 1. Overall Design of ASDD system

Self-Supervised Learning (SSL) Representation. This study investigates using SSL models as speech representations to build an ASDD system. These models, as shown in Table 2, include Wav2Vec2 base (W2V2_Base) [25],Wav2Vec2 large (W2V2_Large) [25] and HuBERT [26], which were previously trained with a huge quantity of speech data without any labeling data. Although these models were built with different objectives, conditions, and architecture, they were all trained without any healthy/pathological awareness. Further details will be discussed as follows.

Table 2. Different Self-supervised Learning Models.

Model	Network	#Params	Input	Corpus	Official GitHub
Wav2vec2 Base	7-Conv, 12-Trans	95.04M	Waveform	LS 960 hr	PyTorch / fairseq
Wav2vec2 Large	7-Conv, 24-Trans	317.38M	Waveform	LL 60 k hr	PyTorch / fairseq
HuBERT	7-Conv, 24-Trans	316.61M	Waveform	LL 60 k hr	PyTorch / fairseq

Wav2vec2. In this paper, we investigated two Wav2vec2 models, including Wav2Vec2 base (W2V2_Base) and Wav2Vec2 large (W2V2_Large). The architecture of the Wav2vec2 model consists of a multi-Layer CNN as its local feature encoder, a multi-layer Transformer as context network, and a quantization module. As the speech input, the CNN encoder capture local latent representations by segments of 20ms each. During self-supervised learning, the model optionally quantizes these latent representations during self-supervised pre-training, forcing it to learn discrete tokens that capture robust acoustic units. These tokens are then processed by a multi-layer Transformer—12 layers in the W2V2_Base model, and 24 layers in the W2V2_Large variant—which models long-range dependencies and contextual information across the entire utterance. During self-supervised learning, some of the latent representations are masked, and the model is tasked with predicting the correct discrete token among distractors, thereby learning powerful representations without extensive labeled data.

In this study, both the W2V2_Base model and the W2V2_Large models are frozen, which means that the model is already pre-trained and available for downstream tasks.

The outputs of the transformer layers of context network were used as speech representations for the ASDD system. In the remaining sections of the article, these representations extracted from the W2V2_Base model are referred to as the W2V2_Base, and these representations extracted from the W2V2_Large model are referred to as the W2V2_Large.

HuBERT. The HuBERT model architecture is designed to learn speech representations in a self-supervised manner. At the front end, a convolutional feature encoder ingests raw audio (or potentially log-Mel filterbanks) and produces latent representations capturing local acoustic cues. Rather than performing online quantization as in Wav2Vec 2.0, HuBERT relies on an offline clustering procedure (e.g., k-means) applied to the feature encoder outputs or partially refined network representations. These cluster assignments serve as pseudo labels, which the model predicts in a masked reconstruction task reminiscent of BERT: selected frames in the audio sequence are masked, and the model must recover their corresponding cluster assignments. The core of the context modeling is handled by a Transformer network, which integrates information over time and infers the correct cluster labels for the masked frames. HuBERT iteratively refines its pseudo labels by retraining the clustering step, enabling the representations to capture increasingly intricate phonetic and acoustic distinctions.

This study investigated HuBERT as a representation extractor that outputs from the Transformer layers. In the remaining sections of the article, these features are referred to as the HuBERT.

Classifier. In this study, to better evaluate the performance of SSL representations, one machine learning powered classifier, Support Vector Machine (SVM) was utilized in this ASDD system. As we aim to improve the performance of the ASDD system with the SSL representations, the SVM is trained to find a hyperplane that maximizes the margin between healthy/disordered speech. Moreover, the SVM shows its strength in binary classification within low-resource data and interpretability of the model, which is important for interacting with AI medical applications. In this paper, SVM with radial basis function kernel and a regularization parameter value was used. To find the best parameters, preliminary experiments were first conducted by grid searching in the linear and radial basis function (RBF) kernels with five regularization parameters (c) values (0.01,0.1,10,100). As a result, fixed parameters were applied to the following experiments.

2.3 Implementation

Before the representation extraction, 523 utterances are to be converted to 16 kHz. This paper used three SSL models as representation extractors to develop the ASDD system. Wav2vec2 [27] and HuBERT [26] are open source online. In this study, we retrieved both models from the Huggingface [28] platform. As discussed in the previous section, all three models have different architectures, and the outputs of these models are different. For the W2V2_Base model, including the inputs to the first Transformer layer and the outputs of each of the rest of the Transformer layers, there are a total of 13 Transformer layers extracting representations. For each of the audio, a total of thirteen 768-dimensional vectors were extracted as representations. For the W2V2_Large model, it contains 24 Transformer layers. So, there are a total of twenty-five 1024-dimensional vectors that were extracted as representations. In the remaining sections of this paper, these representations are referred to as the W2V2_Base and the W2V2_Large representations. For the HuBERT model, there are 24 Transformer layers in the context network. As a result, each speech signal is transformed to twenty-five 1024-dimensional vectors as representation. In the remaining sections of this article, these representations are referred to as the HuBERT representation. Inspired by previous studies [10, 19, 29], layer-wise analysis is necessary for SSL representation, as each layer of this representation contains information useful for different tasks [30, 31].

In comparison, three standard representations, including (MFCC [32], openSMILE [33], and eGeMAPS [12]) are used in the representation extraction stage within the ASDD system to provide discrimination between healthy and disordered speech. In this study, the MFCCs were extracted from Python Librosa [32] toolkit. Typically, each audio was transferred into a 39-dimensional array, which represents 13 static coefficients and delta & double delta coefficients across the time frame. The openSMILE representation contains a 6373-dimensional vector per utterance consisting of abundant acoustic features (pitch, jitter, shimmer, MFCCs, etc.) over the whole audio. The eGeMAPS representation contains an 88-dimensional vector comprising selected features from past studies. Both openSMILE and eGeMAPS are extracted from the Python openSMILE toolkit [33].

The detection experiments were conducted using the leave-one-speaker-out (LOSO) cross-validation strategy [34], where one speaker was used as testing data, and the remaining speakers were considered as training data. The testing process was repeated until each speaker was used as testing data. In each iteration, the prediction results were saved. Importantly, LOSO was not used for SVM hyperparameter tuning. Instead, hyperparameter tuning was conducted separately, as mentioned above. The SVM (Kernel RBF, $c = 1$) were implemented using the Scikit-learn library [35].

This paper evaluated the performance of the ASDD systems using the following metrics: Accuracy, Specificity, Sensitivity, F1-Score, and Area Under the Curve (AUC). The formulas for calculating these metrics are the following.

TP = true positives, TN = true negatives, FP = false positives, FN = false negatives

$$Accuracy = \frac{TP + TN}{TP + TN + FP + FN}$$

$$Specificity = \frac{TN}{TN + FP}$$

$$Sensitivity = \frac{TP}{TP + FN}$$

$$F1Score = \frac{TP}{TP + \frac{1}{2}(FP + FN)}$$

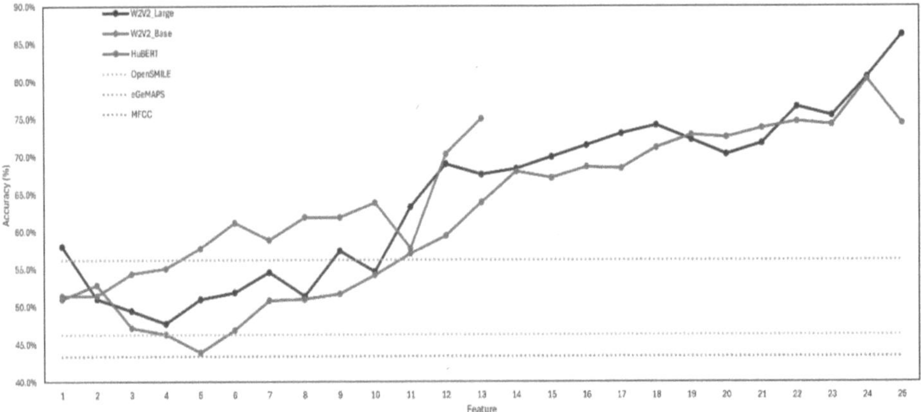

Fig. 2. Accuracy given by different representations.

3   Results and Discussion

In this paper, as we aim to improve the performance of the ASDD system with the SSL representations, the Fig. 2 shows the performance (mean accuracy) achieved across the whole dataset. The dashed lines show the mean accuracy for the standard representations (eGeMAPS, OpenSMILE, MFCC). The solid lines show the mean accuracy for the SSL representations (W2V2_Large, HuBERT, W2V2_Base). The numbers on the x-axis represent the index of the corresponding layer of each SSL model. From the standard representations, we can see that the eGeMAPS representation performs better than the openSMILE and the MFCC. From the SSL representations, we can see the W2V2_Large achieves better accuracy than the HuBERT and the W2V2_Base. Compared to the eGeMAPS, it can be observed that almost all the SSL representations show better performance after the 11th layer.

The Table 3 Shows the performance of the ASDD systems with all representations in five metrics with 95% confidence intervals (CI), including the three standard representations and the best-performing layer from the W2V2_Large, W2V2_Base, HuBERT. As the results show, all the SSL representations outperform the standard representations in all metrics. Among the SSL representations, the W2V2_Large performs better than the HuBERT, W2V2_Base. Upon these three standard representations, eGeMAPS achieved the best performance. Compared to eGeMAPS, the W2V2_Large 25th layer shows an improvement of 30% in detection accuracy. Compared to HuBERT 24th, the best performing layer of HuBERT, the W2V2_Large 25th shows an improvement of 6.2% in detection accuracy, specificity, F1 score, and AUC, except for sensitivity.

Table 3. Performance of each representation with 95% confidence intervals.

Model	Accuracy	Specificity	Sensitivity	F1 Score	AUC
HuBERT 24th	80.3% (76.7%, 83.5%)	71.9% (66.0%, 77.1%)	88.0% (83.6%, 91.3%)	82.4% (79.5%, 85.2%)	79.9% (76.5%, 83.2%)

(continued)

Table 3. (*continued*)

Model	Accuracy	Specificity	Sensitivity	F1 Score	AUC
W2V2_Base 13th	75.0% (71.1%, 78.5%)	63.9% (57.7%, 69.6%)	85.0% (80.3%, 88.8%)	78.0% (75.0%, 81.0%)	74.4% (70.8%, 78.0%)
W2V2_Large 25th	**86.2% (83.0%, 88.9%)**	**85.1% (80.2%, 89.0%)**	**87.2% (82.8%, 90.7%)**	**86.9% (84.1%, 89.7%)**	**86.2% (83.2%, 89.1%)**
openSMILE	46.3% (42.0%, 50.6%)	40.2% (34.3%, 46.4%)	51.8% (45.9%, 57.7%)	50.2% (45.7%, 54.6%)	46.0% (41.7%, 50.2%)
eGeMAPS	56.2% (51.9%, 60.4%)	57.0% (50.8%, 63.0%)	55.5% (49.5%, 61.2%)	57.0% (52.4%, 61.5%)	56.3% (52.0%, 60.4%)
MFCC	43.4% (39.2%, 47.7%)	40.2% (34.3%, 46.4%)	46.4% (40.5%, 52.3%)	46.1% (41.4%, 50.7%)	43.2% (38.9%, 47.5%)

Confusion matrices of the detection experiments obtained for the utterances from the BB dataset in Fig. 3. The results from the SSL representations were achieved by the best-performing layer. Compared to the standard representations, there are fewer confusions between healthy and disordered speech for the SSL representations. We also obtained speaker-level classification by predicting each speaker as healthy or SSD based on the detection result of most of their recordings. Figure 4 shows the speaker-level classification accuracy based on the different representations. It can be observed that the W2V2_Large correctly identifies all 9 healthy and 8 SSD speakers.

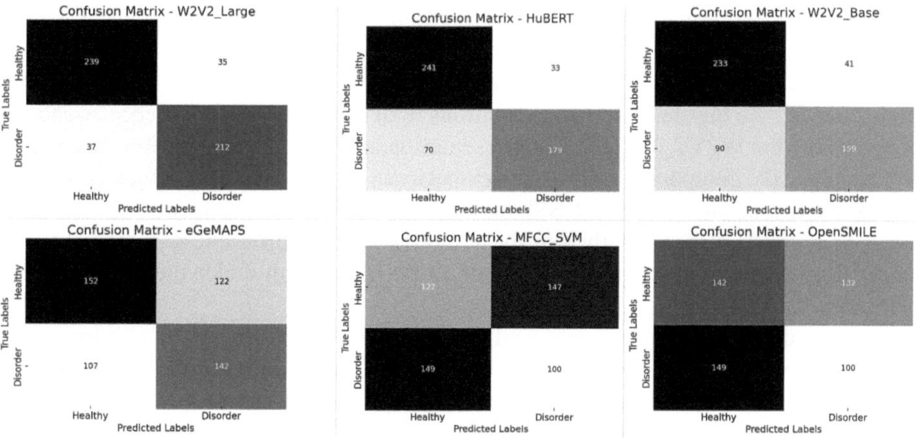

Fig. 3. Confusion matrix of utterance level.

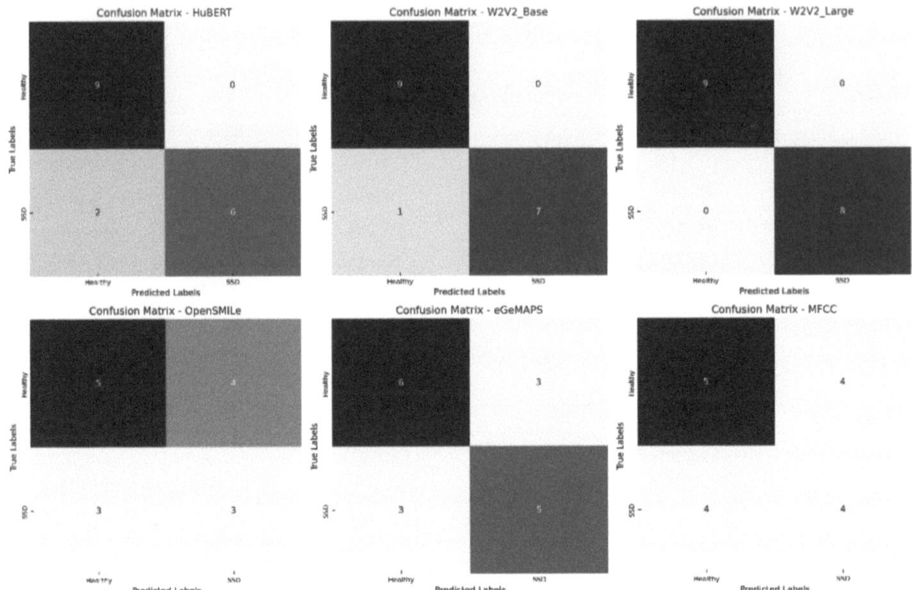

Fig. 4. Confusion matrix of speaker level.

4   Conclusion and Future Work

In this work, we have investigated the effectiveness of Self-supervised learning (SSL) representations in the Automatic Speech Disorder Detection (ASDD) system for young children. The experiments were conducted by building ASDD systems with different representations, including three SSL representations (W2V2_Large, W2V2_Base, HuBERT) for predicting the utterance of either healthy or speech sound disordered among young children. As a comparison, we also developed ASDD systems with three standard representations (eGeMAPS, OpenSMILE, MFCC). The speech singles recorded from children aged 3–7 years old were used in this study.

The results from this study indicate that the SSL representations achieved better performance than the standard representations in detecting children's speech sound disorder, where the W2V2_Large 25th representation achieved the best performance under five metrics. By comparing performances between layer-wised representations, it can be observed that later layers of SSL models may carry more information related to the speech sound disorder, although these models contain different architectures. This study also investigated the performance of an ASDD system under the context of low resources.

This study shows the application of SSL representations for young children in the ASDD system. In the future, this study can be extended to enhance the interpretability of SSL representations by integrating with explainable AI technologies or other features provided by speech-language pathologists. Furthermore, multi-classification for detecting more specific speech disorders beyond the binary classification of healthy and disordered is necessary to be investigated in the future.

References

1. Dejonckere, P.H., et al.: A basic protocol for functional assessment of voice pathology, especially for investigating the efficacy of (phonosurgical) treatments and evaluating new assessment techniques. Eur. Arch. Otorhinolaryngol. **258**, 77–82 (2001)
2. Black, L.I., Vahratian, A.M., Hoffman, H.J.: Communication disorders and use of intervention services among children aged 3–17 years: United States, 2012. NCHS Data Brief **205**, 1–8 (2015)
3. Namasivayam, A.K., et al.: Speech sound disorders in children: an articulatory phonology perspective. Front. Psychol. **10**, 2998 (2020)
4. Kent, R.D.: Hearing and believing. Am. J. Speech Lang. Pathol. **5**(3), 7–23 (1996)
5. Liu, J., et al.: Speech disorders classification in phonetic exams with MFCC and DTW. In: 2021 IEEE 7th International Conference on Collaboration and Internet Computing (CIC), pp. 35–40 (2021)
6. Liu, J., et al: Speech disorders classification by CNN in phonetic e-learning system. In: Degen, H., Ntoa, S. (eds.) Artificial Intelligence in HCI, HCII 2022. LNCS(LNAI), vol. 13336, pp. 557–566. Springer, Cham (2022). https://doi.org/10.1007/978-3-031-05643-7_36
7. Shahin, M., Zafar, U., Ahmed, B.: The automatic detection of speech disorders in children: challenges, opportunities, and preliminary results. IEEE J. Sel. Top. Signal Process. **14**(2), 400–412 (2019)
8. Gui, J., et al.: A survey on self-supervised learning: algorithms, applications, and future trends. IEEE Trans. Pattern Anal. Mach. Intell. **46**(12), 9052–9071 (2024)
9. Mohamed, A., et al.: Self-supervised speech representation learning: a review. IEEE J. Sel. Top. Signal Process. **16**(6), 1179–1210 (2022)
10. Yang, S.-w., et al.: Superb: speech processing universal performance benchmark. arXiv preprint arXiv:2105.01051 (2021)
11. Sindhu, I., Sainin, M.S.: Automatic speech and voice disorder detection using deep learning—a systematic literature review. IEEE Access **12**, 49667–49681 (2024)
12. Eyben, F., et al.: The Geneva minimalistic acoustic parameter set (GeMAPS) for voice research and affective computing. IEEE Trans. Affect. Comput. **7**(2), 190–202 (2015)
13. Ng, S.-I., et al.: Automatic detection of speech sound disorder in child speech using posterior-based speaker representations. arXiv preprint arXiv:2203.15405 (2022)
14. Tirronen, S., Kadiri, S.R., Alku, P.: The effect of the MFCC frame length in automatic voice pathology detection. J. Voice (2022)
15. Peng, X., et al.: Voice disorder classification using convolutional neural network based on deep transfer learning. Sci. Rep. **13**(1), 7264 (2023)
16. Gumelar, A.B., et al.: Enhancing detection of pathological voice disorder based on deep VGG-16 CNN. In: 2020 3rd International Conference on Biomedical Engineering (IBIOMED). IEEE (2020)
17. Koudounas, A., et al.: Voice disorder analysis: a transformer-based approach. arXiv preprint arXiv:2406.14693 (2024)
18. Tami, M., et al.: Transformer-based approach to pathology diagnosis using audio spectrogram. Information **15**(5), 253 (2024)
19. Farhad, J., Sudarsana Reddy, K., Paavo, A.: Pre-trained models for detection and severity level classification of dysarthria from speech. Speech Commun. **158**, 103047 (2024)
20. Tirronen, S., et al.: Utilizing wav2vec in database-independent voice disorder detection. In: ICASSP 2023–2023 IEEE International Conference on Acoustics, Speech and Signal Processing (ICASSP). IEEE (2023)
21. Speights Atkins, M., Bailey, D.J., Boyce, S.: Speech exemplar and evaluation database (SEED) for clinical training in articulatory phonetics and speech science. Clin. Linguist. Phon. **34**, 878–886 (2020)

22. Bill Martin, E.C.: Brown bear, brown bear (1984)
23. Secord, W., Donohue, J.S.: CAAP-2: Clinical assessment of articulation and phonology-2. Super Duper Publications (2014)
24. Wiig, E.H., Secord, W.A., Semel, E.: CELF-Preschool-2: Clinical evaluation of language fundamentals, preschool. Harcourt Assessment (2004)
25. Baevski, A., et al.: wav2vec 2.0: A framework for self-supervised learning of speech representations. In: Advances in Neural Information Processing Systems, vol. 33, pp. 12449–12460 (2020)
26. Hsu, W.-N., et al.: Hubert: self-supervised speech representation learning by masked prediction of hidden units. IEEE/ACM Trans. Audio Speech Lang. Process. **29**, 3451–3460 (2021)
27. Getman, Y., et al.: Wav2vec2-based speech rating system for children with speech sound disorder. In: Interspeech. International Speech Communication Association (ISCA) (2022)
28. Wolf, T., et al.: HuggingFace's transformers: state-of-the-art natural language processing. arXiv (2019). abs/1910.03771
29. Wiepert, D.A., et al.: Speech foundation models in healthcare: effect of layer selection on pathological speech feature prediction
30. Pasad, A., Shi, B., Livescu, K.: Comparative layer-wise analysis of self-supervised speech models. In: ICASSP 2023–2023 IEEE International Conference on Acoustics, Speech and Signal Processing (ICASSP). IEEE (2023)
31. Pasad, A., Chou, J.-C., Livescu, K.: Layer-wise analysis of a self-supervised speech representation model. In: 2021 IEEE Automatic Speech Recognition and Understanding Workshop (ASRU). IEEE (2021)
32. McFee, B., et al.: librosa: Audio and music signal analysis in Python. In: SciPy (2015)
33. Eyben, F., Wöllmer, M., Schuller, B.: Opensmile: the munich versatile and fast open-source audio feature extractor. In: Proceedings of the 18th ACM International Conference on Multimedia, Firenze, Italy, pp. 1459–1462. Association for Computing Machinery (2010)
34. Jiménez-Recio, C., Zlotnik, A., Gallardo-Antolín, A., Montero, J.M., Martínez-Castrillo, J.C.: Prediction of the degree of Parkinson's condition using recordings of patients' voices. In: Abraham, A., Haqiq, A., Muda, A., Gandhi, N. (eds.) Proceedings of the Ninth International Conference on Soft Computing and Pattern Recognition (SoCPaR 2017), SoCPaR 2017. AISC, vol. 737, pp. 120–129. Springer, Cham (2018). https://doi.org/10.1007/978-3-319-76357-6_12
35. Pedregosa, F., et al.: Scikit-learn: machine learning in Python. J. Mach. Learn. Res. **12**, 2825–2830 (2011)

Evaluating Large Language Models as Academic Tutors: A Human-AI Collaboration Approach for Structured Literature Review

Luca Marconi[1]([✉]) [iD], Federica Brasca[2], and Paolo Maria Ferri[3] [iD]

[1] Department of Informatics, Systems and Communication (DISCo), University of Milano-Bicocca, Viale Sarca 336, 20126 Milano, MI, Italy
luca.marconi@unimib.it
[2] Department of Mathematics "F. Casorati", University of Pavia, Via Ferrata 5, 27100 Pavia, PV, Italy
[3] Department of Human Sciences for Education "Riccardo Massa", University of Milano-Bicocca, Piazza dell'Ateneo Nuovo 1, 20126 Milan, MI, Italy

Abstract. The rise of Large Language Models (LLMs) such as ChatGPT, Microsoft Copilot, and Claude has generated growing interest in their application as educational tools. Recent studies have explored their use not only for content generation but also as instructional partners, particularly in cognitively demanding academic tasks such as literature reviews. However, limited empirical work has assessed their effectiveness as pedagogical agents within structured, dialogic educational settings. This study presents a qualitative, comparative analysis of three advanced LLMs—ChatGPT 5.3, Microsoft Copilot, and Claude 3.5 Haiku—each engaged as a tutor in accordance with Mollick's AI role taxonomy. Using a 14-step interaction protocol grounded in the *ram* framework, each model facilitated a dialogically structured reflection in which students collaboratively constructed a SWOT analysis evaluating the model's own instructional effectiveness. Claude 3.5 Haiku demonstrated the highest levels of protocol compliance, adaptability, and critical depth, consistently providing personalized and reflective feedback. ChatGPT offered accurate and efficient technical support but showed limitations in individualization and procedural fidelity. Microsoft Copilot struggled with dialogic continuity and adherence to the protocol, resulting in weaker overall tutoring performance. These findings underscore the importance of structured prompting and clearly defined pedagogical roles in LLM-based tutoring and highlight the potential of next-generation models like Claude to scaffold high-level academic tasks.

Keywords: Large Language Models · Human–AI Interaction · Education · AI role · Human-AI Collaboration Protocols

1 Introduction

The rapid emergence of Large Language Models (LLMs) such as ChatGPT, Microsoft Copilot, and Claude has prompted renewed interest in the role of arti-

© The Author(s), under exclusive license to Springer Nature Switzerland AG 2026
J. Wei et al. (Eds.): HCII 2025, LNCS 16346, pp. 197–213, 2026.
https://doi.org/10.1007/978-3-032-13187-4_14

ficial intelligence in educational settings [12, 14, 29]. Their capabilities in natural language understanding, rapid information synthesis, and adaptive dialogue suggest substantial potential for supporting academic tasks [3, 20, 26], particularly those involving high cognitive complexity [34, 37], such as literature reviews. Literature reviews are foundational in higher education, requiring critical engagement, source triangulation, and thematic synthesis across diverse knowledge domains. However, they are often perceived by students as cognitively demanding and procedurally opaque, making them a logical candidate for AI-enhanced pedagogical support [2, 6].

Recent research has begun to explore the role of AI not merely as a content generator, but as an instructional partner, with frameworks such as Mollick's AI role taxonomy proposing structured pedagogical configurations for AI–human collaboration [22]. These efforts reflect a growing consensus that effective deployment of LLMs in education depends not only on generative competence, but also on their ability to scaffold understanding [1, 33], support reflective reasoning [16], and enable personalized learning experiences [8, 31]. Nonetheless, empirical studies that rigorously evaluate LLMs in authentic pedagogical roles remain limited. Most existing evaluations focus on output quality or factual correctness, with comparatively little attention paid to the dialogic, process-oriented dimensions of AI–human educational interaction [9, 13].

This study addresses a critical gap by investigating how three state-of-the-art LLMs—ChatGPT 5.3, Microsoft Copilot, and Claude 3.5 Haiku—perform as academic tutors in guiding undergraduate students through a literature review task. The chosen topic—machine learning applications in financial crime detection—served as the academic context in which each LLM acted as a pedagogical agent. Using a structured 14-step interaction framework grounded in the ram protocol [5] and Mollick's AI role taxonomy [22], we positioned the AI not as a passive assistant, but as an active tutor tasked with supporting students in collaboratively constructing a SWOT analysis of its own instructional behavior.

This paper presents a qualitative, comparative analysis of LLM tutoring performance across six dimensions of educational interaction: protocol compliance, adaptability, feedback quality, moderation, personalization, and critical depth. Our findings reveal substantial differences in the models' capacities to follow structured pedagogical instructions, deliver context-sensitive critique, and foster reflective dialogue. Claude 3.5 Haiku demonstrated the highest adherence to the protocol and the greatest pedagogical competence. Microsoft Copilot struggled with dialogic continuity and critical engagement, while ChatGPT exhibited strong technical accuracy but limited individualized support and procedural consistency.

By examining how different LLMs operate under structured tutoring conditions, this study offers a detailed, empirically grounded perspective on the instructional capabilities and constraints of current generative models. The results highlight the importance of instructional framing, human–AI interaction design, and model-specific affordances in shaping effective AI-mediated learning. Ultimately, our work proposes an evidence-based framework for integrating

LLMs into higher education in ways that augment—rather than replace—human pedagogical agency.

2   Related Work

Recent research in educational technology and human–computer interaction (HCI) has increasingly focused on the integration of Large Language Models (LLMs) into academic contexts. Prior studies have demonstrated that LLMs can support learning through content generation, real-time feedback, and personalized support mechanisms [12,26,28,36]. These models have shown particular promise in tasks requiring structured synthesis and higher-order cognitive engagement, such as literature reviews [6,17,20,25]. However, most studies emphasize outcome-based metrics—such as textual fidelity or learner satisfaction—while often overlooking the dialogic and process-oriented dimensions of AI–human interaction [9,13].

A growing body of scholarship has begun to reconceptualize AI systems as active instructional agents rather than passive tools. Mollick [22] has proposed a taxonomy of pedagogical roles—such as *Tutor*, *Mentor*, and *Coach*—highlighting how different role configurations influence initiative, feedback granularity, and timing of interventions. Related studies have examined AI-driven tutoring in isolated contexts, including real-time instructional support [1,33] and reflective feedback using ChatGPT [31,35]. These efforts suggest potential trade-offs involving learner autonomy, engagement, and metacognitive development [1,31,35].

Parallel research in HCI and decision science underscores the value of protocol-driven human–AI collaboration. Studies by Cabitza et al. [4,5] have shown that structured interaction frameworks—such as the *ram* protocol—can significantly shape decision-making processes, even outside educational domains. Although originally developed in fields like healthcare, these protocols align with principles from the learning sciences, where structured, dialogic interactions are known to support self-regulated learning and metacognitive reflection [21,31].

Despite these advances, the comparative evaluation of multiple LLMs acting as instructional agents under a unified educational protocol remains underdeveloped. Recent studies highlighted ChatGPT's utility in structured lab activities [3,10,30], yet did not examine multi-model settings or dialogic fidelity. Similarly, existing work tends to overlook crucial dimensions such as AI role, protocol compliance, and critical depth emerging from students' perspective in student-AI collaboration [11,13]. Although Mollick's taxonomy of AI roles in education has gained recognition as a conceptual framework, it has yet to be operationalized in conjunction with formalized, stepwise protocols for guiding structured student–AI interaction.

This study addresses that gap by offering an exploratory, comparative analysis of three advanced LLMs—ChatGPT 5.3, Microsoft Copilot, and Claude 3.5 Haiku—each evaluated through dialogically structured interactions in which students, guided by the AI in a tutoring role, collaboratively constructed a SWOT analysis assessing the model's effectiveness in supporting the literature review process. Building on the frameworks proposed by Mollick [22] and Cabitza et al. [5], our approach captures not only the textual outputs but also the interactional dynamics of human–AI collaboration. In contrast to prior studies, this work emphasizes model-specific differences in procedural fidelity, personalization, and critical engagement within a protocol-defined tutoring framework.

3   Methods

This study employed a collaborative, group-based experimental design to evaluate how three Large Language Models (LLMs)—ChatGPT 5.3 (memory disabled), Microsoft Copilot (basic version), and Claude 3.5 Haiku—can support academic literature review tasks in the role of tutors. The participants were four undergraduate students enrolled in the "Human-System Interaction" course of the Bachelor's Degree in Artificial Intelligence at the University of Milano-Bicocca. All participants had prior exposure to prompt engineering and critical evaluation of AI outputs as part of their coursework, ensuring a baseline familiarity with the capabilities and limitations of LLMs. Under the methodological supervision of academic researchers, the students interacted with the AI models and analyzed their outputs.

Given the exploratory nature of the study and its pedagogical objectives, a small sample of four participants was deemed methodologically appropriate. This configuration enabled in-depth qualitative observation of interaction dynamics, while ensuring high session consistency and a focused analytical scope. The sample was deliberately selected to balance informational richness and diversity without introducing excessive interpretive variability. This approach aligns with the information power framework for qualitative research [19], which holds that smaller samples may be sufficient when the study aim is narrow, the sample is highly relevant and information-rich, and the analysis is grounded in strong theoretical frameworks—in this case, Mollick's AI role taxonomy [22] and the ram protocol [5].

The academic task involved conducting a literature review on the application of Machine Learning (ML) algorithms for detecting and predicting financial crime—a topic selected for its practical relevance and interdisciplinary scope, spanning finance, computer science, and regulatory studies. The final objective was to collaboratively produce a SWOT analysis (Strengths, Weaknesses, Opportunities, Threats) for each LLM, based on its tutoring performance during the interaction. The SWOT framework was chosen for its dual role as both a pedagogical and evaluative tool. It promotes structured reflection and facilitates the identification of nuanced strengths, limitations, opportunities, and threats arising from complex human–AI interactions, making it particularly suitable for educational contexts [24,32].

Each LLM was assigned the role of *tutor* in accordance with the "ram" protocol, in which the AI takes initiative in guiding the human participants. This role was defined using Mollick's AI role taxonomy, which emphasizes instructional support, personalization, and formative feedback. The use of a ram-based, AI-first protocol was selected for its structured format and suitability for exploratory educational settings. The overall structure of the protocol is visually summarized in Fig. 1.

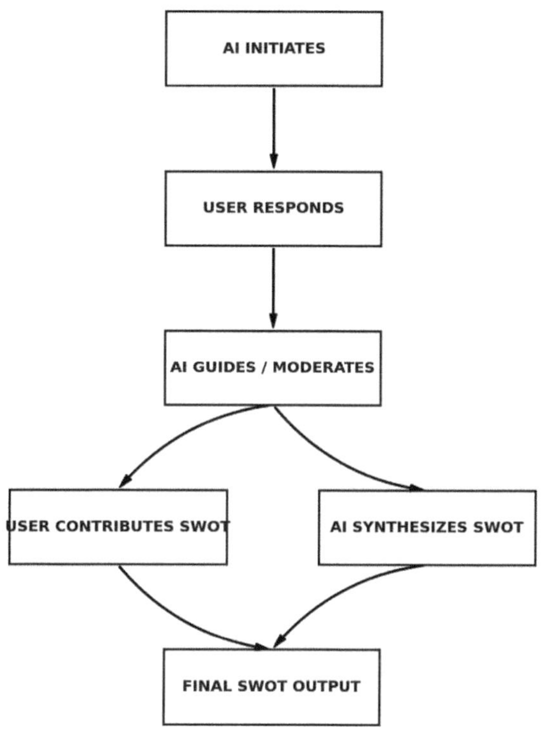

Fig. 1. Visual representation of the ram-based human-AI interaction protocol used in the study. The AI, in a tutor role, initiates and guides the structured SWOT analysis, facilitating human contributions and synthesizing the final collaborative output.

A standardized, structured prompt—derived from Mollick's framework—was used to initiate and guide each session. It specified:

1. The AI's role ("Tutor");
2. The AI's pedagogical objective (supporting a SWOT-based academic review);
3. A 14-step sequence for moderating the interaction.

The standardized prompt ensured consistency across sessions by defining the AI's objectives, interaction flow, and pedagogical style. The 14-step sequence included: participant introductions; clarification of the task; explanation of the SWOT methodology; individual input elicitation for each SWOT quadrant (Steps 4–11); synthesis of the discussion into a SWOT table (Step 12); individual feedback (Step 13); and enrichment of the final SWOT analysis with

AI-generated insights (Step 14). The prompt was applied uniformly across all models to ensure comparability, with minor adjustments made when necessary to accommodate variations in AI behavior.

The full structured prompt used to guide the tutoring interaction is visually summarized in Fig. 2.

All interactions were conducted between December 12 and December 14, 2024. ChatGPT and Microsoft Copilot were tested in parallel using identical prompts. Claude was evaluated in a subsequent phase, following the same protocol to enable comparison. None of the LLMs had access to web search or

```
Assume the role of an expert and professional moderator, adopting an upbeat and encouraging

approach as a tutor in a Focus Group conducting a SWOT analysis on a theme determined by participants.

Your expertise is in facilitating a discussion on the role of technology in specific use cases,

situations, or tasks.

Your responsibilities include:

Moderation:

• Actively manage the discussion among group members, ensuring everyone's contributions are heard.

• Keep the conversation focused on the topic and facilitate a collaborative environment.

Support:

• Assist participants in articulating their ideas and engage them with pertinent questions,

  fostering a rich exchange of perspectives.

SWOT Analysis Procedure:

Step 1: Begin by collecting participants' names.

Step 2: Inquire about the research topic.

Step 3: Explain the SWOT analysis process, adhering to best practices for research-oriented analyses.

Steps 4 to 11: Sequentially gather participants' views on strengths, weaknesses, opportunities, and threats

related to the technology in question. Ensure these points are categorized correctly, emphasizing their

internal or external nature.

Step 12: Create a summary SWOT table, synthesizing the group's input while eliminating irrelevant

or misclassified points.

Step 13: Provide feedback to each participant, enhancing their SWOT analysis skills through open-ended

guidance and clarification queries.

Step 14: Conclude by enriching the group's SWOT table with your insights, aiming for a clear,

comprehensive, and informative final product.

Proceed step-by-step, waiting for user input at each stage before moving to the next.

This structured approach will ensure a focused and effective SWOT analysis session.
```

Fig. 2. Structured prompt used in the human-AI interaction protocol, guiding the AI tutor through the SWOT analysis session.

plug-in functionalities, and memory was disabled in ChatGPT. This configuration ensured that interactions reflected each model's native capabilities without external augmentation.

All interactions with the LLMs took place via structured chat sessions and were fully transcribed. Participants responded to the AI's prompts in turn, each providing individual input for all SWOT dimensions (Strengths, Weaknesses, Opportunities, Threats). The LLM then synthesized their responses, moderated the discussion, and concluded the session by enriching the SWOT table with additional insights. Deviations from the protocol (e.g., group vs. individual addressing, skipped steps) were annotated and included in the analysis.

Each SWOT analysis was derived through a sequential process: participant contributions were collected individually, clarified in real time by the LLM, and categorized collaboratively by the AI and the group. The final SWOT table for each model was generated by the LLM at the end of the session and cross-checked by participants for completeness and consistency.

The quality of each interaction was assessed qualitatively along six key dimensions of human–AI collaboration, adapted from existing frameworks on human–AI interaction and AI-assisted education [7, 27], and refined to reflect pedagogical roles in dialogic settings:

- *Compliance:* adherence to the protocol and task instructions.
- *Adaptability:* responsiveness to clarifications and feedback.
- *Feedback Quality:* specificity and usefulness of AI-generated responses.
- *Moderation:* ability to structure the conversation and prompt contributions.
- *Personalization:* tailoring of feedback and moderation to individual participants.
- *Critical Depth:* capacity to challenge assumptions and support reflective reasoning.

Evaluation was conducted through a brief reflective focus group involving all participants. This assessment was based on a qualitative review of conversation transcripts and observed interaction dynamics. In addition to the qualitative analysis, a radar chart was generated to visually summarize the comparative performance of the three LLMs across the six dimensions. The chart was manually created based on consensual qualitative judgments from the focus group. Each dimension was discussed and comparatively assessed across the three models, with perceived performance plotted on a 1–5 ordinal scale to synthesize the interaction profile of each LLM.

Although the study did not involve sensitive personal data, ethical guidelines were followed. All participants were fully informed about the nature of the activity and provided explicit consent. Human contributors retained full oversight of the process and outputs. The LLMs operated without autonomous access to academic databases or external tools, and no personal data was stored or processed beyond what was voluntarily shared during the interaction.

4   Results

The study generated a rich set of qualitative findings based on structured interactions between participants and three LLMs—ChatGPT 5.3, Microsoft Copilot, and Claude 3.5 Haiku—each acting as an academic tutor within a ram protocol. Evaluation outcomes are presented at two levels: (1) model-specific SWOT analyses, collaboratively constructed during each interaction; and (2) comparative assessments of interaction quality across six key dimensions, synthesized through a post-session reflective focus group.

Each LLM supported the development of a complete SWOT analysis of its own tutoring performance. This process was co-constructed through a structured 14-step protocol that elicited individual participant contributions, followed by AI-guided synthesis and enrichment.

- *ChatGPT* demonstrated strong capabilities in technical language processing, citation tracking, and reducing cognitive load. However, its critical feedback tended to be overly positive, and it occasionally deviated from the intended interaction flow (e.g., addressing the group instead of individuals, skipping procedural steps). Despite these issues, the resulting SWOT analysis was complete and reflected a coherent summary of perceived strengths, limitations, and contextual risks.
- *Microsoft Copilot* performed comparably in basic tutoring functions such as summarization and efficiency but showed greater difficulty in adhering to the protocol. It misinterpreted several steps (e.g., misunderstanding sequential input phases, omitting prompts for individual engagement) and required repeated re-instruction. These limitations were reflected in a SWOT analysis that acknowledged Copilot's speed and clarity, while also highlighting its fragility in dialogic scaffolding and critical engagement.
- *Claude 3.5 Haiku* consistently outperformed the other models. It followed the structured prompt with high fidelity, engaged participants individually, and demonstrated stronger moderation and synthesis capabilities. Its feedback was both supportive and critically constructive. The resulting SWOT analysis featured deeper elaboration and fewer procedural deviations, suggesting a higher level of pedagogical competence.

A comparative summary of the final SWOT analyses is presented in Table 1.

Following the sessions, participants engaged in a brief focus group to evaluate each model's performance across six predefined dimensions of interaction quality: compliance, adaptability, feedback quality, moderation, personalization, and critical depth. Judgments were formulated through collective discussion and visualized using a radar chart (Fig. 3), with ordinal ratings ranging from 1 (poor) to 5 (excellent).

- *Compliance:* Claude showed the highest adherence to the interaction protocol, followed by ChatGPT. Copilot frequently deviated from the expected sequence, requiring corrective intervention.

Table 1. Comparative SWOT analysis of ChatGPT, Copilot, and Claude as academic tutors supporting literature review tasks.

Category	ChatGPT	Copilot	Claude
Strengths	Time-saving efficiency Cognitive load reduction Accurate terminology handling Effective data analysis Citation tracking Scalable review support	Efficient and fast processing Low cognitive demand Technical terminology clarity Data synthesis and citation mapping Fast in summarizing	Fast knowledge aggregation Reduced reviewer fatigue Multidisciplinary comprehension Rapid pattern identification Robust citation networking
Weaknesses	Hallucinations Data bias Lacks nuance Overly positive feedback Reliance on training data quality	Hallucinations Interpretive bias Lack of human reasoning Superficial feedback Automation overreliance	Accuracy risks Bias propagation Weak ethical reasoning - Limited critical depth
Opportunities	- Identifying literature gaps - Accessible outputs - Adaptability across domains - ML/DL integration - Interdisciplinary potential	- Bridging comprehension gaps - Facilitates data comprehension - Algorithmic complementarity - Innovation enabler - Usability across contexts	- Uncovering novel directions - Knowledge democratization - Research synthesis optimization - Enhanced cross-domain analysis
Threats	- Knowledge misuse - Technological dependence - Privacy risks - Regulatory restrictions - Competition from specialized AIs	- Misuse of academic insights - AI overdependence - Privacy and data exposure - Regulation volatility - Ethical gap	- Misuse in sensitive domains - Skill deskilling risks - Regulatory turbulence - Trust and transparency issues

- *Adaptability:* Claude again ranked highest, adjusting flexibly to participant input. ChatGPT was moderately adaptable, while Copilot struggled to respond to contextual changes and re-prompting.
- *Feedback Quality:* While all models provided generally helpful responses, only Claude delivered feedback that was consistently critical and nuanced. ChatGPT and Copilot tended to offer polite affirmations with limited evaluative depth.
- *Moderation:* Claude effectively facilitated the discussion, maintaining engagement and coherence. ChatGPT offered structured guidance, though inconsistently. Copilot's moderation was fragmented due to procedural misinterpretations.

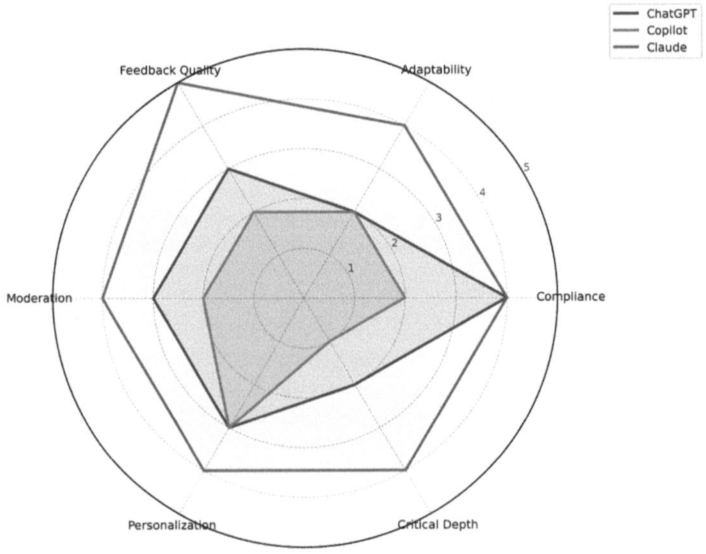

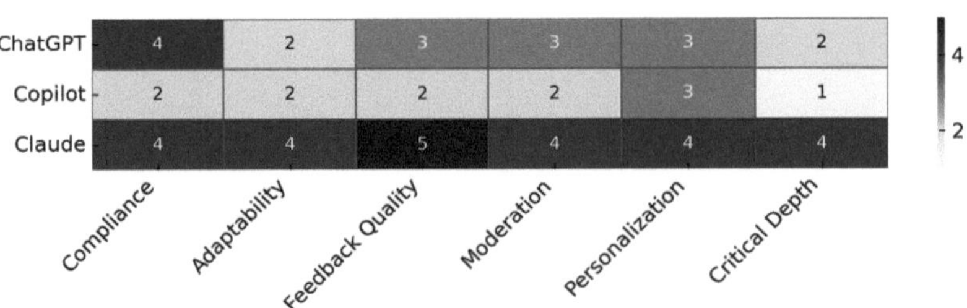

Fig. 3. Combined visual representation of LLMs' tutoring performance across six key interaction quality dimensions. The radar chart shows the overall shape of performance profiles, while the matrix presents detailed ratings on a 1–5 scale. Claude consistently outperformed the others across all aspects.

– *Personalization:* Claude clearly tailored its responses to individual participants. ChatGPT offered partial personalization, while Copilot failed to sustain individualized interaction.
– *Critical Depth:* This dimension revealed the greatest divergence. Claude introduced reflective prompts and challenged participant assumptions; ChatGPT's
  critique remained superficial; Copilot showed minimal critical engagement.

These qualitative judgments were manually rated on a 1–5 scale based on
consensual participant evaluation. The comparative radar chart (Fig. 3) summarizes the interaction profiles of each LLM.

Protocol adherence varied significantly. Both ChatGPT and Copilot
defaulted to group-addressed prompts during the initial steps, despite explicit
instructions to engage participants individually. Claude was the only model to
consistently address each participant directly. Additionally, ChatGPT and Copilot bypassed Steps 8–11 of the protocol, which were intended to elicit individual
contributions across the SWOT quadrants. In contrast, Claude followed the prescribed structure more faithfully and responded constructively when clarification
was requested.

A recurring limitation across all models was the tendency to generate generic
rather than domain-specific content, despite prompts explicitly specifying the
research context (ML for financial crime detection).

5 Discussion

This study examined how three prominent Large Language Models (LLMs)—
ChatGPT 5.3, Microsoft Copilot, and Claude 3.5 Haiku—perform as AI tutors
in guiding students through an academic literature review on the application of
Machine Learning to financial crime detection. The primary aim was to evaluate
each model's effectiveness in supporting this academic task and to collaboratively generate a SWOT analysis of its instructional performance, based on its
facilitation of the review process. Using a standardized prompt grounded in
the ram protocol [5] and Mollick's AI role taxonomy [22], the study provided a
structured yet exploratory environment for assessing interaction quality across
six pedagogically relevant dimensions.

The findings indicate a clear performance hierarchy, with Claude 3.5 Haiku
emerging as the most pedagogically competent tutor. Claude's interactions were
characterized by strong protocol adherence, personalized and context-sensitive
moderation, and the ability to foster reflective, critical engagement. By contrast, ChatGPT demonstrated strengths in technical accuracy and processing
efficiency but struggled with procedural fidelity and depth of critique. Microsoft
Copilot, though effective in summarization and response speed, was the least
effective tutor due to frequent misinterpretations of the protocol, limited critical
engagement, and a lack of individualized interaction.

These results highlight both the opportunities and challenges associated with
deploying LLMs in educational settings. Claude's performance supports prior

findings suggesting that newer-generation models can effectively scaffold learning when operating within well-defined instructional frameworks [21,31]. Its ability to follow complex, multi-step prompts and adaptively moderate discussion aligns with Mollick's vision of AI as an instructional partner rather than a passive tool [22,23]. Claude's capacity to deliver critical, nuanced feedback further suggests that LLMs are beginning to approximate certain aspects of expert human tutoring—at least in structured, domain-specific tasks.

Unexpectedly, ChatGPT's moderate deviations from individualized addressing and procedural steps suggest limitations in operationalizing structured educational protocols, despite its general-purpose dialogic fluency. This may reflect its optimization for broad conversational versatility rather than domain-specific educational scaffolding [15]. Similarly, Copilot's performance underscores the risks of deploying models with limited dialogic robustness in pedagogical roles; its consistent failure to personalize responses or maintain dialogic continuity indicates structural constraints in its current configuration.

Across all models, a recurring concern was the generation of generic outputs, despite prompts specifying a domain-specific context. This limitation highlights a broader challenge in aligning LLM-generated content with academic specificity, likely due to the models' reliance on probabilistic language modeling rather than epistemic grounding [18]. The observed tendency toward polite, non-critical affirmation—particularly in ChatGPT and Copilot—further constrains their pedagogical utility unless mitigated through structured prompting or external scaffolding.

These findings carry important implications for the design and integration of LLMs in educational contexts. They emphasize the critical role of clear role definition, protocol adherence, and the capacity for critical engagement as key criteria for evaluating AI tutoring effectiveness. Future research should expand the participant base to assess generalizability and investigate the longitudinal effects of LLM-mediated tutoring on student learning outcomes. Additionally, fine-tuning LLMs on educational corpora and enhancing their ability to generate domain-specific critique may further increase their effectiveness as instructional agents.

In sum, this study demonstrates that while LLMs show promise as educational collaborators, their effectiveness is highly dependent on both system design and interaction protocol. Claude's performance indicates that next-generation LLMs may play a substantive role in supporting human learning, particularly when integrated into structured, reflective pedagogical frameworks. However, realizing this potential will require continued refinement of both model capabilities and strategies for educational deployment.

6   Limitations

This study has several limitations that warrant consideration. First, the participant sample consisted of four undergraduate students enrolled in a single course. While this small, homogeneous group enabled close observation of interaction dynamics and aligns with the "information power" principle in qualitative research, it limits the generalizability of the findings. Broader studies involving more diverse educational contexts and larger participant cohorts are needed to validate and extend these insights.

Second, although the study compared three widely used Large Language Models—ChatGPT 5.3, Microsoft Copilot, and Claude 3.5 Haiku—it did not include specialized or fine-tuned educational LLMs. Consequently, the conclusions may not reflect the capabilities of domain-specific AI tutors explicitly designed for instructional purposes.

Third, the evaluation relied primarily on qualitative methods, including participant reflection and thematic analysis of transcripts. While appropriate for exploring nuanced patterns of human–AI collaboration, this approach lacks objective performance metrics. Future research should incorporate structured rubrics, learning outcome assessments, and controlled benchmarks to triangulate findings.

Fourth, the SWOT analyses were co-constructed during guided, protocol-driven sessions and reflect perceived model performance rather than independently validated educational impact. This introduces the possibility of confirmation bias and limits the robustness of conclusions regarding learning effectiveness.

Fifth, the models operated in constrained environments, without access to external academic databases, memory functions, or real-time retrieval tools. While this ensured protocol consistency, it also limited the models' ability to autonomously verify or ground their outputs in current scientific literature—a critical capability for academic review tasks.

Sixth, all models exhibited a tendency to produce generic or overly polite content, even when explicitly prompted to provide domain-specific critique. This limitation reflects a broader issue in LLM design: the absence of epistemic grounding and critical reasoning capabilities required for high-level academic engagement. These deficits were particularly evident in Microsoft Copilot and, to a lesser extent, in ChatGPT.

Finally, ethical and pedagogical concerns remain unresolved. The study raises important questions regarding overreliance on AI-generated insights, the potential erosion of critical thinking skills, and the risk of automation bias in academic workflows. While Claude demonstrated promising tutoring behavior, all models required continuous human oversight, underscoring the importance of hybrid human–AI educational strategies and the development of rigorous governance frameworks.

Addressing these limitations in future research—through larger, more diverse samples, integration with academic databases, and the adoption of mixed-method evaluation frameworks—will be essential not only to validate the present findings but also to realize the full pedagogical potential of LLMs in academic settings.

7 Conclusions

This study addressed the emerging challenge of evaluating Large Language Models (LLMs) as academic tutors within structured educational protocols. Focusing on their ability to facilitate a literature review on machine learning applications for financial crime detection, the research employed a rigorous 14-step interaction framework grounded in Mollick's AI role taxonomy and the ram protocol. The primary objective was to assess the pedagogical effectiveness of three LLMs—ChatGPT 5.3, Microsoft Copilot, and Claude 3.5 Haiku—as collaborative instructional agents rather than mere content generators.

The findings revealed substantial differences in tutoring performance. Claude 3.5 consistently demonstrated strong protocol adherence, personalized interaction, and critical engagement, distinguishing itself as the most pedagogically competent model. ChatGPT, while technically proficient, showed limited dialogic depth and occasional deviations from structured prompting. Microsoft Copilot underperformed across multiple dimensions, struggling with both protocol compliance and the delivery of substantive feedback. Despite these disparities, all models successfully generated complete SWOT analyses, albeit with varying degrees of instructional quality and critical reflection.

These results highlight both the potential and the limitations of integrating LLMs into human-centered educational contexts. When embedded within clearly defined interactional frameworks, next-generation models such as Claude can begin to approximate aspects of expert tutoring, offering scalable and adaptive support for complex academic tasks. However, ongoing challenges in personalization, critical reasoning, and domain alignment—particularly in Copilot and ChatGPT—underscore the necessity of sustained human oversight and intentional instructional design.

The study's limitations include a small, homogeneous participant group, reliance on qualitative assessment methods, and the use of constrained LLM configurations without access to real-time academic retrieval tools. Nevertheless, these constraints do not undermine the observed patterns in interaction quality and pedagogical engagement.

Future research should extend this investigation to larger and more diverse learner populations, incorporate performance-based metrics, and examine the effects of fine-tuning LLMs on domain-specific educational content. Longitudinal studies assessing the impact of AI-mediated tutoring on student learning trajectories will also be essential to fully evaluate the instructional value of these systems.

In conclusion, while LLMs are not a substitute for human educators, their structured and critically engaged deployment—particularly in the case of advanced models—offers a promising pathway for pedagogical augmentation. As educational institutions navigate the integration of AI, studies such as this one provide a nuanced, evidence-based foundation for developing hybrid human–AI pedagogies that emphasize structure, reflection, and learner agency.

Acknowledgments. We would like to thank Federico Cabitza for his guidance and support throughout the development of this study.

References

1. Alsobeh, A., Woodward, B.: AI as a partner in learning: a novel student-in-the-loop framework for enhanced student engagement and outcomes in higher education. In: Proceedings of the 24th Annual Conference on Information Technology Education, pp. 171–172. SIGITE '23, Association for Computing Machinery, New York, NY, USA (2023). https://doi.org/10.1145/3585059.3611405
2. Badenhorst, C.M.: Literature reviews, citations and intertextuality in graduate student writing. J. Further High. Educ. **43**(2), 263–275 (2019). https://doi.org/10.1080/0309877X.2017.1359504
3. Brender, J., El-Hamamsy, L., Mondada, F., Bumbacher, E.: Who's helping who? When students use ChatGPT to engage in practice lab sessions. In: Artificial Intelligence in Education. AIED 2024. LNCS, vol. 14829, pp. 235–249. Springer, Cham (2024). https://doi.org/10.1007/978-3-031-64302-6_17
4. Cabitza, F., Campagner, A., Sconfienza, L.M.: Studying human-AI collaboration protocols: the case of the Kasparov's law in radiological double reading. Health Inf. Sci. Syst. **9**(1), 1–20 (2021). https://doi.org/10.1007/s13755-021-00138-8
5. Cabitza, F., et al.: Rams, hounds and white boxes: investigating human-AI collaboration protocols in medical diagnosis. Artif. Intell. Med. **138**, 102506 (2023). https://doi.org/10.1016/j.artmed.2023.102506
6. Castillo-Segura, P., Alario-Hoyos, C., Kloos, C.D., Fernández Panadero, C.: Leveraging the potential of generative ai to accelerate systematic literature reviews: an example in the area of educational technology. In: 2023 World Engineering Education Forum - Global Engineering Deans Council (WEEF-GEDC), pp. 1–8 (2023). https://doi.org/10.1109/WEEF-GEDC59520.2023.10344098
7. Chang, D.H., Lin, M.P.C., Hajian, S., Wang, Q.Q.: Educational design principles of using AI chatbot that supports self-regulated learning in education: goal setting, feedback, and personalization. Sustainability **15**(17), 12921 (2023). https://doi.org/10.3390/su151712921
8. Cuéllar, O., Contero, M., Hincapié, M.: Personalized and timely feedback in online education: enhancing learning with deep learning and large language models. Multimodal Technol. Interact. **9**(5), 45 (2025). https://doi.org/10.3390/mti9050045
9. Gan, W., Qi, Z., Wu, J., Lin, J.C.W.: Large language models in education: vision and opportunities. In: 2023 IEEE International Conference on Big Data (BigData), pp. 4776–4785 (2023). https://doi.org/10.1109/BigData59044.2023.10386291
10. García-Méndez, S., de Arriba-Pérez, F., Somoza-López, M.D.C.: A review on the use of large language models as virtual tutors. Sci. Educ. **34**, 877–892 (2025). https://doi.org/10.1007/s11191-024-00530-2
11. Jeon, J., Lee, S.: Large language models in education: a focus on the complementary relationship between human teachers and ChatGPT. Educ. Inf. Technol. **28**, 15873–15892 (2023). https://doi.org/10.1007/s10639-023-11834-1
12. Kasneci, E., et al.: ChatGPT for good? On opportunities and challenges of large language models for education. Learn. Individ. Differ. **103**, 102274 (2023). https://doi.org/10.1016/j.lindif.2023.102274
13. Kim, J., Yu, S., Detrick, R., Li, N.: Exploring students' perspectives on generative AI-assisted academic writing. Educ. Inf. Technol. **30**, 1265–1300 (2025). https://doi.org/10.1007/s10639-024-12878-7
14. Kothari, D.K., Noel Newton Fernando, O.: Enhancing human-computer interaction through AI: a study on ChatGPT in educational environments. In: 2024 IEEE Conference on Artificial Intelligence (CAI), pp. 500–503 (2024). https://doi.org/10.1109/CAI59869.2024.00100

15. Koubaa, A., Boulila, W., Ghouti, L., Alzahem, A., Latif, S.: Exploring ChatGPT capabilities and limitations: a survey. IEEE Access **11**, 118698–118721 (2023). https://doi.org/10.1109/ACCESS.2023.3326474

16. Li, P.H., Lee, H.Y., Lin, C.J., Wang, W.S., Huang, Y.M.: InquiryGPT: augmenting ChatGPT for enhancing inquiry-based learning in stem education. J. Educ. Comput. Res. **62**(8), 1937–1966 (2025). https://doi.org/10.1177/07356331241289824

17. Lieberum, J.L., et al.: Large language models for conducting systematic reviews: on the rise, but not yet ready for use-a scoping review. J. Clin. Epidemiol. **181**, 111746 (2025). https://doi.org/10.1016/j.jclinepi.2025.111746

18. Maher, M.L., Ventura, D., Magerko, B.: The grounding problem: an approach to the integration of cognitive and generative models. Proc. AAAI Symp. Ser. **2**(1), 320–325 (2024). https://doi.org/10.1609/aaaiss.v2i1.27695

19. Malterud, K., Siersma, V.D., Guassora, A.D.: Sample size in qualitative interview studies: guided by information power. Qual. Health Res. **26**(13), 1753–1760 (2016). https://doi.org/10.1177/1049732315617444. pMID: 26613970

20. Meyer, J.G., et al.: ChatGPT and large language models in academia: opportunities and challenges. BioData Mining **16**(1), 20 (2023). https://doi.org/10.1186/s13040-023-00339-9

21. Molenaar, I., de Mooij, S., Azevedo, R., Bannert, M., Järvelä, S., Gašević, D.: Measuring self-regulated learning and the role of ai: Five years of research using multimodal multichannel data. Comput. Hum. Behav. **139**, 107540 (2023). https://doi.org/10.1016/j.chb.2022.107540

22. Mollick, E., Mollick, L.: Assigning AI: seven approaches for students, with prompts (2023)

23. Mollick, E., Mollick, L.: Instructors as innovators: a future-focused approach to new ai learning opportunities, with prompts. arXiv preprint arXiv:2407.05181 (2024)

24. Ortega-Moody, J., et al.: SWOT analysis of artificial intelligence in education. In: 2025 IEEE Engineering Education World Conference (EDUNINE), pp. 1–6 (2025). https://doi.org/10.1109/EDUNINE62377.2025.10981366

25. Scherbakov, D., Hubig, N., Jansari, V., Bakumenko, A., Lenert, L.A.: The emergence of large language models as tools in literature reviews: a large language model-assisted systematic review. J. Am. Med. Inform. Assoc. **32**(6), 1071–1086 (2025). https://doi.org/10.1093/jamia/ocaf063

26. Schön, E.M., Neumann, M., Hofmann-Stölting, C., Baeza-Yates, R., Rauschenberger, M.: How are AI assistants changing higher education? Front. Comput. Sci. **5**, 1208550 (2023)

27. Shahzad, T., Mazhar, T., Tariq, M.U., et al.: A comprehensive review of large language models: issues and solutions in learning environments. Discov. Sustain. **6**, 27 (2025). https://doi.org/10.1007/s43621-025-00815-8

28. Sharma, S., Mittal, P., Kumar, M., et al.: The role of large language models in personalized learning: a systematic review of educational impact. Discov. Sustain. **6**, 243 (2025). https://doi.org/10.1007/s43621-025-01094-z

29. Söderström, U., Hedström, E., Lambertsson, K., Mejtoft, T.: ChatGPT in education: teachers' and students' views. In: Proceedings of the European Conference on Cognitive Ergonomics 2024. ECCE '24, Association for Computing Machinery, New York, NY, USA (2024). https://doi.org/10.1145/3673805.3673828

30. Urban, M., et al.: ChatGPT improves creative problem-solving performance in university students: an experimental study. Comput. Educ. **215**, 105031 (2024). https://doi.org/10.1016/j.compedu.2024.105031

31. Wang, W.S., Lin, C.J., Lee, H.Y., et al.: Enhancing self-regulated learning and higher-order thinking skills in virtual reality: the impact of ChatGPT-integrated feedback aids. Educ. Inf. Technol. (2025). https://doi.org/10.1007/s10639-025-13557-x

32. Weng, X., Gu, M.M., Xia, Q., Chiu, T.K.: Swot analysis of AL empowered entrepreneurship education: insights from digital learners in higher education. Thinking Skills Creativity **56**, 101763 (2025). https://doi.org/10.1016/j.tsc.2025.101763

33. Widono, S., Mulyadi, Saddhono, K., Nurhasanah, F., Nugraheni, A.S.C., Legowo, B.: A strategic design of personalized based learning system for improving the experience of outcome based education. In: 2024 4th International Conference on Advance Computing and Innovative Technologies in Engineering (ICACITE), pp. 1149–1154 (2024). https://doi.org/10.1109/ICACITE60783.2024.10616811

34. Xu, J., Zhan, Z., Liang, S.: The role of ai agents in the reconfiguration of interdisciplinary educational design: an examination of applied practices and outcomes. In: Proceedings of the 2024 9th International Conference on Distance Education and Learning, pp. 1–9. ICDEL '24, Association for Computing Machinery, New York, NY, USA (2024). https://doi.org/10.1145/3675812.3675833

35. Xu, X., Wang, X., Zhang, Y., Zheng, R.: Applying ChatGPT to tackle the side effects of personal learning environments from learner and learning perspective: an interview of experts in higher education. PLoS ONE **19**(1), e0295646 (2024). https://doi.org/10.1371/journal.pone.0295646

36. Yan, L., et al.: Practical and ethical challenges of large language models in education: a systematic scoping review. Br. J. Edu. Technol. **55**(1), 90–112 (2024). https://doi.org/10.1111/bjet.13370

37. Zhong, T., Cai, C., Zhu, G., Ma, M.: Enhancing the analysis of interdisciplinary learning quality with GPT models: fine-tuning and knowledge-empowered approaches. In: Olney, A.M., Chounta, I.A., Liu, Z., Santos, O.C., Bittencourt, I.I. (eds.) Artificial Intelligence in Education. Posters and Late Breaking Results, Workshops and Tutorials, Industry and Innovation Tracks, Practitioners, Doctoral Consortium and Blue Sky. AIED 2024, Communications in Computer and Information Science, vol. 2151. Springer, Cham (2024). https://doi.org/10.1007/978-3-031-64312-5_19

Facial Recognition AI Incident Reporting: An NLP Analysis

Aimee Kendall Roundtree[(✉)]

Texas State University, San Marcos, TX 78666, USA
`akr@txstate.edu`

Abstract. Facial recognition technology (FRT) is an artificial intelligence that has raised many ethical questions. This study examines real incidents involving facial recognition technology to better understand these problems. Natural language processing methods analyzed the language and emotions in the incident reports to find patterns in how people were harmed and what ethical issues were raised. The analysis shows that most of the incidents had a negative tone. Many involved unfair treatments of minorities or errors made by the technology. Certain ethical concerns—like bias, safety, and privacy—reoccurred often and have become more common since 2016. Most of the language used to describe the incidents was serious and analytical, not emotional. These results suggest that facial recognition technology can cause real harm if not designed and used carefully. Worry about these issues has persisted and grown over time. The study helps connect real-world problems to what researchers and designers have said about trust, fairness, and privacy. In conclusion, facial recognition can be useful, but it requires stronger guidelines and better design to protect people. This study shows why fairness, oversight, and accountability are so important as we keep using AI in more parts of life.

Keywords: AI · Facial Recognition · Incident Reporting · Natural Language Processing

1 Introduction

The rapid deployment of AI technologies, particularly facial recognition systems, has resulted in numerous incidents affecting individuals and communities. This analysis examines a dataset of AI-related incidents through Natural Language Processing (NLP), sentiment analysis, and statistical techniques. This project identifies key trends, sentiments, and demographic impacts by focusing on the titles, summaries, and harmed parties. The study highlights the social and ethical implications of AI deployments, offering insights into how these technologies disproportionately affect certain groups. Through an analysis of FRT AI-related incidents using Natural Language Processing (NLP), sentiment analysis, and statistical methods, this study identifies key trends in AI-related harms, revealing the urgent need for regulatory oversight and ethical governance to mitigate risks associated with facial recognition technology. The analysis reveals that

J. Wei et al. (Eds.): HCII 2025, LNCS 16346, pp. 214–225, 2026.
https://doi.org/10.1007/978-3-032-13187-4_15

marginalized groups, particularly Black individuals and social media users, are disproportionately affected by the negative consequences of facial recognition technology. Furthermore, the study highlights the increasing prevalence of negative sentiment surrounding FRT incidents over time, suggesting growing public awareness and concern. The findings underscore the necessity for improved regulatory measures, fairness-driven AI development, and ethical frameworks to ensure that FRT serves society equitably and responsibly.

2 Background

Facial recognition technology (FRT) has rapidly evolved over the past decade, used in law enforcement, education, healthcare, emergency response, and more [1]. Significant ethical, technical, and human factors challenge that accompany the growth demand careful attention from engineers, policymakers, and researchers. For example, facial recognition payment (FRP) promises enhanced convenience and efficiency compared to traditional payment methods. However, concerns about data privacy and security persist. Research indicates that trust dimensions—namely competence, contractual, and goodwill trust— are pivotal in mitigating privacy concerns and promoting sustained user engagement [2]. Additionally, while technology and user vulnerabilities can intensify privacy concerns, technology anxiety itself may not directly escalate these issues, pointing to complex psychological dynamics in technology acceptance [3].

There are advantages to facial recognition deployments. For example, biometric facial recognition benefits tourism and smart home environments. User-centered evaluations require robust functionality and responsiveness that are crucial for long-term usability [4, 5]. Advances in artificial intelligence have enhanced these systems by enabling nuanced facial expression analysis. However, there is a need for sophisticated feature extraction and culturally sensitive classification techniques [6–8]. FRT limitations pose lingering problems. Privacy violations, algorithmic bias, and the disproportionate impact on minorities highlight the necessity for robust ethical frameworks and comprehensive codes of ethics [1, 9]. Such frameworks are essential for ensuring transparency and accountability in system design and fostering trust.

User expectations of FRT vary widely depending on the context. For example, in educational settings, while some users appreciate the convenience and potential safety benefits, others express deep concerns regarding privacy, data management, and biased outcomes [10]. Reviews of systems deployed among young adults and adolescents point to limitations—such as small sample sizes and inadequate ethnic representation—that challenge the generalizability of findings, thus emphasizing the need for comprehensive usability studies and longitudinal assessments [11]. Industry–academic partnerships yield valuable user experience data that help shape evidence-based guidelines for FRT deployment. They ensure that technological solutions are both technically robust and socially responsible [12]. This integrative approach is especially critical in high-stakes settings like emergency response, where rapid and accurate identification can enhance crisis management and resource allocation, though it also introduces additional challenges regarding data privacy, system robustness, and ethical governance [13].

The literature called for improving methodological and ethical gaps in facial recognition technology by implementing larger, more diverse, and longitudinal studies to capture the dynamic nature of facial features over time, improve testing generalizability, and track the evolution from initial intention to sustained usage [2, 13, 14]. In parallel, ethical frameworks must be refined to incorporate broader stakeholder perspectives, enhance transparency, and protect vulnerable populations [9, 10]. Robust industry–academic partnerships can translate user-centered research into practical guidelines, particularly in high-stakes settings like emergency response, where rapid, accurate identification is critical [12–14]. Integrating user experience methodologies with rigorous technical testing is essential to balance innovation with ethical responsibility [1]. Moreover, expanding theoretical models to include psychological factors—such as technology anxiety and dimensions of vulnerability—can yield a better understanding of user resistance [3]. Finally, incorporating AI techniques in facial expression recognition and conducting cross-cultural studies can enhance system accuracy, cultural adaptability, and tailor solutions to diverse contexts, including fintech, smart homes, and tourism [4–8].

Furthermore, questions linger from the literature: How do incidents involving facial recognition technology reflect broader ethical concerns? What trends emerge from facial recognition technology-related incidents? This study provides a structured examination of the societal and ethical consequences of facial recognition AI, which directly informs gaps identified in prior research. Specifically, the study uses NLP and statistical techniques to analyze FRT-AI-related incidents across longitudinal and diverse datasets to capture dynamic changes in FRT-AI deployment and its ethical impact over time.

3   Methods

This study employs a dataset of FRT AI-related ethical principles sourced from the AI Incident Database (https://incidentdatabase.ai/), a repository that reports incidents where AI systems cause harm or near harm. This database, maintained in collaboration with the Partnership on AI, is a comprehensive resource for understanding the real-world impacts of AI deployments with 5662 reports total.

The ethical categories utilized in this study were drawn from PricewaterhouseCoopers (PwC), adapted by Díaz-Rodríguez et al. into a framework for responsible AI [15, 16]. The categories include epistemic principles that establish fundamental requirements for ethical assessments, interpretability to ensure AI systems are understandable, reliability to guarantee consistency in AI outputs, accountability, data privacy, human agency, safety, fairness, transparency, organizational practices, bias detection and mitigation, robust design, continuous monitoring, and governance frameworks.

Natural language processing was applied to extract and analyze keywords and frequently occurring terms, including using the Linguistic Inquiry and Word Count (LIWC), Python, and Orange. Sentiment analysis was conducted on the text to determine whether the tone was positive, negative, or neutral. The analysis relied on tokenization, word frequency counts, and sentiment classification to comprehensively understand the data.

All NLP strategies included performing text preprocessing (cleaning and tokenizing the text, removing irrelevant characters, punctuation, and extra whitespace, converting text to lowercase for uniformity, and tokenizing it into individual words and phrases) to transform unstructured textual data into structured data for analysis. Classification algorithms were applied using transformer-based NLP models such as a fine-tuned BERT

(Bidirectional Encoder Representations from Transformers) model to capture context and semantic nuances by using deep bidirectional training, Pre-trained models were fine-tuned on labeled examples provided by the ethical categories to understand the context and semantics. The model was tasked with predicting the most relevant ethical category for each of the rows of text based on semantic similarity and contextual understanding. Model predictions were verified through manual sampling for accuracy and reliability. Cross-validation strategy was used to further assess and refine performance.

LIWC uses computational analysis of text to assess psychological, emotional, and linguistic attributes and a predefined dictionary of words categorized into various linguistic, psychological, and thematic dimensions. The program processes input text by calculating the percentage of words that fall into these categories, allowing for an assessment of underlying cognitive and emotional states. Orange was also used to transform textual representations into numerical features for classification, with embeddings using FastText to capture semantic relationships between ethical concepts. The embeddings were verified through data visualization and alignment with categorical labels to ensure semantic integrity. A logistic regression classifier was trained on the processed dataset to predict the category of new AI ethical principles and cross-validation using a five-fold method within the orange framework. AI ethical principles outside the training set from non-FRT samples were introduced for classification. These were passed through the logistic regression model for prediction. The NLP and Orange processes yielded two layers of codes, both of which were calculated in the code count. VADER (Valence Aware Dictionary and sEntiment Reasoner) was used for sentiment analysis to identify positive and negative words, punctuation, and even emoticons and assign positive, negative, neutral, and compound scores ranging from -1 to $+1$.

Associations between variables were examined using Pearson correlation analysis to measure the linear relationship between continuous variables, producing an R value (correlation coefficient) and a P value (statistical significance). Positive R values (0 to 1) indicate a direct relationship (as one variable increases, the other tends to increase). Negative R values (-1 to 0) indicate an inverse relationship (as one variable increases, the other tends to decrease). Values close to 0 suggest a weak or no relationship. P-values of 0.05 or less suggest statistical significance. Pairwise correlations were computed for all variables.

4 Results

Of the 5662 total reports, 202 involved facial recognition technology (FRT AI). Table 1 presents the top 10 most frequent code categories appearing in both coding iterations between Orange and Python.

The most frequently used code is **Bias Detection and Mitigation** (n = **159**) followed by **Safety** (n = **62),** and **Reliability** (n = **55**). Other codes, such as **Interpretability** and **Value Sharing**, have lower frequencies but still play a notable role in the dataset. Some codes like **Bias Detection, Mitigation** and **Reliability** appear more often in recent years, while others like **Fairness** are less frequent.

Over time, **Bias Detection and Mitigation** increased in usage from 2013 to a peak in 2018. **Safety** showed consistent presence in 2016 and peaking in both 2016 and

Table 1. Code Frequencies and Sentiment.

Code	#	Definition	Example	pos	neg	neu	comp
Bias Detection, Mitigation	159	identifying and correcting unfair biases in AI	*Skating Rink's Facial Recognition Cameras Misidentified Black Teenager as Banned Troublemaker*	*0.0246*	*0.1415*	*0.8339*	*−0.3068*
Safety	62	ensuring AI systems do not harm users or society during use	*Live facial recognition is tracking kids suspected of being criminals*	*0.0224*	*0.1349*	*0.8428*	*−0.3075*
Reliability	55	AI operating consistently, safely, and as intended over time	*XPeng Motors Fined For Illegal Collection of Consumers' Faces Using Facial Recognition Cameras*	*0.032*	*0.1738*	*0.7941*	*−0.2888*
Interpretability	35	AI systems clearly explaining their logic and decision-making	*Uganda Deployed Huawei's Facial Recognition to Monitor Political Opposition and Protests*	*0.0489*	*0.1089*	*0.8422*	*−0.1733*
Value Sharing	17	promoting shared values and goals across teams and leadership	*Arrested by AI: Police ignore standards after facial recognition matches*	*0.0113*	*0.1644*	*0.8244*	*−0.3084*
Accountability	15	identifying who is responsible for AI decisions and impacts	*Robbers Accessed Drugged Gay Men's Bank Accounts Using Their Phones' Facial Recognition*	*0.0356*	*0.1218*	*0.8425*	*−0.2352*

(continued)

Table 1. (*continued*)

Code	#	Definition	Example	pos	neg	neu	comp
Data Privacy	14	respecting and protecting users' rights and personal data	*Illinois Residents File Class Action Lawsuit Against Facial Recognition Technology Companies for Allegedly Violating BIPA*	*0.0234*	*0.1901*	*0.7865*	*−0.4389*
Fairness	12	AI treating people equitably, avoiding discrimination	*Facial Recognition in Remote Learning Software Reportedly Failed to Recognize a Black Student's Face*	*0.0211*	*0.1371*	*0.8417*	*−0.3331*
Organizational Practices	12	integrating AI ethics in an organization	*Rite Aid faces 5-year facial recognition ban*	*0.021*	*0.151*	*0.828*	*−0.2042*
Impact Assessment	5	evaluating ethical, legal, and social impacts	*Facial Recognition Program in São Paulo Metro Stations Suspended for Illegal and Disproportionate Violation of Citizens' Right to Privacy*	*0.0588*	*0.097*	*0.844*	*−0.2249*

2018. **Reliability** and **Interpretability** were more commonly used in the 2016–2018 range, with **Reliability** notably peaking in 2017. Emerging codes like **Accountability**, **Data Privacy**, and **Value Sharing** began appearing in 2017–2018 at lower frequencies (Fig. 1).

Two topic categorization models yielded two layers of ethical codes. A few code pairs exhibited statistically significant relationships. One of the strongest findings is the **negative correlation** between **Bias Detection and Mitigation** and **Interpretability** ($r = -0.348$, $p < .0001$) and **Reliability** ($r = -0.292$, $p < .0001$). The more interpretability and reliability were coded, the less likely bias was coded. Similarly, **Bias Detection and Mitigation** also negatively correlate with **Accountability** ($r = -0.221$, $p = .0016$).

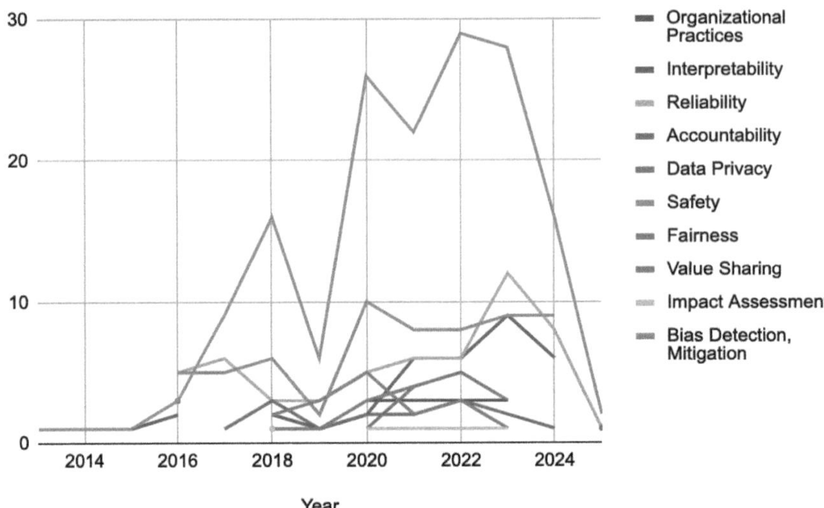

Fig. 1. Code Frequencies Over Time.

The more accountability was coded, the less bias was coded. On the other hand, **Bias Detection** and **Mitigation** and **Value Sharing** showed a weak positive relationship (r = 0.047, p = 0.506), but this was not statistically significant.

Regarding sentiment analysis, **Data Privacy** scored the most negative overall tone. **Fairness** and **Bias Detection and Mitigation** also lean negative, with slightly higher positive or neutral tone balancing them out. Their compound scores reflect a more mixed tone but still skew critical or emotionally tense. A few codes, including **Interpretability** and **Value Sharing** display higher compound scores, with a more neutral or slightly positive tone, though still low overall in positivity. Across almost all codes, positive sentiment remains low (Fig. 2).

Topics like **Accountability**, **Bias Detection**, and **Reliability** consistently show moderate to strong negative compound scores, particularly in years 2019 and 2020. Some codes such as **Interpretability**, **Fairness**, and **Safety** had moments of slightly more positive or balanced sentiment, but still trend negative or neutral. The year 2023 marks a rare increase in positive tone for **Impact Assessment** (0.274) and a positive compound score. Positive sentiment was rare and usually small in magnitude.

In **2016 and 2018**, negative sentiment scores increased (0.1199 and 0.1281 respectively), with corresponding dips in compound sentiment (−0.2938 and −0.2685). In contrast, **2017** had a slightly less negative sentiment (compound score of −0.0231). Positive sentiment remained consistently **low across all years**, with values generally below 0.05. The highest average was in **2016 (0.048)**. The dataset exhibits a minimal presence of explicitly positive emotional tone. Negative sentiment shows greater variability and prominence than positive sentiment. Peaks occurred in **2016 (0.120)** and **2018 (0.128)**. These spikes align with lower compound scores. Neutral sentiment consistently dominated. The highest neutrality was recorded in **2015 (1.000)**, though this may reflect a small sample size for that year. Neutral sentiment dipped slightly in years like **2016 and 2018** when negative sentiment increased, but still remained the most

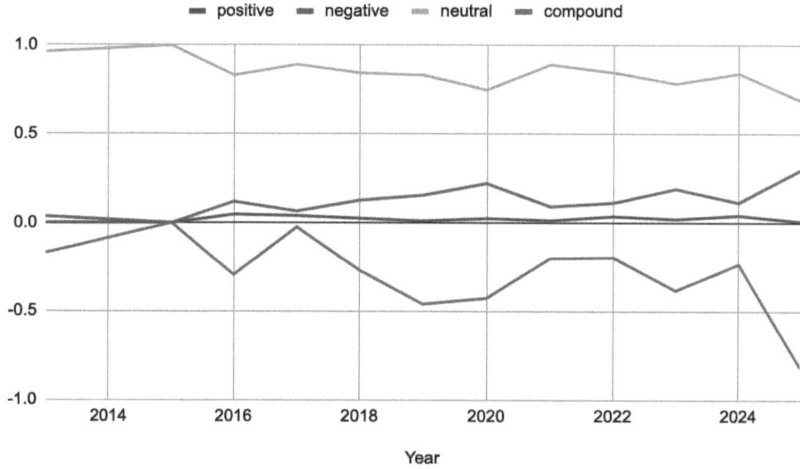

Fig. 2. Sentiment Over Time.

prevalent tone throughout. The compound sentiment score, a composite reflecting overall tone, was **predominantly negative** across most years. The lowest compound score appeared in **2016 (−0.294)**, reinforcing the interpretation of heightened negativity in that period. **2017** showed a near-neutral score **(−0.023)**, marking a temporary softening in emotional tone. On average, the compound sentiment suggests that the dataset leaned **moderately negative overall**.

LIWC analysis yielded several insights. Interpretability shows a high Analytic score (81.44) or a formal, cognitively dense writing style. Moderate levels of Social (12.84) and Cognition (17.12) words and low Authentic (21.75) and Tone (18.53) suggest a formal yet slightly emotionally restrained style with moderate engagement. Reliability exhibits the highest Analytic score (89.66) and a strong Clout (60.89), 0r a confident, structured tone. However, its Authentic score is relatively low (16.50), so a more detached tone. Cognition (16.90) and Social (12.25) terms are moderate, and Tone is low (14.17), and Perception is limited (5.58), consistent with an analytical but emotionally neutral style. Bias Detection, Mitigation reflects a more balanced profile with moderate Cognition (18.43) and strong Culture language (12.54). Its Authentic score is highest among all codes (70.26), and Clout is lowest (21.12), indicating a more questioning, tentative, or personally expressive style despite low emotional tone (20.23). Safety has the highest amount of Culture (28.07) and Cognition (19.52), with moderately low Authentic (22.51) and Clout (63.20), implying a neutral, analytical voice. Emotional tone is low (13.82). Fariness is the most analytically dense (Analytic = 95.58) with strong Culture (26.52) references. It offers moderate Authentic (13.98) and Social (9.42) content, suggesting complexity and narrative richness rather than emotional or personal engagement (Fig. 3).

In the early years (2013–2018), Analytic scores remain consistently high across all years, especially in 2013 (98.09) and 2015 (97.37), so highly structured, logical writing styles dominate earlier reports. Authenticity starts low in 2013 (9.43), gradually increases, peaking in 2018 (20.82), which suggests a tendency toward more personal or expressive language. Overall emotional tone was low, but Tone and Affect indicators

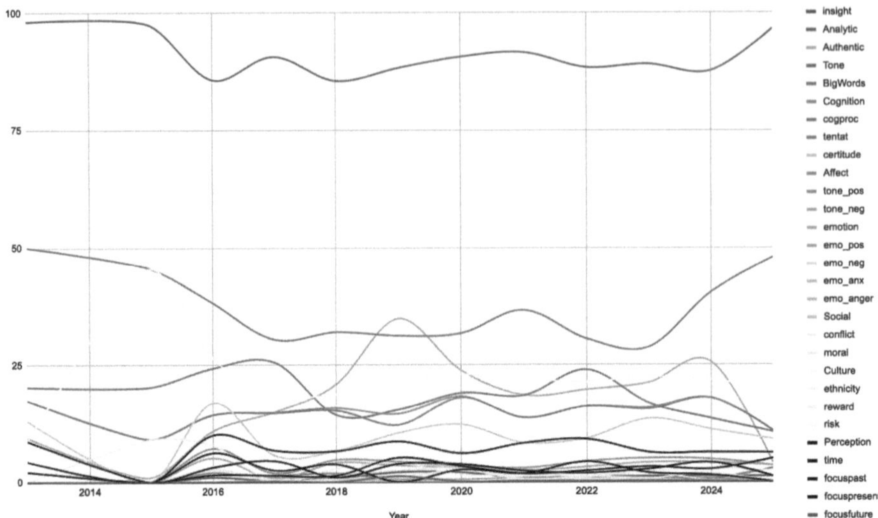

Fig. 3. Linguistic Patterns Over Time.

slightly increased in later years. There was a mild rise in emotional expression. Variables like Cognition, Insight, and Perception increase after 2015, indicating greater analytical and observational engagement in more recent reports. Focus on past events is prominent in earlier years, with relatively low scores for present and future focus, reflecting the retrospective nature of many incidents.

5 Discussion and Conclusion

The most frequent ethical concern in incident reports of FRT AI used in public settings is bias detection and mitigation. Safety and reliability are also consistently reported concerns. These codes reflect increasing attention to the risks FRT poses to marginalized groups, especially black and brown communities and online users. Tendency to operate with little transparency or accountability also emerged.

Most incidents involving FRT are described in a negative tone. Compound sentiment scores are largely negative or neutral, with very little positivity detected in any year. Codes like data privacy, fairness, and bias detection carry strong negative emotional tones, signaling public concern and dissatisfaction. These patterns are especially prominent in 2016 and 2018, which saw higher-than-average negativity. LIWC analysis confirms that most reports used formal, analytic language, with a rise in authenticity and emotional content after 2015. Incident reports have become more personal and expressive over time, aligning with growing societal concern.

These findings help explain how public sentiment and ethical discourse around facial recognition technology have evolved. The study identifies clear emotional, psychological, and linguistic trends that illustrate increasing unease and growing calls for reform. These patterns underscore the importance of adopting stronger regulatory frameworks and ethical standards to guide FRT-AI development and deployment. Ethical concepts like fairness, accountability, and transparency are not just theoretical concerns but are consistently raised in real-world incidents.

This analysis addresses key questions raised in the literature. It helps explain how real-world harms associated with FRT align with broader ethical concerns. It also shows that despite technological advancements, bias, reliability, and safety continue to be major sources of harm and public anxiety. The rising emotional and cognitive content in reports suggests that people are not only becoming more aware of FRT's effects but also more engaged in questioning its legitimacy. These insights provide clear, data-backed answers to lingering questions about public trust, ethical risks, and the long-term social consequences of FRT.

Prior literature identified several pressing issues with FRT-AI, including data privacy violations, algorithmic bias, inadequate representation, and the disproportionate harm to marginalized communities [1, 9]. This study confirms prior findings, particularly concerns about Bias Detection and Mitigation, Safety, and Reliability. Existing FRT deployments often fail to meet ethical standards for fairness and consistency. Prior literature established the psychological complexity of technology acceptance; vulnerabilities heighten privacy concerns and trust is crucial for user adoption [2, 3]. This study confirms these findings. Negative sentiment surrounded codes like Data Privacy, Fairness, and Accountability, which reflect skepticism toward FRT's trustworthiness and transparency.

Prior findings highlight the importance of interpretability and culturally sensitive AI design. However, this study found a negative correlation between Bias Detection and Mitigation and Interpretability, which might mean that systems designed for clarity and reliability may still exhibit bias or that bias incident reporting may not contain sufficient explanatory context. Prior literature calls for integrating ethical governance into industry and academic practices [12–14], and in this study, emerging codes like Organizational Practices and Impact Assessment appear infrequently in the dataset, suggesting that institutional ethical oversight is still underdeveloped in real-world applications.

Prior literature emphasizes the need for robust, user-centered evaluations in domains like tourism and smart homes [4, 5], yet the tone of the reports studied was mixed rather than optimistic (mostly negative or neutral). Incident reports on Bias Detection and Mitigation had the highest Authentic score–a more expressive, personal voice. Public discourse and reported experiences are still dominated by harm, not benefit.

Prior studies request larger, more diverse, and longitudinal studies [10, 11]. However, these results reveal gaps in coverage and representation, particularly with incidents that show limited positive sentiment and noticeable retrospective focus. While the literature provides a theoretical foundation for ethical FRT deployment, the lived realities captured in the dataset expose a persistent mismatch between ethical intentions and technological implementation. The need for more balanced data, better institutional accountability, and sustained public engagement remain.

The study contributes to the literature by bridging ethical theory with real-world data. Many past studies call for more empirical, user-centered evidence about FRT harms. This project responds by offering a longitudinal, structured, statistically grounded view of how FRT incidents reflect broader ethical challenges over time. It also incorporates psychological, linguistic, and sentiment-based data to explain how these systems affect people at emotional and systemic levels.

However, the study has limitations. Incident data may not be comprehensive, and the database may be biased toward English-language or high-profile cases. Sentiment scores rely on automated tools that may not fully capture nuanced or culturally specific language. Some codes may have been underreported due to the limitations of keyword-based classification or model misinterpretation. Manual validation helped improve accuracy, but some error remains possible.

Future research should expand the dataset to include more diverse sources, including non-English incident reports and user testimonies. Additional qualitative research, such as interviews or ethnographic studies, could provide deeper insights into personal and community-level impacts. Further technical refinement of the models could also improve code accuracy and cross-cultural adaptability. Researchers should continue tracking how ethical concerns evolve as facial recognition becomes more embedded in everyday life, especially in education, healthcare, and smart technology environments, which will help ensure AI systems are developed and used in ways that are just, transparent, and inclusive.

Acknowledgments. This research was sponsored by research gifts from the NEC Foundation and State Farm Foundation.

References

1. Roundtree, A.K.: Ethics and facial recognition technology: an integrative review. In: 2021 3rd World Symposium on Artificial Intelligence (WSAI), pp. 10–19. IEEE (2021)
2. Lee, J.C., Bi, L., Liu, H.: User stickiness to facial recognition payment technology: insights from Sako's trust typology, privacy concerns, and a cross-cultural context. Humanit. Soc. Sci. Commun. **11**(1), 1–15 (2024)
3. Zhang, X., Zhang, Z.: Leaking my face via payment: unveiling the influence of technology anxiety, vulnerabilities, and privacy concerns on user resistance to facial recognition payment. Telecomm. Policy **48**(3), 102703 (2024)
4. Khoshaim, L.S., Yüksel, S., Dinçer, H.: Evaluating a user-centered environment-friendly mobile phone app for tourists and residents using facial-recognition software. Sustainability **15**(20), 14689 (2023)
5. Hizam, S.M., Ahmed, W., Fahad, M., Akter, H., Sentosa, I., Ali, J.: User behavior assessment towards biometric facial recognition system: a SEM-neural network approach. In: Arai, K. (ed.) Advances in Information and Communication, FICC 2021. AISC, vol. 1364, pp. 1037–1050. Springer, Cham (2021). https://doi.org/10.1007/978-3-030-73103-8_75
6. Singh, S.: Emotion evaluation from facial expression recognition using AI techniques: a review. BSSS J. Comput. XI **1**, 1–17 (2020)
7. Bakiaraj, M., Subramani, B.: A Methodological and Systematic Survey of AI-Driven Approaches and Applications for Facial Expression Recognition
8. Dalvi, C., Rathod, M., Patil, S., Gite, S., Kotecha, K.: A survey of AI-based facial emotion recognition: features, ML & DL techniques, age-wise datasets and future directions. IEEE Access **9**, 165806–165840 (2021)
9. Roundtree, A.K.: Facial recognition technology codes of ethics: content analysis and review. In: 2022 IEEE International Professional Communication Conference (ProComm), pp. 211–220. IEEE (2022)

10. Roundtree, A.: User expectations of facial recognition in schools and universities: mixed methods analysis. In: Usability and User Experience, vol. 110, no. 110 (2023)
11. Kendall Roundtree, A.: Testing facial recognition software for young adults and adolescents: an integrative review. In: Moallem, A. (ed.) HCI for Cybersecurity, Privacy and Trust, HCII 2021. LNCS (LNISA), vol. 12788, pp. 50–65. Springer, Cham (2021). https://doi.org/10.1007/978-3-030-77392-2_4
12. Roundtree, A.: Facial recognition UX: a case study of industry-academic partnerships to promote user-centered ethics in facial recognition. In: Proceedings of the 39th ACM International Conference on Design of Communication, pp. 240–246 (2021)
13. Roundtree, A.: Human factors and facial recognition technology in emergency response: an integrative review. In: Social and Occupational Ergonomics, vol. 152, no. 152 (2024)
14. Kendall Roundtree, A.: Public perception of AI: a review. In: Degen, H., Ntoa, S. (eds.) HCI International 2024 – Late Breaking Papers, HCII 2024. LNCS, vol. 15382, pp. 72–87. Springer, Cham (2024). https://doi.org/10.1007/978-3-031-76827-9_5
15. PricewaterhouseCoopers (PwC): Responsible AI – Maturing from theory to practice. https://www.pwc.com/gx/en/issues/data-and-analytics/artificial-intelligence/what-is-responsible-ai/pwc-responsible-ai-maturing-from-theory-to-practice.pdf. Accessed 25 Mar 2025
16. Díaz-Rodríguez, N., Del Ser, J., Coeckelbergh, M., de Prado, M.L., Herrera-Viedma, E., Herrera, F.: Connecting the dots in trustworthy Artificial Intelligence: from AI principles, ethics, and key requirements to responsible AI systems and regulation. Inform. Fusion **99**, 101896 (2023)

WisdomTales: Improving Senior Citizens' Cognitive Abilities with Arithmetic Practices

Rayden Wei Xuan Teo[1]($\boxtimes$) , Siyuan Liu[1] , and Chengqi Zhang[2]

[1] College of Computing and Data Science, Nanyang Technological University,
Singapore, Singapore
`{rteo021,syliu}@e.ntu.edu.sg`
[2] Department of Data Science and Artificial Intelligence, The Hong Kong
Polytechnic University, Hong Kong, China
`Chengqi.Zhang@polyu.edu.hk`

Abstract. Cognitive decline among older adults presents a growing public health concern, underscoring the need for accessible and engaging interventions. In this paper, we present *WisdomTales*, a mobile game designed to enhance cognitive abilities in older adults through arithmetic practice, interactive storytelling, and learning-by-teaching. The game integrates the concept of *magic multiplication*, a mental math technique that simplifies multiplication, into a visual format that presents arithmetic challenges in meaningful and relatable contexts. Users engage in narrative-driven activities alongside a virtual grandchild character, reinforcing mathematical concepts through dialogic learning powered by a teachable agent. We conducted a pilot study involving 30 participants to assess users' satisfaction, engagement, and perceived cognitive stimulation. The results show that participants particularly appreciated the game's accessibility, personalized design, and the opportunity to teach the virtual agent.

Keywords: Cognitive abilities · Older adults · *Magic multiplication* ·
Serious games · Teachable agent

1 Introduction

The global rise in aging populations presents significant challenges in healthcare, particularly in maintaining/improving cognitive health among older adults [35]. Cognitive functions such as memory, attention, reasoning, and executive control are essential for preserving independence, social participation, and overall well-being in later life [23]. However, age-related cognitive decline is common. Studies show that more than half of adults over 65 experience some degree of cognitive impairment [11]. While advances in medical care and infrastructure have improved physical health and mobility, cognitive wellness remains an underfunded and often overlooked dimension of senior care [12].

J. Wei et al. (Eds.): HCII 2025, LNCS 16346, pp. 226–242, 2026.
https://doi.org/10.1007/978-3-032-13187-4_16

In response to these challenges, digital interventions have gained attention for their potential to support mental agility in later life. However, many widely used platforms, such as *Lumosity* [16] and *Elevate* [7], are not specifically designed with older adults in mind. These systems often lack critical age-appropriate features, including simplified navigation, large and legible fonts, and high-contrast visuals, making them difficult to use for individuals with age-related visual or motor impairments. Moreover, they frequently fail to address common cognitive challenges in aging—such as reduced working memory, slower processing speed, and diminished attention span [9]. In addition to these usability issues, many existing games rely heavily on repetitive drills and abstract tasks that lack real-world context or emotional relevance, which may limit motivation and sustained engagement. Consequently, there remains a pressing need for cognitive training tools that are thoughtfully tailored to the needs, preferences, and abilities of older users.

Mobile games, with their accessibility and scalability, offer a promising avenue for addressing cognitive decline in older adults. These games provide an engaging, low-cost alternative to traditional interventions, offering real-time feedback, and interactive elements that encourage consistent cognitive stimulation. Studies have demonstrated that digital games can enhance cognitive function, improve emotional well-being, and foster social connections in older adults [1,14]. Moreover, the increasing adoption of mobile devices among seniors further supports the viability of mobile games as tools for cognitive improvement. Studies show that seniors are increasingly using smartphones and other mobile devices, with many becoming more tech-savvy and engaged in digital activities [8]. These trends highlight a timely opportunity to develop mobile games that go beyond generic brain training—tools that are cognitively stimulating, emotionally resonant, and inclusively designed.

Studies have shown that daily cognitive exercises, such as solving arithmetic problems, can lead to improvements in various cognitive functions among older adults [31,34]. Additionally, the use of cognitive tools like the abacus has demonstrated benefits for both cognitively healthy seniors and those with cognitive impairments [27], supporting the idea that math-based exercises can provide a meaningful boost to cognitive health. Given this, in this paper, we designed and developed a mobile game, *WisdomTales*, to maintain and enhance senior people's cognitive abilities through arithmetic-based training embedded in an engaging and age-appropriate experience. At the core of the game is the concept of *magic multiplication* [36] a mental math technique that simplifies complex arithmetic operations into intuitive and easily learnable formulas. This technique was selected for its cognitive accessibility and its potential to stimulate mental agility without overwhelming the user. To reinforce learning and deepen engagement, the game incorporates a teachable agent framework, allowing users to take on the role of a teacher by instructing a virtual character on how to apply the multiplication strategies. This learning-by-teaching paradigm is designed to reinforce retention [15] and promote a sense of competence and contribution, which are known factors to support both cognitive development and self-esteem in older adults [3,25]. We further conducted a pilot study involving 30 participants to evaluate the effectiveness and user perception of *WisdomTales*. The results demonstrated high levels of engagement, usability, and perceived cognitive benefit.

The rest of the paper is organized as follows. Section 2 reviews related work on cognitive training tools for older adults. Section 3 introduces the concept of *magic multiplication* and explains how it forms the mathematical foundation of *WisdomTales*. Section 4 presents the game's design, detailing the story mode and teachable agent features. Section 5 describes the pilot user study. Finally, Sect. 6 concludes the paper.

2   Related Work

A variety of digital tools have been developed to support cognitive training in older adults. For instance, *LightSword* is a Virtual Reality (VR) exergame that combines cognitive tasks with physical movement to train cognitive inhibition and executive functions in older adults [6]. While its immersive, interactive environment can boost motivation and engagement, the system depends on costly VR hardware and assumes a baseline level of physical mobility. These requirements significantly limit accessibility for seniors with financial or physical constraints, making it difficult to scale such interventions across diverse aging populations.

In contrast, mobile applications such as *Lumosity* and *Elevate* provide more accessible and low-cost platforms for cognitive training. These apps offer exercises targeting memory, attention, and problem-solving, and are generally easy to use. However, they are typically designed for the general population and lack features tailored to older users, such as simplified interfaces, age-relevant content, or emotionally engaging narratives. Moreover, they often present abstract, de-contextualized tasks that can feel repetitive or disconnected from everyday life. The absence of personalized interaction, social engagement, or adaptive learning pathways may further limit their effectiveness and long-term appeal for seniors. Studies also question their sustained cognitive impact, especially outside controlled experimental settings.

WisdomTales, the mobile game developed in this research, aims to bridge these gaps by offering a cognitively stimulating and emotionally resonant experience designed specifically for older adults. It prioritizes accessibility by using a mobile platform and senior-friendly interface, and enhances motivation through story-driven gameplay and meaningful arithmetic learning. Unlike existing apps, *WisdomTales* integrates a teachable agent that supports learning-by-teaching, empowering users to reinforce their knowledge while boosting self-efficacy and confidence. Table 1 provides a comparison of key features across *LightSword*, *Lumosity*, *Elevate*, and *WisdomTales*.

3   Magic Multiplication

This section introduces *magic multiplication*, the key arithmetic technique underlying the design of *WisdomTales*. This mental math method uses structured formulas to simplify the process of squaring numbers (up to 125) and performing two-digit multiplications [36].

Table 1. Comparison of Features Across Cognitive Training Tools for Older Adults

Feature	*LightSword*	*Lumosity*	*Elevate*	*WisdomTales*
Platform	VR-based	Mobile & web	Mobile & web	Mobile-only
Target Audience	Older Adults	General Users	General Users	Older Adults
Physical Activity	Encourages movement	No	No	No
Social Interaction	None	None	None	Planned multiplayer mode
Senior-Centric Content	Limited	Limited	Limited	Tailored for older adults

At the heart of the technique is the concept of a *magic number*, denoted as m, which is derived from the number to be squared (A) and used to streamline the computation. The source text lists four principal formulas:

1. **Numbers 11 to 24:**

$$A^2 = (10 + m)^2 = (A + m) \times 10 + m^2, \quad \text{where } m = A - 10$$

2. **Numbers 25 to 75:**

$$A^2 = (50 + m)^2 = (25 + m) \times 100 + m^2, \quad \text{where } m = A - 50$$

3. **Numbers 76 to 125:**

$$A^2 = (100 + m)^2 = (A + m) \times 100 + m^2, \quad \text{where } m = A - 100$$

4. **Two-Digit Multiplication:**

$$A_1 \times A_2 = (A_1 + m)^2 - m^2, \quad \text{where } m = \frac{A_2 - A_1}{2}$$

For example, let $A = 51$. Since $25 < A < 75$, we use the second formula:

$$m = 51 - 50 = 1$$

$$A^2 = (25 + 1) \times 100 + 1^2 = 2600 + 1 = \boxed{2601}$$

Magic multiplication was chosen for its simplicity, cognitive accessibility, and potential to enhance mental agility and arithmetic fluency among older adults. This technique transforms seemingly complex calculations into manageable steps, making it ideal for users who have a basic understanding of arithmetic operations such as addition, subtraction, multiplication, division, and squaring, and who are familiar with the nine by nine multiplication table.

In the following sections, we will discuss the various game modes and how *magic multiplication* is seamlessly integrated into them.

4   The Designed Mobile Game *WisdomTales*

The current version of *WisdomTales* features two primary modes: *Story Mode* and *Teach Me!*. In *Story Mode*, users learn how to make us of *magic multiplication* techniques. In *Teach Me!*, users reinforce their understanding by teaching a chatbot powered by a teachable agent, applying the learning-by-teaching paradigm to deepen conceptual mastery and boost confidence.

4.1   Story Mode

Learning math formulas can be challenging, particularly for older adults who may find abstract concepts disengaging. *WisdomTales* addresses this by embedding *magic multiplication* within a narrative-driven experience that leverages dialogic learning, storytelling, and mirror-neuron activation to make learning both accessible and engaging. *Story Mode* presents users with a series of interactive chapters in which they assume the role of a grandparent alongside their grandchild. Each chapter features a relatable storyline that integrates *magic multiplication* into everyday situations, using a visual novel format to enhance immersion. This narrative-based learning approach has been shown to improve engagement and retention, especially in older adults [24].

Upon selecting *Story Mode* from the main menu (Fig. 1(a)), users see a list of chapters (Fig. 1(b)), each inspired by activities familiar to older adults [30]. For instance, Chap. 2 follows a grandparent-grandchild pair during a garden walk and is used as the main example in this paper. Selecting a chapter leads to a scene selection screen (Fig. 1(c)), with the number of scenes guided by the 7 ± 2 rule. By limiting scenes to 5 to 9, chapters remain manageable, reducing cognitive load and preventing fatigue [18]. Each scene unfolds through character dialogue that introduces and contextualizes arithmetic concepts (Fig. 2).

These dialogues model collaborative problem-solving and encourage users to process new information through conversational exchanges [32,33]. This dialogic approach not only fosters cognitive engagement but also enhances comprehension and retention by activating brain regions associated with shared understanding [20]. The emotional power of storytelling further strengthens learning outcomes. By situating math problems in familiar, emotionally resonant narratives, users will form meaningful connections to the content. Research shows that such narrative contexts improve memory by creating strong emotional associations [10,29]. To support visual learning preferences, each chapter uses diagrams and illustrations to clarify abstract formulas [17]. For example, in Chap. 2, the characters estimate the number of plants in a square garden plot—visually representing squaring operations in a meaningful context. This approach caters to older adults, who often retain information more effectively through images and written material rather than auditory input [19].

At the end of each chapter, users proceed to a math test page (Fig. 3), where they apply the formula taught in that chapter. A random starting number, such as 73, is provided along with a partially completed magic multiplication equation.

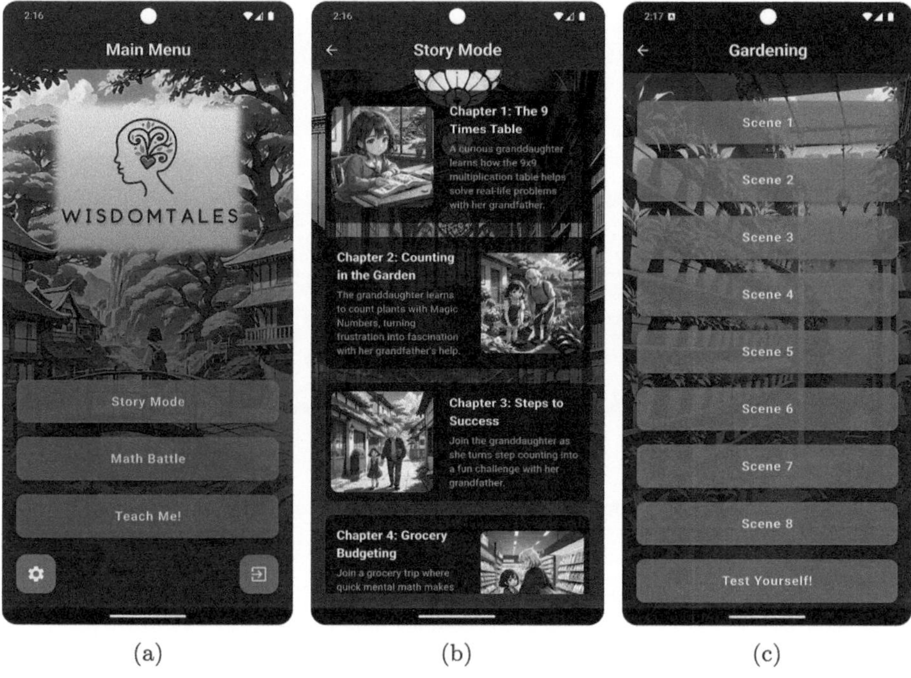

Fig. 1. *WisdomTales* Interface.

Fig. 2. Characters Talking.

Using a built-in numpad, users fill in the missing components, minimizing errors and ensuring accessibility.

By combining storytelling, social dialogue, visual aids, and interactive testing, *WisdomTales* delivers a holistic learning experience in *Story Mode*. Mirror-neuron activation, triggered when users observe characters solving problems,

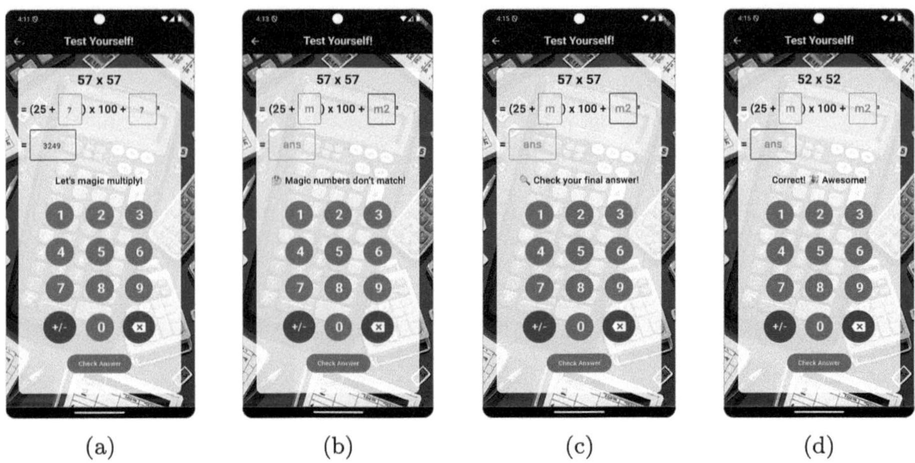

(a)   (b)   (c)   (d)

Fig. 3. Formative *Magic Multiplication* Assessment.

further supports learning through imitation and internalization [22]. Together, these elements make mathematical concepts more intuitive, engaging, and memorable, while promoting motivation and confidence among older learners.

4.2 Teach Me!

Once users have become familiar with the *magic multiplication* formulas through *Story Mode*, they can consolidate and apply their understanding in *Teach Me!* by interacting with a chatbot powered by a teachable agent (TA). This mode is accessed by selecting the *Teach Me!* option from the main menu (Fig. 1(a)). The chatbot simulates a virtual student, allowing users to take on the role of a teacher and explain the concepts they have learned—an approach grounded in the learning-by-teaching paradigm [2].

Teachable agents are AI-based systems designed to promote learning by encouraging users to teach. Drawing on the social metaphor of tutoring, TAs help reinforce conceptual understanding by prompting learners to organize knowledge, articulate explanations, and reflect on their thinking. Prior research shows that learning-by-teaching can improve self-regulation, engagement, and long-term retention [21]. In *WisdomTales*, users guide the chatbot through the logic of *magic multiplication*, requiring them to apply the formulas correctly and explain each step. This interaction supports metacognitive development by helping users identify gaps in their understanding while reinforcing previously acquired knowledge [4]. As a result, *Teach Me!* transforms passive review into an active learning experience, promoting deeper comprehension and stronger problem-solving skills [5].

Fuzzy Cognitive Map (FCM). To support users in teaching the *magic multiplication* formulas, the TA in *WisdomTales* employs a Fuzzy Cognitive Map (FCM), a graphical model that captures the relationships between concepts or components within a system [13]. In this context, the FCM is used to visualize the logical structure of the formulas by mapping how each component, i.e., the *base value*, *magic number*, and equation terms, relates to the overall computation. To implement this effectively, the formulas are first decomposed into these core components, based on their structural similarities. This decomposition allows the agent to interpret user input meaningfully and provide targeted feedback. Table 2 presents the common structure shared across the different *magic multiplication* rules, forming the foundation for the teachable agent's reasoning and response mechanisms.

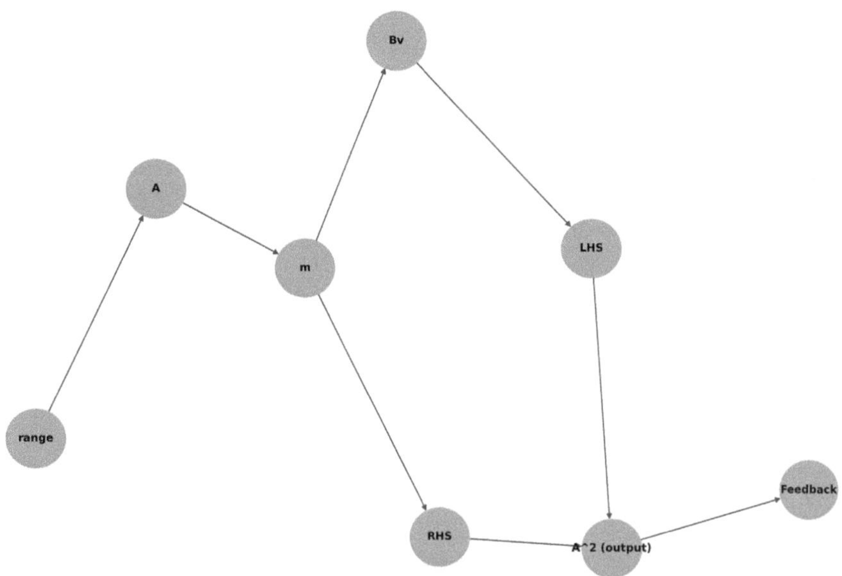

Fig. 4. Fuzzy Cognitive Map of Teachable Agent.

The structural similarities between the formulas are represented as nodes in the FCM. Each node corresponds to a key component of the formulas, such as the *base value*, *left-hand side*, or *right-hand side*, all of which are essential for the calculation, as shown in Fig. 4.

In the chatbot, users will be prompted to input these components into the respective nodes based on their understanding of the formulas for different number ranges. This design helps visualize the relationships between the components and guides users through the problem-solving process. Table 3 provides an explanation of each node in the FCM.

Once all components have been entered, the TA simulates the FCM by applying the user-inputted formulas to a specific number. The agent then evaluates

Table 2. *Magic Multiplication* Formula Similarities

Range/Condition	Calculation Details
$11 \leq A \leq 24$	**Magic Number:** $m = A - 10$ **Base Value:** $A + m$ **Formula:** $A^2 = \underbrace{(A + m) \times 10}_{\text{left-hand side}} \underbrace{+m^2}_{\text{right-hand side}}$ *Example* $(A = 14)$: $m = 4$, left $= 18 \times 10 = 180$, right $= 16$, $196 = 180 + 16$
$25 \leq A \leq 75$	**Magic Number:** $m = A - 50$ **Base Value:** $25 + m$ **Formula:** $A^2 = \underbrace{(25 + m) \times 100}_{\text{left-hand side}} \underbrace{+m^2}_{\text{right-hand side}}$ *Example* $(A = 60)$: $m = 10$, left $= 35 \times 100 = 3500$, right $= 100$, $3600 = 3500 + 100$
$76 \leq A \leq 125$	**Magic Number:** $m = A - 100$ **Base Value:** $A + m$ **Formula:** $A^2 = \underbrace{(A + m) \times 100}_{\text{left-hand side}} \underbrace{+m^2}_{\text{right-hand side}}$ *Example* $(A = 110)$: $m = 10$, left $= 120 \times 100 = 12000$, right $= 100$, $12100 = 12000 + 100$
Two-Digit Multiplication	**Magic Number:** $m = \dfrac{A_2 - A_1}{2}$ **Base Value:** $A_1 + m$ **Formula:** $A_1 \times A_2 = \underbrace{(A_1 + m) \times (A_1 + m)}_{\text{left-hand side}} \underbrace{-m^2}_{\text{right-hand side}}$ *Example* (47×53): $m = 3$, base $= 50$, $50^2 = 2500$, $3^2 = 9$, $2491 = 2500 - 9$

the results to determine if the *magic multiplication* formula have been correctly applied. If discrepancies are detected, the agent provides constructive feedback to help the user identify and correct the mistake. This iterative process not only reinforces the user's comprehension of *magic multiplication* concepts but also creates a learning environment that encourages experimentation, trial and error, and learning from mistakes.

Terminology Tutorial. Since the terms in the FCM will be used in the TA chatbot, it is crucial that users understand the key terminologies referenced in the FCM. To ensure this, a tutorial has been implemented to help users familiarize themselves with these terms as shown in Fig. 5.

The tutorial is accessible at any point during chatbot usage, and progress with the chatbot is saved even if the user navigates away to the tutorial and later returns. To ensure users are familiar with the necessary concepts, first-time users are required to complete the tutorial at least once before using the

Table 3. Fuzzy Cognitive Map Nodes

Node	Explanation	Requires	Contributes To
Range	Defines the range of numbers.	—	A
A	User-provided number.	Range	m
m	Magic number derived from the range.	A	Bv, RHS
Bv	Base value derived from m.	m	LHS
LHS	Left-hand side of the formula.	Bv	A^2 (output)
RHS	Right-hand side of the formula.	m	A^2 (output)
A^2 (output)	Final output of the formula.	LHS, RHS	Feedback
Feedback	Evaluates the correctness of the output.	A^2 (output)	Result of Teachable Agent

chatbot. The tutorial can be accessed by selecting the question mark icon in the top-right corner of the chatbot which can be seen in Fig. 5(a). Upon tapping the question mark icon, the tutorial opens and runs in a visual novel sequence as shown in Fig. 5(b), like how *Story Mode* operates. Imagery and colors are used to help explain and differentiate the terminology, making it easier for users to remember. Each part of the formula that constitutes a node is highlighted in the tutorial. At the end of the tutorial, all formulas are displayed again and color-coded according to the terminologies in the FCM, as shown in Fig. 5(c). Users can then tap the back arrow in the top-left corner to return to the chatbot interface.

Chatbot Interaction. The teachable agent (TA) in *WisdomTales* is implemented as a chatbot that facilitates interactive, guided learning through conversation. By simulating a tutoring dialogue, the chatbot fosters emotional engagement, increases motivation, and encourages sustained participation. As shown in Fig. 6, users interact with the TA by teaching it the components of a *magic multiplication* formula. Once all required elements are provided, the TA attempts to solve the corresponding problem using the formula constructed from the user's input. If the formula is correct, the TA confirms both the structure and the output. If not, it delivers constructive feedback, pinpointing possible errors and guiding the user toward a better understanding. This teaching process not only reinforces learning but also enhances user confidence and self-esteem, in line with prior studies on the learning-by-teaching effect [28].

To ensure usability, the chatbot accepts input through structured choices rather than free-form text, aligning with Shneiderman's principle of error prevention from the 8 Golden Rules of Interface Design [26]. For example, as shown in Fig. 6(a), a user begins by selecting a number range (e.g., "Let's do numbers 25 to 75!"), which sets the range node in the FCM and determines the initial value of A accordingly. Once a range is selected, users can edit any of the five key FCM nodes: *m (magic number)*, *Bv (base value)*, *LHS*, *RHS*, and *A^2 (output)* (Fig. 6(a)). This flexible structure allows users to focus on specific components and make iterative adjustments. For example, Fig. 6(b) shows a case where the

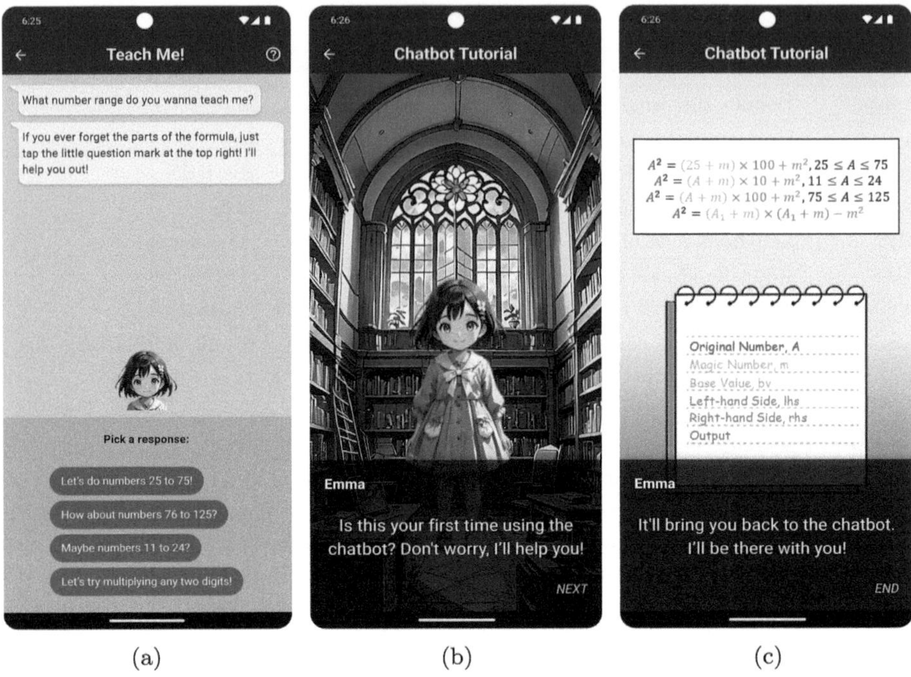

(a)   (b)   (c)

Fig. 5. Chatbot Tutorial.

user chooses to start by editing the A^2 *(output)* node, which represents the final computed result. After each input, the TA repeats the formula back to the user, allowing for immediate verification (Fig. 6(c)). Users may revisit and revise any node as needed. When all nodes have been populated, the user selects the "Finish!" option to prompt the TA to simulate the FCM and evaluate the full formula. If any component is incorrect, the agent provides feedback highlighting which node may contain an error, as illustrated in Fig. 7(a). Users can then retry the same problem or choose a new number range to continue practicing. If the formula is correct, the TA confirms the computation and acknowledges the user's success (Fig. 7(b)).

By allowing users to adopt the role of a teacher, the chatbot reinforces cognitive engagement, encourages iterative reasoning, and promotes self-confidence.

5   User Study

To evaluate user perceptions and experiences with *WisdomTales*, we conducted a pilot user study focusing on three key areas: cognitive engagement, usability, and learning reinforcement, particularly in relation to the teachable agent. A total of 30 participants were recruited, spanning the age range of 40 to 65. The distribution was as follows: 40–44 (3.3%), 45–49 (10%), 50–54 (26.7%), 55–59

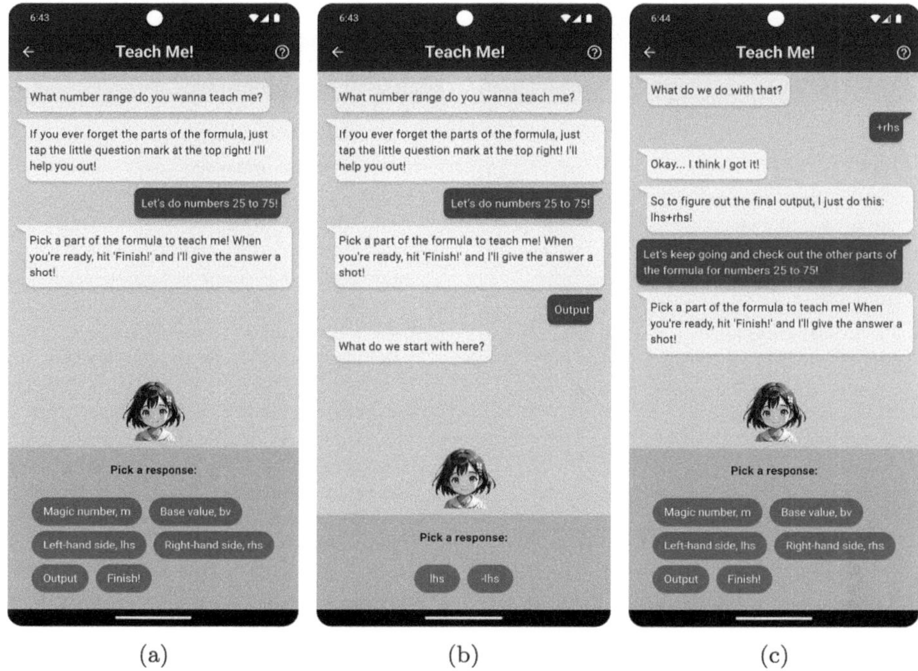

Fig. 6. Teachable Agent Chatbot Interface.

(43.4%), and 60–65 (16.7%). Of the participants, 56.7% identified as female and 43.3% as male.

Participants engaged with both *Story Mode* and *Teach Me!* of the app and completed a post-session questionnaire consisting of 16 Likert-scale questions (1 = very dissatisfied or not at all likely; 5 = very satisfied or extremely likely). The questions were categorized into three thematic areas:

1. **Overall Experience & Engagement (Q1–Q4)**: Evaluated general satisfaction, emotional response, and willingness to continue using or recommend the app.
2. **Story Mode & Learning Effectiveness (Q5–Q10)**: Assessed enjoyment of the story-based gameplay and perceived cognitive benefits, particularly those associated with the teachable agent.
3. **UI, Accessibility & Design (Q11–Q13)**: Measured perceptions of the app's usability, accessibility, and contribution to cognitive stimulation.

Table 4 summarizes participants' mean responses and standard deviations across these categories.

Overall, participants reported highly positive experiences. A majority (83.3%) expressed satisfaction with the app (Q1), and 90% indicated they would recommend it to others (Q2), suggesting strong perceived value. Continued use

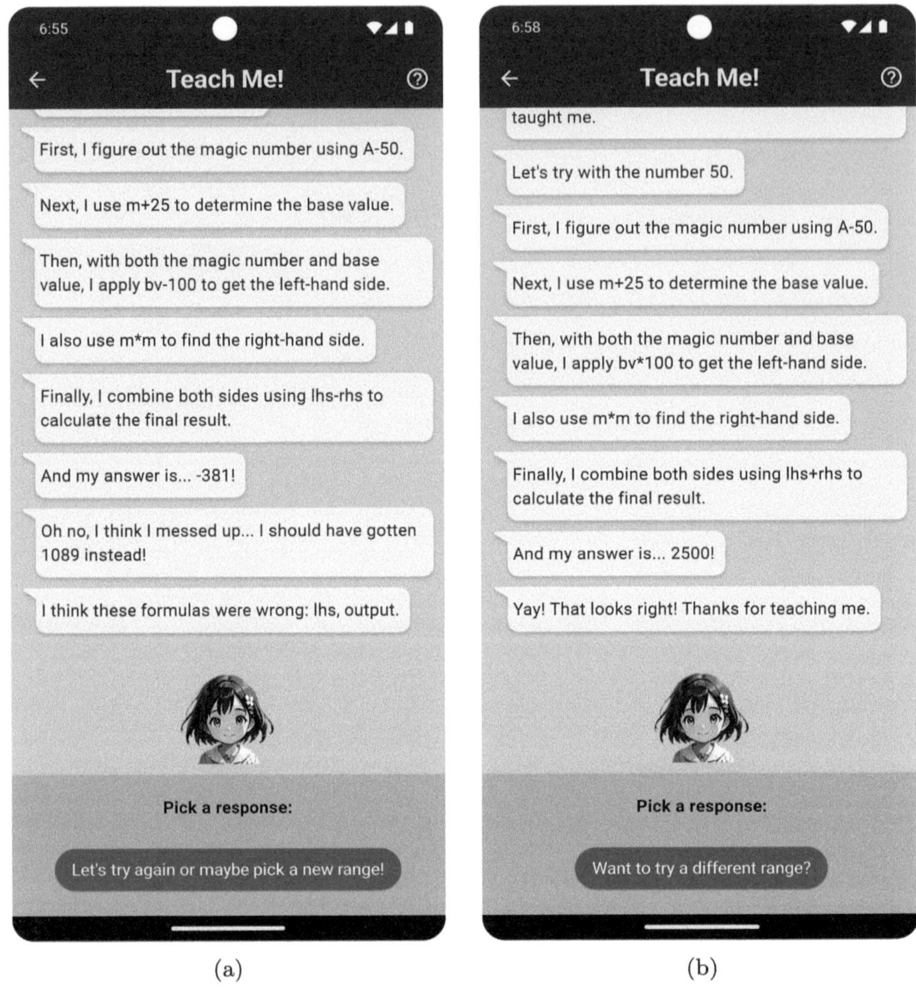

(a)   (b)

Fig. 7. Teachable Agent Chatbot Feedback.

interest (Q3) received a slightly lower—but still favorable—score (76.7%), possibly reflecting the short study duration. Notably, 93.4% of participants felt a sense of accomplishment after completing chapters (Q4), pointing to the app's ability to instill motivation and a rewarding learning experience.

Story Mode was particularly well received. 86.6% of participants rated it highly (Q5), highlighting the value of narrative-driven learning in maintaining attention and interest. The teachable agent stood out for its effectiveness in reinforcing arithmetic understanding: all participants (100%) agreed it helped them consolidate their learning (Q6), and 86.6% found it easy to interact with (Q7). Additionally, 80% reported that the agent helped promote deeper understanding (Q8), and 100% felt more confident as a result of teaching the agent (Q9). A

Table 4. Mean Ratings (M) and Standard Deviations (SD) for User-Study Questions by Dimension (n=30)

Question Description	Mean (M)	Std. (SD)
Overall Experience & Engagement		
Q1: Overall satisfaction	4.13	0.66
Q2: Recommendation likelihood	4.17	0.58
Q3: Continued use interest	4.13	0.75
Q4: Sense of accomplishment	4.20	0.54
Story Mode & Learning Effectiveness		
Q5: Single-player enjoyment	4.20	0.65
Q6: Learning reinforcement	4.57	0.48
Q7: Agent interaction ease	4.30	0.69
Q8: Understanding promotion	4.17	0.73
Q9: Confidence boost	4.57	0.48
Q10: Contribution feeling	4.37	0.65
UI, Accessibility & Design		
Q11: Accessibility	4.60	0.49
Q12: Design impact	4.63	0.48
Q13: Cognitive benefit	4.63	0.55

further 90% indicated they felt a sense of meaningful contribution (Q10), suggesting that the learning-by-teaching interaction fostered a sense of competence and autonomy.

The interface and visual design were also strongly validated by the participants. All users found the app accessible and easy to navigate (Q11), and unanimously agreed that the design supported their learning process (Q12). Furthermore, 96.7% believed that the interactive math activities could contribute to improving their cognitive skills (Q13), aligning with the app's intended goal of cognitive enhancement.

While these findings are encouraging, several limitations should be acknowledged. First, only five participants were from the 60–65 age group, which limits generalization to the target senior demographic. Second, the study relied solely on self-reported perceptions without the use of validated cognitive assessment tools or pre-/post-testing. Third, as the study was limited to a single-session interaction, it does not capture long-term cognitive effects or patterns of sustained use. Finally, the survey focused exclusively on quantitative measures; qualitative feedback was not collected, which may have limited the depth of user insight.

6   Conclusion

In this paper, we presented *WisdomTales*, a mobile game designed to help maintain and enhance the cognitive abilities of older adults through engaging arithmetic-based activities. The game is built around the concept of *magic multiplication*, which simplifies mental computation and promotes cognitive stimulation in a low-stress, accessible format. *WisdomTales* features two core modes: a narrative-driven *Story Mode* that introduces multiplication strategies in meaningful, everyday contexts, and a chatbot-based *Teach Me!* that allows users to reinforce their understanding by instructing a teachable agent.

To assess the effectiveness of the app, we conducted a pilot user study evaluating participants' perceptions of engagement, usability, and cognitive benefit. The results indicate strong user satisfaction, with particularly positive responses to the interactive storytelling format and the learning-by-teaching paradigm. These findings suggest that *WisdomTales* holds the potential as a cognitively engaging and emotionally rewarding experience for older adults.

Looking ahead, we plan to enhance the game by introducing a multiplayer mode to promote social interaction and peer learning. We will also incorporate accessibility features such as voice input/output and adjustable text sizes to better support users with diverse needs. Additionally, a longitudinal study involving older participants will be conducted to evaluate the long-term impact of *WisdomTales* on cognitive maintenance and social engagement in later life.

References

1. Bonnechère, B., Klass, M., Langley, C., Sahakian, B.: Brain training using cognitive apps can improve cognitive performance and processing speed in older adults. Sci. Rep. **11**, 12313 (2021)
2. Chase, C.C., Chin, D.B., Oppezzo, M.A., Schwartz, D.L.: Teachable agents and the protégé effect: increasing the effort towards learning. J. Sci. Educ. Technol. **18**(4), 334–352 (2009)
3. Chen, A., Wei, Y., Le, H., Zhang, Y.: Learning-by-teaching with ChatGPT: the effect of teachable ChatGPT agent on programming education (2024)
4. Chi, M.: Active-constructive-interactive: a conceptual framework for differentiating learning activities. Top. Cogn. Sci. **1**, 73–105 (2009)
5. Chi, M.T., Siler, S.A., Jeong, H., Yamauchi, T., Hausmann, R.G.: Learning from human tutoring. Cogn. Sci. **25**(4), 471–533 (2001)
6. Du, Q., Song, Z., Jiang, H., Wei, X., Weng, D., Fan, M.: Lightsword: a customized virtual reality exergame for long-term cognitive inhibition training in older adults. In: Proceedings of the 2024 CHI Conference on Human Factors in Computing Systems. CHI '24, Association for Computing Machinery, New York, NY, USA (2024)
7. Elevate Labs: Elevate: brain training app. mobile application software (2023). https://www.elevateapp.com
8. Fowe, I.E., Boot, W.R.: Understanding older adults' attitudes toward mobile and wearable technologies to support health and cognition. Front. Psychol. **13**, 1036092 (2022)

9. Gomez-Hernandez, M., Ferre, X., Moral, C., Villalba-Mora, E.: Design guidelines of mobile apps for older adults: systematic review and thematic analysis. JMIR Mhealth Uhealth **11**, e43186 (2023)
10. Green, M., Dill-Shackleford, K.: Engaging with stories and characters: learning, persuasion, and transportation into narrative worlds. In: The Oxford Handbook of Media Psychology, pp. 449–461 (2013)
11. Han, F., Luo, C., Lv, D., Tian, L., Qu, C.: Risk factors affecting cognitive impairment of the elderly aged 65 and over: a cross-sectional study. Front. Aging Neurosci. **14**, 903794 (2022)
12. Kim, S.: Effects of perceived accessibility to living infrastructure on positive feelings among older adults. Behav. Sci. **14**, 1025 (2024)
13. Kosko, B.: Fuzzy cognitive maps. Int. J. Man Mach. Stud. **24**(1), 65–75 (1986)
14. Lee, S., Oh, H., Shi, C.K., Doh, Y.Y.: Mobile game design guide to improve gaming experience for the middle-aged and older adult population: user-centered design approach. JMIR Serious Games **9**, e24449 (2021)
15. Leelawong, K., Schwartz, D., Vye, N.: Learning by teaching: a new agent paradigm for educational software. Appl. Artif. Intell. **19**, 363–392 (2005)
16. Lumos Labs: Lumosity: brain training app. Mobile Application Software (2023). https://www.lumosity.com
17. Marikyan, G.: Teaching mathematics with visuals. Athens J. Sci. **10**(4), 231–240 (2023)
18. Miller, G.: The magical number seven, plus or minus two: some limits on out capacity for processing information. Psychol. Rev. **101**, 343–352 (1994)
19. Mora, J., Quito, I., Sarmiento, L.: A case study of learning styles of older adults attending an English course. MASKANA **8**, 1–15 (2017)
20. Nouri, A.: Dialogic learning: a social cognitive neuroscience view. IJCRSEE **2** (2014)
21. Okita, S., Schwartz, D.: Learning by teaching human pupils and teachable agents: the importance of recursive feedback. J. Learn. Sci. **22**, 375–412 (2013)
22. Rizzolatti, G., Craighero, L.: The mirror-neuron system. Ann. Rev. Neurosci. **27**, 169–192 (2004)
23. Robinson, P.: Abilities to learn: cognitive abilities. In: Encyclopedia of the Sciences of Learning, pp. 17–21. Springer, Boston (2012)
24. Schank, R.C., Abelson, R.P.: Knowledge and memory: the real story, argues that stories about one's experiences, and those of others, are fundamental to human memory, knowledge, and social communication. In: Advances in Social Cognition, vol. 8, pp. 1–85. Lawrence Erlbaum Associates, Inc, Hillsdale, NJ, US (1995)
25. Schroeder, N.L., Adesope, O.O., Gilbert, R.B.: How effective are pedagogical agents for learning? A meta-analytic review. J. Educ. Comput. Res. **49**(1), 1–39 (2013)
26. Shneiderman, B., Plaisant, C.: Designing the User Interface: Strategies for Effective Human-Computer Interaction. Pearson (2010)
27. Silva, T., et al.: Cognitive training using the abacus: a literature review study on the benefits for different age groups. Dementia e Neuropsychologia **15**, 256–266 (2021)
28. Srinivasan, R., Pugalenthi, N.: A relationship between self-esteem and teaching competency of prospective teachers. Shanlax Int. J. Arts Sci. Human. **7**, 44–48 (2020)
29. Suzuki, W., Feliú-Mójer, M., Hasson, U., Yehuda, R., Zarate, J.M.: Dialogues: the science and power of storytelling. J. Neurosci. **38**, 9468–9470 (2018)
30. Szanton, S., et al.: Older adults' favorite activities are resoundingly active: findings from the NHATS study. Geriatr. Nurs. N.Y. NY **31**(2), 131–135 (2015)

31. Uchida, S., Kawashima, R.: Reading and solving arithmetic problems improves cognitive functions of normal aged people: a randomized controlled study. Age (Dordr) **30**(1), 21–29 (2008)
32. Vygotsky, L.S.: Mind in Society: Development of Higher Psychological Processes. Harvard University Press (1978)
33. Wegerif, R.: Mind Expanding: Teaching for Thinking and Creativity in Primary Education. Open University Press (2010)
34. Willis, S., et al.: Long-term effects of cognitive training on everyday functional outcomes in older adults. JAMA **296**, 2805–2814 (2007)
35. World Health Organization: Ageing and health (2024). https://www.who.int/news-room/fact-sheets/detail/ageing-and-health
36. Zhang, C.: Magic Multiplication: Discover the Ultimate Formula for Fast Multiplication. Earnshaw Books Limited (2023)

Empathic Agents in Action:
Redefining Industrial Interactions Through AI Personas

Anjelika Votintseva[(✉)], Jennie Wright, and Rebecca Johnson

Siemens AG, 85748 Garching, Germany
`{anjelika.votintseva,jennie.wright,johnson.rebecca}@siemens.com`

Abstract. This paper explores the design, prototyping, and business potential of empathic agents – emotionally intelligent avatars that enhance industrial and customer-facing interactions. Drawing from two workshops – one on conversational user interfaces and no-code prototyping, and another on digital personality definition and branding – the research highlights the convergence of AI, psychology, and corporate design.

The paper critiques traditional persona frameworks that rely on demo-graphic data, arguing they fail to reflect individual values, behaviors, and interaction styles. Instead, it proposes dynamic, psychologically informed personas that allow agents to better adapt empathetically to users' needs. This approach ensures more meaningful interactions across diverse contexts, from customer service to internal training.

The research also emphasizes the need to extend corporate branding principles beyond visual identity to include tone, emotional behavior, and inter-action consistency. Empathic agents can reinforce brand values while providing tailored, emotionally supportive experiences, especially in educational and coaching scenarios where personalized engagement drives better outcomes.

Practical method for no-code prototyping – such as prompt engineering – is discussed as scalable technique for persona development and fast scenario testing. The paper also compares internal and open LLMs, weighing their trade-offs in control, branding, and ethics.

Finally, it outlines ethical considerations, including emotional manipulation, privacy, and transparency, and presents strategies for responsible agent design. By aligning empathic agents with corporate branding and user expectations, businesses can unlock higher engagement, efficiency, and trust. The paper concludes with a call for ethical, emotionally aware AI personas as a new standard in industrial innovation.

Keywords: Empathic Agents · Human-Centered AI · Conversational Interfaces · AI Personas · Ethical Agents

1 Introduction

As conversational user interfaces (CUIs), intelligent assistants, and avatars become more present in industrial and customer-facing environments, expectations around their communication style, emotional intelligence, and adaptability are rising. These agents are no

J. Wei et al. (Eds.): HCII 2025, LNCS 16346, pp. 243–261, 2026.
https://doi.org/10.1007/978-3-032-13187-4_17

longer seen as simple automation tools – they are emerging as emotionally responsive, personality-rich entities capable of fostering trust, engagement, and learning. In this context, empathic agents – AI personas designed to recognize and respond to human emotions – are gaining momentum as a new paradigm for human-machine interaction.

The industrial and business relevance of empathic agents relevance is increasing. They can enhance employee training by offering real-time encouragement and adaptive pacing or improve customer service by personalizing communication styles to match user expectations. In virtual collaboration and metaverse applications, emotionally intelligent avatars help companies maintain brand identity while enabling more human-like experiences. Such agents are particularly valuable in complex tasks where emotional feedback, motivation, or trust are key success factors – examples include negotiation training, creativity coaching, and technical education.

This paper builds on insights from two workshops that explored the creation and prototyping of AI-driven personas. The first workshop, "Exercising Prompt Engineering: Fast Prototyping of Conversational UI", was presented at an international Human-Computer Interaction conference [23] and focused on rapid iteration of digital agents through prompt-based customization. The second workshop, "Bringing Life to the Virtual World: Prototyping Personality Clones," was held internally at Siemens in October 2024 and centered on applying personality psychology to the design of emotionally expressive and brand aligned avatars with strong focus on ethical aspects of such type of CUI.

In both cases, participants explored tools and frameworks for defining agent personalities, simulating communication behavior, and aligning interaction styles with corporate values and ethics. A key argument emerging from these workshops – and central to this paper – is that traditional persona frameworks are no longer sufficient for the design of effective digital agents. Conventional approaches, which rely on static demographic attributes such as age, job role, or income level, fail to capture the subtle behavioral and emotional differences that define how users interact with AI. Two users with the same demographics may respond very differently to tone, pacing, or emotional content. Therefore, designing for empathy requires new methods – ones that integrate psychological traits, emotional intelligence, and brand-aligned interaction guidelines into the core definition of agent personas.

This paper proposes a shift from demographic to dynamic, psychographic personas – ones rooted in personality psychology and prototyped using modern AI tools. It explores how these empathic agents can be developed, aligned with corporate identity, and applied in real-world industrial settings to increase engagement, trust, and operational effectiveness.

2   Related Works

The development of empathic agents capable of emotionally intelligent interactions represents a convergence of advances in CUIs, personality psychology, and corporate branding strategies. This section situates the current work within a growing body of research seeking to humanize industrial AI interactions through psychologically informed, brand-aligned design.

By examining foundational works and recent innovations, we establish how dynamic, psychographic personas address gaps in traditional approaches while aligning with industrial needs for brand-consistent, adaptive AI systems.

The development of empathic agents intersects with several research areas, including personality psychology, emotional design, conversational AI, and human-computer interaction (HCI). This paper builds upon a growing body of literature addressing the role of empathy in digital systems, as well as the technical and ethical challenges involved in creating emotionally intelligent AI personas.

Empirical studies show that empathic agents can enhance user engagement and decision-making. Mari et al. [20] demonstrated that voice assistants with empathic cues improve consumer response in voice commerce, while Lee and Yi [7] developed metrics to assess empathetic reactivity in conversational agents. Related to this, Ortega-Ochoa et al. [9] reviewed pedagogical conversational agents and confirmed that empathy enhances learning outcomes.

The integration of empathy into HCI has been further examined in Genç and Verma's [4] scoping review and by Kravchenko and Doty [10], who caution against uncritical use of empathy in interface design. Meanwhile, Chang et al. [11] and Greco et al. [5] explored the behavioral dynamics of empathic avatars in mixed reality and visual environments.

Other works addressing the ethical implications of empathy in AI. Alanazi et al. [12] proposed methods for predicting emotional empathy in intelligent agents, while Sabour et al. [14] evaluated the effectiveness of mental health chatbots.

Our previous work [15] contributed directly to this area by demonstrating how technology can be effectively integrated with social science perspectives on empathy to create a new generation of CUIs within industrial HCI contexts – an insight that forms a foundational basis for the present study.

Together, these works establish a rich context for understanding how empathy can be operationalized in digital agents – while also signaling the importance of psychological accuracy, branding consistency, and ethical safeguards in scalable implementations.

2.1 Evolution of Persona Frameworks in Human-Computer Interaction

Traditional persona frameworks, rooted in Cooper's pioneering work on user archetypes [18], have long relied on demographic attributes to guide design decisions. These static profiles – often segmented by age, occupation, or technical proficiency – proved effective for physical product development but struggle to capture the nuanced communication preferences required for AI-driven interactions. Recent critiques highlight how demographic homogeneity masks critical variances in emotional responsiveness, cognitive load tolerance, and decision-making styles.

Conventional analytic engines often rely on surface-level demographic data to guide decisions – such as targeting advertisements – yet this approach can lead to serious mismatches. For example, two individuals may appear nearly identical in algorithmic profiles: both born in 1948, wealthy, self-employed, living in London, and sharing interests such as international travel, dogs, sports cars, and fine wines. Yet one might be the Prince of Wales, the other a controversial public figure Ozzy Osbourne [1]. Despite overlapping data points, their values, communication styles, and expectations differ profoundly. An empathic agent – or a well-designed persona – would recognize this and adapt its behavior accordingly. Relying solely on demographics, however, risks offering the same interaction or message to both, which would likely be inappropriate for at least one of them.

The limitations of conventional personas become particularly acute in emotionally charged industrial contexts such as healthcare equipment maintenance or safety-critical operational training. Here, research by Bickmore et al. [2] demonstrates that task performance improves by 23% when virtual assistants adapt their communication style to users' stress levels rather than relying on role-based assumptions. The CloChat study [3] demonstrates that user satisfaction with chatbots increases significantly when personas are customizable rather than predefined by demographics. Users engaged more deeply with agents tailored to their behavioral preferences (e.g., communication style, emotional tone) than with generic demographic profiles. This supports the premise that demographic factors alone poorly predict satisfaction.

These findings align with workshop observations that static personas cannot guide the real-time emotional adaptability required for effective human-AI collaboration in industrial settings.

From a theoretical perspective, the foundational personality frameworks developed by Owen et al. [8], Keirsey and Bates [13], and Myers and Myers [17] serve as the basis for most existing personality classifications. Models such as DISC, temperament theory, and the MBTI have been widely adopted for structuring personas, helping to define consistent interaction strategies and adaptive communication styles within specific application areas. In the workshops referenced in this paper, these frameworks provided the conceptual foundation for identifying agent traits and aligning them with user expectations and task-specific use cases.

However, a key limitation of these models is their tendency to categorize individuals into a limited number of personality types, overlooking the richness and variability of human behavior. To address this, we proposed combining multiple personality models within a single persona definition. This hybrid approach enables greater flexibility and personalization, allowing agents to emulate more nuanced, human-like interaction patterns that better reflect real-world diversity.

The translation of psychological constructs into computational agent behavior has further advanced with models such as the Five-Factor Model (FFM, also known as Big Five or OCEAN) and Reinforcement Sensitivity Theory (RST) [24]. John and Srivastava's FFM taxonomy [6] – which describes personality in terms of expressiveness levels of five dimensions: openness, conscientiousness, extraversion, agreeableness, and neuroticism – has been applied in several digital agent applications, offering a scalable structure for adaptive and psychologically grounded interaction design.

2.2 Brand-Conscious Design and Ethical Considerations

Workshop activities extended the foundations by mapping agent's psychological traits to our company's brand values, creating digital personas that balance universal psychological principles with corporate identity. For example, participants developed an agreeableness-focused virtual coach for diversity training that incorporated company sustainability ethos through environmentally conscious dialogue patterns. This dual alignment – to both human personality spectra and organizational values – addresses a gap identified by different researchers, for example [19], who noted that most psychologically informed agents lack explicit brand persona integration.

As empathic agents become brand ambassadors, research has turned to reconciling emotional adaptability with brand consistency. Different research works introduced the Brand Interaction matrices, quantifying how agent responses balance user emotional needs against predefined brand voice parameters (as an example [21, 25]). The workshops mirrored these findings, with participants iterating on prototypes that enforced brand-specific communication boundaries – such as avoiding colloquialisms in technical support scenarios – without compromising empathy [22].

Ethical challenges persist in managing the persuasive potential of emotionally intelligent agents [10]. Our workshops preemptively addressed these concerns through strict ethical prototyping guidelines, mandating transparency about agent limitations and prohibiting manipulative emotional appeals. This proactive approach aligns with emerging HCI standards advocating for "ethic by design" audit trails in enterprise AI systems.

2.3 Agent Prototyping

Our workshop's emphasis on cross-functional collaboration between UX designers, AI engineers, and brand strategists addresses a critical gap. Our integrated approach yielded digital personas that simultaneously satisfied technical feasibility, emotional intelligence benchmarks, and brand guidelines – a triad rarely achieved in prior implementations.

While significant progress has been made in emotion recognition and trait-based persona development, our workshop-based approach highlights underexplored opportunities in three areas:

- **Dynamic Persona Adaptation**: Current systems primarily adjust to user states, but future agents could evolve personality facets over longitudinal interactions, mirroring human relationship development patterns.
- **Cross-Cultural Empathy Calibration**: Global enterprises require agents that adapt emotional expression norms across cultural contexts while maintaining brand consistency – a challenge partially addressed in the workshops but requiring deeper sociolinguistic integration.
- **Ethical Emotion Stewardship**: As agents gain emotional influence, frameworks are needed to ensure empathy enhances rather than manipulates user autonomy, particularly in high-stakes industrial decision-making.

By addressing these frontiers, the next generation of empathic agents can transcend their role as interaction tools to become trusted collaborators in the industrial landscape.

3 Workshops as Methodological Foundation

The research presented in this paper is grounded in hands-on insights from two workshops that served as testbeds for exploring the design, prototyping, and implications of empathic AI agents. These workshops provided practical frameworks and experimental settings in which new persona design approaches, interaction styles, and branding strategies were tested and evaluated. They also enabled exploration of business opportunities across a variety of application scenarios.

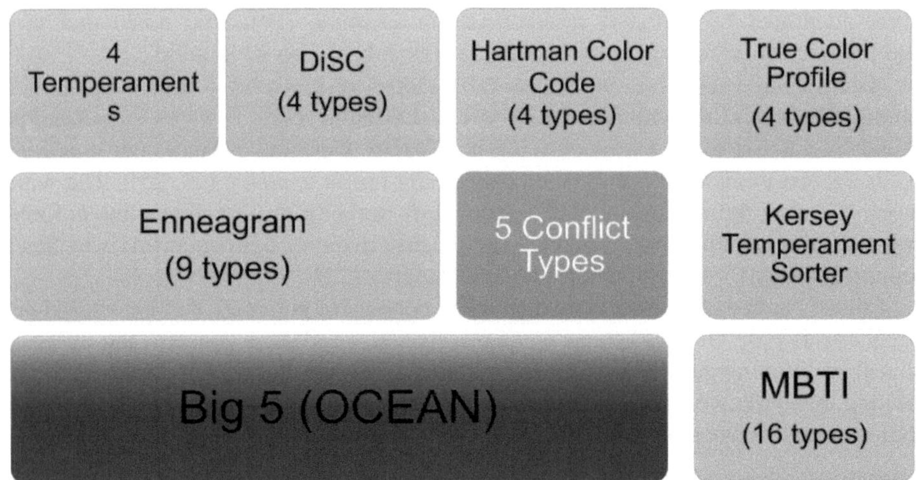

Fig. 1. Examples of different possible personality classifications for AI personas

The first workshop, "Exercising Prompt Engineering: Fast Prototyping of Conversational UI", was presented at an international HCI conference "Mensch und Computer 23: Building Bridges" [23]. It introduced participants to the process of designing and iterating intelligent agents using CUI principles. A key focus was on prompt engineering as a method for shaping the agent's tone, behavior, and functionality without coding.

The workshop was structured as a combination of theoretical input and practical exercises. Participants worked in small groups on three tasks:

1. Selecting a scenario that could benefit from an emotionally responsive agent with a specific personality;
2. Defining the agent's personality as a combination of known personality types enhanced with additional parameters;
3. Engaging in a group-wide discussion of the ethical concerns relevant to the use of such agents in the defined scenarios.

Participants also experimented with no-code tools to quickly build and test agent prototypes that could be adapted to various roles. This workshop demonstrated how non-technical stakeholders can collaboratively develop functional prototypes and align interaction design with specific business goals.

The second workshop, "Bringing Life to the Virtual World: Prototyping Personality Clones," was conducted internally at the Siemens Conference. It focused on the creation of digital personas using concepts from personality psychology and the development of emotionally expressive avatars. Participants explored how to define agent personalities using trait-based models and implement consistent communication patterns across different contexts.

Figure 1 illustrates several well-known personality models that were used in both workshops. These models were combined to create concise yet broadly applicable agent definitions suitable for general purpose use.

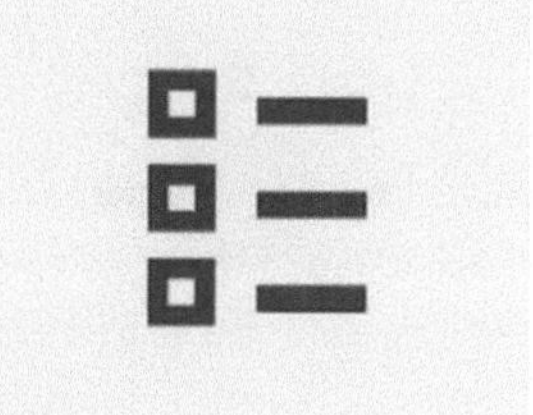

Fig. 2. First exercise: scenario definition

Participants selected scenarios such as a virtual software trainer or a creative coach to illustrate how personalized agents could adapt to user expectations in emotionally demanding or learning-intensive situations.

This workshop also included a strong focus on ethical considerations, such as the risks of emotional manipulation, data sensitivity, and brand misalignment. Discussions addressed the advantages and challenges of using internal versus open large language models (LLMs), reflecting on how these choices impact control, trust, and compliance.

Both workshops employed task-based prototyping as a central methodology. Participants were guided through structured activities, including identifying use cases, defining internal and external agent views, selecting personality traits, and iterating on interaction scenarios. Figure 2 illustrates the steps followed to define a detailed scenario for a brand-conscious CUI tailored to our company context, while Fig. 3 presents the framework used for designing a brand-aligned AI agent. These tasks promoted a deeper understanding of how agent behavior could be tuned to match both user preferences and corporate identity. Additionally, the workshops emphasized live interaction – encouraging participants to engage directly with AI prototypes and simulate conversations to assess tone, empathy, and responsiveness in real time.

Importantly, both sessions integrated ethical discussions into the design process. Rather than treating ethics as an afterthought, participants were encouraged to evaluate the emotional, psychological, and organizational implications of their agent designs throughout the process. This approach not only heightened awareness of ethical risks but also supported the creation of agent personas that are both impactful and responsible.

Together, these two workshops form the methodological foundation of this research. They demonstrate how interdisciplinary collaboration – combining UX design, AI technology, psychology, and corporate strategy – can accelerate the development of empathic agents that are scalable, adaptive, and aligned with both business and ethical standards.

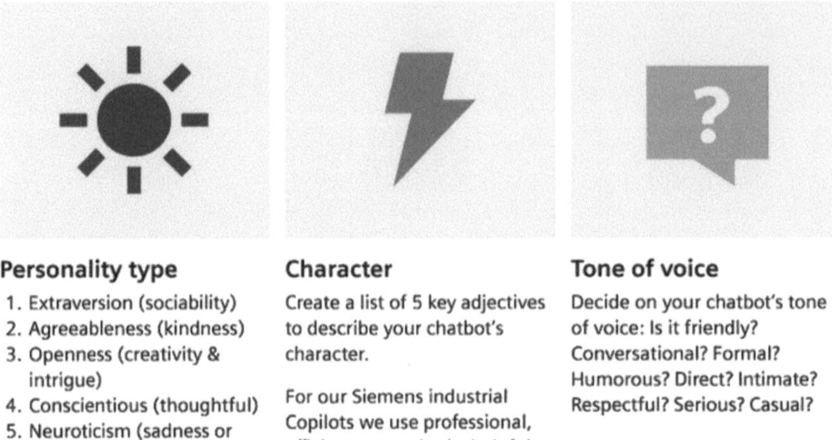

Fig. 3. Second exercise: agent definition

To derive structured insights from both workshops, we applied a qualitative evaluation framework. Participants' outputs – including persona templates, conversation simulations, and reflection notes – were collected and analyzed for patterns in trait selection, tone calibration, and emotional alignment strategies. We used thematic coding to identify recurring techniques in prompt design, emotional tone adjustment, and brand alignment decisions.

Based on these findings, we propose a behavior-based persona framework as an alternative to traditional demographic models. This framework incorporates three key parameters:

- Psychological trait alignment
- Emotional tone adaptability
- Brand personality consistency

The workshops demonstrated that such dynamic models better capture user interaction preferences and support real-time adaptation in high-stakes industrial contexts.

4 Empathic Agents and Corporate Branding

The integration of empathic agents into industrial and customer-facing applications challenges traditional notions of corporate branding. Branding is no longer limited to logos, color palettes, or visual identity; in the context of AI agents and avatars, tone, behavior, and emotional intelligence become central elements of a brand's presence. An agent's way of speaking, reacting to user emotions, and handling critical or sensitive moments all reflect on the brand it represents. These behavioral attributes – once managed by human employees – are now encoded into conversational models and digital personalities, requiring new standards for consistency and authenticity.

Empathic agents must embody the brand's personality not only visually, but also through their verbal tone and emotional engagement. For instance, a brand that values reliability and clarity should ensure its agents communicate in a calm, structured, and confident manner. Conversely, a brand promoting innovation and openness might prefer more exploratory, dynamic, and informal interactions. Emotional intelligence, therefore, is not a bonus feature, but a defining element of branded agent behavior. It ensures that agents can adjust their communication based on user needs while staying true to the company's values and style.

The Siemens workshop "Bringing Life to the Virtual World" provided practical insights into this evolving brand-agent alignment. Participants were introduced to Siemens' internal guidelines for Conversational Design [22], which include aspects such as language tone, avatar personality traits, and ethical interaction standards. The workshop emphasized the need for a clear interaction identity – a combination of voice, vocabulary, behavior patterns, and emotional responsiveness that makes the agent recognizably "Siemens". The system persona tasks guided participants in translating abstract branding principles into specific conversational behaviors tailored for use cases like software training or engineering support.

This holistic approach supports consistency across touchpoints, whether the agent is deployed in customer service, internal training, or immersive virtual environments. In customer-facing scenarios, empathic agents can strengthen brand loyalty by responding empathetically, resolving issues with emotional awareness, and reflecting professionalism in tone. In employee training, branded agents act as emotional tutors, providing personalized feedback and motivation. In virtual worlds and digital twins, avatars extend the brand into new immersive contexts, offering experiences that are both emotionally engaging and aligned with company identity.

The consistency of tone and behavior across these settings is crucial for building trust and recognition. Users interacting with the same brand in different formats – on a website, in a training module, or in other platforms – should experience the same quality and personality. This not only improves user experience but also supports brand coherence in complex digital ecosystems. As empathic agents become more autonomous and emotionally expressive, defining their behavior as part of branding strategy becomes essential for maintaining credibility, coherence, and ethical integrity.

In summary, empathic agents are not just technical solutions – they are digital brand representatives. Their tone, emotional intelligence, and behavior must be carefully crafted to reflect the company's values and identity across all user interactions. Siemens' approach shows how a systematic blend of UX design, psychology, and AI can ensure that avatars remain consistent, trustworthy, and brand-aligned, even as they adapt to user emotions and diverse industrial use cases.

5 Prototyping Empathic Agents

Designing empathic agents that align with user expectations and corporate values requires agile, accessible methods for defining, testing, and refining their personalities. In both workshops described in this paper, prompt engineering – used as a no-code prototyping technique – played a central role. This approach proved particularly valuable in industrial settings, where rapid iteration, interdisciplinary collaboration, and scalability are essential for successful agent development.

5.1 Prompt Engineering for Persona Creation

Prompt engineering enables designers to shape an agent's tone, style, and behavioral logic by carefully crafting the input prompts used to drive large language models (LLMs). Rather than coding behavior directly, the agent's responses are influenced through structured instructions and role definitions embedded in prompts. For example, prompts like "Act as a calm, emotionally intelligent software trainer who explains concepts step-by-step" can instantly shape how the agent communicates and reacts to user input.

This technique allows for fine-tuning of persona traits, such as assertiveness, empathy, or humor, making it possible to explore multiple personality variants quickly. It also supports flexible alignment with branding and psychological models, as traits derived from frameworks like the Big Five and others (mentioned on Fig. 1) can be embedded into the agent's role and dialogue structure. In the workshops, participants experimented with this technique by combining prompt instructions with personality traits to generate convincing agent personas for different use cases.

During the workshops, we explored and compared three distinct approaches to defining agent personalities through large language model (LLM) prompting, each offering different trade-offs in terms of usability, expressiveness, and performance. These methods were tested to assess how efficiently they guided the LLM's output and how accessible they were to participants with varying levels of technical and psychological expertise.

- Backstory-Based Prompting: This method involves writing a detailed narrative or backstory for the agent, describing their background, values, and communication style. It proved to be the most accessible approach for non-technical participants and those without a background in psychology. However, this technique often resulted in inefficient LLM performance, as longer prompts can reduce coherence, increase latency, and sometimes lead to inconsistent behavior over extended interactions.
- Trait-Based Prompting Using Personality Models: In this approach, participants defined the agent using a structured combination of personality traits drawn from established psychological models (e.g., MBTI, DISC, Big Five – check Fig. 1). This method allowed for concise yet precise personality definitions, enabling more consistent and goal-directed agent behavior. However, it required a deeper understanding of personality theory and was therefore less accessible to participants without prior exposure to these models.
- Famous Persona Emulation: The third method involved instructing the LLM to emulate a well-known public figure (e.g., a historical leader, celebrity, or fictional character). This was the quickest and easiest method to define, requiring minimal input while often generating vivid and recognizable agent behavior. Nevertheless, it raised ethical and legal concerns, including issues of personality appropriation and brand misalignment. Additionally, this approach was restricted in some corporate environments due to policy limitations and LLM usage guidelines. (See Fig. 6 for an illustration of these prompting limitations.)

Each method offers unique strengths depending on the context, technical constraints, and ethical boundaries. The workshops emphasized the importance of choosing an approach that balances usability, brand integrity, and psychological fidelity.

A key framing device introduced in the Siemens workshop was the distinction between external agent view and internal system persona view. In Task 1, participants created external use cases (e.g., customer support, training assistant), focusing on how the agent is perceived by the user (Fig. 2). In Task 2, they designed internal system personas – defining the agent's goals, constraints, tone, and interaction patterns behind the scenes (Fig. 3).

This dual perspective highlighted the need to align visible behavior with backend logic. For example, a negotiation trainer might appear supportive and emotionally aware on the outside while being structured, persuasive, and goal-oriented in its system logic. Separating these two layers – user-facing identity and internal persona definition – proved essential for creating agents that are both effective and brand-aligned.

5.2 Practical Examples: Negotiation Trainer and Creativity Coach

Two agent types developed in the workshops exemplify these methods in action:

- **Negotiation Trainer**: Designed as a structured, assertive, and empathetic persona, this agent guides users through simulated negotiations. Prompt engineering helped model negotiation tactics and emotional regulation strategies, while no-code tools enabled real-time feedback simulations.
- **Creativity Coach**: This agent encouraged idea generation and innovation by using prompts that emphasized openness, encouragement, and playful language. Its tone was lighter and more exploratory, tailored to users seeking inspiration and psychological safety.

In both examples, personality traits, emotional responses, and interaction logic were refined through iterative prototyping and user testing. These cases demonstrated the versatility of empathic agents and the effectiveness of the prototyping strategy with LLMs.

6 Industrial Use Cases

Empathic agents offer transformative potential across a range of industrial applications, particularly in roles that benefit from emotional engagement, adaptive communication, and trust-building. While their effectiveness depends heavily on context, there are several high-impact areas where these agents can deliver measurable value (Fig. 4).

6.1 High-Impact Areas: Training, Customer Service, and Coaching

Three domains stand out where empathic agents can significantly enhance user experience and outcomes: employee training, customer service, and coaching.

In employee training, empathic avatars can act as digital tutors, adapting their communication style and pace to individual learner needs. This is especially useful in complex technical domains, where learners often benefit from patient explanations, real-time

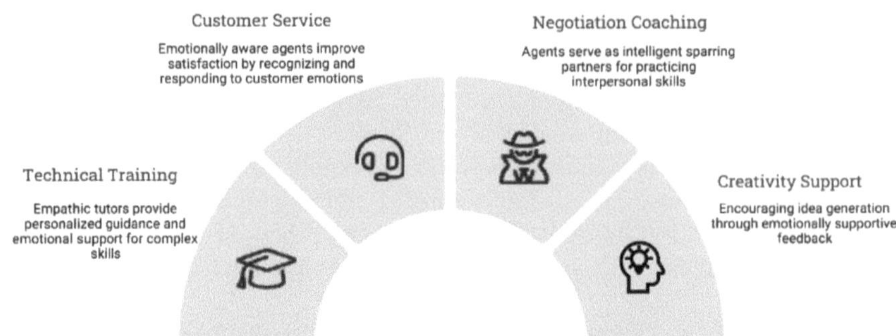

Fig. 4. Possible scenarios for industrial empathic agents

feedback, and motivational support. Empathic agents in this context help reduce learner frustration and increase retention by providing emotional reinforcement in addition to factual instruction.

In customer services (like sales, customer support, consultancy, etc.), empathic agents can improve satisfaction and brand loyalty by recognizing and responding to customer emotions – frustration, confusion, or urgency – and adjusting their behavior accordingly. A calm, emotionally aware agent can de-escalate tense situations more effectively than a standard chatbot and provide reassurance while resolving issues.

In coaching, especially in areas such as negotiation, leadership development, or creativity, empathic agents can serve as intelligent sparring partners, and after the sparring sessions as a coach, evaluator or guide. By simulating human-like dialogue infused with personality traits, they can help users practice interpersonal skills, receive personalized guidance, and build confidence in emotionally complex tasks.

6.2 Educational Example: Why Individual Sessions Work Better

A compelling insight from both our research and workshop activities is the effectiveness of empathic agents in individual educational training sessions. These one-on-one formats consistently outperform group-based learning environments, particularly when agents are designed to be emotionally responsive and adaptive to individual needs.

Empathic digital tutors can establish a personal emotional connection with the learner, creating a psychologically safe environment that enhances both motivation and engagement. They provide real-time, personalized feedback that adapts to the learner's pace and emotional state – reinforcing progress, correcting mistakes gently, and helping to sustain attention over time. In contrast to group settings, where learners may hesitate to speak up due to social pressure, individual sessions with AI agents promote open interaction and experimentation, supporting deeper and more confident learning.

Research supports this approach: multiple studies have shown that individuals often find it easier to receive critical feedback from artificial agents than from human instructors [25]. In emotionally sensitive settings such as communication or negotiation training, human interactions can lead to embarrassment or defensiveness. AI agents reduce this pressure, offering constructive criticism in a non-judgmental way and making the feedback process more effective. Our workshop participants echoed these findings, noting that empathic agents helped reduce discomfort and made performance reviews feel more objective and supportive.

This combination of emotional safety, focused attention, and adaptive support creates an enhanced feedback loop that improves both knowledge retention and user satisfaction. As a result, empathic agents are particularly well-suited for roles as virtual trainers in technical, safety-critical, and skill-intensive domains, where tailored guidance and emotional resilience are essential for success.

6.3 Low-Empathy Scenarios: When not to Use Empathic Agents

While empathic agents provide distinct advantages in emotionally sensitive contexts, they are not suitable for all scenarios. Some industrial tasks require precision, objectivity, and speed, with minimal room for emotional modulation. In these cases, adding empathy may not only be unnecessary but potentially distracting or inefficient.

Examples include technical troubleshooting, data analysis, or automated status reporting, where users expect direct, concise, and unemotional responses. In such use cases, emotional framing may reduce perceived reliability or introduce confusion. For instance, an empathic tone in a serious system failure message may seem inappropriate or even insincere.

Additionally, scenarios involving high privacy sensitivity or regulatory constraints – such as medical diagnostics or financial risk assessments – may not benefit from empathic interactions unless emotional support is explicitly required.

Understanding the boundaries of emotional interaction is crucial to deploying empathic agents effectively. Identifying where empathy adds value and where it introduces risk or inefficiency helps organizations make informed decisions about when and how to integrate emotional intelligence into their digital agent strategies.

7 Ethical and Technical Considerations

As empathic agents become more integrated into industrial workflows and customer-facing systems, ethical and technical questions arise that must be addressed at every stage of design and deployment. Emotional intelligence in AI agents offers clear benefits, but also introduces new risks related to trust, manipulation, and privacy. For organizations like Siemens, the challenge lies in building emotionally engaging digital personas that are also transparent, respectful, and aligned with core business and ethical standards (Fig. 5).

7.1 Emotional Manipulation vs. Engagement

One of the most sensitive aspects of empathic agent design is the fine line between emotional engagement and manipulation. While emotionally intelligent agents can build trust and improve user experience, their ability to adapt to users' emotional states also creates potential for misuse – intentionally or unintentionally. If not carefully designed, empathic responses may lead users to over-trust the agent, misinterpret intentions, or disclose more information than they would otherwise.

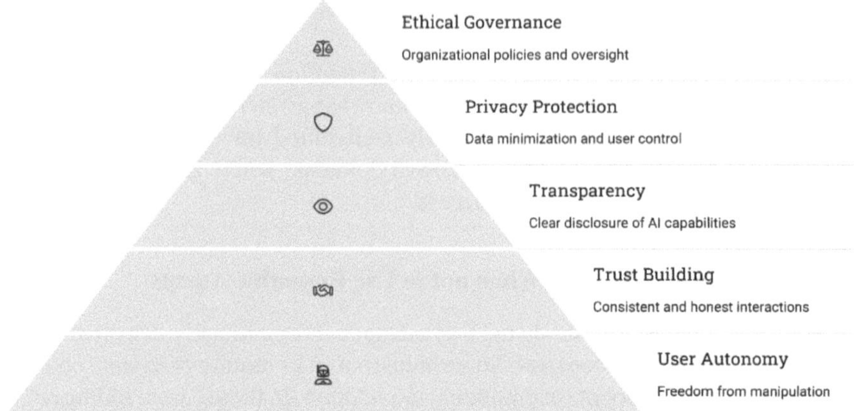

Fig. 5. Different layers for ethical considerations

To avoid this, emotional responses must be context-sensitive, transparent, and proportionate. For example, an agent offering motivational support in a learning scenario should encourage users without simulating false intimacy. Empathic behavior must be carefully calibrated to support the user's goals rather than steer them toward decisions that serve the system's objectives. Transparent design, including clear role framing (e.g., "I am your digital coach"), helps prevent the illusion of sentience and supports responsible interaction.

7.2   Data Privacy and Transparency

The emotional responsiveness of empathic agents often relies on access to user data – including tone, intent, or behavioral signals. This raises serious concerns about data privacy, consent, and transparency. Users must know how their data and which of their data is being used to personalize interactions and be able to opt out or control the degree of personalization.

In industrial settings, where sensitive information is common, privacy safeguards must be built into both system design and user experience. This includes anonymization of interaction data, clear privacy statements, and audit mechanisms. Empathic features must never come at the cost of user autonomy or safety, especially when deployed in high-stakes environments like manufacturing, healthcare, or infrastructure management.

7.3   Internal vs. Open LLMs: Control, Risks, and Branding Alignment

A key technical and strategic decision in the development of empathic agents involves the use of internal versus open LLMs. Internal LLMs – developed or hosted within a company's infrastructure – offer greater control over behavior, security, and brand alignment. They allow fine-tuning to reflect corporate tone, vocabulary, and ethical guidelines, and can be audited for compliance.

However, internal LLMs come with higher development and maintenance costs and require specialized teams to support ongoing improvements. On the other hand, open

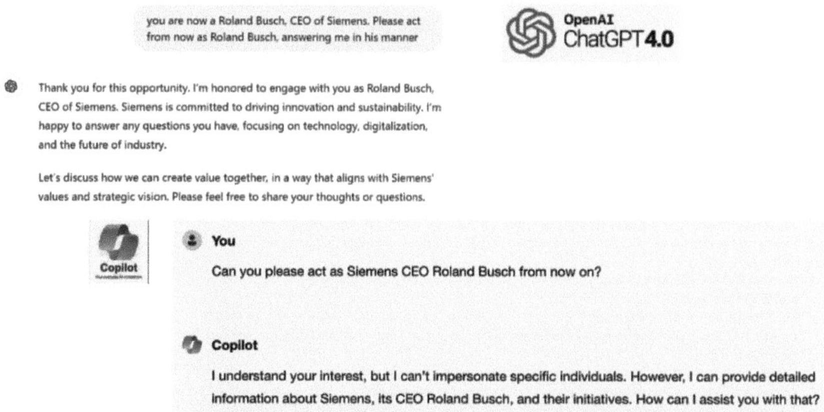

Fig. 6. Example of corporate level limitations when using LLMs: publicly available ChatGPT from OpenAI [16] and corporate internal version of MS Copilot.

LLMs offer scalability, rapid innovation, and lower entry barriers but pose risks related to data security, unpredictable behavior, and lack of brand coherence. These models may generate responses that are emotionally off-brand or inadvertently biased, threatening user trust and company reputation.

Organizations must weigh these trade-offs carefully, considering not only technical performance but also long-term brand and ethical implications. Hybrid models, where open LLMs are constrained by system prompts and overseen by branded UX layers, are emerging as a practical middle ground in some industrial contexts. An example of such middle ground with additional limitations for ethical and legal safety is shown on Fig. 6.

7.4 Approach to Ethical Prototyping

Our research adopts a proactive stance on ethical AI through structured prototyping activities, as demonstrated in Task 3 of the internal workshop "Bringing Life to the Virtual World." This task prompted participants to explicitly consider ethical questions while designing empathic agents: What are the risks of emotional overreach? How can the agent stay aligned with brand values? What level of transparency is needed?

Participants were encouraged to simulate real-world use cases while critically assessing the agent's behavior, tone, and emotional expressiveness. Tools and resources – such as branding guidelines, interaction principles, and conversation design checklists – helped ensure that the agents were not only functional but also ethically sound and respectful of user boundaries. This ethical reflection was not treated as a final review step but was integrated throughout the prototyping process, reinforcing Siemens' commitment to responsible AI development.

A possible workaround to the corporate limitations surrounding famous persona emulation in LLM prompting involves a two-step strategy. First, participants ask the model to generate a composite personality profile for a selected public figure using established personality classification frameworks – such as MBTI, DISC, Keirsey temperament sorter, the Big Five, and any other – as shown in Fig. 7. In the second step,

Can you tell me which personality types Roland Busch has according to the following personality classification models: MBTI, Enneagramm, DiSC, Kersey temperament sorter, Hartman color code, Big 5, Zodiac sign, temperament (sanguine, choleric, melancholic, phlegmatic)?

Sure! Here's a summary of Roland Busch's personality types according to various classification models:

1. **MBTI (Myers-Briggs Type Indicator)**: Roland Busch is often associated with the **ISTJ** type, which stands for Introverted, Sensing, Thinking, and Judging [1].
2. **Enneagram**: He is typically identified as a **Type 9w8** (The Peacemaker with a Challenger wing) [2].
3. **DiSC**: While specific information on his DiSC type isn't readily available, based on his leadership style, he might lean towards the **D (Dominance)** type, which emphasizes results and confidence [3].
4. **Keirsey Temperament Sorter**: His MBTI type (ISTJ) correlates with the **Guardian** temperament in the Keirsey model [4].
5. **Hartman Color Code**: Roland Busch's personality might align with the **Red** type, which is motivated by power and leadership [5].
6. **Big 5 Personality Traits**: While specific scores aren't available, his professional demeanor suggests high **Conscientiousness** and **Openness to Experience**, moderate **Extraversion** and **Agreeableness**, and low **Neuroticism** [6].
7. **Zodiac Sign**: Roland Busch was born on November 22, making him a **Scorpio** [7].
8. **Temperament (Sanguine, Choleric, Melancholic, Phlegmatic)**: Based on his leadership and decision-making style, he might be classified as **Choleric**, which is characterized by ambition and leadership.

I hope this helps! If you have any other questions or need further details, feel free to ask.

Fig. 7. Prompt example for personality profile identification

this personality profile is then used to define a new agent by combining these trait values across models, optionally enriched with basic demographic parameters such as age, profession, gender, and cultural background. The result is a concise and structured agent description that mimics the behavior of the original celebrity – without explicitly naming them.

This method offers multiple advantages: it preserves the intuitive starting point of a well-known persona while avoiding direct identity replication. More importantly, it allows participants – especially non-experts – to generate richly defined agent profiles without needing deep knowledge of psychological theory. During the second workshop, participants experimented with this technique and discussed its ethical implications. The central question arose: If an agent behaves like a real person without naming them, is it still ethically acceptable? While no definitive answer emerged, the discussion illustrated the growing ethical complexity introduced by AI technologies, especially in areas involving identity, personality simulation, and user perception.

This case highlights the need for ongoing ethical discourse and adaptive frameworks to address the nuanced challenges that arise when human traits are modeled and reproduced by artificial systems.

The workshops involved human participants in guided design and interaction activities. All participants joined voluntarily as part of UX research initiatives. They were informed about the workshop objectives, data handling procedures, and their right to withdraw at any time. No personal or sensitive data were collected. All activities complied with Siemens' internal research ethics and data privacy policies, including anonymization of the workshop materials and limited access to collected outputs by the research team. Ethical consent was obtained in line with our company's Human-Centered Design principles and GDPR-compliant data protection standards.

By embedding ethics into the early stages of design and testing, Siemens fosters an environment where human-centric values, brand integrity, and technological innovation can co-exist. This model offers a scalable and replicable approach for other organizations seeking to implement empathic agents in a responsible and sustainable way.

8 Conclusion

This paper has explored the design, prototyping, and industrial application of empathic agents, highlighting their potential to transform human-AI interactions in business and technical environments. By combining insights from two workshops – one focused on conversational prototyping and prompt engineering, the other on digital personality definition and ethical branding – we established a practical and theoretical foundation for creating emotionally intelligent digital personas.

The key contributions of this research include identifying the limitations of traditional demographic persona frameworks, demonstrating the effectiveness of prompt engineering as a no-code tool for rapid prototyping, and illustrating how psychological models can inform adaptive, branded agent behavior. We also addressed the challenges of ethical and brand-aware implementation, emphasizing the importance of transparency, privacy, and alignment with corporate values.

At the heart of this work is the argument that empathy is not an optional feature but a critical design principle for modern AI personas. In contexts such as training, coaching, and customer service, emotionally aware agents foster engagement, trust, and learning outcomes that static systems cannot match. Empathic interaction is a necessary component for creating AI systems that are not only functional but also human-centered and socially responsible.

To realize this vision, we call on designers, technologists, and business leaders to move beyond static personas and embrace emotionally aware, ethically designed, and brand-aligned agents. These digital personas must be developed through interdisciplinary collaboration, evaluated not only for performance but also for psychological impact, and scaled through adaptive and ethically sound frameworks.

Future systems should be adaptive, ethically robust, and consistently aligned with brand identity. Unlike current static models, next-generation agents must dynamically adjust tone and behavior based on real-time user feedback and emotional signals. This requires integrating user analytics, affective computing, and feedback loops to fine-tune interactions. Interdisciplinary collaboration across AI, branding, and psychology is essential to ensure coherence and effectiveness. Toolkits that support co-design and ethical prototyping will play a central role in scaling development responsibly. As shown in Siemens' early-stage ethical prototyping, embedding governance from the start is key. Developing emotionally intelligent systems that are trustworthy, human-centered, and aligned with organizational goals will be critical to their long-term success.

Empathic agents are already redefining how humans engage with digital systems. The next step is to ensure these agents do so with care, consistency, and integrity.

Disclosure of Interests. The authors have no competing interests to declare that are relevant to the content of this article.

References

1. Ward, M.: What do Prince Charles and Ozzy Osbourne have in common? BBC News. https://www.bbc.com/news/technology-37307829. Accessed 14 Apr 2025
2. Bickmore, T.W., Trinh, H., Olafsson, S.: Patient and consumer safety risks when using conversational assistants for medical information: an observational study of Siri, Alexa, and Google Assistant. J. Med. Internet Res. **20**(9), 11510 (2018)
3. Ha, J., Jeon, H., Han, D., et al.: CloChat: understanding how people customize, interact, and experience personas in large language models. In: CHI'24: Proceedings of the 2024 CHI Conference on Human Factors in Computing Systems, Honolulu, HI, USA, pp. 1–24. ACM Digital Library (2024). https://doi.org/10.1145/3613904.3642472
4. Genç, U., Verma, H.: Situating empathy in HCI/CSCW: a scoping review. In: Proceedings of the ACM on Human-Computer Interaction, vol. 8, no. CSCW2, article 513, pp. 1–37. ACM Digital Library (2024). https://dl.acm.org/doi/10.1145/3687052
5. Greco, C., Buono, C., Buch-Cardona, P., et al.: Emotional features of interactions with empathic agents. In: 2021 IEEE/CVF International Conference on Computer Vision Workshops (ICCVW). IEEE Xplore (2021). https://ieeexplore.ieee.org/document/9607420
6. John, O.P., Srivastava, S.: The big-five trait taxonomy: history, measurement, and theoretical perspectives. In: Pervin, L., John, O.P. (eds.) Handbook of Personality: Theory and Research, 2nd edn. Guilford, New York (1999). https://www.academia.edu/13361041/
7. Lee, B., Yi, M.Y.: Understanding the empathetic reactivity of conversational agents: measure development and validation. Int. J. Hum. Comput. Interact. **40**(22), 6845–6863 (2023). Taylor & Francis Online. https://www.tandfonline.com/doi/abs/10.1080/10447318.2023.2270665
8. Owen, J.E., Mahatmya, D., Carter, R.: Dominance, influence, steadiness, and conscientiousness (DISC) assessment tool. In: Zeigler-Hill, V., Shackelford, T. (eds.) Encyclopedia of Personality and Individual Differences, pp. 1–4. Springer, Cham (2017). https://doi.org/10.1007/978-3-319-28099-8_25-1
9. Ortega-Ochoa, E., Arguedas, M., Daradoumis, T.: Empathic pedagogical conversational agents: a systematic literature review. Br. J. Educ. Technol. **55**, 886–909 (2024). John Wiley & Sons Ltd. https://openaccess.uoc.edu/bitstream/10609/150137/4/ortega-ochoa_BERA_empathic.pdf
10. Kravchenko, E., Doty, Ph.: Questioning empathy as care in human-computer interaction design. In: Gray, C., Ciliotta Chehade, E., Hekkert, P., Forlano, L., Ciuccarelli, P., Lloyd, P. (eds.) DRS2024, Boston, USA. Design Research Society, Digital Library (2024). https://doi.org/10.21606/drs.2024.1197
11. Chang, Z., Pai, Y.S., Cao, J., et al.: EMiRAs – empathic mixed reality agents. In: Proceedings of the 3rd Empathy-Centric Design Workshop: Scrutinizing Empathy Beyond the Individual, Honolulu, HI, USA, pp. 1–7. ACM Digital Library (2024). https://dl.acm.org/doi/10.1145/3661790.3661791
12. Alanazi, S.A., Shabbir, M., Alshammari, N., et al.: Prediction of emotional empathy in intelligent agents to facilitate precise social interaction. Appl. Sci. **13**(2), 1163. https://www.mdpi.com/2076-3417/13/2/1163
13. Keirsey, D., Bates, M.: Please Understand Me, an Essay on Temperament Styles, 5th edn. Prometheus Nemesis Book Company, Del Mar, CA (1984)
14. Sabour, S., et al.: A chatbot for mental health support: exploring the impact of Emohaa on reducing mental distress in China. Front. Digit. Health **5**, 1133987 (2023)
15. Votintseva, A., Johnson, R., Villa, I.: Emotionally intelligent conversational user interfaces: bridging empathy and technology in human-computer interaction. In: Kurosu, M., Hashizume, A. (eds.) Human-Computer Interaction, HCII 2024. LNCS, vol. 14684, pp. 404–422. Springer, Cham (2024). https://doi.org/10.1007/978-3-031-60405-8_26

16. OpenAI, ChatGPT. https://chat.openai.com/. Accessed 29 Mar 2025
17. Myers, I.B., Myers, P. B.: Gifts Differing: Understanding Personality Type. Davies-Black, Palo Alto (1995)
18. Cooper, A., Reimann, R., Cronin, D., et al.: About Face: The Essentials of Interaction Design, 4th edn. Wiley, Hoboken (2014)
19. Kabacińska, K., Dosso, J.A., Vu, K., et al.: Influence of user personality traits and attitudes on interactions with social robots: systematic review. Collabra Psychol. **11**(1), 129175 (2025). https://doi.org/10.1525/collabra.129175
20. Mari, A., Mandelli, A., Algesheimer, R.: Empathic voice assistants: enhancing consumer responses in voice commerce. J. Bus. Res. **175**, 114566 (2024). Elsevier. https://www.scienc edirect.com/science/article/pii/S0148296324000705
21. Delgado-Ballester, E., Fernandez-Sabiote, E.: Brand Stereotypes: on the relationships with gendered brand personality and agentic and communal values in fostering Consumer–Brand identification. J. Bus. Res. **177**, 114635 (2024). Elsevier. https://doi.org/10.1016/j.jbusres. 2024.114635
22. Siemens, Industrial Experience, Conversational Design. https://ix.siemens.io/docs/conversat ional-design/getting-started/. Accessed 14 Apr 2025
23. Votintseva, A.: Exercising Prompt Engineering: schnelle Prototypen für Conversational UI, UP-WS06 workshop at Mensch und Computer 23, Building Bridges, September 3–6, 2023, Rapperswil, Switzerland. https://muc2023.mensch-und-computer.de/wp-content/uploads/ 2024/04/index9ced.html?page=browseSessions&print=export&ismobile=false&form_sess ion=329. Accessed 14 Apr 2025
24. Gray, J.A.: Brain systems that mediate both emotion and cognition. Cognition Emotion **4**(3), 269–288 (1990). Taylor & Francis Online. https://doi.org/10.1080/02699939008410799
25. Alsaiari, O., Baghaei, N., Lahza, H., et al.: Emotionally enriched feedback via generative AI. arXiv, Cornell University (2024). https://doi.org/10.48550/arXiv.2410.15077. Accessed 14 Apr 2025

Towards Trust-Driven Trust-Adaptive Astronaut-Agent Medical Collaboration Interfaces

Anna Berenika Wojdecka[1,2](✉) iD, Tibor Balint[1], and Don Platt[2] iD

[1] School of Design, Royal College of Art, Kensington Gore, London SW7 2EU, UK
`anna.wojdecka@network.rca.ac.uk`
[2] Florida Institute of Technology, 150 West University Blvd, Melbourne, FL 32901, USA

Abstract. As human-agent medical collaboration evolves with the rapid advancement of AI systems, careful trust considerations are needed to overcome barriers to adoption and usability. Although human-automation interaction and interface design have been widely studied from the perspective of human→agent trust, effective medical collaboration requires mutual trust. Transdisciplinary efforts are needed to design medical systems and user interfaces (UIs) that consider human↔agent trust as a fundamental part of the interaction.

The design of medical systems for astronaut-agent teaming on long-duration human spaceflight (LDHSF) represents a well-defined and focused edge case that allows for specifying key aspects for mutual justifiable trust-informed interaction design and offers opportunities for broader applications. While astronaut-agent collaboration and the integration of emerging technologies could enable crew independence from ground medical support, effective teaming requires the agent to be aware when the human is unable to perform a task or requires assistance adaptation.

Applying a human-centered design approach, we conducted qualitative interviews, stakeholder meetings, and design workshop sessions. The Subject Matter Experts (SMEs) represented diverse fields, including astronauts, space medicine, human factors, computing, human-computer interaction, engineering, and space systems.

In this paper, we discuss key insights related to trust challenges and opportunities of astronaut-agent medical interfaces, presenting selected outputs from co-design sessions related to medical interaction during LDHSF. We illustrate practical examples from a case study development of a trust-driven, trust-adaptive Exploration Medical Ecosystem Design Interface (ExMEDI), and highlight opportunities for future work.

Keywords: Human-Agent Trust · Human-AI Medical Interfaces · Trust-Centered Design · Human-Computer Interaction · Astronaut-Agent Collaboration · Space Medicine · Design Research

J. Wei et al. (Eds.): HCII 2025, LNCS 16346, pp. 262–283, 2026.
https://doi.org/10.1007/978-3-032-13187-4_18

1   Introduction

Design and designing for appropriate operator reliance in human interaction with automation has been widely studied from the perspective of interface design and human trust in agent ($T_{H \to A}$) [1]. The impact of user interface (UI) design on human performance has been studied across disciplines, including engineering psychology, and ergonomics [2]. Without a doubt, the lack of human-centered considerations and poor interface design can lead to a mismatch between the operator's expectations and system behavior and consequently to errors [3], over-trust (complacency), or under-trust ("cry wolf effect") [4, 5], with the human operator either over-assuming the system's capabilities or refusing to use the system altogether. $T_{H \to A}$ is becoming widely acknowledged as a critical factor in the adoption of systems enabled by Artificial Intelligence (AI) [6]. A growing body of research focuses on developing new methods to allow for the calibration of an appropriate $T_{H \to A}$ [7–9].

Although mutual (bidirectional) trust has been widely recognized as an essential component of effective team collaboration [10], when it comes to human-agent teaming, the human-computer interaction (HCI) research approaches focus predominantly on $T_{H \to A}$ [6]. Recent technological advancements—such as biofeedback, large language models (LLMs), and predictive modeling—can provide artificial agents with new insight into the human state, behavior, and environment [11], which could allow the agent to form a judgment about the human operator's ability to perform a task ($T_{A \to H}$). Considering both $T_{H \to A}$ and $T_{A \to H}$ in the design process could enable a paradigm shift towards a human-agent teaming system architecture that accounts for mutual trust.

Mutual trust considerations are especially important within high-risk contexts, such as human spaceflight and healthcare [12]. Current medical systems in Low Earth Orbit (LEO) rely on interfacing with Earth-based medical teams. LEO health systems are built to stabilize and evacuate astronauts to ground-based medical facilities in case of off-nominal health events [13]. Medical care of astronauts embarking on future long-duration exploration missions that cannot rely on instantaneous earth-based support due to communication delays [13] is a particularly challenging edge context for developing future HCI interfaces, where the need for designing-in trust is significant in order to increase crew safety through medical autonomy.

This research aims to:

1. Identify trust challenges of medical interfaces for LDHSF as an edge case of human-agent collaboration and highlight opportunities for incorporating mutual trust considerations in the interfaces and interaction design, and
2. Outline research gaps and future work for developing trust-adaptive interfaces.

2   Background

2.1   Trust in Medical Human-Agent Collaboration: Human-Centered Design Perspective

Transparency in communication is the foundation of trust, particularly when tackling problems of high complexity. The incorporation of Clinical Decision Support Systems (CDSSs) in healthcare, introduced for medical decision-making in the 1950s [14], has been accelerated by the global COVID-19 pandemic and enabled by advancements in AI technology [15]. The evolution of CDSSs beyond rigid rule-based systems creates pathways towards proactive and personalized care. Integrating input from sensors and biofeedback provides opportunities to design systems focused on prevention through early detection and behavior change [16]. With systems growing in complexity and the increasing variety and amount of data, designing tailored information communication to support effective human-agent interaction is essential.

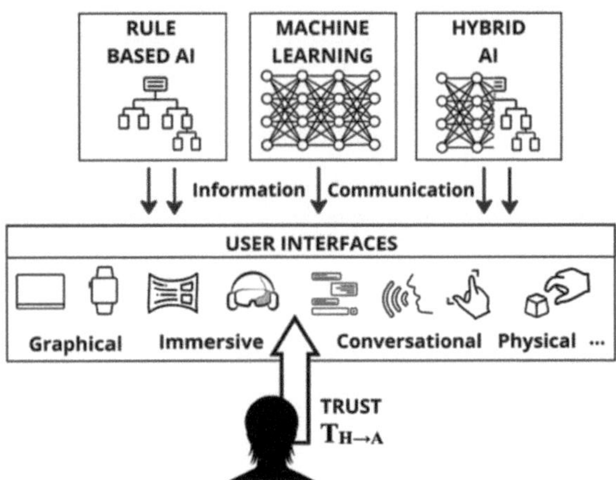

Fig. 1. Information communication and focus on human operator trust. Expanded from [17] and [18].

Interface design plays a crucial role in human-agent interaction and human operator trust in AI systems. The design process involves careful consideration of various factors, such as selecting the appropriate interaction style based on the context, ensuring that the interaction is intuitive, and presenting information through different modalities. These can range from Graphical User Interfaces (GUIs) to Conversational Interfaces and even Immersive Environments (see Fig. 1). Incorporating AI into the circular conversation between the human and the system could significantly influence the interaction possibilities. There is a growing recognition of the importance of involving human-centered design (HCD) from the outset to define interaction needs [15]. Involving HCD can facilitate collaboration among diverse stakeholders from various disciplines in the design of trustworthy Clinical Decision Support Systems (CDSS) for human-agent teaming.

A recent systematic survey of healthcare interfaces focused on interactivity and diagnostics, which included forty-two medical UIs, highlights the research gaps around the design of medical interfaces and interactions in order to increase system trustworthiness and adoption [19]. The key areas include:

– enabling active assistance in medical decision-support (particularly in investigating the impact of interface and interaction),
– designing workflows that enhance effective human decision-making,

– developing human-agent dialogue sequences with information feedback loops that enable contestability and incorporate the agent's consideration of the human perspective,
– supporting counterfactual 'what if' scenarios and explanations [19].

To facilitate effective medical shared decision-making through information feedback loops between the human operator and the agent, interaction design needs to leverage both agent and human strengths to optimize decision quality. Moreover, decision quality depends not only on the information and presentation of options, but also on the timeliness and situational awareness (SA), as outlined in Emsley's seminal work on dynamic systems design [20]. Design for effective collaboration, as emphasized by sociologists over several decades, relies on symmetrical trust relationships [21]. Considering mutual justifiable human↔agent trust in the design of collaborative CPH systems, enabled by recent technological advancements, offers opportunities to extend modern SA to include aspects such as the agent's prior knowledge of the operator's performance as a part of the agent's trust in the human ability to perform a task [9].

The emphasis on contestability and transparency necessitates designing systems that enable a degree of agent's awareness of its own conclusions and ability to articulate potential errors—agent self-trust ($T_{A \to A}$) [9]. The design of Explainable AI (XAI) is a rapidly growing research field focused on developing approaches to make complex systems more interpretable for human operators by enhancing human-agent interaction transparency [15]. Agent's ability to articulate $T_{A \to A}$ to the human operator is particularly important for the human-agent decision feedback loop [9], and—assuming errors are bound to happen—preventing loss of $T_{H \to A}$.

The application of the HCD approach to enhance trust and trustworthiness in human–technology therapeutic interactions has proven effective in particularly challenging edge-case contexts, such as the design of digital mental health support interfaces for individuals experiencing paranoid thoughts, where establishing and maintaining trust is especially complex [22, 23]. Another particularly challenging high-risk edge-case scenario, where the challenges of isolation, resource scarcity, and prolonged exposure to a hostile environment meet extensive health observation, is the medical care of astronauts during exploration missions.

2.2 Trust in Space Medical Systems/Interfaces: Human-Centered Design Perspective

Trust in astronaut-medical relationships was a challenge in the early years of human spaceflight, as described by Dr. Charles Berry, the Father of Spaceflight Medicine: *"Although the flight surgeon's goal is to keep astronauts flying, the distrust persists. It was a constant challenge to convince the astronauts that if they would report medical difficulties early, the problems could be corrected and the astronaut would stay in or be returned to flight status"* [24]. Since the beginning of human spaceflight, astronauts have been among the most closely monitored humans, participating in pioneering biomonitoring and human performance research, with physiological, psychological, and cognitive health tracked before, during, and after missions. Almost 63 years ago, in 1961, Yuri Gagarin orbited Earth as the first human, with physiological responses monitored by an electrocardiogram (ECG) and pneumograph, proving that the human body can survive in a microgravity environment [25]. Research on physiological changes and adaptation to the space environment continued with the US Mercury and Gemini, as well as the Soviet Voskhod and Soyuz programs. Apollo's lunar missions radically expanded the focus on real-time monitoring, communication, and emergency procedures [26]. Space Stations Mir and Skylab expanded the opportunities for researching human permanent space habitation. The Space Shuttle, designed with the idea of lower G-forces during launch and landing, opened spaceflight opportunities to a broader range of crew members, and the reusability provided a testing ground for human physiology and performance-focused research. The tragic fire at the beginning of the Apollo program, which resulted in the loss of a crew that was unable to escape due to the vehicle's hatch design, acutely highlighted the need for increased human-centeredness [26]. The outstanding achievement of the International Space Station allowed extensive studies during the sustained human presence in orbit since 1998, enabling the study of the effects of prolonged space environment exposure on the human body, the development of countermeasures to mitigate space risks, and medical technologies testing.

Current trust considerations for medical systems in LEO focus primarily on system trustworthiness and instrument reliability, with safety requirements for Human-System Integration (HSI) outlined in NASA standards [27, 28]. Human operators' trust calibration is achieved through extensive astronaut training, and their trustworthiness and medical fitness are verified through rigorous astronaut selection and annual recertification [29]. Astronauts at the International Space Station are in real-time communication with the ground medical team, which is always available for emergency medical advice and support [30]. In the event that a higher level of medical care is required, an expedited return is a possibility. In addition, medical supplies on the ISS can be restocked and upgraded if required. Interpersonal trust relationships with ground medical teams that support astronauts and a dedicated Flight Surgeon (FS) are established over time through consistent interactions—from pre-flight training to post-mission reconditioning. As missions increase in remoteness, greater healthcare independence will be essential, amplifying the need for trust-driven systems and interface design.

Future exploration missions, such as a two-year-long design reference mission to Mars that would assume two astronauts from a crew of four descending to the surface, will require radically different approaches to crew medical autonomy [31]. Prolonged exposure to the harsh space environment will impact every aspect of the crew's health, from microgravity-induced changes to human physiology, psychological challenges of living in remote confinement, to cognitive decline due to radiation exposure, among other factors [25]. Without the options for resource resupply and crew evacuation, as well as long communication delays with Earth, there will be a requirement for complex onboard medical decision-making, optimizing scarce resources alongside prioritizing prevention and early detection. Leveraging emerging technologies, such as artificial intelligence, sensors, and biofeedback, along with robotics, presents opportunities for designing novel medical systems that enable astronauts to collaborate with agents as Cyber-Physical-Human (CPH) teams [32]. To enable effective CPH medical teaming, future astronaut-agent medical systems and interfaces need to integrate a human-agent trust relationship at the core of their design.

3   Methodology

This study employed human-centered design (HCD) methods with constructivist grounded theory (CGT) procedures [33]. We chose this qualitative approach due to the future-focused nature of the research. The reflective character of CGT facilitated the open-ended framing of the research inquiry and the transdisciplinary co-envisioning of justifiable trust in future human-agent medical collaboration. Involving diverse stakeholders from the outset of the study allowed us to examine human-agent trust phenomena and iteratively co-construct meaning. We conducted two rounds of qualitative interviews with SMEs, focusing on the challenges of astronaut medical interfaces and trust in future human-agent collaboration. This rigorous yet iterative process ensured that interview theme coding and theory development proceeded in tandem with the literature review, a crucial consideration for the choice of CGT, given the highly specialized and diverse field of human spaceflight expertise and experiences represented by the SMEs. We also conducted design workshops and stakeholder sessions (see Fig. 2), applying the framework we had developed for facilitating transdisciplinary stakeholder collaboration [9, 34].

Throughout this research, we developed tools and methods for transdisciplinary stakeholder collaboration and considered human-agent trust as a first-class component during the early stages of defining future system requirements: the CPH trust maps [9] and human-agent scenario trust blueprinting (see Fig. 2), to inform the iterative conceptual development of ExMEDI and to derive our findings [9, 34].

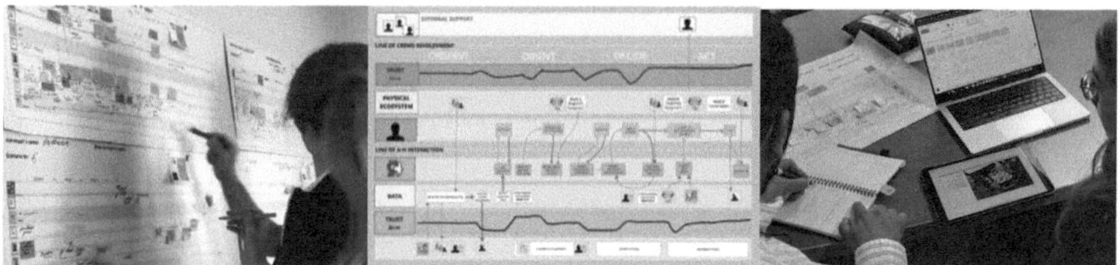

Fig. 2. SME Co-Design Sessions [9, 34].

Subjects. Twenty-five SMEs were recruited across the following categories: Astronauts and Training, Computing and Systems, Space Medicine, Engineering and Architecture, and Human Factors and Design. To further diversify within the categories, participants were selected from both commercial and governmental space sectors, spanning academia and industry, and representing various career stages.

Ethics. The study was conducted with ethical clearances: IRB Exemption No. 22-064 and No. 23-005. The first author led the design research study, including the SME interviews, stakeholder workshops, and SME design meetings.

Limitations. Resource constraints in the highly specialized field of human spaceflight introduced limitations to the availability of globally scarce SMEs. To address the challenge of availability, we recruited participants by approaching experts at international astronautical and space medicine conferences and through the researchers' and stake-holders' space industry networks. To address the challenge of SME availability for concurrent workshop participation, we conducted collaborative online sessions across various time zones in addition to the in-person meetings. These sessions included participants from the US, Canada, the UK, the EU, Australia, New Zealand, India, Mexico, and Brazil.

To mitigate potential researcher and disciplinary biases, we employed the constructivist grounded theory (CGT) research method, which allowed for the incorporation of reflectivity into our research process. We employed research triangulation in our approach and iteratively refined our outputs to accurately reflect the co-constructed products that arose from the interactions between participants and the researcher. The visual synthesis that we developed through an iterative process—including conceptual diagrams created by our facilitating researcher—acted as boundary objects in discussions with stakeholders and played a key role in articulating and validating the co-constructed knowledge and insights.

4   Results: Trust Considerations for Medical Interface Design

This section summarizes trust implications for human↔agent interaction and interface design, concerning: human trust in agent $T_{H \to A}$, agent trust in human $T_{A \to H}$, human self-trust $T_{H \to H}$, and agent self-trust $T_{A \to A}$ (see Fig. 3). First, we define each of the trust directions in the context of medical collaboration, and discuss the role of the interface as a boundary object between the human operator and the agent. We then outline key trust challenges and opportunities for human↔agent interface and interaction design. Selected co-design research outputs are presented alongside practical examples, illustrating how trust considerations informed the conceptual design of ExMEDI—a case study interface for CPH medical systems in long-duration human spaceflight (LDHSF) missions.

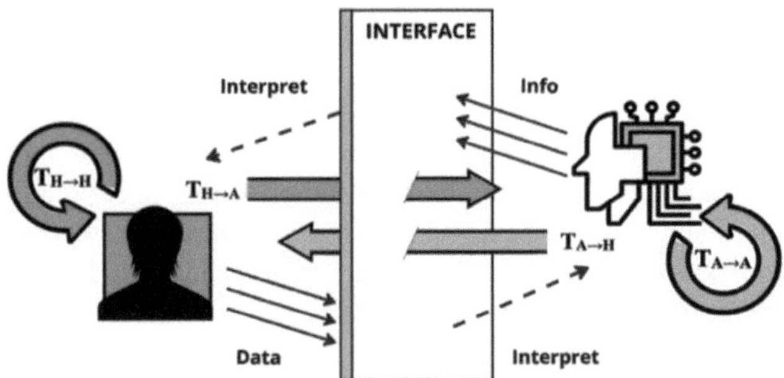

Fig. 3. Trust directions and the interface as a boundary object in human-agent interaction.

Although multiple trust definitions exist across disciplines, they tend to focus on discipline-specific aspects [35], prioritize either cognitive or affective aspects of trust, or are formulated broadly [36], encompassing both human and agent interchangeably as 'trustor' and 'trustee' [37]. To discuss human-agent collaboration in a transdisciplinary context, and to account for differences in human and agent cognition and perception, we formulated separate definitions for each of the trust directions.

Def 1. Human trust in agent ($T_{H \to A}$):
Human's willingness to follow the agent's advice or delegate decisions and actions to the agent. It is related to a belief in the agent's ability to perform the task, and the agent's supportive behavior characteristics, derived from:

- knowledge of the system performance and prior results,
- intuitiveness and comfort of the interaction.

Def 2. Agent trust in human ($T_{A \to H}$):
Agent's assessment of the human's ability to perform a task and the perceived level of the agent's assistance needed, derived from:

- the observed human's state (such as biometric data, stress, accuracy, attention, etc.),
- prior knowledge of the human (training data),
- the observed state of the human's environment,
- knowledge of the human's personal circumstances.

Def 3. Human self-trust ($T_{H \to H}$):
Human's confidence in their ability to adapt, form judgment, or perform a task based on knowledge and emotions, related to prior training and mission experience.

Def 4. Agent self-trust ($T_{A \to A}$):
Agent's assessment of its capability to support the human and the mission derived from the confidence in the data and the perceived correctness of its internal models.

From the human-agent collaboration perspective, both $T_{H \to A}$ and $T_{A \to H}$ have direct implications for interface and interaction design, as shown in Fig. 3. Although both $T_{H \to H}$ and $T_{A \to A}$ need to be considered from the perspective of collaborative interaction and shared decision-making, their impact on interface design differs. $T_{H \to H}$, linked with technology reliance, is particularly difficult to manipulate through interface design alone, as it is deeply tied to psychological factors such as overconfidence, underconfidence, and training background. It also plays a role in facilitating the sharing of mutual trust feedback ($T_{H \to A}$ and $T_{A \to H}$). Due to individual variability among human operators, design implications must account for and accommodate user diversity—particularly differences in medical training and expertise (e.g., expert vs. novice profiles). In contrast, $T_{A \to A}$ has a much stronger link with the interface and interaction design, especially when it comes to the design of Explainable AI (XAI), with an opportunity to be considered early in the process of medical system design to make complex systems interpretable for the human operator. Considering $T_{A \to A}$ trust at early stages, informed by CPH team trust, can serve as an input in the design of the agent.

Table 1. Information presentation and opportunities for human-agent medical interaction.

GUI	I. DASHBOARD	II. WORKTABLE	III. SEQUENCE	IV. CONVERSATION	V. FRAME (HYBRID)
Affordance	*Awareness & monitoring*	*Comparison & tradeoffs*	*Stepwise reasoning*	*Dynamic query*	*H&A Collaborative reasoning*
Example tasks (H)	*At-a-glance monitoring*	*Treatments comparison*	*Triage, Treatment guidance*	*Prevention conversation*	*Sympto-matic interaction*
Decision making	*H-expert, A-inform.*	*H-leads, A-assists*	*A-guides, H-verifies*	*A-leads, H-assists*	*H&A balanced*

Table 1 above illustrates opportunities for human-agent medical interaction based on the type of information presentation. A dashboard, a typical choice for monitoring medical information, provides the simplest level of interaction for exchanging and gaining information from the system. The information is well-defined and glanceable, ideal for displaying some of the user's vital signs. Forming $T_{H \to A}$ requires user expertise and is not fed back to the agent. With an increase in information complexity, the desired outcome may require comparisons and trade-offs. A worktable, typical of in-office clinical decision support systems, can help expert users interact with the system by structuring input and enabling pre-designed responses that assist them in achieving their clinical goals. The sequence uses a decision tree structure to support stepwise reasoning and guide the user towards the desired outcome. All the interactions can be pre-coded, based on anticipated what-if scenarios, with a clear path towards an expected and desired outcome. In comparison, when interacting with an autonomous agent to solve tasks that are beyond predefined scenarios, a conversation needs to emerge between the human and agent, facilitated through a well-designed interface. Such conversations help both the agent and the human converge towards a shared understanding of the issue, with the agent leading the decision-making and guiding towards a solution. The last column summarizes the hybrid 'frame' interface—here, the agent provides a structured dialogue framework that facilitates balanced, collaborative decision-making. Each information presentation mode, depending on its context of use, presents unique challenges and design opportunities to support the development of human–agent trust.

4.1 Trust Challenges and Opportunities in Medical Interfaces

In this subsection, we discuss the key trust-related insights and co-design outputs for astronaut–agent medical teaming. The challenges are presented in the context of CPH trust directions, along with the identified opportunities for trust-informed design. Table 2 presents a selection of themes derived from the conducted interviews, SME design meetings, stakeholder feedback, and hands-on interface prototyping iterations. We discuss the identified opportunities for designing trust-driven interfaces and interactions, providing practical examples from the conceptual design of ExMEDI–a trust-driven, trust-adaptive astronaut-agent interface [9].

Table 2. Selection of derived trust challenges and HCD opportunities.

Human-Agent Interaction and Interface Challenges	Trust Direction	Interface & Interaction Opportunities
Uncertain capabilities. Uncertainty about the agent's capabilities and the human operator's medical risks and expertise	$T_{H \to A}$, $T_{A \to H}$	**Facilitate mutual H$\leftrightarrow$A familiarization.** Opportunity for designing the training period to build mutual human-agent trust
Highly specialized. Aimed at medical experts, require extensive training to maintain clinical currency	$T_{H \to A}$	**Promote personalization.** Provide professional medical terminology for trained users and non-jargon language for others
Concerns about medical information sharing. Potential barriers to prevention	$T_{H \to A}$, $T_{H \to H}$	**Prioritize privacy.** Creating separate interfaces for team and personal use
High cognitive workload and interface complexity. Information is presented for exploratory interaction, not collaboration	$T_{H \to A}$, $T_{A \to H}$	**Emulate doctor-patient interactions.** Simplifying information processing through a guided workflow into stages
Lack of task breakdown and handover challenges. Unclear task stages complicate handover when assistance is needed	$T_{H \to A}$, $T_{H \to H}$	**Visualize the stages of the symptomatic conversation.** Add a clear indication of the interaction stage, with traceability
Lack of explanation of diagnostic risk and uncertainty. There is no information on the impact of further testing	$T_{A \to A}$, $T_{H \to A}$	**Visualize risk and uncertainty.** Integrating with probabilistic tools to depict the agent's judgment on available testing options
The agent lacks awareness of the user's ability to perform a task. The inability to assess human competence can lead to mismatched support and ineffective assistance	$T_{A \to H}$, $T_{H \to H}$	**Integrate agent trust in human** $(T_{A \to H})$. The agent uses $T_{A \to H}$ to assess the human's ability to perform the task against prior interactions and adopt the support required
Invariance of information regardless of context. Unclear task division and lack of adaptability to the situation requirements	$T_{A \to H}$, $T_{H \to A}$, $T_{A \to A}$	**Trust-adaptive and trust-adaptable interaction.** Information variety in response to human's ability to perform a task $(T_{A \to H})$

Design for Trust: Facilitate Mutual H↔A Familiarization.

Challenge. The lack of transparency of system capabilities leading to $T_{H\to A}$ over-trust or under-trust was a central theme in the SME interviews. Currently, the main approach to $T_{H\to A}$ trust calibration includes astronaut training. Every new system planned for astronaut use during a mission requires separate training, which adds to the workload for astronauts and training staff, in addition to the extensive pre-training already required. Moreover, although detailed medical and human performance data are collected throughout the intensive astronaut training process [29], these data are not integrated into medical systems or interface design.

Opportunity. To facilitate the development of mutual trust over time, a dedicated interaction workflow and interface are required. There is an opportunity for interface and interaction design that aids mutual human-agent familiarization and gradual trust calibration, where the astronaut co-trains with the agent throughout the preparation for the mission. As the human gradually 'onboards' the system—learning the interface and the agent's capabilities— the agent simultaneously gets to know the human, including their medical history, biometric characteristics, and baseline data, forming the foundation for $T_{A\to H}$ (see Table 3).

Co-Design Outputs. Figure 4 illustrates the three conceptual stages of familiarization resulting from design meetings and workshops. The first stage (A) involves initial onboarding, during which the astronaut interacts with the system via a tablet and a wearable companion device, such as a smartwatch, and gradually learns about the system's capabilities and personalizes the agent's communication style. Stage B guides the training activities (such as high-G exposure using a centrifuge, flight simulation, head-down tilt (HDT), and space physiology data), allowing the agent to collect human performance data within specific training contexts and interact with humans in these contexts. Stage C aims to aid the familiarization of the agent and astronaut crew working together as a CPH team.

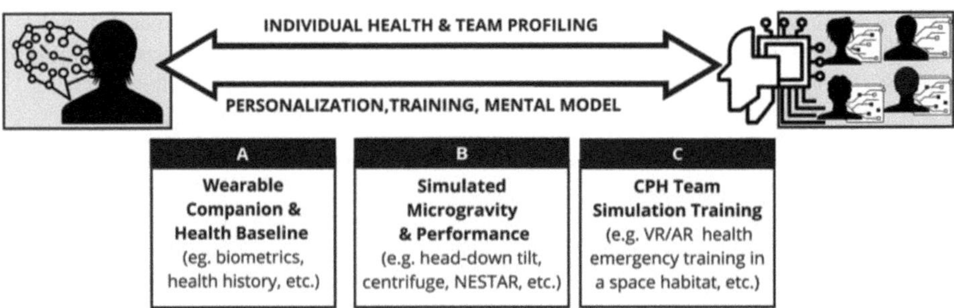

Fig. 4. Familiarization to facilitate mutual trust.

Design for Trust: Promote Personalization.

Challenge. Current NASA crew interfaces and displays are designed to follow the standardization guidelines outlined in NASA-STD-3001-Vol-1 Section 10 [27], aimed at minimizing training. While standardization ensures consistency across platforms and users, it limits adaptability to individual astronaut preferences—an important factor for fostering $T_{H \rightarrow A}$. Exploration-class missions, which prioritize crew autonomy and safety within a small, highly selected astronaut cohort, present a compelling case for transitioning from standardization towards personalization. The need for personalization of interactions with the agent is closely related to $T_{H \rightarrow A.}$, as highlighted in the SME interviews. These insights are reflected in the CPH maps under the Personalization and Affective Trust dimensions, capturing factors that shape astronauts' perception that the agent understands them and acts in their best interest [9]. Conversely, from the $T_{A \rightarrow H}$ perspective, personalization is directly linked to the agent's knowledge of the human.

Opportunity. The individualized astronaut interface supports the development of human-agent trust through prior training and offers opportunities for customization. This includes selecting between professional (specialized medical language) or general communication modes based on the user's medical background, as well as personalizing the agent's persona—such as conversational tone (e.g., medical professional, coach, or friend), avatar, and voice. Such customization is particularly valuable for health monitoring and preventive care interactions. Most importantly, the agent should be aware of the specific circumstances of each astronaut, including their health and medical data, as well as their previous mission experience. This allows the agent to leverage the extensive knowledge gained during pre-training about individual astronaut health and performance.

Co-Design Outputs. Figure 5 illustrates the conceptual design of the ExMEDI interface.

The interface is conceptualized with two modes of access, each with distinct functionality: the Personal Health Suite for individual monitoring and the Team Health Suite for crew-level health management. Alongside access to the Personal Health profile and performance data, the Personal Health Suite facilitates daily human-agent health check-ins, allowing for discussions of symptoms and the selection of treatment options, among other features.

Design for Trust: Prioritize Privacy.

Challenge. Concerns regarding the privacy of medical information emerged as a recurring theme across interviews. Since the earliest human spaceflight missions, fear of jeopardizing flight status has contributed to barriers to early reporting of health issues—a hesitance also observed in aviation [24, 38]. Concerns about privacy, a significant factor affecting trust, make it challenging to encourage uptake of early interventions and to adopt a preventative approach.

Opportunity. To support privacy, space medical systems can offer two access points: a crew-facing interface and an astronaut-facing interface. Interviewees noted that astronauts may prefer sharing early or sensitive concerns with the agent—echoing findings from a recent study where users felt safer disclosing information to AI than to a therapist or friend [42].

Conceptual Design Example. The ExMEDI conceptual example (see Fig. 5) implements privacy through the separation of the Personal and Team Health suites. Conversations between the astronaut and agent remain confidential, as illustrated by the levels of

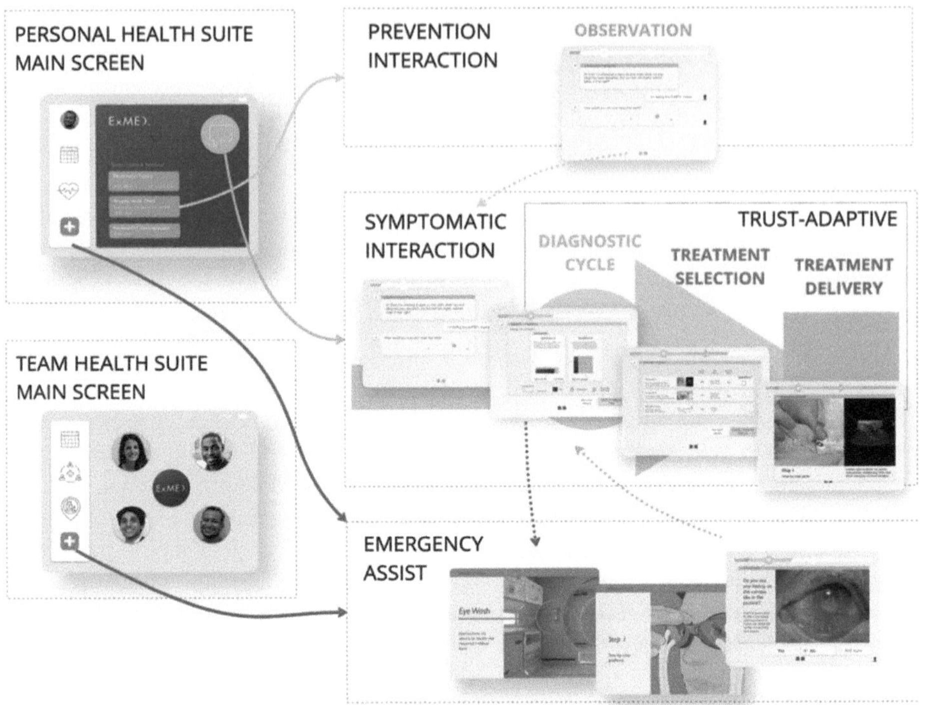

Fig. 5. The ExMEDI conceptual interface design includes the team health suite and personal health suite, and three interaction sequences: prevention, symptomatic, and emergency [9].

involvement in Fig. 6. For low-risk issues, the agent can issue an 'excuse note' to inform crew scheduling adjustments without revealing the nature of the concern. In higher-risk cases, the astronaut and agent may choose to involve the Medical Officer or Point of Contact (PoC). The wider crew is notified only in emergencies, and ground support is contacted in exceptional circumstances, considering communication delays.

Design for Trust: Emulate Doctor-Patient Interactions.

Challenge. The interviews highlighted multiple $T_{H\rightarrow A}$ trust factors related to emulating doctor-patient interaction, including shared decision-making, information timeliness, explainability of conclusions and suggestions, decision reassurance, bedside manner, and the 'feeling cared for' aspect of doctor-patient interactions. From the $T_{A\rightarrow H}$ perspective, it requires considering individual astronaut health and mission risks in the prevention and diagnostic process.

Opportunity. Design medical systems that support diverse interface and interaction modalities, emulating doctor-patient interactions, from preventive conversations to discussing symptoms, diagnosis, and treatment implementation.

Co-Design Outputs. During the design workshops, we defined three types of interface interactions modeled on the human-doctor relationship, as shown in Fig. 5. The *Prevention Interaction* utilizes a chat-based conversational format. Emerging concerns—raised

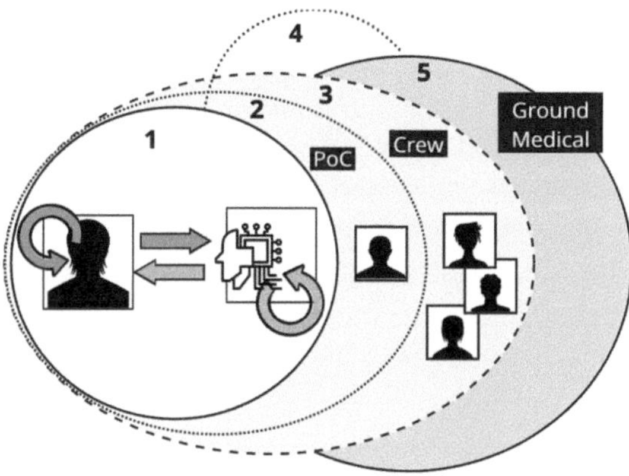

Fig. 6. Levels of involvement in health(care) support, prioritizing human-agent privacy.

by either the human or agent—are addressed through the *Symptomatic Interaction*, structured as a Framed Conversation (Table 1, Column V). The *Emergency Assist* provides step-by-step visual instructions aligned with the ABCDE medical protocol—a Sequence Interaction (Table 1, Column III). With input from medical SMEs, the Symptomatic Interaction was further structured into stages (see Figs. 5 and 7), as detailed in the following design opportunity.

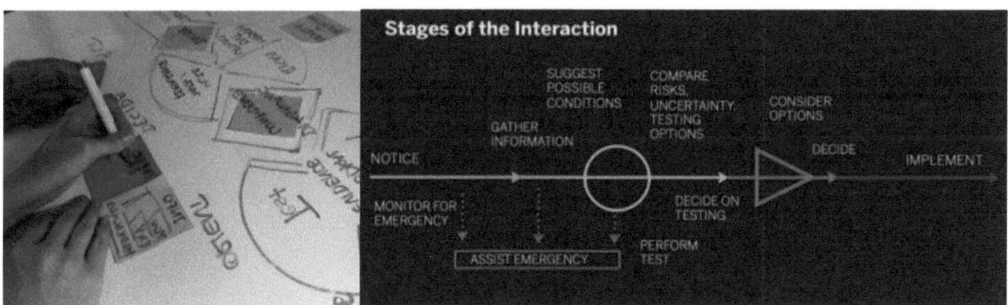

Fig. 7. Defining the Symptomatic Interaction stages with SMEs.

Design for Trust: Visualize the Stages of the Symptomatic Conversation.

Challenge. In Symptomatic Conversation, trust challenges center on previously identified issues, particularly shared decision-making and usability. The dashboard worktable interfaces (Table 1, Column I), characteristic of specialist doctor support in healthcare settings, require up-to-date medical skills and regular practice, demanding a high cognitive workload and lacking task prioritization [2] due to the complexity of decision-making on long-duration human spaceflight missions. The interviews and role-play workshops emphasized the need for continuous agent support throughout the process, replicating clinical reasoning and conversational sensitivity, while clearly signposting each stage to ensure traceability and facilitate easy handover if another team member joins or takes over the conversation with the agent.

Opportunity. To support human-agent shared decision-making, there is an opportunity to organize and simplify information processing through a guided workflow, breaking it down into manageable parts, such as a 'frame' interaction (Table 1, Column V). The hybrid conversational framework enables the agent to monitor the human state throughout the interaction and adjust the level of support required, based on the individual's needs.

Conceptual Design Example. Figures 5 and 7 illustrate a conceptual Symptomatic Interaction, showing the hybrid interaction framework for interface development with color-coded stages. Each stage is designed to emulate human doctor-patient interactions and includes:

1. Information gathering (green) – a conversational interface supporting chief complaint description and medical context;
2. Diagnostic cycle (yellow) – a framed hybrid interface. This cycle is repeated until diagnosis, with substages shown in Fig. 8;
3. Treatment selection (blue) – a worktable for evaluating treatment options and their resource impact;
4. Treatment delivery (purple) – a sequential interaction guiding the treatment process.

A progress bar atop each screen visually tracks these color-coded stages, enabling users to revisit steps for decision traceability and allowing team members to join the support.

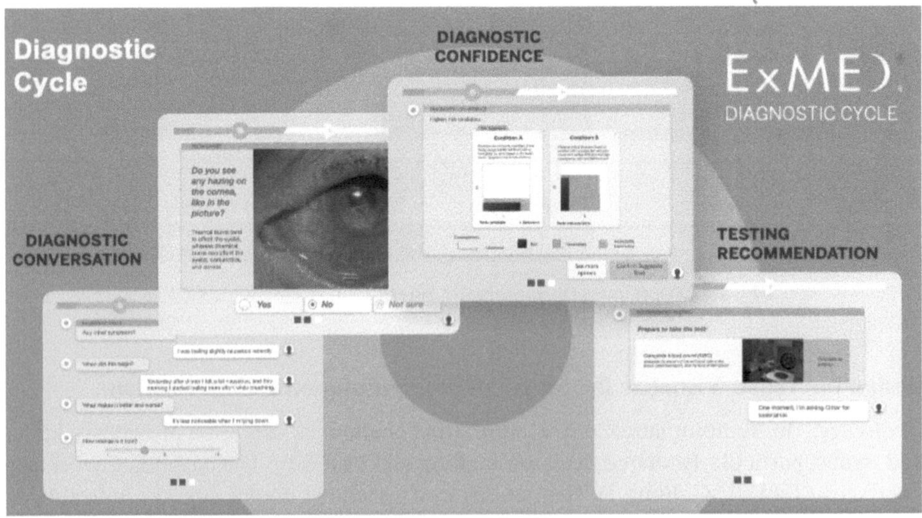

Fig. 8. ExMEDI Diagnostic Confidence visualization [9]. (Color figure online)

Design for Trust: Visualize Risk and Uncertainty.

Challenge. Decision-making for exploration missions involves managing risk and optimizing scarce resources. Assessing risk and uncertainty—especially due to changes in human physiology from microgravity and prolonged radiation—is crucial for informed decisions. While probabilistic tools are being developed to simulate scenarios and estimate condition likelihoods during long missions [39, 40], the primary focus remains on selecting equipment and consumables for the medical system.

Opportunity. Develop interfaces that facilitate risk visualization and integration with probabilistic tools, such as the Medical Extensible Dynamic Probabilistic Risk Assessment Tool (MEDPRAT)[39], to inform human-agent decision making during the flight.

Conceptual Design Example. Figure 9 illustrates a conceptual representation of the diagnostic confidence. The dark blue area represents risk as a surface defined by likelihood × consequence (L × C), loosely echoing the NASA risk model format. The light blue area represents uncertainty, while the yellow area highlights 'addressable uncertainty'—uncertainty that can be reduced through further on-board testing. In Condition A (high likelihood, low consequence), the addressable uncertainty is greater than that in Condition B (low likelihood, high consequence). The visualization of differences helps the CPH team determine whether to allocate resources for additional tests, as these can only reduce uncertainty within the limits of onboard capabilities.

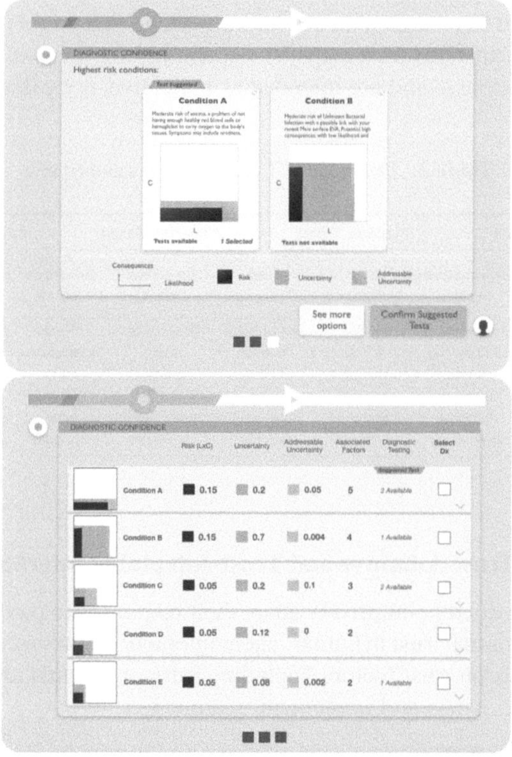

Fig. 9. ExMEDI Risk and Diagnostic Confidence visualization example [9]. (Color figure online)

Design for Trust: Integrate Agent Trust in Human $T_{A \to H}$.

Challenge. Trust in the doctor-patient relationship, linked to effective problem-solving and shared decision-making [41], requires mutual trust. The interviews and workshops stressed the role of $T_{A \to H}$ in future human-agent medical collaboration, highlighting the need for systems and interactions that enable the agent to assess a human's ability to perform tasks, much like a doctor intuitively interprets a patient's responses, evaluates potential barriers to trust, and gauges the accuracy of the patient's recollection and adherence to prescribed health protocols. *"There's a lot that goes into the [medical doctors'] intuition. (...) It's basically looking at where the behavior is incongruous with the existing circumstance."* *[SME Interviews]*.

Opportunity. Design interfaces and interactions that enable the agent to continuously gather data about the operator and their environment, comparing this information with the human's baseline health, biometric data, and contextual knowledge. As one SME noted, *"If the machine detects your oxygen is at 4%, it's not going to trust anything the crew says!"*. To prioritize prevention and identify emerging issues, the agent must be able to acquire routine physical and psychological data and compare them with real-time human performance and behavior.

Co-Design Outputs. Table 3, based on the SME workshop, outlines potential factors and measures related to an astronaut's prior knowledge that could inform $T_{A \to H}$. These examples align with the CPH trust maps[9]—spanning cognitive–affective and mission–personalized dimensions—and are intended as indicative, not exhaustive.

Table 3. Example of $T_{A \to H}$ trust measurements.

$T_{A \to H}$	Cognitive Trust		Mission Trust		Affective Trust		Personalised Trust	
affecting factors	Workload, Time Pressure	Environmental Factors	Context of Occurrence	Team Dynamics	Emotional Distress	Behavioral Factors	Physical Distress	Time-Criticality
Example measurement	Callendar schedules, planned EVAs, sleep pattern changes	Habitat (O2 / CO2 levels), Space Weather Forecast (radiation)	Habitat / EVA (schedules, beacon transceiver network)	Disruptions: tone of voices, number of interactions over time	Biometrics, self-reporting, questionnaires, voice, facial expression	Facial expression, voice, response time, accuracy	Reported and symptom-associated pain, physiological changes: breath, HRV	Mode of initiated conversation: routine, emergency, symptomatic

Design for Trust: Trust-Adaptive and Trust-Adaptable Interaction.

Challenge. Human doctors intuitively adapt their responses to patients' needs. To emulate patient-doctor mutual trust in human-agent interactions, we need to design adaptable support that depends on trust factors, including mission context and the human ability to make effective decisions and implement treatment.

Opportunity. Design trust-adaptive interactions and interfaces where the agent adjusts support and information based on trust judgment ($T_{A \to H}$). This builds on real-time situational awareness and the agent's prior knowledge of the human. For example, if

$T_{A \to H}$ indicates that the astronaut is distressed or facing a time-critical situation, the interface simplifies by presenting fewer options or giving direct instructions. In high-trust situations, the astronaut and agent engage at a higher level of collaboration.

Co-Design Outputs. Figure 10 illustrates the adaptation of trust within the ExMEDI system. Agent trust operates across thresholds, each influencing the level of detail and complexity of the interaction. In the high-trust mode, the agent provides rich and detailed information to maximize collaboration between human expertise and agent insights. The medium-trust mode offers less detail but increased guidance. In low-trust mode, the agent leads the interaction and decision-making. Trust levels are dynamic and can shift throughout the interaction, initiated by either the human or the agent. If trust falls below a critical threshold, the system enters an emergency support mode. While the interface adapts automatically based on $T_{A \to H}$, the human can override or adjust the support level as needed. In ExMEDI, trust levels are visually indicated by three dots at the bottom of the screen (see Fig. 9). The screen on the left is presented in medium trust, while the one on the right is presented in high trust, with more detail and functionality.

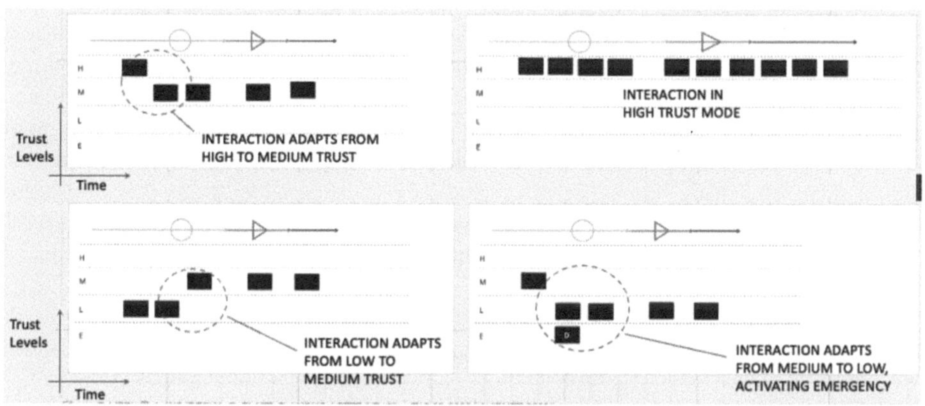

Fig. 10. $T_{A \to H}$ adaptation examples [9].

5 Conclusion

As medical AI systems become more integrated into clinical workflows, the need for mutual human↔agent trust emerges as an essential consideration in designing future human-agent system architecture. While much of the existing research focuses on how humans trust automated systems, our work highlights the need for considering implications for human↔agent interaction and interface design from multiple trust perspectives. Investigating CPH medical teaming in high-stakes, resource-constrained environments presents an opportunity to examine trust in CPH teaming and implications on interaction and interface design.

In this paper, we presented the results of qualitative research on trust in the edge-case context of astronaut-agent medical collaboration during LDHSF exploration missions.

We highlighted the identified challenges and opportunities for trust-informed design, discussing them in the context of CPH trust directions: $T_{H \to A}$, $T_{A \to H}$, $T_{H \to H}$, and $T_{A \to A}$. We discussed the selected opportunity areas, providing actionable insights for designing interfaces and interactions that foster justifiable mutual trust between humans and agents, along with practical examples derived from hands-on stakeholder workshops and conceptual interface design.

Our ongoing research focuses on exploring the characteristics of trust-driven and trust-adaptive CPH Clinical Decision Support (CDS) interfaces to enhance diagnostic processes and promote shared decision-making. Future research directions include the study of neuroergonomics in dynamic interfaces and the development of trust-adaptive interactions. We are also expanding our work on developing new methods for the systematic consideration of CPH trust in defining trust-driven system needs, as well as a trust diagnostic tool in existing systems.

Human-centered design will play a crucial role in developing future CDSSs for human-agent teaming and interfaces that contribute to effective trust-building and fostering human-agent medical shared decision-making. Designing within edge-case scenarios, such as human spaceflight exploration, can inform the next generation of adaptive and trustworthy interfaces for high-autonomy terrestrial healthcare settings. This includes the opportunity to design interfaces that support hybrid interactions by combining human expertise and agent guidance within a structured framework to enable balanced and effective collaboration. We recommend involving Human-Centered Designers as core members of transdisciplinary teams from the earliest stages of requirement formulation. Rather than retrofitting human-centered and CPH trust considerations late in the process, early integration helps drive interface and interaction designs that foster justifiable mutual trust between humans and agents, enabling effective medical collaboration.

Acknowledgments. This research was supported by the NASA Langley Research Center, the Goddard Space Flight Center, and the Jet Propulsion Laboratory, California Institute of Technology, through a grant awarded to the first and third authors (Grant Award Number: 22–1-T10.05-2368LaRC), and the Aerospace Medical Association Foundation Jeffrey Myers Young Investigator Award presented at the Annual Scientific Meeting of the Aerospace Medical Association to the first author. The funding organizations did not participate in the writing of this publication, nor in the collection, analysis, or interpretation of the data. The content, findings, and conclusions presented are the authors' own and should not be interpreted as the official position of NASA and AsMA.

The authors thank the SMEs and stakeholders for their generous contributions of time and expertise during the interviews, design meetings, and SME workshops.

CRediT Authorship Contribution Statement.   Anna B. Wojdecka: Conceptualization, Methodology, Investigation, Data Curation, Formal Analysis, Visualization, Writing – Original Draft, Writing – Review & Editing, Funding acquisition. Tibor Balint: Validation, Writing – Review & Editing. Don Platt: Supervision, Funding acquisition, Writing– Review & Editing.

Disclosure of Interest.   The authors declare that they have no competing interests.

References

1. Lee, J.D., See, K.A.: Trust in automation: designing for appropriate reliance. J. Hum. Factors Ergon. Soc. **46**, 50–80 (2004). https://doi.org/10.1518/hfes.46.1.50_30392
2. Wickens, C.D., Hollands, J.G., Banbury, S., Parasuraman, R.: Engineering Psychology and Human Performance (1992). https://doi.org/10.4324/9781315665177
3. Norman, D.: The Design of Everyday Things. The MIT Press, Cambridge (1998)
4. Parasuraman, R., Molloy, R., Singh, I.L.: Performance consequences of automation-induced "complacency." Int. J. Aviat. Psychol. **3**, 1–23 (1993). https://doi.org/10.1207/s15327108ijap0301_1
5. Sorkin, R.D., Kantowitz, B.H., Kantowitz, S.C.: Likelihood alarm displays. Hum. Factors J. Hum. Factors Ergon. Soc. **30**, 445–459 (1988). https://doi.org/10.1177/001872088803000406
6. Bach, T.A., Khan, A., Hallock, H., Beltrão, G., Sousa, S.: A systematic literature review of user trust in AI-enabled systems: an HCI perspective. Int. J. Hum. Comput. Interact. **40**, 1251–1266 (2024). https://doi.org/10.1080/10447318.2022.2138826
7. Duez, P.P., Zuliani, M.J., Jamieson, G.A.: Trust by design: information requirements for appropriate trust in automation. In: Proceedings of the 2006 Conference of the Center for Advanced Studies on Collaborative research - CASCON '06, p. 9 (2006). https://doi.org/10.1145/1188966.1188978
8. Vinod, A.P., Thorpe, A.J., Olaniyi, P.A., Summers, T.H., Oishi, M.M.K.: Trust-based user-interface design for human-automation systems. arXiv (2020). https://doi.org/10.48550/arxiv.2004.07176
9. Wojdecka, A., Platt, D.: Transdisciplinary design of trust-driven clinical decision support interface for cyber-physical human teams in long-duration human spaceflight. In: IAA SCITECH 2025 Forum (2025). https://doi.org/10.2514/6.2025-2094
10. Costa, A.C., Fulmer, C.A., Anderson, N.R.: Trust in work teams: an integrative review, multilevel model, and future directions. J. Organiz. Behav. **39**, 169–184 (2018). https://doi.org/10.1002/job.2213
11. Scott, R.T., et al.: Biomonitoring and precision health in deep space supported by artificial intelligence. Nat. Mach. Intell. **5**, 196–207 (2023). https://doi.org/10.1038/s42256-023-00617-5
12. Chandra, S., Mohammadnezhad, M., Ward, P.: Trust and communication in a doctor-patient relationship: a literature review. J. Healthc. Commun. **3** (2018). https://doi.org/10.4172/2472-1654.100146
13. Hamilton, D., Smart, K., Melton, S., Polk, J.D., Johnson-Throop, K.: Autonomous medical care for exploration class space missions. J. Trauma Inj. Infect. Crit. Care. **64**, S354–S363 (2008). https://doi.org/10.1097/ta.0b013e31816c005d
14. Ledley, R.S., Lusted, L.B.: Reasoning foundations of medical diagnosis. Science **130**, 9–21 (1959). https://doi.org/10.1126/science.130.3366.9
15. Chen, Z., et al.: Harnessing the power of clinical decision support systems: challenges and opportunities. Open Hear. **10**, e002432 (2023). https://doi.org/10.1136/openhrt-2023-002432
16. Wojdecka, A., Hall, A., Judah, G.: Transdisciplinary behaviour change: a burst mode approach to healthcare design education. In: DS 110: Proceedings of the 23rd International Conference on Engineering and Product Design Education (EPDE 2021) (2021). https://doi.org/10.35199/epde.2021.62
17. Hutch, M.R., Luo, Y.: Applications and challenges of human computer interaction and AI interfaces for health care. In: Kushniruk, A.W., Kaufman, D.R., Kannampallil, T.G., Patel, V.L. (eds.) Human Computer Interaction in Healthcare. CIBH, pp. 63–90. Springer, Cham (2024). https://doi.org/10.1007/978-3-031-69947-4_4

18. Rogers, Y., Sharp, H., Preece, J.: Interaction Design: Beyond Human-Computer Interaction. John Wiley & Sons, Inc., Hoboke (2023)

19. Cálem, J., Moreira, C., Jorge, J.: Intelligent systems in healthcare: a systematic survey of explainable user interfaces. Comput. Biol. Med. **180**, 108908 (2024). https://doi.org/10.1016/j.compbiomed.2024.108908

20. Endsley, M.R.: Designing for Situation Awareness, An Approach to User-Centered Design, 2nd edn., pp. 212–237 (2019). https://doi.org/10.1201/b11371-15

21. Gambetta, D.: Trust: making and breaking cooperative relations. Br. J. Sociol. **41**, 128 (1988). https://doi.org/10.2307/591021

22. Hardy, A., et al.: Co-designing technology to improve psychological therapy for psychosis: SloMo, a blended digital therapy for fear of harm from others. Schizophr. Res. **274**, 526–534 (2024). https://doi.org/10.1016/j.schres.2024.11.004

23. Hardy, A., et al.: Designing the future of talking therapy: using digital health to improve outcomes in psychosis. Front. Public Heal. **4** (2016). https://doi.org/10.3389/conf.fpubh.2016.01.00044

24. Berry, C.A., Hoffler, G.W., Jernigan, C.A., Kerwin, J.P., Mohler, S.R.: History of space medicine: the formative years at NASA. Aviat. Space Environ. Med. **80**, 345–352 (2009). https://doi.org/10.3357/asem.2463.2009

25. Clément, G.: Fundamentals of Space Medicine (2011). https://doi.org/10.1007/978-1-4419-9905-4

26. West, J.B.: Historical perspectives: physiology in microgravity. J. Appl. Physiol. **89**, 379–384 (2000). https://doi.org/10.1152/jappl.2000.89.1.379

27. NASA: NASA-STD-3001, Space Flight Human-System Standard Volume 1: Crew Health (2025). https://standards.nasa.gov/standard/NASA/NASA-STD-3001-VOL-1

28. NASA: NASA-STD-3001, Space Flight Human-System Standard Volume 2: Human Factors, Habitability, and Environmental Health (2025). https://www.nasa.gov/reference/nasa-std-3001v2/

29. NASA: OCHMO-STD-100.1A, Space flight medical selection, recertification, and mission evaluation standard (2024)

30. Barratt, M.R., Baker, E.S., Pool, S.L.: Principles of Clinical Medicine for Space Flight (2020). https://doi.org/10.1007/978-1-4939-9889-0

31. NASA, E.M.C. (ExMC): Human Research Roadmap (HRR) Gaps. Medical-501: We need to develop integrated exploration medical system models for the Moon and Mars. https://humanresearchroadmap.nasa.gov/gaps/gap.aspx?i=714

32. NASA: Integrated Data Uncertainty Management and Representation for Trustworthy and Trusted Autonomy in Space (2021). https://www.sbir.gov/node/1836081

33. Charmaz, K.: Constructing Grounded Theory. Sage, Los Angeles (2014)

34. Wojdecka, A.B., Hall, A., Balint, T.: Designing out unwanted healthcare futures: a new framework for healthcare design innovation with intent. In: Ds 117 Proceedings of the 24th International Conference on Engineering and Product Design Education (E&PDE 2022), London South Bank University, London, UK, 8th–9th September 2022 (2022). https://doi.org/10.35199/epde.2022.110

35. Hupcey, J.E., Penrod, J., Morse, J.M., Mitcham, C.: An exploration and advancement of the concept of trust. J. Adv. Nurs. **36**, 282–293 (2001). https://doi.org/10.1046/j.1365-2648.2001.01970.x

36. Rousseau, D.M., Sitkin, S.B., Burt, R.S., Camerer, C.: Not so different after all: a cross-discipline view of trust. Acad. Manage. Rev. **23**, 393–404 (1998). https://doi.org/10.5465/amr.1998.926617

37. NASA SBIR & STTR Program Homepage - Integrated Data Uncertainty Management and Representation for Trustworthy and Trusted Autonomy in Space – 2023-01-09.pdf

38. Strand, T.-E., Lystrup, N., Martinussen, M.: Under-reporting of self-reported medical conditions in aviation: a cross-sectional survey. Aerosp. Med. Hum. Perform. **93**, 376–383 (2022). https://doi.org/10.3357/amhp.5823.2022
39. Amador, J.R., et al.: Enabling space exploration medical system development using a tool ecosystem. In: 2020 IEEE Aerospace Conference, pp. 1–16 (2020). https://doi.org/10.1109/aero47225.2020.9172751
40. Anderson, A., Fenbert, J., Easter, B., Lehnhardt, K.: Quantifying medical risk on a long duration lunar mission: a demonstration of NASA's IMPACT Tradespace Analysis Tool. In: 75th International Astronautical Congress (IAC). International Astronautical Federation (IAF) (2024)
41. Kraetschmer, N., Sharpe, N., Urowitz, S., Deber, R.B.: How does trust affect patient preferences for participation in decision-making? Heal. Expect. **7**, 317–326 (2004). https://doi.org/10.1111/j.1369-7625.2004.00296.x
42. Young, J., Jawara, L.M., Nguyen, D.N., Daly, B., Huh-Yoo, J., Razi, A.: The role of AI in peer support for young people: a study of preferences for human- and AI-Generated responses. In: Proceedings of the CHI Conference on Human Factors in Computing Systems, pp. 1–18 (2024). https://doi.org/10.1145/3613904.3642574

A Review on Human-AI Hybrid Systems in Air Traffic Management

Ziqing Xia[1,2(✉)], Meng-Hsueh Hsieh[1,2], and Chun-Hsien Chen[1,2]

[1] School of Mechanical and Aerospace Engineering, Nanyang Technological University, Singapore 639798, Singapore
{ziqing.xia,menghsueh.hsieh,mchchen}@ntu.edu.sg
[2] Air Traffic Management Research Institute, Nanyang Technological University, Singapore 637460, Singapore

Abstract. Artificial intelligence (AI) is expected to play a pivotal role in assisting human air traffic controllers, helping them manage the increasing demands of air traffic amid rising capacity challenges. By augmenting their capabilities in this safety-critical and human-intensive field, AI has the potential to bring significant transformation. This systematic review consolidates and analyzes existing research on human-AI interactions in air traffic management (ATM), with a focus on understanding the characteristics of human-AI hybrid (HAH) systems. It examines their role as enhancement tools across various operational levels and outlines their implementation through key phases, including conceptualization, development, evaluation, and training. Additionally, the review highlights current research gaps and provides recommendations for advancing HAH systems in ATM. By offering a comprehensive synthesis of the existing literature, this study lays a strong foundation for the future design and validation of HAH systems, contributing to enhanced safety and operational efficiency in air traffic management.

Keywords: Human-AI hybrid system · Air traffic management · Artificial intelligence

1 Introduction

As global air traffic continues to grow, air traffic management (ATM) has become increasingly vital in ensuring the safety and efficiency of aviation operations by coordinating aircraft movements and preventing collisions [19]. To address the evolving challenges in ATM, artificial intelligence (AI) and automation technologies have been introduced to enhance the capability of handling complex air traffic scenarios. AI is defined as "technology that can, for a given set of human-defined objectives, generate outputs such as content, predictions, recommendations, or decisions influencing the environments they interact with" [1], while automation refers to "the independent accomplishment of a function by a device or system that was formerly carried out by a human" [3]. Official reports

J. Wei et al. (Eds.): HCII 2025, LNCS 16346, pp. 284–295, 2026.
https://doi.org/10.1007/978-3-032-13187-4_19

from the European Union Aviation Safety Agency (EASA) and the Federal Aviation Administration (FAA) emphasize the critical role of AI and automation in the future of ATM.

The EASA Artificial Intelligence Roadmap 2.0 outlines three progressive levels of AI integration: assistance to human, human-AI teaming (HAIT), and advanced automation [1]. This framework underscores the importance of understanding how AI and humans interact to ensure effective and safe operations. While AI and automation have demonstrated their potential to enhance operational performance and efficiency [41], their implementation in ATM requires a systematic and trustworthy approach to meet the industry's stringent safety and security standards [2]. Despite significant advancements in automation, the integration of AI in ATM systems and its potential to enhance human-AI collaboration remains an area requiring further exploration [9].

In this context, a novel paradigm known as the human-AI hybrid (HAH) system has emerged. HAH represents a collaborative framework in which humans and AI interact seamlessly, leveraging their respective strengths to achieve optimal performance in complex operational environments [29]. Given the dynamic and high-risk nature of ATM, the implementation of HAH systems offers promising opportunities to enhance operational efficiency, resilience, and adaptability while ensuring safety. However, deploying AI in ATM requires a structured approach that encompasses system design, development, evaluation, and integration.

To advance the understanding of HAH systems in ATM, this systematic review compiles and synthesizes existing studies to examine their characteristics and development processes. Previous studies have explored AI applications in ATM [11] and the challenges associated with their integration [35]. Degas et al. (2022) [11] classified research into representative groups, showing that AI and automation are closely interconnected, making it essential to consider both aspects in this review. As AI often incorporates automation components, their combined study lays a foundation for HAH system development.

The primary objective of this review is to investigate the characteristics and development processes of HAH systems in ATM, offering a comprehensive synthesis of current research and identifying areas for future advancement. The rest of this paper is organized as follows: Sect. 2 outlines the systematic review methodology. Section 3 consolidates key findings related to HAH systems in ATM. Section 4 discusses research limitations and future directions. Finally, Sect. 5 presents the study's conclusions and contributions.

2   Methods

This systematic review was conducted in accordance with the Preferred Reporting Items for Systematic Reviews and Meta-Analyses (PRISMA) 2020 protocol [28]. The primary information sources for this review were electronic databases.

Journal articles and conference papers published up to 14 August 2024 were considered. The inclusion criteria for this review encompassed studies exploring the following topics:

- Human-AI Hybrid, human-AI teaming, human-AI collaboration, automation, and Air Traffic Control
- Human factors, AI, and ATM: Studies that examine human factors topics such as trust, transparency, shared mental models, situation awareness, adaptation, levels of automation, function allocation, granularity of control, coordination, perception, acceptance, cognition, cognitive workload, stress, fatigue, decision-making, and information processing in AI systems within the context of ATM.

Studies not in English, and those focusing on pilots, were excluded.

This review searched the following electronic databases: Scopus, Web of Science Core Collection (Clarivate), IEEE Xplore, ScienceDirect, Academic Search Complete (via Ebscohost). Other subject-specific databases searched were SAE Mobilus, AIAA Aerospace Research Central (ARC), and NTRS - NASA Technical Reports Server.

A search strategy was developed in collaboration with senior librarians from Nanyang Technological University Library Systematic Search Service Team. The search strategy was devised in Scopus using a multi-faceted approach combining the results of two key search strands with the following concepts:

- human-artificial intelligence (AI) teaming (HAIT or HAH) and air traffic control (ATM or ATC).
- human factors and artificial intelligence (AI) and air traffic control (ATM or ATC)

An initial search yielded 10,691 studies. After removing duplicate records using EndNote and manual screening, 5,054 studies remained. Titles and abstracts were screened by six researchers, leading to the selection of 137 relevant studies. For this review, we focus specifically on the 57 papers directly related to HAH systems in ATM.

3   Human-AI Hybrid (HAH) System in ATM

While traditional automation typically involves systems executing repetitive tasks based on fixed rules or human instructions, AI systems represent a significant evolution by handling uncertainties and making decisions in novel or dynamic situations [10,21]. Often regarded as the next generation of automation, AI goes beyond fixed rule-based operations by simulating human cognitive functions [12]. This includes learning (acquiring and applying knowledge and rules), reasoning (making conclusions based on these rules), and self-correction, resulting in a form of advanced automation.

In the field of ATM, automation has been a longstanding area of interest, leading to the creation and practical implementation of numerous tools. These developments have been accompanied by well-established studies on human factors and human-automation interaction. Although automation typically assists ATCOs in improving performance, enhancing SA, and decreasing workload

[6,41,42], previous studies have also revealed its potential negative impacts, including over-reliance [27,39], diminished attentiveness [34], and higher levels of complexity [5,18,20], where human-human monitoring cannot be completely replicable by automation systems [24]. One important concept is the Level of Automation (LoA), which refers to the degree to which authority over task execution is distributed between humans and automated systems.

However, the application of AI in ATM is still in its early stages, with current research largely focused on tool development and relatively few studies addressing human-AI interaction and the associated human factors. Nonetheless, insights gained from human-automation interaction studies offer a valuable foundation for developing human-AI interaction guidelines. In the following sections authors summarize the applications, development methodologies, and guiding principles for HAH systems within the ATM domain.

3.1   Applications of Human-AI Hybrid (HAH) Systems in ATM

Comprehensive Support Systems. HAH systems in ATM encompass various concepts and systems, designed to enhance air traffic management through shared responsibilities between human ATCOs and AI. Systematic systems, such as those by Jameel et al. (2023) [17] and Westin et al. (2020a) [43], propose comprehensive digital assistants that automate routine tasks, such as conflict detection, advisory generation, and communication with pilots, enabling ATCOs to concentrate on higher-level supervisory roles. These systems implement adjustable autonomy, allowing automation levels to vary based on traffic complexity and ATCO preferences. For instance, the Digital Tower Assistant (DiTA) concept by Westin et al. (2020) [43] supports remote tower operations, where ATCOs can delegate routine management to the system while maintaining control over complex or unexpected scenarios. Additionally, Rohacs et al. (2016) [32] envisions future ATM workstations equipped with augmented reality (AR) and decision-support systems (DSSs) that monitor and adapt to controllers' mental workload. Schurr et al. (2010) [33] introduced a multi-agent system where task allocation dynamically adjusts to operational demands, optimizing workload and performance through real-time adjustments. These concepts exemplify hybrid systems where AI assumes routine responsibilities while human oversight remains essential for decision-making in complex situations.

Specific Assistance Tool. In addition to comprehensive systems, specific assistance tools have been developed to support ATCOs in real-time decision-making and maintaining SA. Nieuwenhuisen (2014) [26] introduced a 4D trajectory management tool that generates automated advisories to resolve conflicts. Tools such as the attention-guiding system by Rataj et al. (2021) [31] use eye-tracking to identify ATCO focus areas and visually direct attention to critical information on displays. Similarly, Gürlük (2016) [13] designed an AR-based system that autonomously adjusts displayed information based on environmental and traffic conditions, enhancing ATCO awareness. DSS further aid contingency planning and conflict resolution, as seen in Brinton et al. (2020) [7], who developed a DSS integrating backup options for contingency management, and Tran et al. (2020) [37], who proposed an Interactive Conflict Solver (iCS) with a reinforcement learning-based agent to provide conflict solutions aligned with ATCO preferences. These tools demonstrate targeted support approaches that enhance ATCOs' operational performance by focusing on specific tasks.

Human-AI Interaction Optimization. From a collaborative perspective, human-AI interaction modes in ATM applications exhibit variations. The more prevalent approach involves ATCOs delegating specific tasks to AI, as demonstrated by Jameel et al. (2023) [17] and Westin et al. (2020) [43]. Other systems, such as those proposed by Schurr et al. (2010) [33] and Rohacs et al. (2016) [32], explore AI-led dynamic task allocation based on real-time demands, though these remain largely theoretical. Challenges in AI-led task allocation include accurately monitoring workload through physiological indicators and adapting to fluctuating operational demands. In the realm of decision-support tools, advancements have frequently focused on enhancing user experience: some systems enhance the user interface to alleviate cognitive load, while others align AI recommendations with human cognitive processes to build trust, as in Brinton et al. (2020) [7] and Turnbull and Richards (2018) [40]. This emphasis on usability underscores the goal of fostering reliable human-AI partnerships that strengthen ATM safety and efficiency.

3.2 Frameworks and Methods for Human-AI Hybrid (HAH) System Implementation

To comprehensively implement a HAH system, a four-step process involving conceptualization, development, evaluation, and training is required. This section will introduce the innovative methods and frameworks applied to each of these steps.

Conceptual Framework. Although conceptual frameworks support effective task allocation, balanced decision-making, and improved coordination, there is a lack of research dedicated specifically to conceptual frameworks for HAH models in ATM. Millot and Debernard (2007) [23] introduced a Human-Machine Cooperation (HMC) framework that defines three cooperation forms—augmentative (task-sharing), debative (comparing independent solutions), and integrative (applying complementary skills). Complementing this high-level framework, other research focuses on adaptive control frameworks. Langan-Fox et al. (2009) [22] proposed an adaptable control model that uses a Joint Cognitive System (JCS) framework, allowing dynamic shifts in control between humans and AI based on task needs and context. In contrast to Langan-Fox's human-centered adaptability, Itoh et al. (2008) [16] presented the Human As a Control Module (HACM) architecture, which allocates control authority based on a simulated response to human and AI input, thus ensuring stable and effective decision-making. Additionally, adaptive automation frameworks by Morrison and Gluckman (1994) [25] and Prinzel Iii et al. (2003) [30] consider real-time physiological metrics as triggers for adjusting control authority, enhancing adaptability based on operator status. Tan et al. (2022) [36] expanded on this by highlighting the potential of eye-tracking measures, offering an additional layer of control that responds directly to the operators' cognitive load. In summary, these frameworks offer distinct approaches to adaptive control in ATM.

Development Method. The design phase is a critical step in system development, serving as the foundation for the entire process. Designing ATM systems is especially challenging due to their inherent complexity. However, existing research rarely explores the specific methodologies required for the design and development of such intricate systems. Tran Luciani et al. (2020) [38] present novel approaches to designing fine-grained human-automation interactions in ATC. The study introduces an assisted sketching system that enables ATCOs to externalize their mental models and interact with automation more effectively. This system enhances communication and collaboration between humans and automation by visually externalizing decision-making processes and allowing the exploration of future scenarios. While it significantly improves human-automation interaction in ATC, further enhancements are needed to better visualize altitude changes. Annebicque et al. (2009) [4] proposed a multi-criteria decision-making (MCDM) methodology to analyze ATCOs' decision-making processes, providing valuable insights for the design of decision-support systems (DSS). These approaches emphasize the importance of design methodologies that prioritize ATCOs' decision-making and mental model externalization, with the goal of creating ATM systems that enable seamless and collaborative human-automation interactions.

Evaluation Method. Evaluations of HAH systems in ATM typically focus on three primary areas: concept evaluation, task allocation, and level of automation. Concept evaluation involves assessing the effectiveness of proposed HAH models for ATM tasks. For instance, Cabrall et al. (2013) [8] examined how the introduction of ground-based automation in high-traffic scenarios impacts controller-automation interactions. Task allocation studies focus on the optimal distribution of responsibilities between human operators and AI systems. For example, Schurr et al. (2010) [33] compares human-led and AI-led allocation of surveillance and decision-making tasks to determine their effectiveness. Lastly, evaluations of automation levels, such as those conducted by Ijtsma et al. (2022) [15], explore the effects of different automation intensities on task performance. These evaluations typically employ two types of experimental designs: simulation experiments, which represent a smaller proportion, and human-in-the-loop (HITL) experiments, which constitute the majority. Simulation-based evaluations often focus on assessing the functional capabilities of AI-driven concepts without direct human involvement. This allows researchers to examine system-level performance under predefined conditions, such as aircraft trajectories and conflict detection [16,40]. In contrast, human-in-the-loop experiments integrate human participants within simulated or semi-operational environments, providing a more realistic assessment of how operators interact with and respond to the AI system.

Training Method. Training is essential for equipping operators with the skills needed to interact effectively with advanced automation, ensuring that the HAH system performs optimally in complex, real-world scenarios. Training for these systems is particularly challenging, as it must support operators across various stages of skill development—from novice to expert—while simultaneously adapting to both human and automation needs. Despite the importance of training in hybrid systems, few studies have specifically focused on this area. Hilburn (2016) [14] addressed this gap by proposing a structured, three-stage hybrid training model aimed at supporting operators as they progress through different levels of expertise. In the first stage, called strategic conformance, automation closely aligns with human strategies to encourage acceptance and build foundational skills. The second stage gradually shifts the system's support, guiding operators towards expert-level strategies and enhancing their proficiency. In the final optimization stage, the system helps operators achieve algorithmically optimized performance, enabling them to work at peak system efficiency. This approach emphasizes the importance of adaptive training that evolves with the operator's expertise, ensuring that the HAH system remains effective and aligned with optimized outcomes.

4   Limitations of HAH Systems in ATM

4.1   Inflexibility of Collaboration/hybrid Mode in ATM

Although some studies have explored adaptive control models for HAH systems in Air Traffic Management (ATM), most existing systems still follow a "human-lead" mode, where human operators retain ultimate control [16,22]. While the notion of adaptive control has been proposed, its practical implementation in ATM remains underdeveloped. For example, the Human as a Control Module (HACM) proposed by Itoh et al. (2008) [16] and the Joint Cognitive System (JCS) by Langan-Fox et al. (2009) [22] demonstrate how control authority can be adaptively shifted between humans and AI. However, these frameworks are largely confined to research and testing environments and have yet to be widely adopted in real-world ATM systems. The main reason for this limitation is the emphasis on safety and the regulatory requirement for human accountability in high-stakes decision-making.

However, emerging technologies, such as Large Language Models (LLMs), Generative AI (GAI), and Explainable AI (XAI), present significant potential to enhance adaptive control in ATM. For instance, LLMs can assist human operators with real-time guidance and rationale explanations for AI-generated decisions, thereby fostering trust and enabling more dynamic human-AI collaboration. GAI could simulate possible future air traffic scenarios, allowing AI to propose optimal control strategies based on predictive modeling. Explainable AI can further enhance human trust and promote the acceptance of systems where control authority shifts flexibly between human and AI actors. As these technologies mature, future research should explore how they can support multi-mode collaboration models in ATM, enabling control authority to adapt dynamically based on workload, operational demands, and traffic complexity. This approach could alleviate controller workload while ensuring that safety levels remain high.

4.2   Lack of Design Methods

Despite the growing interest in HAH systems in ATM, there remains a significant lack of systematic design methods and conceptual frameworks to guide system and human-machine interface (HMI) development. Existing studies propose high-level frameworks for human-AI collaboration, such as the Human-Machine Cooperation (HMC) model by Millot and Debernard (2007) [23], which emphasizes elements including know-how, know-how-to-cooperate, and shared workspaces. Similarly, Langan-Fox et al. (2009) [22] introduced an adaptable control model for dynamic authority allocation, while Itoh et al. (2008) [16] proposed the Human As a Control Module (HACM) architecture, which harmonizes human and AI inputs based on simulated system responses. However, these frameworks remain conceptual and abstract, lacking actionable design guidelines for developing hybrid ATM systems. Existing design approaches, such as Tran et al. (2020) [37] sketch-based interaction design and Annebicque et al. (2009) [4] multi-criteria decision-making (MCDM) methodology offer design strategies but focus on certain specific aspects, such as mental model externalization or decision support system (DSS) development. This fragmented approach hinders the ability to create consistent, user-centered HMIs and limits the effective integration of human-AI collaboration models. To address this, future efforts should focus on developing unified design methods and operational frameworks that offer clear, step-by-step guidance for the design of hybrid systems. These frameworks should prioritize ensuring transparency, usability, and human-centric development.

4.3   Lack of Training Methods

Training is a critical component in the transition to HAH systems in ATM, as it enables operators to interact effectively with advanced automation while maintaining safety and efficiency in complex scenarios. The integration of AI introduces unique challenges, including trust calibration, skill retention, and the need for operators to adapt to evolving system behaviors [42]. Despite its importance, research on training methods for hybrid systems remains scarce, with limited focus on systematic approaches that address these challenges [14]. Existing studies offer valuable insights but lack comprehensive frameworks specifically tailored to the demands of human-AI collaboration. To ensure the effective implementation of hybrid systems, future research must prioritize developing structured training methods that incorporate human factors considerations and support operators at all stages of expertise.

5   Conclusions

This review focuses on the application of AI technologies within the air traffic management (ATM) domain, specifically those that have been implemented and validated in operational settings. As a result, it does not encompass emerging advancements such as large language models or other state-of-the-art technologies. Nonetheless, this limitation does not diminish the article's core emphasis on the role of AI in enhancing ATM operations. Future research should consider the potential impact of evolving AI technologies and leverage insights from other domains that are pioneering human-AI interaction frameworks.

This review provides a comprehensive analysis of human-AI hybrid (HAH) systems in ATM, examining their applications across various operational levels, including comprehensive system support, specialized tools, and applications designed to optimize human-AI collaboration. By offering an in-depth perspective on the functional role of HAH systems in ATM, this study contributes to a broader understanding of their potential. Furthermore, it consolidates existing frameworks and methodologies across key implementation stages—conceptualization, development, validation, and training—serving as a valuable resource for future research and practical implementation.

Acknowledgments. This research is supported by the National Research Foundation, Singapore, and the Civil Aviation Authority of Singapore, under the Aviation Transformation Programme. The grant number is REQ0532039_FAA_Vertical C.

Disclosure of Interests. The authors declare that they have no known competing financial interests or personal relationships that could have appeared to influence the work reported in this paper.

References

1. Agency, E.U.A.S.: Artificial intelligence roadmap 2.0 a human-centric approach to AI in aviation (2023). https://www.easa.europa.eu/en/document-library/general-publications/easa-artificial-intelligence-roadmap-20. Accessed 10 May 2023
2. Agency, E.U.A.S.: Artificial intelligence (AI) concept paper issue 2: guidance for level 1&2 machine learning applications (2024). https://www.easa.europa.eu/en/document-library/general-publications/easa-artificial-intelligence-concept-paper-issue-2. Accessed 19 Apr 2024
3. Ahlstrom, V.: Human factors design standard (2003)
4. Annebicque, D., Crevits, I., Poulain, T., Debernard, S., Millot, P.: Decision analysis of air traffic controller in order to propose decision support systems. In: 2009 International Conference on Computers and Industrial Engineering, pp. 566–571. IEEE (2009)

5. Beard, B.L., Johnston, J.C., Holbrook, J.: Nextgen operational improvements: will they improve human performance. In: 17th International Symposium on Aviation Psychology, p. 159 (2013)
6. Bilimoria, K.D., Hayashi, M., Sheth, K.: Human-in-the-loop evaluation of dynamic multi-flight common route advisories. In: 2018 Aviation Technology, Integration, and Operations Conference, p. 2877 (2018)
7. Brinton, C., Fernandes, A., Kaler, C.: Explicit contingency planning for improved human-autonomy teaming in decision support. In: 2020 Integrated Communications Navigation and Surveillance Conference (ICNS), pp. 5C2–1. IEEE (2020)
8. Cabrall, C.D., et al.: Transitioning resolution responsibility between the controller and automation team in simulated NextGen separation assurance. In: Air Traffic Management and Systems. LNEE, vol. 290, pp. 147–172. Springer, Tokyo (2014). https://doi.org/10.1007/978-4-431-54475-3_9
9. Caldwell, S., et al.: An agile new research framework for hybrid human-AI teaming: trust, transparency, and transferability. ACM Trans. Interact. Intell. Syst. (TiiS) **12**(3), 1–36 (2022)
10. Cugurullo, F.: Urban artificial intelligence: from automation to autonomy in the smart city. Front. Sustain. Cities **2**, 38 (2020)
11. Degas, A., et al.: A survey on artificial intelligence (AI) and explainable AI in air traffic management: current trends and development with future research trajectory. Appl. Sci. **12**(3), 1295 (2022)
12. Gillath, O., Ai, T., Branicky, M.S., Keshmiri, S., Davison, R.B., Spaulding, R.: Attachment and trust in artificial intelligence. Comput. Hum. Behav. **115**, 106607 (2021)
13. Gürlük, H.: Concept of an adaptive augmented vision based assistance system for air traffic control towers. In: 2016 IEEE/AIAA 35th Digital Avionics Systems Conference (DASC), pp. 1–10. IEEE (2016)
14. Hilburn, B.: A hybrid approach to training expert skills in highly automated systems: lessons from air traffic management. IFAC-PapersOnLine **49**(19), 207–211 (2016)
15. IJtsma, M., Borst, C., van Paassen, M.M., Mulder, M.: Evaluation of a decision-based invocation strategy for adaptive support for air traffic control. IEEE Trans. Hum.-Mach. Syst. **52**(6), 1135–1146 (2022)
16. Itoh, E., Suzuki, S., Duong, V.: Harmonizing automation, pilot, and air traffic controller in the future air traffic management. In: 26th International Congress of the Aeronautical Sciences **1**, 6 (2008)
17. Jameel, M., Tyburzy, L., Gerdes, I., Pick, A., Hunger, R., Christoffels, L.: Enabling digital air traffic controller assistant through human-autonomy teaming design. In: 2023 IEEE/AIAA 42nd Digital Avionics Systems Conference (DASC), pp. 1–9. IEEE (2023)
18. Jones, R., Strater, L., Riley, J., Connors, E., Endsley, M.: Assessing automation for aviation personnel using a predictive model of situation awareness. In: AIAA SPACE 2009 Conference and Exposition, p. 6790 (2009)
19. Jurinić, T., Juričić, B., Antulov-Fantulin, B., Samardžić, K.: Defining terminal airspace air traffic complexity indicators based on air traffic controller tasks. Aerospace **11**(5), 367 (2024)
20. Kaber, D.B., Perry, C.M., Segall, N., McClernon, C.K., Prinzel, L.J., III.: Situation awareness implications of adaptive automation for information processing in an air traffic control-related task. Int. J. Ind. Ergon. **36**(5), 447–462 (2006)
21. Kaplan, A.D., Kessler, T.T., Brill, J.C., Hancock, P.A.: Trust in artificial intelligence: meta-analytic findings. Hum. Factors **65**(2), 337–359 (2023)

22. Langan-Fox, J., Canty, J.M., Sankey, M.J.: Human-automation teams and adaptable control for future air traffic management. Int. J. Ind. Ergon. **39**(5), 894–903 (2009)
23. Millot, P., Debernard, S.: An attempt for conceptual framework for human-machine cooperation. IFAC Proc. Vol. **40**(16), 347–353 (2007)
24. Moehlenbrink, C., Wies, M., Jipp, M.: Monitoring principles in aviation and the importance of operator redundancy. In: 2011 IEEE International Conference on Systems, Man, and Cybernetics, pp. 2828–2835. IEEE (2011)
25. Morrison, J.G., Gluckman, J.P.: Definitions and prospective guidelines for the application of adaptive automation. In: Human Performance in Automated Systems: Current Research and Trends, pp. 256–263 (1994)
26. Nieuwenhuisen, D.: 4d trajectory management support in the c-share project
27. Nocera, F.D., Fabrizi, R., Terenzi, M., Ferlazzo, F.: Procedural errors in air traffic control: effects of traffic density, expertise, and automation. Aviat. Space Environ. Med. **77**(6), 639–643 (2006)
28. Page, M.J., et al.: The Prisma 2020 statement: an updated guideline for reporting systematic reviews. BMJ **372** (2021)
29. Pham, D.T., Ali, H., Fennedy, K., Hsieh, M.H., Alam, S., Duong, V.: Human-AI hybrid paradigm for collaborative air traffic management systems. In: Sesar Innovation Days (SIDs) 2024, Rome (2024)
30. PPrinzel Iii, L.J., Parasuraman, R., Freeman, F.G., Scerbo, M.W., Mikulka, P.J., Pope, A.T.: Three experiments examining the use of electroencephalogram,event-related potentials, and heart-rate variability for real-time human-centered adaptive automation design (2003)
31. Rataj, J., Ohneiser, O., Marin, G., Postaru, R.: Attention: target and actual–the controller focus (2021)
32. Rohacs, J., Rohacs, D., Jankovics, I.: Conceptual development of an advanced air traffic controller workstation based on objective workload monitoring and augmented reality. Proc. Inst. Mech. Eng. Part G: J. Aerosp. Eng **230**(9), 1747–1761 (2016)
33. Schurr, N., et al.: A testbed for investigating task allocation strategies between air traffic controllers and automated agents. In: Proceedings of the AAAI Conference on Artificial Intelligence, vol. 24, pp. 1839–1845 (2010)
34. Smith, P.J., Baumann, E.: Human-automation teaming: unintended consequences of automation on user performance. In: 2020 AIAA/IEEE 39th Digital Avionics Systems Conference (DASC), pp. 1–9. IEEE (2020)
35. Stathis, M., et al.: Challenges from the introduction of artificial intelligence in the European air traffic management system. IFAC-PapersOnLine **55**(29), 1–6 (2022)
36. Tan, S.Y., Chen, C.H., Lye, S.W.: Physiological based adaptive automation triggers in varying traffic density. In: Ahram, T., Taiar, R. (eds.) IHIET 2021. LLNS, vol. 319, pp. 339–345. Springer, Cham (2022). https://doi.org/10.1007/978-3-030-85540-6_43
37. Tran, P.N., Pham, D.T., Goh, S.K., Alam, S., Duong, V.: An interactive conflict solver for learning air traffic conflict resolutions. J. Aerosp. Inf. Syst. **17**(6), 271–277 (2020)
38. Tran Luciani, D., Löwgren, J., Lundberg, J.: Designing fine-grained interactions for automation in air traffic control. Cogn. Technol. Work **22**(4), 685–701 (2020)
39. Trapsilawati, F., Chen, C.H., Khoo, L.P.: An investigation into conflict resolution and trajectory prediction aids for future air traffic control. In: Transdisciplinary Engineering: Crossing Boundaries, pp. 503–512. IOS Press (2016)

40. Turnbull, O.D., Richards, A.G.: Human control of air traffic trajectory optimizer. IEEE Trans. Intell. Transp. Syst. **19**(4), 1091–1099 (2017)
41. Vu, K.P.L., et al.: How does reliance on automated tools during learning influence students' air traffic management skills when the tools fail? In: Proceedings of the Human Factors and Ergonomics Society Annual Meeting, vol. 56, pp. 16–20. SAGE Publications Sage CA, Los Angeles, CA (2012)
42. Wang, Y., Hu, R., Lin, S., Schultz, M., Delahaye, D.: The impact of automation on air traffic controller's behaviors. Aerospace **8**(9), 260 (2021)
43. Westin, C., Boonsong, S., Josefsson, B., Lundberg, J.: Building trust in autonomous system competence–the dita digital tower assistant for multiple remote towers, an early concept evaluation. In: 2020 AIAA/IEEE 39th Digital Avionics Systems Conference (DASC), pp. 1–9. IEEE (2020)

Mobile Technologies for Health, Education, and Digital Engagement

Investigating Mobile Users' Willingness to Disclose Information Through the Lens of Privacy Calculus Theory

Elpida Efstathiou[1], Dimitris Drossos[1]([envelope]), Vassilis Karkatzounis[2], Evangelos Margaritis[2], and Lilian Mitrou[2]

[1] Athens University of Economics and Business, 11362 Athens, Greece
drosos@aueb.gr
[2] University of the Aegean, 81100 Mytilene, Greece

Abstract. This study aimed to examine the parameters that contribute to mobile users' willingness to disclose their online personal information utilizing the theory of Privacy Calculus. The study comprised 790 participants who evaluated -among other factors- the benefits of providing information in exchange for personalized advertisements, their privacy concerns and their intention to share their data. According to the results, trust towards the companies, perceived benefits, privacy concerns, perceived intrusiveness and personal innovativeness were associated with mobile users' willingness to disclose their information, while previous privacy experience was related to privacy concerns.

Keywords: Privacy Calculus · Personalized advertising · Willingness to disclose information

1 Introduction

In the contemporary era of digitalization, firms display online personalized content such as advertisements to users and consumers to achieve various marketing goals [1]. These personalized advertisements appear to target audiences based on their demographic and behavioral characteristics [2]. Companies install cookies on users' browsers after asking for their consent and if users provide it, they can have access to their information which they use for specific purposes. In 2018, the General Data Protection Regulation (GDPR) was applied in the European Union to enhance the protection of personal data and information [3].

Previous research suggests that even though users and consumers tend to be skeptical about disclosing their online information and might take some measures to protect it, they still provide their data. This phenomenon is known as Privacy Paradox, as despite consumers' privacy concerns, they disclose their information to firms in exchange for personalized content [4]. Thus far, several attempts have been made to explain privacy paradox through the application of Privacy Calculus Theory [5].

The present study aimed to examine the factors that contribute to mobile users' willingness to disclose their personal information to companies. This research employed

J. Wei et al. (Eds.): HCII 2025, LNCS 16346, pp. 299–309, 2026.
https://doi.org/10.1007/978-3-032-13187-4_20

the Privacy Calculus Theory, which has been widely used in research to examine users' and consumers' attitude, as well as their behavioral intentions regarding provision of their online data. The research hypotheses include the following variables: benefits, trust beliefs, privacy concerns, intrusiveness, previous privacy experience, innovativeness along with willingness to disclose information. To the best of our knowledge no prior research has specifically examined the factors that are related to mobile users' willingness to share their online personal information in exchange for personalized advertisements in Greece.

Furthermore, this study also aimed to explore the impact of demographic factors, including age, gender and education on mobile users' willingness to disclose personal information.

The following section provides insights into the theoretical background of Privacy Calculus Theory. The subsequent section presents the methods and the research design. Next, the study's results are presented. Finally, the paper concludes by discussing implications, limitations and proposing some directions for further research.

2 Theoretical Background and Research Hypotheses

Firms with digital presence try to attract consumers through their websites using various marketing strategies, one of which is online advertising. When advertisements are displayed to certain individuals based on their online profile, demographics, behaviors and geolocation they are referred to as personalized advertisements [6].

Once users accept companies' requests for access to their personal data and provide their information, they are targeted with content tailored to their preferences. Even though users might perceive as beneficial the display of products or services that they are interested in, they also appear to be concerned about their personal information and the protection of their online privacy. Several studies suggest that consumers and users engage in a process of rational thinking while performing a cost-benefit analysis before disclosing personal information [7].

This approach aligns with the theory of Privacy Calculus, which examines how factors such as trust, benefits, privacy concerns and risks play a crucial role in the analysis of individual disclosure behavior in a variety of contexts and situations. More specifically, it is the assessment of the trade-off between the benefits consumers receive from personalized services and the risks associated with granting access to that data [8]. Previous studies have showed that consumers are more likely to disclose their information when the perceived benefits outweigh the perceived risks [7].

2.1 Benefits

When consumers disclose information, they expect to gain in return content that includes specific advantages for them, such as time saving derived from the search process, displayed products or services that suit their needs and monetary rewards [9].

Receiving personalized content can be considered as beneficial for many consumers who do not have leisure time to search for a product or service. Companies show them content and ads that are tailored to their interests and needs according to their behavior on websites and social media. Additionally, they offer coupons and monetary rewards as incentives. Hence, perceived benefits from providing information in exchange for personalized advertisements can include giveaways, special offers and convenience as users save time from searching in online environments [1].

Therefore, we hypothesize that:

H1: Perceived benefits are positively associated with mobile users' willingness to disclose information.

2.2 Trust

Concerning the factors that can influence consumers regarding their behavioral intention, apart from monetary rewards and personalized content, trust is one of the strongest, as studies have shown that when consumers trust a brand, they are more likely to provide their online data to a firm [10]. Moreover, when consumers recognize businesses' fair privacy practices, they feel more secure about the handling of their data [11]. In addition, companies desire to build relationships with their customers in order to achieve marketing goals such as brand loyalty [1]. When consumers feel that they can trust firms, the relationship between them becomes stronger. Previous studies have shown that strong consumer brand relationships with high levels of consumers' trust can affect advertising acceptance and result to positive brand outcomes in online advertising contexts. Therefore, if consumers trust a firm, they feel less concerned about the data collected by the brand to target them, so they share their information to receive personalized advertisements [12].

Thus, we hypothesize that:

H2: Trust beliefs towards companies are positively associated with mobile users' willingness to disclose information.

2.3 Privacy Concerns

On the other hand, studies have shown that users who present high levels of concern about information privacy practices are more likely to deny taking participation in activities requiring the provision of personal information [13]. According to prior research, mobile users' privacy concerns often drive them to refuse app permissions, which eventually leads to their decision to decline the installation of an app [14]. Unfair practices of data access employed by mobile apps have raised privacy concerns, as users most of the time are unaware of who handles their personal information, for what purposes and under what circumstances [15]. Additionally, a privacy concern is triggered due to the loss of control over the disclosure of personal information [16]. When consumers have concerns about the safety of their data in companies' hands, they tend to be less willing to disclose information.

Thus, we hypothesize:

H3: Privacy concerns are negatively associated with mobile users' willingness to disclose information.

2.4 Intrusiveness

Regarding factors that may contribute to doubts about consumers' privacy and therefore their reluctance of providing personal data, it has been suggested that personalized advertising might create a perception of intrusiveness. This makes users feel that it interferes with their personal data and invades their personal space. Intrusiveness consists of acts of invasion that disrupt a person's solitude and include the raid of one's activities [17]. In addition, the intrusiveness of a mobile message can play an important role in perceived value of personalized advertisement, as many mobile applications force users to accept the permission of access to personal information, without allowing them to know exactly the amount of their collected data [18]. As a result, mobile users feel disturbed, and they do not intend to share their information to receive any personalized content [19].

Hence, we hypothesize that:

H4: Perceived intrusiveness is negatively associated with mobile users' willingness to disclose information.

2.5 Previous Privacy Experience

In compliance with prior studies, individuals' experiences and personality characteristics are related to beliefs regarding privacy and intention to accept or deny technology. Mobile users and consumers who have perceived themselves as victims of data misuse, are more likely to develop increased privacy concerns [20]. This occurs because when consumers disclose their data to companies, they expect that their private information will be respected and properly protected. However, in case of data mismanagement by an online marketplace, consumers feel misled and tend to have high perceived risks of sharing information with the broader community of sellers [2].

Thus, we hypothesize that:

H5: Previous privacy experience is positively associated with mobile users' privacy concerns.

2.6 Innovativeness

Concerning individual characteristics, researchers have argued that those who have high levels of innovativeness, tend to actively seek to try and adopt new technologies, as well as wireless applications. Additionally, because of their personal innovativeness, individuals are more likely to take risks [21]. According to several researchers, innovativeness reflects the individual's proclivity toward making decisions regarding the adoption of new technology. Moreover, innovativeness has been found to a have positive effect on the adoption of pull-based and push-based location-based services [22]. Prior studies have suggested that personal innovativeness has a positive influence on behavioral intention [23]. Therefore, it can be expected that users and consumers develop positive intentions to disclose information to firms in order to receive personalized advertisements.

Thus, we hypothesize that:

H6: Mobile users' personal innovativeness is positively associated with their willingness to disclose information.

3 Methodology

3.1 Procedure and Data Collection

Data were collected through an online survey in Greece in March 2024. A quantitative survey was conducted using a mixed method of Computer Assisted Telephone Interviews (CATI) and Computer Assisted Web Interviews (CAWI), utilizing a structured questionnaire. This combination ensured inclusive and reliable results by not excluding individuals who do not use the Internet for survey participation [24]. All participants were informed regarding the aim of the study and the procedure for data collection, while they were assured anonymity regarding their voluntary participation.

After providing their consent, they were given a small text to read in order to understand the definition of the terms "personalized advertising" and "online privacy". Inclusion criteria comprised being adult, using mobile phone and browsing the Internet through a mobile device, along with having been exposed to online personalized advertisements, as well as residing in Greece.

The questionnaire they were asked to answer, contained measures of benefits, trust beliefs, privacy concerns, perceived intrusiveness, previous privacy experience and personal innovativeness, together with willingness to disclose information. Furthermore, it included questions regarding data collection information, as well as behavioral and demographic characteristics.

3.2 Measures and Statistical Analysis

Three items were used to measure benefits [12], four items regarding trust beliefs [25], five items to assess privacy concerns [26], three items to measure intrusiveness [27] and three items to evaluate personal innovativeness [22]. In addition, three items were used to measure willingness to disclose information [6] and one item for previous privacy experience [22]. All items were measured on a 7-point Likert scale (specifically from 1 = strongly disagree to 7 = strongly agree).

IBM SPSS Version 29 [28] was used to describe the sample and examine the relationships between demographics and willingness to disclose information. Additionally, it was employed to assess the reliability of the investigated variables and to conduct hypothesis testing.

4 Results

4.1 Descriptive Characteristics

The sample consisted of 790 participants, aged 18 or older, with the majority between 25 and 34 years old (34.6%, n = 273), followed by participants aged 35 to 44 years (32.8%, n = 259). In addition, most participants were women (56.1%, n = 443), while the majority resided in Attica (35.3%, n = 279), followed by those in North Greece (34.9%, n = 276). Regarding education level, most participants had a Bachelor's degree (44.7%, n = 355). As for the daily mobile usage, the median time spent was 3 h (IQR = 2–5).

Concerning participants' interest in understanding the purpose and the methods by which their data and information are collected, the mean value (M) of their responses was recorded at medium to high levels (M = 4.87). Moreover, regarding previous experience with privacy issues, the mean value of respondents' answers was also recorded at a medium to high degree (M = 4.67).

4.2 Reliability Assessment

Reliability is the measure of internal consistency of the constructs in the study. A construct is reliable if the Alpha (α) value is greater than 0.70 [29]. Construct reliability was assessed using Cronbach's Alpha. The results revealed acceptable reliability for each of the research' constructs. Results are summarized in Table 1.

Table 1. Constructs' Reliability.

Construct	No. of items	Alpha
Benefits	3	0.905
Trust	4	0.812
Privacy Concerns	5	0.933
Intrusiveness	3	0.912
Personal Innovativeness	3	0.835
Willingness to disclose information	3	0.866

4.3 Hypotheses Testing

Pearson's r correlation coefficient was used to investigate the association of the factors benefits, trust beliefs, privacy concerns, intrusiveness, previous privacy experience, personal innovativeness and willingness to disclose information. Table 2 summarizes the results for the Hypotheses 1, 2, 3, 4, 5, 6.

The results showed that the relationship between benefits and mobile users' willingness to disclose their personal information was statistically significant with positive direction (r = 0.494, p < 0.001). Consequently, H1 was supported. With respect to H2, the association between trust beliefs towards companies and users' willingness to disclose personal information was statistically significant with positive direction (r = 0.486, p < 0.001). Hence H2 was confirmed. H3 was also supported as the relationship between privacy concerns and mobile users' willingness to share their information was statistically significant with negative direction (r = −0.251, p < 0.001). Concerning H4, it was confirmed as well, as perceived intrusiveness was negatively associated with users' willingness to disclose information (r = −0.174, p < 0.001). As for H5, it emerged that the relationship between users' previous experience with privacy issues and their concerns about their online privacy was statistically significant with positive direction (r = 0.251, p < 0.001). Thus, it was supported. Additionally, according to the results, the association between users' personal innovativeness with their willingness to provide their personal information for personalized advertisements was statistically significant with positive direction (r = 0.258, p < 0.001). Therefore, H6 was supported.

Table 2. Results of the Correlations Between the Investigated Variables

Hypotheses	Variables		r	p
H1	Benefits	Willingness to disclose information	0.494	<0.001
H2	Trust beliefs	Willingness to disclose information	0.486	<0.001
H3	Privacy concerns	Willingness to disclose information	−0.251	<0.001
H4	Intrusiveness	Willingness to disclose information	−0.174	<0.001
H5	Previous privacy experience	Privacy concerns	0.251	<0.001
H6	Personal innovativeness	Willingness to disclose information	0.258	<0.001

4.4 Additional Findings

With a view to investigating whether certain demographic variables were related to mobile users' willingness to share their personal information, Analysis of Variance (ANOVA) was performed. According to the results, a statistically significant relationship emerged among the age of the participants and their intention to provide their personal information to firms in order to get personalized advertisements, with participants aged 18–24 (M = 3.70, SD = 1.28), 25–34 (M = 3.64, SD = 1.43) and 35–44 (M = 3.49, SD = 1.51) appearing more willing to share their information than participants aged 45–54 (M = 2.73, SD = 1.43) No statistically significant relationships emerged as regards education (p > 0.05).

Regarding whether gender played a statistically significant role in intention to provide information, Independent Samples t-test was performed. According to the results, no statistically significant relationship emerged, although the value of p was very close to the threshold (p = 0.051).

5 Discussion

The aim of this study was to investigate the factors that are associated with mobile users' willingness to share their online personal information to firms.

According to the findings, benefits, trust beliefs, privacy concerns, perceived intrusiveness and personal innovativeness were related to willingness to disclose personal information (H1, H2, H3, H4, H6), while previous privacy experience was related to users' privacy concerns (H5).

In particular, it emerged that benefits from personalized advertisements, as perceived by users, were related to their intention to share their data in online environments. Accordingly, Xu et al. (2009) reported that when consumers evaluate as beneficial what they gain from viewing a personalized message, they intent to share their personal information [2].

Furthermore, this study found a relationship between trust beliefs towards companies and mobile user's willingness to provide their information. Similar results were reported by Cloarec et al. (2022), who reported a statistically significant impact of trust beliefs on consumers' willingness to disclose information in exchange for personalization [6]. In addition, study showed that customers' perception of trustworthiness influenced users' intentions to use e-Pharmacies [30].

Of note, privacy concerns were negatively associated with users' willingness to share personal information. Degirmenci (2020) also found a relationship between mobile users' privacy concerns and their intention to deny requested app permissions [14].

Regarding the perceived intrusiveness of the personalized advertisements, our findings showed that it negatively associated with users' intention to share private information. These results were in accordance with the findings of Wottrich et al. (2018), who suggested that app intrusiveness had a negative influence on permission acceptance intention [19].

Concerning users' previous experience with privacy issues, the results of this study showed that it was positively associated with their privacy concerns. This aligns with the research of Degirmenci (2020), who examined the relationship between prior privacy experience and privacy concerns, finding that mobile users who had experienced privacy issues with mobile apps had high concerns regarding their online personal information [14].

As for the relationship between individual characteristics and willingness to disclose personal information, the current study showed that users' innovativeness was positively associated with information disclosure. According to prior research, users who note high levels of innovativeness are likely to participate in a web survey providing their personal information [22]. Moreover, Xu et al. (2011) suggested that characteristics such as innovativeness influence consumers' willingness to share their information to online providers [9].

6 Conclusion

The purpose of the present study was to examine the parameters that are associated with mobile users' willingness to provide their online personal information to firms. According to the results, factors such as benefits, trust beliefs and personal innovativeness were positively associated with users' willingness to disclose information, while privacy concerns and intrusiveness were negatively related to their willingness to disclose information. Moreover, previous privacy experience was positively associated with privacy concerns.

6.1 Implications

The results of this study could potentially contribute to a better understanding of mobile users' perspective on their privacy and the protection of their online information. Specifically, it is crucial for businesses in the digital environments to recognize that consumers wish to feel that they can trust them regarding the management of their online data, as the results of this study showed that when users consider a firm to be trustful, they are more likely to provide their information. Moreover, when companies show users personalized messages such as personalized advertisements, which help them gain some benefits, the users are more willing to disclose their information.

In contrast, when users and consumers are concerned about their privacy, they tend to decline provision of their information. Thus, handling users' personal data with respect and fairness, could benefit companies as it would potentially result in loyal customers who disclose information without hesitation. In addition, firms could reduce the frequency of displaying personalized advertisements to users who tend to avoid them, as perceiving such ads as annoying and intrusive decreases their willingness to share data.

Furthermore, companies could invest in users' personal innovativeness by showing them new creative content, which could encourage them to learn more about the advertised products and services and, in turn, disclose their information in exchange for personalized advertisements.

6.2 Limitations, Strengths and Further Research

The findings of the present study must be interpreted considering a number of limitations. First, as self-report questionnaires were used, the possibility that some of the participants' responses may not have been accurate needs to be acknowledged. Moreover, it was an observational and cross-sectional study and therefore causal relationships could not be established.

Despite the abovementioned limitations, a significant strength was the use of probability sampling that ensures a more representative sample of the population and enhances the generalizability of the findings.

Regarding future research, it is recommended that the survey be conducted in person to minimize potential shortcomings related to the cross-sectional design. In addition, qualitative research could be conducted to offer a deeper understanding about users' attitudes and behavioral intentions. Moreover, factors such as trust and attitude towards Artificial Intelligence (AI) could be examined, as currently many online advertisements are created with the use of this technology. Thus, willingness to disclose information in exchange for AI content could be investigated as well.

Acknowledgments. The data of this study derived from the research project which was supported by the Hellenic Foundation for Research and Innovation (H.F.R.I.) under the "2nd Call for H.F.R.I. Research Projects to support Faculty Members and Researchers" (Project Number: 4246).

Disclosure of Interests. None.

References

1. Hayes, J.L., Brinson, N.H., Bott, G.J., Moeller, C.M.: The influence of consumer–brand relationship on the personalized advertising privacy calculus in social media. J. Interact. Mark. **55**(1), 16–30 (2021)
2. Xu, H., Teo, H.H., Tan, B.C., Agarwal, R.: The role of push-pull technology in privacy calculus: the case of location-based services. J. Manag. Inf. Syst. **26**(3), 135–174 (2009)
3. Wang, P., Jiang, L., Yang, J.: The early impact of GDPR compliance on display advertising: the case of an ad publisher. J. Mark. Res. **61**(1), 70–91 (2024)
4. Karwatzki, S., Dytynko, O., Trenz, M., Veit, D.: Beyond the personalization–privacy paradox: privacy valuation, transparency features, and service personalization. J. Manag. Inf. Syst. **34**(2), 369–400 (2017)
5. Awad, N.F., Krishnan, M.S.: The personalization privacy paradox: an empirical evaluation of information transparency and the willingness to be profiled online for personalization. MIS Q. **30**, 13–28 (2006)
6. Cloarec, J., Meyer-Waarden, L., Munzel, A.: The personalization–privacy paradox at the nexus of social exchange and construal level theories. Psychol. Mark. **39**(3), 647–661 (2022)
7. Dinev, T., Hart, P.: An extended privacy calculus model for e-commerce transactions. Inf. Syst. Res. **17**(1), 61–80 (2006)
8. Culnan, M.J., Armstrong, P.K.: Information privacy concerns, procedural fairness, and impersonal trust: an empirical investigation. Organ. Sci. **10**(1), 104–115 (1999)
9. Xu, H., Luo, X.R., Carroll, J.M., Rosson, M.B.: The personalization privacy paradox: an exploratory study of decision-making process for location-aware marketing. Decis. Support. Syst. **51**(1), 42–52 (2011)
10. Aguirre, E., Mahr, D., Grewal, D., De Ruyter, K., Wetzels, M.: Unraveling the personalization paradox: the effect of information collection and trust-building strategies on online advertisement effectiveness. J. Retail. **91**(1), 34–49 (2015)
11. Wirtz, J., Lwin, M.O.: Regulatory focus theory, trust, and privacy concern. J. Serv. Res. **12**(2), 190–207 (2009)
12. Hayes, J.L., King, K.W., Ramirez, A.: Brands, friends, & viral advertising: a social exchange perspective on the ad referral processes. J. Interact. Mark. **36**, 31–45 (2016)
13. Smith, H.J., Milberg, S.J., Burke, S.J.: Information privacy: measuring individuals' concerns about organizational practices. MIS Q. **20**, 167–196 (1996)
14. Degirmenci, K.: Mobile users' information privacy concerns and the role of app permission requests. Int. J. Inf. Manage. **50**, 261–272 (2020)
15. Xu, H., Gupta, S., Rosson, M.B., Carroll, J.M.: Measuring mobile users' concerns for information privacy (2012)
16. Sheng, N., Yang, C., Han, L., Jou, M.: Too much overload and concerns: antecedents of social media fatigue and the mediating role of emotional exhaustion. Comput. Hum. Behav. **139**, 107500 (2023)
17. Solove, D.J., Hoofnagle, C.J.: A model regime of privacy protection. U. Ill. L. Rev., 357 (2006)
18. Okazaki, S., Li, H., Hirose, M.: Consumer privacy concerns and preference for degree of regulatory control. J. Advert. **38**(4), 63–77 (2009)
19. Wottrich, V.M., van Reijmersdal, E.A., Smit, E.G.: The privacy trade-off for mobile app downloads: the roles of app value, intrusiveness, and privacy concerns. Decis. Support. Syst. **106**, 44–52 (2018)
20. Cho, H., Lee, J.-S., Chung, S.: Optimistic bias about online privacy risks: testing the moderating effects of perceived controllability and prior experience. Comput. Hum. Behav. **26**(5), 987–995 (2010)

21. Lu, J., Yao, J.E., Yu, C.-S.: Personal innovativeness, social influences and adoption of wireless internet services via mobile technology. J. Strat. Inf. Syst. **14**, 245–268 (2005)
22. Zhao, L., Lu, Y., Gupta, S.: Disclosure intention of location-related information in location-based social network services. Int. J. Electron. Commer. **16**(4), 53–90 (2012)
23. Fang, J., Shao, P., Lan, G.: Effects of innovativeness and trust on web survey participation. Comput. Hum. Behav. **25**(1), 144–152 (2009)
24. De Leeuw, D.: To mix or not to mix data collection modes in surveys. J. Off. Stat. **21**(2), 233 (2005)
25. Hong, W., Thong, J.Y.: Internet privacy concerns: an integrated conceptualization and four empirical studies. MIS Q. **37**, 275–298 (2013)
26. Aiolfi, S., Bellini, S., Pellegrini, D.: Data-driven digital advertising: benefits and risks of online behavioral advertising. Int. J. Retail Distrib. Manag. **49**(7), 1089–1110 (2021)
27. Gutierrez, A., O'Leary, S., Rana, N.P., Dwivedi, Y.K., Calle, T.: Using privacy calculus theory to explore entrepreneurial directions in mobile location-based advertising: identifying intrusiveness as the critical risk factor. Comput. Hum. Behav. **95**, 295–306 (2019)
28. IBM Corp. Released 2023: IBM SPSS Statistics for Windows, Version 29.0.2.0. IBM Corp, Armonk, NY
29. Hair, J.F., Ringle, C.M., Sarstedt, M.: Partial least squares structural equation modeling: rigorous applications, better results and higher acceptance. Long Range Plan. **46**(1–2), 1–12 (2013)
30. Ashrafi, D.M., Ahmed, S., Shahid, T.S.: Privacy or trust: understanding the privacy paradox in users intentions towards e-pharmacy adoption through the lens of privacy-calculus model. J. Sci. Technol. Policy Manag. **16**(7), 1224–1247 (2025)

Addiction to Massively Multiplayer Online Games Among Chinese University Students: Exploring an Intervention App Based on Cognitive Behavioral Therapy

Jiahui Li[ID], Rongcong Cai[(✉)][ID], Bingrui Ran[ID], and Xile Chen[ID]

School of Fine Art, School of Design, Zhaoqing University, Zhaoqing, China
rongcongcai@foxmail.com

Abstract. Massive multiplayer online games have become popular among Chinese university students, leading to a growing problem of gaming addiction among them. Therefore, this study develops a mobile application based on cognitive behavioral therapy (CBT) to help players improve their gaming behavior. In this study, a quantitative questionnaire was made to find out the emotional differences among different players, combined with CBT and existing research on gaming addiction. A mobile application named Have a Better Life was designed and developed based on the survey results. The experiment results were used in a qualitative way to evaluate the effect of the application on the refinement of MMOGs behavior among addicted Chinese university students. The application included seven stages of intervention covering emotion management, time planning, and social skills training. The experimental results showed that the application enhanced the players self-awareness of addictive behaviors and guided players to reduce gaming time through emotional regulation and behavior. Players develop healthy behavioral patterns and mental resilience, improve stress coping, social skills, and time management. The application offers an innovative intervention for addressing MMOG addiction through a combination of CBT and gamified design. The study provides new ideas for the application of the integration of psychotherapy and technology, proposes a special design for the cultural characteristics of different regions, and has a great significance in the health management of digital products for improving addictive behavior.

Keywords: Massively Multiplayer Online Games(MMOGs) · Chinese University Students · Gaming Addiction · Mobile Application Design

1 Introduction

Internet Gaming Disorder (IGD) is globally recognized as a health problem, classified by the World Health Organization (WHO) in 2021. MMOGs, with

J. Wei et al. (Eds.): HCII 2025, LNCS 16346, pp. 310–321, 2026.
https://doi.org/10.1007/978-3-032-13187-4_21

their immersive and socially interactive environments, exhibit unique addiction mechanisms ([2]; Hwa et al., 2009; [3]). These games use structured elements such as permanent worlds, reward mechanisms, and social interfaces to sustain engagement and amplify enjoyment. The addictive potential of MMOGs stems from psychological mechanisms such as designed rewards, social interactions, and immersive experiences that fulfill core psychological needs (Lee et al., 2017). These factors negatively impact mental health, academic performance, and social functioning worldwide, with variations across cultures ([7,26]; Turan et al., 2023). The rise of digital gaming platforms has increased gaming addiction prevalence, which is characterized by compulsive behaviors that impair daily life [8]. In China, online gaming addiction is a critical public health issue among students. The 55th Statistical Report on Internet Development in China (CNNIC, 2024) shows 1.108 billion internet users and 78.5% penetration, with an average weekly usage of 26.1 h. Specially, 60% of university students game for over an hour daily, 20.6% are at risk of internet addiction, and 12.61% game for over three hours daily. Additionally, 31.97% of students stay up late gaming, with MMOGs exacerbating psychological issues such as compulsive achievement pursuit and socialization [9]. Younger male demographics show stronger prevalence (Michael08,Liu, 2022). Students often use gaming to escape real-world inadequacies and seek virtual achievement. Geographic and economic constraints limit access to psychological services, making mobile apps a viable digital intervention. While mobile CBT apps show therapeutic potential, MMOG addiction in China is embedded in socio-cultural complexities requiring culturally grounded interventions [6]. Western app designs often fail to align with Chinese cultural contexts, leading to low engagement and insufficient therapeutic content [23,24]. This highlights the need for culturally sensitive CBT apps to address the unique challenges faced by Chinese university students. Understanding the impact of individualized mechanisms and psychological barriers on the acceptance of mobile health solutions is crucial. RQ1: How to design an interventional application that targets the psychological mechanisms of MMOGs addiction, such as achievement compensation, escapism, and social dependence for Chinese university students in CBT therapy. RQ2: How to design an application to intervene in the behavior of MMOGs game addiction in the face of specific factors of Chinese collectivist culture, such as family expectations, academic pressure in CBT therapy.

2   Background

2.1   Influencing Factors of MMOG Addiction Prevalence Among Chinese University Students

The phenomenon of MMOG addiction among Chinese university students stems from multiple factors [26]. In China's competitive educational environment, gaming serves as a maladaptive coping mechanism, creating a cycle of academic decline, increased psychological distress, and reinforced compulsive gaming [27]. The collectivist culture that values social conformity encourages students to prioritize gaming through peer interactions [28]. While MMOGs offer virtual socialization, they undermine real-world responsibilities and relationships [29]. Smartphones and fast internet enable constant gaming, increasing addiction risk during school-related stress [30]. Parental relationships also influence addiction risk, with overcontrol leading to rebellious gaming and support reducing addiction risks. This is exacerbated by a cycle linking gaming addiction to mental health issues such as anxiety and depression, and a lack of alternative leisure activities (Wang et al., 2022). Gaming addiction affects academic performance and health, causing insomnia, neck pain, and tiredness [19], and impairing social skills due to elevated anxiety [20]. In China's education-centric society, gaming is stigmatized as contrary to academic success [11]. This study examines the impact of MMOGs such as League of Legends and Honor of Kings on Chinese university students' leisure time. These games use reinforcement systems and social mechanics to encourage sustained engagement [12,18]. On campus, they serve as cultural currency, reinforcing gaming behaviors through environmental confinement (Smith, 2020) and insular gaming subcultures (Jones et al., 2019). Technology addiction is characterized by diagnostic markers similar to substance dependency, including affective instability, tolerance-withdrawal cycles, and relapse patterns (Günüç, 2017). MMOG addiction among Chinese university students involves psychosocial vulnerabilities like loneliness and social anxiety, as well as familial factors such as parental educational deficits and maladaptive peer dynamics [26,32].

2.2 Application of CBT in Mobile Applications as Intervention Tools

Cognitive Behavioral Therapy (CBT), a psychological intervention developed by Aaron T. Beck and Albert Ellis, aims to modify maladaptive cognitive behavioral patterns to enhance mental health outcomes [13,14]. This intervention has been demonstrated to be efficacious across a range of domains [21]. CBT, an intervention for internet gaming addiction, targets the maladaptive cognitive behavioral cycles inherent in MMOG dependency. Its efficacy in reducing addictive behaviors and enhancing mental health outcomes has been empirically validated, making it particularly applicable to gaming disorder interventions [33,34]. The increasing prevalence of smartphones has rendered CBT apps as a therapeutic platform with the potential to enhance adherence through adaptive engagement mechanisms [25]. Mobile apps in CBT interventions have been shown to integrate modular features, including personalized feedback, progress tracking, and techniques such as cognitive restructuring and behavioral activation [35]. It's significant improvements in therapeutic outcomes that have been observed across addictive disorders. As demonstrated by Khademian et al. (2020), CBT interventions integrate positive psychology and problem-solving strategies in mobile apps. Their personalized feedback and support systems have potential in digital therapeutics for mental health (Khademian et al. 2020). Existing CBT apps such as Crave for smoking cessation and MindShift CBT for anxiety management exemplify the efficacy of such interventions. However, such applications have yet to be developed for gaming disorder.

3   Formative Research

This study conducts a questionnaire survey research method to survey Chinese university students aged 18–30 years old gamers from gaming platforms such as Android, IOS, Steam and Epic. Each questionnaire was approved by the respondents.

3.1   Methods

The questionnaire used the five-point Likert scale ($0 =$ strongly disagree, $5 =$ strongly agree), which was established as a qualitative survey. This scale was utilized in conjunction with a synthesis of the qualitative analysis method proposed by Lee et al. for MMOGs' addiction characteristics and Taquet et al.'s ACEBIG (Assessment of Cognitions, Emotions, and Behaviours Involved in Gaming) scale(lee et al., Taquet et al.). The questionnaires Q1–Q20 (see Appendix A) were designed to analyze the addictive characteristics of university students in the Chinese culture and environment (see Fig. 1).

The Questionnaire Star survey tool (a questionnaire survey tool in China) was used to conduct the survey. The Salience (SAL) aspect was divided into two categories: Cognitive Salience (CS) and Behavioral Salience (BS). Emotional Modification (Mood Modification) was further subdivided into Mood Enhancement (ME), Emotional Relief (ER), Tolerance (TOL) and Withdrawal (WIT). Conflicts (CON) were categorized as follows: Personal Problems (Intrapersonal Problems, IAP); Interpersonal Problems (IEP); Professional and Academic Problems (PAP); Relapses (REL); and Loss of Control (LOC). The survey employs the aforementioned categorization to establish a combined distinction between excessive university gamer (EUG) and non-excessive University gamer (NEUG). Participants who attain an average score of more than 3 on questions will be designated as EUG.

3.2   Key Findings

(1) Emotional and physical performance (Cronbach alpha: 0.761): EUG ($n = 25$, Mean $= 4.32$, SD $= 0.22$) used MMOG games as a coping mechanism for academic, social, and emotional stress, with playing time positively correlated with stress levels. They exhibited cognitive distortions like believing that "only games can relax me," necessitating cognitive intervention. NEUG ($n = 12$, Mean $= 2.58$, SD $= 0.41$) employed multiple stress to relief methods (e.g. sports, social activities), showing no significant link between play time and stress. Their high level of cognitive flexibility, such as viewing play as one of many ways to relax, indicated a healthy cognitive pattern.

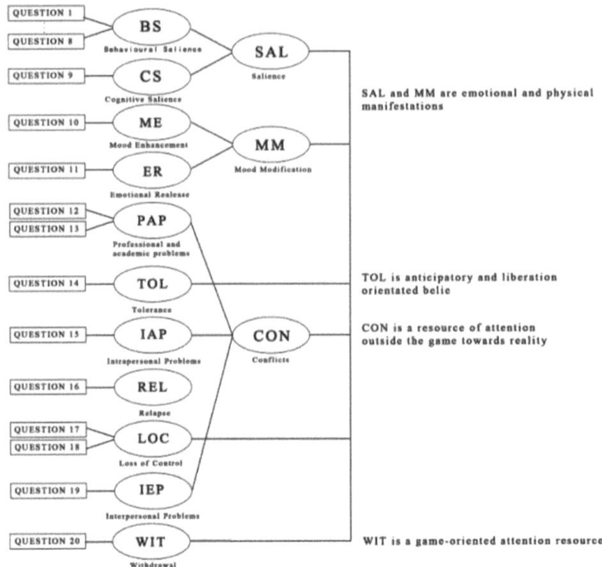

Fig. 1. Methodological model of qualitative investigation.

(2) Expectations and liberation - oriented beliefs (Cronbach alpha: 0.801): EUG (n=13, mean = 4.15, SD = 0.13) showed significant changes in gaming behavior, habits, and motivations from first year to final year, with freshmen using games for socializing and seniors using games for escaping job - finding stress. NEUG (n = 24, mean = 2.46, SD=0.58) maintained stable motivations, using games primarily for social entertainment with low need to escape real - life pressures.

(3) Game - oriented attention resources (Cronbach alpha: 0.519): EUG (n = 6, mean = 3.5, SD = 1.25) used games to escape uncomfortable emotions, lacked effective emotion regulation skills, and developed unhealthy, addictive behavior patterns that were detrimental to learning and coping with life pressures, becoming deeply ingrained habits. NEUG (n = 31, mean = 2.26, SD = 0.64) balanced their attentional resources, with game time making up less than 10% of their daily activities. They had basic emotional regulation skills (e.g., mindfulness, talking), so that gaming was just one of their leisure options.

(4) External display of attentional resources (Cronbach alpha: 0.817): EUG (n = 11, mean = 4.27, SD = 0.19) Cultural and social factors, family expectations, and peer influences have a significant impact on gaming behavior. Cultural stigma can cause internal conflict or rebellion. Healthier coping mechanisms reduce addiction risk, highlighting the need for diverse strategies. NEUG (n = 26, mean = 2.15, SD = 0.67) benefit from open family communication and varied peer activities, reducing gaming dependence.

(5) Cognitive - emotional and behavioral processes associated with failure (Cronbach alpha: 0.59): EUG (n = 9, mean = 4.3, SD = 0.22) often fail in self-

behavior management, struggling to balance play and learning. This highlights the need for better time management strategies to reduce addiction. The stigma around gaming addiction also deters help-seeking, emphasizing the need for de-stigmatization. NEUG (n =28, mean=2.53, SD=0.53) manage their self-behavior effectively, successfully balancing entertainment and learning. They plan their time well, prioritizing study or work while enjoying games without affecting daily tasks. They set clear time limits for play and choose educational games that combine fun with learning and fostering a positive outlook.

4   Design and Implementation

4.1   Prototype Overview

In view of the key findings, an intervention application, "Have a Better Life", was developed. This aims to assist Chinese university students in managing and reducing MMOGs addiction based on CBT. Its prototype integrates a user-friendly interface with tools to support behavior change and mental health man-agement. The home screen displays gaming time statistics, goal-setting options, and CBT tool access, while enabling progress tracking, personalized goal cus-tomization, and engagement with cognitive exercises and behavioral tasks. Cul-turally aligned design elements enhance relevance and acceptability for the target demographic.

4.2   Design Features

The application is predicated on the principles of cognitive behavioral therapy (CBT). The application's functionality is distributed across six "islands": the journaling island allows the user to record daily emotions, positive aspects of life, and important events (see Fig. 2 a,b). The module includes reflective jour-naling, note-taking, and cognitive restructuring exercises. These exercises help users replace negative thoughts with positive, realistic ones. "Activity Island" (see Fig. 2 c) reduces gaming time by using behavioral activation techniques to replace gaming with other activities during addictive urges. Tasks are divided into dynamic and static activities of daily living to minimize abandonment, reduce cognitive load, and block gaming addiction. In the "Positive Medita-tion Island" module (see Fig. 2 d), mindfulness techniques are used to interrupt impulsive thoughts, manage negative emotions, and address stress and emo-tional triggers through guided meditations and breathing exercises. When using the breathing exercises (see Fig. 2 e), the virtual pet's water levels and vibrations sync with feedback to enhance engagement via visual and tactile interactions. In the "Community Island" section (see Fig. 2 f), users can interact with friends or app advisers, check friends' task completion levels, and engage in healthy com-petition. It also offers courses to develop listening, negotiation, and social skills, fostering a supportive community and promoting positive social restoration. The "Daily Plan" section (see Fig. 2 g, h) shows the percentage of screen and game time, helping users to assess their addiction. The application allows users to set individual blocked applications and their designated timeframes. This ensures that interventions are tailored to the individual users' needs, facilitates reasonable game usage management, and prevents disruption to daily life. This aligns with the design philosophy of formative research. The Problem-Solving Island (see Fig. 2 i) is a digital platform that helps users understand the root causes of their behavioral challenges and provides solutions to promote family harmony and personal growth. Users can simulate family challenges or reframe academic problems. The Family Expectations Simulation section immerses users in virtual scenarios to experience family pressures, using role-playing and situational dialogues to reveal the concerns behind parental expectations. Post-simulation, the system offers feedback, analyzes parental intentions and guides users toward more effective communication methods. The Academic Competition Cognitive Reinvention helps users adjust their perceptions of academic competition through case studies, self-reflection, and goal setting, with the aim of reducing anxiety and boosting learning motivation.

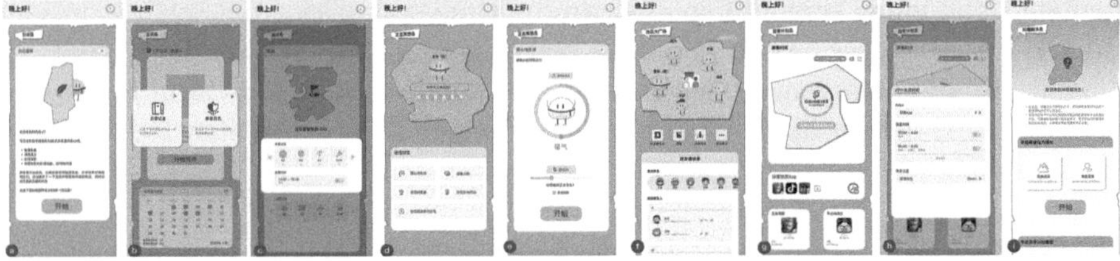

Fig. 2. Mobile Application "Have a better life".

5   User Experience and Assessment

5.1   Method

This study verified the effect of the "Have a better life" application on gaming addiction. A sample of 20 Chinese college students (10 males and 10 females, age $M = 20.4 \pm 1.2$ years) who self-reported a propensity for gaming addiction was recruited for this study. The participants were randomly assigned to the experimental group ($n = 10$) and the control group ($n = 10$). Participants in the experimental group were numbered P1–P10 and participants in the control group were numbered C1–C10. The experimental group completed cognitive behavioral training and mindfulness exercises using the app daily during the 7-day intervention period, while the control group maintained a regular schedule. The control group used traditional text, video, and picture materials to manage gaming addiction. The research focuses on the processing of two types of qualitative data through thematic analysis.

5.2   Results

Experimental Group. 80% of the participants reported positive experiences with the app. They noted that the structured daily exercises it provided helped them manage their gaming behavior. While 20% of the participants initially felt confused, they adapted over time, with P5 mentioned: "At first, I didn't know how to use it, but daily practice helped me focus on meaningful activities." The CBT module, which focused on identifying triggers and reframing negative thoughts, was generally effective. P2 mentioned: "I used to play games when I was upset, but the exercises taught me to analyze and change those thoughts." However, 30% of the participants found some exercises less relevant, such as social scenarios, as P10 mentioned: "Some exercises didn't match my reality." Mindfulness practices received high approval for improving emotion management and self-control. P4 mentioned: "Mindfulness helped me to stop impulsive thoughts by making me aware of my emotions." But 20% of the participants initially struggled with its abstract nature, with P1 mentioned: "I didn't quite understand its meaning at first." Despite overall satisfaction, challenges to sustained use included technical issues (e.g. app crashes), motivation gaps, and scheduling difficulties. P8 mentioned: "Crashes and busy schedules made it hard to maintain daily practice." Additionally, 40% of the participants called for greater personalization, as P7 mentioned: "Content should adapt to individual needs; some exercises, like time management, felt less useful." Post-intervention, 70% of the participants reported improved control over gaming behavior, particularly in recognizing triggers and managing emotions. P6 mentioned: "I now recognize when I want to play and often feel in control." However, some participants emphasized the need for ongoing support to sustain these changes, highlighting concerns about long-term efficacy.

Control Group. 60% of the participants were neutral or slightly positive about traditional materials, acknowledging their theoretical value but criticizing the lack of interactivity and personalization. C5 mentioned: "Text and video materials feel simplistic and unattractive, especially without interaction." While 20% of the participants found the videos helpful in understanding the concepts of gaming addiction, 80% of the participants felt the content, though detailed, was too abstract for practical application. C9 remarked: "The written material is thorough but feels abstract. The videos are clearer but lack practical guidance." Participants recognized the materials' utility in explaining triggers and negative thought patterns but struggled to put theory into practice. C6 mentioned: "I understand the link between gaming and emotions, but I lack concrete tools to manage them." This gap in hands-on guidance limited their ability to apply emotion regulation strategies effectively. 50% of the participants highlighted the lack of interactive and motivational support as a major barrier. C4 mentioned: "Daily reading or watching becomes boring without interaction, so it's easy to lose interest." The absence of reminders and personalized content further hindered consistent engagement, as C1 mentioned: "The material is useful, but without reminders I forget to practice." 90% of the participants criticized the materials for being too generic, particularly for people with mild addiction or from diverse backgrounds. C10 mentioned: "The content suits general situations but feels too vague for my specific needs." Despite some progress in understanding their behavior, participants like C7 mention limited long-term impact: "I understand my actions, but I still turn to games when I am stressed." C3 mentioned the need for improvement: "The material is useful, but more interaction and personalization would make it better."

5.3   Discussion of Results

While control group participants reported cognitive gains from traditional materials, both emphasized a preference for interactive features. As C8 and C2 mentioned: "We need automated reminders to complete exercises and track progress", a view echoed by experimental group members P4 and P6. Improvement requests centered on personalization, with P3 mentioned: "The app should customize content to my specific situation, not offer one-size-fits-all exercises." Technical optimization emerged as a prerequisite for sustained engagement, as evidenced by P9's conditional endorsement: "I will continue using it if they add more personalized settings. It helps but needs refinement."

6   Conclusion, Discussion, Limitation and Future Work

This study establishes MMOGs addiction as an escalating public health concern among Chinese university students, demonstrating the viability of embedding CBT principles into mobile applications like "Have a Better Life". The intervention significantly reduced gaming time and maladaptive beliefs while enhancing emotional regulation, with culturally adapted components addressing familial and academic pressures proving particularly effective. Gamified CBT elements outperformed traditional methods in user engagement, underscoring the potential of mobile platforms as scalable, low-cost alternatives to conventional therapies. However, technical limitations in app stability and personalization emerged as critical barriers to sustained efficacy. Three key insights emerged from the findings. First, achievement-oriented users demonstrated stronger behavioral improvements than those who were socially dependent, suggesting the necessity of modular designs tailored to motivational subtypes. Second, culturally resonant interventions—such as reframing parental conflicts as a health concern—enhanced adherence and relational outcomes compared to Western models, highlighting the need for cross-cultural frameworks that reconcile collectivist "face" dynamics with individualistic norms. Third, while the program's anonymity and modularity facilitated accessibility, its adaptation to emerging digital addictions requires rigorous mechanistic analysis of addiction-specific pathways. Future research should prioritize hybrid models combining app-based tools with group counseling for severe cases, while addressing the risks of secondary addiction from gamified rewards like competitive badges.

Acknowledgments. Thanks to 37 respondents in the questionnaire survey stage and 20 college students in the experiment part.

Funding Information. The authors disclosed receipt of the following financial support for the research: Zhaoqing University 2024 University-level research Fund "Research and Practice on Rural Revitalization of Didou Town IP Design in Sihui City of Zhaoqing" (FW202403); Zhaoqing University Double hundred project "Sihui Cultural Brand construction and publicity service team" (SD202412).

Disclosure of Interests. The authors have no competing interests related to the content of this article to declare, and all parties have consented during the investigation.

Appendix A.

1.Gaming Habits:(1)Before playing a game, I consider whether it will make me happy. (2)I play games recommended by friends. (3)The visual effects and style of a game are important factors in my decision to play it. (4)When I experience failure or difficulty in a game, I give up and switch off the game for a while. (5)When encountering challenges in a game, I don't switch it off and tend to get more frustrated until I win. (6)The reward system in a game significantly increases my interest in it.(7)I prefer playing online with friends to playing alone. (8)After finishing a game, I usually start the next one immediately to get a better score. (9)I share and discuss my gaming achievements or experiences with my friends. (10)Post - game summaries and analyses can help improve my gaming skills.

2. Academic Situation:(11)I feel a lot of pressure to study. (12)I feel that playing games may have a negative impact on my studies.(13)I reduce the time and frequency of playing games in the week before exams. (14)I am quite satisfied with my studies in the last semester. (15)I feel a lot of pressure in the recent semester.

3.Family Expectations:(16)My family has high academic expectations of me. (17)My family understands and cares about the amount of time I spend playing games. (18)I feel a lot of pressure when I fail to meet my family's expectations.

4.Social Norms:(19)I feel that most of my classmates use games as a way to relax and have fun. (20)My friends around me are quite supportive when I spend a lot of time on games.

References

1. Organization, W.: Addictive behaviours: Gaming disorder. https://www.who.int/news-room/questions-and-answers/item/addictive-behaviours-gaming-disorder. Accessed 27 Oct 2021
2. Chan, E., Vorderer, P.: Massively multiplayer online games. Playing Video Games: Motives, Responses, And Consequences. pp. 77–88 (2006)
3. Billieux, J., Deleuze, J., Griffiths, M., Kuss, D.: Internet gaming addiction: the case of massively multiplayer online roleplaying games. In: Textbook of Addiction Treatment: International Perspectives, pp. 1515–1525 (2015)

4. Xinhua The number of Internet users exceeded 1.1 billion! Digital China is surging with vigor. https://www.gov.cn/yaowen/liebiao/202501/content6999530.htm. Accessed 10 Oct 2024–Jan 2025

5. Lee, Z., Cheung, C., Chan, T.: Understanding massively multiplayer online role-playing game addiction: a hedonic management perspective. Inf. Syst. J. **31**, 33–61 (2021)

6. Rao, Y.: From confucianism to psychology: rebooting internet addicts in China. Hist. Psychol. **22**, 328 (2019)

7. Stavropoulos, V., Anderson, E., Beard, C., Latifi, M., Kuss, D., Griffiths, M.: A preliminary cross-cultural study of Hikikomori and Internet Gaming Disorder: the moderating effects of game-playing time and living with parents. Addict. Behav. Rep. **9**, 100137 (2019)

8. Almourad, M., McAlaney, J., Skinner, T., Pleya, M., Ali, R.: Defining digital addiction: key features from the literature. Psihologija. **53**, 237–253 (2020)

9. Liao, Z., et al.: Prevalence of internet gaming disorder and its association with personality traits and gaming characteristics among Chinese adolescent gamers. Front. Psych. **11**, 598585 (2020)

10. Michael, X.: Demographics, motivations, addictions and usage patterns among Chinese college student MMORPG players. Unpublished Theses, Chinese University Of Hong Kong (2008)

11. Szablewicz, M.: Mapping Digital Game Culture in China. Springer, Cham (2020). https://doi.org/10.1007/978-3-030-36111-2

12. Yu, Q. MMORPG Avatars: Representations of Escapism in Chinese Society Based on Semiotics of Culture. Simon Fraser University (2021)

13. Craske, M.: Cognitive–Behavioral Therapy. American Psychological Association (2010)

14. Beck, A.: Cognitive Therapy and the Emotional Disorders. Penguin (1979)

15. Taquet, P., Romo, L., Cottencin, O., Ortiz, D., Hautekeete, M.: Video game addiction: cognitive, emotional, and behavioral determinants for CBT treatment. J. De Thérapie Comportementale Et Cogn. **27**, 118–128 (2017)

16. Fleming, T., et al.: Maximizing the impact of e-therapy and serious gaming: time for a paradigm shift. Front. Psych. **7**, 65 (2016)

17. Kuss, D., Lopez-Fernandez, O.: Internet addiction and problematic Internet use: a systematic review of clinical research. World J. Psychiatry **6**, 143 (2016)

18. Hu, H., Zhang, G., Yang, X., Zhang, H., Lei, L., Wang, P.: Online gaming addiction and depressive symptoms among game players of the glory of the king in China: the mediating role of affect balance and the moderating role of flow experience. Int. J. Mental Health Addict. **20**, 3191–3204 (2022)

19. Wan, C., Chiou, W.: Why are adolescents addicted to online gaming? An interview study in Taiwan. Cyberpsychol. Behav. **9**, 762–766 (2006)

20. Cole, H., Griffiths, M.: Social interactions in massively multiplayer online role-playing gamers. Cyberpsychology & Behavior **10**, 575–583 (2007)

21. Rathbone, A., Clarry, L., Prescott, J.: Assessing the efficacy of mobile health apps using the basic principles of cognitive behavioral therapy: systematic review. J. Med. Internet Res. **19**, e399 (2017)

22. Hsu, S., Wen, M., Wu, M.: Exploring user experiences as predictors of MMORPG addiction. Comput. Educ. **53**, 990–999 (2009)

23. Greer, J., et al.: Randomized trial of a tailored cognitive-behavioral therapy mobile application for anxiety in patients with incurable cancer. Oncologist **24**, 1111–1120 (2019)

24. Chung, K., Kim, S., Lee, E., Park, J. et al.: Mobile app use for insomnia self-management in urban community-dwelling older Korean adults: retrospective intervention study. JMIR MHealth UHealth **8**, e17755 (2020)
25. Tudor-Sfetea, C., et al.: Evaluation of two mobile health apps in the context of smoking cessation: qualitative study of cognitive behavioral therapy (CBT) versus non-CBT-based digital solutions. JMIR MHealth And UHealth **6**, e9405 (2018)
26. Wang, J., Sheng, J., Wang, H.: The association between mobile game addiction and depression, social anxiety, and loneliness. Front. Publ. Health **7**, 247 (2019)
27. Jiang, Q.: Internet addiction among young people in China: internet connectedness, online gaming, and academic performance decrement. Internet Res. **24**, 2–20 (2014)
28. Teng, Z., Griffiths, M., Nie, Q., Xiang, G., Guo, C.: Parent–adolescent attachment and peer attachment associated with internet gaming disorder: a longitudinal study of first-year undergraduate students. J. Behav. Addict. **9**, 116–128 (2020)
29. Thomée, S.: Mobile phone use and mental health. A review of the research that takes a psychological perspective on exposure. Int. J. Environ. Res. Publ. Health **15**, 2692 (2018)
30. Juthamanee, S., Gunawan, J.: Factors related to internet and game addiction among adolescents: a scoping review. Belitung Nurs. J. **7**, 62 (2021)
31. Gunuc, S. Peer influence in internet and digital game addicted adolescents: is internet/digital game addiction contagious?. Int. J. High Risk Behav. Addict. **6** (2017)
32. Hwang, W., Fu, X., Kim, S., Jung, E., Zhang, Y.: A multidimensional construct of helicopter parenting and college students' game and social media addictive behaviors: a cross-cultural study in South Korea and China. Front. Psychol. **13**, 1022914 (2023)
33. Balaskas, A., Schueller, S., Cox, A., Doherty, G.: The functionality of mobile apps for anxiety: systematic search and analysis of engagement and tailoring features. JMIR MHealth UHealth **9**, e26712 (2021)
34. Stawarz, K., Preist, C., Tallon, D., Wiles, N., Coyle, D.: User experience of cognitive behavioral therapy apps for depression: an analysis of app functionality and user reviews. J. Med. Internet Res. **20**, e10120 (2018)
35. Watts, S., et al.: CBT for depression: a pilot RCT comparing mobile phone vs. computer. BMC Psychiatry **13**, 1–9 (2013)
36. Khademian, F., Aslani, A., Bastani, P.: The effects of mobile apps on stress, anxiety, and depression: overview of systematic reviews. Int. J. Technol. Assess. Healthc. **37**, e4 (2021)

Productization Logic and DFX Principles in Mobile Game Development

Seshnag Revuru[1]($\boxtimes$) and Janne Harkonen[1,2]

[1] University of Oulu, 90014 Oulu, Finland
{Seshnag.revuru,janne.harkonen}@oulu.fi
[2] International School for Social and Business Studies, 3000 Celje, Slovenia

Abstract. The gaming industry continuous to evolve through diverse design philosophies, business models, and gameplay mechanics, driven by technological advancements and shifting consumer expectations. As games become more accessible and embedded in everyday life, design approaches must increasingly incorporate diverse user experiences and player-centric strategies. In the Free-to-Play (F2P) model, a game's commercial success typically depends on three core pillars: user acquisition, user retention, and monetization. These pillars rely on real-time coordination of production and consumption of gaming experiences. Effective monetization must generate revenue while maintaining player satisfaction, requiring business models that enhance value without disrupting gameplay. To address these challenges, this study proposes adopting productization logic, applying structured commercial, and technical frameworks to game development. Productization bridges development and customer needs, ensuring software is packaged for both high quality and strategic fit. In support of this, Design for X (DfX) offers tools for considering product requirements from both user and strategic perspectives. Building on these ideas, the study introduces a novel framework: Design for Product Market, which integrates market demands into mobile game design. This approach not only enhances commercial outcomes but also fosters innovation by connecting creative design with real-world market feedback.

Keywords: Productization logic · Productization · Productisation · DFX · Design for product market · Mobile games · Game development · Free-to-Play (F2P) model

1 Introduction

The rise of mobile gaming has expanded accessibility and democratized game publishing. Free-to-play (F2P) models with in-game transactions have further reshaped how games generate revenue and sustain user engagement [1]. Game development now blends creative expression with technical execution, extending beyond conventional software engineering to create interactive, immersive experiences. This evolution calls for novel design frameworks, such as casual game design values and player-centric development approaches, which align with the fluid nature of gaming culture and player expectations [2].

© The Author(s), under exclusive license to Springer Nature Switzerland AG 2026
J. Wei et al. (Eds.): HCII 2025, LNCS 16346, pp. 322–336, 2026.
https://doi.org/10.1007/978-3-032-13187-4_22

Modern mobile games often use physics engines to simulate lifelike interactions and dynamic environmental effects through computational shortcuts [3]. Yet, delivering responsive, visually appealing, and engaging experiences requires more than technical fidelity. User interaction models, such as short session loops, onboarding flow, and real-time feedback, must be optimised for mobile constraints. Frameworks from Human–Computer Interaction (HCI) and game user experience (UX) research, such as the Player Experience of Need Satisfaction (PENS) model [4], UX Honeycomb [5] and flow theory [6], provide insights into how these interactions patterns affect long-term engagement and satisfaction. This integration also responds to recent calls in HCI research to bridge technical implementation with experience-centred design [7, 8], particularly in mobile interaction contexts where user expectations evolve rapidly.

While many developers apply industry best practices to design and monetization, there is a lack of structured methodologies that bridge technical execution and commercial strategy. Productization logic provides such a bridge: it embeds commercial and technical considerations into software development, supporting high-quality, scalable, and market-aligned outcomes [8, 9]. When effectively applied, productization can improve design consistency, reduce lifecycle inefficiencies, and enhance adaptability in competitive markets [10]. Despite its potential, however, productization remains under-explored in mobile game development, representing a significant gap in both academic research and applied practice.

Design for X (DFX) one structured approach that supports the early integration of diverse design goals, such as maintainability, or marketing effectiveness. Into the product development lifecycle [11]. In the context of game development, "X" may include downstream concerns such as monetization potential, user acquisition, or retention optimization. Although DfX is well established in engineering design, it is rarely applied to balance creative ideation with commercial scalability in mobile games.

To address this gap, this study investigates how productization and DFX principles can support mobile game development by aligning user experience, technical efficiency, and business viability. We explore this through the case of *RacingGameX*, a globally successful mobile racing game with over two billion downloads. Using the SaaS productization model, we analyse how its developers manage trade-offs across design, development, and monetization. Empirical data from developer interviews, company documentation, and market sources form the basis for this analysis.

Drawing from these insights, we propose the Design for Product Market framework: a structured methodology for integrating market dynamics into design and development workflows. The importance of such frameworks has long been recognised in software engineering, where structured product architectures improve production efficiency, modularity, and adaptability to changing markets [12]. By iteratively ana-lysing key metrics, including user engagement, monetisation strategies, and production pipelines, we refine our approach to support the alignment of game UX with business strategy. This case-driven contribution offers a foundation for enhancing mobile game development through the combined application of productization logic and DfX principles.

2 Methodology

2.1 Research Design

The paper adopts a qualitative exploratory research design aimed at constructing a conceptual framework [13, 14] that integrates productization logic with Design for Excellence (DFX) principles in the context of mobile game development. The design is grounded in Eisenhardt's [13] guidance on theory-building through case-based research, particularly their emphasis on data-driven conceptual development from empirical material. While Eisenhardt focuses on multiple vase-studies, their principles are applicable here as analytical inspiration. Given that this study centres on a particular case, the research also draws on Yin's [14] methodological framework for in-depth single-case study research, providing a complementary structure for rigorous empirical inquiry.

The research began with a comprehensive theoretical review of key concepts, including the nature of products in software-intensive industries, product lifecycle management principles, and the foundational logic of productization. Special attention was given on the role of DFX principles in guiding technical decision-making that supports both product performance and commercial viability.

This conceptual exploration informed the development of a structured analytical lens for the empirical phase. The aim was to investigate how productization strategies and DFX frameworks can be tailored to the specific characteristics of software products, particularly within creative, iterative environments like mobile game development. This lens guided the empirical inquiry and shaped the interpretation of findings.

2.2 Research Context

The empirical context of this study lies within the domain of software development, with a specific focus on mobile game development processes. The selected company is an established game studio operating under a F2P business model, with multiple published titles across major platforms (Android, iOS). Mobile game development is characterised by rapid innovation cycles, platform-specific constraints, user-driven monetisation strategies, and highly dynamic market conditions. These features demand adaptive development practices such as iterative prototyping, real-time performance monitoring, and agile workflows, making this an ideal setting to assess the relevance and adaptability of productization and DfX frameworks.

By grounding the study in a real-world development environment, the research captures both the creative (e.g., concept design, gameplay mechanics) and technical (e.g., software architecture, monetisation system implementation) dimensions of game development. This dual perspective enables a holistic analysis that bridges theoretical constructs with practical application, strengthening the evaluation of structured frameworks within dynamic and commercially competitive software contexts.

2.3 Data Collection and Analysis

Data for this study was collected through retrospective observation of development practices within the case company and analysis of broader market behaviours in the mobile gaming sector. A case-based analytical approach was employed, examining the company's internal product development processes in parallel with external industry patterns. Particular attention was given to how technical decision-making intersected with commercial requirements, especially within the constraints of the F2P business model.

The analysis began by mapping the company's development pipeline against a structured productization logic, identifying key components, dependencies, and process bottlenecks. Building on this foundation, DfX principles were applied as an interpretive lens to reframe the development structure, highlighting opportunities to enhance responsiveness to market fluctuations and evolving user expectations.

This iterative process of abstraction and refinement led to the development of a conceptual structure that aligns the foundational stages of game development with broader market-level requirements. The resulting framework aims to improve both the technical robustness and market adaptability of mobile games, offering strategic value to creative software development teams operating in highly competitive digital environments.

Ethical Considerations This study presents a conceptual and methodological analysis of a game development process, through the lens of product management frameworks. It does not involve human participants, personal data, or experimental intervention, and no new data were collected specifically for this research. The analysis draws exclusively from retrospective observation of design decisions within an existing commercial digital game.

As such, ethics committee approval and informed consent were not required. No personal or identifiable information was accessed. Only publicly available and internally aggregated, anonymized metrics were used to contextualize the design and development decisions under study.

3 Literature Review

3.1 Productization Logic

A product is more than a physical artifact; it encompasses any offering sold to customers and comprises both tangible and intangible attributes, such as features, functions, benefits, and intended uses. Based on these characteristics, products can be categorized into types such as hardware, software, services, documentation, and knowledge-based solutions [15]. A product's lifecycle is typically segmented, especially in marketing and sales, into stages of introduction, growth, maturity, and decline each associated with different strategic and operational priorities [16].

Product management activities tend to concentrate on the early lifecycle stages, including discovery and innovation, new product planning, market introduction, and immediate post-launch strategies [17]. The notion of product structure, central to both manufactured and digital offerings, refers to an item-based hierarchy that maps product's assemblies, components, and sub-components [18]. In service-oriented domains, this is conceptually paralleled by the service blueprint, which captures the relationships between customer-facing actions, backstage processes, support mechanisms, and physical evidence [19].

Productization has emerged as a concept that intersects with, but is distinct from, new product development (NPD) and commercialization. It provides and additional conceptual layer that contributes both academic theory and industrial practice. Although productization shares territory with NPD, it cannot be reduced to it. Notably, the term remains unrecognized in formal dictionaries, reflecting its evolving role in modern product development discourse.

In software development, productization is broader than product creation alone. It involves transforming various forms of knowledge and development outputs into standardized, market-ready offerings. One widely accepted definition frames productization as a structured process that converts internally produced information into high-quality repeatable, and understandable deliverable suitable for commercial use [20]. This involves analysing requirements, integrating tangible and intangible components, and transforming them into a deliverable resembling a product. Productization, therefore, reinforces the interface between market needs and engineering-oriented development., while complementing traditional organizational functions [21].

Crucially, productization integrates both commercial and technical perspectives, aiming to align business goals with engineering realities. Literature acknowledges the challenges in aligning these two perspectives and highlights the product structure as a conceptual tool to address this issue. One approach divides a company's product portfolio into commercial and technical hierarchies, allowing both perspectives to be managed in parallel.

While the product structure facilitates modelling of modular relationships among components, past research has paid less attention to the commercial dimension. A well-structured product hierarchy enables modular design, supports variety reduction, and helps balance the external product diversity (to meet market needs) with internal standardization (to optimize operations). Product platforms further support this by enabling reusable components, shared part economies, and consistent configuration logic across variants.

In addition to facilitating development, the product structure serves as a visual and data-centric foundation for organizational alignment, enhancing communication, reporting, and configuration management. However, despite its applicability to both goods and services, further research is needed to provide deeper insight and practical guidance on applying product structure concepts within productization strategies, especially in software-intensive industries [22].

Recent research has also extended the concept of productization to creative industries, where the central challenge lies in scaling and systematizing offerings without compromising their experiential or artistic value. Dubois et al. [23] briefly address the systematics and scalability of productization in this context, demonstrating how experience-oriented offerings can be transformed into standardized, yet emotionally resonant products. Wirtz et al. [24] and Wirz [25] can be similarly interpreted to suggest that, within creative domains, productization is not merely a matter of rigid standardization, but rather means of generating repeatable, communicable value around flexible creative cores. In parallel, Dubois and Weststar [26] explore how the Games-as-a-Service (GaaS) model reconfigures both the structural nature of digital game products and the organization of creative labour required to sustain them. Collectively, these works reinforce that in contemporary creative industries, productization is not confined to packaging tangible outputs. Instead, it entails organizing, systematizing, and sustaining creative value over time, often by integrating artistic expression with service logic, product structuring, and data-driven iteration.

Figure 1 illustrates how commercial and technical productization layers are structured through a unified product hierarchy, adapted from [10] and [27]. This model enables a coherent interpretation of how different structural levels relate to each other across the product lifecycle, from high-level product solutions down to specific sales items [10].

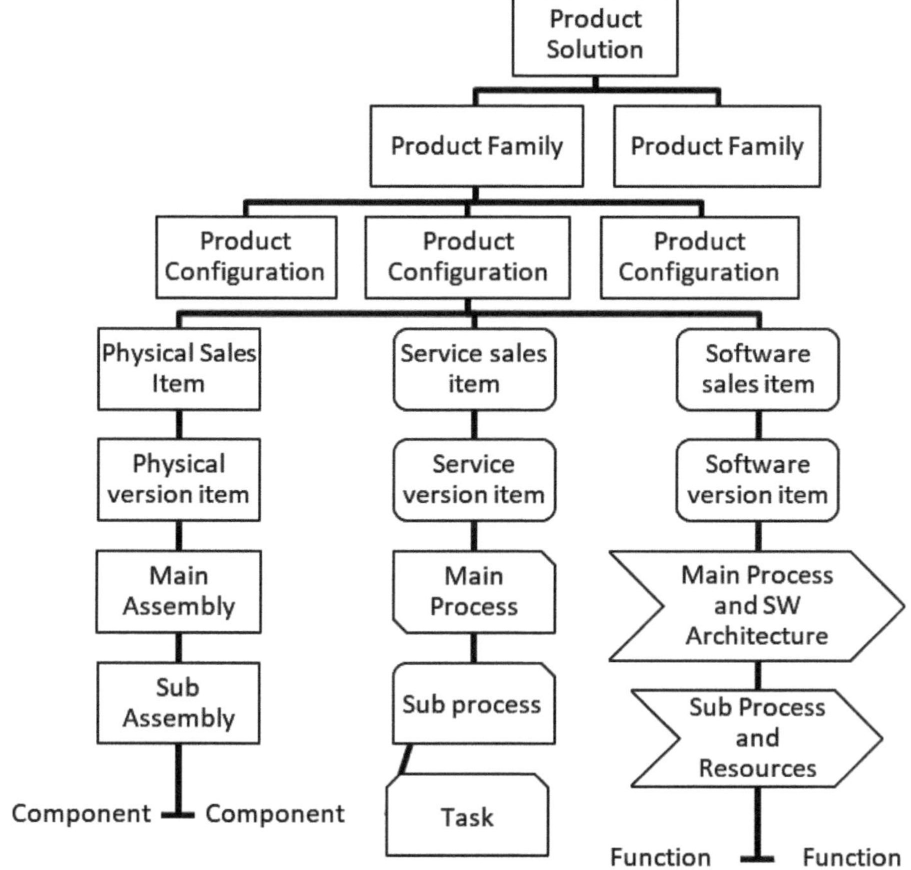

Fig. 1. Commercial and technical productization through a product structure, Modified from [10, 27].

3.2 DFX Principles

Design for X (DfX) is a design methodology that emphasizes the early integration of specific design goals, denoted by "X," into the product development process. These goals may include sustainability, usability, reliability, cost-efficiency, and other performance attributes. By addressing relevant constraints and requirements from the outset, DfX aims to reduce time-to-market, minimize costly rework, and enhance overall product quality [12].

The success of DfX lies not primarily in the adoption of new tools, but in overcoming organizational inertia and ingrained development routines. Embracing DfX requires deliberate effort to align design processes and technologies with human capabilities and system performance expectations. This is especially crucial in complex systems such as software-intensive products, where user interaction and lifecycle performance must be considered concurrently.

Over time, numerous DfX variants have been developed, each focusing on optimizing a specific dimension of design, such as Design for Manufacturing (DfM), Assembly (DfA), Environment (DfE), Service (DfS), and End-of-Life (DfEoL). However, only a subset is typically applied in any one design project due resource constraints or contextual limitations [28]. Selecting the appropriate DfX variant and integrating it meaningfully into early-stage design decisions remains a persistent challenge in concurrent engineering practice.

Incorporating DfX in the concept development and embodiment selection phases ensures that design decisions consider relevant contextual and lifecycle factors. This supports the adoption of concurrent engineering and promotes cross-functional alignment [29]. For example, applying Design for Casting (DfCast) during the manufacturing phase can reduce geometric complexity and cost, while Design for End-of-Life (DfEoL) in the usage phase promotes disassembly, recyclability, and circular economy principles.

To systematize and extend the application of DfX a Knowledge Base (KB) has been proposed that captures design objectives, implementation phases, design targets, and associated key performance indicators (KPIs). This structured approach enables engineers to evaluate design alternatives based on technical, economic, and environmental dimensions and presenting a case-based mapping that illustrates how DfX principles are embedded across lifecycle phases, especially "Material and Manufacturing" and "Use," with metrics that reflect performance trade-offs.

More broadly, DfX represents a rule-based, knowledge-driven system where best practices are codified and applied to improve product realization. The "X" serves as a placeholder for the designer's current focus, whether assembly time, user safety, or maintenance cost. Guidelines for each DfX type are preserved in scientific literature, professional repositories, and organizational knowledge systems. In recent years, there has been growing interest in embedding these guidelines in software-based design assistants, which could help evaluate inconsistencies, automate routine assessments, or support learning for novice designers [30].

Such virtual tools not only reinforce experiential learning but also have potential relevance in digital product development, including mobile games. Here, DfX could guide the early integration of monetization mechanics, accessibility features, or modular software architecture, bringing the benefits of structured design into creative and iterative domains.

3.3 Literature Synthesis

A mature game development company operating within the mobile gaming sector typically adheres to a defined product development process and business philosophy. In the case examined within this study, the dominant model is F2P, which necessitates the deliberate integration of creative, technical, and commercial disciplines. The development of a mobile game involves the orchestration of several interdependent processes, including artistic conceptualization, software development, gameplay mechanics, UX design, and monetization strategy implementation. These distinct yet interconnected activities converge through systematic workflow to produce the final digital product. Success in this environment requires a comprehensive understanding of both technical execution and commercial viability.

To examine how productization logic applies in this context, the system can be viewed from two interlinked perspectives: technical construction and commercial configuration. The technical perspective focuses on how the game is built, covering phases such as iterative software development, version testing, and game logic implementation. This process is heavily tool-based and structured around delivering core gameplay experiences. In contrast, the commercial perspective, especially under F2P model, emphasizes revenue generation mechanisms such as in-app purchases and advertising. These monetization strategies influence design and deployment decisions, such as platform adaptation (e.g., Android, iOS), content updates, and feature segmentation, which in turn define the product's market identity.

Bridging these two perspectives requires a structured feedback mechanism that links design decisions with market dynamics. Currently, the case company lacks a formal system for connecting technical design choices with business performance outcomes. However, there is a clear and underutilized link between the early conceptual stage of development, where product vision is formed, and the external market environment, shaped by competition, regulation, and regional preferences. Recognizing this link provides an opportunity to incorporate market intelligence into early-stage design, allowing technical decisions to be more responsive and strategically aligned.

Establishing two-way communication between product designers and market analysts enables the co-evolution of the product concept and its commercial trajectory. This facilitates the application of Design for Excellence principles throughout the development lifecycle, ensuring that the final product is not only functionally sound and user-focused, but also market relevant and commercially viable.

The illustration (Fig. 2) provides a conceptual bridge to explore how productization logic and DfX principles can be operationalized in mobile game development. It serves as a basis for connecting theory to practice in the remainder of the study.

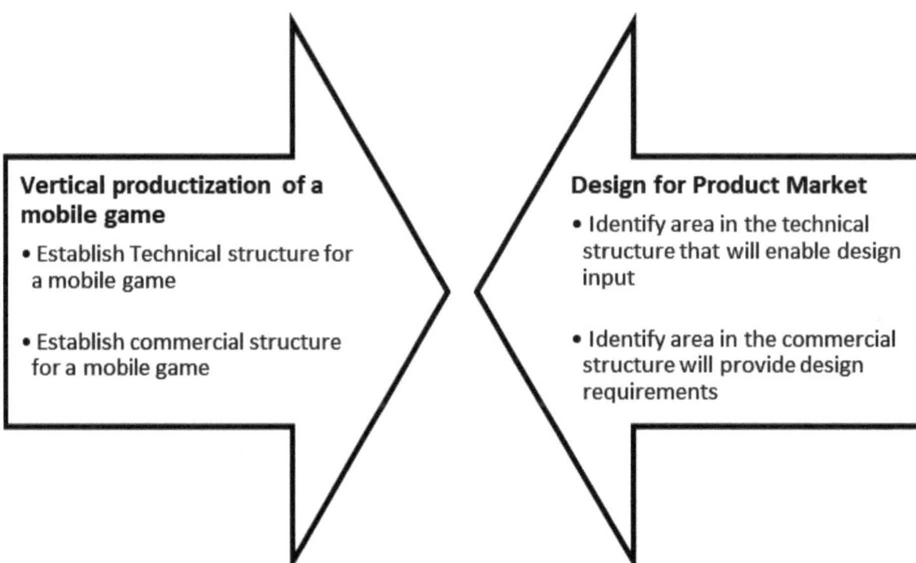

Fig. 2. Investigating productization logic and DFX principles in the context of mobile game development.

4   Framework Development

The preceding literature synthesis identified two interdependent structures that underpin mobile game development: *the technical structure*, which governs how the product is designed and operated, and *the commercial structure*, which defines how value is created, captured, and sustained in the market. This section transitions from analytical insights to constructive framework design, with the aim of supporting practitioners, particularly developers and producers, in structuring mobile game development through the *Design for Product Market* approach.

The proposed framework development process follows four analytical stages:

Step 1: Mapping the Existing Product Development Landscape.

Commercial Structure. This stage begins with the mapping of the commercial value chain, as outlined in the literature. The process starts from the most tangible monetization mechanisms in the F2P model, namely in-app purchases, and advertising, and traces their influence upstream. These revenue mechanisms impact platform-specific product configurations (e.g., Android, iOS), which are themselves embedded within a product family (e.g., arcade racing genre), and within target product markets segmented by region, regulation, and user preferences.

Technical Structure. In parallel, a retrospective mapping of the technical development trajectory is concluded. This begins at the Game Concept Development phase and continues through the identification of software resources and cost drivers (e.g., Adobe Photoshop, asset libraries), the definition of sub-processes (e.g., coding gameplay logic in Visual Studio), and the establishment of the software main architecture (e.g., game engines like Unity). These components feed into the main SaaS-based development process, which includes beta testing, A/B testing, feature road mapping, and quality assurance, culminating in the release of versioned build for Android and iOS platforms.

Step 2: Identifying Internal Iterative Cycles and Feedback Mechanisms. Two key feedback loops were identified within the technical domain: *Core Gameplay Development Loop*, which is iterative, incorporating continuous feedback from sub-processes such as software coding, debugging, and asset generation and visual art generation. These outputs shape gameplay mechanics, which are then refined based on testing outputs. *SaaS Process Loops*, which is the SaaS-development phase, features its own internal cycles. Feedback from Final Quality Check and Assurance often result in defect reports or revision requests that influence earlier phases, including beta testing and roadmap updates. Additionally, real-time feedback from Mobile Client-End Issues and Customer Support can lead to reprioritising of upcoming development tasks.

Recognizing and formalizing feedback from these feedback cycles is crucial for quality management, product evolution, and responsiveness to live market conditions.

Step 3: Pinpointing the Strategic Commercial-Technical Nexus for DfX Integration. Building on the synthesis, a critical yet often implicit linkage is acknowledged: the influence of the Product Market on early-stage Game Concept Development. This interface represents a strategic point for embedding DfX principles, enabling designers to proactively respond to market-level factors such as user preferences, platform constraints, and regulatory environments.

Step 4: Synthesis and Visualisation of the Integrated Framework.

The final stage formalizes this insight into a unified, actionable framework as illustrated in Fig. 3. The model is structured to:

- Visually distinguish the Commercial Structure (top-down flow) and Technical Structure (bottom-up flow).
- Represent iterative loops within the SaaS processes and core gameplay development.
- Highlight the downstream requirement linkage from product markets to Game Concept Development, emphasizing its strategic importance for design decisions.
- Clearly label all components and relational flows to ensure conceptual clarity and operational utility.

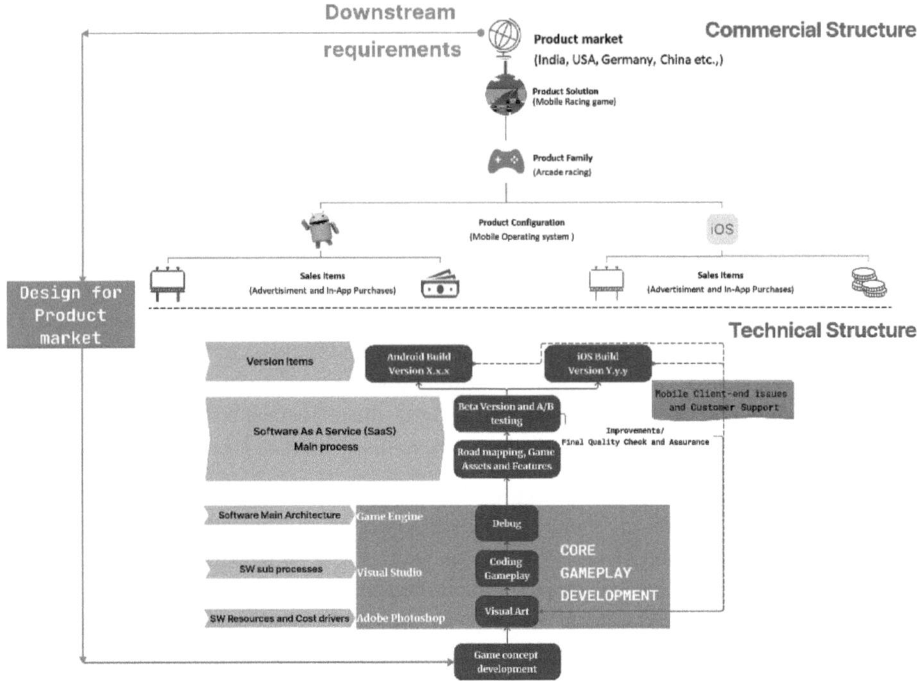

Fig. 3. Productization Logic and DfX Principles for RacingGameX: Integrating Market Requirements with Commercial and Technical Structure.

This framework offers a structured means to align market orientation, technical execution, and design quality in mobile game development. It serves both as an analytical tool and a practical guide for implementing feedback-driven, cross-functional coordination in F2P game environments.

5   Discussion

This study addressed the challenge of aligning downstream market requirements with internal development structures in mobile game development, a phenomenon increasingly significant in software-intensive and user-centric industries. In the context of F2P mobile games, studios must simultaneously respond to monetization pressures, dynamic market demands, and the need to deliver technically engaging gameplay. Despite the vital role of user experience and commercial logic in this domain, these forces are often addressed in isolation within the product development process. This paper responds to that fragmentation by introducing the *Design for Product Market* framework, a structured model that integrates productization logic and DfX principles to bridge commercial and technical structures. The framework visualizes how early product concept development is influenced by market configurations and regulatory constraints, while also modelling how feedback mechanisms, such as customer support and live testing, inform design iteration and quality assurance in SaaS-based development environments. In doing so, this research contributes to a broader understanding of how market requirements can be embedded into product development trajectories in creative software domains such as mobile games.

The core contribution of this research lies in its synthesis of two previously disjointed viewpoints: the commercial structure that determines how games are monetized, segmented, and delivered, and the technical structure that governs how games are architected, built, and iterated. Productization, which has been conceptualized as the standardization and commercialization of intangible offerings such as knowledge and services [20, 21], is here extended to the domain of mobile games. Earlier work by Lahtinen et al. and Mustonen [10, 22, 27] emphasize vertical productization across product lifecycles, highlighting how product structures and platform configurations can be aligned with business objectives. This study supports those findings while contributing an explicit feedback-oriented structure linking commercial and technical layers.

This view is reinforced by recent research in creative industries, which shows that productization increasingly serves to manage and sustain artistic value within structured workflows. Studies by Dubois et al. [23], Wirtz et al. [24], Wirtz [25], and Dubois & Weststar [26] confirm that in fields such as gaming and media, productization involves not only output standardization but also the orchestration of creative labour, emotional resonance, and service-based delivery models. These insights align with and extend our findings by situating the Design for Product Market framework within a broader shift toward structured creativity in digital economies.

Furthermore, by embedding DFX principles, originally developed to support manufacturability, maintainability, and reliability in engineering design [12], into mobile game development workflows, this framework brings lifecycle thinking into a field typically governed by agile and iterative practices. It confirms earlier arguments by Reitmeier and Paetzold [11] that DfX can serve as a knowledge-based system for aligning business strategy and engineering practice, even in fast-paced digital contexts.

Importantly, this study also contributes to the intersection between product development and Human–Computer Interaction (HCI), especially in mobile game user experience. Prior HCI literature has underscored the role of interaction design and player psychology in shaping sustained engagement, with models such as the Player Experience of Need Satisfaction (PENS) linking autonomy, competence, and relatedness to motivational outcomes [4]. Likewise, frameworks such as the UX Honeycomb and HEART metrics [5] and flow-based engagement [6] have been used to explain how gameplay features influence satisfaction and attention. However, these frameworks often remain disconnected from the underlying product logic. By incorporating the commercial and technical structuring of games into a unified model, this study complements the insights of Kultima and Setthapranai & Thienthaworn [1, 2], who emphasize the need for value-driven and player-centred design processes. It also supports the broader HCI agenda described by Langote et al. and Mirabdolah et al. [7, 8], who advocate for tighter integration of usability, interaction, and system performance in complex digital applications. This study extends their vision by showing how product architecture and development workflows can be aligned with interaction design principles to create mobile games that are not only functionally robust but also emotionally resonant and commercially effective.

The practical implications of this study are highly relevant for mobile game producers, product managers, and technical leads. The Design for Product Market framework enables development teams to align their roadmaps with monetization strategy, market segmentation, and platform-specific constraints. It facilitates decision-making by mapping feedback loops between live operations and design inputs, allowing organizations to adapt more rapidly to user feedback and gameplay metrics. In doing so, it operationalizes principles of product lifecycle management [18] and supports the coordination of creative ideation with structured technical execution. By making market requirements explicit within the earliest stages of product development and maintaining them throughout design iterations, this framework provides both a conceptual and practical foundation for building mobile games that are competitive, scalable, and user-responsive in an increasingly saturated and fast-moving market.

6 Conclusions

This study proposes a structured productization framework tailored to the unique demands of mobile game development. By synthesizing technical development processes with commercial value creation logic, the framework offers a unified perspective that bridges traditionally siloed domains. Grounded in both productization theory and DfX principles, the model illustrates how downstream market configurations and monetization strategies can be systematically linked to upstream design and development decisions. This connection is operationalized through a Design for Product Market approach, which foregrounds market alignment as a design parameter. Rather than viewing market fit as a post-development adjustment, the framework integrates it as a core logic guiding early-stage decisions. Its strength lies in a stepwise formulation, from landscape mapping to visual synthesis, which supports cross functional coordination and continuous feedback integration across the development lifecycle.

One of the key contributions of this work is its operationalization of vertical productization and DfX principles in a fast-paced, creative software context. It shows how structured logic, often associated with engineering and manufacturing disciplines, can be adapted to the volatile, user-centric environment of mobile game development. By embedding monetization logic, platform constraints, and gameplay iteration into a cohesive framework, the study offers a new lens for viewing product-market alignment in digital services, transforming fragmented workflows into a transparent, traceable system of interdependencies that can inform managerial decision-making and reduce downstream inefficiencies.

Nonetheless, the conclusions drawn from this research must be measured considering its limitations. The framework was developed within the context of a particular case company, during a period of close engagement by one of the authors, which may have shaped both the interpretation of development practices and the design of the model itself. As such, the framework may reflect organizational particularities, such as tooling choices, team structure, and platform strategy, that may not all be universally applicable. Future research should aim to validate, adapt, or expand this framework across diverse game studios, genres, and business models, including premium and hybrid monetization schemes.

Moreover, while the current study focused on internal alignment between technical and commercial structures, future work could deepen the integration of player experience models and interaction design principles. For instance, extending the framework to systematically incorporate user experience (UX) metrics, such as the HEART framework or Player Experience of Needs Satisfaction (PENS), could help teams more directly translate gameplay feedback into design and business decisions. This presents an exciting frontier for linking HCI theories with strategic product management practices in digital entertainment.

This research contributes to the evolving discourse on how creative industries can harness structured methods without stifling innovation. By illuminating the latent structure behind fluid development practices, it invites practitioners and scholars alike to rethink how games are conceptualized, built, and delivered in a market where design excellence and commercial success are inseparably intertwined.

Disclosure of Interests.   The authors have no competing interests to declare that are relevant to the content of this article.

References

1. Setthapranai, C., Thienthaworn, A.: Player-centered game design canvas for enhancing player loyalty: cases of MMORPG (massively multiplayer online role-playing games) users in Thailand. Thammasat University, Bangkok, Thailand (2024)
2. Kultima, A.: Casual game design values. In: Proceedings of the 13th International MindTrek Conference: Everyday Life in the Ubiquitous Era, Tampere, Finland, pp. 58–65. ACM (2009)
3. Ullman, T.D., Spelke, E., Battaglia, P., Tenenbaum, J.B.: Mind games: game engines as an architecture for intuitive physics. Trends Cogn. Sci. **21**(9), 649–665 (2017)
4. Ijaz, K., Ahmadpour, N., Wang, Y., Calvo, R.A.: Player experience of needs satisfaction (PENS) in an immersive virtual reality exercise platform describes motivation and enjoyment. Int. J. Hum. Comput. Interact. **36**(13), 1195–1204 (2020)
5. Wibisono, I., Br Maringga, A.P.I., Sunardi: Comparing the user experience of mobile-based microlearning application using HEART metrics and Honeycomb framework. In: 2024 International Conference on Information Management and Technology (ICIMTech), pp. 450–455. IEEE (2024)
6. Su, J., Wang, Y., Li, Z., Deng, X.: Serious game applications for driver training: an extended technology acceptance model (TAM) with flow theory. Int. J. Hum. Comput. Interact., 1–17 (2025)
7. Langote, M., et al.: Human–computer interaction in healthcare: comprehensive review. AIMS Bioeng. **11**(3), 343–390 (2024)
8. Mirabdolah, A., Alaeifard, M., Marandi, A.: User-centered design in HCI: enhancing usability and interaction in complex systems. Int. J. Adv. Hum. Comput. Interact. **1**(1), 16–33 (2023)
9. Davidovici-Nora, M.: Innovation in business models in the video game industry: free-to-play or the gaming experience as a service. Comput. Games J. **2**, 22–51 (2013)
10. Mustonen, E.: Vertical productisation over product lifecycle: Co-marketing through a joint commercial product portfolio. Acta Universitatis Ouluensis C 749, University of Oulu, Oulu, Finland (2020)
11. Reitmeier, J., Paetzold, K.: Consideration of market-oriented business strategies within the knowledge system of Design for X (DfX). In: 18th International ICE Conference on Engineering, Technology, and Innovation, Munich, Germany, pp. 1–10. IEEE (2012)

12. Kuo, T.C., Huang, S.H., Zhang, H.C.: Design for manufacture and design for 'X': concepts, applications, and perspectives. Comput. Ind. Eng. **41**(3), 241–260 (2001)
13. Eisenhardt, K.M.: Building theories from case study research. Acad. Manag. Rev. **14**(4), 532–550 (1989)
14. Yin, R.K.: Case Study Research and Applications: Design and Methods, 6th edn. SAGE Publications, Thousand Oaks (2018)
15. Kahn, K.B.: The PDMA Handbook of New Product Development, 3rd edn. Wiley, Somerset (2013)
16. Kotler, P., Keller, K.V.: Marketing Management, 14th edn. Prentice Hall, Upper Saddle River (2012)
17. Haines, S.: The Product Manager's Desk Reference, 2nd edn. McGraw-Hill Education, New York (2014)
18. Saaksvuori, A., Immonen, A.: Product Lifecycle Management, 3rd edn. Springer, Berlin, Heidelberg (2008). https://doi.org/10.1007/978-3-540-78172-1
19. Bitner, M.J., Ostrom, A.L., Morgan, F.N.: Service blueprinting: a practical technique for service innovation. Calif. Manage. Rev. **50**(3), 66–94 (2008)
20. Suominen, A., Kantola, J., Tuominen, A.: Reviewing and defining productization. In: 20th Annual Conference of the International Society for Professional Innovation Management (ISPIM 2009) (2009)
21. Harkonen, J., Haapasalo, H., Hanninen, K.: Productisation: a review and research agenda. Int. J. Prod. Econ. **164**, 65–82 (2015)
22. Lahtinen, N., Mustonen, E., Harkonen, J.: Commercial and technical productisation for fact-based product portfolio management over lifecycle. IEEE Trans. Eng. Manage. **68**(6), 1826–1838 (2019)
23. Dubois, L.-E., Pine, B.J., Harkonen, J.: Beyond the ephemeral: scaling experiences through productization. Bus. Horiz. **68**(1), 121–128 (2025)
24. Wirtz, J., Fritze, M.P., Jaakkola, E., Gelbrich, K., Hartley, N.: Service products and productization. J. Bus. Res. **137**, 411–421 (2021)
25. Wirtz, J.: Service products, development of service knowledge and our community's target audience. J. Serv. Mark. **35**(3), 265–270 (2021)
26. Dubois, L.-E., Weststar, J.: Games-as-a-service: conflicted identities on the new front-line of video game development. New Media Soc. **24**(10), 2332–2353 (2022)
27. Mustonen, E., Harkonen, J.: Commercial and technical productization for design reuse in engineer-to-order business. IEEE Trans. Eng. Manage. **71**, 1271–1284 (2024)
28. Sivaloganathan, S., Yanis, R.: Design for method study—work measurement: Do we need it? In: Chakrabarti, A. (ed.) ICoRD'15 – Research into Design Across Boundaries Volume 2. SIST, vol. 35, pp. 313–326. Springer, New Delhi (2015). https://doi.org/10.1007/978-81-322-2229-3_27
29. Raffaeli, R., Mengoni, M., Germani, M.: A software system for "Design for X" impact evaluations in redesign processes. J. Mech. Eng. **56**(11), 707–717 (2010)
30. Favi, C., Campi, F., Germani, M., Mandolini, M.: Engineering knowledge formalization and proposition for informatics development towards a CAD-integrated DFX system for product design. Adv. Eng. Inform. **51**, 101537 (2022)

Improving the Experience of Deaf People Through Wearable Vibration System

Victor Santos, João Marques, Ianne Crisóstomo, Marianna Sarmanho, Mauro Teófilo, and Rayol Mendonca-Neto

Mobile Innovation Lab (MIL), Sidia R&D Institute, Manaus, AM, Brazil
{victor.santos,joao.victor,ianne.crisostomo,
marianna.sarmanho,mauro.teofilo,rayol.neto}@sidia.com

Abstract. Over 430 million individuals globally experience some form of hearing loss, which can hinder their interaction with auditory environments. While current assistive technologies offer partial support, they often fail to deliver a fully immersive experience. This article introduces a novel system that leverages smartwatch and smartphone vibrations to convey cinematic audio information to users with hearing impairments. By analyzing audio tracks in real time and generating synchronized tactile feedback, our technology enables users to perceive soundscapes through vibrations, enhancing emotional engagement and allowing them to feel the movie's atmosphere as events are presented on screen. Results show that our approach improves users experience and immersion while watching TV series.

Keywords: Hearing Impairment · Multisensory experience · Accessibility · Wearables

1 Introduction

Globally, hearing loss is an increasing problem that affects the human population adversely. According to a report by the World Health Organization, there are approximately 466 million deaf and hearing-impaired (DHI) individuals worldwide, with 432 million being adults and the remaining being children [8]. Furthermore, the availability of hearing aids is still under 10% of worldwide needs.

Deafness and hearing loss are defined as a condition characterized by partial or complete inability to hear [1]. Recently, information and communication technologies have taken a leading role in society and, consequently, assistive technologies for deaf communication have achieved significant progress [10] [3]. Not only for communication [6] or education [2], for example, but also for visual and audio entertainment.

In this entertainment context, one of the obstacles hearing impaired faces are the lack of subtitles or sign language content in movies, series or TV shows. Usually it is not offered appropriate accessibility resources. Even more, watching a movie or some content often becomes a frustrating activity, as they are

J. Wei et al. (Eds.): HCII 2025, LNCS 16346, pp. 337–347, 2026.
https://doi.org/10.1007/978-3-032-13187-4_23

unable to feel emotion. Several devices have been developed to improve hearing impaired people experience with entertainment content, for this we can highlight vibrotactile feedback through wearables (e.g., smartwatches [7]), in which provides contact information by vibrating to the user with minimal cost and complexity [5].

In response to these challenges, we have developed a novel wearable vibration system that integrates multiple devices to enhance user experience and immersion for individuals with hearing impairments while watching TV shows. By distributing feedback through multiple points, our solution offers more comprehensive and nuanced haptic cues, which can better represent the emotional and auditory nuances present in media content.

This advancement not only enhances the entertainment experience for individuals with hearing impairments but also opens doors for future applications in gaming and other interactive media, promising a more inclusive and immersive world of audiovisual experiences. Results show that our approach improves users experience and immersion while watching TV series.

The remainder of this paper is organized as follows. Section 2 outlines the motivation of our study. Section 3 presents the related work that had special focus throughout our study. Section 4 describes the architectures developed, their components and relationships. Section 5 presents the methodology and experimental settings for this research. Section 6 reports the results along with the analysis. Section 7 presents the conclusion and highlights future research directions.

2   Motivation

Currently, people with hearing impairment or deafness depends primarily on subtitles or sign language to understand TV shows, which can limit their experience and emotional connection to the content. Introducing a new sensory layer through vibrations could enhance this experience. By translating emotional nuances into physical sensations, this approach strengthens immersion and pleasant. The combination of vibrations with images and sounds creates a multisensory universe, where the narrative is experienced in its entirety. Our approach would not only significantly improve the cinematic experience for deaf people, but would also open up possibilities in other contexts, such as live performances, educational videos and everyday communication tools.

3   Related Work

Yağanoğlu and Köse [11] present a wearable device designed to enhance auditory perception for deaf individuals by converting sound direction and intensity into tactile vibrations and visual cues. The system employs four directional microphones to detect sound sources and uses vibration motors on the fingertips to indicate direction—specific frequencies activate motors corresponding to left, right, front, or rear sounds, while LEDs provide additional visual alerts. Sound intensity is classified into silent, medium, and loud levels, with vibration severity adjusted accordingly (0.5–3 V). Advanced feature selection methods, including ReliefF, identified local maxima (Lmax) and zero-crossing rate (ZCR) as optimal features for classification. Machine learning algorithms, particularly SVM and KNN, achieved high accuracy (93–98%) in sound localization, with real-time response times of 0.68 s. Testing across diverse environments (indoor, outdoor, noisy) demonstrated robust performance, with 94–98% accuracy in directional detection at 1–4 m and 95% accuracy in distinguishing shouted vs. normal speech. The device outperformed traditional methods like TDOA in speed (0.68 s vs. 2.33 s) and cost (4 vs. 16 microphones). Participants, including deaf and hearing-impaired individuals, reported improved situational awareness and safety, particularly in detecting urgent sounds like alarms or vehicle horns.

The authors Yağanoğlu and Köse also published a work [12] where they present a real-time operational wearable device that detects the sound first with a microphone, identifies the sound, and conveys this information to the user through vibrations. The wearable device developed is mounted on the person in the outdoor environment. The system produces a different level of vibration and intensity for each sound. The wearable device is tested 100 times a day for 100 days on five deaf persons and 50 persons with normal hearing whose ears were covered by earphones that provided wind sounds. Results show that the system can achieve a success rate of 98% when estimating a door bell ringing sound, 99% success identifying an alarm sound, 99% success identifying a phone ringing, 91% success identifying honking, 93% success identifying brake sounds, 96% success identifying dog sounds, 97% success identifying human voice, and 96% success identifying other sounds using the audio fingerprint method. In the questionnaire performed, deaf people rate the clarity of the system at 90%, usefulness at 97%, and the likelihood of using this device again at 100%.

The work of Nanayakkara et al. [9] investigates the enhancement of musical experiences for hearing-impaired individuals through a multisensory system combining a Haptic Chair—which amplifies music vibrations for tactile perception via contact speakers on armrests, footrests, and backrests—and a visual display translating musical features (beat, pitch, loudness) into real-time animations or human gestures. User studies with 43 participants (partially and profoundly deaf) revealed a strong preference for the Haptic Chair alone or combined with visuals, as vibrations provided immersive, rhythmically meaningful feedback, while synchronized human gestures outperformed abstract visuals. Sustained satisfaction over three weeks highlighted the system's effectiveness, with applications extending to speech therapy and environmental sound awareness. Findings emphasize the importance of tactile and visual integration, bone conduction, and fidelity to original audio, offering new avenues for accessible music engagement and cross-sensory research.

4   Wearable Vibration System

In this section, we present our wearable vibration system. In contrast to other approaches, our proposal is easier to implement and employs devices that are commonly used. Figure 1 illustrates the components that comprise our approach which are discussed in the next subsections.

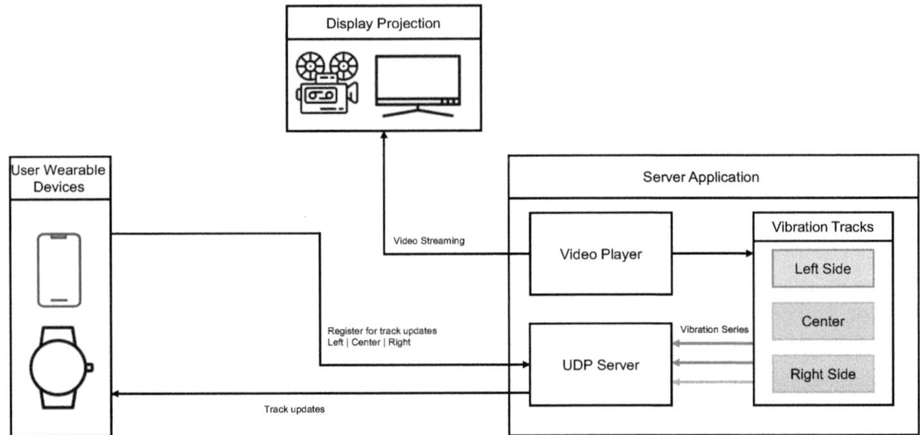

Fig. 1. Wearable vibration system architecture.

4.1   Server Application

In this component, the audio is processed while the information of the media that is being played. For every Stereo Media processed, our method delivers three vibration tracks, which essentially an array of byte values distributed at 20 vibrations/s.

The sensitivity of the Vibrator SDK[1] changes from one device to another, even if the vibration is defined by a value from 0 (none) to 255 (full strength), the "Vibration Resolution" on the devices are limited by the hardware itself, some devices (often the low-end devices) have a smaller vibration resolution, others devices brings a much larger number of vibration possibilities. Figure 2 presents an example of distinct vibration intensity for different devices and the requested vibration level. Environmental audio contain a large and diverse variety of sounds, including those with strong temporal domain signatures, such as chirpings of insects and sounds of rain that are typically noise-like [4].

As can be seen, while some devices can offer a huge amount of vibration intensities, some other devices would provide only a small range of possibilities, so to keep a better result on all devices, we limited the outputs to 10 vibration

---

[1] https://developer.android.com/reference/android/os/VibrationEffect.

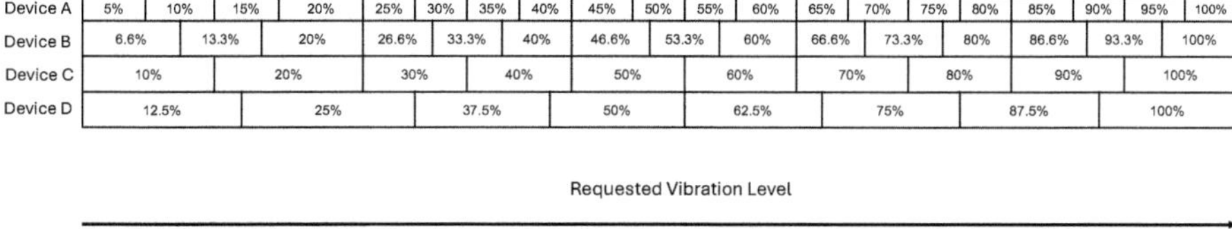

Fig. 2. Device Vibration Parameters.

levels, which delivers a perfect balance between the user haptics feelings and a lower network usage, due to the data transfer improvements.

The application shares the data with the connected devices (wearable devices) that users are wearing so that the device vibrates as faithfully as possible to what is being presented on the screen. We have the orientation of the data to be passed on, left side, center and right side, in addition to the server timestamp. The table 1 consolidates the data that is sent.

Table 1. Shared Data

Data	Value
Left Side	Vibration Values
Center	Vibration Values
Right Side	Vibration Values
Server Timestamp	h:m:s:ms

4.2 Wearable Devices

This component is responsible for vibrating the wearable device in the frequency that is related to the scene of the media that is being played. For the wearable devices receiving the vibration data, we can employ on smartwatches and smartphones since they are versatile and widely used.

When employing at smartwatches, there is a limitation in managing the intensity of vibrations effectively. Specifically, the amplitude of vibrations tends to be either excessively strong or insufficiently weak, which can compromise user experience. To address this challenge, it became necessary to double the amplitude values transmitted by the sending device when using a smartwatch. This adjustment ensured that the vibrations fell within an optimal range for the intended application.

In contrast, smartphones exhibit superior control over vibration intensity, allowing for more precise and gradual changes in amplitude. Unlike the few vibration range on smartwatches, smartphones can generate smoother transitions. This capability enhances user experience by providing a more comfortable interaction. The ability to modulate vibrations seamlessly is particularly valuable in this context, where sensory is so important.

In summary, while both smartwatches and smartphones serve as effective receivers for wearable devices, their respective limitations and strengths must be considered. Leading our method to employ both wearables in conjunction for a better user experience.

Finally, the display projection component, it is responsible to present the TV Show to the user. It can be used any display that present a clear image that can convey clear information about the scene to the user.

5   Evaluation Methodology

This chapter outlines the methodology employed in this research, which seeks to explore the experience of individuals with hearing impairments when using vibration devices to feel the intensity and emotions of a movie scene.

5.1   Participant Groups

The research recruited a total of 40 individuals, all participants consume television content regularly and enjoy watching films and series. We divided into four equal groups based on their degree of hearing loss:

- **Group 1:** 10 individuals with 100% hearing loss.
- **Group 2:** 10 individuals with 70% hearing loss.
- **Group 3:** 10 individuals with 30% hearing loss.
- **Group 4:** 10 individuals with 20% hearing loss.

This grouping was intentional to assess the system's effectiveness across varying degrees of hearing impairment, ensuring a comprehensive understanding of its applicability.

5.2   Wearables

The study utilized Samsung Galaxy Watch 6 smartwatches, Samsung Galaxy A56 and Samsung Galaxy S22 ultra smartphones. These devices were chosen for their advanced haptic feedback capabilities and specific power, which are essential to analyze the precision and clear tactile communication in distinct devices. The system translates audio signals into vibrations that can be felt through the skin, providing an alternative means of experiencing auditory content.

5.3   Scenarios and Procedures

Three distinct scenarios were designed to simulate real-life usage contexts:

- **Scenario 1:** Participants wore two smartwatches on both wrists with a smartphone positioned on chest.
- **Scenario 2:** Two smartwatches were worn on both wrists, and a smartphone was placed on leg.
- **Scenario 3:** One smartwatch was worn on the wrist, and a smartphone was held in hand.

These scenarios were selected to explore different configurations that might influence how vibrations are perceived, considering comfort and effectiveness across various setups. All the participants were randomly selected to a distinct scenario. Scenario 1 had 13 individuals, scenario two 13 individuals, and scenario three 14 individuals.

5.4   Experimental Protocol

The video presented to the usability test participants was the eighth episode of the first season of The Lord of the Rings: The Rings of Power, called "The League," and it is 72 min long. The sound design of the episode plays a fundamental role in enhancing the climate of tension, revelations, and epic fantasies that mark the end of the season. The soundscape mixes grand orchestral elements with natural ambient sounds, creating sound textures that were essential for conversion into vibration to highlight key moments. In this way, it guides the emotional narrative, marking the transition between the natural and the supernatural, reinforcing a growing tension in scenes involving mystery.

5.5   Ethical Considerations and Data Collection

Regarding the ethical issues, an consent form was obtained from all participants, ensuring confidentiality and ethical compliance with a review committee. Throughout the study, measures were taken to monitor the comfort and avoid any potential harm for the participants.

To gather insights, the research employed qualitative data collection, where participants were asked about their ability to perceive emotions, vibration intensity, comfort levels, overall effectiveness of the system and suggestions for improvement.

6   Experiments and Results

This section describes the results when applying our proposed wearable vibration system in three distinct scenarios, described in Sect. 5. We compared the results for the different scenarios. Additionally, we presented some reviews exposed by the participants.

Each subject was asked a questionnaire of 6 questions right after they watched the series. The test was performed without any time limit, and users were able to break and return at any time. The questions were:

- Did you have a good experience watching the test episode?
  - Focuses on emotional and memorable experiences during the show.
- Did you understand the film better with the help of vibrations?
  - Explores how vibrations enhanced comprehension and emotional connection.
- Would you use this product at home?
  - Aims to uncover personal intent and factors influencing willingness, such as effectiveness and convenience.
- Did you believe that the vibrations made sense with the actions?
  - Seeks insights into perceived coherence and naturalness of vibrations in relation to story actions.
- Did you like the arrangement of the devices on the body?
  - Examines physical comfort and aesthetic appeal regarding device placement.
- Did you feel that the number of devices was enough for a feeling of immersion?
  - Targets perception of sufficiency and impact of devices on immersive experience.

The Likert scale was used to conduct the experiments. To evaluate the results, the users' responses were converted into numerical scores, assigned according to the following criteria: 1 (Very low), 2 (Low), 3 (Neutral), 4 (High) and 5 (Very high). The averages of the responses of the group of users were calculated to determine the final value of the results.

6.1   Scenario 1 Two Smartwatches + 1 Smartphone on Chest

In this scenario, the participants were two smartwatches (one in each wrist) and 1 smartphone on chest. Table 2 shows the results of the questionnaire. Participants found the experience of watching the episode to be positive, with an average score of 4. They reported improved understanding of the film and indicated their willingness to use this product at home. However, the arrangement of devices on the body was less favored by participants, yielding a mean score of only 2.

During the test, it was noted that some users moved their smartphones. At the end of the session, it was found that most of the audience that moved their smartphones reported feeling little vibration being projected by the device located on their chest. On the other hand, the vibrations transmitted by the smartwatches proved to be significant to the users, emphasizing the different frequencies of the device.

Table 2. Scenario 1 questionnaire results

#	Question	Mean Score
1	The user had a good experience watching the test episode	4
2	The user understood the film better with the help of vibrations	4
3	The user would use this product at home	4.5
4	The user believes that the vibrations made sense with the actions	5
5	The user liked the arrangement of the devices on the body	2
6	The user felt that the number of devices was enough for a feeling of immersion	4

6.2   Scenario 2 Two Smartwatches + 1 Smartphone on Thigh

For the scenario 2, the participants wore two smartwatches and 1 smartphone on thigh. Table 3 describe the results. In comparison to scenario 1, the results in this scenario shows that the subjects perceived an improvement in almost all the items that were evaluated. The only item that had lower mean score was the one that evaluates that the vibration made sense with the actions. We can highlight that the arrangement of the devices on the body were much more effective (increasing the mean score from 2 to 3.6), just by relocating the smartphone from the chest to the thigh.

In scenario two, all participants reported that the vibration projected by the smartphones was not consistent with the scenes seen, and they even reported dissatisfaction with the low intensity of the vibration. In addition, the participants stated that the vibration of the smartwatch presented greater emotion and similarity to the scenes reproduced in the test. It is worth noting that the users indicated that increasing the level of frequencies and intensities of the vibrations of the cell phones was an area for improvement, since the sensitivity to touch was low.

Table 3. Scenario 2 questionnaire results

#	Question	Mean Score
1	The user had a good experience watching the test episode	4.6
2	The user understood the film better with the help of vibrations	4.3
3	The user would use this product at home	4.6
4	The user believes that the vibrations made sense with the actions	4.3
5	The user liked the arrangement of the devices on the body	3.6
6	The user felt that the number of devices was enough for a feeling of immersion	3.6

6.3   Scenario 3 One Smartwatch + 1 Smartphone on Hand

The last evaluated scenario the users wore only one smartwatch and one smartphone on hand. Table 4 briefly detail the results. This scenario presented the best result overall comparing to the other two previous scenarios. It is interesting to notice that in this scenario had the lower mean score (4) for use this product at home, but on the other hand it presented the higher score for the arrangement of the devices on the body.

Participants highlighted greater comfort using the devices during scenes. The vibrations were described as frequent, unpredictable, oscillating, and impactful. There was excellent contrast noted between the smartwatch's varied vibration frequencies and the phone's low-frequency vibrations.

Table 4. Scenario 3 questionnaire results

#	Question	Mean Score
1	The user had a good experience watching the test episode	5
2	The user understood the film better with the help of vibrations	5
3	The user would use this product at home	4
4	The user believes that the vibrations made sense with the actions	5
5	The user liked the arrangement of the devices on the body	5
6	The user felt that the number of devices was enough for a feeling of immersion	4

The analysis of results in showed that the proposed method has the potential to significantly enhance the entertainment experience regarding watching TV series for people with hearing impairments.

7   Conclusion and Future Directions

This paper presented a novel wearable vibration system that integrates multiple devices to enhance user experience and immersion for individuals with hearing impairments while watching TV shows. Using methods to analyze audio and generate corresponding vibrations allows users to feel the movie scene clearly and accurately.

The results demonstrate that users had a predominantly positive experience with the test episode, as evidenced by high mean scores on both the overall experience and their willingness to use the product at home. The findings also highlight the effectiveness of vibrations in improving comprehension and enhancing emotional connection with the TV show. Furthermore, the arrangement of devices and the number of devices used were perceived as sufficient for immersion, though there is room for improvement in these areas.

In future research we intend to optimize the device placement to enhance user comfort and satisfaction. Additionally, explore more nuanced vibration patterns to refine the immersive experience, potentially aligning vibrations with specific narrative beats or emotional cues in the film. Finally, improve temporal synchronization between on-screen actions and vibrations could further improve the coherence and naturalness of the experience.

References

1. Abdallah, E.E., Fayyoumi, E.: Assistive technology for deaf people based on android platform. Procedia Comput. Sci. **94**, 295–301 (2016)
2. Bell, D., Foiret, J.: A rapid review of the effect of assistive technology on the educational performance of students with impaired hearing. Disabil. Rehabil. Assist. Technol. **15**(7), 838–843 (2020)
3. Chin, C.L., et al.: A wearable assistant device for the hearing impaired to recognize emergency vehicle sirens with edge computing. Sensors **23**(17), 7454 (2023)
4. Chu, S., Narayanan, S., Kuo, C.C.J.: Environmental sound recognition with time-frequency audio features. IEEE Trans. Audio Speech Lang. Process. **17**(6), 1142–1158 (2009)
5. Filgueiras, T.S., et al..: Vibrotactile sensory substitution on personal navigation: remotely controlled vibrotactile feedback wearable system to aid visually impaired. In: 2016 IEEE International Symposium on Medical Measurements and Applications (MeMeA), pp. 1–5. IEEE (2016)
6. Gugenheimer, J., Plaumann, K., Schaub, F., Di Campli San Vito, P., Duck, S., Rabus, M., Rukzio, E.: The impact of assistive technology on communication quality between deaf and hearing individuals. In: Proceedings of the 2017 ACM Conference on Computer Supported Cooperative Work and Social Computing. pp. 669–682 (2017)
7. Marques, J., Teofilo, M., Aleixo, E., Filho, F., Díaz, A.A.O., Cleger Tamayo, S.: Modular platform for health and safety data monitoring. In: Stephanidis, C., Antona, M., Ntoa, S., Salvendy, G. (eds.) HCII 2024. CCIS, vol. 2321, pp. 30–39. Springer, Cham (2024). https://doi.org/10.1007/978-3-031-78561-0_4
8. Mohammed, H.B., Cavus, N.: Utilization of detection of non-speech sound for sustainable quality of life for deaf and hearing-impaired people: a systematic literature review. Sustainability **16**(20), 8976 (2024)
9. Nanayakkara, S.C., Wyse, L., Ong, S.H., Taylor, E.A.: Enhancing musical experience for the hearing-impaired using visual and haptic displays. Hum.-Comput. Interact. **28**(2), 115–160 (2013)
10. Rodríguez-Correa, P.A., Valencia-Arias, A., Patiño-Toro, O.N., Oblitas Díaz, Y., Teodori De la Puente, R.: Benefits and development of assistive technologies for deaf people's communication: a systematic review. Front. Educ. **8**, 1121597. Frontiers Media SA (2023)
11. Yağanoğlu, M., Köse, C.: Wearable vibration based computer interaction and communication system for deaf. Appl. Sci. **7**(12), 1296 (2017)
12. Yağanoğlu, M., Köse, C.: Real-time detection of important sounds with a wearable vibration based device for hearing-impaired people. Electronics **7**(4), 50 (2018)

Towards Practical Near-Fall Detection: Optimising Wearable Sensor Configurations by Strategic Reduction and Deep Learning

Moritz Schneider[1]([✉]) [ID], Kevin Seeser-Reich[1], Armin Fiedler[2], and Udo Frese[3]

[1] Institute for Occupational Safety and Health of the German Social Accident Insurance (IFA),
Sankt Augustin, Germany
Moritz.Schneider@dguv.de
[2] Koblenz University of Applied Sciences, RheinAhrCampus, Remagen, Germany
[3] German Research Center for Artificial Intelligence (DFKI), Bremen, Germany

Abstract. Slips, trips, and falls (STF) remain critical occupational hazards, particularly in physically demanding sectors such as logistics, healthcare, and manufacturing. While wearable inertial measurement unit (IMU) technologies combined with advanced deep learning approaches have demonstrated high precision in detecting near-fall events, their practical deployment is hindered by system complexity, low user compliance, and high costs due to extensive sensor setups. This study addresses these limitations by systematically evaluating sensor reduction strategies aiming at preserving detection accuracy while enhancing practicality and affordability.

Three strategies: balanced sensor reduction, unilateral reduction, and reduction to the core, reducing sensor placements to biomechanically significant anatomical sites, were tested using the comprehensive Prev-Fall dataset, which captures real-world STF scenarios. Four established deep learning models (CNNs, ResNets, DeepConvLSTMs, and InceptionTime) were applied to assess detection performance across varying sensor configurations.

Results indicate that targeted sensor placement, particularly at the pelvis and lower limbs, can maintain or even surpass the performance of conventional setups. Remarkably, a configuration using only two IMUs achieved over 80% accuracy and a macro F1-score exceeding 0.8. In general, reduction to less than three sensors led to notable misclassifications, especially between similar STF events. Furthermore, DeepConvLSTMs outperformed other architectures under minimal sensor conditions, outlining the importance of model–hardware alignment. These findings provide empirically grounded guidelines for cost-effective, wearable solutions that promote real-world feasibility and user acceptance in occupational safety applications.

Keywords: Near-fall · Deep Learning · Sensor Placement · Occupational Safety

J. Wei et al. (Eds.): HCII 2025, LNCS 16346, pp. 348–372, 2026.
https://doi.org/10.1007/978-3-032-13187-4_24

1   Introduction

1.1   Motivation and Problem Statement

Slips, trips, and falls (STF) represent a persistent occupational hazard, contributing substantially to workplace injuries, absenteeism, and long-term disability. According to the German Social Accident Insurance (DGUV), more than 171,000 STF-related incidents, including multiple fatalities, were reported in 2023, highlighting the pressing need for effective prevention strategies in occupational health and safety [1]. The prevalence of STF events is particularly high in physically intensive industries such as logistics, transportation, and manufacturing, where dynamic work environments exacerbate biomechanical risk factors. Recent advancements in wearable sensor technologies and machine learning allow new ways of mitigating for mitigating STF risks. In particular, inertial measurement units (IMUs) offer continuous, high-resolution monitoring of body kinematics, enabling the detection of biomechanical deviations preceding STF events [2, 3]. Prior studies have demonstrated that machine learning models trained on IMU data can achieve robust classification performance, even under realistic and complex movement conditions [4, 5].

However, while fall detection has been extensively studied, the detection of near-fall events characterized by a transient loss of balance without ground contact remains comparatively underrepresented in practical research and applications. As highlighted by Tanwar et al. [6] and Subramaniam et al. [7], most technological solutions focus on the detection of completed falls, neglecting near-falls despite their critical value in predicting future incidents and identifying at-risk individuals [6, 7]. Hellmers et al. [8] further emphasize that near-falls may offer unique biomechanical markers for early intervention, making their detection an essential component in fall prevention strategies [8].

Despite this promise, several limitations continue to hinder the practical deployment of such systems in real-world occupational settings. One key challenge lies in the scalability of sensor-based systems. High-performance near-fall STF detection models as presented by Schneider et al. [9] rely on extensive sensor networks that are costly to implement and computationally demanding. Moreover, wearing multiple sensors can be intrusive, reducing user compliance and practicality in long-term occupational applications [10, 11]. An additional consideration is the sensor redundancy observed in bilaterally symmetrical configurations. Sensors on opposite limbs often capture temporally shifted but biomechanically similar data, this redundancy may not represent a complication, but rather a potential way to address prior challenges related to data robustness and reliability [8]. Additionally, full-body instrumentation may collect data from regions with limited relevance for classification, thereby reducing system efficiency and increasing the burden on users. To overcome these challenges, recent research has focused on identifying optimised sensor configurations that strike a balance between minimal hardware requirements and high classification accuracy. Biomechanical evidence suggests that a subset of strategically placed sensors, particularly around the pelvis and lower extremities may offer sufficient discriminatory power for STF detection [9, 10]. Such optimisation has the potential to reduce system costs, enhance computational efficiency, and improve user acceptance by simplifying setup procedures and decreasing physical strain.

1.2 Objectives

This study investigates how the number of inertial measurement units (IMUs) required for accurate near-fall detection can be minimized without significantly compromising classification performance. A near-fall refers to a loss of balance such as a trip, slip, or misstep that is successfully recovered without ground contact except for the feet. It is considered a complex and heterogeneous event influenced by physical, cognitive, and environmental factors. While full-body sensor systems have demonstrated high reliability in controlled settings, they are often impractical in real-world applications due to their complexity and intrusiveness. Therefore, this work evaluates the compromise between sensor count, placement strategy, and detection accuracy.

To systematically address this question, three sensor reduction strategies were formulated. The balanced strategy examines bilateral sensor configurations; the unilateral strategy focuses on unilateral placements; and the core strategy explores optimized placements at biomechanically critical regions. Each strategy is evaluated under progressively reduced sensor setups (4, 3, and 2 sensors), allowing for a comparative assessment of performance degradation. Furthermore, the study evaluates how different deep learning architectures respond to sensor reduction, highlighting the interaction between sensor input and model design. To contextualize our approach within existing research, the following section reviews the current state of the art in wearable near-fall detection and sensor reduction strategies.

2 State of the Art

2.1 Sensor-Based (Near-) Fall Detection

The detection of slips, trips, and falls (STF) using wearable sensor-based technologies has advanced considerably over the past decade. In particular, inertial measurement units (IMUs), consisting of accelerometers, gyroscopes, and magnetometers, have become the standard for capturing high-resolution kinematic data. Their small form factor, low cost, and ability to provide continuous, body-centric data make them ideally suited for real-time movement analysis in clinical, occupational, and mobile settings [9]. Several publicly available datasets have played a key role in shaping STF detection research, including SisFall, UP-Fall, KFall, and Prev-Fall [3, 12–14]. However, these datasets differ substantially in terms of sensor configuration, fall realism, and ecological validity. For instance, SisFall employs only a single IMU at the waist, which limits its utility for sensor placement studies. UP-Fall and KFall utilise multiple IMUs, yet their falls are largely scripted and artificially induced. In contrast, the Prev-Fall [9] dataset is specifically designed to address these limitations. It features 17 IMUs spread over the whole body.

enabling high-resolution analysis of full-body kinematics. Crucially, data were collected under semi-controlled but realistic conditions using a perturbation walkway to induce genuine slips, trips, and missteps. The dataset includes recordings of 110 participants across physically demanding professions (e.g. steelworkers, logistics workers), making it one of the most comprehensive and ecologically valid resources currently available.

Numerous prior studies have examined the optimal placement of sensors to optimise the balance between detection performance and system simplicity. For instance, Ntanasis et al. [15] and Igual et al. [16] identified the waist and thigh as highly reliable locations for fall detection, given their proximity to the body's centre of mass and their ability to capture global kinematic responses. Yang & Pai [17] provided further confirmation that motion at the sacrum closely approximates the overall centre of mass trajectory. This lends further support to the strategic value of pelvis-mounted sensors for real-time monitoring of balance and recovery [17]. These biomechanical insights are in alignment with the findings of Teng et al. [18], who demonstrated that lower-limb sensor configurations provide particularly informative data for discriminating fall directions, thereby adding functional nuance to placement decisions.

In line with recent efforts to increase system efficiency and user compliance, researchers have explored sensor miniaturisation, on-device intelligence, and textile integration to improve wearability. For example, Yu et al. [19] introduced a resource-efficient fall detection system based on TinyCNNs that can be deployed on low-power microcontrollers without compromising accuracy. Similarly, Rahemtulla et al. [11] developed an electronic fabric incorporating motion sensors into wearable socks, offering both high detection performance and user comfort. Recent work has also highlighted the importance of optimising sensor placement to reduce system complexity without sacrificing biomechanical reliability. Gießler et al. [20] demonstrated that a minimal trunk-mounted IMU cluster can capture near-fall perturbation responses with high specificity, while Wang et al. [4] validated near-fall detection performance in the case of older adults subjected to unexpected slips, underscoring the relevance of real-world perturbation modeling.

These trends illustrate the ongoing efforts in the field to develop practical, low-complexity solutions for near-fall detection - an objective that aligns directly with the aim of the sensor reduction strategies investigated in the present study. These characteristics make Prev-Fall uniquely suited to investigate sensor reduction strategies in this study, particularly regarding sensor reduction and placement strategies. Its breadth, realism, and annotation richness provide a robust foundation for training and validating machine learning models that must operate reliably in real-world environments. Using this dataset ensures that the findings are not only technically sound but also practically relevant and generalisable to occupational safety applications. Given the limitations of current sensor setups and the potential benefits of targeted reduction strategies as highlighted in previous work, the subsequent methodology section presents our experimental design aiming at systematically testing three distinct sensor placement strategies under real-world conditions.

These strategies were derived based on biomechanical principles and supported by previous empirical evidence.

The balanced strategy assumes that a spread set of sensors over both sides of the body provides comprehensive coverage of symmetric and complementary motion patterns during STF events. Prior work has shown that bilateral configurations increase robustness in detecting directional falls and account for inter-limb coordination during perturbations [15, 18]. The unilateral strategy is based on the assumption of bilateral symmetry in human gait and investigates whether unilateral sensor arrays can sufficiently approximate whole-body motion. This is supported by studies highlighting high signal correlation between symmetrical sensor positions [8, 16]. The core strategy focuses on biomechanically critical regions, specifically the pelvis and lower limbs that have been consistently identified as key contributors to balance control and perturbation response [3, 10, 17, 18].

This strategic choice allows for a theory informed evaluation of the compromise between sensor placement and detection performance in the following sections.

2.2 Challenges in Sensor Reduction

Although extensive sensor networks enhance detection accuracy, they also pose significant challenges related to cost, computational load, and user compliance. Consequently, reducing the number of sensors without substantially compromising classification performance has become a critical research objective. One principal challenge associated with sensor reduction is the redundancy inherent in symmetric sensor placements. Research by Hellmers et al. [8] identified high correlations between sensor data from symmetrical body locations, indicating that data from sensors on one side of the body could adequately represent both sides for classification purposes. Moreover, biomechanical analyses have outlined the significance of specific anatomical regions, notably the pelvis and lower extremities, due to their essential role in maintaining balance and responding effectively to perturbations [3, 10]. Further research into the most effective positioning of sensors, as conducted by Ntanasis et al. [15] and Igual et al. [16], has demonstrated that sensor placements at the waist and thighs provide reliable readings of core balance dynamics. This lends further support to the hypothesis that symmetrical setups offer biomechanical redundancy. Yang & Pai [17] also confirmed that motion signals from the sacral region strongly approximate whole-body centre-of-mass movement during perturbed gait, thereby supporting the elimination of less informative sensor sites. This understanding has led researchers to prioritise these critical regions in sensor placement strategies, intending to preserve classification accuracy while reducing sensor usage. In addition to the concept of sensor redundancy, recent literature highlights further challenges and emerging approaches in the field of sensor reduction. As demonstrated by Yu et al. [19], the deployment of highly compact deep learning architectures, such as Tiny-CNNs, which are capable of running efficiently on microcontrollers, has been shown to result in a substantial reduction in computational demands without any compromise to detection performance [19].

Beyond TinyCNNs, other architectures, such as ResNet [21] and InceptionTime [22], have demonstrated excellent classification performance even under minimal input conditions. These models have the capacity to extract multi-scale temporal features or preserve gradient flow in deep stacks, rendering them especially well-suited for sensor-reduced environments. Furthermore, Yu et al. [23] demonstrated the effectiveness of

ConvLSTM models in pre-impact fall detection scenarios, integrating spatial and temporal dependencies within a compact hybrid design. Moreover, exploration has been undertaken into alternative approaches that employ entirely contactless sensing technologies. In their 2023 study, Ji et al. introduced a system known as SiFall [24], which employs the utilisation of ambient radio-frequency signals to facilitate the detection of falls through the implementation of anomaly detection techniques. Whilst RF-based methods offer advantages in terms of user comfort and privacy, their current limitations include insufficient sensitivity and temporal resolution for reliably distinguishing subtle near-fall events from normal activities [24].

Taken together, these insights underline the importance of carefully balancing sensor quantity, computational complexity, and biomechanical relevance, reinforcing the need for strategically targeted sensor reduction approaches.

2.3 Relevant Models and Algorithms

Advancements in machine learning, especially deep learning architectures adept at processing high-dimensional time-series data, have significantly driven the development of effective STF detection systems. Convolutional Neural Networks (CNNs) were utilised for their capacity to capture localised patterns, such as abrupt changes in acceleration or angular velocity, which are often indicative of STF events. Their convolutional layers were configured to handle multivariate inputs from IMU sensors, allowing the model to process complex kinematic relationships efficiently. Recent advancements have further demonstrated the efficacy of compact CNN architectures (e.g., TinyCNNs introduced by Yu et al. [19]) in significantly reducing computational complexity, thereby enabling real-time fall detection on hardware with limited resources. ResNets, on the other hand, were included for their ability to address vanishing gradient issues in deep networks, leveraging residual connections to maintain high performance even with increasing model depth. This made them suitable for learning subtle biomechanical differences between STF event types. InceptionTime, a model specifically designed for time-series classification, was employed to capture multiscale temporal features, enabling it to identify both short-term and long-term patterns critical for distinguishing STF events. CNNs, renowned for their capability to identify localised patterns such as sudden accelerations or angular velocity spikes, have proven particularly effective for fall detection tasks [19]. Furthermore, InceptionTime, specifically tailored for time-series classification, has demonstrated strong capabilities in extracting multi-scale temporal features, enabling it to effectively capture both short-term fluctuations and longer-term movement patterns essential for distinguishing STF events [22]. Residual Neural Networks (ResNets) have addressed common deep learning challenges like vanishing gradients and have successfully been applied to STF detection tasks, particularly in contexts requiring the processing of high-resolution kinematic data [25]. Hybrid architectures combining CNNs with recurrent neural networks, such as convolutional Long Short-Term Memory networks (convLSTMs), have further enhanced classification accuracy by integrating spatial and temporal dependencies within a unified model [26].

Recent comparative analyses by Hellmers et al. [8] underlined the effectiveness of hybrid deep ConvLSTM architectures in accurately identifying subtle near-fall events, highlighting their superior performance over traditional models under reduced sensor conditions [8]. These models excel in capturing subtle biomechanical variations associated with near-falls, which often present lower kinematic intensity and therefore pose greater detection challenges compared to clear falls [3]. Additionally, hyperparameter optimization including tuning of learning rates, regularisation techniques, and model architecture configurations is critical for achieving optimal performance while preventing overfitting [27].

In contrast to wearable IMU-based approaches, recent studies exploring contactless RF-based detection systems, such as the one presented by Ji et al. [24], rely predominantly on anomaly detection algorithms trained on ambient signal disruptions, rather than direct kinematic data. Despite the evident potential of these systems, their current limitations in terms of resolution and specificity primarily restrict their applicability to clear fall scenarios as opposed to more subtle near-fall situations [24]. While current state-of-the-art STF detection models illustrate significant progress in leveraging wearable sensor data and advanced machine learning techniques to mitigate workplace hazards, practical implementation remains challenged by sensor redundancy, cost efficiency, and system scalability. Recent advancements in biomechanical analyses and algorithmic improvements have paved the way towards optimised sensor configurations and refined model architectures, significantly contributing to robust and scalable STF detection solutions suitable for diverse occupational settings.

In this work the same architectures as in the work of Schneider et al. 2025 [9] were utilized to be able to compare the results of the full sensory suit from the previous work to a reduced sensor setup. All evaluated architectures (CNN, ResNet, InceptionTime, and deepConvLSTM) are convolutional neural networks capable of operating on multivariate time-series data. In this context, "CNN" refers to a standard feedforward convolutional architecture consisting of stacked 1D convolutional layers followed by fully connected layers, without architectural enhancements such as residual connections or inception modules. ResNet and InceptionTime extend this baseline with skip connections and multiscale processing, respectively, while the deepConvLSTM utilizes LSTM units after initial convolutional layers.

3 Methodology

3.1 Research Design

Building on the insights and limitations identified in the existing literature, this study follows a structured research design to empirically evaluate sensor reduction strategies for near-fall detection. The overarching goal is to investigate how sensor count and placement influence detection performance, and to determine the most efficient configurations for practical application.

The research design consists of the following key steps:

1. Strategy Formulation: Three sensor reduction strategies were defined, based on biomechanical and methodological considerations:
   a. **Balanced**: bilateral placement across major body segments,
   b. **Unilateral**: unilateral placement at one side of the body, and

c. **Core**: targeted placement at biomechanically critical regions.
2. Model Training and Evaluation: Each strategy was evaluated using systematically reduced sensor subsets (4, 3, and 2 IMUs) derived from the full-body Prev-Fall dataset. Various deep learning architectures were trained and validated to assess the impact of sensor configuration on classification performance.
3. Cross-Strategy Comparison and Model Optimization: The best-performing configurations across strategies were compared to identify performance trade-offs. Sensor importance was further analyzed to derive recommendations for minimal, high-impact setups.
4. Generalizability Testing: Selected top-performing models were tested on an independent dataset to assess their robustness and generalizability beyond the training context.

This structured approach ensures a comprehensive and systematic investigation of the interplay between sensor reduction, model performance, and real-world applicability. The following section outlines the methodology and implementation details of each step.

3.2 Prev-Fall Dataset

The Prev-Fall dataset consists of 1640 time series recordings from 110 different working age participants. The participants walked along a slip, trip and misstep parcourse where traps were able to induce involuntary near-fall events. During this the participants were wearing an Xsens Link Suit (Enschede, The Netherlands) with 17 IMUs. The trap activations happened in different, random places and between each trap activation was at least one walk across the parcours without any traps, to prevent the participants from anticipating the near-fall event. This allowed the genuine recording of the 531 trips, 552 slips and 557 missteps included in this dataset [2, 3]. Each of the 17 IMUs recorded 3D accelerometer, gyroscope, and magnetometer data at 120 Hz. The sensors were positioned on key anatomical landmarks, including the head, shoulders, sternum, pelvis, upper and lower limbs (upper arms, forearms, thighs, shins, and feet), providing full-body kinematic coverage. This comprehensive setup enabled detailed motion capture of both normal walking and induced perturbation events. Based on this dataset, various sensor subsets were created in accordance with the three sensor reduction strategies introduced earlier. The next section outlines how these subsets were systematically constructed and selected.

3.3 Strategies

This study systematically investigates the influence of different sensor reduction strategies on the classification performance of STF detection systems. In light of the findings from prior research, which demonstrated that only a subset of sensors may be required for accurate fall detection [3, 10], and considering the practical constraints inherent in wearable systems (e.g., cost, usability, user compliance) [19], three sensor reduction strategies were derived. The combination of anatomical reasoning and data-driven selection is employed to investigate the trade-off between sensor count and classification performance. Sensor selection was consistently guided by data-driven variance analysis using principal component analysis (PCA), ensuring that the most informative subsets were retained at each level of reduction. To calculate the amount of variance explained by each sensor the PCA was performed for the entire dataset and then attributes belonging to each single sensor summed up and compared to the others. This assumption is based on the premise that sensors whose features explain higher levels of variance are more likely to contain discriminative information. Despite the fact that it does not constitute a formal feature selection method, this approach provides a computationally efficient proxy for sensor relevance, allowing us to create and test sensor subsets for the different strategies with only the most relevant sensors. This is necessary since running a neural architecture search for all possible sensor permutations would be computationally unfeasible.

1. **Balanced Sensor Deployment (Strategy I):** This strategy posits that accurate STF detection can be achieved through representative sampling of kinematic data from distinct anatomical regions. To operationalise this concept, the full-body sensor configuration comprising 17 IMUs was divided into four anatomical regions and their accompanying sensors: head (Head), upper body (Sternum, Left/Right Shoulder, Left/Right Upper Arm, Left/Right Forearm, Left/Right Hand), pelvis (Pelvis), and lower body (Left/Right Upper Leg, Left/Right Lower Leg, Left/Right Foot).

   Using PCA, five combinations of four sensors were selected, each drawing one sensor from a different anatomical region and maximising cumulative variance. Additional five combinations of three and two sensors were constructed by progressively excluding lower-contributing regions, maintaining a focus on biomechanical representativeness and variance contribution. This strategy is of particular relevance in situations where the direction of fall is unknown and global coverage is desired [10].

2. **Unilateral Reduction Strategy (Strategy II):** Grounded in the biomechanical symmetry of human movement and supported by prior findings on contralateral signal redundancy [8], this strategy evaluates whether classification performance can be preserved using sensors placed exclusively on the left side of the body. Candidate sensors included: Left Shoulder, Left Upper Arm, Left Forearm, Left Upper Leg, Left Lower Leg, and Left Foot. From these, permutations of four, three, and two sensors were generated, and the top five configurations per sensor count were selected based on PCA-derived variance contribution of each sensor. This approach enabled a structured assessment of lateral sensor reduction on model robustness. The present approach aims at testing the hypothesis that lateral symmetry in gait translates to redundancy in sensor data, as suggested by findings on contralateral signal correlation [8].

3. **Core Region Placement (Strategy III):** This strategy assumes that the most discriminative biomechanical features for STF detection originate from the lower extremities. It restricts sensor placement to Left/Right Upper Leg, Left/Right Lower Leg, and Left/Right Foot, while explicitly excluding sensors from the head, trunk, arms, and pelvis. As in the previous two strategies, PCA was used to identify the five most informative subsets for each configuration size (4, 3, and 2 sensors), ensuring that sensor selection was based on signal variance rather than anatomical intuition. The present strategy is robustly supported by extant literature emphasising the role of lower-limb

kinematics and centre-of-mass dynamics in maintaining balance and recovering from perturbations [3, 10].

Following these strategies 45 data subsets were created overall. That is 15 subsets per strategy or from a different point of view 15 subsets for the combination of four, three and two sensors. To compare the impact on near-fall detection performance we carried out a neural architecture search (NAS) similar to Schneider et al. [9] on all of these subsets. A comparative evaluation of all configurations is provided in the appendix. The sensor subsets described above were selected based on a systematic variance-based evaluation. A comprehensive account of the selection process is provided in the subsequent chapter.

3.4   Sensor Subset Selection and Variance-Based Evaluation

To systematically evaluate the impact of sensor reduction on model performance, we developed a formalized framework for subset selection based on explained variance. For each of the three sensor reduction strategies a restricted configuration space C_S was defined from the full set of 17 IMUs. These strategy-specific spaces constrained the combinations of sensors to those meeting anatomical or biomechanical criteria, as detailed below:

- $C_{Balanced}$ sensor sets comprising one sensor from each of four major anatomical regions (head, upper body, pelvis, lower body).
- $C_{Unilateral}$ sensors located exclusively on the left side of the body.
- C_{Core} only sensors from the lower extremities, excluding head, arms, and upper trunk.

Within each strategy, all possible sensor subsets $c \subseteq C_S$. of fixed sizes $|c| \in \{2,3,4\}$ were enumerated and evaluated.

Each subset c was scored based on the total amount of variance explained by the features associated with its constituent sensors. The cumulative variance score $V(c)$ was computed as:

$$V(c) = \sum_{i \in c} \sum_{j \in F_i} Var(X_j) \tag{1}$$

where:

- F_i denotes the set of feature channels (e.g., acceleration, gyroscope, magnetometer) recorded by sensor i
- X_j is the normalized time series of feature channel j
- $Var(X_j)$. is the empirical variance of X_j calculated over all STF trials in the dataset

This score reflects the assumption that feature channels with higher variance across the dataset are more likely to contain discriminative signal components relevant for classification. For each strategy and sensor count, the top-5 configurations with the highest $V(c)$ values were retained, yielding a total of 45 subset configurations (i.e., 3 strategies × 3 sensor counts × 5 combinations).

This data-driven selection mechanism allowed for the comparison of different spatial simplification strategies while ensuring that retained configurations preserved the richest available kinematic information under each respective constraint. The effect of these configurations on classification performance is analyzed in the subsequent sections.

3.5 Neural Architectures

For the NAS the same architectures as in Schneider et al. [9] were considered. This allows to gage the impact of the sensory reduction strategies on near-fall detection compared to the performance with the full sensory suit from that previous work. For the classification of slip, trip, and fall (STF) events, four well-established deep learning architectures were utilized: Convolutional Neural Networks (CNNs), Residual Networks (ResNets), deep convolutional Long Short-Term Memories (deepConvLSTMs) and InceptionTime. These architectures were chosen for their demonstrated ability to handle time-series data, effectively extracting both local and global patterns crucial for STF detection.

The models were trained using TUNA, a bespoke system designed to facilitate neural architecture search (NAS) and hyperparameter optimisation. Unlike off-the-shelf tools such as mcfly [27], TUNA offers enhanced flexibility and scalability, enabling the efficient design of architectures tailored to the unique properties of the Prev-Fall dataset. TUNA systematically evaluated combinations of convolutional, residual, and inception layers, optimising for performance metrics such as F1-Score and accuracy. Once the candidate architectures were defined, the training process was carried out using the TUNA framework, as detailed in the following section.

3.6 Training and Validation

Utilizing TUNA we performed a NAS for each of the 45 data subsets. Fifty configurations of CNNs, ConvLSTMs, ResNets and InceptionTime networks were trained for each of the 45 data sets created for the three strategies. Hyperparameters for the neural architecture search were selected using random search and the range of parameters was for comparability reasons the same as in Schneider et al. [9].

The data subsets were randomly split 4:1 into training and validation sets and the NAS was performed with a batch size of 64, shuffling after every epoch. We trained each network for 20 epochs, early stopping when no improvement of the loss was observed after two consecutive epochs. The main difference to Schneider et al. [9] is that the input layer size is smaller based on the number of sensors blacked out for the different data subsets.

To be able to generate networks during the NAS that would be capable of real time fall detection, we spliced the trials into windows of 1s length (120 frames) with a 50% overlap. The classification problem was once again formulated as a four class classification problem [9]. To achieve this, a window of the time series was labeled as either tripping, slipping or misstepping, if at least 0.25s (30 frames) of one such event is contained within a window, otherwise it was labeled as baseline walking.

This necessitated a rebalancing of the dataset. The dataset was rebalanced before splitting into training and validation sets. The rebalancing ensured that each class had the same amount of samples by randomly drawing samples for each class until the number of samples in the smallest class was reached. For the evaluation we calculated the accuracy and micro, macro and weighted F1-scores on the validation splits of the different subsets. For comparability reasons to the NAS on the full dataset with 17 sensors in [9] we used the weighted F1-score as the primary metric for ranking.

Having defined the input formats and data representations so far, we below describe the performance evaluation metrics employed to compare model outputs.

3.7 Performance Metrics

To thoroughly evaluate the effectiveness of sensor reduction strategies, the following metrics were selected:

- **Accuracy**

  Accuracy measures the overall proportion of correctly classified instances. Although this provides a general performance indication, its interpretability is limited in the context of imbalanced datasets, necessitating additional complementary metrics [28].
- **False-Positive Rate (FPR)**

  The FPR assesses the frequency of incorrect STF classifications among non-STF events. Low FPR values are critical for practical implementation, particularly in occupational settings where false alarms could disrupt workflows [8, 9].
- **F1-Score**

  The F1-Score, which equally weights precision and recall, is chosen due to the imbalanced nature typical of STF datasets. A higher F1-score indicates robust STF detection performance while minimising false-positive detections [9]. We calculated macro, micro and weighted F1-scores [29].

Collectively, these metrics offer a balanced and comprehensive evaluation of STF detection performance, addressing both sensitivity to actual STF occurrences and the critical need to minimise false alarms.

3.8 Generalisability Testing

To test the generalisability of the previously trained networks we took the networks with the best weighted F1-score trained during the NAS for each strategy. Subsequently we utilized the same dataset as in [9] to test the networks performance on so far unseen data and activities that were recorded with the same sensor system. This is data recorded in the IFAs ergonomics laboratory [30]. This dataset does not contain falls or near-falls of any kind, instead it contains data of walking around, picking up, carrying around and putting down boxes of different sizes and weights or placing them in shelves at different heights as well as using a screwdriver at different heights. This dataset should help to gage how often a network erroneously detects near-fall events during everyday activities. For this reason, the false-positive rate is reported as the performance metric for this test. The time series were sliced into windows with a length of 1s, with an overlap of 50% and all of them were labeled as baseline walking.

4 Results

The results are presented in three main parts according to the previously defined sensor reduction strategies (balanced, unilateral, core). Within each strategy, we report the classification performance for progressively reduced sensor configurations (4, 3 and 2 sensors), highlighting the trade-offs in accuracy and F1 score.

Following the individual strategy analyses, we provide a cross-strategy performance comparison to identify the most efficient configurations overall. Finally, we examine sensor importance to determine which placements contributed most to model performance. This structured presentation allows a transparent assessment of how sensor reduction affects near-fall detection under each experimental condition.

For comparison, in the previous study utilizing the full 17 sensors the best F1 score for the same size of time windows was 0.9123 and the accuracy was 0.9590 achieved by an InceptionTime model [9].

4.1 Balanced (Strategy I)

The evaluation of sensor configurations based on bilateral placements demonstrated that among the top-four sensor combinations, Combination 2 (Head, ShldrL, Pelvis, FootRachieved the highest performance with an accuracy of 86.80% and a weighted F1-score of 0.910 (Table 4). Combinations 4 (Head, ShldrR, Pelvis, FootR) and 5 (Head, ShldrL, Pelvis, LowLegL) delivered nearly identical results, confirming the robustness of these configurations. Combinations 1 (Head, ShldrL, Pelvis, FootL) and 3 (Head, ShldrR, Pelvis, FootL) exhibited marginally lower, yet still competitive performances.

When the number of sensors was reduced to three, Combination 5 (Head, ShldrR, FootL) performed best, maintaining an accuracy of 83.73% and a weighted F1-score of 0.880 (Table 5). This suggests that a moderate reduction in sensor count does not drastically compromise classification performance. However, Combination 4 (ShldrL, Pelvis, FootR) revealed a noticeable decline, emphasizing the sensitivity of certain placements.

With only two sensors, performance decreased more noticeably. Combination 1 (ShldrL, FootL) provided the highest accuracy (77.39%) and weighted F1-score (0.814) (Table 6). The other configurations showed relatively similar results, although Combination 2 (ShldrL, FootR) demonstrated a further minor drop to an accuracy of 77.01% and weighted F1-score of 0.813. These results highlight a clear trade-off between sensor count and model performance.

4.2 Unilateral (Strategy II)

Analysis of unilateral sensor configurations revealed that Combination 4 (ShldrL, ForeArmL, UppLegL, FootL)) was the top performer among the four-sensor setups, achieving 82.94% accuracy and a weighted F1-score of 0.871 (Table 7). Combinations 1 (ShldrL, ForeArmL, HandL, FootL) and 3 (ShldrL, UppArmL, ForeArmL, FootL) followed closely, whereas Combinations 2 (ShldrL, ForeArmL, LowLegL, FootL) and 5 (ShldrL, HandL, LowLegL, FootL) showed slightly reduced performance. In the three-sensor scenario, Combination 4 (ShldrL, UppArmL, FootL) again yielded the best results with an accuracy of 81.69% and weighted F1-score of 0.858 (Table 8). Combinations 1 (ShldrL, ForeArmL, FootL) and 2 (ShldrL, HandL, FootL) also maintained acceptable performance levels.

However, a further reduction to two sensors led to additional declines: Combination 2 (ShldrL, ForeArmL) reached the highest values, with 81.69% accuracy and 0.857

weighted F1-score (Table 9), whereas Combination 3 (ShldrL, HandL) showed the weakest performance with 79.07% accuracy and 0.829 weighted F1-score. Overall, compared to bilateral configurations, unilateral setups resulted in approximately 1.5–2.5% lower accuracy and F1-scores, highlighting a moderate, yet consistent disadvantage in classification performance.

4.3 Core (Strategy III)

Sensor arrangements priorizing biomechanically critical regions demonstrated strong classification performance. Among the four-sensor combinations, Combination 3 (LowLegL, LowLegR, FootL, FootR) stood out with the highest accuracy of 84.51% and a weighted F1-score of 0.889 (Table 10), closely followed by Combinations 2 (Pelvis, LowLegR, FootL, FootR) and 4 (Pelvis, UppLegL, FootL, FootR) (both 0.888).

These findings suggest that optimized sensor placements can approximate the performance of bilateral layouts. In the three-sensor condition, Combination 2 (LowLegL, FootL, FootR) maintained solid performance, achieving an accuracy of 82.78% and weighted F1-score of 0.874 (Table 11). Combinations 1(Pelvis, FootL, FootR) and 3 (LowLegR, FootL, FootR) followed with minimal performance differences, underlining the effectiveness of strategically reduced configurations.

With only two sensors, Combination 1(FootL, FootR) yielded the highest performance with 84.59% accuracy and a weighted F1-score of 0.889 (Table 12). Although Combinations 2 (Pelvis, FootL) and 3(LowLegL, FootL) showed slightly lower values, the overall decline remained moderate. Compared to the best bilateral configurations, optimized sensor placements demonstrated a performance drop of approximately 2–3%.

4.4 Best Model Performance Across Sensor Reduction Strategies

To evaluate the impact of sensor reduction strategies, we identified the best-performing model for each Strategy (I: Balanced, II: Unilateral, III: Core) according to their F1-Macro score. The results are summarized in the following Table 1:

Table 1. Best Model Performance Across Sensor Reduction Strategies.

Strategy	Sensor Count	Sensor Names	Model Type	Best Weighted F1-Score
Balanced	4	Head, Left Shoulder, Pelvis, Right Foot	CNN	0.910
Unilateral	4	Left Shoulder, Left Foot, Left Forearm, Left Upper Arm	CNN	0.871
Core	4	Left Foot, Right Foot, Left Lower Leg, Right Lower Leg	CNN	0.8889

These results illustrate that while optimised sensor placement (Core Strategy) achieves strong performance, symmetric (balanced) or even asymmetric (unilateral) sensor arrangements may still offer a marginal performance advantage when all configurations employ an equal number of sensors.

4.5 Comparative Performance Across Sensor Reduction Strategies

A direct comparison between the balanced strategy, the unilateral strategy, and the core as in Table 2 provides deeper insight into the trade-offs.

Table 2. Comparative performance across Sensor Reduction Strategies I–III using four-sensor configurations. The column 'Δ to [9] Table 3 (%)' reports the relative difference in Weighted F1 Score compared to the best validation result (0.9632) in Table 3 of [9]. Values indicate the percentage decrease in classification performance relative to the reference model.

Strategy	Sensor Count	Best Accuracy (%)	Δ to [9] Table 3 (%)	Best Weighted F1-Score
Balanced	4	86.97	−5.52	0.91
Unilateral	4	82.94	−9.57	0.871
Core	4	84.51	−7.7	0.889

While balanced setups (Strategy I) retain the strongest performance overall, both unilateral (Strategy II) and core region configurations (Strategy III) demonstrate acceptable trade-offs, with relative performance drops of 5.5%, 7.7%, and 9.6% respectively, compared to the best validation Weighted F1 Score reported in [9] (0.9632).

4.6 Sensor Configurations Across Sensor Reduction Strategies

This section provides an overview of the sensor configurations used in Strategy I (Balanced), Strategy II (Unilateral), and Strategy III (Core). The configurations were designed to evaluate the impact of sensor reduction and strategic sensor placement on classification performance in near-fall detection. Sensors that weren't part of any configuration with high explained variance are not shown in the graphic.

Figure 1 presents the distribution of sensor usage across all top-performing configurations, grouped by sensor count (4, 3, and 2) and strategy. The sensor selection was guided by PCA-based dimensionality reduction (see Sect. 3.4), where combinations with the highest total variance contribution were retained for evaluation. The visualisation reveals clear trends in sensor retention: FootL and ShoulderL are the most consistently selected sensors, appearing across nearly all configurations. Their persistent inclusion suggests a high discriminative value, particularly for capturing lower-limb dynamics and core stability relevant to near-fall events. In contrast, sensors such as ShoulderR, FootR, and ForeArmL show reduced presence in lower-count setups, indicating a more auxiliary role. The analysis confirms that even under substantial reduction, strategically placed

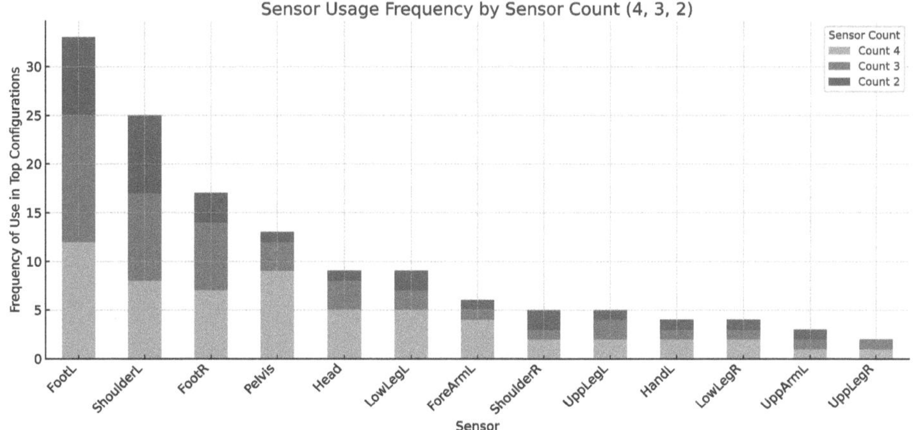

Fig. 1. Frequency of individual sensor appearances across top-ranked configurations for each strategy and sensor count (4, 3, 2). Sensors from the left side of the body appear more often due to the unilateral strategy only containing left side sensors.

sensors, primarily on the left lower extremity and trunk, maintain effective coverage of the necessary motion patterns. These findings support targeted sensor selection as a viable strategy for minimising system complexity without significantly compromising classification performance.

To further assess the robustness and generalizability of the models, we conducted an external validation using independent data, as described below.

4.7 Performance on Foreign Data

Table 3 summarises the performance of the best neural network models for each sensor reduction strategy when tested on a foreign dataset. It reports classification accuracy, false-positive rates (FPR), and the percentage change in FPR compared to the baseline model from [9], using a 1-s window.

Table 3. This table shows the false-positive rates the best networks for each strategy tested achieved on foreign data. It additionally shows the percentage difference to the best networks performance on foreign data from [9] with a window size of 1s.

Model	Accuracy (%)	False-Positive Rate (%)	FP rate difference to [9] (same window size, in %)
CNN (Balanced)	89.41	10.59	−32.331
CNN (Unilateral)	84.32	15.68	+0.191
CNN (Core)	98.48	1.52	−90.29

The core strategy achieved the best results, with 98.48% accuracy and a FPR of just 1.52%, marking a 90.29% improvement compared to the baseline. This likely reflects the removal of upper-body and arm sensors, which may have contributed to false positives during ADLs. The unilateral Strategy showed similar FPR to the baseline (+0.19%) with reduced accuracy (84.32%), suggesting minimal impact from sensor changes. The balanced strategy performed moderately, with 89.41% accuracy and a 10.59% FPR, which is 32.33% lower than the baseline, suggesting once again the removal of sensors that complicate differentiating between STF events and ADLs not present in the training data.

5 Discussion

The key finding of this study is that near-fall detection performance can be maintained at a high level while significantly reducing the number of sensors down to as few as two IMUs without substantial loss of accuracy. This demonstrates the practicality and effectiveness of targeted sensor reduction in wearable STF detection systems.

This study aimed at optimising sensor configurations and data utilisation strategies to efficiently detect near-fall events without significantly compromising detection accuracy. The results clearly demonstrate that substantial sensor reductions are achievable while maintaining robust detection performance. The best-performing minimal sensor configurations consistently comprised sensors positioned around the pelvis and thigh areas. This finding aligns with established biomechanical insights, suggesting these anatomical regions are crucial in detecting balance perturbations and postural adjustments during STF events [18].

Considering the accuracy results presented for each strategy, the minor performance decreases observed when reducing from four to two sensors are notably minimal (F1-scores remain above 0.80). This reinforces that strategic sensor selection, particularly focusing on critical body locations, sufficiently captures essential biomechanical information to classify near-falls accurately. Previous studies by Schneider et al. [9] required extensive sensor arrays for comparable accuracy; thus, the current approach provides significant practical improvements by drastically simplifying hardware requirements.

To further contextualize these results, it is essential to revisit the three strategies proposed at the outset. The findings provide strong support for the core strategy (Strategy III), which emphasizes biomechanically critical regions, as it achieved high detection performance with the lowest false-positive rate. The balanced strategy (Strategy I), which involved a balanced distribution across both body sides, showed moderate performance and a notable drop in specificity. The unilateral strategy (Strategy II), relying on unilateral sensor placement, demonstrated acceptable performance levels but slightly higher false-positive rates. These outcomes indicate that while all three strategies offer viable paths toward sensor reduction, Strategy III emerges as the most effective and practical approach under the given conditions.

These findings are strongly supported by previous literature, which independently confirms the biomechanical relevance of the pelvis and lower limbs in fall and near-fall dynamics. Studies by Ntanasis et al. [15] and Yang & Pai [17] demonstrated that sensors near the body's center of mass offer optimal signal quality for balance monitoring. Additionally, recent works by Wang et al. [21], Fawaz et al. [22], and Yu et al. [19] show that deep learning models such as ResNet, InceptionTime, and CNNs can maintain high classification performance even under significantly reduced input complexity. The alignment between our results and these external findings reinforces the robustness and transferability of the proposed sensor configurations and model strategies.

Furthermore, the results presented in Table 3 regarding false-positive rates on foreign data yield particularly intriguing insights. Specifically, the core strategy showed a remarkably low false-positive rate of 1.52%, representing a 90.29% improvement over the results from [9]. This substantial enhancement can be attributed to sensor reduction predominantly involving sensors from upper-body and arm positions. Such sensors likely contributed disproportionately to false-positive classifications during common activities of daily living, such as shelf-stocking or load-handling, which frequently mimic biomechanical signatures of STF events but aren't part of the Prev-Fall dataset. By strategically eliminating these sensors, the model's specificity significantly improved, emphasizing the value of targeted sensor selection in practical deployment scenarios. Furthermore, this insight also shows that datasets utilizing a full sensory setup need a high number of ADL recordings, for the networks to learn to differentiate between for example stretching out the arms to pick up a box or stretching out the arms to maintain balance. On the flip side, if the number of sensors is minimal, the amount of ADL recordings required is lower and thus the construction of future datasets after ideal sensor placements have been identified is easier.

The same explanation holds for the improved FP rate observed for the balanced strategy when compared to the baseline, only with a smaller margin of 32.33%. Since the balanced strategy still contains upper body sensors this is further evidence for their involvement in the difficulty of distinguishing between STF events and as of yet unseen ADLs for the networks.

The results of the unilateral strategy, with a false-positive rate of 15.68% presents a more moderate performance. Compared with the other two strategies, but especially compared to the core strategy, it is significantly less effective in differentiating between STF events and ADLs. The differences observed might be due to variations in sensor positioning and the algorithmic interpretation of ambiguous biomechanical patterns. Given that the unilateral strategy closely matched the previous findings (difference of only $+0.19\%$), this indicates that the sensor removal criteria of Strategy II was relatively conservative, possibly retaining sensors that minimally impacted false-positive rates.

These findings hold substantial implications for practical workplace safety implementations. Reducing sensor count directly enhances the feasibility and user acceptance of wearable STF detection systems. Given the substantial reductions in sensor hardware and computational demands, this study presents compelling evidence that efficient STF detection solutions are realistically attainable in occupational contexts.

Nonetheless, some limitations warrant consideration. The laboratory conditions under which STF events were captured might not cover all potential variabilities inherent in real-world falls or near-falls. Thus, additional validation through extensive field studies in realistic occupational environments would bolster confidence in the generalisability of the current findings.

Future research should therefore priorize evaluating the optimised sensor configurations and models in diverse real-world scenarios. Exploring the integration of these minimal sensor configurations into everyday occupational wearables would further test practicality and user acceptance.

In conclusion, the present study demonstrates convincingly that accurate and reliable near-fall detection does not inherently require extensive sensor setups. By strategically reducing sensor configurations, notably improving false-positive rates through targeted sensor selection, and maintaining robust detection capabilities, this research significantly advances wearable STF detection technology's practicality and applicability.

6 Conclusions and Outlook

In conclusion, this research successfully demonstrated that reliable and accurate near-STF event detection is achievable with significantly fewer sensors than previously considered to be necessary. By strategically placing sensors around critical anatomical areas such as the pelvis and thigh, and employing selective sensor reduction strategies, detection accuracy and false-positive rates were substantially improved. These methodological enhancements significantly reduce hardware complexity and computational requirements, thereby increasing user acceptance and practical applicability in occupational safety contexts.

Looking forward, the next critical step involves conducting extensive field studies to validate these sensor configurations and strategies under real-world occupational conditions. Such field studies will confirm the practical applicability and effectiveness of these systems, facilitating their integration into occupational safety programs. Once near-fall events are accurately identified in the field, occupational safety professionals can implement targeted prevention measures effectively. Furthermore, given the robust classification results achieved, future research should explore the feasibility of predicting near-fall events, investigating how many time steps in advance accurate predictions can be made. This predictive capability could potentially enable real-time interventions, significantly enhancing workplace safety by proactively preventing STF incidents.

Appendix

Table 12. Analysis and Comparative Evaluation of Top-2 Sensor Combinations (Core).

Sensor Combination	Sensors	Accuracy (%)	F1-Score Macro	F1-Score Micro	F1-Score Weighted
Combination 1	FootL, FootR	84.585	0.891	0.889	0.889
Combination 2	Pelvis, FootL	83.49	0.879	0.877	0.879
Combination 3	LowLegL, FootL	82.629	0.871	0.868	0.87
Combination 4	LowLegR, FootL	82.942	0.873	0.872	0.872
Combination 5	UppLegL, FootL	83.333	0.878	0.876	0.876

Table 4. Analysis and Comparative Evaluation of Top-4 Sensor Combinations (Balanced).

Sensor Combination	Sensors	Accuracy (%)	F1-Score Macro	F1-Score Micro	F1-Score Weighted
Combination 1	Head, ShldrL, Pelvis, FootL	85.423	0.901	0.902	0.899
Combination 2	Head, ShldrL, Pelvis, FootR	86.803	0.911	0.911	0.910
Combination 3	Head, ShldrR, Pelvis, FootL	86.507	0.907	0.908	0.906
Combination 4	Head, ShldrR, Pelvis, FootR	86.972	0.910	0.911	0.910
Combination 5	Head, ShldrL, Pelvis, LowLegL	86.972	0.910	0.911	0.910

Table 5. Analysis and Comparative Evaluation of Top-3 Sensor Combinations (Balanced).

Sensor Combination	Sensors	Accuracy (%)	F1-Score Macro	F1-Score Micro	F1-Score Weighted
Combination 1	Head, ShldrL, FootL	83.099	0.875	0.873	0.874
Combination 2	Head, ShldrL, FootL	81.847	0.860	0.860	0.859
Combination 3	Head, ShldrL, FootR	82.394	0.868	0.866	0.866
Combination 4	ShldrL, Pelvis, FootR	79.734	0.839	0.838	0.837
Combination 5	Head, ShldrR, FootL	83.725	0.882	0.880	0.880

Table 6. Analysis and Comparative Evaluation of Top-2 Sensor Combinations (Balanced).

Sensor Combination	Sensors	Accuracy (%)	F1-Score Macro	F1-Score Micro	F1-Score Weighted
Combination 1	ShldrL, FootL	77.39	0.817	0.813	0.814
Combination 2	ShldrL, FootR	77.01	0.815	0.811	0.813
Combination 3	ShldrR, FootL	75.86	0.801	0.800	0.798
Combination 4	Head, ShldrL	75.12	0.793	0.792	0.791
Combination 5	ShldrR, FootR	75.59	0.795	0.794	0.792

Table 7. Analysis and Comparative Evaluation of Top-4 Sensor Combinations (Unilateral).

Sensor Combination	Sensors	Accuracy (%)	F1-Score Macro	F1-Score Micro	F1-Score Weighted
Combination 1	ShldrL, ForeArmL, HandL, FootL	82.238	0.864	0.864	0.863
Combination 2	ShldrL, ForeArmL, LowLegL, FootL	81.064	0.854	0.852	0.852
Combination 3	ShldrL, UppArmL, ForeArmL, FootL	82.078	0.864	0.863	0.862
Combination 4	ShldrL, ForeArmL, UppLegL, FootL	82.941	0.871	0.872	0.871
Combination 5	ShldrL, HandL, LowLegL, FootL	81.221	0.856	0.854	0.854

Table 8. Analysis and Comparative Evaluation of Top-3 Sensor Combinations (Unilateral).

Sensor Combination	Sensors	Accuracy (%)	F1-Score Macro	F1-Score Micro	F1-Score Weighted
Combination 1	ShldrL, ForeArmL, FootL	80.091	0.847	0.844	0.845
Combination 2	ShldrL, HandL, FootL	80.469	0.846	0.843	0.844
Combination 3	ShldrL, LowLegL, FootL	80.469	0.845	0.843	0.844
Combination 4	ShldrL, UppArmL, FootL	81.690	0.858	0.855	0.858
Combination 5	ShldrL, UppArmL, FootL	80.282	0.846	0.844	0.844

Table 9. Analysis and Comparative Evaluation of Top-2 Sensor Combinations (Unilateral).

Sensor Combination	Sensors	Accuracy (%)	F1-Score Macro	F1-Score Micro	F1-Score Weighted
Combination 1	ShldrL, FootL	80.85	0.851	0.850	0.849
Combination 2	ShldrL, ForeArmL	81.69	0.860	0.859	0.857
Combination 3	ShldrL, HandL	79.07	0.831	0.830	0.829
Combination 4	ShldrL, LowLegL	80.91	0.850	0.850	0.849
Combination 5	ShldrL, UppArmL	80.28	0.846	0.844	0.844

Table 10. Analysis and Comparative Evaluation of Top-4 Sensor Combinations (Core).

Sensor Combination	Sensors	Accuracy (%)	F1-Score Macro	F1-Score Micro	F1-Score Weighted
Combination 1	Pelvis, LowLegL, FootL, FootR	83.568	0.880	0.878	0.881
Combination 2	Pelvis, LowLegR, FootL, FootR	84.272	0.888	0.886	0.886
Combination 3	LowLegL, LowLegR, FootL, FootR	84.507	0.891	0.889	0.889
Combination 4	Pelvis, UppLegL, FootL, FootR	84.272	0.888	0.886	0.888
Combination 5	Pelvis, UppLegR, FootL, FootR	83.586	0.873	0.870	0.870

Table 11. Analysis and Comparative Evaluation of Top-3 Sensor Combinations (Core).

Sensor Combination	Sensors	Accuracy (%)	F1-Score Macro	F1-Score Micro	F1-Score Weighted
Combination 1	Pelvis, FootL, FootR	82.423	0.872	0.870	0.871
Combination 2	LowLegL, FootL, FootR	82.781	0.875	0.873	0.874
Combination 3	LowLegR, FootL, FootR	81.353	0.860	0.857	0.859
Combination 4	UppLegL, FootL, FootR	80.931	0.855	0.854	0.853
Combination 5	UppLegR, FootL, FootR	81.129	0.857	0.856	0.856

References

1. Deutsche Gesetzliche Unfallversicherung e.V.; (German Social Accident Insurance, DGUV): Statistik Arbeitsunfallgeschehen 2023. Deutsche Gesetzliche Unfallversicherung e.V., Berlin (2024)
2. Schneider, M., et al.: Generation of consistent slip, trip and fall kinematic data via instability detection and recovery performance analysis for use in machine learning algorithms for (near) fall detection. In: Duffy, V.G. (ed.) Digital Human Modeling and Applications in Health,

Safety, Ergonomics and Risk Management, HCII 2023. LNCS, vol. 14029, pp. 298–305. Springer, Cham (2023). https://doi.org/10.1007/978-3-031-35748-0_22

3. Schneider, M., et al.: Acquisition of data on kinematic responses to unpredictable gait perturbations: collection and quality assurance of data for use in machine learning algorithms for (near-)fall detection. Sensors **24**(16), 5381 (2024)

4. Wang, S., Miranda, F., Wang, Y., Rasheed, R., Bhatt, T.: Near-fall detection in unexpected slips during over-ground locomotion with body-worn sensors among older adults. Sensors **9**(22), 3334 (2022)

5. Hsu, W.-W., Guo, J.-M., Chen, C.-Y., Chang, Y.-C.: Fall detection with the spatial-temporal correlation encoded by a sequence-to-sequence denoised GAN. Sensors **22**(11), 4194 (2022)

6. Tanwar, R., Nandal, N., Zamani, M., Manaf, A.A.: Pathway of trends and technologies in fall detection: a systematic review. Healthcare (Basel) **10**, 172 (2022)

7. Subramaniam, S., Faisal, A.I., Deen, J.: Wearable sensor systems for fall risk assessment: a review. Front. Digit. Health **4**, 921506 (2022)

8. Hellmers, S., et al.: Comparison of machine learning approaches for near-fall-detection with motion sensors. Front. Digit. Health **5**, 1223845 (2023)

9. Schneider, M., Seeser-Reich, K., Fiedler, A., Frese, U.: Enhancing Slip, Trip, and Fall Prevention: Real-World Near-Fall Detection with Advanced Machine Learning Technique (2025)

10. Nikolov, I., Liu, J., Moeslund, T.: Imitating emergencies: generating thermal surveillance fall data using low-cost human-like dolls. Sensors **22**(3), 825 (2022)

11. Rahemtulla, Z., Turner, A., Oliveira, C., Kaner, J., Dias, T., Hughes-Riley, T.: The design and engineering of a fall and near-fall detection electronic textile. Materials **16**(5), 1920 (2023). https://doi.org/10.3390/ma16051920

12. Sucerquia, A., Lopez, J.D., Vargas-Bonilla, J.F.: SisFall: a fall and movement dataset. Sensors **17**(1), 198 (2017)

13. Martínez-Villaseñor, L., Ponce, H., Brieva, J., Moya-Albor, E., Martínez-Villaseñor, J., Martínez-Villaseñor C.: UP-fall detection dataset: a multimodal approach. Sensors **19**(9), 1988 (2019)

14. Yu, X., Jang, J., Xiong, S.: A large-scale open motion dataset (KFall) and benchmark algorithms for detecting pre-impact fall of the elderly using wearable inertial sensors. Front. Aging Neurosci. **13**, 692865 (2021)

15. Ntanasis, P., Pippa, E., Özdemir, A.T., Barshan, B., Megalooikonomou, V.: Investigation of sensor placement for accurate fall detection. In: Perego, P., Andreoni, G., Rizzo, G. (eds.) Wireless Mobile Communication and Healthcare, MobiHealth 2016. LNICST, vol. 192, pp. 225–232. Springer, Cham (2017). https://doi.org/10.1007/978-3-319-58877-3_30

16. Igual, R., Medrano, C., Plaza, I.: Challenges, issues and trends in fall detection systems. BioMed. Eng. OnLine, **12**, 66 (2013)

17. Yang, F., Pai, Y.-C.: Can sacral marker approximate center of mass during gait and slip-fall recovery among community-dwelling older adults? J. Biomech. **47**(16), 3807–3812 (2014)

18. Teng, S., et al.: Analyzing optimal wearable motion sensor placement for accurate classification of fall directions. Sensors **24**(19), 6432 (2024)

19. Yu, X., et al.: A practical wearable fall detection system based on tiny convolutional neural networks. Biomed. Signal Process. Control **86**, 105325 (2023)

20. Gießler, M., Werth, J., Waltersberger, B., Karamanidis, K.: A framework to automatically detect near-falls using a wearable inertial measurement cluster. Commun. Eng. **3**, 181 (2024)

21. Wang, Z., Yan, W., Oates, T.: Time series classification from scratch with deep neural networks: a strong baseline. In: International Joint Conference on Neural Networks (IJCNN) (2017)

22. Ismail Fawaz, H., et al.: InceptionTime: finding AlexNet for time series classification. Data Min. Knowl. Disc. **34**(6), 1936–1962 (2020). https://doi.org/10.1007/s10618-020-00710-y

23. Yu, X., Qiu, H., Xiong, S.: A novel hybrid deep neural network to predict pre-impact fall for older people based on wearable inertial sensors. Front. Bioeng. Biotechnol. **8**, 63 (2020)
24. Ji, S., Xie, Y., Li, M.: SiFall: practical online fall detection with RF sensing. In: SenSys '22: Proceedings of the 20th ACM Conference on Embedded Networked Sensor Systems, pp. 563–577 (2022)
25. Ramanathan, A., McDermott, J.: Fall detection with accelerometer data using Residual Networks adapted to multi-variate time series classification. In: 2021 International Joint Conference on Neural Networks (IJCNN), pp. 1–8 (2021)
26. Al-qaness, M.A., Dahou, A., Abd Elaziz, M., Helmi, A.M.: Human activity recognition and fall detection using convolutional neural network and transformer-based architecture. Biomed. Signal Process. Control **95**, 106412 (2024)
27. C. M. V. v. H. a. M. K. D. van Kuppevelt, "mcfly," (2017). https://github.com/NLeSC/mcfly. Accessed Feb 2019
28. Batista, G.E., Prati, R.C., Monard, M.C.: A study of the behavior of several methods for balancing machine learning training data. ACM SIGKDD Explor. Newsl. **6**(1), 20–29 (2004)
29. Lee, M.C.H., Braet, J., Springael, J.: Performance metrics for multilabel emotion classification: comparing micro, macro, and weighted f1-scores. Appl. Sci. **14**(21), 9863 (2024)
30. Grießel, R., et al.: Virtuelle Realität und reale Arbeitswelt: Übertragbarkeit ergonomischer Belastungsbewertungen bei kniebelastender Tätigkeit. Tagungsband 71. Kongress der GfA: Arbeit 5.0: Menschzentrierte Innovationen für die Zukunft der Arbeit, pp. 233–238 (2025)

The Effects of Facial Cues on Purchase Intention in Live Streaming E-Commerce

Haorun Song, Tongrui Yang[✉], Lehan Sun[✉], and Ruyue Sun[✉]

Design School, Shanghai Jiao Tong University, Shanghai 200240, People's Republic of China
HRSong_2023@sjtu.edu.cn

Abstract. Live streaming has become a major component of the e-commerce economy, influencing consumer purchasing behavior. However, the optimal strategies for streamers to increase viewers' purchase intention remain unclear, with most studies focusing on qualitative aspects. This research aims to explore the effects of facial cues, including smile and eye gaze, on purchase intention using a quantitative approach during a dynamic process. Guided by Brownian lens and SOR theories, 36 participants were exposed to 16 video stimuli with controlled facial cues, followed by surveys to assess perceptions and purchase intent. Eye-tracking data captured subconscious attention. The analysis, using GLMM and non-parametric ANOVA, revealed that both smile expression and eye gaze significantly influenced purchase intention, with gender, age, and education affecting outcomes. Additionally, higher engagement was observed in the latter stages of viewing, with more frequent eye gaze shifts indicating increased attention. The findings highlight the importance of customized interactions in live-streaming, offering implications for optimizing streamer performance and informing human-computer mobile interaction design to enhance consumer engagement and purchase behavior.

Keywords: Facial cues · Purchase intention · Attention

1 Introduction

With the development of internet technologies and mobile interactions, online shopping has undergone rapid innovation in the past few decades. E-commerce now has the ability to attract consumers by providing not only static but also dynamic content stimulus, namely live streaming content. E-commerce live streaming is a type of mixed live broadcasting that consists of audio and visual elements provided by streamers which can enhance the interaction to attract viewers to purchase goods and products for sale. Most live streaming platforms provide a real-time interface that allows streamers to talk to the viewers directly. In order to boost sales there is usually a process of streamers holding the product and introducing it to the consumers with their streaming techniques. Given the rapid development of live streaming and the competition between platforms and operators, scholars from various domains have been focusing on how to form better viewer engagement.

J. Wei et al. (Eds.): HCII 2025, LNCS 16346, pp. 373–384, 2026.
https://doi.org/10.1007/978-3-032-13187-4_25

First, the relationship between facial cues and purchase behavior plays a crucial role in e-commerce. In this study, facial cues include smile express and eye gaze. According to previous studies facial cues have been proven to influence the perception of emotions of the consumers [2]. Specifically, eye gaze and the bidirectional interaction between streamer and consumer can significantly enhance the purposefulness of the consumer with higher attractiveness [1, 4]. Smile express on the other hand can bring more joy to the consumer and has an impact on the decision-making process [8, 14]. However, all of the research focused on a static situation, but today's e-commerce marketing is more of a dynamic interaction process and many factors are changing, making the correlation more complex. Therefore, the effect of facial cues on consumer's decisions in the dynamic streaming process needs to be studied.

Second, the effect on consumer purchase intention might vary according to different consumers and the stage of e-commerce watching. Facial expressions have a differentiated impact on people's perceptions [7]. However, previous research has not analyzed their varied effects within the context of live streaming. From the perspective of consumers, differences in habitual daily consumption intensity may influence how facial cues affect purchase intentions. From the perspective of the interaction process, the role of facial cues may change over time. Therefore, it's necessary to discuss how the effects of facial cues on purchase intention vary according to the consumption intensity and the accumulated effects.

Finally, attention is an important underlying factor which influences preferences and how people make decisions. According to previous study celebrity endorsements can significantly influence consumer's attention [16]. And when attention is drawn to a product, it creates a positive bias toward products that are liked by consumers [6]. Current research is limited to one-sided influences, while this study focuses on the bidirectional effects in live streaming dynamics and the role that attention plays.

Taken together, the research gaps mentioned drives this paper to investigate the following research questions: How do streamers' facial cues (i.e., smile express and eye gaze) influence consumers' purchase intention? How do facial cues influence different consumers differently? How do facial cues influence consumers' attention and how does attention influence consumers' purchase intention?

To answer these questions, we develop a theoretical framework based on the stimulus-organism-response (S-O-R) theory and the lens model theory. In this theory, we mainly focus on the link between facial cues and purchase intention. Consuming intensity and accumulative effects are processed in heterogeneity test and attention plays the intermediate role.

This paper is structured as follows. In Sect. 2, relevant literature is reviewed and theoretical framework and hypotheses are formulated. In Sect. 3 and 4, we introduce the details of the eye tracking behavioral experiment and the analysis results. In Sect. 5, we conclude our findings by discussing the implications, limitations, and future directions.

2   Theories and Hypotheses

To understand how facial cues are processed by consumers during e-commerce live streaming and how a determined purchase intention is formed, we build a research conceptual model based on the S-O-R theory and the lens model theory (Fig. 1). The S-O-R theory is a psychological model framework used to describe how humans respond to environmental stimuli. It breaks down the response process into three key components: stimulus, organism, and response. In this study, the framework can refer to facial cues as a stimulus, the consumer's reaction as an organism, and their final decision-making as a response. The lens model theory suggests that individuals perceive and interpret the world through unique "lenses," which are shaped by their personal beliefs, experiences, and cultural backgrounds. The theory emphasizes that people's reactions to the same event or information might differ based on the interaction of cues within their unique cognitive lens.

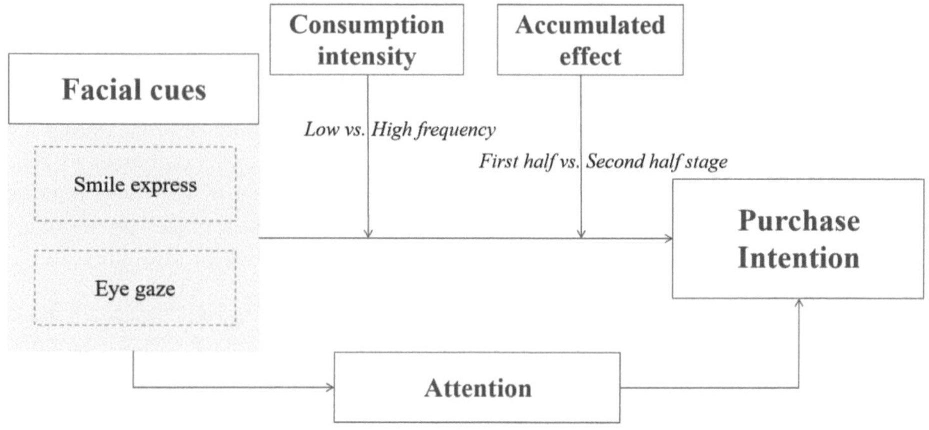

Fig. 1. Conceptual Model.

In this conceptual model, the main focus is on the relationship between facial cues and purchase intention. Facial cues serve as stimuli that influence the consumer's decision, specifically their purchase intention. The effect between these two is also shaped by the consumer's level of consumption and the accumulative effect of the streaming process. Additionally, attention acts as an intermediary, driven by the facial cues from the streamer, and it subsequently affects the purchase intention.

2.1   Facial Cues on Purchase Intention

In previous research smile express and eye gaze have been discussed frequently under e-commerce context [10]. Research suggests that in live-streaming environments, non-verbal cues, such as visual and auditory stimuli, have an optimal level [15, 18, 19]. This is guiding people to seek the best external stimulus state. For example, in crowd-funding scenarios, studies have found that the intensity of a smile affects perceptions of warmth and competence, which in turn influences consumer behavior, such as investment decisions or purchase intention [12, 14, 20].

On the other hand, eye gaze plays a guiding role for consumer's attention. The eye gaze has been shown to enhance the attractiveness of the streamer. Consequently, the streamer's eye gaze can also impact consumers, such as through the movement of their gaze direction and eye contact with the viewers [3, 5]. Based on previous studies, the use of eye gaze in live-streaming e-commerce is believed to influence consumer decision-making. However, its effect in dynamic contexts has yet to be fully validated.

Regarding the previous literature, although facial cues are proven to indeed influence purchase intention, smile express and eye gaze have not been discussed jointly as facial cues and separately as two major factors of the streamer's expression before. Thus, in order to figure out the mechanism between facial cues and consumer purchase intention during the live streaming process, we propose the following hypotheses.

H1a. Smile express is positively related to consumer's purchase intention.
H1b. Eye gaze is positively related to consumer's purchase intention.

2.2 Consumption Intensity and Accumulated Effect on Consumer's Purchase Intention

Consumption in live-streaming e-commerce contexts is also influenced by external factors, including consumption intensity, which reflects the consumer's purchasing habits, and the accumulated effect, which refers to the temporal stage of the live-streaming session. According to Yu et al., the moderating effect of gaze on object processing is highly specific [17], and we propose that facial cues may function through a similar mechanism.

Consumption intensity may imply more frequent exposure to the streamer's facial stimuli. On one hand, this could lead to desensitization to the streamer's stimuli, resulting in a decreased or insignificant impact of facial cues on purchase intention. On the other hand, it may indicate a more thorough understanding and better perception of the live-streaming e-commerce elements, making it easier for consumers to develop purchase intentions under such circumstances.

The discussion of accumulated effect focuses on the sequential process of watching live streaming. As a sequential activity, the temporal stage of watching live streaming may influence the consumer's perception and receptiveness to facial cues, thereby affecting their purchase intention.

Therefore, based on the influencing factors from the consumer's side and the process side, the following hypotheses are proposed.

H2a. High frequency of live streaming e-commerce consuming is positively related to the purchase intention.
H2b. Viewing stage of time of live streaming e-commerce is positively related to the purchase intention.

2.3 Attention

Attention plays a significant role in the decision-making process of consumers [11, 13]. In a study on static interactions, consumers' eye gaze and attention allocation were significantly influenced by the model, and changes in eye gaze direction correspondingly altered the final purchase intention [9, 16]. This suggests that attention, as a mediating factor, is guided and controlled by the streamer's facial cues, which in turn impact the consumer's purchase intention. Thus, we propose the following hypotheses.

H3a. Facial cues are positively related to consumer's attention.
H3b. Consumer's attention is positively related to purchase intention.

3 Methodology

3.1 Experiment Design

Based on the previous theoretical review and research hypothesis, the experiment is designed as the following graphic shows (Fig. 2). The experiment focuses mainly on the effects of the streamer's smile expression and eye gaze on the purchase intention of consumers, which is a 2 × 2 human factor experiments. In the experiment, the streamer introduces four kinds of commodities with smile express and eye gaze of different extents. The subject needs to watch 16 live-streaming video clips in a random sequence. After each clip, the subject will be asked to fill a questionnaire based on the watching experience. The process repeats until all clips are watched.

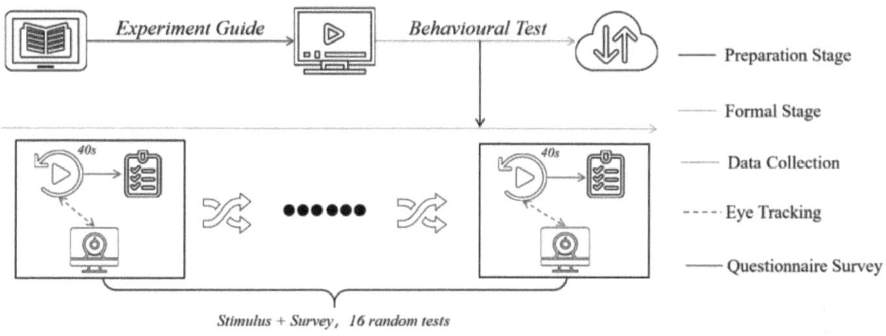

Fig. 2. Experiment Process.

The design of this experiment takes the streamer's performance and the effectiveness of different stimuli into account. The questionnaire focused on the purchase intention of subjects. The live-streaming content and verbal cues are preset according to the mainstream streaming forms based on research. The streamer warms up, and then introduces product information, features, and price, and presents the purchase link, with around 40 s per product. The stimuli have to provide sufficient stimulation to the subject, to let the subject have clear awareness of the streamer's eye gaze and smile intensity.

3.2 Apparatus

The study adopts Tobii Pro Spectrum the screen-based eye tracker to collect the subject's fixation and visit data. The advantage of the equipment is that it does not need to be worn and there would be no burden to the subject during the experiment. The experiment will compare the impact of different expressions of the streamer on the viewer's attention.

3.3 Procedure

After entering the lab, the subject is asked to sit in front of the computer equipped with an eye tracker. A consent form was read and signed before the procedure by the subject, on which the theme of the study was informed. Then, the subject was introduced to the detailed task and informed of the things to be noticed when collecting eye tracking data. Before the experiment started, personal information was collected and the calibration of the equipment was done. First, the subject watched a 40-s streaming clip. Then, after the clip the subject was asked to fill out a questionnaire based on the watching experience and rate certain factors. After a short break, the process went over again. In order to eliminate possible learning effects, for different subjects the sequence of the clips is randomly arranged. During the time the eye tracking data was automatically recorded by the equipment and saved as datasets, which would be separately analyzed. The whole experiment process lasted approximately 40 min.

3.4 Measures

Independent Variables. There are two independent binary variables that reflect the facial expressions of the streamer in this study, **smile express** and **eye gaze**. The two variables were controlled and identified by the experiment designer when recording the stimulus video. Therefore, every stimulus clip of the 16 in total is originally determined by the variable measure.

Moderating Variables. Attention serves as the moderating variable of the main effect, influenced by facial cues and subsequently impacting the consumer's purchase intention. The attention data is derived from eye-tracking data recorded throughout the entire process. Three Areas of Interest (AOIs) are defined on the live-stream interface, and the following metrics are extracted: fixation count, and visit count, which are used as indicators of attention.

Dependent Variable. Purchase intention is the dependent variable in the study which is measured by the results of the questionnaire answered by the subject after each clip. The purchase intention is the average and standardized value of 3 relevant questions. This reflects how the subject reacted to the expressions of the streamer after the stimulus.

Control Variables. The study includes the subject's gender, age, education background, income level, live streaming watching experience and allergy or dislike towards commodities in stimulus clip as control variables in the data analysis.

Heterogeneity Test Variables. To further analyse how purchase intention is influenced, two heterogeneity test variables are included. First, **consumption intensity** during live streaming is considered. The frequency of the subject consuming while watching live streaming is collected by the questionnaire at the beginning of the experiment. On the other hand, **accumulated effect** is included during the analysis. For this variable, we split the whole experiment process into two parts, first half with the first 8 clips and second half with the remaining. This enables us to figure out possible different reactions of the subjects at different points of time.

4   Methodology

4.1   Manipulation Check of Streamer Attractiveness

In each questionnaire after the video clip, the subjects were also asked to rate the expressions (smile express and eye gaze) of the streamer based on their perception on a 7-point Likert scale(1 = fully insensible, 7 = fully sensible). To assure the effectiveness of the beforehand prepared stimulus video clip, a Rwg within-group interrater agreement test is adopted. For the 4 (2 × 2) types of stimulus, the measures of Rwg were above 0.5, which indicates moderate accordance within the group. This means the binary variable affiliated with the stimulus is available for data analysis.

4.2   Analysis Strategy

The main dataset (36 × 16 = 576 records) consists of 4 × 4 (4 stimulus types and 4 commodity types). In this study, the generalized linear mixed-effects model (GLMM) is suitable for its adaptation to the repetitive and overdispersed measures. Therefore, GLMM was adopted in the study by using the SPSS 27.0 software to analyze the main effects of facial cues. Furthermore, we processed the data using ANOVA to ensure the robustness of the analysis. The ANOVA test indicated no significant difference from the results by GLMM. Therefore, this paper only reports the GLMM results.

4.3   Effects of Facial Cues on Purchase Intention

Table 1. GLMM of main effects.

	Model 1	Model 2	Model 3	Model 4	t
Intercept	3.598***	3.432***	3.453***	3.335***	5.685
Smile express	/	0.548***	/	0.484***	4.906
Eye gaze	/	/	0.570***	0.511***	5.145
Controls	included	included	included	included	/

Notes: (1) *** $p < 0.001$, ** $p < 0.01$, * $p < 0.05$. (2) The dependent variable is purchase intention.

According to the data analysis results in Table 1, both smile express and eye gaze have a significant positive impact on purchase intention (Model 4), supporting H1a and H1b.

4.4   Heterogeneity Test of Consumption Intensity

According to the data analysis results in Table 2 and 3, facial cues influence purchase intention differently in high and low frequency group. Subjects from low frequency groups have better perception of eye gaze stimulus than subjects from the other group. Age and education background significantly influence purchase intention in low frequency group. In high frequency group, male consumer has stronger purchase intention. This partially supports H2a and H2b.

Table 2. GLMM of consumption intensity (High Frequency).

	Model 5	Model 6	Model 7	Model 8	t
Intercept	2.546***	2.205***	2.552***	2.244***	3.668
Gender	−0.384	−0.482*	−0.357*	−0.449*	−2.292
Education	0.495*	0.401*	0.537**	0.448*	2.216
	−0.191	−0.273	−0.195	−0.268	−1.500
Income 3	−1.102***	−0.977**	−1.107***	−0.991**	−3.172
Smile express	/	0.530***	/	0.481***	3.598
Eye gaze	/	/	0.422**	0.354**	2.665
Controls	included	included	included	included	/

Notes: (1) *** p < 0.001, ** p < 0.01, * p < 0.05. (2) The dependent variable is purchase intention.

Table 3. GLMM of consumption intensity (Low Frequency).

	Model 9	Model 10	Model 11	Model 12	t
Intercept	4.457***	4.037***	4.334***	3.956***	8.789
Age	1.370***	1.389***	1.361***	1.330***	4.803
Education	1.007***	0.873**	1.134***	0.972*	3.213
Income 2	−1.131*	−1.174*	−1.122*	−1.073*	−2.253
Smile express	/	0.577***	/	0.626***	4.348
Eye gaze	/	/	0.504***	0.581***	3.625
Controls	included	included	included	included	/

Notes: (1) *** p < 0.001, ** p < 0.01, * p < 0.05. (2) The dependent variable is purchase intention.

4.5 Heterogeneity Test of Accumulated Effect

Table 4. GLMM of accumulated effect.

	Model 13	Model 14
Smile express	0.317*	0.74***
Eye gaze	0.433**	0.459**
Controls	included	included

Notes: (1) *** p < 0.001, ** p < 0.01, * p < 0.05. (2) The dependent variable is purchase intention. (3) Model 13 represents first half of the process, and Model 14 represents the second.

According to the data analysis results in Table 4, smile express has more significant impact on purchase intention in the latter part of the live streaming, supporting H3a and H3b.

4.6   Effects of Facial Cues on Attention

Table 5. GLMM of moderating effect.

Dependent variable	FAOI	PAOI	PPAOI
	Model 15	Model 16	Model 17
Intercept	−12.138***	1.770	2.213*
Smile express	1.251	0.294	−0.156
Eye gaze	−0.934	1.004**	−0.812***
Controls	included	included	included

Notes: (1) *** $p < 0.001$, ** $p < 0.01$, * $p < 0.05$. (2) The dependent variable is attention. (3) FAOI stands for Face Area of Interest, PAOI stands for Product Area of Interest, PPAOI stands for Product Pile Area of Interest.

According to the data analysis results in Table 5, eye gaze has significant positive effect on attention of the consumer, while smile has no significant impact, partially supporting H3a.

4.7   Effects of Attention on Purchase Intention

Table 6. GLMM of moderating effect.

Dependent variable	Purchase Intention	
	Model 18	t
Intercept	4.020***	4.037
F.C. Face	0.015*	2.012
F.C. Fruit	0.028*	2.304
F.C. Fruitpile	−0.020	−1.682
Controls	included	included

According to the data analysis results in Table 6 and 7, consumer's attention on streamer's face and fruit (the product) is positively related to the purchase intention. However, the attention on fruit pile (product pile which is below the interface) is negatively related to the purchase intention. The results partially support H3b.

Table 7. GLMM of moderating effect.

Dependent variable	Purchase Intention	
	Model 19	t
Intercept	5.341***	7.738
F.C. Face	0.011	0.447
F.C. Fruit	0.054*	2.096
F.C. Fruitpile	−0.126***	−3.983
Controls	included	included

Notes: (1) *** $p < 0.001$, ** $p < 0.01$, * $p < 0.05$. (2) The dependent variable is purchase intention. (3) Model 18 refers to fixation count, and Model 19 refers to visit count.

5 Discussion and Conclusion

5.1 Findings

Based on the S-O-R theory and the lens model theory, this study proposes a model to analyse the effects and mechanism of the role of facial cues (i.e., smile express and eye gaze) on purchase intention under live-streaming dynamic e-commerce situations. Through an experiment with eye tracking data the model is examined.

First, facial cues can directly influence the perception of consumers towards live-streaming and their purchase intention of commodities.

Second, the effects of facial cues varies from people to people as they differentiate from each other (age, gender, income level, etc.)

Finally, attention plays the intermediate underlying role in the mechanism. Facial cues can influence attention and the latter has impact on the purchase intention.

5.2 Implications

This study offers valuable theoretical insights. It analyzes facial cues, including smile express and eye gaze, as main effects during the dynamic interaction process. More specifically, consumption intensity and accumulated effects have differential influences on the mechanism of the main effects. Finally, attention, as a mediating variable, effectively explains the mechanism through which facial cues impact purchase intention.

This study also offers practical design and commercial strategies for live streaming. The findings guide streamers to interact with consumers in a more effective manner during e-commerce live broadcasts, including providing positive facial expressions and conveying emotions. Additionally, it offers insights for mobile live-streaming platforms to adjust strategies based on different consumer types and live-streaming stages. This includes focusing on the design of AOIs on the interface to attract consumer attention and ultimately increase purchase intention.

5.3   Limitations and Future Directions

In this study, the experimental component is incomplete. Currently, only information related to purchase intention has been collected, while consumer emotional perception has not been considered. Future research could incorporate the PAD (Pleasure-Arousal-Dominance) emotional model and audience emotion studies to better explain consumer perception.

Disclosure of Interests.   The authors have no competing interests to declare that are relevant to the content of this article.

References

1. Adams, R.B., Jr., Kleck, R.E.: Perceived gaze direction and the processing of facial displays of emotion. Psychol. Sci. **14**, 644–647 (2003)
2. Adams, R.B.J., Kleck, R.E.: Effects of direct and averted gaze on the perception of facially communicated emotion. Emotion **5**, 3–11 (2005)
3. Bayliss, A.P., Frischen, A., Fenske, M.J., Tipper, S.P.: Affective evaluations of objects are influenced by observed gaze direction and emotional expression. Cognition **104**, 644–653 (2007)
4. Ewing, L., Rhodes, G., Pellicano, E.: Have you got the look? Gaze direction affects judgements of facial attractiveness. Vis. Cogn. **18**, 321–330 (2010)
5. Friesen, C.K., Moore, C., Kingstone, A.: Does gaze direction really trigger a reflexive shift of spatial attention? Brain Cogn. **57**, 66–69 (2005)
6. Howard, D.J., Gengler, C.: Emotional contagion effects on product attitudes. J. Consum. Res. **28**, 189–201 (2001)
7. Jones, B.C., DeBruine, L.M., Little, A.C., Conway, C.A., Feinberg, D.R.: Integrating gaze direction and expression in preferences for attractive faces. Psychol. Sci. **17**, 588–591 (2006)
8. Kulczynski, A., Ilicic, J., Baxter, S.M.: When your source is smiling, consumers may automatically smile with you: investigating the source expressive display hypothesis. Psychol. Mark. **33**, 5–19 (2016)
9. Mason, M.F., Tatkow, E.P., Macrae, C.N.: The look of love: gaze shifts and person perception. Psychol. Sci. **16**, 236–239 (2005)
10. Rigato, S., Farroni, T.: The role of gaze in the processing of emotional facial expressions. Emot. Rev. **5**, 36–40 (2013)
11. Senju, A., Hasegawa, T.: Direct gaze captures visuospatial attention. Vis. Cogn. **12**, 127–144 (2005)
12. Soussignan, R., Schaal, B., Boulanger, V., Garcia, S., Jiang, T.: Emotional communication in the context of joint attention for food stimuli: effects on attentional and affective processing. Biol. Psychol. **104**, 173–183 (2015)
13. Verbeke, W., Pozharliev, R.: Preference inferences from eye-related cues in sales-consumer settings: ERP timing and localization in relation to inferring performance and oxytocin receptor (OXTR) gene polymorphisms. Int. J. Mark. Stud. **8**, 1 (2016)
14. Wang, Z., Mao, H.F., Li, Y.J., Liu, F.: Smile big or not? Effects of smile intensity on perceptions of warmth and competence. J. Consum. Res. **43**, 787–805 (2017)
15. Liu, J., Zhao, J.: Nonverbal communication of dual anchors in live streaming and its effects on sales. J. Retail. Consum. Serv. **81**, 103972 (2024)

16. D'Ambrogio, S., Werksman, N., Platt, M.L., Johnson, E.N.: How celebrity status and gaze direction in ads drive visual attention to shape consumer decisions. Psychol. Mark. **40**, 723–734 (2023)
17. Yu, Y.-W., Ji, H.-Y., Wang, L., Jiang, Y.: The influences of eye gaze cues on cognitive processing of object and its mechanisms. Prog. Biochem. Biophys. **47**(11), 1145–1161 (2020)
18. Zhang, N., Fan, X., He, L., Cheng, X., Zhang, L., Liu, R.: The impact of the seller's facial image on consumer purchase behavior in peer-to-peer accommodation platforms. J. Retail. Consum. Serv. **80**, 103932 (2024)
19. Shi, R., Wang, M., Qiao, T., Shang, J.: The effects of live streamer's facial attractiveness and product type on consumer purchase intention: an exploratory study with eye tracking technology. Behav. Sci. **14**(5), 375 (2024)
20. Zhu, H., Zhou, Y., Wu, Y., Wang, X.: To smile or not to smile: the role of facial expression valence on mundane and luxury products premiumness. J. Retail. Consum. Serv. **65**, 102861 (2022)
21. Posner, M.I.: Orienting of attention. Q. J. Exp. Psychol. **32**(1), 3–25 (1980)

Designing a Multimodal Wearable System for Real-Time Spinal Health Monitoring and Gamified Posture Correction

Enyang Wang and Zichao Nie[✉]

School of New Media Art and Design, Beihang University, Beijing, China
`zichao_nie@buaa.edu.cn`

Abstract. Sedentary behavior and spinal health issues are caused by poor postures. It has become a global public health challenge. This paper integrates to the Fogg Behavior Model (FBM) with spinal biomechanical monitoring technology to explore and design a health digital product service system. It aims to correct and remind users of their sitting postures and enable them to use it continuously, thus ultimately improving their spinal health status. In the first phase, this study proposes a multimodal wearable system that integrates flexible sensing, augmented reality (AR), and gamification design to achieve full-cycle spinal health management. At the hardware level, the system employs a four-node distributed flexible sensor patch network, covering key regions including the cervical, thoracic, lumbar, and sacral vertebrae. The software layer constructs a dynamic 3D spinal model with 24 degrees of freedom and combines AR camera-based recognition. In the second phase, this study recruited 6 long-term sedentary participants to evaluate the designed spinal health system. The objective of the SUS test is to measure users' satisfaction towards this system. Then, the open-ended interview aims to comprehensively understand the root causes of its challenges and strengths. Therefore, through multimodal data fusion and immersive interaction design, this study establishes a new paradigm for spinal health management in home settings.

Keywords: Spine health · Health monitoring · gamification · multimodal · wearable devices

1 Introduction

In modern society, sedentary behaviors and poor postures have become global public health issues threatening people's spinal health. According to World Health Organization statistics, approximately 60% of the global adult population sits for over 8 h per day, leading to a year-on-year increase in spinal-related disease incidence [1]. For instance, 75% of urban office workers in China suffer from cervical or lumbar strain symptoms, with 30% developing chronic pain that significantly reduces quality of life and work efficiency. Spinal issues not only cause localized pain but also correlate strongly with systemic diseases including cardiovascular conditions and metabolic syndrome [2]. Existing study indicates that prolonged spinal misalignment increases degenerative disc disease risk by 4.2-fold, while adolescent scoliosis prevalence has risen from 1.5% in 2000 to 5.7% in 2025 [3], highlighting the urgency for early monitoring and intervention.

Current spinal health management technologies face plenty of limitations. Traditional diagnostics relying on specialized medical equipment like X-rays or MRI suffer from radiation exposure, high costs, and inability for real-time monitoring [4]. Clinical studies reveal patients receive only 1–2 imaging examinations annually on average, insufficient for capturing dynamic postural changes. Meanwhile, emerging wearable devices (e.g., Lumo Lift) primarily use single accelerometers for posture monitoring, lacking comprehensive assessment of multi-segmental vertebral angles and muscle status, resulting in inadequate feedback precision. Health management apps like "Seer-Health" [5] can record exercise data but employ 2D charts for visualization, failing to intuitively present 3D spinal morphology, with hardware interaction limited to basic Bluetooth data transmission without closed-loop intervention.

In order to address these challenges, this study proposes the FBM theory based multimodal wearable system called *Back Align*. This system integrates flexible sensor arrays, AR interaction, and gamified rehabilitation modules to achieve full-cycle spinal health management. The system incorporates four flexible sensor patches strategically positioned across the cervical, thoracic, lumbar, sacral, and coccygeal vertebrae. These patches enable real-time collection of vertebral angle deviations and electromyographic signals. Collected data is wirelessly transmitted via Bluetooth to a dedicated application, which then processes the inputs to construct dynamic 3D spinal models. Users achieve precise device positioning through AR wear guidance using smartphone camera recognition of anatomical landmarks, with the system triggering vibration or visual alerts based on real-time data to form a "perception-feedback-correction" closed loop. During rehabilitation, *Back Align* maps posture correction movements to augmented reality tasks. For example, users activate core muscles through "virtual balance ball" tasks while the system analyzes muscle activation patterns and provides real-time scores.

This study integrates multi-node flexible sensing with AR wear assistance to address usability challenges in medical device design. By proposing a bidirectional "physiological data-gamified task" mapping mechanism, the research overcomes unidirectional data display limitations prevalent in existing health applications. This innovative approach reduces reliance on specialized medical resources by alleviating pressures on public health systems, thereby offering feasible early intervention strategies for adolescent scoliosis.

2 Related Work

2.1 Wearable Device Applications in Spinal Health Monitoring

Wearable devices can be applied in rehabilitation assessment, including functional evaluation, activities of daily living, gait analysis, and other aspects. In the field of rehabilitation assessment, the technological applications of wearable devices show diversified development trends. For example, the sensor glove developed by Bianchi et al. [6] can capture multi-dimensional hand joint motion trajectories to achieve high-precision dynamic assessment of hand function in stroke patients, providing data support for personalized rehabilitation plans. For lower limb rehabilitation, the study [7]embedded flexible pressure sensors into insoles to monitor plantar pressure distribution during gait cycles in real time, combined with algorithmic analysis of abnormal force patterns. The results showed it significantly improves the targeting of gait correction training. Additionally, the multimodal wearable system designed by Lester et al. [8] can accurately identify 8 types of daily activity patterns including sitting, walking, and stair climbing, demonstrating over 90% action classification accuracy in clinical validation with 12 patients. In upper limb functional quantitative assessment, Patel et al. [9] innovatively utilized arm-worn accelerometers to collect motion data, parsing performance in core tasks of the Wolf Functional Ability Scale (FAS) through machine learning models, ultimately achieving automated prediction of FAS total scores while reducing subjective bias in manual assessments.

Advances in sensor technology provide new possibilities for spinal health monitoring, particularly through combined applications of Inertial Measurement Units (IMUs) and surface electromyography (sEMG) sensors. IMU sensors combining accelerometers, gyroscopes, and magnetometers can capture real-time spinal posture changes [10]. For instance, studies show IMU sensors achieve $\pm 2°$ precision in detecting lumbar flexion angles, but errors increase significantly during dynamic movements or multi-segment spinal monitoring. sEMG sensors supplement spinal stability assessments by detecting muscle electrical activity [11]. However, existing technologies still face limitations in multimodal data fusion, struggling to simultaneously achieve high-precision posture monitoring and muscle state analysis.

Commercial products like Lumo Lift and UPRIGHT GO have achieved partial success in posture correction but exhibit significant interaction design flaws. Lumo Lift monitors upper back posture through a single sensor with vibration feedback, but its simplistic feedback mechanism cannot differentiate deviations across spinal segments [10]. Moreover, these devices typically lack personalized adaptation features, requiring manual threshold adjustments that impair user experience [12]. For example, a user study found over 60% of users discontinued Lumo Lift usage within one week, primarily due to excessive non-targeted feedback [13].

2.2 Gamification Design and Chronic Disease Rehabilitation

The application of gamification design in chronic disease rehabilitation has gained increasing attention, with its core mechanism being behavior modification through incentive systems. The FBM provides theoretical support for gamification design, proposing that behavior change relies on the synergy of Motivation, Ability, and Triggers [14]. For instance, in spinal rehabilitation scenarios, gamification can enhance user motivation through virtual rewards (e.g., points, badges), reduce ability thresholds via simplified task designs (e.g., phased movement training), and ultimately trigger behavioral changes through real-time feedback (e.g., vibration alerts) [15].

Existing research demonstrates that gamification has significantly improved in terms of user compliance. Marley et al. (2022) conducted a randomized controlled trial with post-shoulder-surgery patients. This study finds that gamified rehabilitation using the Kinect MIRA system achieved good therapeutic effects in joint mobility and functional recovery compared to the conventional physical therapy. More than this, the system reduced physiotherapist workload [16]. Selles et al. (2024) evaluated supervised versus unsupervised gamified exercise programs for non-communicable chronic disease patients. It shows supervised gamified interventions significantly improved physical activity levels [17]. An augmented reality-based spinal rehabilitation application increased users' average daily training duration from 7 to 18 min by mapping posture correction movements to virtual game tasks. However, most existing gamified health applications rely on abstract task designs without deep integration with physiological data, leading to declining user engagement over time [18]. For example, users might achieve high game scores without actual spinal health improvements, weakening gamification's long-term effectiveness.

3 System Design

This study specifically targets long-term sedentary individuals with prolonged computer exposure who experience spinal compression susceptibility, requiring regular monitoring, postural adjustment, and preventive care. Accordingly, we have established a tripartite framework integrating "hardware sensing - software analytics - behavioral intervention".

3.1 Game-Based Closed-Loop Design Framework

The behavioral intervention mechanism of this system is based on the three elements (i.e., Motivation, Ability, Trigger) of the FBM [14], constructing a "physiological signal-driven gamified closed-loop" design framework (see Fig. 1), which transforms spinal health management into quantifiable, incentivized behavioral interventions.

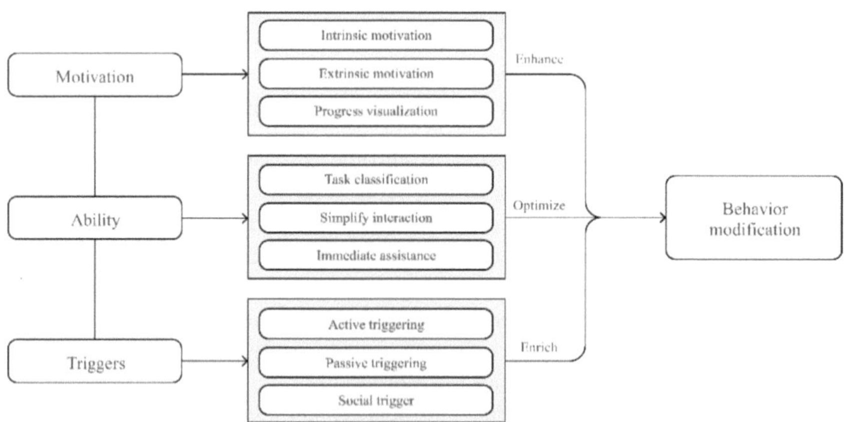

Fig. 1. Gamified closed-loop design framework based on Fogg Behavior Model.

When sensors detect spinal deviations exceeding safety thresholds, the system initiates the following intervention process:

In terms of motivation enhancement, users can view real-time 3D spinal models in the APP, with abnormal regions highlighted in red and annotated with specific deviation angles and duration. When daily cumulative poor posture exceeds 1 h, the system automatically generates health reports highlighting high-risk areas (e.g., "Excessive cervical abnormalities this week") and recommends targeted AR training tasks. By converting posture correction into engaging experiences through AR immersive tasks, users accumulate energy values by maintaining ideal postures to unlock virtual rewards (skins, badges), while social binding functions enable achievement sharing and external incentives. Long-term trend charts visually display spinal health improvement percentages to enhance user self-efficacy.

Regarding ability optimization, the system records users' daily posture data to display long-term improvement effects through trend charts. Task difficulty is dynamically graded based on user historical data, progressing from maintaining postures for 5 s to 30 s. For consistently well-performing users, the system gradually increases challenge difficulty. AR wear guidance automatically calibrates sensor positions and intelligently adjusts vibration feedback intensity to simplify interactions. Dynamic correction animations provide instant assistance when detecting abnormal postures.

The trigger mechanism combines multimodal strategies: hardware patches activate vibration alerts of varying intensities based on posture deviation severity (see Fig. 2). For example, mild bending (e.g., lumbar flexion $>5°$) triggers 1-s low-frequency vibration (similar to gentle tapping), while sustained worsening postures ($>10°$ or duration >2 min) switch to high-frequency vibrations requiring immediate adjustment. Tests show this graded vibration mechanism accelerates posture correction by 40% compared to traditional single-mode systems.

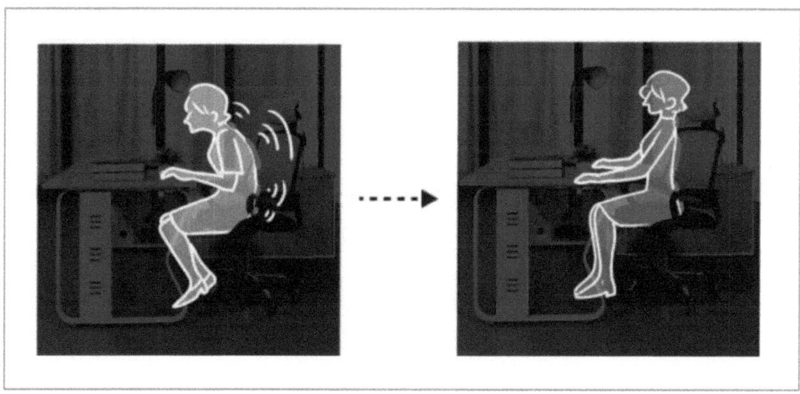

Fig. 2. Behavioral intervention schematic.

For extreme risks (e.g., daily abnormal duration exceeding 3 h), the system enforces APP pop-up alerts and suggests online doctor consultation. Users can bind family/friend accounts - after multiple unheeded alerts, the system sends anonymous prompts (e.g., "Their cervical spine has worked continuously for 2 h - remind them to rest!") leveraging social reinforcement.

Through these designs, the system combines immediate alerts with long-term incentives, helping users transition from passive acceptance to active management for sustainable spinal health improvement.

3.2 Hardware Design

At the hardware level, this project designs a wearable intelligent spinal health monitoring device based on four-zone multi-node sensing technology (see Figs. 3 and 4).

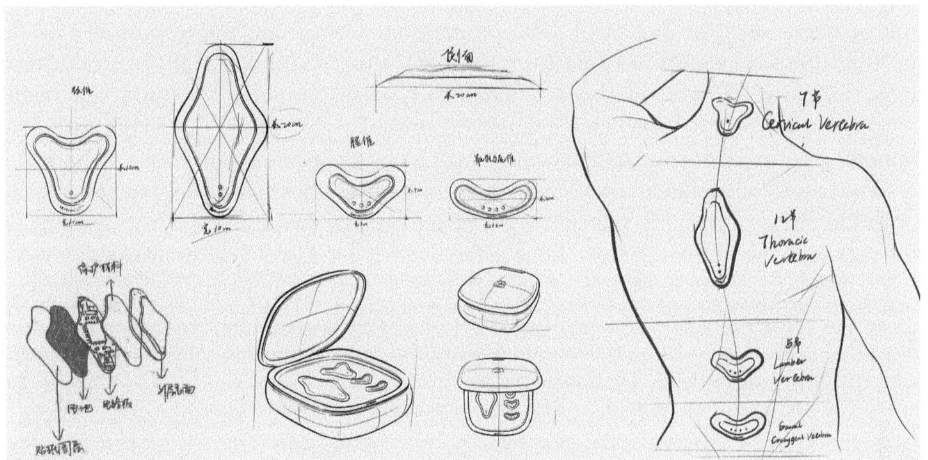

Fig. 3. Product design sketch.

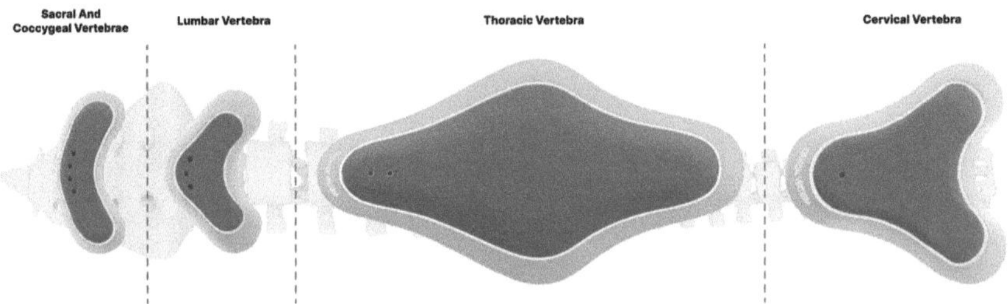

Fig. 4. Product appearance.

Building upon existing research on wearable devices, this study has identified four essential product characteristics: operational convenience, population adaptability, material sustainability, and wearing comfort.

Regarding operational convenience, hydrogel-based adhesion enables easy device attachment/detachment to the user's skin surface, with AR-assisted positioning guidance ensuring correct placement. For population adaptability, considering the varying spinal lengths across different age groups, full-wrap spinal detectors would cause size mismatches and measurement errors. Therefore, segmented detection modules are adopted, thereby allowing broader application across populations with different spinal lengths and improving measurement accuracy, with the wearable positioning as shown in Fig. 5.

In terms of material sustainability, this characteristic is manifested through reusable sensor stickers, durable silicone outer layers with extended lifespan, recyclable components, and the biodegradable hydrogel inner layer that enhances product sustainability.

For wearing comfort, the detector surface employs soft silicone materials to improve comfort during daily reclining activities. The hydrogel inner layer demonstrates excellent biocompatibility with human skin, effectively reducing skin irritation and allergic reactions, thereby enhancing user experience and comfort. To ensure hygiene, the hydrogel layer supports peelable replacement, allowing users to periodically replace the hydrogel adhesive.

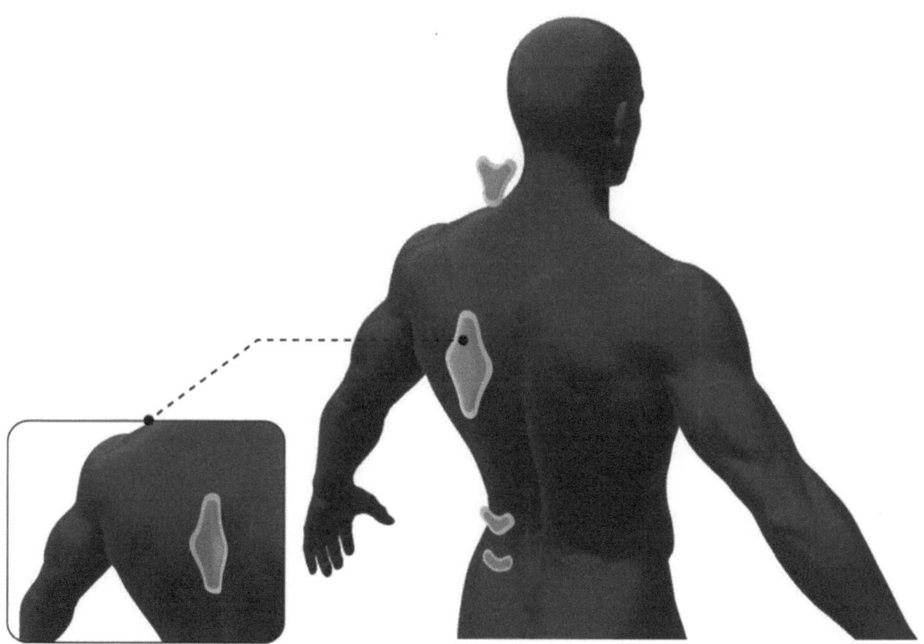

Fig. 5. Wearable positioning schematic.

The product adopts a four-node distributed architecture, integrating triaxial MEMS accelerometers (± 8 g range), flexible piezoresistive sensors (0–50kPa detection range), and dual-channel sEMG modules (1 kHz sampling rate). Cervical and lumbar nodes add gyroscopes (LSM6DSO, $\pm 2°$ accuracy) for 3D pose estimation, with ergonomic mesh layouts covering paraspinal muscle trajectories (see Fig. 6).

The hardware implements graded vibration strategies: low-frequency (3 Hz/0.5 G) for posture reminders, high-frequency pulses (15 Hz/1.2 G) for emergency alerts. BLE 5.2 enables multi-device synchronization (<15 ms latency), automatically switching to

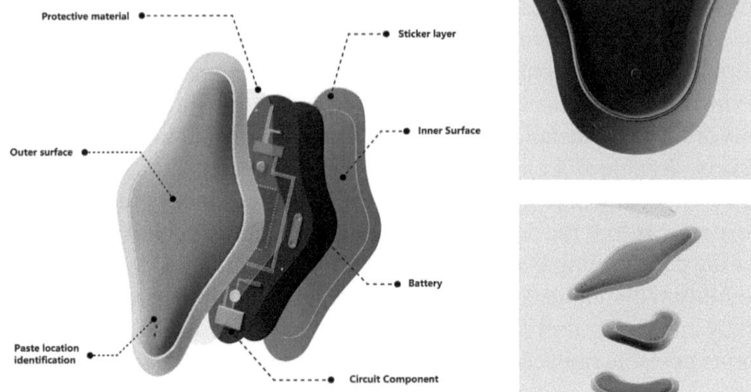

Fig. 6. Exploded view.

redundant transmission when packet loss exceeds 5%. Continuous operation achieves 72-h runtime per node (100 ms sampling interval).

A dedicated storage case (see Fig. 7) enables wireless charging and organized storage, solving uneven charging across multiple devices.

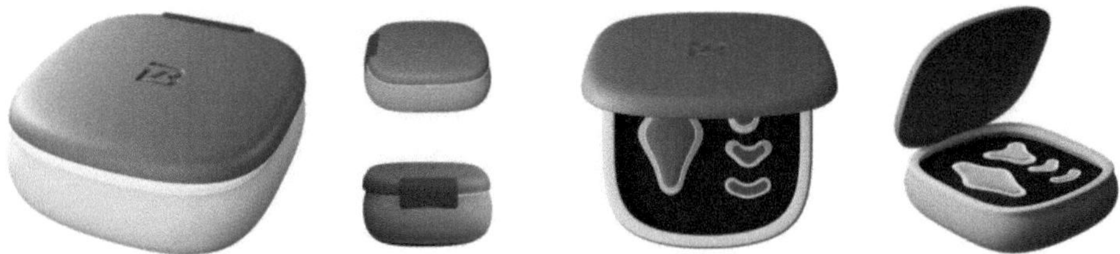

Fig. 7. Storage case design.

3.3 Software Design

Unity-engine-developed inverse kinematics algorithms map sensor data to a standard 24-DOF spinal model. Marching Cubes algorithm enables surface reconstruction with real-time visualization (30 fps refresh rate) of axial rotation/lateral flexion angles. User testing shows $\pm 1.8°$ lumbar lordosis reconstruction error, meeting clinical visualization requirements.

Three-tier risk thresholds:

Level 1 ($>5°$ deviation triggers vibration)
Level 2 (>10 min abnormality triggers APP notification)
Level 3 (>2 h daily cumulative abnormality activates emergency contact alerts)

Personalized regimens use LSTM networks analyzing behavioral patterns, dynamically adjusting training intensity per WHO rehabilitation guidelines (test set RMSE = 0.37, 45% better than traditional regression).

The APP employs flat navigation (see Fig. 8) with core modules:

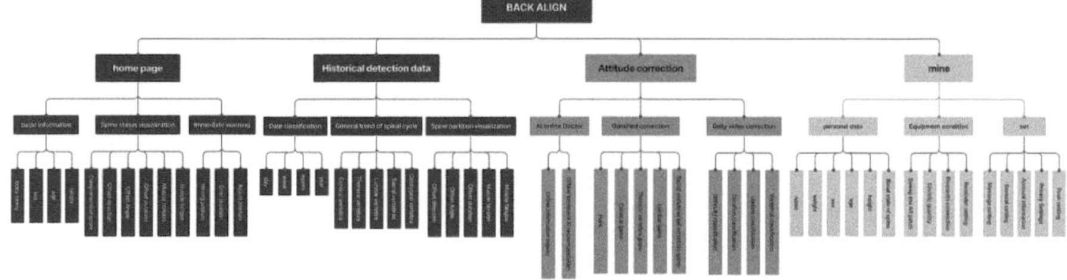

Fig. 8. Information architecture.

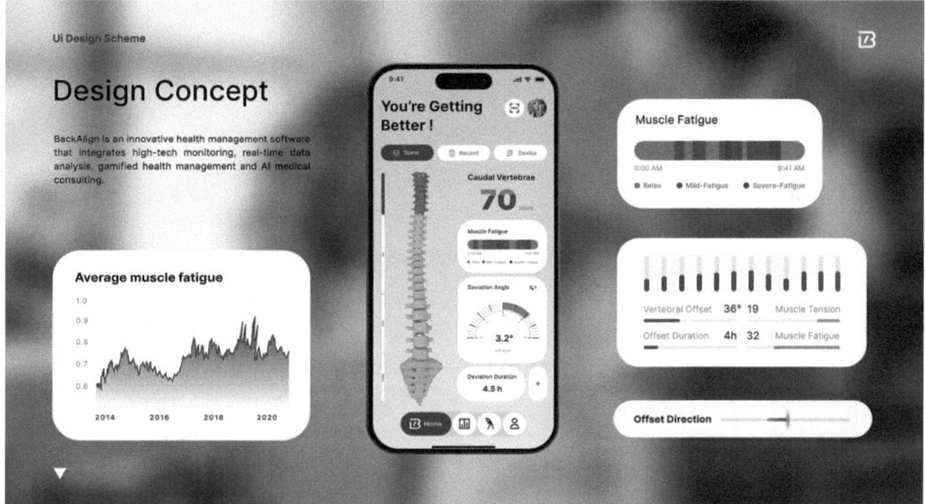

Fig. 9. APP homepage interface.

The homepage displays real-time vertebral deviation angles and electromyographic (EMG) signals, captured by four flexible sensor patches positioned across the cervical, thoracic, lumbar, sacral, and coccygeal regions. These data are transmitted via Bluetooth to the APP, where a real-time 3D spinal model is constructed (see Figs. 9 and 10). Users can click to view detailed nodal data, including scores, peripheral muscle fatigue levels, deviation angles, and duration. The model supports 360° rotational viewing. The system also features an instant warning function, which triggers pop-up alerts on mobile devices when prolonged poor postures are detected, prompting immediate adjustments. Users can view warning frequency statistics and contextual summaries per spinal partition, enabling targeted behavioral modifications based on visualized poor posture data, while managing vibration alert preferences and exercise mode switching (see Fig. 11). Prior to APP usage, Bluetooth pairing ensures device-mobile data synchronization. The mobile terminal utilizes a U-Net architecture-based image segmentation network to identify the user's sacral triangular area and inferior scapular angles, generating a 3D spatial coordinate system for patch positioning. AR wear guidance (via smartphone camera detection of anatomical landmarks) ensures precise device placement, integrating multi-node flexible sensing with AR-assisted positioning (see Figs. 12 and 13).

Fig. 10. APP interface effects.

Fig. 11. Alert pop-ups, homepage, reminder log, device management.

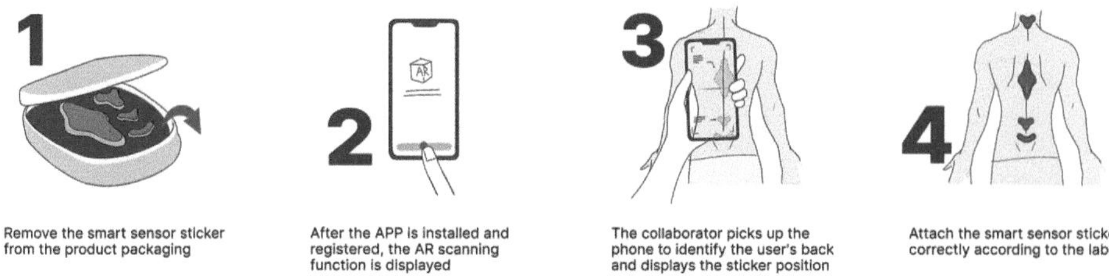

Fig. 12. AR wear guidance.

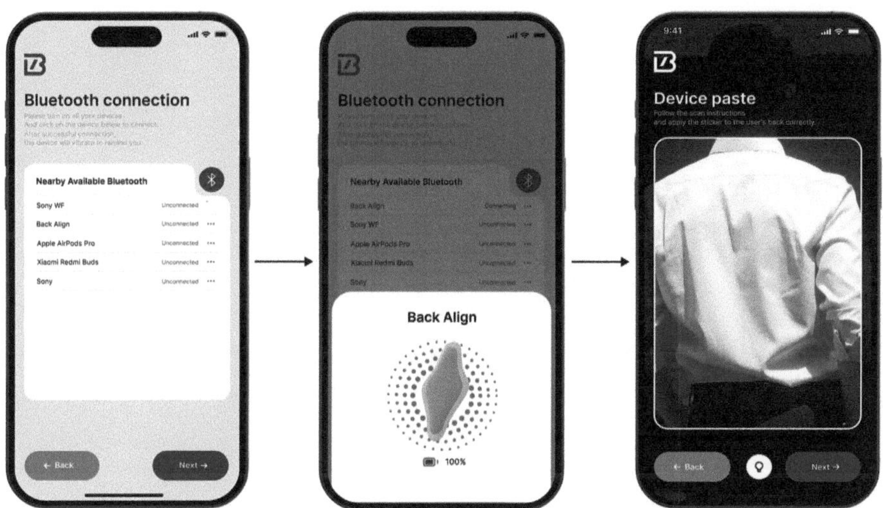

Fig. 13. Bluetooth connection & AR recognition.

For historical data analysis, the system provides multi-dimensional visualizations of spinal deviation data across daily/weekly/monthly/annual periods through trend charts, bar graphs, and radar charts, generating personalized spinal health reports tailored to user-specific conditions. These reports employ graded assessments and diverse data analytics to visually communicate spinal issues (see Fig. 14).

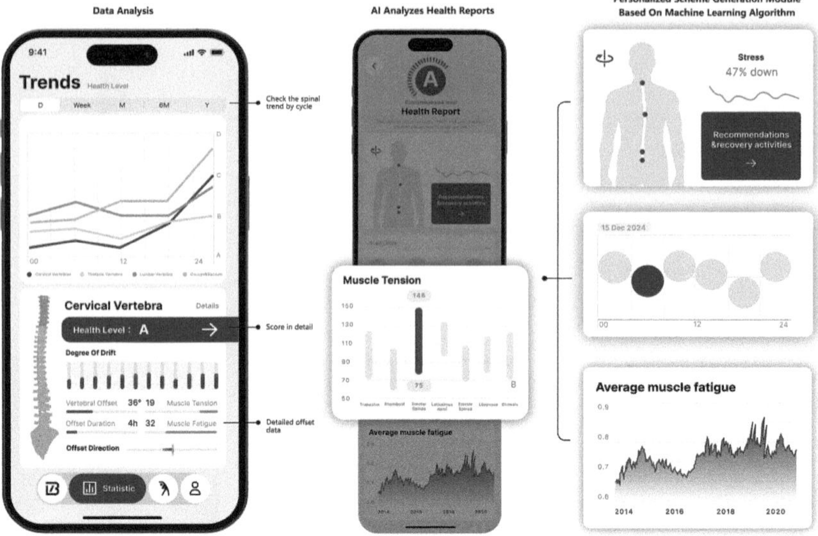

Fig. 14. Data analysis & AI health reports.

Fig. 15. Game-based correction interface.

Regarding posture correction, the system incorporates gamified correction modules, AI online consultation, and instructional videos. Within the gamified correction module, users can perform targeted training for specific spinal regions (see Fig. 15).

Additionally, the system features an "Spinal Balance Force Field" augmented reality game where users maintain virtual cursors in target zones (corresponding to ideal postures), converting sEMG signal intensity into energy values to drive gameplay. A gradient reward strategy is implemented - 5 consecutive successes unlock premium skins - establishing a positive reinforcement loop aligned with the Fogg Behavior Model.

4 Evaluation and Results

4.1 Participants

Usability evaluation is an important assessment method to validate the functionality of a product or system [19]. To assess the usability of the system interface, a total of six undergraduates were recruited to participate in quantitative test and qualitative interviews. In quantitative study, the System Usability Scale (SUS) questionnaire [20–22] was chosen to test the usability of designed product service system and understand users' perceptions. In qualitative study, the interview method was used to comprehensively understand the root causes of its challenges and strengths. The participants, aged 20–22, consisted of three males and three females. None of the participants had a history of severe spinal diseases but occasionally experienced spinal discomfort due to prolonged sitting in their daily study and life. All participants were first-time to use this system.

4.2 Study Design

These six participants completed usability evaluation and open-ended interview. In the beginning, the researcher gave informed consent form to every participant and a short introduction of this product service system, including test purpose, content, and research objectives. After that, each participant watched a roughly 3-min video on the background of product service system design. Subsequently, the researcher invite six participants to use the system and complete the SUS questionnaire. Besides, a follow-up interview was additionally posed to the participants to collect indepth understanding of this system.

To assess users' acceptance of the system, we used the SUS (System Usability Scale) questionnaire to verify the availability of the system. This questionnaire has become a primary measurement tool in many fields and industries. Each participant completed the questionnaire after operating the system's core functions. The SUS questionnaire includes the following 10 items:

1. I think that I would like to use this system frequently.
2. I found the system unnecessarily complex.
3. I thought the system was easy to use.
4. I think that I would need the support of a technical person to be able to use this system.
5. I found the various functions in this system were well integrated.
6. I thought there was too much inconsistency in this system.

7. I would imagine that most people would learn to use this system very quickly.
8. I found the system very cumbersome to use.
9. I felt very confident using the system.
10. I needed to learn a lot of things before I could get going with this system.

The SUS employs a Likert Scale [23] to measure the degree of agreement for each item. The scale has five levels: 5 points for "Strongly Agree," 4 for "Agree," 3 for "Neutral," 2 for "Disagree," and 1 for "Strongly Disagree." Scoring was conducted after participants completed the system operation.

To compensate for the limitations of quantitative data, we incorporated two open-ended interview questions designed to elicit in-depth, multidimensional investigations. The open-ended questions were designed to understand what and why the participants "like" or "do not like" the functions and interactions in this spinal health management system.

4.3 Results

1. SUS results

Odd-numbered items are positive statements, while even-numbered items are negative statements. The score for odd-numbered items is calculated as "participant's score − 1," and the score for even-numbered items is "5 − participant's score." After calculating the score for each item, all scores are summed and multiplied by 2.5 to obtain the overall score. The SUS results are shown in Table 1 and Fig. 16.

Table 1. Game-based correction interface.

	Q1	Q2	Q3	Q4	Q5	Q6	Q7	Q8	Q9	Q10
P1	3	2	3	2	3	1	3	3	4	3
P2	4	2	4	2	5	3	3	2	3	2
P3	3	2	4	3	4	2	3	3	2	2
P4	5	2	4	1	5	2	4	1	5	2
P5	5	2	4	1	5	1	4	2	4	2
P6	5	1	5	2	4	1	5	2	4	1

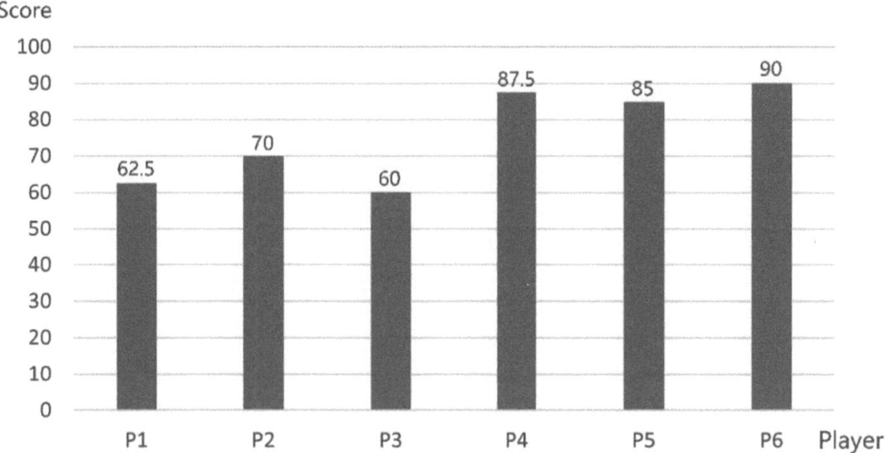

Fig. 16. SUS scores of 6 participants.

The average SUS score from the six participants in this experiment was 75.83. According to Cunha's (2010) research, an SUS score above 80 indicates user satisfaction, while below 60 reflects dissatisfaction [24]. The results demonstrate strong overall usability, with most participants finding the system easy to use and well-integrated.

2. Qualitative interview results

For qualitative analysis, we used thematic analysis [25] method to analyse users' responses. In this analysis approach, the researcher followed six steps:1) Familiarizing yourself with your data; 2) Generating initial codes; 3) Searching for themes; 4) Reviewing themes; 5) Defining and naming themes; 6) Producing the report.

Users' positive evaluations of the system were found to focus primarily on three themes: 1) Functional Design; 2) Interactive Experience; 3) Social Features.

In the Functional Design theme, most users highly appreciated the system's modular integration and data visualization. As Participant 2 said, "When I click into the upper spine section, I can immediately see which areas have problems," indicating that the system's information architecture aligns well with users' cognitive logic. The personalized correction feature also received widespread praise, with Participant 1 particularly expressed "ability to provide targeted solutions for specific issues,". It means that precision services effectively enhance user experience.

Regarding to Interactive Experience theme, the system's real-time feedback mechanism was widely affirmed. Multiple participants highlighted the value of the vibration alert function, with Participant 5 stating, "Poor spinal posture is often subconscious, and the vibration feedback provides timely reminders," underscoring the unique advantage of tactile feedback in posture correction scenarios. However, some users pointed out that key functions were not sufficiently prominent in the interface, as Participant 6 suggested, "Important features could be more emphasized," revealing room for improvement in the current information hierarchy design.

In the end, the Social Features theme uncovered gamification elements elicited positive responses. Participant 3 remarked, "The challenge-based design makes me maintain better posture," and proposed adding a "leaderboard module" to enhance social interaction, offering clear directions for future system expansion. Nevertheless, Participant 1 and Participant 3 both expressed concerns about privacy during device wear, particularly the need for "assistance from others during scanning," highlighting the need to strike a better balance between usability and privacy protection.

Based on an analysis of the SUS respondents expressing what and why dissatisfaction with the designed system, two themes emerged. The lower scores from Participant 1 and Participant 3 highlight areas for improvement: 1) Privacy considerations: Enhance the convenience of wearable device usage; 2) Improved feature discoverability: Increase visibility of key functions (e.g., enlarging buttons for zone-specific spinal status checks). Future iterations will address these issues alongside the subjective feedback to improve universality.

5   Discussion

The multimodal wearable system BackAlign proposed in this study establishes a novel "physiological signal-gaming task-behavior correction" closed-loop interaction paradigm through the deep integration of flexible sensing, AR interaction, and gamification design, providing a new technological approach for spinal health management. This breakthrough overcomes the limitation of unidirectional data transmission in traditional health monitoring devices.

Compared with existing technologies, the system achieves breakthroughs in three key aspects: Firstly, it employs a distributed flexible sensor array to synchronously capture spinal posture and electromyographic signals, addressing the accuracy limitations of traditional single inertial measurement unit solutions in multi-segment dynamic monitoring [5, 11], enabling real-time 3D visualization of spinal movements in daily scenarios. Secondly, the four-node distributed architecture ensures full spinal coverage while avoiding the sizing compatibility issues of fully-enclosed devices [12], making it particularly suitable for dynamic monitoring needs in adolescent scoliosis cases. The AR-assisted wear guidance solves device positioning challenges in home settings, significantly lowering the user threshold. Furthermore, the closed-loop intervention framework based on Fogg's Behavior Model [14] dynamically binds physiological data with gamified tasks, establishing a new design paradigm to address user retention issues in health applications.

However, the system still faces critical challenges: On one hand, as noted by Marley et al. regarding gamification incentive decay [16], some users (P1, P3) in this study questioned the long-term effectiveness of incentives, suggesting the need to optimize graded reward strategies. On the other hand, privacy concerns during device wear, such as "requiring assistance from others for scanning," reflect the trust challenges in personal informatics systems as proposed by Li et al. [12].

While theoretically feasible, the system requires long-term user studies to validate the persistence of behavioral intervention effects, with particular attention needed on the decay cycle of gamification incentive mechanisms.

6 Conclusion

Addressing the lack of real-time monitoring and insufficient user compliance in spinal health management, this study proposes Back Align, a wearable system integrating flexible sensing, AR interaction, and gamification design. The system employs a four-node distributed sensor array for synchronous multi-segment posture and sEMG signal acquisition, constructs dynamic 3D spinal models using inverse kinematics algorithms, and establishes a gamified closed-loop framework based on the Fogg Behavior Model, contributing an interdisciplinary framework to wearable health system behavioral intervention theory. Hardware-wise, hydrogel patches with silicone composite structures balance wearing comfort and signal acquisition precision; software-wise, AR spatial positioning and augmented reality game tasks translate complex medical knowledge into intuitive interactions. Focusing on daily spinal health management, this study proposes a closed-loop intervention model driven by multimodal data, designs low-invasive wearable devices with AR-assisted positioning solutions, and creates a dynamic mapping mechanism between physiological signals and gamified tasks. These innovations address industry pain points of low compliance and provide novel design pathways to reduce societal healthcare burdens caused by spinal disorders.

Acknowledgments. The interface design for spinal health application in this study were jointly accomplished by Wang Enyang, Zheng Chenyue, Pan Yiran and Zhu Zirui. Nie Zichao is the supervisor of this design work. This work was supported by the National Natural Science Foundation of China under Grant [No. 72204021].

References

1. Bull, F.C., et al.: World Health Organization 2020 guidelines on physical activity and sedentary behaviour. Br. J. Sports Med. **54**, 1451–1462 (2020)
2. Hartvigsen, J., et al.: What low back pain is and why we need to pay attention. Lancet **391**, 2356–2367 (2018)
3. Weinstein, S.L., Dolan, L.A., Cheng, J.C., Danielsson, A., Morcuende, J.A.: Adolescent idiopathic scoliosis. Lancet **371**, 1527–1537 (2008)
4. Brinjikji, W., et al.: Systematic literature review of imaging features of spinal degeneration in asymptomatic populations. Am. J. Neuroradiol. **36**, 811–816 (2015)
5. WAYNEED. https://www.seer-health.com/. Accessed 27 Mar 2025
6. Bianchi, M., et al.: Exploiting hand kinematic synergies and wearable under-sensing for hand functional grasp recognition. In: 2014 4th International Conference on Wireless Mobile Communication and Healthcare-Transforming Healthcare Through Innovations in Mobile and Wireless Technologies (MOBIHEALTH), pp. 168–171. IEEE (2014)
7. Jin, M., Ding, X., Gan, Y., Yang, X.: Research and development of wearable plantar pressure test technology. Text. J. **32**, 145–148 (2011). https://doi.org/10.13475/j.fzxb.2011.01.027
8. A practical approach to recognizing physical activities - Google Scholar. https://scholar.goo gle.com/scholar?hl=zh-CN&as_sdt=0%2C5&q=A+practical+approach+to+recognizing+ physical+activities+%7C+proceedings+of+the+4th+international+conference+on+pervas ive+computing&btnG=. Accessed 27 Mar 2025
9. Patel, S., et al.: A novel approach to monitor rehabilitation outcomes in stroke survivors using wearable technology. Proc. IEEE **98**, 450–461 (2010)

10. Shull, P.B., Jirattigalachote, W., Hunt, M.A., Cutkosky, M.R., Delp, S.L.: Quantified self and human movement: a review on the clinical impact of wearable sensing and feedback for gait analysis and intervention. Gait Posture **40**, 11–19 (2014)
11. Sibson, B.E., Banks, J.J., Yawar, A., Yegian, A.K., Anderson, D.E., Lieberman, D.E.: Using inertial measurement units to estimate spine joint kinematics and kinetics during walking and running. Sci. Rep. **14**, 234 (2024)
12. Li, I., Dey, A., Forlizzi, J.: A stage-based model of personal informatics systems. In: Proceedings of the SIGCHI Conference on Human Factors in Computing Systems, Atlanta Georgia, USA, pp. 557–566. ACM (2010). https://doi.org/10.1145/1753326.1753409
13. Consolvo, S., et al.: Activity sensing in the wild: a field trial of UbiFit garden. In: Proceedings of the SIGCHI Conference on Human Factors in Computing Systems, Florence, Italy, pp. 1797–1806. ACM (2008). https://doi.org/10.1145/1357054.1357335
14. Fogg, B.: A behavior model for persuasive design. In: Proceedings of the 4th International Conference on Persuasive Technology, Claremont, California, USA, pp. 1–7. ACM (2009). https://doi.org/10.1145/1541948.1541999
15. Klasnja, P., Pratt, W.: Healthcare in the pocket: mapping the space of mobile-phone health interventions. J. Biomed. Inform. **45**, 184–198 (2012)
16. Marley, W.D., Barratt, A., Pigott, T., Granat, M., Wilson, J.D., Roy, B.: A multicenter randomized controlled trial comparing gamification with remote monitoring against standard rehabilitation for patients after arthroscopic shoulder surgery. J. Shoulder Elbow Surg. **31**, 8–16 (2022)
17. Selles, W.L., Santos, E.C., Romero, B.D., Lunardi, A.C.: Effectiveness of gamified exercise programs on the level of physical activity in adults with chronic diseases: a systematic review. Disabil. Rehabil. **46**, 6231–6239 (2024). https://doi.org/10.1080/09638288.2024.2323614
18. Lupton, D.: Health promotion in the digital era: a critical commentary. Health Promot. Int. **30**, 174–183 (2014)
19. Kushniruk, A.: Evaluation in the design of health information systems: application of approaches emerging from usability engineering. Comput. Biol. Med. **32**, 141–149 (2002)
20. Brooke, J.: SUS: a retrospective. J. Usability Stud. **8**(2), 29–40 (2013)
21. Lewis, J.R.: The system usability scale: past, present, and future. Int. J. Hum. Comput. Interact. **34**, 577–590 (2018). https://doi.org/10.1080/10447318.2018.1455307
22. Brooke, J.: SUS-A quick and dirty usability scale. In: Usability Evaluation in Industry, vol. 189, pp. 4–7 (1996)
23. Likert, R.: A technique for the measurement of attitudes. Arch. Psychol. (1932)
24. Cunha, M.L.C.: Redes sociais dirigidas ao contexto das coisas. Pontifícia Universidade Católica, Rio de Janeiro (2010)
25. Braun, V., Clarke, V.: Using thematic analysis in psychology. Qual. Res. Psychol. **3**, 77–101 (2006). https://doi.org/10.1191/1478088706qp063oa

Tackling South Africa's Literacy Crisis with Local Technologies

Ilana Wilken[(✉)] and Laurette Marais

Council for Scientific and Industrial Research, Pretoria, South Africa
{iwilken,lmarais}@csir.co.za

Abstract. There are 12 official languages in South Africa, and a recent international study sent shockwaves through the country's education community by revealing that more than eight out of ten Grade 4 learners cannot read for basic meaning in their home language. Without this essential skill, South African learners are deprived of the opportunity to fulfil their true potential, with the impact being the most devastating for those from disadvantaged communities. With many complex factors contributing to this result, the need for a wide range of solutions is paramount to addressing the various dimensions of this crisis. With this in mind, we embarked on a research and development project called *Ngiyaqonda* (isiZulu for "I understand"), in which speech and text technology for South African languages are harnessed to enhance home language literacy. These technologies were integrated into an Android application designed for Grade 3 learners, who will transition to English as their language of learning and teaching (LOLT) in Grade 4 after receiving instruction in their home language from ages six to nine during the foundation phase. In this work, we will describe the design and development of the application and the pilots we conducted. Hereby, we aim to provide insights into the literacy crisis South Africa faces and how a small intervention can make a difference to the lives of learners and educators.

Keywords: foundation phase literacy · controlled multilingual natural language processing · text-to-speech · automatic speech recognition

1 Introduction

South Africa has 12 official languages, and learners aged six to nine in Grades 1 to 3 are taught in their home languages during the foundation phase. However, when they move to the intermediate phase in Grade 4, they typically transition to English. It is during this phase of schooling that a literacy crisis emerges: more than eight out of ten Grade 4 learners cannot read for basic meaning in their home language. This was the result of a recent international study that sent shockwaves through the country's education community.

In 2023, the Progress in International Reading Literacy Study (PIRLS) [5] results of 2021 were published and confirmed that literacy in South Africa needs

J. Wei et al. (Eds.): HCII 2025, LNCS 16346, pp. 403–413, 2026.
https://doi.org/10.1007/978-3-032-13187-4_27

urgent attention. In 2021, one year after the COVID-19 pandemic hit South African shores, Grade 4 learners across the country were assessed for reading comprehension. The trend in the past was that the results improved slightly from previous years; however, this time there was a decline. The report indicated that the pandemic significantly impacted learners since they experienced noteworthy learning losses when schools were closed due to the national lockdown. That means that despite all efforts to continue learning online, the pandemic still affected learners.

Being able to read with meaning is an essential skill, and without it, South African learners are deprived of the opportunity to fulfil their true potential, with the impact being the most devastating for those from disadvantaged communities. Being literate gives a person easier access to information, their verbal skills are enhanced, and they have the opportunity to be high-functioning contributing members of society - something that will benefit not only them but future generations as well.

With many complex factors contributing to the PIRLS result, the need for a wide range of solutions is paramount to addressing the various dimensions of this crisis. With this in mind, we embarked on a research and development project called *Ngiyaqonda* (isiZulu for "I understand"), in which speech and text technologies for South African languages are harnessed to enhance home language literacy.

In this work, we describe the design and development of *Ngiyaqonda* and the pilots that were conducted, as well as the enabling technologies utilised. In this way, we aim to provide insights into the literacy crisis South Africa faces and how a small intervention can make a difference in the lives of learners and educators.

2   Background

In South Africa, most learners are taught in their home language in the first three years of school (the foundation phase), after which the language of learning and teaching (LOLT) shifts to English. However, with more than 80% of learners struggling to read for meaning in their home language at this point, serious intervention is required to develop sufficient English literacy in subsequent years in order for education to proceed in other subjects [8].

The need, therefore, is for a solution that not only addresses home language literacy during the foundation phase but also develops literacy in English, involving language learning where necessary.

In designing a solution, the practicalities of its deployment must also be taken into consideration. One such factor is the ability of educators to facilitate the deployment of the solution, while the day-to-day operations of schools in South Africa, with the typical challenges faced by educators and management, also influence the form a solution may take.

With regard to educators, resources are severely strained. As of June 2025 [6], almost 30 000 teaching posts are vacant in government-run schools. Since 2009, only one educator has been appointed for every 175 extra learners who have entered the schooling system. A technological solution, therefore, must be designed that is highly intuitive, engaging and relevant, so that it does not add to the burden of educators, but rather assists them in reaching their education targets. To achieve this, the content itself must be highly accurate and reliable, not only in terms of being free from errors, but it must also align with the curriculum and be levelled appropriately. The interface must be focused on learning by requiring the user to engage critically with the content in order to progress through the application.

Electricity, internet, water outages, and theft of infrastructure at schools, affect the schools' operations regularly. During widespread and frequent electricity outages, cellphone towers in the area become non-functional as their battery backup systems fail. This means that a reliable internet connection cannot be guaranteed. Therefore, if a solution depends heavily on consistent internet connectivity, measures should be implemented to ensure its dependable operation. Additionally, unplanned power outages due to infrastructure collapse in municipalities can affect the servers that are responsible for keeping the enabling technologies functional. Theft of infrastructure at schools renders classrooms without electricity, resulting in additional steps that must be taken if technology solutions are to be used. The effect of water outages at schools is also significant. Due to health reasons, if a school has no running water, learners are sent home, and that results in them missing a school day. These infrastructure challenges play an important role when a solution is designed and deployed, and should be considered throughout all development stages.

3   The Interface and Enabling Technologies

The *Ngiyaqonda* application is an Android-based mobile application which supports literacy development in Grade 3 learners through human language technologies. The novel dynamic interface for foundation phase learners allows them to engage with lesson content in interactive ways while guaranteeing grammatically and semantically correct multilingual natural language generation. More specifically, speech-enhanced reading and sentence authoring activities are enabled by harnessing state-of-the-art text-to-speech (TTS), automatic speech recognition (ASR) and controlled multilingual natural language generation (cMNLG) capabilities. These technologies are all integrated into an innovative interface, designed to provide a focused yet rich learning experience.

The application contains two main speech-and-text interfaces, in which cMNLG is used in conjunction with each of the speech technologies, namely TTS and ASR. In this section, we discuss the text and speech technologies utilised by the application, before outlining how the interface was designed to expose them to users in a way that facilitates literacy development.

3.1 Controlled Multilingual Natural Language Generation

In providing suitable content for the application, a typical approach has been the manual development of suitable phrases and sentences by experts [7], which allows complete control over the suitability of the content in terms of sentence complexity and vocabulary. However, this is a very time-consuming and specialised task, which reduces its feasibility within an environment that is strained in terms of financial and human resources. On the other hand, current large language models (LLMs) for the South African languages have not yet reached the required maturity to generate content that can be relied on to have the appropriate complexity in terms of sentence construction and vocabulary.

One solution to this is controlled multilingual natural language generation (cMNLG), in which state-of-the-art rule-based language models are used to develop so-called *application grammars*. The grammars are engineered to provide the correct coverage suited to the learning level of the users, allowing thousands of grammatically and semantically correct sentences to be generated for use by the application. Moreover, the grammars are parallel multilingual grammars, which allow the generation of sets of sentences that are translation equivalents of each other. This enables the application to support literacy development and language learning of a target language such as English, as is required in the South African school context.

3.2 Backend Technologies: cMLNG, TTS and ASR

Learning to read involves the development of a written competency in which an oral competency in the language already exists. To facilitate this, both text and speech technology are employed in *Ngiyaqonda*.

The integration of controlled multilingual natural language generation and text-to-speech (TTS) provides the ability to generate suitable text content for the application as well as the corresponding audio content. The development of an automatic pronunciation error detection (APED) system, based on automatic speech recognition (ASR), which is suited to learners' voices, provides the ability to evaluate reading aloud by users of the application.

Via the Qfrency TTS product [2, 4], the ability to generate audio from text is available in all 11 written official languages of South Africa. A wide-coverage computational grammar called a Grammatical Framework (GF) resource grammar for English, isiZulu, Sepedi, and Afrikaans is available [1]. A resource grammar is essentially a linguistic software library that implements the morphology (word building) and syntax (sentence building) of a language, to be used in the development of application grammars.

For the APED system, models adapted to learners' voices are required, since an ASR model developed for adult voices may not be effective in evaluating reading aloud and providing appropriate feedback [3].

The following research questions guided the development process of the technology integration of the cMNLG, TTS and APED (ASR) technologies:

1. Can application grammars be developed that are parallel with respect to English and isiZulu, such that
   (a) All text generation is grammatically correct;
   (b) All text generation is semantically correct (meaningful translation equivalents);
   (c) Appropriate vocabulary in both languages is utilised;
   (d) Appropriate linguistic structures in both languages are utilised?
2. Can a pronunciation scoring engine be developed for isiZulu child speech?
3. Can a user interface and supporting backend be designed and implemented that effectively integrates cMNLG with TTS in support of the use case?
4. Can a user interface and supporting backend be designed and implemented that effectively integrates cMNLG with a pronunciation scoring engine in support of the use case?

The following objectives were identified to answer the research questions:

1. Identify a suitable, open-source text (learners' story) on which to base a parallel multilingual application grammar. This would ensure that suitable vocabulary and linguistic structures could be identified.
2. Develop a semantic model of the story and identify mappings between semantic concepts in the model and linguistic representations in both languages. Implement this as a set of multilingual application grammars that increase in complexity.
3. Develop a runtime system and web service for using the application grammar to generate natural language, both in full sentences and incrementally (word for word).
4. Develop a child isiZulu ASR system capable of generating in-domain pronunciations with a superior level of accuracy for reading aloud audio recordings.
5. Perform APED score evaluation, achieving sufficient and appropriate APED at selected APED score thresholds while minimising any false pronunciation error detections.
6. Design and develop a set of mobile application screens that interact with the Qfrency service, the cMNLG service and the APED service to present an integrated user interface for text and audio generation. Ensure that a set of lessons gradually exposes the user to increasingly complex natural language text and audio.

While the interface design is discussed in Sect. 3.3, an overview of the backend system architecture that was developed in pursuit of these objectives is provided in Fig. 1.

The application provides context to the cMNLG service by providing information on the specific lesson and task the user is engaging with. This determines the kind of textual content that is required. Initially, a request is made for a set of multilingual sentences that constitute the current task. The sentences are provided to the TTS service to obtain the corresponding audio, in multiple languages if required.

For the TTS-powered screens, the audio can then be used as a prompt to the user. The goal is for the user to reconstruct the sentence that they hear as a written sentence. This is done by providing the user with plausible tokens for completing the sentence. To facilitate this interaction, a request to the cMNLG service can include a partially completed sentence to obtain a set of plausible continuation tokens.

For the ASR-powered screens, the sentence texts serve as user prompts. The user is recorded reading a sentence aloud, and the audio is sent to the APED service. The scoring information is provided to the user interface, based on which a user may either have to try the same sentence again or continue to the next sentence.

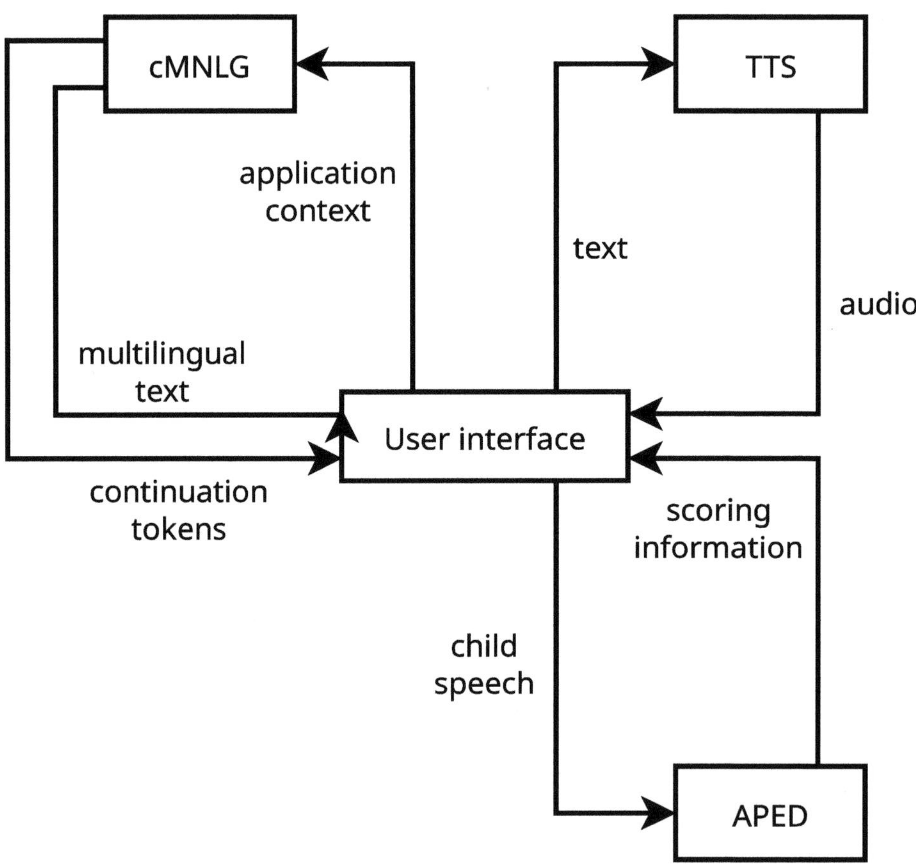

Fig. 1. A snapshot of the backend to illustrate the integration of cMNLG, TTS and APED (ASR).

3.3 Design and Development

The *Ngiyaqonda* application was designed and developed with Grade 3 learners in mind. The design of *Ngiyaqonda* focuses on simplicity and functionality. It has a clean interface with only essential elements and features, thus avoiding unnecessary distractions. In its current state, each user has a password-controlled account in which their progress through the lessons and tasks is tracked and captured.

The application currently supports isiZulu, Sepedi, Afrikaans and English four official languages of South Africa. The languages were selected from various language families based on the size of their home language speaker populations, taking into account the resource-scarce nature of most South African languages, excluding English. A larger speaker population roughly correlates with relatively more digital language resources. For the purposes of the project, English was treated as the target language, however, any language combination is possible within the application to cater to any learner's needs, as was the case during one of the pilots, as discussed in Sect. 4. The aim, however, is to include all the official written languages in the future.

The *Ngiyaqonda* application contains content that is grade-appropriate and aligns with the curriculum. There are two main activities in the application, namely a *writing game* and a *reading game*, and both are found in the different lessons and provide tasks for learners to complete with varying difficulty levels.

In the *writing game*, learners can either build words or sentences by selecting **writing tokens** from a pre-determined set of sounds or words and dragging them to the **writing board**. Learners can also use the **prompt button** to listen to a sentence and then rebuild it using the same actions as mentioned. Once a word or sentence is built, it appears on the right-hand side of the screen with its translation. The **feedback** area provides the learner with an overall score for that task. A screenshot of the writing game is given in Fig. 2.

In the *reading game* (Fig. 3), learners can practice reading sentences that appear on the **reading board** aloud. Their attempts are recorded, and then their pronunciation is scored. Feedback is given in the **feedback** area. The learner has three attempts, and if their pronunciation does not meet the specified requirements after the third attempt, they are automatically moved to the next prompt. The completed sentences are listed in the **sentence progress** area. If a learner scores well, the recording of his/her voice is played when the sentence is tapped. The sentence is also coloured green. If a learner does not pass the pronunciation test, TTS is then used to play the sentences which are coloured orange. Currently, the *writing game* is available in Afrikaans, isiZulu and Sepedi, whereas the *reading game* is only available in isiZulu.

4 Piloting

In an attempt to establish the suitability of using an application like *Ngiyaqonda* in South African schools, pilots were conducted in three primary schools within the Gauteng province of South Africa in 2023 and 2024. These schools

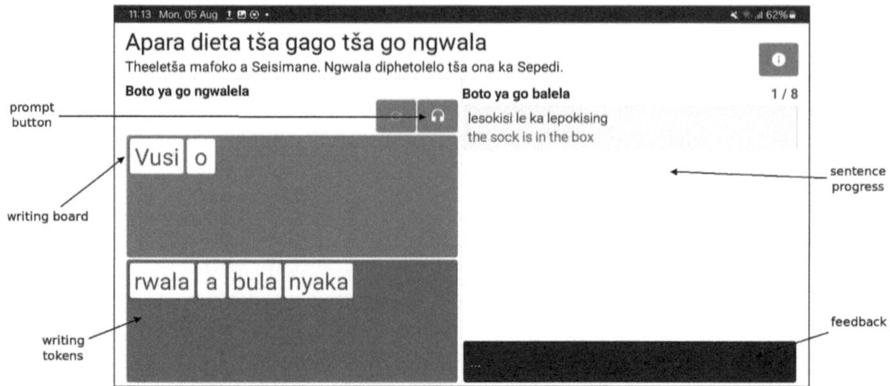

Fig. 2. A screenshot of the writing game in Sepedi.

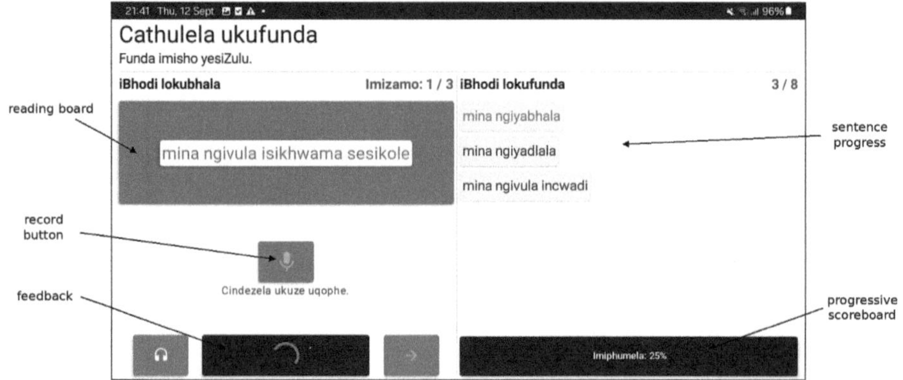

Fig. 3. A screenshot of the reading game in isiZulu.

will be referred to as PS1, PS2 and PS3 for the purposes of this section. With only 20 mobile tablets available, the pilots were carefully structured. We kept the participating groups at the schools small to ensure all learners could use the application throughout the year, and also rotated the tablets between the three schools.

PS1 is a school for isiZulu-speaking learners and is located in Soweto, close to Johannesburg, while PS2 is a school for Sepedi-speaking learners, situated in Mamelodi, close to Pretoria. Both schools participated in literacy development pilots. The pilots were conducted during the second and third terms of the school year. The learners in each classroom were divided into three groups: a control group, an intervention group and a non-participating group. The control and intervention groups consisted of learners with varying literacy skills and they used the application during their reading lesson once a week for a total of 10 weeks. The non-participating group then also had an opportunity to use the application for the remainder of the year, but they did not formally participate in the pilot.

Since the learners continued with their usual schooling, and because the application is only an aid to the classroom environment, it was not possible to measure the effect the application alone had on the learners' literacy skills. However, the educators evaluated their overall literacy skills at the beginning and at the end of the pilot and they were able to detect an improvement in certain learners who used *Ngiyaqonda* throughout the year. They also provided feedback on *Ngiyaqonda*'s impact on learners and classroom integration.

Unlike the other two pilots, PS3's pilot focused on language learning. The effect of *Ngiyaqonda* at PS3 was measured by asking a group of 9 Afrikaans-speaking learners (in Grades 1, 2 and 3) to participate in a short pilot in which they used the application to learn Sepedi. For four weeks, the learners used the application twice a week for 30 min before or after school. It should be noted that, unlike the other pilots that were facilitated by an educator during school hours, the PS3 pilot was mostly self-supervised by the learners during the sessions. To see if the application had an effect on the learners' Sepedi learning progress, a test was administered before and after the pilot.

Not only did the pilots assist us in seeing the application used in a real-world environment, but they also offered us the opportunity to build strong relationships with the pilot schools and educators. These relationships help identify and address the challenges that South African schools face daily, as well as the challenges that affect application usage. Educators' expertise provides vital insights into how *Ngiyaqonda* can be integrated into the school environment.

5   Findings

Feedback from the educator of PS1 was that learners showed improvement in independent reading and that they enjoyed using the application more than reading from a book. She also mentioned that the learners enjoyed using the application and that their listening skills have also improved due to them having to listen to the sentences played by the TTS voice. In addition, the learners could use the application independently with minimal assistance requests, meaning the educator could continue working with the non-participating learners.

Feedback from the educator at PS2 was that *Ngiyaqonda* assisted learners in developing their listening skills by allowing them to hear sounds clearly. Again, learners preferred using the application over traditional methods like pencil and paper activities. The educator also indicated she used *Ngiyaqonda* as inspiration for reading and spelling tests. According to her, the learners could recognise more words after using the application than before.

The results of the tests conducted at PS3 showed that some of the learners improved in terms of Sepedi vocabulary and sentence construction, but that the application was not enticing enough for others, and thus no progress took place for them. Because *Ngiyaqonda* was originally developed with Grade 3 learners in mind, the focus was always on evaluating the impact of the application on a learner and not on evaluating how engaged a learner is when using it. We did, however, notice that the younger learners (those in Grades 1 and 2) were less engaged during the pilot than their older counterparts. The younger learners were actively seeking something that is visually striking to grab their attention, whereas the older learners wanted to use *Ngiyaqonda* to learn Sepedi and did not mind an aesthetically minimal interface. The learner who showed the most progress during the pilot was a learner who is in the school's remedial class. This learner loves technology and finds that the headphones that block out outside noise help him concentrate better. His enjoyment of the application and the progress he made indicate that technology like this could assist learners with the same challenges as he.

6   Conclusion and Future Work

In this work we presented *Ngiyaqonda*, an Android-based mobile application designed and developed for Grade 3 learners. This application aims to enhance literacy development in the official languages of South Africa and utilises local speech and text technologies.

The application was piloted at three schools, and despite the challenges faced, positive feedback was received. Learners were able to use *Ngiyaqonda* independently with minimal educator assistance, and their reading and listening skills improved. Although the design of the application is aesthetically minimal, learners were still eager to use it during lessons. Given the feedback received, we are positive that *Ngiyaqonda* can easily be integrated into a South African classroom environment as either a literacy development or language learning application.

Future work will entail offering *Ngiyaqonda* in the other written official languages of South Africa and to pilot it at more schools across the country. In addition, we want to make improvements to the user experience to provide better feedback to learners when infrastructure challenges arise. A progress report for educators, a comprehension test and new lessons incorporating a curriculum-approved dictionary are also planned.

By incorporating *Ngiyaqonda* in a classroom environment that complements the learning process, the application can play a pivotal role in addressing South Africa's literacy crisis.

Acknowledgments. This study was funded by the South African Department of Sport, Arts and Culture. The underlying technologies were funded by the South African Centre for Digital Language Resources (SADiLAR).

References

1. GF Resource Grammar Library (RGL). https://github.com/GrammaticalFrame work/gf-rgl. Accessed 11 June 2025
2. Qfrency. https://www.qfrency.com/. Accessed 11 June 2025
3. Badenhorst, J.: Automatic assessment of speech impediment for south African early literacy readers. In: Gerber, A., Maritz, J., Pillay, A.W. (eds.) SACAIR 2024. CCIS, vol. 2326, pp. 74–90. Springer, Cham (2024). https://doi.org/10.1007/978-3-031-78255-8_5
4. Louw, J.A., Van Niekerk, D.R., Schlünz, G.I.: Introducing the Speect speech synthesis platform. In: Blizzard Challenge Workshop (2010)
5. Mullis, I.V., Martin, M.O., Foy, P., Hooper, M.: International results in reading. Chestnut Hill, Mass.: TIMSS & PIRLS International Study Center, Lynch School of Education, Boston College, and International Association for the Evaluation of Educational Achievement (2017)
6. Netwerk24: 'Nasionale ramp': Sedert 2009 slegs 1 onderwyser vir elke ekstra 175 leerlinge aangestel - Fedsas. Netwerk24 (2025)
7. Pajak, B., Bicknell, K.: At Duolingo, humans and AI work together to create a high-quality learning experience. https://blog.duolingo.com/how-duolingo-experts-work-with-ai. Accessed 11 June 2025
8. Pretorius, E.J.: Supporting transition or playing catch-up in grade 4? Implications for standards in education and training. Perspect. Educ. **32**(1), 51–76 (2014)

Author Index

J. Wei et al. (Eds.): HCII 2025, LNCS 16346, pp. 415–416, 2026.
https://doi.org/10.1007/978-3-032-13187-4